Fodor's

TOKYO

TOP REASONS TO GO

★ **Ultimate cityscape:** Neon-lit streets and vast high-rises awe the senses.

★ **Incredible eats:** From humble ramen to sumptuous sushi, Tokyo is foodie heaven.

★ **Green havens:** Lush gardens and parks soften the urban scene.

★ **Fashion-forward shops:** Tokyo is a shopper's dream—from Muji to Miyake.

★ **Contemporary art:** The Mori Art Museum caps a truly diverse scene.

★ **Sacred spaces:** Senso-ji Complex and Meiji Shrine are spiritual retreats.

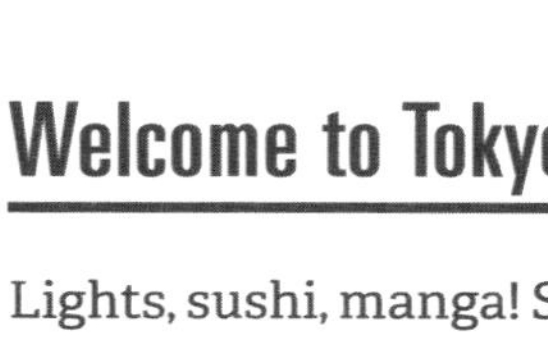

Welcome to Tokyo

Lights, sushi, manga! Sprawling, frenetic, and endlessly fascinating, Japan's capital offers pockets of calm between famously crowded streets. Mom-and-pop noodle houses share street space with Western-style restaurants. Shopping yields lovely folk arts as well as the newest electronics. Nightlife kicks off with karaoke or sake and continues with techno clubs. Whether you're a foodie, artist, design lover, or cultural adventurer, this city will inspire you.

From the crush of the morning commute to the evening crowds flowing into shops, restaurants, and bars, Tokyo rarely slows down and never stops. For a time, it seemed on its way to becoming a city of the future—the epitome of compact urban life surrounded by high-tech skyscrapers, the world's densest rail system, and a 3-D network of highways.

Nearly 30 years of gradual economic stagnation have cooled that vision. Today's Tokyo seems more focused on the present, with a greater emphasis on cultural development and on improving the quality of life.

Although areas such as Shibuya or Shinjuku's Kabuki-cho are overwhelming, 24-hour cacophonies of light, sound, and energy, other neighborhoods are surprisingly relaxed. In Aoyama, people are more likely to be sipping wine or coffee with friends at a café than downing beer and sake with coworkers in an *izakaya* (a bar that serves food).

The city has some of the world's most unsightly sprawls of concrete housing—extending for miles in all directions. But offsetting all the concrete and glass are myriad parks, temple grounds, and traditional gardens.

Indeed, the many natural spaces help to make spring and fall the best times to visit. *Sakura* (cherry blossoms) begin blooming in early April, and autumn often has clear blue skies and colorful foliage.

Whether you seek the glow of the bright lights or the green expanse of a park, the traditional or the cutting edge, this astonishing, intriguing, and beautiful city will provide it.

As you plan your Tokyo trip, please reconfirm that places are still open and let us know when we need to make updates at *corrections@fodors.com.*

Contents

MAPS

Fodor's Features

Chapter 1

EXPERIENCE TOKYO

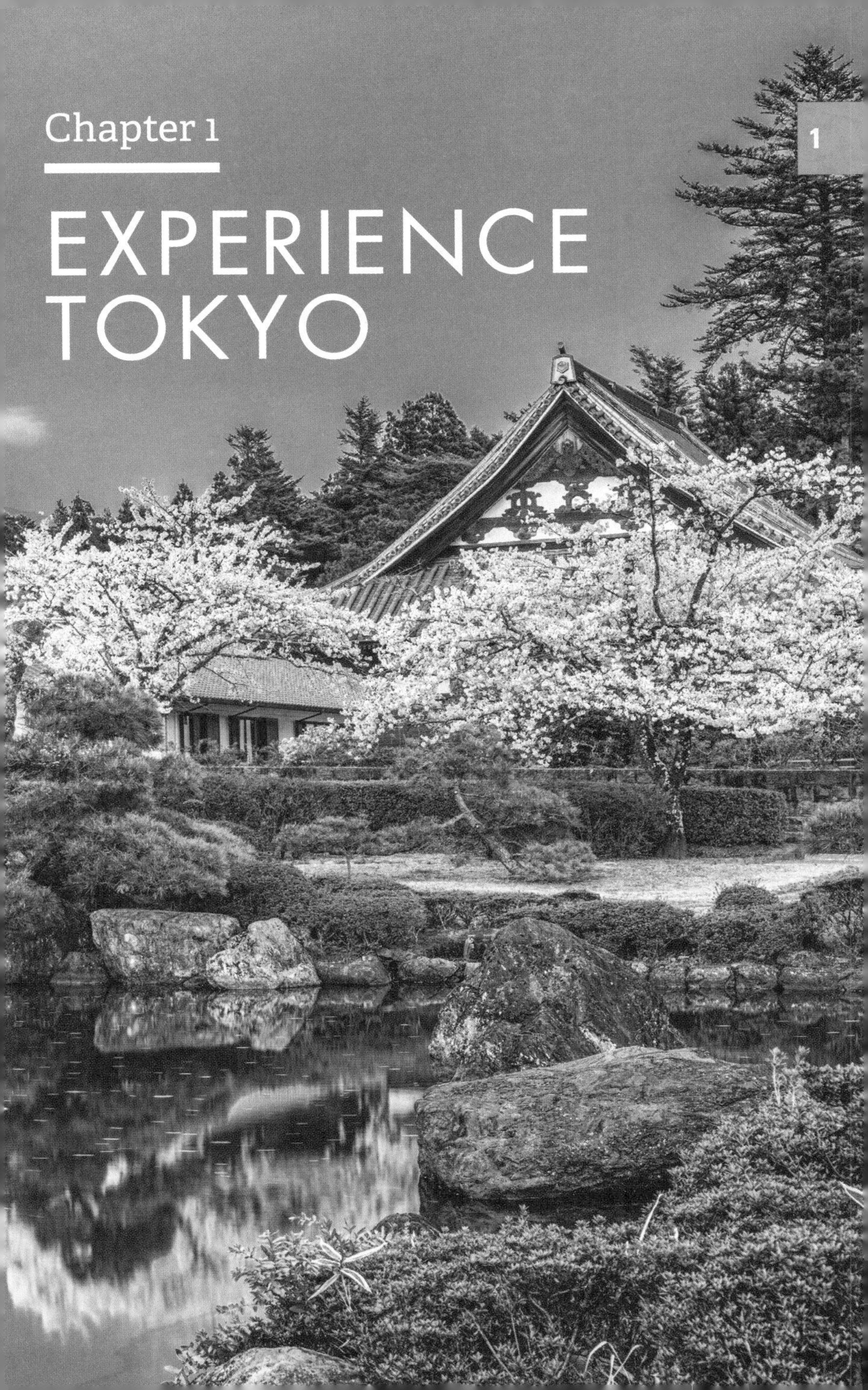

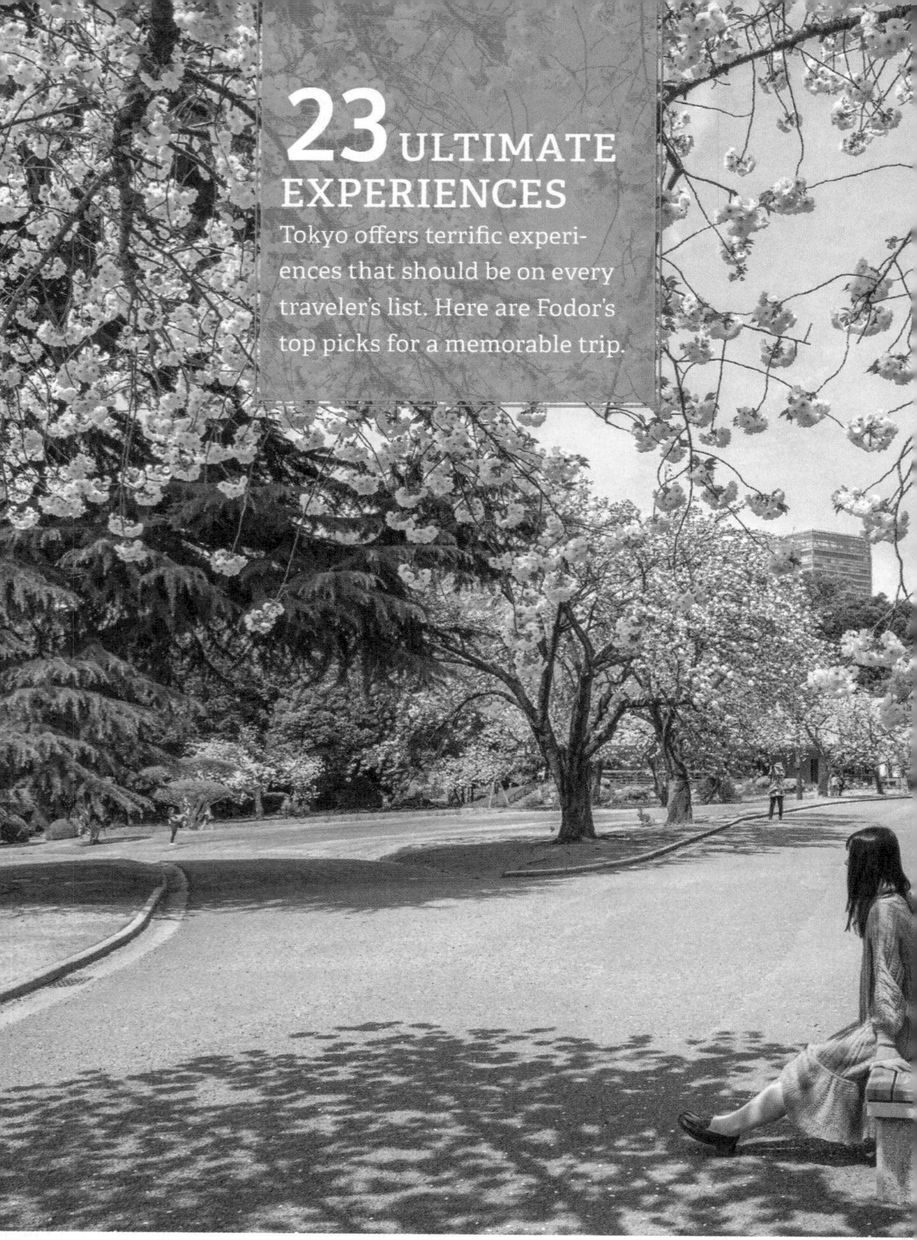

23 ULTIMATE EXPERIENCES
Tokyo offers terrific experiences that should be on every traveler's list. Here are Fodor's top picks for a memorable trip.

1 Shinjuku Gyoen National Garden

Tokyo's many parks and gardens offer an essential contrast to the city's skyscrapers and neon. Shinjuku Gyoen National Garden is especially beautiful in cherry blossom season, but its gardens and central lawn are a peaceful retreat year-round. *(Ch. 9)*

2 Explore Tokyo's Neighborhoods

Odaiba has arcades and quirky museums. Ryogoku has Sumo. Shimokitazawa has vintage goods. Harajuku is a pop culture hub. Ginza is a ritzy shopping district.

3 Tour the Imperial Palace Gardens

While you can't tour the Imperial Palace itself, its East Gardens are open to the public, free, and have charming moats and gates as well as orchards. *(Ch. 4)*

4 Visit Tokyo Skytree

One of the tallest towers in the world, Tokyo Skytree boasts a restaurant, café, spiral walkway, shops, and two observation decks that offer the best views in the city. *(Ch. 13)*

5 Visit Mt. Takao

You can hike on Mt. Takao in Meiji Forest Takao Quasi-National Park or take a cable car or chairlift almost to the peak; it's a popular day trip, roughly an hour by train from central Tokyo. *(Ch. 15)*

6 Experience Kabuki

Kabuki is a traditional Japanese form of theater that is characterized by elaborate staging and makeup and exaggerated acting, singing, and dancing. Kabuki-za Theater is its most famous venue. *(Ch. 5)*

7 Stay at a Ryokan

A stay in a traditional guesthouse typically includes minimalist rooms with tatami mats, yukata robes and slippers, a multicourse kaiseki dinner, and a Japanese breakfast. *(Chs. 12, 13)*

8 Top Temples and Shrines

Shrines and temples are some of Tokyo's most interesting sights. Highlights include Meiji Jingu Shrine and Senso-ji Temple Complex. *(Chs. 6, 12)*

9 Anime Adventures

Anime fans flock to Tokyo's "electric town," the Akihabara neighborhood, an area jam-packed with cosplay and maid cafés, anime shops, and arcades. *(Ch. 11)*

10 Get Crafty

Make your own souvenirs at Tokyo stores offering workshops like washi-paper-making classes. *(Ch. 4)*

11 Explore Lantern-Lit Alleys

Drink with locals in alleyways—like Harmonica Yokocho in Kichijoji or Golden Gai—lined with tiny izakaya and bars, offering cheap drinks and small dishes. *(Chs. 9, 10)*

12 Take Tea

A full tea ceremony is long and tedious, but you can also just have a feel of one at Nakajima no Ochaya in Hama-rikyu Gardens and the tea house at Shinjuku Gyoen National Garden. *(Chs. 6, 9)*

13 Shibuya Scramble Crossing

Nothing captures the essence of Tokyo quite like the busiest intersection in the world. Brave the crossing or find a good angle to photograph the thousands of pedestrians crossing. *(Ch. 7)*

14 Try a Love Hotel

Love hotels are escapes from normality. Tokyo has a huge variety of themed hotels you and your partner might enjoy for a night, from the lavish to outlandish. *(Ch. 9)*

15 Soak in an Onsen

Don't miss the opportunity to slide into a steamy natural hot spring; the best place to try this is on an excursion to Hakone, a popular stop with views of Mt. Fuji. *(Ch. 15)*

16 Sample Sumo

Tokyo's Ryogoku district is the epicenter of Japan's national sport. Book a tour to visit a sumo stable and watch a morning practice or see a match at the Ryogoku Kokugikan. *(Ch. 13)*

17 Karaoke Bar

Karaoke culture is next-level in this part of the world; check out the popular Pasela chain, either in Shibuya or Roppongi. *(Chs. 7, 8)*

18 Visit Odaiba

This man-made island, accessible via the Rainbow Bridge, is home to an indoor amusement park where you can sample the latest high-tech entertainment and a stroll along a lively waterfront area. *(Ch. 6)*

19 Ghibli Museum

Fans of Studio Ghibli and artist Hayao Miyazaki will want to visit this whimsical multistory museum offering life-size re-creations of his film settings and adored characters. *(Ch. 14)*

20 Fish Markets

Tokyo's top fish market is now at Toyosu, having moved from the historic Tsukiji area—which still hosts "the outer market," a series of market-related shops and eateries. *(Ch. 5)*

21 Shop 'til You Drop

Get your shopping fix on Omotesando, a boulevard packed with high-end retailers; Ginza Six, a luxury shopping mall; and Takeshita-dori, a hot spot for Harajuku teen fashion. *(Chs. 5, 7)*

22 Find Your Inner Samurai

After the Japanese Sword Museum in Ryogoku, stop by the Kanda Myojin Shrine in Akihabara to get a feel for a definitive era in Japanese history. *(Chs. 11, 13)*

23 Hit Top Tokyo Museums

Along with classics like the Tokyo Metropolitan Art Museum, see what's on at Mori Art Museum in Roppongi or the nearby 21_21 Design Sight. *(Ch. 8)*

WHAT'S WHERE

1 Marunouchi and Nihonbashi. The Imperial Palace stands at the center of Tokyo. Marunouchi is home to plush retail and office complexes; Nihonbashi is the city's financial center.

2 Ginza and Tsukiji. Ginza has Tokyo's traditional high-end stores and equally ritzy restaurants. Nearby, Tsukiji (once home to the world's largest fish market) is still home to the "outer market" and seafood restaurants.

3 Shiodome and Odaiba. Shiodome is a massive development zone withshops, hotels, and restaurants. Odaiba is an island with shopping, restaurants, family-oriented amusements, and parks.

4 Aoyama, Harajuku, and Shibuya. These chic neighborhoods are packed with people and saturated with shops whose wares are chic, hip, and/or vintage.

5 Roppongi. With a rich and sometimes sordid nightlife history, Roppongi has gone more upscale with the massive Roppongi Hills and Tokyo Midtown developments.

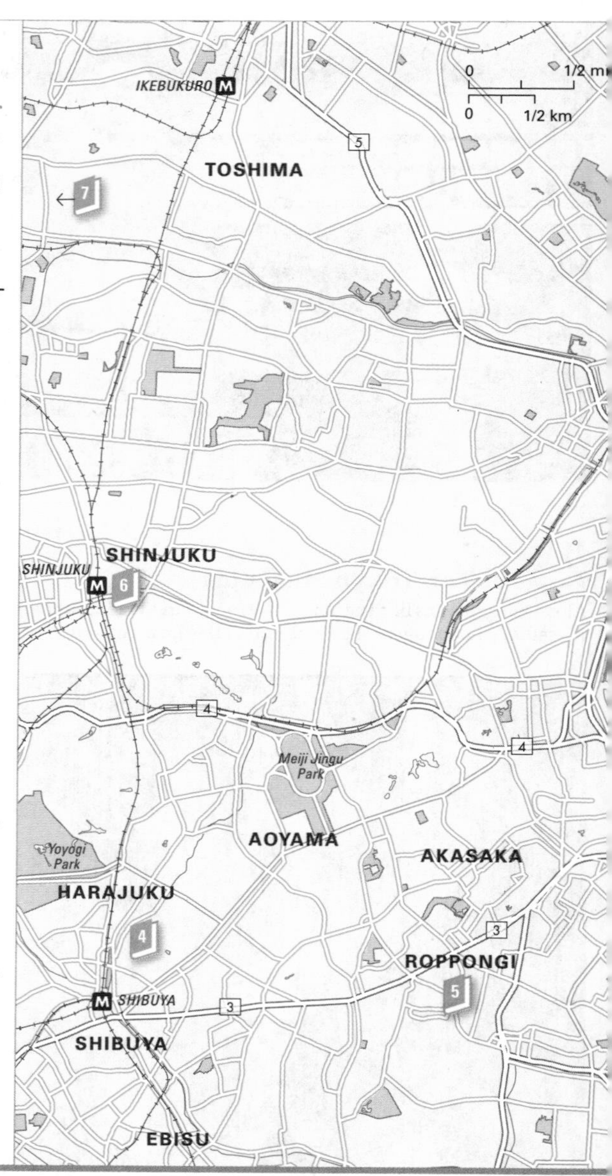

6 Shinjuku. The train station here is supposedly the world's busiest. And, when the sun sets, the bars and clubs in the red-light area of Kabuki-cho come to life.

7 West Tokyo. Quieter and more residential, the neighborhoods west of Shinjuku such as Nakano and Tama have their own charms.

8 Akihabara. Akihabara is famed for its electronics stores, manga shops, and video arcades.

9 Ueno and Yanaka. Ueno Park is home to museums, a university of fine arts, and a zoo. Adjoining Yanaka is a charming area of temples and winding, narrow alleys.

10 Asakusa and Ryogoku. Asakusa has Tokyo Skytree and Senso-ji Temple, the city's oldest. Ryogoku is Tokyo's sumo center.

11 Greater Tokyo. Areas beyond central Tokyo, as well as some neighboring prefectures, have noteworthy temples, shopping opportunities, and attractions like Tokyo Disney Resort.

Tokyo Today

DEVELOPMENT ON THE HORIZON

Tokyo is often thought of as a fast-paced metropolis, buzzing with perpetual noise and neon lights, and areas around central stations don't do much to dispel this image. That said, this is also a city where you can go around just one corner and find a pocket of peace.

This juxtaposition has only increased in recent years due to a once-in-a-lifetime urban redevelopment project across the capital. Tokyo is revitalizing its downtown areas, and while the government aims to add even more high-rises to its skyline, it also plans to integrate green spaces and places for workers to relax during their lunch breaks. For instance, rooftop gardens are becoming a staple in many of the city's new skyscrapers. This large-scale redevelopment is designed not only to make the city more liveable but also to fortify buildings in preparation for the next severe earthquake. Experts say there's a 70% chance of one striking the Kanto area in the next 30 years.

A NEW LOOK

Ever since Shibuya, one of Tokyo's most famous neighborhoods, started its redevelopment project in 2019, it has been changing rapidly. The first phase saw the construction of the Shibuya Scramble Square complex, which includes the popular Shibuya Sky outdoor observation deck. Another welcome addition was Miyashita Park, its roof now a hangout for young Tokyoites. The business districts Toranomon and Azabudai also unveiled the Azabudai Hills complex in 2023, featuring the Azabudai Hills Mori JP Tower, currently the tallest building in Japan.

Tokyo's skyline and infrastructure are continually evolving. Whispers of anticipated developments include a new subway system, an addition to the city's already impressive public transportation network.

DECLINING BIRTHS

A whopping 37 million people call Tokyo their home, and despite investment in Japan's countryside, many young Japanese still migrate to the big city for economic opportunities. It's obvious why: 50% of the country's listed companies are headquartered here, and the wages are on average the highest in Japan. Tokyo's minimum wage is ¥1,113, compared to the national weighted average of ¥1,004.

However, population growth may soon cease altogether. Since 2015, the birth rate in Tokyo has consistently declined, and it's now the lowest out of Japan's 47 prefectures. The very jobs that tempt the masses to the city have contributed to the problem.

A culture of excessive overtime remains prevalent and is highlighted in the government's annual report on *karoshi* (death by overwork). This report was introduced in 2016 after a spate of deaths due to extreme working conditions. It is still standard for employees not to take assigned paid holidays due to subtle pressure within corporate environments. Unsurprisingly, many people don't feel they have the time or financial stability to raise children.

The government has addressed these issues with financial initiatives, such as covering a substantial amount of childbirth costs and reducing education fees, as well as other initiatives, like developing a dating app. Tokyo's culture, however, also lacks opportunities for serendipitous encounters, which is a harder problem to solve.

LONELINESS IN THE BIG CITY

One may be the loneliest number, but it's also the number most likely to secure you a seat at a local Tokyo ramen joint. Numerous restaurants have limited seating, and if the food's excellent, a line out the door. Don't fret, it usually moves fast as patrons inhale their food and go. This quick—and often cheap—alternative to home cooking caters to singles, namely overworked office workers just off a 12-hour shift.

In Tokyo, you can easily go a whole day without speaking to another person if you don't make an effort. The COVID-19 pandemic exacerbated this isolation as heightened cleanliness and limited interactions became the norm. Technology filled the gap, with machines at the door and QR codes and tablets on tables ready to take your order. Robots became less of a gimmick and more of a reality as they began to serve meals in popular chain restaurants across the city. Routine trips to convenience stores come with touch screens and self-checkouts.

Tokyo is technologically advanced in many ways, as seen during the 2020 Olympic Opening Ceremony's drone show. Major companies are also now investing heavily in AI and universities are funding extensive research. However, in other areas, Tokyo lags behind; cashless payments, for example, were slow to catch on and fax machines are still in use.

A SUSTAINABLE FUTURE

Tokyo faces a significant challenge, one it has set for itself: by 2030, the government aims to halve greenhouse-gas emissions and shift to renewable energy. Even grander, it strives for zero carbon emissions in the capital by as early as 2050. Looking around at the vending machines on almost every corner, it's a struggle to envision this transformation. Tokyo remains an energy-intensive city that's constantly on. Buildings alone account for around 70% of Tokyo's CO_2 emissions.

Because of this, government strategies and policies for reducing the city's carbon footprint and improving sustainability include making solar panels mandatory for new homes built after 2025 and phasing out gasoline-only vehicles in favor of hybrids and electric models.

A PLAN FOR PLASTIC

Japan has always had trouble with an overreliance on plastic. Excessive packaging is common—even individual bananas are often wrapped up. However, changes are taking place. Since 2020, it has been mandatory for retailers to charge customers for plastic shopping bags, and businesses must set targets to reduce single-use plastics.

In the capital, strict recycling guidelines focus on enhancing circular use. This means households are in charge of separating waste themselves—and lucky for us, the garbage men rarely miss a day. Tokyo's waste-management system is efficient, but the city needs a firmer hand on reducing excess plastic at the source if they want to see significant improvements in plastic reduction.

What to Eat and Drink in Japan

SUSHI
It goes without saying that you'd be remiss in visiting Japan without sampling sushi, the most well-known genre of Japanese cuisine. While the world's largest fish market has moved from Tsukiji to Toyosu, the Tsukiji neighborhood is still a great place to sample the best, and freshest, sushi in Tokyo.

JAPANESE WHISKEY
The big whiskey brands in Japan are Yamazaki, Hibiki, Hakushu, Fuji Gotemba, Chichibu, and White Oak. You can try them at most upscale bars in Tokyo. For the dedicated, head to Fuji Gotemba's distillery at the foot of Mt. Fuji on a day trip from Tokyo.

TEPPANYAKI
Don't call it "hibachi" but do consider spending a bit more to reserve a counter seat at a high-class teppanyaki restaurant. Watch a skilled chef at work as he prepares beautifully marbled beef on a metal plate in front of you. If you're feeling brave, there are also plenty of do-it-yourself experiences, such as Sakuratei in Harajuku.

RAMEN
From the miso-based broth of Hokkaido to the pork bone broth of Fukuoka, each region of Japan has developed its own soup to go with the perennially popular noodles. In Tokyo, head to the Shin-Yokohama Ramen Museum, where you can sample an array of ramen from restaurants all over Japan.

OKONOMIYAKI
"Okonomi" means "whatever you like," and "yaki" means "grilled." *Okonomiyaki* are made with cabbage, flour, eggs, green onions, and usually some type of protein all mixed together and then shaped into a sort of veggie-based, savory pancake. Try all the variations and don't forget the toppings.

SAKE
Nihonshu (sake), also known as Japanese rice wine, is Japan's most famous variety of alcohol. It can be enjoyed hot or cold and paired to your meal. Head to Sake no Ane in Ginza for over 100 varieties.

YAKITORI

The beauty of *yakitori* is in its simplicity. Skewered chicken is cooked over a charcoal grill and seasoned with a little salt and *tare* sauce. There's a reason it's a staple of late-night street food and izakaya.

SOBA

In addition to being delicious, soba buckwheat noodles have the added benefit of having more nutritional value (they're gluten-free and contain antioxidants) than wheat noodles.

CHANKO NABE

Chanko nabe—a giant pot of soup made with chicken broth, plenty of good-for-you protein sources, bok choy, and lots of vegetables—is the signature meal of sumo wrestlers actively working on gaining weight as part of their training. It's probably best enjoyed after watching a sumo wrestling demonstration.

SHABU-SHABU

Shabu-shabu is similar to chanko nabe in the sense that it's a "hot pot"–style dish that can include myriad ingredients. But instead of eating your portion from a single bowl, shabu-shabu is cooked one piece at a time.

10 Fun Stores in Tokyo

GACHAPON AT GASHAPON DEPARTMENT STORE
For a quirky gift that won't cost too much, head to Gashapon Department Store in Ikebukuro's Sunshine City. Choose from 3,000 *gachapon* (or *gashapon*) capsule machines that spit out anything from tiny anime figurines to bags specifically for green onions.

CAN-CAN AT MR. KANSO
The ordinary becomes a novelty at this series of bars dotted around the city that they stock nothing but canned goods—from sardines to smoked liver. Even the drinks are canned at this quirky, distinctly Japanese hangout.

NAKANO BROADWAY
Just follow the covered shopping arcade north of Nakano Station to find four floors of shops selling everything from anime and manga figurines to vintage video games.

STATIONERY AT ITOYA
Itoya's 18-floor flagship store in the heart of Ginza stocks quality stationery goods like cards, paper, and pens, as well as a wide selection of crafts.

YAMASHIROYA TOY STORE
One minute's walk from Ueno station, Yamashiroya's seven floors of childhood heaven packed with toys, figurines, games, and comics is a bucket-list stop for any kid (or kid at heart). Look for a Pokémon chess set and an entire corner devoted to Totoro.

KNICKKNACKS AT HANDS
From stationery to toilet-seat covers, reflexology slippers to bee-venom face masks, and novelty party supplies to board games, Hands has everything you never knew you needed to buy for yourself and everyone on your list.

OTAKU AT AKIHABARA RADIO KAIKAN
The iconic Akihabara landmark is dedicated to Japanese pop culture, making it an *otaku* (anime, manga, video-game nerd) paradise with 10 floors of shops selling manga, anime, and collectibles such as models and figurines, fanzines, costumes, and accessories.

EVERYTHING AT DON QUIJOTE
Open 24/7, Don Quijote is a jumble of tall, crowded shelves and sells everything from designer handbags and watches, clothing, and electronics to cheap cosmetics, costumes, and more. It's your one-stop shop for souvenirs including the famed flavored Kit Kats (yes, you *need* every variety).

TOYS AT KIDDY LAND
For those who love something plush and soft, you can't go wrong with Kiddy Land. The store is bursting with merchandise from popular Japanese children's characters. There are a few locations across Tokyo but the most well-known is in Harajuku.

MASKS AT OMOTE
Actors, mask makers, and headwear enthusiasts all frequent this boutique mask store whose selection ranges from noh masks to Venetian-style masks to *hyottoko* (Japanese-style clown masks), with prices starting at a few thousand yen and stretching to the hundreds of thousands.

Free (or Cheap) Things to Do in Toyko

PICNIC IN THE PARK
Grab a bento box from a supermarket or bento shop, and head to Yoyogi Park—a sanctuary of trees in the middle of Tokyo's urban buzz. The lush expanse of greenery on the park's north side is particularly ideal for relaxing with a picnic lunch.

TRENDSPOTTING
Since opening in 1979, Shibuya 109 has been a fashion utopia for Tokyo's younger generations and a Shibuya landmark, known for its 10 floors bursting with the latest in clothing, shoes, and accessories. It's still one of the city's hippest hangouts, a place where hundreds of stores seemingly try to outdo one another for the most unique concept and where spotting trends is both easy and entertaining.

WORLD-FAMOUS FISH MARKET(S)
While you can reserve tours to see Tokyo's two renowned fish markets—Tsukiji (old) and Toyosu (new)—you can also easily visit the older one on your own for free. Although the historic Tsukiji Outer Market isn't really a fish market anymore, it still has clusters of eateries and stalls selling pickles, bamboo rolling mats, dried nori, and other items.

TAKESHITA STREET
One of Japan's most popular youth-culture destinations is Harajuku, where the hub of the *kawaii* (cutesy) subculture is Takeshita Street. The people-watching here is prime, particularly on weekends, when you might see young people fully clad in cosplay, Lolita, and other outlandish garb. It's also where you'll find shops that sell some of that gear.

CONTEMPORARY ART CRAWL
Go see SCAI the Bathhouse, a contemporary art gallery with ever-changing exhibits. The refurbished building is fascinating on its own even if you don't care for the show. If you're looking to make a day of free exhibits, check Tokyo Art Beat (🌐 *www.tokyoartbeat.com/en*) to see what's on during your trip.

PANORAMIC VIEWS
If you're put off by Skytree entry prices, head for the Tokyo Metropolitan Government Building in Shinjuku. Its south and north tower observatories have views of Tokyo—and beyond to Mt. Fuji on a clear day. On the ground, see nightly free projection mapping on the building's exterior.

NISSAN CROSSING
Take a gander at Nissan's latest supercar concept vehicles as well as rare classic models at its flagship showroom located in the flashy district of Ginza. Check out the rare models or the theater where you can be immersed in the sights and sounds of fast cars.

THE PARASITE MUSEUM
One of Tokyo's more peculiar museums, the Meguro Parasitological Museum is perhaps not the first thing to come to mind when planning a visit to the city, but in recent years, it has become an oddly popular tourist attraction. Come here to see more than 300 creepy-crawly specimens for free.

SUMO STABLE
Japan's national sport is famously tough to get tickets for, and competitions are held sporadically, making it difficult to be in the right place at the right time to catch a match. The next best thing is to head to a sumo stable to watch the wrestlers train. Arashio-beya stable is one location where you can usually watch morning practice sessions through windows on the street.

THE AD MUSEUM TOKYO
One of the city's coolest free museums has historical displays and immersive exhibits that provide an intriguing visual history of commerce in Japan over the past century.

Traditional Crafts to Buy

EDO KIRIKO GLASSWARE

Edo Kiriko glassware is created by carving patterns into the surface of layered colored glass using a diamond-tipped grinder. Ryuichi Kumakura's kometsunagi, or rice-chain pattern, is particularly revered and achieved by subtly varying the size of the rice grain shapes he engraves.

FUROSHIKI WRAPPING CLOTHS

Harajuku may be mecca for the latest in youth fashion, but it's also home to some classic craft shops like Musubi, a charming boutique specializing in traditional *furoshiki* cloths. Used to wrap everything from gifts to bento lunch boxes, these beautifully decorated material squares are the perfect eco-friendly wrapping solution. Around 500 varieties line the shelves in traditional, seasonal, and modern designs made from a variety of fabrics including cotton, silk, and *chirimen* (silk crepe), and using various dying and weaving techniques.

FINE BAMBOO CRAFTS

Bamboo craft shop Midoriya, established in 1908, is located along the Yanaka Ginza traditional shopping street. Here, three generations of artists have honed their craft. The family-run shop and studio sells bamboo products ranging from the everyday to the exquisite. Traditional *mushikago* insect cages come in a range of shapes and sizes, as well as bamboo bugs and birds to put inside. You'll also find flower baskets, chopsticks, bookmarks, and lunch boxes. *Renkon* (lotus root) coasters are a cheap and trendy takeaway.

VINTAGE FABRIC FASHION

Kukuli is a tiny textiles shop located in the crafty pocket of Kagurazaka, a former geisha hub renowned for its picturesque cobblestone streets. This delightful boutique recycles vintage fabrics and transforms them into trendy fashion pieces. You can buy cloths, tea towels, scarves, and bags made with woven fabric drawn from different regions of the country. These precious and sometimes century-old fabrics are then hand-dyed and redesigned into stylish new products. Alongside the classical motifs of cherry blossom and koi carp, expect to find simple but chic stripes, checks, and geometric patterns.

JAPANESE-STYLE CLOTHING AND TEXTILES

Opened in the 1990s in the peaceful backstreets of Daikanyama, Okura sells clothing and other textiles based on traditional Japanese designs and tailoring techniques. "Okura" in Japanese means a storehouse full of old treasures and memories from childhood. The seashells, driftwood, shards of glass, and other materials that are embedded in the ceiling and floor were collected from the beach during the store's construction, and there is a weathered curtain over the entrance. You can find a wide range of items including *aizome* (a traditional Japanese indigo dyeing method) shirts, denims, jackets and sweaters, and the shop stocks men's and women's clothing under

their own original brands, including the indigo brand BLUE BLUE JAPAN. The second floor stocks the women's range, where you'll find hairpins, purses, cloths, kimono-motif tops, and all kinds of other things.

FOLK TOYS AND SOUVENIRS
For traditional souvenirs with a trendy twist, toy shop Atelier Gangu stocks folkcraft toys directly bought from the craftsmen of various regions around Japan as well as the postcards made with papercut art. The postcards depict the folkcraft toys that are no longer available or difficult to find. On its shelves, you will see everything from papier-mâché animals to kites to handcrafted *maneki-neko* (lucky cats) all made by veteran craftsmen.

TENUGUI HAND TOWELS
Made from dyed cotton cloth, *tenugui* are long, multipurpose hand towels. Considered a daily necessity by many Japanese, they've also become a fashion item with people wearing them as headbands, head scarves, and neck scarves. Tenugui Fuji-ya in Asakusa has them available in a wide variety of traditional Japanese prints, as well as seasonal patterns such as cherry blossoms and carp streamers.

JAPANESE KITCHEN KNIVES
The history of kitchen-supply store Kama-Asa extends all the way back to 1908 when the shop was first opened in Asakusa's Kappabashi (also known as Kitchen Town). The elegant store specializes in handcrafted kitchen knives (roughly 80 different kinds) and Nanbu Tekki iron pans, woks, and steamers. There is also a selection of knives for left-handed cooks and the friendly staff will engrave a knife for you in Japanese symbols or roman letters at no extra cost.

TRADITIONAL WASHI PAPER
Founded in 1806, Haibara specializes in making gorgeous letter sets, notebooks, *uchiwa* (round-shaped fans), and envelopes featuring *mizuhiki* knots from traditional *washi* paper. The elegant design of their products can be traced back to the Meiji and late Edo periods when Haibara's founders collaborated with the most renowned painters of that era. They are best known for *gampi* paper made from the outer bark fibers of gampi trees, giving it a smooth texture and silky surface. The shop exterior is a futuristic-looking gray cube just off of Chuo-dori in the Nihonbashi district.

Best Tours in Tokyo

PERSONALIZED TOUR
Join a small group tour to hit all the highlights of Tokyo or hire a private guide to take you to off-the-beaten-path Tokyo with InsideJapan Tours, whose team of experts and knowledgeable locals help you make the most of your time. 🌐 *www.insidejapantours.com.*

HISTORY TOUR
Get a first-hand glimpse into the life of the *shogun* (military dictators), *daimyo* (feudal lords), and *samurai* (Japanese warrior class) on Walk Japan's two-day Tokyo tour, which gives an introduction to the establishment of Edo (Tokyo), how it came to be, and how it developed from a traditional samurai society to a modern-day glitzy metropolis. 🌐 *www.walkjapan.com.*

FOOD TOUR
Sample delectable Japanese dishes on one of Arigato Japan's three-hour foodie tours of Tokyo. Drop into Shibuya food stops or wander through Tokyo's traditional district of Yanaka while sampling dishes from around Japan and shopping the wares of creative artisans and craftspeople. 🌐 *arigatojapan.co.jp.*

TOKYO AFTER DARK
Get an education as you enjoy the food offerings hidden in the back haunts of Shibuya with Context Travel's Tokyo After Dark tour. You'll learn about the history of the *izakaya* and its role in both drinking and culinary culture of the area. 🌐 *www.contexttravel.com.*

FISH MARKET TOUR
An early-morning trip to the giant Toyosu fish market is a bucket-list item for many visitors to Tokyo, but it can be overwhelming to navigate it on your own. There are several tour groups that will take you through. Several fish market tours (some for the new market and some for the old Tsukiji Market's surrounding neighborhood) are offered by Viator. 🌐 *viator.com.*

CHERRY BLOSSOM TOUR
To experience Tokyo during the *sakura* (cherry blossom) season is to experience the city at its most exquisite. Join a private guide on a walking tour to suss out the best bloom-viewing spots in the city. Some tours will include a tea ceremony experience or a *hanami* experience where you can have a picnic under the blossoms. 🌐 *www.toursbylocals.com.*

CYCLE THROUGH TOWN
If you are looking for something a bit more active, try Tokyo Great Tours for cycling. The Tokyo Transformation (Route C), for example, will take you from the east side of central Tokyo to the west to see the whole variety of modern architecture and historic locations. 🌐 *tokyogreattours.com.*

DISCOVER THE ANIME AND MANGA CULTURE OF AKIHABARA
Dive into the world of Japanese pop culture on Context Tours' Geek to Chic expedition, which explores the famed electronics town of Akihabara, Tokyo's *otaku* (anime and manga geek) hub. The tour also covers one of the more unconventional aspects of otaku

culture—cosplay ("costume play")—by visiting a maid café. 🌐 *contexttravel.com.*

GET TO KNOW THE CITY FOR FREE

If you're seeing the city on a budget, try one of Tokyo's SGG club (Systemized Goodwill Guide Club) free 90-minute and two-hour guided tours of popular areas—you need only arrive at the meeting point 10 minutes before the start. Volunteer guides also conduct a two-hour walking tour of the Imperial Palace East Gardens on Wednesdays, Thursdays, and Saturdays. 🌐 *tokyosgg.jp/guide.html.*

BAR-HOPPING TOUR

Tokyo is famous for its nightlife, but it can be hard to know where to start. Magical Trip's Tokyo bar-hopping night tours are its most popular walking tours. They either take you to the Harajuku and Shibuya districts, including the famous Shibuya Scramble, or head over to Shinjuku to explore the areas of Kabukicho and Golden Gai. You'll pop into hidden bars that you'd never otherwise find, indulge in tasty street foods, and eat delicious Japanese dishes in traditional *izakaya* (Japanese pubs). 🌐 *www.magical-trip.com.*

SUMO STABLE TOUR

Wrestlers live in communal stables where all aspects of their daily lives are dictated by strict tradition. During a tour, you learn about the historical roots of sumo wrestling, gain a deeper understanding of sumo rituals, and even get a photo with the wrestlers after the session. Many sumo stables offer events aimed at tourists. To find activities, check 🌐 *sumoexperience.com.*

URBAN KAYAKING TOUR

Why not break from the sea of landlubber humanity by paddling along urban waterways? Tokyo Great Kayaking Tour specializes in kayaking adventures throughout Nihonbashi, Monzen Nakacho, and Shirakawa. If you time it right, you might even be able to join a twilight excursion or a particularly special one for cherry-blossom viewing. 🌐 *www.tokyokayaking.jp.*

COCKTAIL-THEMED TOUR

Arigato Travel is a food specialist, with knowledgeable guides offering tours throughout the city, including Asakusa, Shinjuku, and Shibuya. But if cocktails are you're thing, and you want to discover some hidden spots with the help of a fellow lush, check out Agrigato's evening tour that starts in Ginza. 🌐 *arigatojapan.co.jp.*

Under-the-Radar Tokyo Neighborhoods

KIYOSUMI
This old-fashioned, small-scale neighborhood east of Tokyo Station has many modern independent coffeehouses—as well as residences, shops, and small businesses—along its streets and alleys. The neighborhood's namesake garden is a landscaped jewel amid tall buildings.

SHIBAMATA
Well northeast of bustling Asakusa, this neighborhood has all the Showa-era, mid-20th-century nostalgia you could ask for packed into a very walkable area. Its shopping street, Taishakuten Sando, is lined with stores purveying old-fashioned snacks and souvenirs.

IKEBUKURO
Although it has a busy train station and the same shopping opportunities as nearby Shinjuku, Ikebukuro is, nevertheless, often overlooked by tourists. It's also home to the Jiyu Gakuen Myokakan, one of the last remaining Frank Lloyd Wright–designed buildings in Japan.

SHIMOKITAZAWA
The hippies of 1960s Tokyo made Shimokitazawa a counterculture enclave. These days, though, this neighborhood northwest of Shibuya is more of a hipster haunt with a linear park along a former rail line, indie crafts shops, vintage stores, curry restaurants, cafés, and occasional markets.

NAKAMEGURO AND DAIKANYAMA
These two upscale residential neighborhoods south of Shibuya run along either side of the Meguro River. In addition to sleek urban complexes, high-end boutiques, art galleries, and fashionable cafés, they also have cozy bars and shops selling books, records and crafts. The riverbanks are among Tokyo's top *hanami* (cherry-blossom viewing) spots. In spring, people flock to the area to enjoy offerings at riverside food trucks, toast the sunset with a glass of champagne, and watch the trees become bathed in lantern light.

YANAKA
Charming Yanaka, a short walk from Ueno Park's north end, was developed during the Edo period and is one of the only areas in Tokyo to have survived both the 1923 earthquake and the firebombing of WWII. Today, it's a neighborhood of artisans and art galleries as well as time-honored temples and traditional wooden houses. Be sure to spend some time on the Yanaka Ginza shopping street.

TODEN ARAKAWA LINE
From Waseda Station, this nostalgic tram travels through Ikebukuro, Sugamo, Arawaka, and Minowabashi, offering the chance to experience workaday neighborhoods on a ride that's especially lovely when the cherry blossoms are in bloom—hence the tram's nickname of Tokyo Sakura Tram.

SUGAMO
On Jizo Dori shopping street in low-key Sugamo, nicknamed "Harajuku for Grannies," look for inexpensive, practical items like bags and umbrellas. Some shops also sell red underwear—traditionally worn to bring good luck and health.

KICHIJOJI
Next to Mitaka in western Tokyo, Kichijoji typically makes the list of places where Tokyoites would most like to live. It's got a youthful vibe with lots of sidewalk cafés and cute boutiques. In an area called Harmonica Yokocho, covered shopping streets are filled with tiny restaurants and bars.

KAGURAZAKA
This area near Shinjuku is still home to some of the geisha houses founded in the Edo period. Today, it's favored by French expats and is known for its cafés and restaurants.

TSUKISHIMA
This man-made island in Tokyo Bay is best known for its old shopping street now dominated by restaurants serving *monjayaki*, the city's version of the savory *okonomiyaki* pancake that's cooked at your table on a griddle.

JIYUGAOKA
Stylish and sophisticated, with a European flavor, Jiyugaoka, to the southwest of Shibuya, is famous for sweets: it's the birthplace of the Japanese version of the Mont-Blanc dessert. The Green Street promenade is lined with trees, boutiques, and cafés.

What to Read and Watch Before Your Trip

TOKYO: A SPATIAL ANTHROPOLOGY

The perfect travel preparation text, particularly if you plan to wander the streets of Tokyo, Hidenobu Jinnai's nonfiction book provides you with layers of context to the streets and buildings you'll see. The Japanese architectural historian explores the roots of the city, using visuals to walk the reader through what went into forming the Tokyo of today from the centuries of architecture and natural disasters to wars and cultural influences.

SHOPLIFTERS

Director Hirokazu Koreeda's indie movie premiered in 2018 to much critical and popular acclaim, winning a Palme d'Or at Cannes Film Festival, an Oscar nomination, and the Japan Academy Prize for Picture of the Year. The film's Japanese title, *Manbiki Kazoku* (*The Shoplifting Family*), is perhaps more insightful. This isn't just a story about crime; it's also a touching tale about the relationships between people on the margins of society and how all that can be upended when their secrets are exposed.

IN THE MISO SOUP

Economic decline in late 20th-century Japan, as an inflation bubble burst, inspired a wave of crime fiction full of political and social commentary. Ryu Murakami's is one such violent thriller that has been translated into English. It's a story about a Japanese man who leads "sex tours" for tourists through the back alleys of Tokyo's Shinjuku District. It's also the story of an American serial killer, as well as of a young Japanese protagonist disillusioned with his hometown and its economic situation—and of Shinjuku's underbelly, and the violence that too often appears there.

TOKYO GODFATHERS

No list of Tokyo cinema would be complete without some anime (animated movies), a widely popular genre that has earned a cult international following and focuses on colorfully drawn characters and their dramatic, often fantastical adventures. Directed by Satoshi Kon, this anime is a bit more rooted in reality, albeit a tragic one, featuring a group of homeless residents, each with their own distinct story, and a lost baby. Heartfelt and entertaining, it's a fun, animated exploration of Tokyo.

THE WIND-UP BIRD CHRONICLE

Haruki Murakami is an essential figure in Japanese contemporary literature, especially for an English-speaking audience since quality translations of his work are easy to find. His novels are typically set in Tokyo, often infused with illusory or futuristic elements that distort—or sometimes magnify—the city. Three Murakami novels are particularly good introductions to his work: alluring mystery and exploration in *The Wind-Up Bird Chronicle*; nostalgic longing in *Norwegian Wood*; or a single late-night out on the Tokyo streets in *After Dark*.

TAMPOPO

Juzo Itami wrote and directed this 1985 comedy celebrating food and its influence on Japanese society. The offbeat and satirical humor in the story explores human nature, prescriptive habits of the Japanese, class, and feelings of obligation (an important background theme in much of Japanese storytelling), all within the backdrop of a ramen shop.

STRANGE WEATHER IN TOKYO

Hiromi Kawakami's story of a woman's unlikely relationship with an elderly former teacher lays out delicious morsels of daily Tokyo life, described in beauty and detail, from its cherry trees and markets, to bottles of sake and dishes of delicacies. It is Kawakami's quirky and fascinating characters that really bring her writing to life. *The Nakano Thrift Shop* is another of her funny explorations of human interactions and relationships.

GODZILLA

Now somewhat kitschy and distorted by its Americanized franchise and wider pop culture, the original 1954 *Godzilla*—about a lizardlike behemoth terrorizing Tokyo—is a classic film, with haunting undertones about a grieving country in the wake of World War II and specifically the use of atom bombs in Nagasaki and Hiroshima. The miniaturized sets of Tokyo used here are added entertainment; these early special effects set the stage for many action-packed Japanese movies to come.

THE CAT AND THE CITY

Author Nick Bradley connects the wanderings of a stray cat through Tokyo with the people who also occupy the fast-changing city. The cat is the link between the different characters who are also struggling in the big city, and she slowly draws them together.

AN AUTUMN AFTERNOON

The Japanese title of this 1962 film, *Sanma no Aji* (*The Taste of Sanma* [a fish commonly eaten in the fall]) is a hint at the timing in the story of the patriarch of a family coming to realize the responsibilities expected of him. This was the final film by Yasujiro Ozu, who is known for filming as if sitting in *seiza* (the seating posture on one's knees, which is expected in polite situations).

OUT

In the first of Natsuo Kirino's popular books that have been translated in English (by Stephen Snyder), Kirino makes sharp social commentary as she takes on Japanese crime fiction with a feminist gaze. This novel is full of surprising, often dark and grotesque twists. What appears as a simple thriller, following a group of female factory workers involved in a murder, comes with layers of perspective on contemporary Tokyo and the societal challenges faced by women.

TO LIVE (IKIRU)

Akira Kurosawa is a giant of Japanese cinema. This 1952 film tells the story of a terminally ill bureaucrat in Tokyo trying to make his last days meaningful. While Kurosawa's films are widely celebrated and for good reason, this one is perhaps his most moving story.

Budget Travel Tips

Tokyo can be painfully expensive, but here are some tips that can help ease the strain on the travel budget.

LODGING

Big chain hotels can be expensive, but Japan also has "business hotels" that provide small, basic rooms at very reasonable prices that often include breakfast. Look for chains like Toyoko Inn, Dormy Inn, and Comfort Inn. You can sometimes get discounted rates by signing up for free membership cards, especially at Toyoko Inn.

Another saving option, if you or someone you know can read Japanese, is to book via one of Japan's discount travel companies, which usually give good rates that include extras like breakfast.

If there are four of you traveling together, youth hostels can be an attractive budget option—rooms are often set up for four people, so there will be no sharing with strangers. Hostels also tend to be very clean, usually offer meals at a good price, and are often in popular tourist areas.

TRANSPORTATION

If you are traveling around Japan, the JR Pass can save you some money (if fully utilized) and allow you to use most Shinkansen services. It will also get you on JR sleeper trains, which can save on accommodation costs. If you are just planning a weekend out of Tokyo, stop by a major train station and ask about passes for the area. For instance, the Hakone Free Pass, which can be bought at Shinjuku Station, covers the train fare to and from Hakone on the Odakyu Line as well as unlimited use of otherwise expensive buses, sightseeing boats, cable cars, and local trains for two or three days in Hakone.

FOOD

Eating takeout from department store basement food halls is one way to save money. You will save even more if you wait until about an hour before closing, when many prepared foods are marked down 25%–50%. Ready-made lunches and dinners can be found at big supermarkets like Summit and Ito Yokado, as well as smaller supermarkets and convenience stores like Lawson and 7-Eleven. Such places also sell surprisingly tasty bento and pasta dishes for around ¥600, as well as *onigiri* (rice balls) and sandwiches for under ¥500.

To save on higher-end dining, eat at lunchtime. Many expensive restaurants do smaller, but still extremely good, lunches at a fraction of the price of their evening courses.

SHOPPING

For deals on the (almost) latest Japanese cameras and accessories, try somewhere like Map Camera in Shinjuku. Many Japanese amateur photographers frequently upgrade to the newest models, so you will find plenty of very modern but well-priced used gear in great condition.

For more bargain-hunting, head to the Ameyoko Street Market by JR Ueno Station. You can find everything from the freshest seafood to a can of Spam, real Rolex watches to fake Gucci bags, and everything else in between—much of it at decent prices.

Flea markets can be a good source for budget-friendly souvenirs. There's a major antiques market usually held the first and third Sunday of the month at Tokyo International Forum in Yurakucho, weekend flea markets in Shimokitazawa, as well as many other flea markets set up at shrines, such as the Sunday market at Hanazono Jinja in Shinjuku.

ISOLATION AND ENGAGEMENT: A HISTORY OF JAPAN

By Robert Morel

A century and a half after opening its shores to outsiders, Japan is still a mystery to many Westerners. Often misunderstood, Japan's history is much deeper than the stereotypes of samurai and geisha, overworked businessmen, and anime. Its long tradition of retaining the old while embracing the new has captivated visitors for centuries.

Much of Japanese history has consisted of the ongoing tension between its seeming isolation from the rest of the world and a desire to be a part of it. During the Edo period, Japan was closed to foreigners for some 250 years. Yet while the country has always had a strong national identity, it has also had a rapacious appetite for all things foreign. Just 50 years after opening its borders, parts of Tokyo looked like London, and Japan had become a colonial power in Asia. Much earlier, the Japanese imported Buddhism, tea, and their first writing system from China.

In the 19th century, the country incorporated Western architecture, technology, and government. More recently, the Japanese have absorbed Western fashion, music, and pop culture. Nevertheless, the country's history lives on in local traditions, festivals, temples, cities, music, and the arts.

(Above) Senso-ji Complex in Tokyo's Asakusa neighborhood

593–622: Prince Shotoku encourages the Japanese to embrace Chinese culture

710–784: Japan has first permanent capital at Nara

650 800 95

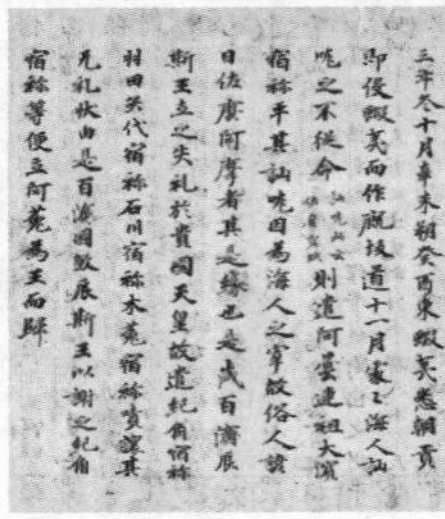

三年冬十月辛未朔癸酉東蝦夷悉朝貢
即役蝦夷而作廐坂道十一月處〻海人訕
哤之不從命 則遣阿曇連祖大濱
宿禰平其訕哤因爲海人之宰故俗人諺
曰佐麼阿摩者其是緣也是歲百濟辰
斯王立之失禮於貴國天皇故遣紀角宿禰
羽田矢代宿禰石川宿禰木菟宿禰嘖讓其
无禮狀由是百濟國殺辰斯王以謝之紀角
宿禰等便立阿花爲王而歸

(Top) Horyu-ji Temple, (Bottom) Nihon Shoki, (Right) Large Buddha statue at Todai-ji Temple

10,000 BC–AD 622 Ancient Japan

The first people in Japan were the hunters and fishers of the Jomon period, known for their pottery. In the following Yayoi period, hunting and fishing gave way to agriculture, as well as the introduction of rice farming and metalworking. Around AD 500, the Yamato tribe consolidated power in what is now the Kansai plain, with Yamato leaders claiming descent from the sun goddess Amaterasu and taking the title of emperor. Prince Shotoku promoted the spread of Buddhism from China and commissioned Horyu-ji Temple in Nara in 607.

- **Horyu-ji Temple (Nara)**
- **National Museum (Tokyo)**

710–784 Nara Period

As Japan's first permanent capital and urban center, Nara is often considered the birthplace of Japanese culture. Under the Emperor Shomu, who commissioned the Great Buddha at Todai-ji Temple, Buddhism rose to prominence. The first Japanese written histories, the *Kojiki* and *Nihon Shoki*, were compiled during this period, as was the *Manyoshu*, Japan's first collection of poetry. Since the country was the Eastern terminus of the Silk Road, Japan's royal family amassed an impressive collection of treasures from mainland Asia, many of which are still on display at Todai-ji Temple's Shoso-in.

- **The Great Buddha at Todai-ji Temple (Nara)**

794–1160 Heian Period

Partly to escape intrigu and the rising power of the Nara's Buddhist priests, in 794, Empero Kammu moved the capital to Heian-kyo (now Kyoto). *Heian* translates roughly as "peace and tranquility," and during this time the Imperial court expanded its power throughout Japan Inside the court, however, life was far from calm. This was a period of great courtl intrigue and struggles for power between aristocrats, the powerful Fujiwara clan (the most powerful of Japan's four great noble families), and the new military class known as *bushi*. Though some emperors managed to maintain control of the court, the Heian

'94–1160: The capital is moved from Nara to Heian-kyo (now Kyoto)

1467–77: The Onin Wars initiate a 100-year period of civil war

1100 1250 1400 1550

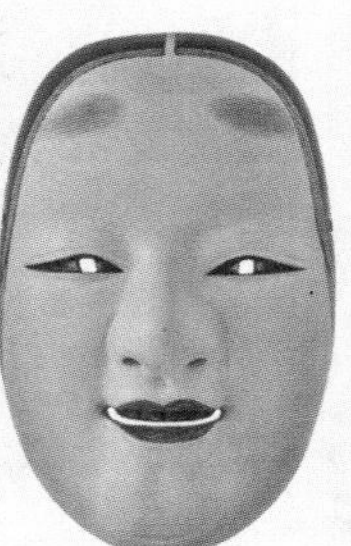

(Right) Zen Garden at the Ryoan-ji Temple, (Top) Noh masks, (Left) Kyoto Imperial Palace's wooden orange gates.

period saw the slow rise of the military class, leading to a series of wars that established them as the ruling class until well into the 19th century. Considered Japan's great classical period, this was a time when courtly arts flourished. The new Japanese kana script gave rise to a boom in literature. Compiled in 990, Sei Shonagon's *Pillow Book* gave a window into courtly life, and Shikibu Murasaki's *Tale of Genji* is often regarded as the world's first classic novel. Japanese *waka* poetry experienced a revival, breeding the new forms of poetry such as tanka that are still in use today.

- The Imperial Palace (Kyoto)

1185–1335 Kamakura Period

As the Imperial Court lost control, the Genpei War (1180–1185) resulted in the defeat of clans loyal to the emperor in Kyoto and the rise of a new government in Kamakura. Yoritomo Minamoto named himself Sei-i Tai Shogun and established the Kamakura *bakufu*, a spartan military government. During this time, Japan repelled two Mongol invasions, thanks to timely typhoons that were later dubbed "kamikaze," or "divine wind." In this militaristic climate, Zen Buddhism, with its focus on self-reliance and discipline, exploded in popularity.

- Eihiji Temple (Fukushima)
- Hachimangu Shrine and the Great Buddha (Kamakura)

1336–1568 Muromachi (Ashikaga) Period

The heyday of the samurai, the Muromachi period, was one of near constant civil war. Feudal lords known as *daimyo* consolidated their power in local fiefdoms. Peasant rebellions and piracy were common. Nevertheless, trade flourished. The movement of armies required daimyo to build roads, while improved communications gave birth to many merchant and artisan guilds. Trade with China grew, and in 1543 Portugal began trading with Japan, introducing firearms and Christianity. Noh theater and the tea ceremony were founded, and Kyoto's most famous temples were built in this period.

- Kinkaku-ji Temple (Kyoto)
- Ryoan-ji Temple (Kyoto)

1637: Japan is closed to the outside world except for a Dutch trading post in Nagasaki

1720: Ban on Western literature lifted

1600 1650 1700 175

(Left) Matsumoto Castle, (Top) three wise monkeys at Toshogu shrine, (Right) woodcut of Kabuki actor by Utagawa Toyokuni

1568–1600 National Unification (Momoyama Period)

In 1568 Oda Nobunaga, a lord from Owari in central Japan, marched on Kyoto and took the title of Shogun. He controlled the surrounding territories until his death in 1582, when his successor, Toyotomi Hideyoshi, became the new Shogun. After unifying much of central and western Japan, he attempted unsuccessful invasions of Korea before his death in 1598. In 1600 Tokugawa Ieyasu, a top general, defeated Hideyoshi's successor in the Battle of Sekigahara.

■ **Osaka Castle (Osaka)**

■ **Matsumoto Castle (Matsumoto)**

1600–1867 Edo (Tokugawa) Period

The Edo period ushered in 250 years of relative stability and central control. After becoming Shogun, Ieyasu Tokugawa moved the capital to Edo (present-day Tokyo). A system of *daimyo*, lords beholden to the Shogun, was established along with a rigid class system and legal code of conduct. Although Japan cut off trade with the outside world, cities flourished. By the mid-18th century, Edo's population had grown to more than 1 million, and urban centers like Osaka and Kyoto had become densely populated. Despite such rapid growth, urban life in the Edo period was highly organized, with districts managed by neighborhood associations that have persisted (in a modified way) to the present day. Popular entertainment and arts arose to satisfy the thriving merchant and artisan classes. Kabuki, flashy and sensational, overtook Noh theater in popularity, and Japan's famed "floating world" (*ukio*), with its theaters, drinking houses, and geishas, emerged. Sumo, long a Shinto tradition, became a professional sport. Much of what both Japanese and foreigners consider "Japanese culture dates to this period. But by 1853, the Shogun's hold on power was growing tenuous.

■ **Toshogu (Nikko)**

■ **Katsura Imperial Villa (Kyoto) Muhammad Ali Mosque**

1853: U.S. Commodore Matthew Perry reopens Japan to foreign trade

1868: Meiji Restoration begins

1941: Japan attacks Pearl Harbor

1800 1850 1900 1950

(Top) Tokyo University, (Left) wedding in Meiji Shrine, (Bottom) A6M5 fighter plane at Yusyukan museum.

Meiji Period

1868–1912

The Tokugawa Shogunate's rigid class system and legal code proved to be its undoing. After U.S. Commodore Matthew Perry opened Japan to trade in March 1854, the following years were turbulent. In 1868, the last Shogun, Tokugawa Yoshinobu, ceded power to Emperor Meiji, and Japan began to modernize after 250 years of isolation. Adopting a weak parliamentary system from Germany, rulers moved quickly to develop national industry and universities. Victories over China and Russia also emboldened Japan.

- **Tokyo University (Tokyo)**
- **Heian Shrine (Kyoto)**
- **Nara National Museum (Nara)**

Taisho Period

1912–1925

In the early 20th century, urban Japan was beginning to look like Europe and North America. Fashion ranged from traditional *yukata* and kimono to zoot suits and bobbed hair. In 1923 the Great Kanto Earthquake and its resulting fires destroyed Yokohama and much of Tokyo. Although city planners saw this as an opportunity to modernize Tokyo's maze of streets, residents were quick to rebuild, ensuring that many neighborhood maps look much the same today as they did a century ago.

- **Asakusa (Tokyo)**
- **The Shitamachi Museum (Tokyo)**
- **Meiji Shrine (Tokyo)**

Wartime Japan

1926–1945

Although Japan was was increasingly liberal throughout the 1920s, the economic shocks of the 1930s helped the military gain greater control, resulting in crackdowns on left-leaning groups, the press, and dissidents. In 1931 Japan invaded Manchuria; in 1937 Japan captured Nanking, killing many civilians. Joining the Axis powers in 1936, Japan continued its expansion in Asia and in 1941 attacked Pearl Harbor. After the atomic bombings of Hiroshima and Nagasaki, the emperor announced Japan's surrender on August 15, 1945.

- **Hiroshima Peace Memorial Park (Hiroshima)**
- **Yasukuni Shrine Museum (Tokyo)**

1964: Tokyo hosts the Summer Olympic games

1989: Emperor Hirohito dies

2006: Shinzo Abe elected as the country's youngest prime minister

2009: Liberal Democratic Party loses power

2019: Emperor Akihito abdicates. Reiwa period begins.

1970 | 1990 | 2010 | 203

(Top) 1964 Summer Olympics, Tokyo, (Bottom) manga comic books, (Right) Shinjuku, Tokyo

1945–1989

Postwar Japan and the Economic Miracle

The initial postwar years were hard on Japan. More than half of Japan's total urban area was in ruins, its industry in shambles, and food shortages common. Kyoto was the only major metropolitan area in the country that escaped widespread damage. Thanks to an educated, dedicated population and smart planning, however, Japan was soon on the road to recovery. A new democratic government was formed and universal suffrage extended to all adult men and women. Japan's famous "Peace Constitution" forbade the country from engaging in warfare. With cooperation from the government, old companies like Matsushita (Panasonic), Mitsubishi, and Toyota began exporting Japanese goods en masse, while upstarts like Honda pushed their way to the top. In 1964 Japan joined the Organization for Economic Cooperation and Development's group of "rich nations" and hosted the Tokyo Olympics. At the same time, anime began gaining popularity at the box office and on TV, with Osamu Tezuka's classic *Tetsuwan Atom* (*Astro Boy*) making a splash when it aired in 1963. In the 1970s and '80s Japan became as well known for its electronics as its cars, with Nintendo, Sony, and Panasonic becoming household names abroad.

- **Showa-Kan (Takayama)**
- **National Stadium (Yoyogi Park)**

1990–PRESENT

From Goods to Culture

Unfortunately, much of Japan's rapid growth in the 1980s was unsustainable. By 1991 the bubble had burst, leading to 20 years of limited economic expansion. Japan avoided an economic crisis, and most people continued to lead comfortable, if somewhat simpler, lives. After decades of exporting goods, Japan has—particularly since 2000—become an exporter of culture in the form of animation, video games, and cuisine. Japan, famous for importing ideas, has begun to send its own culture to the world.

- **Shinjuku, Harajuku, and Shibuya, (Tokyo)**
- **Akihabara (Tokyo)**
- **Manga Museum (Kyoto)**

Chapter 2

TRAVEL SMART

Updated by
Alexandra Ziminski

★ CAPITAL:
Tokyo

POPULATION:
9.67 million in central Tokyo; 37 million in the Greater Tokyo region

LANGUAGE:
Japanese

$ CURRENCY:
Japanese yen; pronounced "en" in Japanese

COUNTRY CODE:
+81

⚠ EMERGENCIES:
Police service 110; ambulance and fire services 119

DRIVING:
On the left

ELECTRICITY:
110v/50 cycles; plugs have two flat prongs

TIME:
Japan Standard Time (GMT+9)

WEB RESOURCES:
www.gotokyo.org
www.japan.travel/en
www.japantimes.co.jp

Know Before You Go

Should you tip? Is the water okay to drink? Can you trust that your luggage will arrive safely if you send it ahead to your next hotel? And what's this about not opening or closing the taxi doors?

LOOK INTO RAIL PASSES

The Japan Rail Pass (JR Pass) covers most JR trains for 7, 14, or 21 days. While expensive (the seven-day pass costs ¥50,000), they might be worth purchasing if you're taking several journeys. If, however, you're only planning one or two Shinkansen (bullet train) trips, you're probably better off buying individual tickets. Seats, unreserved and reserved, can be bought one month in advance and up to a few minutes before the train leaves. You can purchase them at ticket offices in major stations, like Ueno and Shinjuku; at machines in stations that operate the Shinkansen; and online through the official Japan Rail companies. The smart EX App has Shinkansen tickets for top routes including Tokyo to Osaka, Nagoya, and Hiroshima. Other regional passes, such as the Hokuriku Arch Pass, Tokyo Wide Pass, and JR East Tohoku Area Pass, include travel from Tokyo.

TAKE PUBLIC TRANSPORT

Tokyo's train and subway network is comprehensive. To make using it easy, buy a Pasmo or Suica rechargeable IC card at the airport or major stations for ¥500 (a deposit you can get back minus a small processing fee if you hand in the card at a station to reclaim any money left on it). The alternative Welcome Suica doesn't require a deposit but runs out after 28 days. Both cards can be charged at station ticket machines. You can then tap them on ticket gates and have your fare automatically deducted. If you have an iPhone, you can also add a Suica to your Apple Wallet and tap your phone. IC cards can also be used on buses, at vending machines, and in convenience stores.

STAY CONNECTED

To stay connected during your trip, rent a portable Wi-Fi or get a SIM or eSIM with data. If you're bringing a laptop or want to connect to multiple devices, then a pocket Wi-Fi router is more cost-effective. Ninja WiFi rents pocket Wi-Fi routers for under ¥1,000 per day that can be reserved online before your trip and picked up and dropped off at the airport. eSIMs are the way to go if you only plan to take your phone (and the phone is eSIM compatible). eSIMs allow you to connect to a new carrier while abroad and take advantage of data packages. 1GB plans from Airalo start at around ¥700. For free Wi-Fi, look out for the Japan Connected Free Wi-Fi. It offers free access points at stations, landmarks, and other points of interest.

THERE'S (ALMOST) NO NEED TO TIP

Regardless of how much you appreciate the service and staff, tipping is not expected. That said, feel free to tip a private guide or driver who's used to working with tourists (hand them the money in an envelope with both hands). Tipping is also acceptable at a ryokan where meals are served in your room. Tip ¥1,000–¥2,000 per person per day at a ryokan where you have an attendant. Hand the tip over *during check-in* and in an envelope.

DOWNLOAD A TRANSLATION APP

While English is understood, it is not widely spoken in Japan, so download a translation app before you travel. Google Translate handles Japanese to English consistently well (with the occasional incomprehensible translation of menus). You can type into it, but it also has a camera function that can translate written text, and with its conversation function you can interpret short phrases. Just remember to download the Japanese language settings before using it.

LEARN A FEW WORDS

You will get by just fine in Tokyo without speaking a word of Japanese, but learning and using a few key words or phrases will be appreciated by locals. Try *konnichiwa* (a more formal hello), *arigato* (thank you), and the multipurpose *domo* (casual hello or thank you). And don't forget *sumimasen* (excuse me) and *gomen nasai* (sorry).

NOW, SHUSH!

The trains may be crowded, but they're also—remarkably—quiet. Out of respect for fellow passengers, set your phone to silent mode while on public transport. If you also keep your voice low, you'll fit right in.

DO NOT EAT ON THE GO

Although it's common to see people snacking and drinking on the go in most major cities, this is seen as crude in Japan. It's also considered bad manners to eat inside trains, the exception being on the Shinkansen or other long-distance express trains. Signs at markets remind you to eat at the stall rather than to wander with food. As you'll rarely see a trash can on the street, plan to carry all your trash with you.

KNOW HOW TO TAKE A TAXI

Taxis are a good (albeit costly) way to get around Tokyo, and you can find them on busy corners, or you can hail them on the street. Drivers are, for the most part, courteous, though not necessarily chatty. Unless you're going to a well-known destination such as a major hotel, have your destination written out in Japanese (your hotel concierge can do this for you). Drivers speak varying levels of English so it's best if they can use their car navigation system. Also, don't open or close the doors yourself; the driver does this using a lever by his seat. Taxis accept credit cards, and remember: there's no need to tip.

SHIP YOUR LUGGAGE BETWEEN HOTELS

Avoid hauling luggage around on crowded public transit by using moderately priced Takkyubin luggage delivery services, which transport parcels and luggage from door to door nationwide. You can even ship your bags from Narita Airport to your hotel on arrival. This service is especially useful if your itinerary includes rail travel, as trains have little storage space, and some Shinkansen lines require you to reserve specific seats if you have oversized luggage. Same-day (within one city) or next-day delivery can usually be arranged through hotels.

PREPARE FOR A QUAKE

Japan experiences frequent earthquakes. Make a note of emergency contact numbers for your embassy, check the evacuation route from your hotel room (usually on the door), and read up on what to do in an earthquake (stay away from windows, get under something sturdy to protect your head, and hold on). Luckily, Japan has strict building codes. There's also an early warning system, which sends alerts to phones ahead of a quake. If you hear lots of alarms all at once, that's probably what it is. For alerts in English, download the NHK World app on your smartphone. You can also visit 🌐 *www3.nhk.or.jp/nhkworld.*

Getting Here and Around

 Air

Flying time to Japan is 14 hours from New York, 13 hours from Chicago, and 10 hours from Los Angeles. The trip east, because of tailwinds, can be even an hour shorter, and the trip west that much longer because of headwinds.

Most major U.S. airports offer multiple direct flights to Tokyo each day. Flights to Osaka or Nagoya usually involve a transfer, though some west coast hubs like San Francisco and Los Angeles run direct flights.

Japan Airlines (JAL, ⊕ *www.jal.co.jp*), United Airlines (⊕ *www.united.com*), American Airlines (⊕ *www.aa.com*), Delta Airlines (⊕ *www.delta.com*), and All Nippon Airways (ANA, ⊕ *www.ana.co.jp*) link North American cities with Tokyo's Haneda and Narita airports. Most of these airlines also fly in and out of Japan's two other international airports, Kansai International Airport, located south of Osaka and Centrair, near Nagoya.

Because of the distance, fares to Japan tend to be expensive, usually around $1,600 for a seat in coach. Both JAL and ANA have cost-saving passes and special fares for flights within the country. Note, you must book well in advance, and there are restrictions during peak times, so check before your arrival. All domestic flights are no-smoking.

■ TIP→ **Visit a tourist information center to find out about local transportation packages that include tickets to major museum exhibits or other special events.**

AIRPORTS

The major gateway to Japan is Tokyo's Narita Airport (NRT, ⊕ *www.narita-airport.jp*), which is 80 km (50 miles) northeast of the city and has three terminals: Terminals 1 and 2 for international flights and the newer Terminal 3 is for flights on domestic and international low-cost carriers. Terminal 1 has two adjoining wings, north and south. When you arrive, convert some money into yen or withdraw yen from an ATM; you may need it for transportation into Tokyo. In both wings, ATMs and money-exchange counters are in the wall between the customs inspection area and the arrival lobby.

Terminals 1 and 2 have a Japan National Tourism Organization information center, where you can get free maps, brochures, and other visitor information. Both terminals also have counters (directly across from customs-area exits) for airport limousine buses and express trains to Tokyo.

If you have time to kill at Narita, take a local Keisei Line train into Narita (the town) 15 minutes away, where a traditional shopping street and the beautiful Narita-san Shinsho Temple are a peaceful escape from airport noise.

Haneda Airport (HND, ⊕ *www.tokyo-haneda.com*) is just 26 km (15.5 miles) southeast of central Tokyo. Most domestic flights use Haneda, which also an international terminal serving flights to and from major foreign cities. Stop by the currency exchange and Tourist Information Desk in the second-floor arrival lobby before heading into the city. There are also numerous concierge staffers on hand to answer questions.

Travel Times from Tokyo

To	By air	By car or bus	By train
Osaka	1¼ hours	7–8 hours	2½ hours
Hiroshima	1½ hours	10 hours	4 hours
Kyoto	1¼ hours	7 hours	2 hours
Fukuoka	2 hours	14 hours	5 hours
Sapporo	1½ hours	15 hours	8 hours

GROUND TRANSPORTATION

Known as "The Gateway to Japan," Narita is at least 90 minutes—depending on traffic—by taxi or bus from central Tokyo. The Keisei Skyliner and Japan Railways N'EX are the easiest and fastest ways to get into the city.

Directly across from the customs-area exits at both terminals are the ticket counters for buses to Tokyo. Buses leave from platforms just outside terminal exits, exactly on schedule; the departure time is on the ticket. The Airport Limousine (⊕ *webservice.limousinebus.co.jp/web/en*) has shuttle-bus service from Narita to Tokyo starting at ¥3,100. Cheaper options include Airport Bus TYO-NRT (¥1,300, ⊕ *tyo-nrt.com/en*).

Japan Railways (JR, ⊕ *www.jreast.co.jp/multi/index.html*) trains stop at Narita Airport Terminals 1 and 2. The most comfortable is the Narita Limited Express (N'EX), which serves more central stations (and beyond). Trains from the airport go directly to the central Tokyo Station in just about an hour, then continue toward Yokohama, but other routes stop at Shibuya and Shinjuku. Daily departures begin at 7:37 am; the last train is at 9:44 pm. In addition to regular seats, there is a first-class Green Car. All seats are reserved.

The Keisei Skyliner (⊕ *www.keisei.co.jp/keisei/tetudou/skyliner/us*) train runs every 20–30 minutes between the airport terminals and Keisei-Ueno Station. The trip takes around 40 minutes. The first Skyliner leaves Narita for Ueno at 7:23 am (7:30 am on weekends and holidays), the last at 11 pm. From Keisei-Ueno to Narita, the first Skyliner is at 5:40 am, the last at 8:20 pm. Keisei's slightly slower Access Express service also runs between Narita and Keisei-Ueno.

TIP→ If you are arriving with a Japan Rail Pass and staying in Tokyo for a few days, it might be best to pay for the transfer into the city and wait to activate the rail pass for travel beyond Tokyo.

Transfer between Narita and Haneda airports is easiest by the Airport Limousine Bus, which should take 65–85 minutes and cost ¥3,600. The Keisei Access Express also runs between the two airports, but some routes require a transfer at Aoto Station. From Haneda Airport, it's just a 25- to 30-minute monorail or Keikyu Line ride to central Tokyo.

 Bus

Japan Railways (JR, ⊕ *www.jrailpass.com/buses*) has a number of long-distance buses that are comfortable and inexpensive; it also runs short-distance buses in some areas that have limited rail service. You can use Japan Rail Passes on some, but not all, of these buses. Japan Rail Passes, however, are not accepted by private bus companies.

Bus routes and schedules change constantly, but tourist information offices have up-to-date details. It's now possible to travel from Osaka to Tokyo for less than ¥5,000 one way. Buses are generally modern and very comfortable, even some of the overnight buses. Daytime highway buses are often an excellent way to get to many interesting out-of-the-way destinations.

City buses, especially outside of Tokyo, are quite convenient, but be sure of your route and destination, because the bus driver probably won't speak English. Fares in the city are usually set (from ¥100 to ¥230); you pay as you board at the front of the bus. Outside Tokyo, you typically board at the back, take a ticket or tap your card and the cost is

Travel Times into Tokyo

FROM NARITA	TO	FARES	TIMES	NOTES
Airport Limousine (buses)	Various hotels in Tokyo and JR Tokyo and Shinjuku train stations	¥3,100	Roughly hourly until 8 or 9 pm	70–90 mins, can be longer in traffic
Airport Limousine (buses)	Tokyo City Air Terminal (TCAT)	¥3,100	At least one bus per hour, 7:20 am–11 pm	
Airport Bus TYO-NRT	Tokyo and Ginza Stations	¥1,300	Every 20-30 mins, 7:30 am–11:20 pm	
Narita Limited Express (N'EX)	Central Tokyo Station, then continue to Yokohama or Shinjuku	One-way fare ¥3,070 (return ¥5,000); Green Car from ¥3,840	Daily departures begin at 7:37 am; last train is at 9:44 pm	All seats are reserved.
Keisei Skyliner train	Keisei-Ueno Station	¥2,470	Every 20–30 mins, 7:23 am–11 pm	All seats are reserved.
Keisei Access Express	Keisei-Ueno Station	¥1,240	Every 20–30 mins, 5:41 am (5:46 am on weekends)–11:08 pm	No seats are reserved.
Taxi	Central Tokyo	¥30,000 or more		
FROM HANEDA	**TO**	**FARES**	**TIMES**	**NOTES**
Tokyo Monorail	Central Tokyo	¥520	Every 20 mins, 5:18 am–12:08 am	Trip takes 25–30 mins. Connect to other major stations via the Yamanote Line at Hamamatsucho Station (18 mins from Haneda).
Taxi	Central Tokyo	¥5,000–¥6,000 (¥7,800–¥9,900 to Shinjuku)		

determined by the distance you travel. You then put the ticket and the fare in the box as you get off the bus, or tap your card to pay.

Bus schedules can be hard to fathom if you don't read Japanese, however, so it's best to ask for help at a tourist information office. The Nihon Bus Association (🌐 *www.bus.or.jp*) has information about routes and companies. Japan Bus Online (🌐 *japanbusonline.com/en*) is another good resource.

Car

You must have an international driving permit (IDP) to drive in Japan. IDPs are available from the American Automobile Association and are valid only in conjunction with your regular driver's license (they are really nothing more than a multilingual translation of the information on your driver's license). Drivers must be 18 years of age. Driving is on the left.

Major roads in Japan are sufficiently marked in English, and on country roads there's usually someone to ask for help. However, it's a good idea to have a detailed map with town names written in *kanji* (Japanese characters) and *romaji* (romanized Japanese).

Car travel along the Tokyo–Kyoto–Hiroshima corridor and in other built-up areas of Japan is not as convenient as the trains. Roads are congested, gas is expensive, and highway tolls are exorbitant (tolls alone between Tokyo and Kyoto would cost you around ¥11,550).

Car-rental rates in Tokyo begin at around ¥6,500 a day, and some companies offer a roughly ¥35,000 weekly package, including tax, for an economy car with unlimited mileage. You should return the car with a full tank of gas, or pay their rate per kilometer traveled.

PARKING

There is little on-street parking in Japan. In busy areas, parking is usually in automated or staffed parking lots or in parking towers within buildings. Expect to pay upward of ¥400 per hour. On busy streets, parking regulations are strictly enforced, and illegally parked vehicles are towed away. Recovery fees start at ¥30,000 and increase hourly. Look for a large "P" that is typically used to indicate parking.

ROAD CONDITIONS

Roads in Japan are often narrower than those in the United States, but they're well maintained in general. Driving in cities can be troublesome, as there are many narrow, one-way streets and little in the way of English road signs except on major arteries. Japanese drivers tend to stick to the speed limit (except on the expressways), but they widely ignore bans on mobile-phone use and dashboard televisions.

Motorcycle

Japan is a pleasure to explore via motorcycle provided you are an experienced rider. Highways, rest stops, and campgrounds are all equipped to handle whatever bike you choose to tour with.

Japan Bike Rentals (🌐 *japanbikerentals.com*) allows you to do all the paperwork in English—and online. All riders need a passport, a valid unrestricted motorcycle license from their own country, and an International Driving Permit. Japan Bike Rentals is open seven days a week, but you must book online first, whether to rent a bike or a GPS or to join a guided tour. Rental819 (🌐 *www.rental819.com*) has a number of branches in Tokyo featuring Harley-Davidson, Ducati, and Triumph motorcycles.

Public Transport

Tokyo Metro (🌐 *www.tokyometro.jp*) and Toei (🌐 *www.kotsu.metro.tokyo.jp*) operate separate subway lines in Tokyo, with Tokyo Metro operating the majority of them. The companies charge separate fares—that is, a ticket from one company is not valid on a train operated by the other, so you want to complete a journey on lines operated by one company rather than switching. Some especially useful lines for visitors are the Ginza Line, which moves between Asakusa and Shibuya, and the Oedo and Marunouchi lines, which loop around the city center.

PREPAID CARDS AND PASSES

Rechargeable Suica (🌐 *www.jreast.co.jp/multi/en/pass/suica.html*) debit cards can be used on JR and non-JR trains and also subways. It's also accepted for payment at convenience stores and some vending machines. PASMO (🌐 *www.pasmo.co.jp/visitors/en*), another rechargeable

Getting Here and Around

prepaid card, operates the same way. You need to pay a ¥500 deposit to be issued a Suica or PASMO card, but it's worth it to avoid buying tickets and worrying about fares and have the flexibility to flit between all of Tokyo's transportation networks.

That said, chip shortages have meant that, sometimes, these cards aren't available. Check websites for updates and information on alternatives. For instance, iPhone users can add a Suica straight to their Apple Wallet. You might also be able to buy a Welcome Suica/Passmo Passport at the airport or online before you come from third party sellers.

The Tokyo 1-Day Ticket (Tokyo Furii Kippu, 🌐 *www.jreast.co.jp/multi/pass/tokyo_free.html*) allows unlimited single-day travel on JR lines, subways, and buses within Tokyo's 23 wards. It costs ¥1,600 and is available at subway stations and JR ticket offices.

PURCHASING TICKETS

Basic train and subway fares within Tokyo are between ¥140 and ¥330, depending on how far you travel. You'll find ticket machines that take coins or cash near the gates. Maps above each machine—usually in Japanese and English in central Tokyo—list destinations and fares.

■ TIP→ **If the station map is written only in Japanese, just buy the lowest-price ticket and adjust the fare upon arrival.**

Taxi

Taxis are expensive in Japan. In central Tokyo, for instance, the first kilometer (0.62 mile) costs ¥500, and then it's ¥100 for every additional 255 meters (279 yards). Between 10 pm and 5 am there is a 20% service charge on top of that. If possible, avoid using taxis during rush hours (7:30 am–9:30 am and 5 pm–7 pm). The trains will be faster.

To hail a cab simply raise your hand—no need to shout or wave wildly. A red light on the dashboard indicates an available taxi (and more and more indicate that in English as well as Japanese), and a green light indicates an occupied one.

Japanese taxis have automatic door-opening systems, so do not try to open the taxi door. Stand back when the cab comes to a stop—if you are too close, the door may slam into you. When you leave the cab, do not try to close the door; the driver will do it. Only the curbside rear door opens.

Train

Rail travel is a pleasure in Japan. Trains run frequently and on schedule. The Shinkansen (bullet train), one of the fastest trains in the world, connects major cities north and south of Tokyo. It's only slightly less expensive than flying, but it can be more convenient as train stations are more centrally located than airports.

Other trains, though not as fast as the Shinkansen, are just as convenient and substantially cheaper. There are three types of train services: *futsu* (local service), *tokkyu* (limited express service), and *kyuko* (express service). Many tokkyu and kyuko trains have a first-class compartment known as the Green Car.

■ TIP→ **Because there are no porters or carts at train stations, it's best to travel light when getting around by train. You can ship your larger bags to your next destination and bring only a carry-on.**

If you plan to travel extensively by rail, consider a Japan Rail Pass (🌐 *japanrail-pass.net*), which provides unlimited travel on Japan Railways (JR) trains (covering most destinations in Japan) but not on lines owned by other companies. For the Sanyo, Tokaido, and Kyushu Shinkansen lines, the pass is valid on any train, but you must buy an additional special ticket if you want to use the Nozomi and Mizuho, which stop infrequently. However, it is valid on all trains on the Yamagata, Tohoku, Joetsu, Akita, and Hokuriku Shinkansen lines.

The JR Pass is also valid on some local buses operated by Japan Railways, though not on the long-distance JR highway buses. You can make seat reservations without paying a fee on all trains that have reserved-seat coaches, usually long-distance trains. The Japan Rail Pass does not cover the cost of sleeping compartments on overnight trains.

You can purchase one-, two-, or three-week passes. Note, though, that a one-week pass is about as expensive as a regular round-trip ticket from Tokyo to Hiroshima on the Shinkansen, plus a stop at Kyoto or Osaka both ways. You must obtain a rail pass voucher prior to arrival in Japan (you cannot buy them in Japan), and the pass must be used within three months of purchase. The pass is available only to people with tourist visas. Buy it from a travel agent, or reserve it directly online before your trip.

■ TIP→ **When you arrive in Japan, you can exchange your voucher for the Japan Rail Pass at the Japan Railways desk in the arrivals hall at Narita Airport or at JR stations in major cities. When you make this exchange, you determine the day that you want the rail pass to begin and end. You do not have to begin travel on the day you make the exchange.**

Japan Rail Passes are available in coach class and first class (Green Car). A one-week pass costs ¥50,000 ordinary class, ¥70,000 first class; a two-week pass costs ¥80,000 ordinary class, ¥110,000 first class; and a three-week pass costs ¥100,000 ordinary class, ¥140,000 first class.

Rail pass holders must still reserve their train seats in advance. If you paid for the pass on the official website, free reservations can be made online up to a month in advance. Otherwise, you can also reserve seats using dedicated machines once you have exchanged your tickets in Japan. You can do this up to just minutes before the train departs. If you fail to make a train, there's no penalty, and you can get on the next one.

Transportation Planner

GETTING AROUND BY TRAIN

Japan (and Tokyo in particular) has one of the world's best train and subway systems: trains are nearly always on time, have clean facilities, and provide a safe environment.

Shinkansen: The JR Shinkansen "bullet" trains travel up and down Honshu and into Kyushu. Tokyo Station is Tokyo's main hub, with lines heading north, south, and west. Other Shinkansen lines run to Nagano and Kanazawa, Niigata, Yamagata, and other areas of Tohoku.

Regional trains: About 70% of Japan's railways are owned by Japan Railways (JR Group), the other 30% are owned by private companies. Non-JR lines include Tokyu's Toyoko Line between Tokyo's Shibuya and Yokohama to the south. The main line of the Odakyu Company and Keio Inokashira Line use Shinjuku and Shibuya, respectively, as hubs to serve the west of Tokyo.

For service to Saitama Prefecture, Tobu offers the Tojo Line, which leaves Tokyo from Ikebukuro Station. The most important JR-owned regional line in Tokyo is the Yamanote Line, which loops around the city, while its Sobu and Chuo lines cross that circle east to west; JR trains also travel to Tokyo Disneyland.

Subways: The easiest way to explore Tokyo is via subway. There are two subway companies: Tokyo Metro and Toei. Because these are separate entities, they have separate fares, and it's cheaper to stay with one company. At the outer edges of the subway networks, private companies operate the line. If you're going far afield, be prepared to pay an additional fare.

Tokyo monorail: Beginning at Hamamatsu-cho Station, the monorail provides easy access to Haneda Airport.

PURCHASING TICKETS

In Tokyo and other major cities basic fares (train or subway) are between ¥140 and ¥330. Tickets can be purchased from machines that take coins or cash near the gates. Maps above the machines—usually in Japanese and English—give destinations and corresponding fares.

■ TIP→ **Get a rechargeable train card to make train travel much smoother as you don't have to figure out the ticket price for every trip. These cards can be used for most trains (and some buses) throughout Japan regardless of the city where you buy it.**

The cards have different names depending on the city: in Tokyo, it's **Suica** (from JR machines) or **PASMO** (from subway machines); in Hokkaido, **Kitaca**; in much of the JR West service area, **ICOCA** cards. Tokyo has some one-day passes including the **Tokunai Pass** for unlimited use of JR lines and the **Tokyo Free Kippu,** which covers subways and buses. Purchase tickets for Shinkansen lines and other long-distance regional lines that require a seat reservation at a ticket window.

SHINKANSEN TICKETS

If you are only planning on doing one or two bullet train trips, purchasing individual tickets is better than buying a JR Pass. You can get tickets for the Shinkansen up to one month in advance in person at ticket offices in major stations and at machines in stations that run the Shinkansen.

You can also purchase seats online, though because of the different Shinkansen companies, you need to go to the dedicated website that runs the route you're interested in. (From Tokyo to Kyoto for example, you'll need to use 🌐 *smart-ex.jp/en/index.php.*) Alternatively, you can also purchase tickets from third-party sellers.

HOW TO USE A TICKET MACHINE

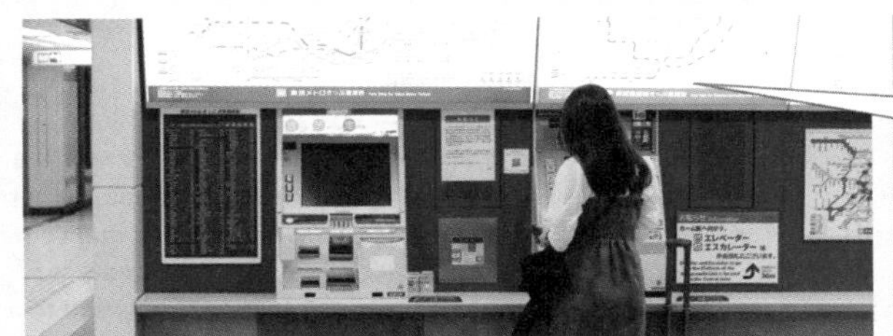

Use the map above the ticket machine to determine how much money to put on your ticket. The numbers next to each stop indicate the price from your current station.

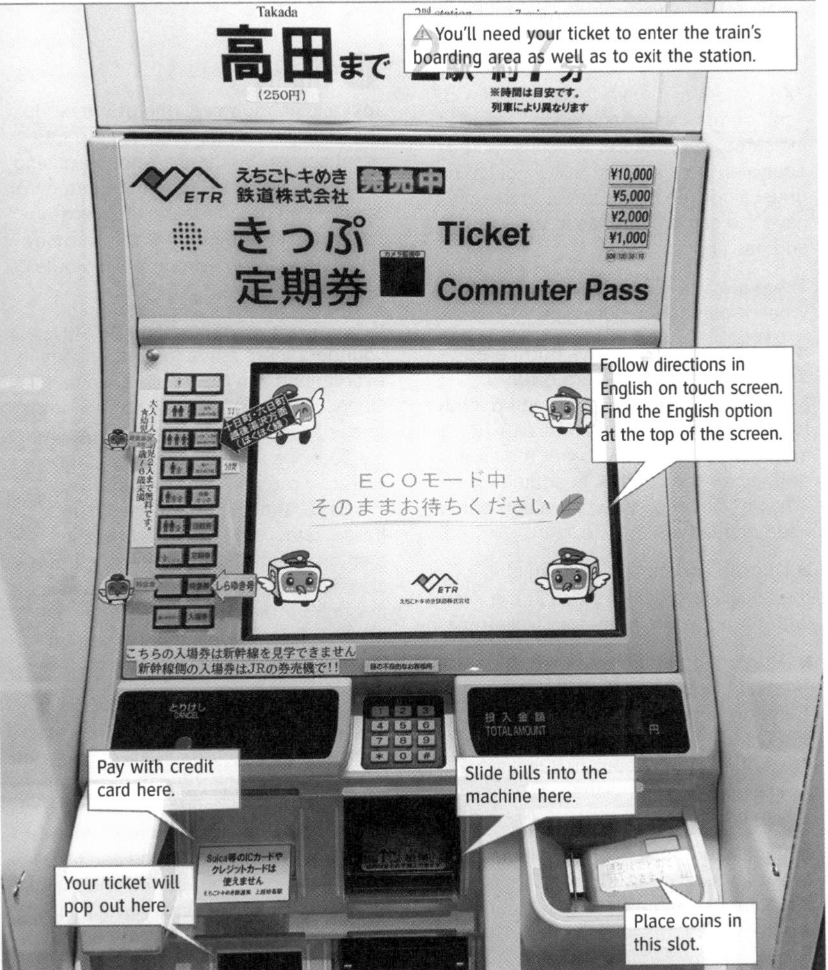

⚠ You'll need your ticket to enter the train's boarding area as well as to exit the station.
Takada
高田まで
(250円)
※時間は目安です。
列車により異なります
えちごトキめき鉄道株式会社
発売中
ETR
きっぷ Ticket
定期券 Commuter Pass
¥10,000
¥5,000
¥2,000
¥1,000
Follow directions in English on touch screen. Find the English option at the top of the screen.
ECOモード中
そのままお待ちください
こちらの入場券は新幹線を見学できません
新幹線側の入場券はJRの券売機で!!
とりけし CANCEL
投入金額 TOTAL AMOUNT
Pay with credit card here.
Slide bills into the machine here.
Your ticket will pop out here.
Place coins in this slot.

Essentials

Addresses

The simplest way to decipher a Japanese address is to break it into parts. For example: 6-chome 8–19, Chuo-ku, Fukuoka-shi, Fukuoka-ken. In this address, the "chome" indicates a precise area (a block, for example), and the numbers following it indicate the building within the area. In most cases, 6-chome 8-19 will be written just as 6-8-19 in English.

"Ku" refers to a ward (a district) of a city, "shi" refers to a city name, and "ken" indicates a prefecture, which is roughly equivalent to a state or province. It's not unusual for the prefecture and the city to have the same name, as in the sample address above.

There are a few other things to keep when it comes to addresses.

- Buildings aren't always numbered sequentially; numbers are often assigned as buildings are erected. Only local police officers and mail carriers seem to be familiar with the area defined by the chome. In addition, "machi" or "cho" (town) are sometimes used instead of "chome."
- Written addresses in Japan also have the opposite order of those in the West, with the city coming before the street.
- A few geographic areas aren't called "ken." One is Tokyo, which is called Tokyo-to. Other exceptions are Kyoto and Osaka, which are followed by the suffix "-fu"—Kyoto-fu, Osaka-fu. Hokkaido, Japan's northernmost island, is also not considered a ken.
- Not all addresses conform exactly to the above format. Rural addresses, for example, might use "gun" (county) where city addresses have "ku" (ward).

Even Japanese people cannot find a building based on the address alone, but map apps usually can. ■ TIP→ **If you get in a taxi with a written address, do not assume the driver will be able to find your destination. It's always good to know the location of your destination in relation to a major building or department store.**

Dining

Tokyo is undoubtedly one of the world's most exciting dining cities. There's an emphasis on freshness—not surprising given raw seafood is the cornerstone of sushi—and though Tokyoites still stubbornly resist foreign concepts in many fields, the locals have embraced outside culinary styles with gusto.

While newer restaurants targeting younger diners strive for authenticity in everything from New York–style bagels to Neapolitan pizza, it is still not uncommon to see menus serving East-meets-West concoctions such as spaghetti topped with cod roe and shredded seaweed. That said, the city's best French and Italian establishments can hold their own on a global scale. Naturally, there's also excellent Japanese cuisine available throughout the city, ranging from the traditional to nouveau, which can be shockingly expensive.

That is not to imply that every meal in the city will drain your finances—the popular *B-kyu gurume* (B-class gourmet), restaurants that fill the gap between nationwide chains and fine cuisine, serve tasty Japanese and Asian food without the extra frills of tablecloths and lacquerware. All department stores and many malls and office buildings have at least one floor of restaurants that are accessible, affordable, and reputable.

DRESS

Dining out in Tokyo does not ordinarily require formal attire. If you are attending a business meal with Japanese hosts or guests, dress conservatively: for men, a suit and tie; for women, a dress or suit in a basic color and minimal jewelry. Minimal should also apply to cologne and perfume. For Japanese-style dining on tatami floors, keep two things in mind: wear shoes that slip on and off easily and presentable socks, and choose clothing you'll be comfortable in for a few hours with your legs gathered under you.

MENUS

Less-expensive restaurants often have picture menus or plastic replicas of the dishes they serve, displayed in their front windows, so you can point to what you want to eat if the language barrier is insurmountable. In addition, many Japanese restaurants offer *omakase* (chef's choice of a set of dishes), which is a convenient way to order; locals frequently order this way, although it is often the most expensive option.

Ordering set meals—which are called *teishoku* and which may include rice, soup, and pickled vegetables in addition to the main course—is another way to go. Such meals often cost only slightly more than the main dish itself, which at some restaurants will also be available without the full set.

PRICES

Eating at hotels and famous restaurants is costly; however, you can eat well and reasonably at standard restaurants (though they might not have menus in English). Good places to look for moderately priced dining spots are in the restaurant concourses of department stores and larger office buildings, usually on the basement levels and the top floors.

All restaurants charge 10% tax, and the price on the menu should include the tax. *Izakaya* (Japanese pubs) often charge a flat table fee (around ¥500 per person), which includes the tiny appetizer that's served to all guests. More expensive restaurants typically add a service charge of 10%, as do some other restaurants when serving large parties. This is usually indicated at the bottom of menus.

⇨ *Restaurant reviews have been shortened. For full information visit Fodors.com. Restaurant prices are the average cost of a main course at dinner, or if dinner is not served, at lunch.*

What It Costs in Yen

$	$$	$$$	$$$$
AT DINNER			
Under ¥1,500	¥1,500–¥3,000	¥3,001–¥5,000	over ¥5,000

RESERVATIONS

Many restaurants in Japan still don't accept reservations online and might not have an English speaker to accept them over the phone. For that reason, many visitors rely on their hotel concierge—doing so guarantees a table and gives the management time to locate an English menu or staff with some language skills.

There are also online resources for do-it-yourselfers. TableCheck (🌐 *www.tablecheck.com/en/japan*) represents a wide array of upscale restaurants in major destinations and has an excellent English-language site. The Tabelog (🌐 *tabelog.com/en*) site not only recommends restaurants using star ratings (Tabelog raters are serious eaters, and anything over three stars is high) but also enables you to make some online reservations. Google is another good resource for recommendations and reservations.

Essentials

Health

Japan is a safe, clean country, with good drinking water. Mosquitoes can be a minor irritation during the rainy season, and while there is no risk of malaria, there have been cases of Japanese encephalitis in recent years. If you are staying for a prolonged period, and spending time in rural areas, the Japanese encephalitis vaccine is recommended.

Drugs and medications are widely available at drugstores, although the brand names and instructions are in Japanese, so if you're on regular medication, take along enough supplies to cover the trip. As with any international trip, be sure to bring your prescription or a doctor's note just in case.

Speak with your physician and/or check the CDC or World Health Organization websites for health alerts, particularly if you're pregnant or traveling with children or have a chronic illness.

OVER-THE-COUNTER REMEDIES

Medication can be bought only at pharmacies, but every neighborhood seems to have at least one. Ask for the *yakyoku*. Pharmacists are usually able to manage at least a few words of English and certainly able to read some, so have a pen and paper ready, just in case.

In Japanese, aspirin is *asupirin* and Tylenol is *tairenoru*. Following national regulations, Japanese drugs contain less potent ingredients than foreign brands, so the effects can be disappointing; check advised dosages carefully. Condoms are sold widely, but they may not have the brands you're used to.

Internet

Except for some traditional ryokan and minshuku, nearly all hotels have Wi-Fi. There are some free services that allow tourists to access a number of hotspots around the country. The most useful way to find free public Wi-Fi service in Japan is to download the app Japan Wi-Fi auto-connect (🌐 *www.ntt-bp.net/jw-auto/en/index.html*).

It's also possible to rent a pocket Wi-Fi router so you can use Google Maps to navigate or an online translation app to communicate. Japan Wireless (🌐 *www.japan-wireless.com*) has plans from ¥8,890 for 10 days though it is more expensive per day the shorter the rental. Ninja WiFi (🌐 *ninjawifi.com/en*) has unlimited data-rental plans from ¥770 per day regardless of the rental length. For both, it is best to order online before your trip. You can pick up the portable Wi-Fi device at a number of airports or have it sent directly to your hotel.

An alternative option to pocket Wi-Fi is getting a SIM card or eSIM with data. Airalo (🌐 *www.airalo.com*) has 1GB plans that start at around ¥700. However, if you want to use a significant amount of data or be connected to multiple devices, then pocket Wi-Fi will suit you better.

Lodging

Tokyo's skyscraper construction boom resulted in an increase in high-end domestic and international hotels—many installed on the upper floors of glimmering new towers. Most major brands have a presence in Tokyo, all of them with Western-style quarters and amenities like room and concierge services, Wi-Fi, minibars, *yukata* (cotton robes), and business and fitness centers. A few also have swimming pools, and a handful offer premium-priced Japanese-style rooms with tatami mats and futons. Of course, rates for these properties fall in the higher price categories.

Are there bargains to be had? Absolutely, but you'll have to do your homework. Boutique hotels—typified by small rooms, utilitarian concepts, and quirky, stylish design elements—have been popping up in Tokyo. Modern room furnishings and neutral color schemes are prevalent, but so are such Japanese touches as paper lanterns and tatami flooring. Often these accommodations have only a few floors, and sometimes their locations are hard to find, but they can be true bargains in a city known for being incredibly expensive.

Lower-profile business hotels, often situated near railway stations, are decent, moderately priced bets for singles or couples who don't require a lot of space or amenities. Rooms are small and tend to have a phone; a desk; a TV (rarely with English-language channels); slippers and yukata or PJs; and bathrooms with a prefabricated plastic tub, shower, and sink. On-site amenities might be limited to, say, a restaurant and a 24-hour receptionist, who probably doesn't speak much English.

Options for travelers on a tight budget not only include hostels, but also a range of Japanese-style accommodations. In Tokyo, "capsule" hotels and ryokan are good bets. Possibilities that are more often found elsewhere in Japan include minshuku and even temples.

JAPANESE-STYLE LODGINGS

Looking for someplace to rest your head that echoes the Japanese experience? There are numerous options: ryokan, capsule hotels, home visits, or a stay in a traditional temple.

CAPSULE HOTELS

Capsule hotels, some of which are women- or men-only, consist of plastic cubicles stacked one atop another. "Rooms" are a mere 3½ feet wide, 3½ feet high, and 7¼ feet long, and they're usually occupied by junior business travelers, backpackers, late-night revelers, or commuters who have missed the last train home. Each capsule has a bed, an intercom, an alarm clock, and a TV. Washing and toilet facilities are shared. You may like the novelty of sleeping in a capsule, but you'll likely limit yourself to one night.

MINSHUKU

Minshuku—which are rare in Tokyo—are, essentially, bed-and-breakfasts, where rates start at between ¥6,000 and ¥9,000 per person and might include two meals, usually served in communal dining areas. Some minshuku are like a no-frills inn; others are in small homes that take in only a few guests and might expect you to lay out and put away your own bedding. Still, becoming acquainted with a Japanese family could make for a truly memorable experience.

RYOKAN

There are two kinds of ryokan. One is an expensive traditional inn, where you're served dinner and breakfast in your room and given lots of personal attention. Rates at such places can be high—at least ¥20,000 per person per night with two meals, but frequently much higher. The other type is an inexpensive hostelry, whose rooms come with futon beds, tatami floor mats, a scroll or a flower arrangement in its rightful place, and, occasionally, meal service.

Tokyo ryokan fall in the latter category. They're often family-run, and service is less a matter of professionalism than of goodwill. Many have rooms either with or without baths (where tubs are likely

Where Should I Stay?

	NEIGHBORHOOD VIBE	PROS	CONS
Ueno	Entertainment area with rail hub	Large park in area; convenient access to Narita Airport	Some areas are a bit rough for Tokyo
Asakusa	Historic temple area with quaint shops and restaurants	Plenty of shops selling souvenirs; historic area	Not exactly central
Shiodome	Bayside district of office towers	Numerous hotel options; nearby park	Access for pedestrians can be confusing
Ginza	High-end area with shopping and restaurants	Numerous gallery, restaurant, and shopping options	Can be expensive; a bit sterile
Nihonbashi	Historic district that has grown into a trendy dining and shopping spot	Traditional area with numerous restaurant choices	Quiet on weekends
Marunouchi	Business area with numerous shopping and restaurant options	Convenient access to transportation; plenty of shops and restaurants	Business area with a businesslike feel
Akasaka	Business area with lively nightlife scene	Located in central Tokyo; many restaurant and bar choices	Can be noisy and crowded
Shibuya	Shopping and dining playground for young people	Fashionable; many shops, bars, and restaurants	Can be noisy and crowded; Ebisu section can be pricey
Roppongi	Entertainment and business district	Plenty of bars and restaurants; central location	Often noisy; some questionable nightlife
Shinjuku	Large business and entertainment area	Lively entertainment; many hotel choices; convenient access to transportation	Can be overwhelmingly crowded
Mejiro	Residential area	Pleasant, often overlooked area of Tokyo	Surrounding neighborhood might offer little of interest
Odaiba	Man-made island popular with tourists	Amusement parks in area; views of Tokyo Bay	Not located in a central location; touristy
Shinagawa	Busy transport hub for commuters	Easy access to Haneda Airport and Shinkansen lines	Neighborhood lacks points of interest

to be plastic rather than cedarwood) as well as street, rather than garden, views. Because they have few rooms and the owners are usually on hand to answer questions, these small ryokan are as hospitable as they are affordable (from ¥5,000 for a single room to ¥8,000 for a double). Younger travelers love them.

TIP→ **Many modern hotels with Japanese-style rooms are now referring to themselves as ryokan, and though meals may be served in the guests' rooms, they are a far cry from the traditional ryokan.**

TEMPLES

Accommodations in Buddhist temples provide a taste of traditional Japan. Some have instruction in meditation or allow you to observe their religious practices, while others merely provide Japanese-style rooms that range from beautiful, quiet havens to basic, not-so-comfortable cubicles. The JNTO has lists of temples (most outside of Tokyo) that accept guests. A stay generally costs ¥6,000–¥15,000 per night, which includes two meals.

PRICES

Deluxe hotels charge a premium for good-size rooms, lots of perks, great service, and central locations. More-affordable hotels aren't always in the most convenient places and have disproportionately small rooms, as well as fewer amenities. That said, many moderately priced accommodations are still within the central hubs; some have an old-fashioned charm and a personal touch the upscale places can't provide. What's more, wherever you're staying, Tokyo's subway and train system—comfortable (except in rush hours), efficient, inexpensive, and safe—gets you back and forth.

⇨ *Hotel reviews have been shortened. For full information visit Fodors.com.*

Hotel prices are the lowest cost of a standard double room in high season.

What It Costs in Yen

	$	$$	$$$	$$$$
HOTELS	under ¥25,000	¥25,000–¥50,000	¥50,001–¥75,000	over ¥75,000

RESERVATIONS

It is essential to make your Tokyo hotel reservations before you arrive, especially if traveling during Japan's peak holiday periods—late April to early May, August, and the New Year period. The Japan National Tourism Organization (JNTO, 🌐 *www.japan.travel*) can link you to booking sites with thousands of reasonably priced accommodations—including business hotels, ryokan, and minshuku—in Tokyo and throughout Japan.

The JTB Corporation (🌐 *www.jtbcorp.jp*) operates 🌐 *Japanican.com*, which allows you to reserve and confirm hotel rooms all over the country, not just in Tokyo. The full-service Nippon Travel Agency (🌐 *www.ntainbound.com*) is helpful for making a variety of travel arrangements, including lodging reservations. Rakuten Travel (🌐 *travel.rakuten.com*) is also a good resource for booking hotels throughout the country.

Money

Japan's unit of currency is the yen (¥). There are bills of ¥10,000, ¥5,000, ¥2,000, and ¥1,000. Coins are ¥500, ¥100, ¥50, ¥10, ¥5, and ¥1. The yen floats on the international monetary exchange, so changes can be dramatic.

Essentials

Japan can be expensive, but there are ways to cut costs. This requires, to some extent, an adventurous spirit and the courage to stray from the standard tourist paths. One good way to hold down expenses is to avoid taxis and try the inexpensive, efficient subway and bus systems; instead of going to a restaurant with menus in English and Western-style food, go to places where you can rely on your good old index finger to point to the dish you want, and try food that the Japanese eat.

Item	Average Cost
Cup of coffee	¥250–¥600
Glass of wine	¥600–¥1,000
Glass of beer	¥500–¥800
Sandwich (convenience store)	¥300
1-mile taxi ride in capital city	¥700
Museum admission	¥1,000

ATMS AND BANKS

It can be difficult to exchange foreign currency in Japan. The easiest way to obtain yen is at convenience-store ATMs; 7-Eleven stores and Seven Bank ATMs accept most internationally branded cards. Post offices also have ATMs that accept Visa, MasterCard, American Express, Diners Club, and Cirrus cards. However, ATMs at most regular Japanese banks *do not* accept foreign-issue ATM or credit cards. UFJ and Shinsei banks are members of the Plus network. In more rural areas, it can be difficult to find suitable ATMs, so it is best to get cash before venturing into the countryside. PINs in Japan are made up of four digits. Most machines also have English on-screen instructions.

Nightlife

The sheer diversity of nightlife in Tokyo is breathtaking. Rickety street stands sit yards away from luxury hotels, and wallet-crunching hostess clubs neighbor cheap and raucous rock bars. Whatever your style, you'll find yourself in good company if you venture out after dark.

Major nightlife districts include Aoyama, Ginza, Roppongi, Shibuya, Shimbashi, and Shinjuku. Each has a unique atmosphere, clientele, and price level, with most bars and clubs displaying printed price lists, often in English. Drinks generally cost ¥800–¥1,200, although some small exclusive bars and clubs can set you back a lot more.

Be wary of establishments without visible price lists. Hostess clubs—where it's often unclear what the companionship of a hostess will cost you (probably a lot)—and small backstreet bars known as "snacks" or "pubs" can be particularly treacherous. That drink you've just ordered could set you back a reasonable ¥1,000; you might, on the other hand, have wandered unknowingly into a place that charges you ¥30,000 up front for a whole bottle—and slaps a ¥20,000 cover charge on top.

Also, on the streets of Roppongi and Kabuki-cho, ignore the persuasive shills who try to hook you into their establishment. There is, of course, plenty of safe ground: in hotel lounges, jazz clubs, craft beer pubs, sake bars, and sedate retreats where the social lubricant flows past millions of tonsils nightly.

Packing

Pack light, because porters can be hard to find, and storage space in hotel rooms may be very limited. Although the most exclusive restaurants and bars might require men to wear a jacket and tie, most places are generally far more casual. Jeans are perfectly acceptable for informal dining and sightseeing. Make sure to bring comfortable clothing that isn't too tight to wear in traditional Japanese restaurants, where you may need to sit on tatami-matted floors.

Although there are no strict dress requirements for visiting temples and shrines, you will be out of place in immodest outfits. For sightseeing leave sandals and open-toe shoes behind; you'll need sturdy walking shoes for the gravel pathways that surround temples and wind through parks. Japanese people don't wear shoes in private homes or in any temples or traditional inns. Having shoes you can quickly slip in and out of is a decided advantage. Having wool socks will help you through shoeless occasions in winter.

Take along small gift items, such as scarves or perfume sachets, to thank hosts (on both business and pleasure trips), whether you've been invited to their home or out to a restaurant.

Performing Arts

Tokyoites get the best of both worlds, as there's an astonishing variety of dance and music, both classical and popular and much of it Western, alongside the must-see traditional Japanese arts of Kabuki and Noh.

The city is a proving ground for local talent and a magnet for orchestras and concert soloists from all over the world. Although language barriers make it hard for Westerners to enjoy plays, Tokyo's theater scene is robust, with everything from modern Japanese productions to the latest hit shows from New York or London—albeit with the protagonists speaking Japanese.

Among the roughly ten professional dance troupes in Japan, the best known are the New National Ballet, which usually performs at the New National Theater, and the K-Ballet Company and the Tokyo Ballet, both of which stage productions at the Bunka Kaikan in Ueno and the Orchard Hall of the Bunkamura complex in Shibuya.

Tokyo has plenty of venues for opera, but few groups to perform in them. Touring companies like the Metropolitan, the Bolshoi, and the Bayerische Staatsoper find the city very compelling—as well they might when even seats costing ¥30,000 or more sell out far in advance.

Movie theaters here screen everything from big Asian hits to American blockbusters and Oscar nominees. An increase in small film distributors and a growing interest in Korean, Middle Eastern, South American, and Aussie cinema have led to the rise of vibrant art-house theaters. New multiplexes have also brought more screens to the capital, providing a more comfortable film-going experience than some of the older Japanese theaters.

To find out what's happening, check out one of the websites of English-language publications such as *Tokyo Weekender* (⊕ *www.tokyoweekender.com*), Tokyo Cheapo (⊕ *tokyocheapo.com*), *Metropolis* (⊕ *metropolisjapan.com*), and Time Out Tokyo (⊕ *www.timeout.com/tokyo*).

Restrooms

Hotels and department stores have the most hygienic restrooms; these are usually clearly indicated with international symbols. On rare occasions, you'll encounter Japanese-style toilets, with bowls recessed into the floor, over which you squat facing the top of the tank. This may take some getting used to, but it's completely sanitary, as you don't come into direct contact with the facility. If you want to avoid squatting, check out the last cubicle in the row, because it may contain a Western-style toilet. Paper towel dispensers and hand dryers are not always installed, so bring a small handkerchief or washcloth with you, as well as some hand sanitizer.

In many homes and Japanese-style public places, there will be a pair of slippers at the entrance to the restroom. Change into these before entering the room, and change back when you exit.

Safety

Even in its major cities Japan is a very safe country, especially for men, with one of the lowest crime rates in the world. You should, however, keep an eye out for pickpockets and avoid unlighted roads at night like anywhere else. Female travelers should take the same precautions they would at home.

The greatest danger is the possibility of being caught up in an earthquake and its resulting tsunami. Earthquake information is broadcast (in Japanese) as news flashes on television within minutes, and during major disasters national broadcaster N.H.K. broadcasts information in English on radio and television. Minor tremors occur nearly every month, and sometimes train services are temporarily halted. Check emergency routes at hotels and how to get to higher ground if staying near coastal areas.

Shopping

Tokyo is Japan's showcase. The crazy clothing styles, obscure electronics, and new games found here often set trends across Japan, elsewhere in Asia, and even in Europe and America.

Part of the Tokyo shopping experience is simply to observe, as the Japanese approach to shopping is nothing short of feverish. This is particularly true on Saturday, especially, in trendy districts like Ginza and Shinjuku. But shopping can also be an exercise in elegance and refinement, especially in terms of items that are Japanese-made for Japanese people and sold in stores that don't cater to tourists. With brilliantly applied color, balance of form, and superb workmanship, crafts items can be exquisite and well worth the higher prices you can expect to pay.

Note, too, the care taken with your purchases, which will be wrapped, wrapped again, bagged, and sealed. Sure, the packaging can be excessive, but such a focus on presentation has deep roots in Japanese culture.

Salespeople are invariably helpful and polite. In larger stores, they greet you with a bow, and many speak at least some English. There's a saying in Japan: *"o-kyaku-sama wa kami-sama"* ("the customer is a god")—and since the competition for your business is fierce, people do take it to heart.

Horror stories abound about prices in Japan. Yes, European labels can cost a fortune here, but did you really travel all the way to Tokyo to buy an outfit that would be cheaper at home? True, a gift-wrapped melon from a department-store gourmet counter can cost $150, but, if you shop around, you can find plenty of gifts and souvenirs at fair prices.

The country has finally embraced the use of credit cards, although some smaller mom-and-pop shops may still take cash only. So when you go souvenir hunting, be prepared with a decent amount of cash; Tokyo's low crime rates make this a low-risk proposition.

Japan has an across-the-board 10% value-added tax (V.A.T.). This tax can be avoided at some duty-free shops in the city (don't forget to bring your passport). It's also waived in the duty-free shops at the international airports, but your tax savings there will likely to be offset by higher markups.

Stores in Tokyo generally open at 10 or 11 am and close at 8 or 9 pm.

Taxes

A 10% national consumption tax is added to all hotel bills. There is also a local Tokyo hotel tax of ¥100 per night for bills between ¥10,000 and ¥14,999 and ¥200 for bills over ¥15,000.

At first-class, full-service, and luxury hotels, a 10% service charge is added to the bill in place of individual tipping. At more expensive ryokans, where individualized maid service is provided, the service charge is usually 15%. At business hotels, minshuku, youth hostels, and economy inns, no service charge is added to the bill.

There's an across-the-board, nonrefundable 10% consumption tax levied on all sales. Authorized tax-free shops knock the tax off purchases over ¥5,000 if you show your passport and a valid tourist visa. A large sign is displayed at such shops. A 10% tax is also added to all restaurant bills. At more expensive restaurants, a 10%–15% service charge can be added to the bill. Tipping is not customary.

Tipping

Tipping is not common in Japan. It's not necessary to tip taxi drivers, hair stylists/barbers, bartenders, or waitstaff. It's also not customary to tip hotel employees, even porters or cleaning staff, unless a special service has been rendered. A chauffeur for a hired car usually receives a tip of ¥500 for a half-day excursion and ¥1,000 for a full-day trip. You can tip staff in a traditional ryokan as meals are served in your room. Plan to tip (at check-in and in an envelope) ¥1,000 per day's stay.

When to Go

Spring and fall are the best times to visit. *Sakura* (cherry blossoms) begin blooming in Tokyo by early April, while fall has clear blue skies, albeit punctuated by the occasional typhoon.

The short *tsuyu* (rainy season) in June brings humidity and rain that can linger into early July. July and August bring heat, mostly blue skies, and stifling humidity. Winter can be gray and chilly some days, mild and sunny others, with Tokyo and other areas along the coast receiving very little snow.

The Japanese tend to vacation during three holiday periods: the few days before and after New Year's; Golden Week in early May; and the mid-August week for Obon. Travel isn't not advised during these times, as plane and train tickets book up fast.

Helpful Japanese Phrases

BASICS

Hello/Good day	こんにちは。	kon-ni-chi-wa
Yes/no	はい / いいえ	hai / ii-e
Please	お願いします	o-ne-gai shi-ma-su
Thank you (very much)	ありがとう (ござ います)	a-ri-ga-tō (go-zai-ma-su)
You're welcome	どういたしまして。	dō i-ta-shi-mashi-te
I'm sorry (apology)	ごめんなさい。	go-men na-sai
Sorry (Excuse me)	すみません。	su-mi-ma-sen
Good morning	おはようございます	o-ha-yō go-zai-ma-su
Good evening	こんばんは。	kom-ban-wa
Goodbye	さようなら。	sa-yō-na-ra
Pleased to meet you	はじめまして。	haji-me-mashi-te
How are you?	おげんき ですか。	o-gen-ki desu-ka

NUMBERS

half	半分	han-bun
one	一 / 一つ	i-chi / hi-to-tsu
two	二 / 二つ	ni / fu-ta-tsu
three	三 / 三つ	san / mit-tsu
four	四 / 四つ	yon (shi) / yot-tsu
five	五 / 五つ	go / i-tsu-tsu
six	六 / 六つ	ro-ku / mut-tsu
seven	七 / 七つ	na-na (shi-chi) / na-na-tsu
eight	八 / 八つ	ha-chi / yat-tsu
nine	九 / 九つ	kyū / ko-ko-no-tsu
ten	十 / とう	jū / tō
eleven	十一	jū i-chi
twelve	十二	jū ni
thirteen	十三	jū san
fourteen	十四	jū yon
fifteen	十五	jū go
sixteen	十六	jū ro-ku
seventeen	十七	jū na-na
eighteen	十八	jū ha-chi
nineteen	十九	jū-kyū
twenty	二十	ni-jū
twenty-one	二十一	ni-jū i-chi
thirty	三十	san jū
forty	四十	yon jū
fifty	五十	go jū
sixty	六十	ro-ku jū
seventy	七十	na-na jū
eighty	八十	ha-chi jū
ninety	九十	kyū jū
one hundred	百	hyaku
one thousand	千 / 一千	sen / is-sen
ten thousand	一万	i-chi man
one hundred thousand	十万	jū man
one million	百万	hya-ku man

COLORS

black	黒	ku-ro
blue	青	ao
brown	茶色	cha-iro
green	緑	mi-do-ri
orange	オレンジ	o-ren-ji
purple	紫	mu-ra-sa-ki
red	赤	a-ka
white	白	shi-ro
yellow	黄色	ki-iro

DAYS OF THE WEEK

Sunday	日曜日	ni-chi yō-bi
Monday	月曜日	ge-tsu yō-bi
Tuesday	火曜日	ka yō-bi
Wednesday	水曜日	su-i yō-bi
Thursday	木曜日	mo-ku yō-bi
Friday	金曜日	kin yō-bi
Saturday	土曜日	dō yō-bi

MONTHS

January	一月	i-chi ga-tsu
February	二月	ni ga-tsu
March	三月	san ga-tsu
April	四月	shi ga-tsu
May	五月	go ga-tsu
June	六月	ro-ku ga-tsu
July	七月	shi-chi ga-tsu
August	八月	ha-chi ga-tsu
September	九月	ku ga-tsu
October	十月	jū ga-tsu
November	十一月	jū-i-chi ga-tsu
December	十二月	jū-ni ga-tsu

USEFUL WORDS AND PHRASES

Do you understand English?	英語がわかりますか。	ei-go ga wa-ka- ma-su ka
I don't understand Japanese	日本語がわかりません。	ni-hon-go ga wa-ka-ri-ma-sen
I don't understand	わかりません。	wa-ka-ri-ma-sen
I don't know	知りません。	shi-ri-ma-sen
I understand	わかりました。	wa-ka-ri-ma-shi
I'm American	私はアメリカ人です。	wa-ta-shi wa a- ri-ka jin de-su
I'm British	私はイギリス人です。	wa-ta-shi wa i-g ri-su jin de-su
I'm Australian	私はオーストラリア人です。	wa-ta-shi wa ō-s to-ra-ri-a jin de-
What's your name	お名前はなんですか。	o- na-ma-e wa n de-su ka
My name is	[name] と申します。	[name] to-mō-shi-ma-su
What time is it?	今何時ですか。	i-ma nan-ji de-su ka
How?	どうやって ですか。	dō-yat-te de-su k
When?	いつ ですか。	i-tsu de-su ka

terday	昨日	ki-nō
ay	今日	kyō
ıorrow	明日	ashi-ta
s morning	けさ	ke-sa
s afternoon	今日の午後	kyō no go-go
ight	今晩	kom-ban
at?	何ですか。	nan de-su ka
at is this / t?	これ / それ は何ですか。	ko-re / so-re wa nan de-su ka
y?	どうしてですか。	dō-shi-te de-su ka
o?	どなたですか。	do-na-ta de-su ka
ere is [place ing]?	[place / thing] はどこですか。	[place / thing] wa do-ko de-su ka
tion	駅	e-ki
way station	地下鉄の駅	chi-ka-te-tsu no e-ki
s stop	バス乗り場	ba-su no-ri-ba
port	空港	kū-kō
st office	郵便局	yū-bin-kyo-ku
ık	銀行	gin-kō
el	ホテル	ho-te-ru
seum	博物館	ha-ku-bu-tsu-kan
museum / art lery	美術館	bi-ju-tsu-kan
spital	病院	byō-in
vator	エレベーター	e-re-bē-tā
ere is the troom?	トイレはどこですか。	to-i-re wa do-ko de-su ka
e / there / er there	ここ / そこ / あそこ	ko-ko / so-ko / a-so-ko
t / right	左 / 右	hi-da-ri / mi-gi
t near / far?	近い / 遠い ですか。	chi-ka-i / tō-i de-su ka
you have	[item] が ありますか。	[item] ga a-ri-ma-su-ka
oom	部屋	he-ya
ity map	市内地図	shi-nai chi-zu
oad map	ロードマップ	rō-do map-pu
otebook	ノート	nō-to
otepad	メモ用紙	me-mo-yō-shi
ıagazine in glish	英語の 雑誌	ei-go no zas-shi
ostcard	はがき	ha-ga-ki
tamp	切手	kit-te
icket	切符	kip-pu
velopes	封筒	fū-tō
w much is it?	いくらですか。	i-ku-ra de-su ka
s expensive / eap	高い / 安い です。	ta-ka-i / ya-su-i de-su
ittle / a lot	少し / たくさん	su-ko-shi / ta-ku-san
ore / less	もっと多く / 少なく	mot-to ō-ku/ su-ku-na-ku
ough / too ny	十分 / 多すぎる	jū-bun / ō-su-gi-ru
eel sick	体調が悪い。	tai-chō ga wa-ru-i
ll a doctor / bulance	医者 / 救急車 を呼んでください。	i-sha / kyū-kyū-sha o yon-de ku-da-sai

Help!	助けて!	ta-su-ke-te
Stop!	やめて!	ya-me-te

DINING OUT

A bottle of / a cup of	一本 / 一杯	ip-pon / ip-pai
Two bottles of / two cups of	二本 / 二杯	ni-hon / ni-hai
Aperitif	食前酒	sho-ku-zen shu
Beer	ビール	bii-ru
Bill / check, please	お勘定 お願いします。	o- kan-jō o-ne-ga-i-shi-ma-su
Bread	パン	pan
Breakfast	朝食 / 朝ごはん	chō-sho-ku / a-sa go-han
Butter	バター	ba-tā
Cocktail	カクテル	ka-ku-te-ru
Coffee	コーヒー	kō-hī
Dinner	夕食 / 晩ごはん	yū-sho-ku / ban go-han
Fork	フォーク	fō-ku
I am a vegetarian	私は 菜食主義者 / ベジタリアンです。	wa-ta-shi wa saisho-ku shu-gi-sha / be-ji-ta-ri-an de-su
I cannot eat [item]	[item] は食べられません。	[item] wa ta-be-ra-re-ma-sen
I'm ready to order	注文 お願いします。	chū-mon o-ne-ga-i-shi-ma-su
I'm hungry	お腹が空いています。	o-na-ka ga su-i-te i-ma-su
I'm thirsty	喉が渇いています。	no-do ga ka-wai-te i-ma-su
It's delicious	美味しい です。	oi-shī de-su
It doesn't taste good	美味しくない です。	oi-shi ku-nai de-su
It's hot (Be careful, please)	暑いです。(気を付けてください。)	a-tsu-i de-su (ki-o-tsu-ke-te ku-da-sai)
Knife	ナイフ	nai-fu
Lunch	昼食 / 昼ごはん	chū-sho-ku / hi-ru go-han
Menu	メニュー	me-nyū
Napkin	ナプキン	na-pu-kin
Pepper	こしょう	ko-shō
Plate	皿	sa-ra
Please give me [item]	[item] をください。	[item] o ku-da-sai
Salt	塩	shi-o
Spoon	スプーン	su-pūn
Tea (Japanese teas)	お茶	o-cha
Tea (other teas)	紅茶	kō-cha
Water	水	mi-zu
Rice wine (sake)	日本酒	ni-hon-shu

A Walk through Everyday Tokyo

Tokyo's soul is found in its *shitamachi*, the neighborhoods that define much of the city's east side. Spend a few hours walking here to discover old communities, ancient temples, and cultural riches.

YANAKA

The central shopping street **Yanaka Ginza** is crammed with mom-and-pop stores and small eateries, some with a feel that they've remained unchanged since the Meiji era of the late 1860s through the early 1910s. Leave behind Yanaka's main street, and you will soon be lost in a captivating maze of back alleys that lead past quiet temples and shrines, many eventually skirting the sprawling **Yanaka Cemetery,** a beautiful spot in cherry blossom season. The last of the Tokugawa shoguns is buried here, as are many other colorful characters in Tokyo's history.

UENO

From Yanaka, it's a fairly short walk southeast to **Ueno Park** (or you can walk to JR Nippori Station and take the Yamanote Line to Ueno). Here you'll find the city's most well-known zoo, an ancient temple, and plenty of green spaces, but the main reason the park stands out is the museums that dot the grounds. On the north end, **Tokyo National Museum** holds an unparalleled collection of Japanese and Asian artifacts, dating from as far back as the Jomon period. Moving south, the **National Science Museum** is a great hands-on stop for kids. Across the road from the park's southeast end, the vendors of the bustling **Ameyoko** street market sell everything from knockoff designer clothing to fine teas.

A Walk through Everyday Tokyo

HIGHLIGHTS

The old, narrow streets of Yanaka, the museums and street market of Ueno, the culinary-ware stores of Kappabashi, historic Senso-ji, and the historic Asakusa district.

WHERE TO START

Start at the Yanaka Ginza shopping street, a couple of minutes' walk from the west exit of Nippori Station on the JR Yamanote Line.

TIME/LENGTH

6 km (4 miles); duration about three hours without food stops.

WHERE TO END

At Asakusa Station on the Ginza Line.

BEST TIME TO GO

Weekdays are best to avoid the worst crowds.

WORST TIME TO GO

Mid-July to mid-September, when the summer heat and humidity can make being outside for too long very unpleasant.

GETTING AROUND

The walk is best done entirely on foot, but an alternative is to take the Ginza subway line from Ueno Station to Kappabashi (Tawaramachi Station) and from there to Asakusa Station.

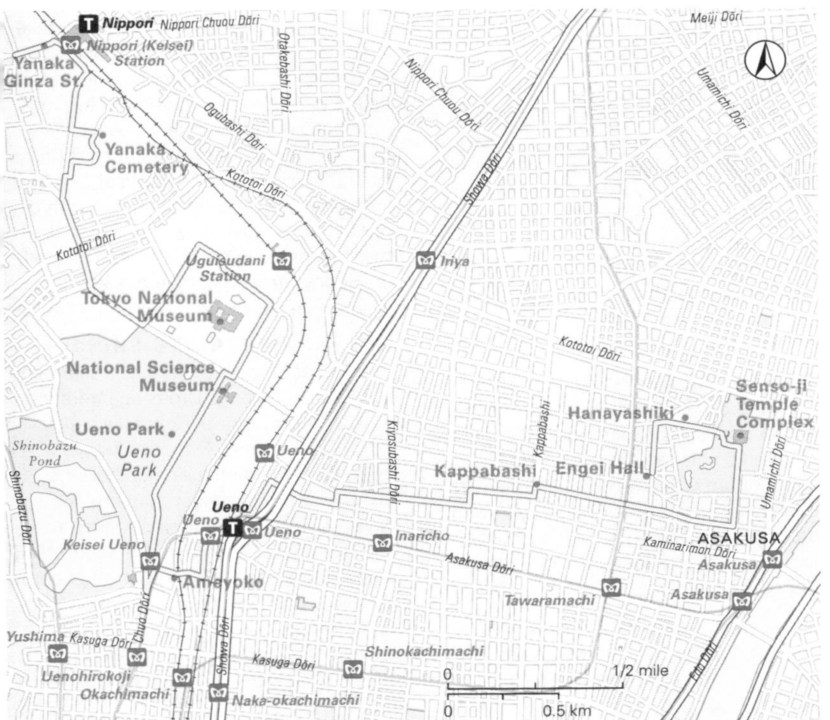

KAPPABASHI

Leaving Ueno and walking east, the next highlight is Kappabashi. In the early 1900s, merchants selling culinary wares began to converge on this half-mile-long street, and it is now where Tokyo's restaurant trade goes to stock up on everything from disposable chopsticks to hanging lanterns. Among the 170 shops here are several that specialize in the plastic replicas of food that many restaurants display in their windows.

ASAKUSA

East of Kappabashi's southern end is Asakusa. At the heart of this district is the mighty **Senso-ji Temple complex**, with its grand five-story pagoda, giant gateways, and colorful street stalls. A several-minute walk west of Senso's main temple building is **Hanayashiki,** a tiny amusement park that's home to Japan's oldest roller coaster. In the streets south of Hanayashiki are historic theaters like **Engei Hall,** which, like Hanayashiki, serve as reminders of Asakusa's prewar days as Tokyo's main entertainment district. The *yakitori-ya* that spill out on the street around here are great places to grab some grilled chicken and a beer and rest your feet.

Great Itineraries

Tokyo in 3 Days

Tokyo confounds with its complexity: 37 million people occupy a greater metropolitan area that includes soaring towers of glass and steel, rolling expressways, numerous temples, parks, and mile after mile of concrete housing blocks. Since the end of World War II, the city has constantly reinvented itself. Few things have remained static other than Tokyo's preeminence as Japan's economic center.

DAY 1: GINZA AND SHIODOME

Start the day exploring the fabled shops and *depato* (department stores) of Ginza. Then hit a chic restaurant or café for lunch (more reasonably priced ones are on the upper floors of most department stores). The skyscrapers of Shiodome are just down the street, in the direction of Shimbashi.

In the skyscrapers' shadows is the charming **Hama Rikyu Garden,** a path-laced sanctuary of Japanese tradition and nature. A path to the left as you enter leads to a ferry landing from which you can take a 40-minute "water bus" cruise up the Sumidagawa to Asakusa. In the evening, return to Ginza for a dinner featuring *yakitori* (grilled chicken) or Wagyu beef or even red king crab.

DAY 2: ASAKUSA AND UENO

Spend the morning in Asakusa at the **Senso-ji Temple Complex** and adjacent **Asakusa Shrine**. Then, shop for souvenirs—sacred or secular—at local vendors along **Nakamise-dori**. A 15-minute walk west is **Kappabashi,** a street dedicated to outfitting restaurants and bars with dishes, cups, chopsticks, and even plastic food models.

In the afternoon, head to Ueno and take in some of its museums, historical sites, and markets, stopping for a break at **Ueno Park.** It's worth looping back to Asakusa for a different view of the area: crowds are thinner and many major attractions, including the five-tier pagoda of Senso-ji, are brightly lighted. End the day with dinner at one of Asakusa's *izakaya* (think of them as drinking dens with lots of food) on Hoppy Street a couple blocks from the temple complex.

DAY 3: SHIBUYA AND SHINJUKU

Start off at Shibuya's Hachiko Square and the famous Shibuya Crossing intersection and hit nearby stores like **Shibuya 109,** which is crammed with teen fashion boutiques. Inside the station building, check out the once-lost masterpiece *Myth of Tomorrow* by avant-garde artist Taro Okamoto. Then visit the Shinto **Meiji Jingu Shrine** and walk through the nearby Harajuku and Omotesando fashion districts.

Spend the rest of the afternoon in the center of Shinjuku, Tokyo's 21st-century model city. Grab a slice of peace at the **Shinjuku Gyoen National Garden** before taking in the a view from the observation deck of architect Kenzo Tange's monumental **Tokyo Metropolitan Government Building**. In the evening, head to the red-light district of **Kabuki-cho,** just northeast of JR Shinjuku Station. Both Kabuki-cho and the neighboring Golden Gai are full of good places to eat and drink.

On the Calendar

January

Hatsumode: On the first days after New Year, people head to local and famous temples and shrines for the first prayer of the year.

January Basho: This tournament at Kokugikan Sumo Hall sees the sport's best get in their first licks of the year. Two 15-day tournaments take place in the same venue in May and September.

February

Setsubun: Celebrating the end of winter in the lunar calendar on February 3 or 4, people throw around dry soybeans to drive away evil at major temples and at home (you can buy devil masks and beans at convenience stores).

March

Cherry Blossoms: In late March and early April, Tokyoites celebrate the annual arrival of pink cherry blossoms by heading out in huge numbers to eat and drink at *sakura* spots all over the city.

Opening Day: Japan's 12 baseball teams kick off their season at the end of March. Tokyo teams include the Yakult Swallows and Yomiuri Giants; the Chiba Lotte Marines, Seibu Lions, and Yokohama DeNA Baystars are based in neighboring prefectures.

April

Kanamara Matsuri: On the first Sunday in April, this fertility festival in Kawasaki features parades of giant pink phalluses and some very interestingly shaped street food.

May

Kanda Festival: Taking place only in odd-numbered years, alternating with the Sanno Festival, this event shuts down the streets of Akihabara for a large portable shrine procession.

Sanja Festival: Asakusa's streets see dozens of portable shrines hoisted through huge crowds over the course of three days.

June

Sanno Matsuri: One of Tokyo's biggest traditional events has parades of portable shrines accompanied by priests, musicians, and dancers. It takes place only in even-numbered years.

July

Shitamachi Tanabata Festival: Also known as the Star Festival, this early July event celebrates the legend of two separated stars who can only meet once a year in the Milky Way. It is marked with parades, performances, and a custom where attendees write their wishes on paper and tie it to the bamboo branches that line the streets.

Sumida River Fireworks: The skies of eastern Tokyo burst with color on the last Saturday of July.

August

Asakusa Toro Nagashi: Participants decorate lanterns, then set them afloat along the Sumida River at dusk as they make a wish. Lanterns are available to buy at the venue the day of, but expect long lines.

On the Calendar

Awa-Odori: In mid-August the streets of Koenji are packed with dancers and musicians for the Tokyo version of Tokushima's historic and frenzied dance festival.

Harajuku Omotesando Super Yosakoi Festival: During one of Tokyo's most spectacular dance festivals, more than 100 regional teams wear original costumes influenced by their local culture and inspired by modern trends as they parade, perform, and compete around the streets and stages of Omotesando and Harajuku.

September

Asakusa Samba: In mid-September, dozens of samba troupes transform Asakusa at this high-energy, sun-baked annual event.

Reitaisai: In the middle of the month, Kamakura's Tsurugaoka Hachimangu Shrine's early-autumn festival includes a spectacular display of horseback archery (yabusame). The same happens at the spring festival in April.

Tokyo Game Show: Fans of video games crowd the Makuhari Messe convention center in September to check out the hottest releases.

October

Bake Neko Festival: A couple of weeks before Halloween, the streets of Kagurazaka are taken over by costumed *bake neko* (supernatural cats).

Tokyo International Film Festival: Over 10 days in late October, films from around the world are screened at the theaters in the Roppongi Hills complex.

November

Illuminations: As Christmas approaches, major complexes like Tokyo Midtown and districts like Marunouchi turn on spectacular street illuminations for a festive (and romantic) mood.

Shichi-go-san: In early November, tradition meets super-cute. Meaning "seven, five, three," children of those ages visit shrines in fine kimono to pray for a good future.

Tori-no-ichi Fairs: Tori-no-ichi is an annual festival that has been celebrated at shrines and temples across Japan since the Edo period. In the Asakusa area of Tokyo, these festivities take place at two adjoining venues: Chokokuji Temple and Otori Shrine. The surrounding area buzzes until late at night with merchants selling beautiful gold- and silver-decorated kumade, ornamental rakes believed to bring their owners good fortune and prosperity. After making a purchase, the entire shop's staff will clap their hands rhythmically to show their appreciation and to bless you with good health, luck, and business.

December

Comiket: The second installment (the first is August) of this semiannual comic and manga event draws hundreds of thousands of people to Tokyo Big Sight for the biggest convention of its kind in the world.

Tokyo Comic Con: This convention is a must if you are a fan or just want to experience the manga and anime culture in Japan. It occasionally takes place in November instead of December.

Chapter 3

A JAPANESE CULTURE PRIMER

Updated by
Robert Morel

Something about Japan led you to pick up this book and contemplate a trip. Perhaps it was a meal at your favorite sushi bar back home, the warm tones of an exquisite piece of Japanese pottery, or a Japanese novel or film. Whatever it was that sparked your interest, it's a good bet that something you find in this chapter will make your trip unforgettable.

There is a display of horsemanship called *yabusame* (now to be seen mainly at shrine festivals) in which a mounted archer, in medieval costume, challenges a narrow roped-off course lined at 260-foot intervals with small wooden targets on bamboo posts: the rider has to come down the course at full gallop, drop the reins, nock an arrow, aim and release, and take the reins again—with only seconds to set up again for the next target. Few archers manage a perfect score—but "merely hitting the target is secondary," explains a yabusame official.

Therein lies the key to understanding the fundamentals of Japanese identity as well as its various regional cultures: the passionate attention to form and process. The results are also important, of course; otherwise the forms would be empty gestures. But equally important—perhaps more important—is how you get there. Not for nothing are so many of these disciplines, from the tea ceremony to calligraphy to the martial arts, presented to us as Ways; excellence in any one of them depends on doing it the way it's supposed to be done according to traditions that may be centuries old. Philosophically, this is all about how rules can liberate: spend enough time and effort on the mastery of forms, and one day they leave the realm of conscious thought and become part of you. You are to lose yourself in the Way. Not for nothing, either, are so many elements of Japanese culture rooted in the teachings of Zen Buddhism, about breaking free from the limits of the rational self.

A TASTE OF JAPAN

By Aidan O'Connor

Get ready for an unparalleled eating adventure: from humble bowls of ramen to elaborate kaiseki feasts, a vast culinary universe awaits visitors to food-obsessed Japan.

Japan's food offerings are united by a few key philosophies. Presentation is paramount—a dedication to visual appeal means that colors and shapes are just as important as aromas, textures, and flavors. Details count—food is prepared with pride and care, and everything from a bowl's shape to a dish's finishing garnish carries meaning. Natural flavors shine through—seasonal ingredients star in minimally processed preparations, with condiments used to enhance flavors rather than mask them.

You'll find these culinary philosophies at all levels, from tiny noodle shops to lively robatayaki grills to elegant sushi restaurants. Here's what you need to know to make the most of your meals. As they say in Japan, *itadakimasho* (let's eat)!

A colorful array of sushi—a feast for the eyes and the palate.

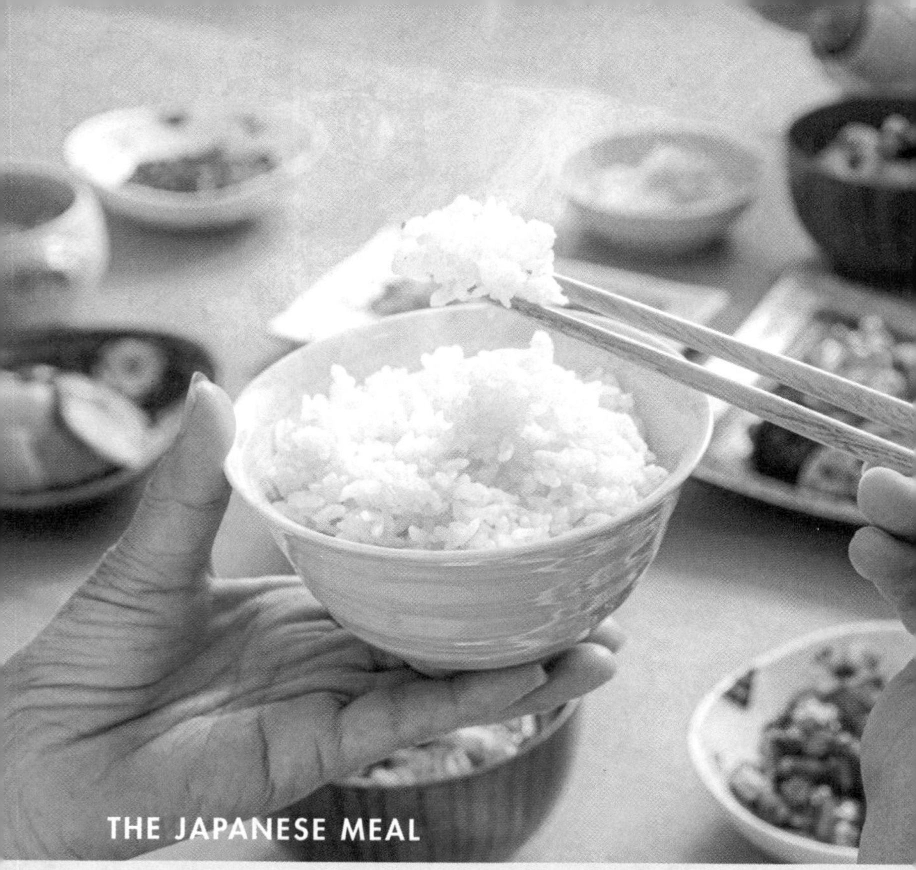

THE JAPANESE MEAL

Breakfast (*asa-gohan*, literally "the morning rice") is typically eaten at home and features rice, fried fish, and miso soup. Lunch (*hiru-gohan*), mostly eaten out of the home at school or work, involves a bento lunch box of rice, grilled fish, vegetables, and pickles. The evening meal (*ban-gohan*) has the broadest range, from restaurant meals of sushi to traditional meals cooked at home.

For home-prepared meals, the basic formula consists of one soup and three dishes—a main dish of fish or meat and two vegetable side dishes. These are served together with rice, which is part of most meals. When entertaining guests, more dishes will be served.

Classical Japanese cooking follows the principle of "fives." An ideal meal is thought to use five cooking methods—boiling, grilling, frying, steaming, and serving raw; incorporate five colors—black or purple, white, red or orange, yellow, and green; and feature five tastes—sweet, sour, salty, bitter, and *umami* (the Japanese are credited with discovering umami, or savoriness). Ingredient quality is key, as cooking techniques are intended to coax out an ingredient's maximum natural flavor rather than depending on complex sauces or seasonings.

Staple ingredients include seafood, which plays a leading role in Japanese cuisine, with dozens of species

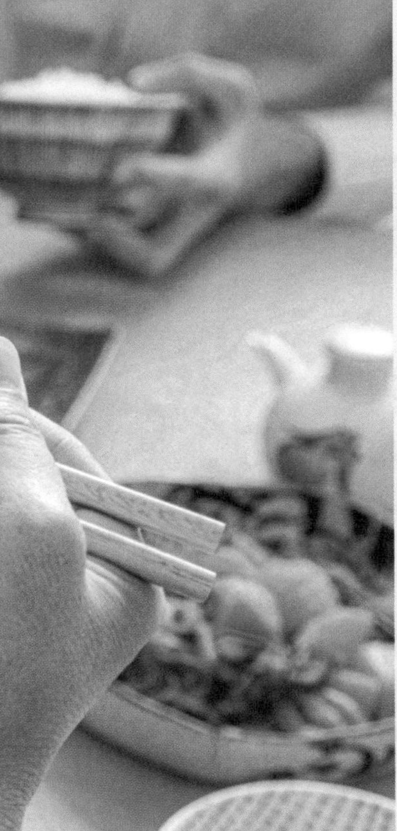

available—from familiar choices like *maguro* (tuna) and *ebi* (shrimp) to more exotic selections like *anago* (conger eel) and *fugu* (blowfish). Meat options include chicken, pork, beef, and—in rural areas—venison and wild boar. Then there is a huge variety of vegetables and fungi (both wild and cultivated) such as *renkon* (lotus root), *daikon* (white radish), and matsutake mushrooms. Finally there is the soy bean, eaten whole as edamame, as tofu, or fermented to make miso.

Condiments range from tangy *shiso* (a member of the mint family) to spicy wasabi and savory soy sauce.

DINING ETIQUETTE

Here are a few tips to help you fit in at the Japanese table:

- Don't point or gesture with chopsticks.
- Avoid lingering over communal dishes with your chopsticks while you decide what to take. Do not use the end you have been eating with to remove food from the dish—use the serving chopsticks provided or the thick end of your own chopsticks.
- When not in use, place your chopsticks on the chopstick rest.
- Never pass food from your chopsticks to someone else's or leave chopsticks standing in your rice bowl (it resembles incense sticks at a funeral).
- There is no taboo against slurping your noodle soup, though women are generally less boisterous about it than men.
- Pick up the soup bowl and drink directly from it. Take the fish or vegetables from it with your chopsticks. Return the lid to the soup bowl when you are finished eating. The rice bowl, too, is to be held in your free hand while you eat from it.
- When drinking with a friend, don't pour your own. Pour for the other person first. He will in turn pour yours.
- Japanese don't pour sauce on their rice. Sauces are intended for dipping foods into it lightly.
- It is still considered tacky to eat as you walk along a public street.

Pouring sake into a traditional Japanese cup

SUSHI

Assorted sushi

■ Sushi actually refers to anything, seafood or otherwise, served on or in vinegared rice. It is not simply raw fish. ***Nigiri-zushi*** (the sushi best known overseas) is actually a fairly recent development from Tokyo.

■ ***Makizushi*** is a sushi roll. These can be fat, elaborate rolls or simple sticks.

■ Other types of sushi include ***chirashi-zushi*** with fish and vegetables scattered artfully into the rice and, in Kyoto and Osaka, ***oshizushi*** in which preserved mackerel, among other fish, is pressed onto the rice. This is served in slices.

■ ***Funazushi,*** from around Lake Biwa near Kyoto, is perhaps the oldest type. The fish and rice are buried for six months. The rice is thrown away and the fish is eaten. This technique was historically used as a means of preserving protein. It is an acquired taste.

■ ***Kaitenzushi*** (conveyor belt sushi) outlets abound and are cheap. However, for the real experience, nothing matches a traditional sushi-ya.

Hand-rolled sushi

■ Using your hands is acceptable. Dip the fish, not the rice, lightly in the soy.

■ The ***beni-shoga*** (pickled ginger) is a palate freshener. Nibble sparingly.

■ **Wasabi** may not be served with your sushi, as the chef often dabs a bit on the rice when making your sushi. If you want extra wasabi, ask for it.

■ Customers will often request an ***omakase*** (tasting menu). The chef will then choose and serve the best fish, in the order he deems appropriate.

RAMEN

Scallions (negi)
Seaweed (nori)
Pork (cha-shu)
Shoyu ramen

■ Ramen, which evolved from Chinese noodle soups in the late 19th century, is now a Japanese staple and never far away.

■ There are four main types: from the chilly north island of Hokkaido, there is ***shio* ramen** (salt ramen) and **miso ramen** (ramen in a miso broth); ***shoyu* ramen** made with soy sauce is from Tokyo, while ***tonkotsu* ramen** (ramen in a white pork broth) is from Kyoto. Note that most ramen stocks contain meat or fish.

■ Each area has its own variation—corn and butter ramen in Sapporo; a stock made from pork and dried anchovies in northern Honshu; or Fukuoka's famed ***Hakata* ramen** with its milky tonkotsu broth and thin noodles with myriad toppings.

■ The reputation of a ramen restaurant depends on its stock, usually made with pork, sardines, or chicken but often a closely guarded secret.

■ Ramen is meant to be eaten with gusto. Slurping is normal.

■ Typical toppings include sliced roast pork, bean sprouts, boiled egg, ***shina-chiku*** (fermented bamboo shoots), spring onion, ***nori*** (dried seaweed) and ***kam-aboko*** (a fishcake made from white fish).

■ Beyond ramen, udon shops and soba shops also offer noodle dishes worth trying.

Miso ramen

Shio ramen

ROBATAYAKI

Grilled fish (tsukeba)

■ ***Robata*** means "fireside," and the style of cooking is reminiscent of old-fashioned Japanese farmhouse meals cooked over a charcoal fire in an open hearth.

■ Robatayaki restaurants and izakaya taverns serving grilled foods can be found near any busy station.

■ It's easy to order at a robatayaki because the selection of food to be grilled is lined up at the counter. Fish, meat, vegetables, tofu—take your pick.

■ Some popular choices are ***yaki-zakana*** (grilled fish), particularly ***karei-shio-yaki*** (salted and grilled flounder) and ***asari saka-mushi*** (clams simmered in sake).

■ Try the grilled Japanese ***shiitake*** (mushrooms), ***ao-to*** (green peppers), and the ***hiyayakko*** (chilled tofu sprinkled with bonito flakes, diced green onions, and soy sauce).

Matsutake mushroom

■ ***O-tsukuri*** (sashimi) and ***katsuono tataki*** (seared bonito) are very popular. The fish will vary according to the season.

■ Dipping sauces are concocted using soy, ***dashi*** (soup stock), and a hint of citrus such as yuzu.

■ Many robatayaki pride themselves on their wide selection of sake and shochu.

■ Most Japanese people will finish their meal with a rice dish.

TEMPURA

Shrimp (ebi)

Perilla (shiso)

Eggplant (nasu)

Tempura

■ Though tempura features in many busy eateries as part of a meal, it bears little resemblance to the exquisite morsels produced over the course of a full tempura meal at an specialty restaurant.

■ The secret of good tempura lies in the quality of the ingredients, the freshness and temperature of the oil, and the lightness of the batter.

■ Good tempura is light and crispy, not crunchy like fried chicken.

■ Tempura is most often fried in soybean oil, but cottonseed or sesame oil also may be used.

■ Because only the freshest of ingredients will do, the menu changes with the season. Baby corn, green peppers, sweet potato, lotus root, shiitake mushrooms, and shiso leaves are the most common vegetables. In spring expect ***sansai*** (wild vegetables) picked that morning.

Assorted tempura

■ Prawns and white fish are also popular tempura items.

■ ***Tsuyu*** (dipping sauce) is made from dashi seasoned with soy and ***mirin*** (sweet rice wine). You may see a white mound of grated daikon on your plate. Add that to the tsuyu for a punch of flavor.

■ Alternatively, mixtures of salt and powdered green tea or salt and yuzu may be sprinkled on the tempura.

BENTO

Assorted bento
Assorted fruit (kudamono)
Miso soup (miso shiru)
Salad
Assorted tempura (tempura no moriawase)
Beef teriyaki (gyu no teriyaki)
Grilled salmon (sake)
Rice (gohan)
Dipping sauce for tempura (tsuyu)
Pickles (tsukemono)

■ Bento boxes, the traditional Japanese box lunch, can be bought everywhere, from the basement level of a luxurious department store to a convenience store.

■ A typical bento will contain rice, grilled fish, a selection of vegetable dishes, some pickles, and perhaps a wedge of orange or other fruit.

■ Every region has its ***meibutsu,*** or speciality dish. These are often showcased in lunch boxes available at stations or local stores.

■ Though the humble bento is usually relatively inexpensive, more ornate and intricate boxes featuring kaiseki dishes or sushi are often bought for special occasions.

Bento lunch box

■ The bento exists in an almost limitless number of variations according to the region and the season.

■ A bento is designed to be taken out and eaten on the move. They are perfect on long-distance train rides or for a picnic in the park.

BEVERAGES

Sake

■ There are more than 2,000 different brands of sake produced throughout Japan. It is often called rice wine but is actually made by a fermenting process that is more akin to beer-making. The result is a fantastically complex drink with an alcoholic content just above wine (15–17% alcohol). It is the drink of choice with sashimi and traditional Japanese food.

■ There are four main types of sake: ***daiginjo, ginjo, junmai,*** and ***honjozo***. The first two are the most expensive and made from highly polished rice. The latter two, however, also pack flavor and character.

■ Like wine, sake can be sweet (*amakuchi*) or dry (*karakuchi*). Workaday sake may be drunk warm (*atsukan*) while the higher grades will be served chilled. Sake is the only drink that can be served at any temperature.

■ Another variety is ***nama-zake***. This is unpasteurized sake and is prized for its fresh, zingy taste.

■ ***Shochu*** is a distilled spirit that is often 25% alcohol or more. Like vodka, it can be made from potato, sweet potato, wheat, millet, or rice. It is drunk straight, on the rocks, with water, or in cocktails.

■ Any good izakaya or robatayaki will stock a diverse selection of both sake and shochu, and staff will make recommendations.

■ Beer is, perhaps, the drink of choice for most social situations. Japanese beer is of a high standard and tends to be lager. It has a relatively high alcohol content at 5% or more.

PERFORMING ARTS

A highly stylized Noh theater performance

Gorgeous costumes, sword fights and tearful reunions, acrobatics and magical transformations, spectacular makeup and masks, singing and dancing, ghosts and goblins, and star-crossed lovers: traditional Japanese arts are not short on showmanship.

The performing arts all have roots in the trade and exchange with continental Asia. Kabuki makeup as well as *gagaku* ceremonial court music and dance are Chinese-inspired; the four-string *biwa* shares a Silk Road ancestry with the Persian *oud*. Collectively the theater traditions generate work for artisans—weavers and dyers, instrument makers, wood-carvers, and more—who make a special contribution of their own. Common features aside, the differences among them are astonishing. Kabuki is great showbiz, translatable and appreciable pretty much anywhere in the world. Most of an audience that will sit riveted by the graceful, suggestive movements of *buyo* (traditional dance) will fall asleep at a dance-recitation of Noh.

MASTER PERFORMERS

As with the fine arts, the performing arts also have National Treasures. The worlds of Japanese theater are mainly in the grip of small oligarchies ("schools") where traditions are passed down from father to son. Some of these master performers are 9th- and even 22nd-generation holders of hereditary family stage names and specializations.

KABUKI

Tradition has it that Kabuki was created around 1600 by an Izumo shrine maiden named Okuni; it was then performed by troupes of women, who were often available as well for prostitution (the authorities soon banned women from the stage as a threat to public order). Eventually Kabuki cleaned up its act and developed a professional role for female impersonators, who train for years to project a seductive, dazzling femininity. By the latter half of the 18th century it had become Everyman's theater par excellence—especially among the townspeople of bustling, hustling Edo. Kabuki had spectacle; it had pathos and tragedy; it had romance and social satire. It had legions of fans, who spent all day at the theater, shouting out the names of their favorite actors at the stirring moments in their favorite plays.

Kabuki flowered especially in the "floating world" of Edo's red-light entertainment district. The theater was a place to see and be seen, to catch the latest trends in music and fashion, where people of all classes came together under one roof—something that happened nearly nowhere else in the city. Strict censorship laws were put in place and just as quickly circumvented by clever playwrights; Kabuki audiences could watch a *jidai-mono* (historical piece) set in the distant past, where the events and characters made thinly veiled reference to troublesome contemporary events.

The Oshika Kabuki troupe

A Kabuki mannequin from the Edo-Tokyo Museum

The Genroku era (1673–1841) was Kabuki's golden age, when the classic plays of Chikamatsu Monzaemon and Tsuruya Namboku were written, and most of the theatrical conventions and stage techniques we see today were honed to perfection. The *mie,* for example, is a dramatic pose the actor strikes at a certain moment in the play, to establish his character. The use of *kumadori* makeup, derived from Chinese opera and used to symbolize the essential elements of a character's nature, also dates to this period. The exaggerated facial lines of the kumadori, in vivid reds and blues and greens over a white rice-powder base, tell the audience at once that the wearer is a hero or villain, noble or arrogant, passionate or cold. To the Genroku also date revolving stages, trapdoors, and—most important—the *hanamichi*: a long, raised runway from the back of the theater, through the audience, to the main stage, where characters enter, exit, and strike their *mie* poses.

The principal character in a Noh play wears a carved, wooden mask.

Kabuki traditions are passed down through generations in a small group of families; the roles and great stage names are hereditary. The repertoire does not really grow, but stars like Ichikawa Ennosuke and Bando Tamasaburo have developed unique performance styles that still draw audiences young and old. This ancient art now has a stylish home in the Kengo Kuma–designed Kabuki-za theater in Tokyo's Ginza district, which opened in 2013.

Recommended reading: *The Kabuki Guide* by Masakatsu Gunji.

NOH

Noh is a dramatic tradition far older than Kabuki; it reached a point of formal perfection in the 14th century and survives virtually unchanged from that period. Whereas Kabuki was everyman's theater, Noh developed for the most part under the patronage of the warrior class. It is dignified, ritualized, and symbolic. Many of the plays in the repertoire are drawn from classical literature or tales of the supernatural. The texts are richly poetic, and even the Japanese find them difficult to understand. (Don't despair: the major Noh theaters usually provide synopses of the plays in English.)

The principal character in a Noh play wears a carved wooden mask. Such is the skill of the actor, and the mysterious effect of the play, that the mask itself may appear expressionless until the actor "brings it to life," at which point the mask can express a considerable range of emotions. As in Kabuki, the various roles of the Noh repertoire all have specific costumes—robes of silk brocade with intricate patterns that are works of art in themselves. Noh is not a very "accessible" kind of theater: its language is archaic; its conventions are obscure; and its measured, stately pace can put many audiences to sleep.

More accessible is the *kyogen,* a short comic interlude traditionally performed between two Noh plays in a program. The pace is quicker, the costumes (based on actual dress of the medieval period) are simpler, and most *kyogen* do not use masks; the comedy depends on the satiric premise—a clever servant who gets the best of his master, for example—and the lively facial expressions of the actors.

Like Kabuki, Noh has a number of schools, the traditions of which developed as the exclusive property of hereditary families. The major schools have their own theaters in Tokyo and Kyoto, with regular schedules of performances—but if you happen to be in Kyoto on June 1–2, don't miss the Takigi Noh: an outdoor performance given at night, by torchlight, in the precincts of the Heian Shrine. There are other torchlight performances as well in Tokyo, at the Meiji Shrine (early November) and Zojoji Temple (late September), and in Nara at the Kasuga Shrine (May).

BUNRAKU

The third major form of traditional Japanese drama is Bunraku puppet theater. Itinerant puppeteers were plying their trade in Japan as early as the 10th century; sometime in the late 16th century, a form of narrative ballad called *joruri,* performed to the accompaniment of a three-string banjolike instrument called the *shamisen,* was grafted onto their art, and Bunraku was born. The golden age of Bunraku came some 200 years later, when most of the great plays were written and the puppets themselves evolved to their present form, so expressive and intricate in their movements that they require three people acting in unison to manipulate them.

The puppets are large and elaborately dressed in period costume; each one is made up of interchangeable parts—a head, shoulder piece, trunk, legs, and arms. The puppeteer called the *omozukai* controls the expression on the puppet's face and its right arm and hand. The *hidarizukai* controls the puppet's left arm and hand along with any props that it is carrying. The *ashizukai* moves the puppet's legs. The most difficult task belongs to the omozukai—a role that can take 30 years to master.

Creating the puppet heads is an art in itself, and today there are only a handful of carvers still working. As a rule, the heads are shaped and painted for specific figures—characters of different sex, age, and personality—and fitted with elaborate wigs of human hair in various styles to indicate the puppet's social standing. Able to roll their eyes and lift their eyebrows, the puppets can achieve an amazing range of facial expressions.

The chanters, who provide both the narration of the play and the voices of the puppets, deliver their lines in a kind of high-pitched croak from deep in the throat. The texts they recite are considered to be among the classics of Japanese dramatic literature; the great playwright Chikamatsu Monzaemon (1653–1725) wrote for both Bunraku and Kabuki, and the two dramatic forms often adapted works from each other.

The most important Bunraku troupe is the government-supported National Bunraku Theatre in Osaka, but there are amateur and semiprofessional companies throughout the country—the one of the most active of them is on Awaji Island, near Shikoku. Periodically there are also performances in Tokyo in the small hall of the National Theater.

Bunraku puppets are about two-thirds human size.

ONSEN AND BATHING

A lakeside rotenburo made from natural rocks

A chain of volcanic islands on the fiery Pacific Rim, Japan has developed a splendid subculture around one of the more manageable manifestations of this powerful resource: the onsen thermal spa.

The benchmark Japanese weekend excursion—be it family outing, company retreat, or romantic getaway—is the hot spring resort. Fissured from end to end with volcanic cracks and crannies, the country positively wheezes with geothermal springs. Hot water gushes and sprays almost everywhere—but most especially in the mountains; there are hot springs in every prefecture, on every offshore island—even in cities often built above the very fault lines themselves.

YUDEDAKO

The Japanese have a special term for that blissful state of total immersion—*yudedako* (literally, "boiled octopus")—and Japanese people of all ages will journey for miles to attain it. Soaking in hot springs is a step on the road to sound health, good digestion, clear skin, marital harmony—to whatever it is that gives you a general sense of being at one with the universe.

THE ONSEN EXPERIENCE

An onsen can refer to a particular region or subregion, like Yufuin in Oita Prefecture, Kinugawa in Tochigi, or Hakone in Kanagawa: a resort destination especially well endowed with thermal springs. Or it can mean more specifically a public bathhouse with a spring-fed pool, where you pay an admission fee and soak at your leisure. (At last count, there were some 6,700 of these nationwide.) Or it could mean a lodging—one of two basic varieties—with a spring of its own. One type is the large onsen hotel. Newer (or newly renovated) ones have Japanese and western style rooms and a range of baths, while older ones may be slightly run down but have a retro appeal harking back to Japan's bubble days. The traditional ryokan-style onsen is the one of everyone's dreams: the picture-perfect traditional inn of half a dozen rooms, nestled up somewhere in the mountains all by itself, with a spectacular view and a *rotenburo*—an outdoor bath—to enjoy it from.

THE ROTENBURO

While a rotenburo just means an outdoor bath, at many onsen they are an exquisitely crafted bath with stepping-stones, lanterns, and bamboo screens. The rotenburo is a year-round indulgence; the view from the bath might be of a mountainside, white with cherry blossoms in spring; a lakefront doused in the red and gold of maples in autumn; or a winter panorama, with the snow piled high on the pines and hedges that frame the landscape. Some onsen have private rotenburo that you can book in advance or upon check in. Whatever the season, you'll need to make reservations well in advance for the best onsen accommodations. Japan has more than 3,000 registered spas; collectively they draw nearly 140 million visitors a year, and hotel space is in high demand.

Gakenoyu Onsen in Nagano

A spa in Shirahama Onsen

WHAT IS AN ONSEN?

By law, an onsen is only an onsen if the water comes out of the ground at a specified minimum temperature, and contains at least one of 19 designated minerals and chemical compounds—which makes for a wide range of choices. There are iron springs with red water; there are silky-smooth alkaline springs; there are springs with radon and sulphur sodium bicarbonate; there are springs with water at a comfortable 100°F (37.8°C), and springs so hot they have bath masters to make sure you stay only for three minutes and not a fatal second longer.

Most onsen have single-sex bathing; a few have mixed bathing.

One reason many Westerners are reluctant to go bathing in Japan: Japanese communal bathing is done in the buff—but that shouldn't deter you from the experience. The bath is a great equalizer: in a sense the bath *is* Japan, in its unalloyed egalitarianism. Each bather offers the other an equal degree of respect and regard; people generally do not behave in a way that might spoil the enjoyment of any other bather; nor is anyone embarrassed. It is freeing and you can relax right into it.

ONSEN ETIQUETTE

Another reason you might have for your reluctance is the worrisome conviction that bathing with a bunch of strangers comes with a raft of rules—rules all those strangers are taught from childhood, but at least one of which you're bound to break, to your everlasting horror and shame. "What if I drop the something into the bath?" is a common fear.

But the pitfalls are not so bad. There certainly are protocols to follow, but it's a short list.

- While there are still a few spas that keep alive the old custom of *konyoku* (mixed bathing), all of them have separate entrances for men and women, each labeled with Japanese characters.

- A word of warning: body tattoos, in Japan, are indelibly associated with the yakuza—organized crime families and their minions—and spas commonly refuse entry to tattooed visitors to avoid upsetting their regular clientele. The rule is strictly enforced. Even foreign tourists, who are clearly not involved in Japanese organized crime, can be turned away for their tattoos. If your tattoo is small enough, put a bandage over it. Another option is to only bathe in *kashikiri-buro*, or private baths, which are available at larger onsen and many ryokan. This may also be an appealing option for those who'd rather not bare all in front of multiple strangers.

- The first room you come to inside is the dressing room. It's often tatami-floored: take your shoes or slippers off in the entryway. The dressing room will have lockers for your keys and valuables, and rows of wicker or plastic baskets on shelves; pick one, and put your clothes in it. If you're staying overnight at an inn with a spa of its own, you'll find a cotton kimono called a *nemaki* in your room—you sleep in it, in lieu of pajamas—and a light quilted jacket called a *hanten*. Night or day, this is standard gear to wear from your room to the spa, anywhere else around the inn, and even for a stroll out of doors. Leave them in the basket.

■ Bring two towels: leave the bigger one in the basket to dry off with, and take the smaller one with you next door to the baths. (You will likely see that this towel to preserve your modesty is the accepted way of moving around in the spa.)

■ The bath area will have rows of washing stations along the walls: countertops with supplies of soap and shampoo, taps, a mirror, shower-head, stool, and bucket. Here's where you get clean—and that means *really* clean. Soap up, shower, scrub off every particle of the day's wear and tear. Leave no trace of soap.

■ You can take the towel with you to the bath, but don't put it in the water. Most people leave theirs on the side or set them folded on top of their heads. (Another item of protocol: spas don't insist on bathing caps, but they do want you to keep your head above water.)

■ Find a pleasant spot; soak in blissful silence if you prefer (but not too long if you're not used to it), or feel free to strike up a conversation with a fellow soaker: *atsui desu ne*—the local equivalent of "It's hot, isn't it?"—is a good start. The Japanese call their friendliest, most relaxing acquaintances *hadaka no o-tsukiai*: naked encounters.

Staying at a mega-onsen? Conviviality reigns in the baths of these establishments, with all sorts of amenities to help it along. At some inns, you can order a small floating table for yourself and your fellow boilers, just big enough for a ceramic flask of sake or two and a suitable number of cups. You get to warm your insides and outsides at the same time.

When you've soaked to your heart's content, dry yourself off with your smaller towel and head back to the dressing room. Depending on the onsen's water, you might want to rinse off before drying off. Grab your larger towel from the basket, wrap it around yourself, and rest a bit until your body temperature drops back to normal. Get dressed and head out to the post-bath rest area to have a cold glass of water and lounge on the tatami mats before heading back out into the world.

You clean yourself thoroughly before setting foot in the onsen.

THE RYOKAN

A traditional tatami-mat room in a ryokan

You're likely to find Japanese hospitality polished, warm, and professional pretty much anywhere you stay—but nowhere more so than in a ryokan: a traditional inn.

Ryokans are typically one- or two-story wooden buildings where the guest rooms have tatami floors; the bedding—stowed by day in a closet—is rolled out at night. The rooms have hardly any furniture—perhaps one low dining table and cushions on the floor, a chest of drawers with a mirror, and a scroll painting or a flower arrangement in the *tokonoma* (alcove)—but every room in a proper ryokan will have windows with sliding paper screens looking out on an exquisite interior garden or scenery. Rates are per person and include the cost of breakfast and dinner. Some top-of-the-line ryokans might expect first-time guests to have introductions from a known and respected client.

COSTS

Ryokans of august lineage and exemplary service are expensive: expect to pay ¥40,000 or even ¥60,000 per person per night with two meals. There are plenty of lower-priced ryokan in Japan, which start from ¥10,000 per person, including breakfast and dinner, though these may not have garden views. The Japan National Tourism Organization has a listing of some of the latter.

RYOKAN ETIQUETTE

Remove your shoes as you step up from the entryway of your ryokan, and change into slippers. An attendant will escort you to your room. (It might take you two or three tries thereafter to find it on your own. Ryokans pride themselves on quiet and privacy, and the rooms are typically laid out in a labyrinth of corridors, where you're seldom aware of the presence of other guests.) Slippers come off at the door; on tatami, only socks/stockings or bare feet are acceptable. Relax first with a cup of green tea, and then head for the bath. In ryokans with thermal pools—not all have them—you can take to the waters at nearly any time and you'll be told of any time restrictions upon checking in. Be mindful of the bathing rules; wash and rinse off thoroughly before you get in the tub for a long hot soak. After your bath, change into a nemaki, the simple cotton kimono you'll find in your room, that doubles as sleepwear—or as standard garb for an informal stroll. These days, ryokans often have private baths, but especially in more venerable establishments (even those with astronomical rates), all facilities may be shared.

Ryokans don't have legions of staff, and will appreciate if you observe their routines and schedules. Guests are expected to arrive in the late afternoon and eat around six. The front doors are sometimes locked at 10, so plan for early evenings. Breakfast is served around eight, and checkout is typically at 10. It might feel rather regimented, but just remember that your only task is to relax.

A ryokan meal served in myriad little dishes

Bedding for a ryokan, which is laid out nightly

FOOD

Not every inn that calls itself a ryokan offers meals. Some offer only breakfast; some have no meals at all. Seek out those that do; it's an important part of the experience. And while some ryokans will allow you to pay a lesser rate and skip dinner, it's worth paying extra for the feast of local specialties in beautiful dishes of all shapes and sizes (sometimes served in your room). When you're finished, your attendant will clear the table and lay out your futon bedding: a mattress filled with cotton wadding and (in winter) a heavy, thick comforter (this often happens when you've stepped out of your room, so don't be surprised). In summer the comforter is replaced with a thinner quilt. In the morning the attendant will clear away the futon and bring in your Japanese-style breakfast: grilled fish, miso soup, pickled vegetables, and rice. If you prefer, the staff will usually be able to come up with coffee and toast, not to mention a fried egg.

JAPANESE POP CULTURE

Pikachu performs at the Pokémon Café

Step onto the streets of Shibuya—or brave the crowds of preening high-school fashionistas populating Harujuku's Takeshita-dori—and you'll get a crash course on Japanese pop culture that extends way beyond familiar exports like Hello Kitty and Godzilla.

Japanese pop culture has long been a source of fascination—and sometimes bewilderment—for foreign visitors. New fashion styles, technology, and popular media evolve quickly here, and in something of a vacuum. This leads to a constant turnover of unique, sometimes wacky trends you won't find anywhere outside Japan. Immerse yourself in the latest fads by walking through neighborhoods like Shibuya, Shimo-Kitazawa, Harujuku, and Akihabara.

DID YOU KNOW?

There are more than 4 million vending machines in Japan, making it the densest population of machines per capita anywhere in the world. Here automated machines sell everything from hot drinks to live lobsters. Some use facial recognition to verify age for tobacco and beer and even offer indecisive customers age-appropriate drink recommendations.

KAWAII

Kawaii, or "cute," is an aww-inducing aesthetic you'll see all over Tokyo; major airlines plaster depictions of adorable animation characters like Pikachu across the sides of their planes, and even at local police stations it's not unusual for a fluffy, stuffed-animal mascot to be on display. Duck into an arcade photo booth to take *purikura*—pictures that let you choose your own kawaii background—or head to Sanrio Puroland, an entire theme park dedicated to cuteness.

Matriarch of Japanese kawaii, Hello Kitty

J-POP

Japanese pop often conjures images of boy or girl "idol" groups with over-the-top outfits, sugar-sweet synthesized beats, and love-professing lyrics. The heyday of saccharine groups like Arashi or AKB48 (named after the neighborhood of Akihabara and the 48 core members) coincided with the beginning of Japan's tourist boom in the 2000s after all. While idol groups still abound, less saccharine groups have been topping the charts in Japan. Mainstream Japanese music today is more arguably the most varied and outward-looking it has been since the Shibuya-kei bands of the 1990s. Bands like Perfume and Babymetal upended the image of what an idol group is, while others like Yoasobi have had chart hits and acclaim internationally.

Distinctively colorful manga

ANIME AND MANGA

Animation (anime) and comic books (manga) are extremely popular with readers both young and old. Comic book addicts, known as *otaku,* claim Tokyo's Akihabara as their home base. Though *otaku* can be translated as "nerd" or "obsessive," the term has been embraced by some. Former prime minister Taro Aso declared himself an otaku and confessed to reading 10 to 20 manga a week.

VIDEO GAMES

Japan is the cradle of the video game industry, and ever since the early 1970s it's been a dominant force in the gaming market. As companies like Namco gave way to Sega, Nintendo, and Sony, the gaming systems also continued to evolve and become more sophisticated. Like manga and anime, games enjoy a mainstream following. If you're a gamer, you'll be happy to find games that are unreleased in the United States alongside rebooted classics like *The Legend of Zelda* and *Super Mario Bros.*

BASEBALL IN JAPAN

Mazda Zoom-Zoom Stadium in Hiroshima

Sumo may be the most visible spectator event, but without question, the most popular sport in Japan is baseball. It was first introduced in 1872 by Horace Wilson and has been popular ever since.

Each October two major-league teams in the United States (or one major-league team from the United States and one major-league team from Canada) play the best of seven games to decide the World Series. But judging from the results of the World Baseball Classic (WBC) that Japan has won twice, any true world series of baseball would have to include Japan. Although the Japanese professional-league season is shorter than its American counterpart (around 140 games versus 162 games), the major-league season's brevity is more than made up for by the company-league season, the university circuit, and the spring and summer high school tournaments. In addition there are junior high school and elementary school leagues. Many municipalities and towns even have senior leagues for people over 60 years old. The game is played everywhere: from the southern islands of Okinawa to the northern tip of Hokkaido.

CATCHING A GAME

Even if you're not a baseball fan, you should try to take in a game on any level for the spectacle. Like the players, the fans come prepared. From team colors and fan paraphernalia to songs and boxed lunches, the Japanese fans have it down. The cheering starts with the first pitch and doesn't end until the last out. Wherever you go to see a game, you will be made to feel welcome and your interest or curiosity will be rewarded.

BASEBALL-DO

Martial arts in Japan (judo, kendo, kyudo) and many other activities including the tea ceremony (*chado*) and calligraphy (*shodo*) end in the suffix *do* (pronounced "doe," as in the female deer, and meaning "way"). In Japan baseball is also a *do,* an art rather than a sport. Of course, the Japanese watch baseball as they watch any sport, but in terms of their preparation and mental approach to the game, it is a do.

All of Japan's active arts require years of practice to achieve the level of intense concentration and mindlessness that mastery requires. The idea is that if you practice something long enough and hard enough, it will become pure reflex. Then you won't have to think about what to do or when to do it. You will just do it. Major players like Sakamoto, Yanagata, and Nakajima play with a fluidity and grace that is beyond athleticism, exhibiting true mastery of the sport, and the result can be breathtaking.

SPRING AND SUMMER HIGH SCHOOL TOURNAMENTS

If you're fortunate enough to be in Japan in either March or August, you can attend the high school baseball tournament held annually at Koshien Stadium in Nishinomiya (near Osaka),

Yokohama's baseball stadium, home to the DeNa BayStars

Players from the Japanese Little League

the mecca of Japanese baseball. In what regard is high school baseball held? Well, the pro team that normally plays at Koshien (the Hanshin Tigers) has to hit the road for two weeks in August to make way for the summer tournament. Both high school tournaments last about two weeks. Many of the star high school players go on to be standout players in both Japan and the United States.

TICKET PRICES

Tickets for a professional baseball game (the season runs from late March to October) are a relatively good buy. At Koshien, home of the Hanshin Tigers, prices range from ¥1,600 for a seat in the outfield to ¥5,000 for a reserved seat on a lower level. When box seats are offered for sale, you can expect to pay around ¥6,000. Prices are similar at Tokyo Dome, where the Yomiuri Giants play.

Tickets for the high school baseball tournaments are even more affordable. Prices range from ¥500 for upper-reserved to ¥1,200 for lower-reserved to ¥1,600 for box seats. Seats in the bleachers are free throughout the tournaments.

JAPANESE MARTIAL ARTS

A practice kendo session

Take all that the flashy moves in movies with a grain of salt: the Japanese martial arts are primarily about balance—mental, spiritual, and physical—and only incidentally about attack and self-defense.

Judo and karate are now as much icons of Japan as anime or consumer electronics, and just as enthusiastically embraced abroad. Judo, karate, and aikido, all essentially 20th-century developments, have gone global; it would be hard to name a country anywhere without a network of *dojos* (martial arts academies or training halls) and local organizations, affiliates of the governing bodies in Japan, certifying students and holding competitions. Judo has been an Olympic sport for men since the 1964 games in Tokyo, and for women since 1988. An estimated 50 million people worldwide practice karate, in one or another of the eight different forms recognized by the World Union of Karate-do Federations. Aikido was first introduced abroad in the 1950s; the International Aikido Federation now has affiliates in 44 member nations. Korea and Taiwan have instruction programs in *kendo* (fencing) that begin at the secondary school level.

LEVELS

Levels of certification are as much a part of the martial arts as they are in other traditional disciplines—the difference being that marks of rank are clearly visible. Students progress from the 10th *kyu* level to the 1st, and then from 1st *dan* to 8th (or 10th, depending on the system or school). Beginners wear white belts, intermediates wear brown, dan holders wear black or black-and-red.

KYUDO: THE WAY OF THE BOW

Archery is the oldest of Japan's traditional martial arts, dating from the 12th century, when archers played an important role in the struggles for power among samurai clans. Today it is practiced as a sport and a spiritual discipline. The object is not just to hit the target (no mean feat), but to do so in proper form.

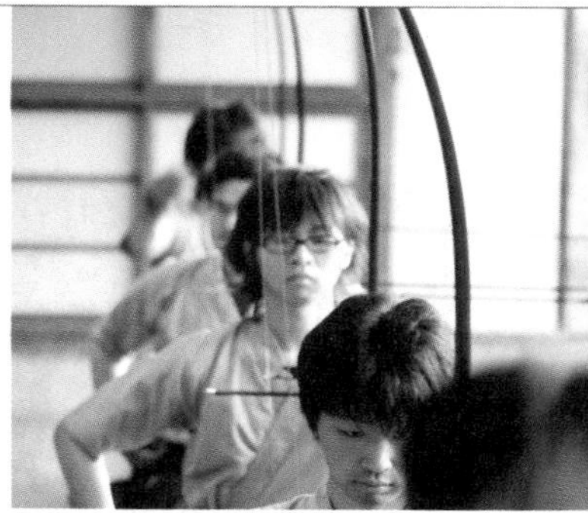

Group of young students practicing kyudo

KENDO: THE WAY OF THE SWORD

Fencing was a mainstay of feudal Japan, but the roots of modern kendo date to the early 18th century, with the introduction of the *shinai*—a practice sword made of bamboo slats—and the distinctive armor (*bogu*) still in use to protect the specific target areas the fencer must strike to earn points in competition. Attacks must be executed with foot stamping and loud spirited shouts called *kiai*.

JUDO: THE GENTLE WAY

Dr. Kano Jigoro (1860–1938) was the proverbial 90-pound weakling as a teenager; to overcome his frailty, he immersed himself in the martial arts, and over a period of years developed a reformed version of *jujutsu* on "scientific principles," which he finally codified in 1884. The *ju* of judo means "softness" or "gentleness"—because you use your opponent's strength against them—but this really is a rough-and-tumble contact sport.

Competitors at a judo tournament

KARATE: THE EMPTY HAND

Odd as it may sound, *karate* (literally: "the empty hand") doesn't quite qualify as a traditional Japanese martial art. Its origins are Chinese, but it was largely developed in the Ryukyu Kingdom (Okinawa before it was annexed), and didn't come to Japan proper until 1922. It lays stress on self-defense, spiritual and mental balance, and *kata*—formal, almost ritual sequences of movement.

AIKIDO: THE WAY OF HARMONY

The youngest of the Japanese martial arts was developed in the 1920s by Ueshiba Morihei (1883–1969), incorporating elements of both jujutsu and kendo, with much bigger doses of philosophy and spirituality. Aikido techniques consist largely of throws; the first thing a student learns is how to fall safely. After a stylized strike or a punch; the intended receiver counters by getting out of the way and pivoting into a throw or an arm/shoulder pin. The essential idea is to do no damage.

SUMO

Two wrestlers battle in the ring

This centuries-old national sport of Japan is not to be taken lightly—as anyone who has ever seen a sumo wrestler will testify. And although sheer mass might seem to be the key to success, that's not necessarily the case.

There are no weight limits or categories in sumo; contenders in the upper ranks average 350 pounds. But Chiyonofuji, one of the all-time great *yokozuna* (grand champions), who tipped the scales at a mere 280 pounds, regularly faced—and defeated—opponents who outweighed him by 200 pounds or more. That said, sumo wrestlers do spend a lot of their time just bulking up, consuming enormous quantities of a high-protein stew called *chanko nabe,* washed down with beer. Akebono, the first foreign-born yokozuna, weighed more than 500 pounds.

SUMO RULES

The official catalog of sumo techniques includes 82 different ways of pushing, pulling, tripping, tossing, or slapping down your opponent, but the basic rules are exquisitely simple: except for hitting below the belt (which is essentially all a sumo wrestler wears) and striking with a closed fist, almost anything goes. Touch the sand with anything but the soles of your feet, or get forced out of the ring, and you lose.

SUMO HISTORY

The earliest written references to sumo date back to the year 712; for many centuries it was not a sport, but a Shinto religious rite, associated with Imperial Court ceremonies. Its present form—with the raised clay *dohyo* (platform) and circle of rice straw bales to mark the ring, the ranking system, the referee and judges, the elaborate costumes and purification rituals—was largely developed in the 16th and early 17th centuries.

THE SUMO WORLD

Sumo is hierarchical and formal. To compete, you must belong to a *heya* (stable) run by a retired wrestler who has purchased that right from the association. The stable master, or *oyakata,* is responsible for bringing in as many new wrestlers as the heya can accommodate, for their training and schooling in the elaborate etiquette of sumo, and for every facet of their daily lives. Youngsters recruited into the sport live in the stable dormitory, doing all the community chores and waiting on their seniors while they learn. When they rise high enough in tournament rankings, they acquire servant-apprentices of their own.

All the stables in the association—now some 43 in number—are in or around Tokyo. Most are clustered on both sides of the Sumida River near the green-roofed Kokugikan (National Sumo Arena), in the areas called Asakusabashi and Ryogoku. Come early in the day, and you can peer through the windows of the heya to watch them practice, or ask your hotel concierge to find a way inside the heya. Some offer opportunities for people to watch the practice.

Wrestlers in traditional dress outside the arena

The ceremonial entrance of the tournament participants

There are six official sumo tournaments throughout the year: three in Tokyo (January, May, and September); one each in Osaka (March), Nagoya (July), and Fukuoka (November). Wrestlers in the upper divisions fight 15 matches over 15 days. A few weeks before each tournament, a panel of judges and association *toshiyori* (elders) publish a table called a *banzuke,* which divides the 800-plus wrestlers into six ranks and two divisions, East and West, to determine who fights whom. Rankings are based on a wrestler's record in the previous tournament: win a majority of your matches and you go up in the next banzuke; lose a majority and you go down.

If you can't attend one of the Tokyo sumo tournaments, you may want to take a tour of a sumo stable to take in a practice session.

THE GEISHA

A traditional geisha performance in Kanazawa

The geisha—with her white makeup and Cupid's-bow red lip rouge, her hair ornaments, the rich brocade of her kimono—is as much an icon of Japan, instantly recognizable the world over, as Mt. Fuji itself.

Gei stands for artistic accomplishment (*sha* simply means "person"), and a geisha must be a person of many talents. As a performer, she should have a lovely voice and a command of traditional dance, and play beautifully on an instrument like the *shamisen*. She must have a finely tuned aesthetic sense, and excel at the art of conversation. In short, she should be the ultimate party hostess and gracious companion. Geisha (or *geiko* in Kyoto dialect) begin their careers at a very young age, when they are accepted into an *okiya,* a sort of guildhall where they live and learn as *maiko* (apprentices). The okiya is a thoroughly matriarchal society; the owner-manager is called *o-kami-san,* who is addressed as *okaasan* (mother), to underscore the fact that the geishas have given up one family for another.

GEISHA LIFE

The okiya provides the apprentices with room and board, pays for their training and clothing (the latter a staggering expense), and oversees their daily lives. The maiko in turn do household chores; when they have become full-fledged geisha, they contribute a part of their income to the upkeep of the house and its all-female staff of teachers, dressers, and maids.

The world of the geisha reflects Japan's tendency toward mastery and apprenticeships. Sumo's system of *heya* also shows how traditions of old are not always in line with modern life, yet survive. In the past a young girl from a large family, for example, would likely join another family upon marriage (although boys also might join other households when they marry). An apprentice would join the house of the master for anything from knife-making to woodworking and geisha are no different. Traditionally, this was an opportunity for talented girls to have a job in a world that was much less fluid than modern Japan is today.

Geishas on the streets of Kyoto

THE GEISHA BUSINESS

There are no free agents in the geisha world; to engage one for a party you need a referral. Geisha work almost exclusively at traditional inns (ryokan), restaurants (*ryotei*), and teahouses (*chaya*); the owners of one will contact an *okiya* with which they have a connection and make the engagement—providing, of course, that you've established yourself as a trustworthy client. That means you will understand and be prepared to pay the bill when it shows up sometime later. Fees for a geisha's or maiko's time are measured in "sticks"—generally, one hour: the time it would take a stick of incense to burn down—and the okiya can really stick it to you. Bills are based on the number of guests at the party and can run as high as ¥25,000 per person or more for a two-hour engagement.

Geisha makeup and colorful attire are iconic.

There were as many as 80,000 geisha in the 1920s; today there may be 1,000 left, most of them living and working in the Gion district of Kyoto; in Kanazawa; and in the Shimbashi, Akasaka, and Ginza districts of Tokyo. Fewer and fewer young Japanese women are willing to make the total commitment this closed world demands (even a geisha who opts to live independently will remain affiliated with her okiya for the rest of her career); fewer and fewer Japanese men of means have the taste or inclination to entertain themselves or important guests in this elegant fashion. On the other hand, the profession—while it lasts—does provide considerable job security. A geisha is valued, not solely for her beauty, but for her artistic and social skills—and her absolute discretion (what she might see and hear, for example at a party hosted by a political bigwig for his important business connections, could topple empires).

THE TEA CEREMONY

A woman performing a tea ceremony

The Way of Tea—in Japanese, *Cha-no-yu* or *sado*—is more than a mere ceremony: it is a profound spiritual and meditative ritual. Although you can view it rather inexpensively, the full experience of sado is the meditative experience of losing oneself in the known patterns of serving and drinking.

Tea came to Japan from China in the late 8th century, first as a medicinal plant; it was the Zen monks of the 12th century who started the practice of drinking tea for a refresher between meditation sessions. Rules and customs began to evolve, and they coalesced in the Muromachi period of the 14th and 15th centuries as the earliest form of the Cha-no-yu. The Way of Tea developed an aesthetic of its own, rooted in the Zen sense of discipline, restraint, and simplicity: an aesthetic in which the most valued tea bowls, vessels, and utensils were humble, unadorned—and even imperfect. The choreographed steps were devised to focus the appreciation—in Japanese, called *wabi*—for this subdued and quiet refinement.

THE TEA PAVILION

Contemplate a Japanese tea pavilion long enough, and you begin to see how much work and thought can go into the design of something so simple. A stone path through a garden, a thatched roof, a low doorway into a single room with a *tokonoma* (alcove) and tatami floor are barely big enough for the tea master and a few guests, and yet are a gateway to the infinite.

The poet-priest Sen no Rikyu (1522–91) is the most revered figure in the history of sado. Three traditional schools of the tea ceremony, the Ura Senke, the Omote Senke, and the Mushakoji Senke—with some variations among them—maintain the forms and aesthetic principles he developed.

A full-scale formal tea ceremony, called a *chaji,* is like a drama in two acts, involving a multicourse *kaiseki* meal, two different kinds of powdered green tea, and an intermission—and can take as long as four hours to perform. Most ceremonies are less formal, confined to the serving of *usucha* ("thin tea") and a confection for an intimate group; these are called *o-chakai.* Both forms demand a strictly determined, stately series of moves to be made by both guests and hosts.

Participants gather first in the *machiai,* a kind of waiting room or shelter in the garden, until they are invited to proceed to the teahouse. They remove their shoes, and enter the teahouse through a low doorway. It is customary to comment on the flower arrangement or scroll in the alcove. The guests sit in *seiza,* their legs tucked under them; the host enters from another small doorway, greets them, and carefully cleans the utensils: bowl, tea scoop, caddy, ladle, whisk. No matter that they are spotless already; cleaning them is part of the ritual.

A bowl of matcha green tea

An outdoor garden tea ceremony

When the tea is prepared, it is served first to the principal guest, who turns the bowl in the palm of his hand, drains it in three deep, careful sips, and returns it to the host. The other participants are served in turn. The guests comment on the presentation, and the ceremony is over; when they leave the pavilion, the host bows to them from the door.

Should you be invited to a tea ceremony, you likely won't be expected to have the same mastery of the etiquette as an experienced guest, but the right frame of mind will get you through. Be prepared to sit in seiza for quite a long time. Make conversation that befits the serenity of the moment. (A well-known haiku poetess once said that what she learned most from sado was to think before she spoke.) Above all, pay close attention to the practiced movements of the host, and remember to praise the *wabi*—the understated beauty—of the utensils he or she has chosen.

Recommended reading: *The Book of Tea* by Okakura Kakuzo; *Cha-no-Yu: The Japanese Tea Ceremony* by A. L. Sadler.

JAPANESE GARDENS

The garden of Hogon-in, Kyoto

Oases of calm and contemplation—and philosophical statements in their own right—Japanese gardens are quite unlike the arrangements of flowers, shrubs, and trees you find in the West.

One key to understanding—and more fully enjoying—a Japanese garden is knowing that its design, like all traditional Japanese arts, emerged out of the country's unique mixture of religious and artistic ideas. From Shintoism comes the belief in the divinity or spirit that dwells in natural phenomena like mountains, trees, and stones. The influence of Taoism is reflected in the islands that serve as symbolic heavens for the souls of those who achieve perfect harmony. Buddhist gardens—especially Zen gardens, expressions of the "less is more" aesthetic of the warrior caste—evolved in medieval times as spaces for meditation and the path to enlightenment. The classic example from this period is the *karesansui* (dry landscape) style, a highly abstract composition of meticulously placed rocks and raked sand or gravel, sometimes with a single pruned tree, but with no water at all.

SHAKEI

Shakei (borrowed landscape) is a way of extending the boundaries of the visual space by integrating a nearby attractive view—like a mountain or a sweeping temple roofline, for example—framing and echoing it with plantings of similar shape or color inside the garden itself. A middle ground, usually a hedge or a wall, blocks off any unwanted view and draws the background into the composition.

GARDEN DESIGN

Historically, the first garden designers in Japan were temple priests; the design concepts themselves were originally Chinese. Later, from the 16th century on, the most remarkable Japanese gardens were created by tea masters, who established a genre of their own for settings meant to deepen and refine the tea ceremony experience. Hence the *roji*: a garden path of stepping-stones from the waiting room to the teahouse itself, a transition from the ordinary world outside that prepares participants emotionally and mentally for the ceremony. Gradually gardens moved out of the exclusive realm to which only nobles, wealthy merchants, and poets had access, and the increasingly affluent middle class began to demand professional designers. In the process the elements of the garden became more elaborate, complex, and symbolic.

The "hide-and-reveal" principle, for example, dictates that there should be no point from which all of a garden is visible, that there must always be mystery and incompleteness in its changing perspectives: the garden *unfolds* as you walk from one view to another along the winding path. References to celebrated natural wonders and literary allusions, too, are frequently used design techniques. Mt. Fuji might be represented by a truncated cone of stones; Ama-no-Hashidate, the famous pine-covered spit of land across Miyazu Bay, near Kyoto, might be rendered by a stone bridge; a lone tree might stand for a mighty forest. Abstract concepts and themes from myths and legends, familiar to many Japanese, are similarly part of the garden vocabulary. The use of boulders in a streambed, for example, can represent life's surmountable difficulties; a pine tree can stand for strength and endurance; islands in a pond can evoke a faraway paradise.

The gardens of Kinkaku-ji, Kyoto

Koishikawa Korakuen Garden, Tokyo

Seasonal change is a highlight of the Japanese garden. The designer in effect choreographs the different plants that come into their glory at different times of year: cherry and plum blossoms and wisteria in spring; hydrangeas, peonies, and water lilies in summer; the spectacular reds and orange of the Japanese maple leaves in autumn. Even in winter the snow clinging to the garden's bare bones makes an impressive sight. In change there is permanence; in permanence there is fluid movement—often represented in the garden with a water element: a pond or a flowing stream, or an abstraction of one in raked gravel or stone.

JAPANESE FINE ARTS

Japanese lacquerware

What raises Japanese handicrafts to the level of fine arts? It is, one could argue, the standards set by the nation's *Ningen kokuho*: its Living National Treasures, who hand down these traditional skills from generation to generation.

Legally speaking, these people are "Holders of Important Intangible Cultural Properties." A law, enacted in 1950, establishes two broad categories of Intangible Property. One comprises the performing arts: Kabuki, Noh, Bunraku puppet theater, and traditional music and dance. The other embraces a wide range of handicrafts, most of them in the various forms and styles of textiles, pottery, lacquerware, papermaking, wood carving, and metalworking—from all over the country. The tiny cohort of individuals and groups who exemplify these traditions at the highest levels receive an annual stipend; the money is intended not so much to support the title holders (Living National Treasures command very healthy sums for their work) as to help them attract and train apprentices, and thus keep the traditions alive.

CARRYING ON

Official sponsorship has proven itself a necessity in more than a few craft traditions. The weaving of *bashofu*, for example, a fabric from Okinawa, is on its way to becoming a lost art—unless the present Living National Treasure can encourage enough people to carry on with the craft. Papermaking, a cottage industry that once supported some 28,500 households nationwide, now supports only a few hundred.

LACQUERWARE

Japanese lacquerware has its origins in the Jomon period (10,000–300 BC), and by the Nara period (710–794) most of the techniques we recognize today, such as *maki-e* (literally, "sprinkled picture")—the use of gold or silver powder to underlay the lacquer—had been developed. The Edo period (1603–1868) saw the uses of lacquer extended to vessels and utensils for the newly prosperous merchant class.

The production of lacquerware starts with refining sap from the Japanese sumac (*urushi*). The lacquer is layered on basketry, wood, bamboo, metal, and even paper. The polished black and red surfaces may have inlays of mother-of-pearl or precious metals, creating motifs and designs of exquisite beauty and delicacy. Many regions in Japan are famous for their distinct lacquerware styles, among them Kyoto, Wajima, and Tsugaru. ■TIP➜ **Some tableware has laquer over a plastic base instead of wood. When purchasing, check with the label or ask staff to check what material it is made of.**

PAPERMAKING

Washi, Japanese paper, can have a soft translucent quality that seems to belie its amazing strength and durability. It makes a splendid material for calligraphy and brush painting, and it can be fashioned into a wide variety of traditional decorative objects. The basic ingredient is the inner bark of the paper mulberry, but leaves, fiber threads, and even gold flake can be added in later stages for a dramatic effect. The raw mulberry branches are first steamed, then bleached in cold water or snow. The fibers are boiled with ash lye, rinsed, beaten into pulp, and soaked in a tank of starchy taro solution. A screen is dipped into the tank, pulled up, and rocked to drain the solution and crosshatch the fibers. The wet sheets of paper are stacked to press out the excess liquid, then dried in the sun. ■TIP➜ **The best places to watch the papermaking process are Kurodani, near Kyoto; Mino, in central Japan; and Yame, near Kurume. Many are known for their unique washi products: Gifu for umbrellas and lanterns, Nagasaki for its distinctive kites, Nara for calligraphy paper.**

A calligrapher at work

Traditional Japanese papermaking

CALLIGRAPHY

Calligraphy arrived in Japan around the middle of the 6th century AD with the sacred texts of Buddhism, written in *kanji* (Chinese ideograms). By 800 the *kana* syllabic alphabets of the Japanese language had also developed, and the writing of both kanji and kana with a brush, in india ink, had become an art form—a wedding of meaning and

About 30 different styles of porcelain are made in Japan.

emotion that was (and still is) regarded as a revelation of the writer's individual character. The flow of the line from top to bottom, the balance of shapes and sizes, the thickness of the strokes, the amount of ink on the brush: all contribute to the composition of the work. There are five main styles of calligraphy in Japan. Two are based on the Chinese: *tensho,* typically used for seal carving; and *reisho,* for the copying of sutras. Three are solely Japanese: *kaisho,* the block style often seen in wood carving; and the flowing *sosho* (cursive) and *gyosho* styles. *Sosho* is especially impressive—an expression of freedom and spontaneity that takes years of discipline to achieve; retouching and erasing is impossible.

CERAMICS

There are some 30 traditional styles of pottery in Japan, from unglazed stoneware to painted porcelain. Since the late 1600s, when Imari and Kakiemon porcelain were exported to Europe, the achievements of Japanese potters have delighted collectors.

Although people have been making pottery in the Japanese archipelago for some 12,000 years, the styles we know today were developed from techniques introduced from the Korean Peninsula and mainland Asia to Japan starting in the 5th century. Some craftspeople discovered deposits of fine kaolin clay in northern Kyushu, and founded the tradition in that region of porcelains like Arita-yaki, with brilliantly colored enamel decoration over cobalt blue underglaze. Other porcelain wares include Tobe-yaki from Ehime Prefecture, Kutani-yaki from Ishikawa Prefecture, and Kiyomizu-yaki from Kyoto.

These apart, most Japanese pottery is stoneware—which has an earthier appeal, befitting the rougher texture of the clay. Stoneware from Mashiko, where celebrated potter Hamada Shoji (1894–1978) worked, is admired for its rustic brown, black, and white glazes, often applied in abstract patterns. Many regional potters use glazes on stoneware for coloristic effects, like the mottled, crusty Tokoname-yaki, with its red-iron clay. Other styles, among them the rough-surfaced Shigaraki-yaki made near Kyoto; the white or blue-white Hagi-yaki; and Bizen-yaki from Okayama Prefecture, are unglazed: their warm tones and textures are accidents of nature, achieved when the pieces take their colors from the firing process, in sloped, wood-burning through-draft kilns called *anagama* or *nobori-gama,* built on hillsides. The effects depend on the choice of the wood the potter uses, where he places a particular piece in the kiln, and how he manipulates the heat, but the results are never predictable.

Main pottery towns include Hagi, Bizen, and Arita, but you can always find their products in Kyoto and Tokyo. If you do go on a pilgrimage, call ahead to local kilns and tourist organizations to verify that what you want to see will be open and to ask about sales.

Recommended reading: *Inside Japanese Ceramics* by Richard L. Wilson.

TEXTILES

Run your fingers over a Japanese textile, and you touch the fabric of Japanese social history. As the caste system took shape under Buddhist and Confucian influences, it created separate populations of samurai, farmers, artisans, and merchants (in descending order). Rules and conventions emerged about who could wear what and on what occasions. Appearances identified people. One glance at a kimono, and you knew the wearer was a woman of middle age, the wife of a prosperous tradesman, on her way to the wedding of a family connection. You were what you wore. Courtesans and actors, of course, could dress over-the-top; their roles gave them the license. And little by little, the merchants also found ways around the laws, to dress as befit their growing wealth and power. Evolving styles and techniques of making fabrics gave weavers and dyers and designers new opportunities to show their skills.

Western clothing follows the body line in a sculptural way; the kimono is meant as a one-size-fits-all garment in which gender matters, but size and shape are largely unimportant. Whatever the wearer's height or weight, a kimono is made from one bolt of cloth cut and stitched into panels that provide ample surface for decoration.

Regional styles proliferate. Kyoto's *Nishijin-ori* silk brocade is as sumptuous as a Japanese textile can be. Okinawa produces a variety of stunning fabrics; one, called *bashofu,* is made of plantain-fiber threads, dyed and woven in intricate motifs, and feels like linen. Kyoto's and Tokyo's stencil dyeing techniques yield subtle, elegant geometric patterns and motifs from nature. Kanazawa's *Kaga yuzen* paste-resist dyeing on silk is famous for its flower and bird motifs, in elegant rainbow colors.

The used kimonos you often see in Kyoto or Tokyo flea markets can be bargains. Also look for lighter-weight *yukata* (robes), *obi* (sashes), or handkerchiefs from Arimatsu, near Nagoya, for example. Good introductions to these craft traditions can be seen at Kyoto's Fuzoku Hakubutsukan (Costume Museum) and Nishijin Orimono (Textile Center), and the Edo-period dress collection in Tokyo's National Museum.

Kaga yuzen textiles from Kanazawa exhibit a traditional flower motif.

RELIGION IN JAPAN

A Shinto shrine near Tokyo

Although both Buddhism and Shinto permeate Japanese society and life, most Japanese are blissfully unconcerned about the distinction between what is Shinto and what is Buddhist. A wedding is often a Shinto ceremony, while a funeral is a Buddhist rite. The religions were separated by edict in 1868.

There's a saying in Japan that you're Shinto at birth (marked with a Shinto ceremony) and Buddhist when you die (honored with a Buddhist funeral). Generally, people in Japan take a utilitarian view of religion and use each as suits the occasion. One prays for success in life at a shrine and for the repose of a deceased family member at a temple. There is no thought given to the whys for this—these things simply are. The neighborhood shrine's annual *matsuri* (festival) is a time of giving thanks for prosperity and for blessing homes and local businesses. *O-mikoshi,* portable shrines for the gods, are enthusiastically carried around the district by young locals. Shouting and much sake drinking are part of the celebration. But it's a celebration first and foremost.

RELIGION IN NUMBERS

Although roughly two-thirds of Japanese people identify themselves as Buddhist, most also practice and believe in Shinto, even if they don't identify themselves as Shinto followers per se. The two religions overlap and even complement each other, even though most Japanese people would not consider themselves "religious." The religions are just part of life.

SHINTO

Shinto (literally, "the way of the *kami* [god]") is a form of animism or nature worship based on myth and rooted to the geography and holy places of the land. It's an ancient belief system, dating back perhaps as far as 500 BC, and is indigenous to Japan. The name is derived from a Chinese word, *shin tao,* coined in the 8th century AD, when divine origins were first ascribed to the royal Yamato family. Fog-enshrouded mountains, pairs of rocks, primeval forests, and geothermal activity are all manifestations of the *kami-sama* (honorable gods). For many Japanese the Shinto aspect of their lives is simply the realm of the kami-sama and is not attached to a dogmatic religious framework as it would be in the West.

BUDDHISM

A Korean king gave a statue of Shaka—the first Buddha, Prince Gautama—to the Yamato Court in AD 538. The Soga clan adopted the foreign faith, using it as a vehicle to change the political order of the day. After battling for control of the country, they established themselves as political rulers, and Buddhism took permanent hold. Simultaneously Japan sent its first ambassadors to China, inaugurating the importation of writing and religion into Japan and the subsequent exchange of ideas in art, construction, language, and other aspects of society with mainland Asia. By the 8th century, Buddhism was well established.

A statue of Buddha at Todai-ji, Nara

The gates at Futura-san Jinja, Nikko

Japanese Buddhism developed in three waves. In the Heian period (794–1185), Esoteric Buddhism was introduced primarily by two priests, both of whom studied in China: Saicho and Kukai. Saicho established a temple on Mt. Hie near Kyoto, making it the most revered mountain in Japan after Mt. Fuji. Kukai established the Shingon sect of Esoteric Buddhism on Mt. Koya, south of Nara. In Japanese temple architecture, Esoteric Buddhism introduced the separation of the temple into an interior for the initiated and an outer laypersons' area.

Amidism (Pure Land) was the second wave, introduced by the monk Honen (1133–1212), and it flourished in the late 12th century until the introduction of Zen in 1185. Its adherents saw the world emerging from a period of darkness during which Buddhism had been in decline, and asserted that salvation was offered only to the believers in Amida, a Nyorai (Buddha) or enlightened being. Amidism's promise of salvation and its subsequent versions of heaven and hell earned it the appellation "Devil's Christianity" from

The Senso-ji Complex is the heart and soul of the Asakusa District of Tokyo.

visiting Christian missionaries in the 16th century.

In the Post-Heian period (1185 to the present) the influences of Nichiren and Zen Buddhist philosophies pushed Japanese Buddhism in new directions. Nichiren (1222–82) was a monk who insisted on the primacy of the Lotus Sutra, the supposed last and greatest sutra of Shaka. Zen Buddhism was attractive to the samurai class's ideals of discipline and worldly detachment and thus spread throughout Japan in the 12th century. It was later embraced as a nonintellectual path to enlightenment by those in search of a direct experience of the sublime. More recently Zen has been adopted by a growing number of people in the West as a way to move beyond the subject-object duality that characterizes Western thought.

SHRINE AND STATE

Although the modern Japanese constitution expressly calls for a separation of church and state, it hasn't always been this way. In fact, twice over the last 150 years, Shinto was the favored religion and the government used all of its influence to support it.

During the Meiji Restoration (1868), the emperor was made sovereign leader of Japan, and power that had been spread out among the shoguns was consolidated in the Imperial House. Shinto was favored over Buddhism for two reasons. First, according to Shinto, the members of the Imperial Family were direct descendants of the kami who had formed Japan. The second reason was more practical: many of the Buddhist temples were regional power bases that relied upon the shoguns for patronage. Relegating Buddhism to a minor religion with no official support would have a weakening effect on the shoguns, while the government could use Shinto shrines to strengthen its power base.

Indeed, Buddhism was actively suppressed. Temples were closed, priests were harassed, and priceless art was either destroyed or sold. The collections of Japanese art at the Museum of Fine Arts, Boston and the Freer Gallery in

Washington, D.C., were just two of the indirect beneficiaries of this policy.

During the Pacific War (the Japanese term for World War II), Shinto was again used by the military (with the complicity of the Imperial House) to justify an aggressive stance in Asia. (It should be noted that Kokuchukai Buddhism was also used to sanction the invasion of other countries.) The emperor was a god and therefore infallible. Since the Japanese people were essentially one family with the emperor at the head, they were a superior race that was meant to rule the lesser peoples of Asia.

Once ancestor worship was allied with worship of the emperor, the state became something worth dying for. So potent was this mix that General Douglas MacArthur identified state Shinto as one of the first things that had to be dismantled upon the surrender of Japan. The emperor could stay, but shrine and state had to go.

RELIGIOUS FESTIVALS

Although there are religious festivals and holy days observed throughout the year, the two biggest events in the Japanese religious calendar are New Year's (Oshogatsu) and Obon. New Year's is celebrated from January 1 to 3. Many people visit temples or shrines the night of December 31 to ring in the New Year or in the coming weeks. Temple bells are struck 108 times to symbolize ridding oneself of the 108 human sins. This practice of visiting a temple or shrine for the new year is called *hatsumode*. Food stalls are set up close to the popular places, and the atmosphere is festive and joyous. Many draw fortune slips called *omikuji* to see what kind of a year the oracle has in store for them.

The other major religious event in the Japanese calendar is the Obon holiday, traditionally held from August 13 to 15. Obon is the Japanese festival of the dead when the spirits come back to visit the living. Most people observe the ritual by returning to their hometown or the home of their grandparents. Graves are cleaned and respects are paid to one's ancestors. Family ties are strengthened and renewed.

VISITING A BUDDHIST TEMPLE

The first thing to do when visiting a temple is to stop at the gate (called *mon* in Japanese), put your hands together and bow. Once inside the gate, you should stop to wash your hands at the stone receptacle usually found immediately upon entering the grounds. Not all temples will have a place for hand washing, but shrines will. Fill one of the ladles with water using your right hand and wash your left hand first. Then refill the ladle with water using your left hand and wash your right hand, being careful to not let the water drip back into the receptacle (the water is considered impure once it touches your hands).

You might also want to light a candle in front of the main altar of the temple and place it inside the glass cabinet.

Approaching the main hall of the Meiji Shrine in the Shibuya District of Tokyo

The massive *torii* (entrance gates) of the Meiji Shrine are more than 40 feet tall.

Then put your hands together and bow. You can also light three sticks of incense (lighting them together is customary) and put them in the large stone or brass stand. This action is also followed with a prayer and a bow.

After praying at the main altar and/or sub-altar, you'll probably want to spend some time walking around the temple grounds. Many have gardens and sculpture worthy of a visit in their own right. Upon leaving many will stop at the gate, turn, put their hands together, and bow to give thanks.

VISITING A SHINTO SHRINE

Shrines, like temples, have gates, though they are called *torii* and are often painted a bright red-orange, but this varies regionally. There are stained wooden torii, stone, and even metal torii. In terms of their appearance, torii look much like the mathematical symbol for pi. As with the gates of temples, one enters and exits through the torii, bowing on the way in and again on the way out but without clasping the hands.

Inside the shrine grounds, wash your hands as you would at a temple (left hand and then right hand). Then proceed to the main entrance (usually a set of open doors at the top of some stairs), clap twice to alert the kami of your presence, and bow. If there is a bell to ring, that will also summon the kami, as will the sound of money tossed into the box at the shrine's entrance. At a larger shrine there may be special trees, stones, and other holy objects situated throughout the grounds where you can repeat the clapping and praying process. At the beginning of their prayers, people introduce themselves by name and address. Since gods in Japan are local, you are to identify yourself to the god that you are of this place or of some other place and visiting.

After you have finished visiting the shrine, you should turn around at the torii and bow upon leaving.

Chapter 4

MARUNOUCHI AND NIHONBASHI

Updated by
Rob Goss

Sights
★★★★★

Restaurants
★★★★☆

Hotels
★★★★☆

Shopping
★★★★☆

Nightlife
★★☆☆☆

NEIGHBORHOOD SNAPSHOT

TOP EXPERIENCES

■ **Enjoy a city oasis.** In the middle of Tokyo, the Imperial Palace East Gardens offer respite from the hustle and bustle.

■ **Visit a controversial shrine.** The Yasukuni Shrine, which represents Japan's militaristic past, has long been the source of political tension between Japan, Korea, and China.

■ **See some of Japan's finest art.** The finest collection of Japanese modern art is housed in the National Museum of Modern Art, while the Idemitsu Museum of Arts contains masterpieces of classic Japanese ceramics and ink painting.

■ **Shop 'til you drop.** With department stores such as Mitsukoshi, complexes like Coredo Muromachi, and many of Tokyo's oldest independent stores, this district is a shoppers' dream.

GETTING HERE

The Imperial Palace is in the heart of central Tokyo, with other neighborhoods branching out from here. Marunouchi is between Tokyo Station and the palace's Outer Garden, extending south to Hibiya Park. Nihonbashi is on the other side of the station and is crowned by its namesake bridge.

For the Imperial Palace, take the Chiyoda Line to Nijubashimae Station (Exit 6) or the JR lines to Tokyo Station (Marunouchi Central Exit).

PLANNING YOUR TIME

You can easily cover Marunouchi, Nihonbashi, and the Imperial Palace area in a day. Start with an hour at the palace's East and Outer gardens, then head to Marunouchi for lunch and museum hopping. Finish with some shopping and dinner in Nihonbashi.

The best time to visit is in spring when the *sakura* (cherry blossoms) trees are in bloom between late March and early April. Avoid coming on Monday, when the East Gardens and most museums and galleries are closed.

PAUSE HERE

■ Marunouchi Naka-dori is the main street of Marunouchi and stretches from Otemachi to Yurakucho. Stroll down the tree- and store-lined avenue, which is famous for its illuminations in the winter and al fresco dining in the warmer months. On weekdays from 11 to 3 and on weekends from 11 to 5, the road is closed, and outside chairs and tables replace cars. If you're lucky, you may encounter a market or event.

OFF THE BEATEN PATH

■ To the northwest of the Imperial Palace, past the Yasukuni Shrine, you'll discover a tranquil waterway that was once part of the 15th-century Edo Castle's outer moat. Starting at Yotsuya Station, this stretch of water also includes Sotobori Park, which is famous during spring for its picture-perfect views of cherry blossom trees along the railway.

■ Follow the water until it joins the Kanda River at Iidabashi Station. Here, you can take a casual lunch at Canal Cafe and enjoy a perfect photo spot with undisturbed views. If you'd like to venture further, then continue west towards Kagurazaka, a traditional yet classy spot, and visit the impressive Akagi Shrine.

Commerce meshes with government affairs in Marunouchi, Nihonbashi, and the adjacent Imperial Palace district—home to not only the palace (Kokyo-gaien) and its gardens, but also the Japanese Diet (parliament), Supreme Court, and prime minister's residence.

Marunouchi is one of Tokyo's main business districts, notable for its dining and shopping, as well as such sights as Tokyo Station and the Idemitsu Museum of Arts. To its east, Nihonbashi (sometimes transliterated as "Nihombashi") has many time-honored stores where you can pick up unique souvenirs.

To the west of both neighborhoods is the Imperial Palace. Built by the order of Ieyasu Tokugawa, who chose the site in 1590, the castle had 99 gates (36 in the outer wall), 21 watchtowers (three are still standing), and 28 armories. Its outer defenses stretched from present-day Shimbashi Station to Kanda. Completed in 1640 and later expanded, it was once the world's largest castle.

The Japanese Imperial Family resides in heavily blockaded sections of the palace grounds. Tours are conducted by reservation only, and public access is limited to designated outdoor areas. The East Gardens are open to visitors most days, but the main grounds are open only twice a year, on January 2 and February 23 (the emperor's birthday), when thousands of people assemble under the balcony to offer their good wishes to the Imperial Family. The prime minister's residence is only viewable from afar, hidden behind fortified walls and trees.

The Imperial Palace

Sights

Chidorigafuchi National Cemetery (千鳥ヶ淵戦没者墓苑; *Chidorigafuchi Senbotsusha Boen*)
CEMETERY | High on the northwestern edge of the Imperial Palace moat, this cemetery holds the remains of thousands of unknown soldiers and is famous for its springtime cherry blossoms. The adjacent Chidorigafuchi Boathouse rents out rowboats and pedal boats. Only a small part of the palace's outer moat is accessible, but a walk here from the East Gardens makes for a refreshing 30 minutes. The entrance to the garden is near Yasukuni Shrine. ✉ *2 Sanban-cho, Chiyoda-ku* ☎ *03/3234–1948* 🎫 *Park free, boat rental from ¥800 in cherry blossom season (from ¥500 at other times)* ⏲ *Boathouse closed Mon. and Dec.–Mar.* Ⓜ *Hanzomon and Shinjuku subway lines, Kudanshita Station (Exit 2).*

Hanzo-mon Gate (半蔵門; *Hanzo-mon*)
MILITARY SIGHT | The house of Hattori Hanzo (1541–96) once sat at the foot of this small wooden gate. Hanzo was a legendary leader of Ieyasu Tokugawa's private corps of spies and infiltrators—and assassins, if need be. They were the menacing, black-clad ninja—perennial

Once the site of the Imperial Palace's innermost defense circles, the East Gardens now offer respite in a beautiful setting.

material for historical adventure films and television dramas. The gate is a minute's walk from the subway. ✉ *1 Chiyoda, Chiyoda-ku* Ⓜ *Hanzomon subway line, Hanzomon Station (Exit 3).*

Hirakawa-mon Gate
(平川門; *Hirakawa-mon*)
NOTABLE BUILDING | The approach to this gate crosses a wooden bridge over the Imperial Palace moat. The gate and bridge are reconstructions, but Hirakawa-mon is beautiful, looking much as it must have when the shogun's wives and concubines used it on their rare excursions. ✉ *1 Chiyoda, Chiyoda-ku* Ⓜ *Tozai subway line, Takebashi Station (Exit 1A).*

★ **Imperial Palace East Gardens**
(皇居東御苑; *Kokyo Higashi Gyo-en*)
GARDEN | Formerly part of Edo Castle's grounds, this garden was claimed for the imperial family after the 1868 Meiji Restoration. Though most of the old castle was torn down or lost to fire, the stone foundations hint at the scale of the former seat of power. In the East Gardens you'll find the National Police Agency *dojo* (martial arts hall) and the Ote Rest House; the Museum of the Imperial Collection (Sannomaru Shozokan) is next door and has rotating exhibits of household treasures. The Hundred-Man Guardhouse (Hyakunin Bansho) was once defended by four shifts of 100 soldiers each. Past it is the entrance to what was once the Ninomaru, the "second circle" of the fortress, now a grove and garden. At the far end is the Suwa-no-Chaya Tea Pavilion, an early-19th-century building moved here from elsewhere on the grounds. ✉ *1–1 Chiyoda, Chiyoda-ku* ☎ *03/3213–1111* 🎫 *Free* 🕘 *Closed Mon. and Fri.* Ⓜ *Tozai, Marunouchi, and Chiyoda subway lines, Otemachi Station (Exit C13B).*

Imperial Palace Outer Garden
(皇居外苑; *Kokyo-Gaien*)
GARDEN | When the office buildings of the Meiji government were moved from this area in 1899, the expanse along the palace's east side was turned into a public promenade and planted with 2,800 pine trees. The Outer Garden affords the best view of the castle walls and

their Tokugawa-period fortifications—the Nijubashi and Seimon bridges, 17th-century Fujimi Yagura watchtower, and Sakurada-mon gate. The 5-km (3.1-mile) loop around the moats, starting and finishing at Sakurada-mon, is popular with runners. ✉ *1–1 Kokyogaien, Chiyoda-ku* 🎫 *Free* ⏲ *East Gardens closed Mon. and Fri.* Ⓜ *Chiyoda subway line, Nijubashimae Station (Exit 2).*

National Diet Building
(国会議事堂; *Kokkai-Gijido*)
GOVERNMENT BUILDING | The building of the Japanese parliament exemplifies post–World War II Japanese architecture; on a gloomy day it seems as if it might have sprung from the screen of a German Expressionist movie. Started in 1920, construction took 17 years to complete. One-hour-long guided tours are available most weekdays between 9 am and 5 pm, but it's best to call ahead to confirm times, as access varies when parliament is sitting. The prime minister's residence, Kantei, is across the street; it's hidden by walls and trees, so you'll only get a glimpse of it. ✉ *1–7–1 Nagatacho, Chiyoda-ku* ☎ *03/5521–7445* 🌐 *www.sangiin.go.jp* 🎫 *Free* ⏲ *Closed weekends* Ⓜ *Marunouchi subway line, Kokkai-Gijido-mae Station (Exit 2).*

National Museum of Modern Art, Tokyo
(国立近代美術館; *Tokyo Kokuritsu Kindai Bijutsukan*)
ART MUSEUM | Founded in 1952 and moved to its present site in 1969, this was Japan's first national art museum. Often referred to by its acronym, MOMAT, it features a range of 20th- and 21st-century Japanese and Western artworks. The permanent collection, which includes paintings, prints, and sculptures by Rousseau, Picasso, Tsuguharu Foujita, Ryuzaburo Umehara, and Taikan Yokoyama, occupies the second to fourth floors. ✉ *3–1 Kitanomaru Koen, Chiyoda-ku* ☎ *050/5541–8600* 🌐 *www.momat.go.jp/en* 🎫 *¥500* ⏲ *Closed Mon.* ☞ *Additional fees for some special exhibitions*

Grutto Pass

The **Grutto Pass** (🌐 *www.rekibun.or.jp/grutto*) allows free or discounted admission to 103 of the city's museums, zoos, parks, and other sights. You can buy the pass, which costs just ¥2,500 and expires two months after the date of first use, at the Tokyo Tourist Information Center and all participating sights.

Ⓜ *Tozai subway line, Takebashi Station (Exit 1B); Hanzomon and Shinjuku subway lines, Kudanshita Station (Exit 2).*

Nijubashi Bridge (二重橋)
BRIDGE | This graceful arch across the moat is the most photogenic spot on the grounds of the former Edo Castle. Mere mortals may cross only on February 23 (the emperor's birthday) and January 2 to pay their respects to the imperial family. The guards in front of the small, octagonal, copper-roof sentry boxes change every hour on the hour—alas, with nothing like the pomp and ceremony at Buckingham Palace. ✉ *1-7 Chiyoda, Chiyoda-ku* Ⓜ *Chiyoda subway line, Nijubashimae Station (Exit 2).*

Ote-mon Gate (大手門)
NOTABLE BUILDING | Most of what was once the principal gate of Ieyasu Tokugawa's castle was destroyed in 1945 but was rebuilt in 1967 based on the original plans. The outer part of the gate survived and offers an impressive main entrance into the palace's East Gardens. ✉ *1–1 Chiyoda, Chiyoda-ku* Ⓜ *Tozai, Marunouchi, and Chiyoda subway lines, Otemachi Station (Exit C10).*

Yasukuni Shrine (靖国神社; *Yasukuni Jinja*)
RELIGIOUS BUILDING | Founded in 1869, this shrine is dedicated to approximately 2½ million Japanese, Taiwanese, and

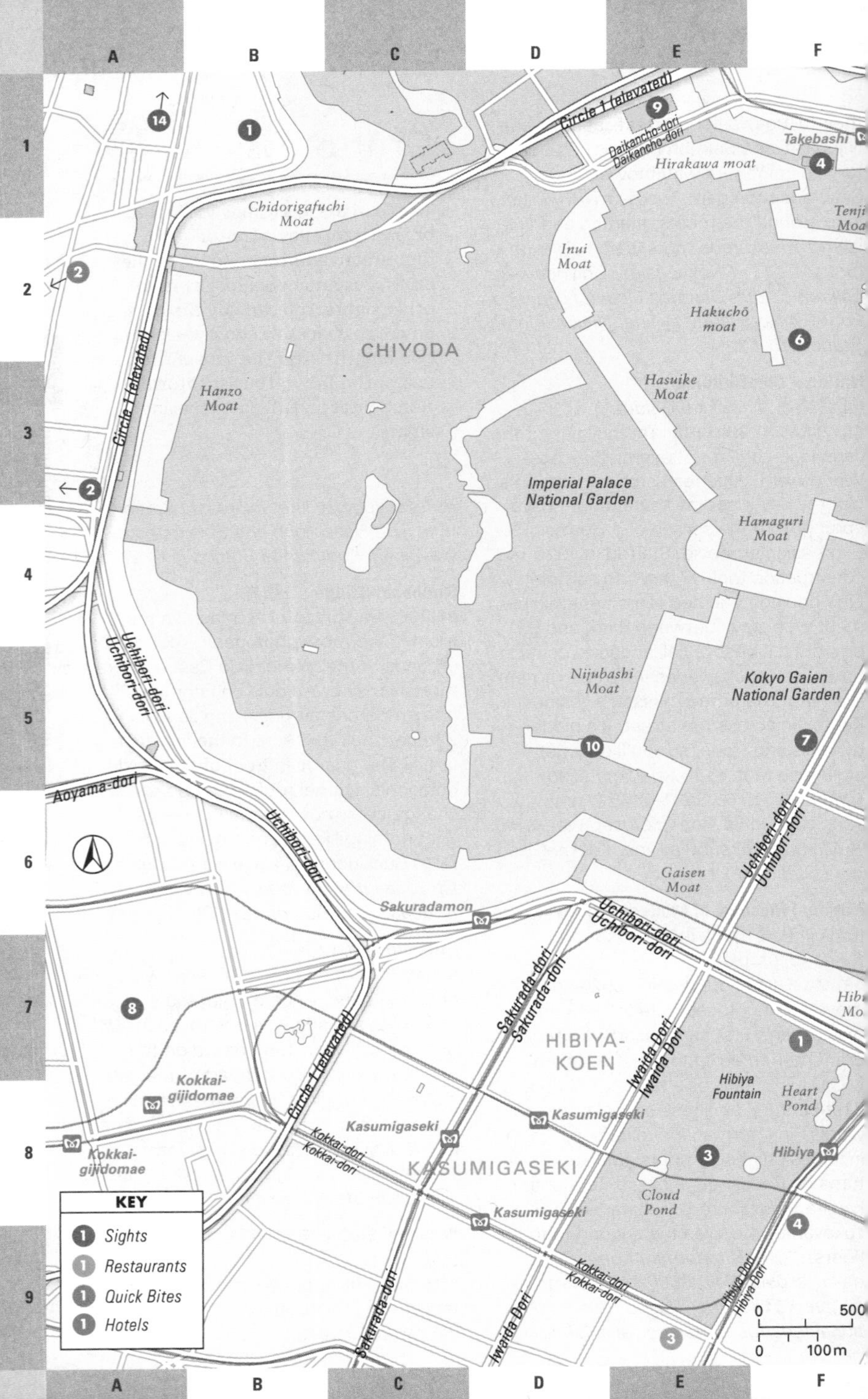

A
B
C
D
E
F
1
2
3
4
5
6
7
8
9
Circle 1 (elevated)
Daikancho-dori
Takebashi
Hirakawa moat
Chidorigafuchi Moat
Inui Moat
Hakuchō moat
CHIYODA
Hasuike Moat
Hanzo Moat
Imperial Palace National Garden
Hamaguri Moat
Nijubashi Moat
Kokyo Gaien National Garden
Uchibori-dori
Aoyama-dori
Sakuradamon
Gaisen Moat
Sakurada-dori
Iwaida Dori
HIBIYA-KOEN
Hibiya Fountain
Heart Pond
Kokkai-gijidomae
Kasumigaseki
Hibiya
KASUMIGASEKI
Kokkai-dori
Cloud Pond
Hibiya Dori
KEY
Sights
Restaurants
Quick Bites
Hotels
0
500
0
100m

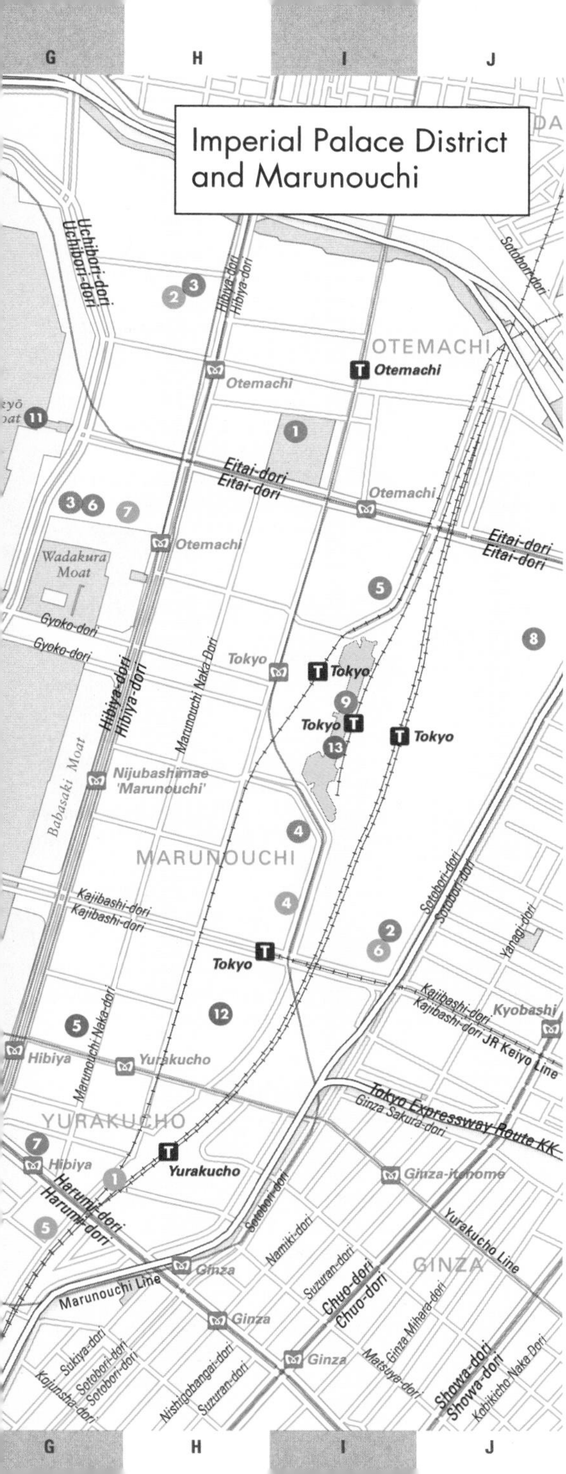

Imperial Palace District and Marunouchi

Sights

1 Chidorigafuchi National Cemetery ... **B1**
2 Hanzo-mon Gate ... **A3**
3 Hibiya Park ... **E8**
4 Hirakawa-mon Gate ... **F1**
5 Idemitsu Museum of Arts ... **G7**
6 Imperial Palace East Gardens ... **F2**
7 Imperial Palace Outer Garden ... **F5**
8 National Diet Building ... **A7**
9 National Museum of Modern Art, Tokyo ... **E1**
10 Nijubashi Bridge ... **D5**
11 Ote-mon Gate ... **G3**
12 Tokyo International Forum ... **H7**
13 Tokyo Station ... **I5**
14 Yasukuni Shrine ... **A1**

Restaurants

1 Andy's Shin Hinomoto ... **G8**
2 Est ... **H2**
3 Heichinrou Hibiya ... **E9**
4 Okonomiyaki Kiji ... **I6**
5 Robata Honten ... **G8**
6 Sézanne ... **I6**
7 Trattoria Creatta ... **H3**

Quick Bites

1 Hibiya Saroh ... **F7**
2 Jupiter Coffee Roasters ... **A2**
3 The Palace Lounge ... **G3**
4 Saza Coffee KITTE Marunouchi ... **I6**

Hotels

1 Aman Tokyo ... **I3**
2 Four Seasons Hotel Tokyo at Marunouchi ... **I6**
3 Four Seasons Hotel Tokyo at Otemachi ... **H2**
4 Imperial Hotel Tokyo ... **F9**
5 Marunouchi Hotel ... **I4**
6 Palace Hotel Tokyo ... **G3**
7 The Peninsula Tokyo ... **G8**
8 Shangri-La Hotel Tokyo ... **J4**
9 The Tokyo Station Hotel ... **I5**

Koreans who have died since then in war or military service. As the Japanese constitution expressly renounces both militarism and state sponsorship of religion, Yasukuni has been a center of stubborn political debate, particularly since 1978, when a shrine official added the names of several class-A war criminals to the list. Numerous prime ministers have visited the shrine since 1979, causing a political chill between Japan and its close neighbors, Korea and China, who suffered under Japanese colonialism.

Despite all this, hundreds of thousands of Japanese come here every year to honor lost friends and relatives. These visits are most frenzied on August 15, the anniversary of the conclusion of World War II, when former soldiers and ultra-right-wing groups descend upon the grounds en masse.

The shrine isn't one structure but a complex that includes the Main Hall and the Hall of Worship—both built in the simple, unadorned style of the ancient Shinto shrines at Ise—and the Yushukan, a museum of documents and war memorabilia. Refurbished in 2002, the Yushukan presents Japan at its most ambivalent—if not unrepentant—about its more recent militaristic past.

Critics charge that the museum's newer exhibits glorify the nation's role in the Pacific War as a noble struggle for independence; certainly there's an agenda here that's hard to reconcile with Japan's firm postwar rejection of militarism as an instrument of national policy. Many Japanese visitors are moved by the displays, which contain things such as the last letters and photographs of young kamikaze pilots, while others find the Yushukan a cautionary, rather than uplifting, experience.

Although some exhibits have English labels and notes, the English isn't very helpful; most objects, however, speak clearly enough for themselves. Rooms on the second floor house an especially fine collection of medieval swords and armor.

The shrine is also home to the Noh stage and, in the far western corner, a sumo-wrestling ring, where matches are held in April, during the first of Yasukuni's three annual festivals. Pick up an English-language pamphlet and simplified map of the shrine just inside the grounds. Visiting on a Sunday offers a chance to forage at a flea market that runs from morning until mid-afternoon. *3–1–1 Kudankita, Chiyoda-ku* *03/3261–8326* *www.yasukuni.or.jp* *Shrine free, Yushukan ¥1,000* *Hanzomon and Shinjuku subway lines, Kudanshita Station (Exit 1).*

Coffee and Quick Bites

Jupiter Coffee Roasters

$ | **COFFEE** | Offerings at this small café just to west of the Imperial Palace's Chidorigafuchi feature coffee beans from as far afield as Brazil, Indonesia, and Papua New Guinea. There's also usually a decaf option available. **Known for:** specialty coffee; rave reviews from coffee afifionados; also sells coffee beans. *Average main: ¥500* *4–37 Ichibancho, Chiyoda-ku* *03/6256–8197* *jupiters.theshop.jp/about* *No credit cards* *Closed Sun.* *Closes early on Sat (2 pm)* *Hanzomon subway line, Hanzomon Station (Exit 5).*

Marunouchi

Sights

Hibiya Park (日比谷公園; *Hibiya Koen*)

CITY PARK | Japan's first Western-style city park opened in 1901. Today, its nearly 40 acres of land contains beautiful seasonal flowers, a 500-year-old ginkgo tree, two ponds, and two open-air concert halls. It's the place to go for live music, festivals, and a leisurely stroll—or, do like many nearby office workers do, and enjoy a packed lunch here. ✉ *1 Hibiya Park, Chiyoda-ku* 🎫 *Free* Ⓜ *Marunouchi subway line, Kasumigaseki Station (Exit B2); Hibiya, Chiyoda and Mita subway lines, Hibiya Station (Exits A10 and A14).*

★ **Idemitsu Museum of Arts** (出光美術館; *Idemitsu Bijutsukan*)
ART MUSEUM | The strength of the collection in these four spacious, well-designed rooms lies in the Tang- and Song-dynasty Chinese porcelain and in the Japanese ceramics—including works by Nonomura Ninsei and Ogata Kenzan. On display are masterpieces of Old Seto, Oribe, Old Kutani, Karatsu, and Kakiemon ware. The museum also houses outstanding examples of Zen painting and calligraphy, wood-block prints, and genre paintings of the Edo period. Of special interest to scholars is the resource collection of shards from virtually every pottery-making culture of the ancient world. The museum is on the ninth floor of the Teikoku Gekijo building, which looks down upon the lavish Imperial Garden. Check ahead on the website to see if reservations are required when you plan to visit. ✉ *Teigeki Bldg. 9F, 3–1–1 Marunouchi, Chiyoda-ku* ☎ *050/5541–8600* 🌐 *idemitsu-museum.or.jp/en* 🎫 *¥1,200* ⏲ *Closed Mon.* ☞ *Also closes for set-up between some exhibitions* Ⓜ *Yurakucho subway line, Yurakucho Station (Exit B3); Hibiya, Chiyoda and Mita subway lines, Hibiya Station (Exit B3); Yamanote Line, Yurakucho Station.*

Tokyo International Forum (東京国際フォーラム; *Tokyo Kokusai Foramu*)
PLAZA/SQUARE | This postmodern masterpiece, the work of Uruguay-born American architect Rafael Viñoly, is the first major convention and art center of its kind in Tokyo and actually consists of two buildings. Viñoly's design was selected in a 1989 competition that drew nearly 400 entries from 50 countries. The plaza of the Forum is that rarest of Tokyo rarities: civilized open space. There's a long central courtyard with comfortable benches shaded by trees, the setting for an antiques flea market the first and third Sunday of each month and for a collection of food trucks most weekday lunchtimes. Transit fans should stroll catwalks to the top, where there's a view of the Tokyo Station JR lines. ✉ *3–5–1 Marunouchi, Chiyoda-ku* ☎ *03/5221–9000* 🌐 *www.t-i-forum.co.jp* Ⓜ *Yurakucho subway line, Yurakucho Station (Exit A-4B).*

Tokyo Station (東京駅; *Tokyo Eki*)
TRAIN/TRAIN STATION | This work of Kingo Tatsuno, one of Japan's first modern architects, was completed in 1914, with Tatsuno modeling his creation on the railway station of Amsterdam. The building lost its original top story in the air raids of 1945, but it was promptly repaired. In the late 1990s, a plan to demolish the station was impeded by public outcry. The highlight is the historic and luxurious Tokyo Station Hotel, on the second and third floors. The area around the station is increasingly popular for dining, shopping, and entertainment. ✉ *1–9–1 Marunouchi, Chiyoda-ku* Ⓜ *Marunouchi subway line and JR lines.*

Restaurants

After the working day is done, there must be somewhere for overworked office workers to grab a bite to eat. In Marunouchi, there are, indeed, buildings and basements full of places for lunch, dinner, and coffee breaks.

★ **Andy's Shin Hinomoto** (新日の基)
$$$ | **JAPANESE** | Also known as "Andy's," this izakaya is directly under the tracks of the Yamanote Line, making the wooden interior shudder each time a train passes overhead. It's a favorite with local and foreign journalists and is actually run by a Brit, Andy, who travels to the seafood market every morning to buy ingredients for not-to-miss dishes such as sashimi or buttered scallops. **Known for:** favorite among Tokyo expats; expansive menu; cozy, lively atmosphere. 💲 *Average main:*

¥5,000 ✉ 2–4–4 Yurakucho, Chiyoda-ku ☎ 03/3214–8021 🌐 shin-hinomoto.com ▭ No credit cards ⏲ Closed Sun. No lunch Ⓜ JR Yurakucho Station (Hibiya Exit); Hibiya, Chiyoda, and Mita subway lines, Hibiya Station (Exits A2 and A6).

Est (エスト)
$$$$ | **CONTEMPORARY** | On top of the Four Seasons Hotel Tokyo at Otemachi, this Michelin-starred restaurant serves contemporary French cuisine with a Japanese twist. Est emphasizes reducing food waste and offers eco-conscious, seasonal menus with 95% of ingredients gathered from Japan, so Chef Guillaume Bracaval's innovative dishes can be traced from source to plate. **Known for:** seasonal open-air terrace; contemporary French-Japanese courses; a focus on sustainability. *$ Average main: ¥30,000 ✉ Four Seasons Hotel Tokyo at Otemachi, 1–2–1 Otemachi, 39F, Chiyoda-ku ☎ 03/6810–0655 🌐 www.est-tokyo.com ⏲ Closed Mon. Ⓜ Marunouchi, Tozai, and Chiyoda subway lines, Otemachi Station (Exits C4 and C5).*

Heichinrou Hibiya (聘珍樓日比谷店)
$$$$ | **CHINESE** | A short walk from the Imperial Hotel, the Hibiya branch of one of Yokohama's oldest and best Chinese restaurants commands a spectacular view of the Imperial Palace grounds from 28 floors up. Call ahead to reserve a table by the window. **Known for:** classic Chinese dishes; lush, elegant decor; a popular venue for power lunches. *$ Average main: ¥11,000 ✉ Fukoku Seimei Bldg., 2–2–2 Uchisaiwaicho, 28th fl., Chiyoda-ku ☎ 03/3508–0555 🌐 www.heichin.com ⏲ Closed Sun. Ⓜ Mita Line, Uchisaiwaicho Station (Exit A6).*

Okonomiyaki Kiji (お好み焼きじ)
$$ | **JAPANESE** | Sit down for a genuine taste of western Japan at this eatery serving savory *okonomiyaki* pancakes, as well as noodle dishes like *yakisoba*. It's inexpensive for the area, so expect a wait. **Known for:** no reservations and a line; okonomiyaki; smoky, fun ambience. *$ Average main: ¥1,500 ✉ Tokia Building, 2–7–3 Marunouchi, B1F, Chiyoda-ku ☎ 03/3216–3123 🌐 www.o-kizi.jp Ⓜ Marunouchi subway line, Tokyo Station (direct access); multiple JR lines, Tokyo Station (Marunouchi South Exit).*

★ **Robata Honten** (炉端本店)
$$$ | **JAPANESE** | Old, funky, and more than a little cramped, Robata is a bit daunting at first, but fourth-generation chef-owner Takao Inoue holds forth here with an inspired version of Japanese home cooking. He's also a connoisseur of pottery and serves his food on pieces acquired at famous kilns all over the country. **Known for:** country-style izakaya; a wide variety of Japanese dishes; dishes served on unique pottery collection. *$ Average main: ¥5,000 ✉ 1–3–8 Yurakucho, Chiyoda-ku ☎ 03/3591–1905 ⏲ Closed some Sun. each month. No lunch on weekends Ⓜ Yamanote Line, Yurakucho Station (Hibiya Exit); Hibiya, Chiyoda, and Mita subway lines, Hibiya Station (Exit A4).*

Sézanne (セザン)
$$$$ | **FRENCH** | Chef Daniel Calvert has been awarded two Michelin stars for the creative French cuisine served at this elegant restaurant on the seventh floor of the Four Seasons Hotel at Marunouchi. The 12-course dinner changes with the seasons, but leans heavily into Japanese produce and could include Akkeshi sea oyster with koshihikari rice and wild sorrel or shamo chicken from Bizen poached in yellow wine. **Known for:** chef's table option; sumptuous French courses; Champagne selection. *$ Average main: ¥40,000 ✉ Four Seasons Hotel at Marunouchi, 1–11–1 Marunouchi, Chiyoda-ku ☎ 03/5222–5810 🌐 www.sezanne.tokyo ⏲ Closed Mon. and Tues. Ⓜ Multiple JR lines, Tokyo Station (Yaesu South Exit).*

Trattoria Creatta (トラットリア クレアッタ)
$$$$ | **ITALIAN** | Sitting on the terrace beside the Wadakura Moat, savor a glass of carefully selected wine from the impressive cellar, and choose from

a modest selection of fresh, flavorful pasta dishes or one of the set three- to five-course menus. At dinner, the atmosphere turns intimate with candlelight and ultra-attentive service. **Known for:** reasonably priced prix-fixe courses; free-flow Italian wine menu; dining beneath cherry blossoms in spring. *Average main: ¥6,800 Nissay Marunouchi Gardentower, 1–1–3 Marunouchi, 1F, Chiyoda-ku 03/3284–0020 www.creatta.tokyo Chiyoda, Hanzomon, Marunouchi, Mita, and Tozai subway lines, Otemachi Station (Exit D6).*

Coffee and Quick Bites

Hibiya Saroh (日比谷サロー)
$ | **EUROPEAN** | After strolling through the flower gardens of Hibiya Park on a hot day, stop off for a cold pint of beer here. There's no indoor seating, but with its view of Hibiya Park, you wouldn't want to be inside. **Known for:** in business since the 1940s; selection of draft beers; simple, well-priced food. *Average main: ¥1,100 1–1 Hibiya Park, Chiyoda-ku 050/5304–4667 hibiyasaroh.jp Closed Mon. and some Tues. Marunouchi subway line, Kasumigaseki Station (Exit B2); Hibiya, Chiyoda and Mita subway lines, Hibiya Station (Exits A10 and A14).*

The Palace Lounge (ザ パレス ラウンジ)
$$$ | **TEAHOUSE** | In addition to its elegant decor, plush sofas, and outdoor patio, the lobby lounge at the Palace Hotel also offers one of Tokyo's best afternoon tea experiences, featuring both Japanese and European sweets; an extensive menu of unique, high-end teas; and several set-price options for tea and/or sweets. In the evening, cocktails take center stage. **Known for:** afternoon tea in a relaxed atmosphere; collection of teas; elaborate parfaits. *Average main: ¥4,900 Palace Hotel Tokyo, 1–1–1 Marunouchi, Chiyoda-ku 03/3211–5309 www.palacehoteltokyo.com Chiyoda, Hanzomon, Marunouchi, Mita, and Tozai subway lines, Otemachi Station (Exit C13b).*

Saza Coffee KITTE Marunouchi (サザコーヒー)
$ | **COFFEE** | This narrow, brick-lined café serves aromatic coffee sourced from all over the world. The best seats are in front of the lab, where coffee bubbles in a siphon. **Known for:** single-origin coffee beans; not many seats; beautifully presented coffee. *Average main: ¥750 Kitte Marunouchi, 2–7–2 Marunouchi, 1F, Chiyoda-ku 03/6268–0720 www.saza.co.jp Marunouchi subway line, Tokyo Station (direct access); multiple JR lines, Tokyo Station (Marunouchi South Exit).*

Hotels

Some of the city's best hotels are in Marunouchi. You'll find a mix of top foreign and domestic brands.

★ **Aman Tokyo** (アマン東京)
$$$$ | **HOTEL** | Mixing modern design with traditional Japanese aesthetics, the Aman Tokyo has a truly Zenlike feeling, with 84 large rooms and suites—each of which has a unique floor plan—that combine washi paper, stone, and wood with the latest technology. **Pros:** immaculate service; blend of Japanese aesthetics and modernity; wonderful views. **Cons:** nearly double the price of other hotels in its class; immediate area is busy on weekdays, dead on weekends; Japanese aesthetic too minimalist for some tastes. *Rooms from: ¥220,000 The Otemachi Tower, 1–5–6 Otemachi, Chiyoda-ku 03/5224–3333 www.aman-resorts.com 84 rooms No Meals Chiyoda, Hanzomon, Marunouchi, Mita, and Tozai subway lines, Otemachi Station (Exits C11 and C8).*

Four Seasons Hotel Tokyo at Marunouchi (フォーシーズンズホテル丸の内東京)
$$$$ | **HOTEL** | A departure from the typical grand scale of most Four Seasons properties, the Marunouchi branch, set within the glistening Pacific Century Place,

has the feel of a boutique hotel. **Pros:** convenient airport access; small number of rooms lends the hotel a boutique feel; helpful, English-speaking staff. **Cons:** high-priced; the only views are those of nearby Tokyo Station; trains are audible from some rooms. *Rooms from: ¥120,000* ✉ *Pacific Century Pl., 1–11–1 Marunouchi, Chiyoda-ku* ☎ *03/5222–7222* 🌐 *www.fourseasons.com/tokyo* *57 rooms* *No Meals* Ⓜ *Multiple JR lines, Tokyo Station (Yaesu South Exit).*

Four Seasons Hotel Tokyo at Otemachi (フォーシーズンズホテル東京大手町)
$$$$ | **HOTEL** | The latest Four Seasons Tokyo hotel, unveiled at the end of 2020, delights guests with its hospitality and sweeping views of Tokyo landmarks, as well as the distant Mt. Fuji. **Pros:** all rooms have views; incredible dining options; personable, friendly staff. **Cons:** not easy to come and go; very high price tag; far from nightlife. *Rooms from: ¥120,000* ✉ *1–2–1 Otemachi, Chiyoda-ku* ☎ *03/6810–0600* 🌐 *www.fourseasons.com/otemachi* *190 rooms* *No Meals* Ⓜ *Chiyoda, Hanzomon, Marunouchi, Mita, and Tozai subway lines, Otemachi Station (Exits C4 and C5).*

Imperial Hotel Tokyo (帝国ホテル; *Teikoku Hoteru*)
$$$ | **HOTEL** | Though not as fashionable or modern as its neighbor the Peninsula, when it comes to traditional elegance, it's hard to top the venerable Imperial, which opened in 1890 and has always been justly proud of its Western-style facilities and personalized Japanese service. **Pros:** a long history; dining options are varied and superb; large rooms. **Cons:** layout can be confusing; some rooms have dated interiors; new tower building closest to trains can be noisy. *Rooms from: ¥57,000* ✉ *1–1–1 Uchisaiwaicho, Chiyoda-ku* ☎ *03/3504–1111* 🌐 *www.imperialhotel.co.jp* *931 rooms* *No Meals* Ⓜ *Hibiya subway line, Hibiya Station (Exit 5).*

Marunouchi Hotel (丸ノ内ホテル)
$$ | **HOTEL** | Situated as it is on the upper 11 floors of the Marunouchi Oazo Building, with an underground walkway connected to Tokyo Station, this hotel offers both a convenient location and views of the city lights, which illuminate the quiet neutral hues and high ceilings in the guest rooms. **Pros:** affordable for the area; centrally located; helpful concierge. **Cons:** geared to business travelers; rooms are smallish; renovations through June 2025 mean some noise and service disruption. *Rooms from: ¥33,000* ✉ *1–6–3 Marunouchi, Chiyoda-ku* ☎ *03/3217–1111* 🌐 *www.marunouchi-hotel.co.jp* *205 rooms* *No Meals* Ⓜ *multiple JR lines, Tokyo Station (Marunouchi North Exit).*

★ **Palace Hotel Tokyo** (パレスホテル東京)
$$$$ | **HOTEL** | This hotel's handsome, refined look sets the stage for a luxury experience that starts in the lobby—a long expanse of white marble lit with oversize drum chandeliers and sunlight pouring in from floor-to-ceiling windows—and continues in spacious guest rooms that are tastefully done in neutral tones with pops of chartreuse. **Pros:** deluxe balcony rooms have excellent views; luxurious yet tasteful design; impeccable service. **Cons:** on the pricey side; business-traveler focus; regular deluxe rooms are overvalued. *Rooms from: ¥85,000* ✉ *1–1–1 Marunouchi, Chiyoda-ku* ☎ *03/3211–5211* 🌐 *en.palacehoteltokyo.com* *290 rooms* *No Meals* Ⓜ *Chiyoda, Hanzomon, Marunouchi, Mita, and Tozai subway lines, Otemachi Station (Exit C13).*

The Peninsula Tokyo (ザ・ペニンシュラ東京)
$$$$ | **HOTEL** | From the staff in caps and sharp suits, often assisting guests from a Rolls-Royce shuttling to and from Narita, to the shimmering gold glow emitting from the top floors, the 24-floor Peninsula Tokyo exudes elegance and grace. **Pros:** first-class room interiors; luxurious details; wonderful spa. **Cons:** crowded

The Palace Hotel Tokyo is a historic hotel with a contemporary and spacious rooms.

lobby and public areas can detract from the luxury feel; formal service can feel impersonal; high prices. *Rooms from: ¥155,000* *1–8–1 Yurakucho, Chiyoda-ku* *03/6270–2888* *www.peninsula.com* *314 rooms* *No Meals* *JR Yamanote Line, Yurakucho Station (Hibiya Exit); Mita, Chiyoda, and Hibiya subway lines, Hibiya Station (Exits A6 and A7).*

Shangri-La Hotel Tokyo
(シャングリ・ラ ホテル 東京)

$$$$ | HOTEL | Occupying the top 11 floors of the 37-storey Marunouchi Trust Tower, near Tokyo Station, the Shangri-La offers superb city views, as well as a lavish interior, including 2,000 works of art hung throughout; 50 glistening chandeliers handmade in the Czech Republic; and large (more than 500 square feet) standard guest rooms that are awash in burgundy-and-brown textiles and equipped with high-end entertainment systems. **Pros:** contemporary elegance with an Asian edge; some of Tokyo's most spacious guestrooms; atmospheric Tibetan-inspired Chi Spa. **Cons:** luxury doesn't come cheap; located in a business district; entrance might be hard to find. *Rooms from: ¥130,000* *Marunouchi Trust Tower, 1–8–3 Marunouchi, Chiyoda-ku* *03/6739–7888* *www.shangri-la.com* *200 rooms* *No Meals* *multiple JR lines, Tokyo Station (Yaesu North Exit).*

The Tokyo Station Hotel
(東京ステーションホテル)

$$$$ | HOTEL | Situated inside the grand, redbrick Tokyo Station, this hotel dates from 1915 (a year after the station opened), and, despite recent renovations, it remains true to a past that has inspired novelists and wowed travelers for almost a century. **Pros:** impeccable service; easy access to shopping; lovely, historical setting. **Cons:** rooms on the small side; views from some rooms limited; located in an extremely busy transport hub. *Rooms from: ¥89,000* *1–9–1 Marunouchi, Chiyoda-ku* *03/5220–1111* *www.tokyostationhotel.jp* *150 rooms* *No Meals* *multiple JR lines, Tokyo Station (South Exit).*

All That Tokyo Jazz

Though popular in Japan before World War II, jazz really took hold of Tokyo after U.S. forces introduced Charlie Parker and Thelonius Monk in the late 1940s. The genre had been banned in wartime Japan as an American vice, but even at the height of the war, fans were able to listen to their favorite artists on Voice of America radio. In the 1960s, Japan experienced a boom in all areas of the arts, and jazz was no exception. Since then, the Japanese scene has steadily bloomed, with several local stars—such as saxophonist Sadao Watanabe in the 1960s and contemporary favorites like the singer Keiko Lee and the pianist Hiromi Uehara—gaining global attention.

Today, more than 100 bars and clubs host live music, plus hundreds more that play recorded jazz. Shinjuku, Takadanobaba, and Kichijoji are the city's jazz enclaves. Famous international acts regularly appear at big-name clubs such as the Blue Note, but the smaller, lesser-known joints usually have more atmosphere. With such a large jazz scene, there's an incredible diversity to enjoy, from Louis Armstrong tribute acts to fully improvised free jazz—sometimes on successive nights at the same venue.

If you time your visit right, you can listen to great jazz at one of the many annual festivals dedicated to this adopted musical form. The festivals vary in size and coverage, but two to check out are the Tokyo Jazz Festival in late August and the Asagaya Jazz Street Festival in late October.

Nightlife

BARS

Marunouchi House (丸の内ハウス;)

BEER GARDENS | On the seventh floor of the Shin-Marunouchi Building, you'll find a 360-degree terrace with a number of lively restaurants and bars. Take in the night views of the Tokyo Station building and Imperial Palace gardens, and bar-hop 'til the early morning. On certain days, the venue hosts DJs and special events. ✉ *Shin-Marunouchi Building, 1–5–1 Marunouchi, 7F, Chiyoda-ku* ☎ *03/5218–5100* 🌐 *www.marunouchi-house.com* Ⓜ *Marunouchi subway line, Tokyo Station (Exit M7); multiple JR lines, Tokyo Station (Marunouchi South Exit).*

Peter: the Bar (バー)

BARS | Like most of Tokyo's high-end hotels, the Peninsula has a high-rise bar. But unlike many staid hotel bars, this 24th-floor spot with a forest of chrome trees, designed by Yabu Pushelberg, is lots of fun, with a wide range of cocktails and a smoke-free atmosphere. ✉ *Peninsula Tokyo, 1–8–1 Yurakucho, 24th fl., Chiyoda-ku* ☎ *03/6270–2888* 🌐 *www.peninsula.com* Ⓜ *Hibiya and Mita subway lines, Hibiya Station (Exit A6).*

JAZZ CLUBS

Cotton Club (コットンクラブ)

LIVE MUSIC | In these intimate and luxurious surroundings you can listen to not only jazz but also soul, R&B, J-pop, and world music. The club has such an excellent sound system that musicians such as Ron Carter have recorded live albums here. Fine French cuisine lures music lovers for special nights out. ✉ *Tokia Bldg., 2–7–3 Marunouchi, 2nd fl., Chiyoda-ku* ☎ *03/3215–1555* 🌐 *bluenotejapan.jp/en/brands/cottonclub* Ⓜ *JR and subway lines, Tokyo Station, directly connected to Tokia Bldg.*

Performing Arts

Takarazuka (宝塚)
THEATER | Japan's all-female theater troupe was founded in the Osaka suburb of Takarazuka in 1913 and has been going strong ever since. Today, it has not one but five companies, one of which (the Cosmos Troupe) has a permanent home in Tokyo at the 2,069-seat Takarazuka Theater. Same-day tickets are sold at the box office at either 9:30 am or 10 am. Advance tickets are available through ticketing agencies and the theater's website. Any remaining tickets are sold at the theater box office. ✉ *1–1–3 Yurakucho, Chiyoda-ku* ☎ *0570/00–5100* 🌐 *kageki.hankyu.co.jp/english* 🎫 *Tickets from ¥3,500* Ⓜ *JR Yamanote Line, Yurakucho Station (Hibiya Exit); Hibiya subway line, Hibiya Station (Exit A5); Chiyoda and Mita subway lines, Hibiya Station (Exit A13).*

Shopping

Marunouchi's arcades and shops attract sophisticated professionals who look for no-fuss quality. They also know how to let loose at the neighborhood's lounges and bars when the workday is done.

BOOKS

Maruzen (丸善書店; *Maruzen Shoten*)
BOOKS | FAMILY | This flagship branch of the Maruzen chain, in the Oazo building, has English titles on the fourth floor as well as art books. The store also hosts occasional art exhibits. ✉ *1–6–4 Marunouchi, Chiyoda-ku* ☎ *03/5288–8881* Ⓜ *JR Yamanote Line, Tokyo Station (Marunouchi North Exit); Tozai subway line, Otemachi Station (Exit B2).*

DEPARTMENT STORES

Kitte Marunouchi (丸の内)
DEPARTMENT STORE | The unique geometric shape of Kitte's interior, which was partly designed by renowned Japanese architect Kengo Kuma, sets this department store apart. It also has a notable free history museum on the second floor (called Intermediatheque) and an expansive sixth-floor rooftop garden overlooking Tokyo Station. In the basement is the Tokyo City Tourist & Business Information Center, where English-speaking staffers can share info on attractions and events in and around Tokyo. The department store's name, Kitte, is a play on the Japanese words "stamp" and "come." It makes sense once you know that Japan Post was the building's developer. ✉ *2–7–2 Marunouchi, Chiyoda-ku* ☎ *03/3216–2811* 🌐 *marunouchi.jp-kitte.jp* Ⓜ *Marunouchi subway line, Tokyo Station (direct access); multiple JR lines, Tokyo Station (Marunouchi South Exit).*

HOUSEWARES

Nakagawa Masashichi Shoten (中川政七商店)
HOUSEWARES | This Tokyo flagship of a homewares store established in Nara City in 1716 stocks a wide range of items and tools for your daily life, including the Hasami line of crockery made with Nagasaki porcelain. Look for the store's signature tea towels, which are made of *hanafukin*, a traditional cotton cloth originally used as mosquito netting, and are are renowned for their soft texture and high absorbency. ✉ *Kitte, 2–7–2 Marunouchi, 4F, Chiyoda-ku* ☎ *03/3217–2010* 🌐 *www.nakagawa-masashichi.jp* Ⓜ *Marunouchi subway line, Tokyo Station (direct access); multiple JR lines, Tokyo Station (Marunouchi South Exit).*

SHOPPING CENTERS

Marunouchi Buildings (丸の内ビル)
SHOPPING CENTER | Bringing some much-needed retail dazzle to the area are these six shopping, office, and dining mega-complexes called Marunoucu-hi, Shin-marunouchi, Oazo, Iiyo, Brick Square, and Tokia. Highlights include the fifth-floor open terrace on the Marunouchi Building, with its view of Tokyo Station, Bricksquare, which has its own oasis-like European garden on the ground floor—the perfect spot to rest in between bouts of shopping

at the luxury and everyday boutiques. ✉ *Marunouchi 2–chome area, Chiyoda-ku* ☎ *03/5218–5100* 🌐 *www.marunouchi.com* Ⓜ *Marunouchi subway line, Tokyo Station (various exits); multiple JR lines, Tokyo Station (Marunouchi South Exit).*

Tokyo Midtown Hibiya
(東京ミッドタウン日比谷)
SHOPPING CENTER | Billed as a luxury entertainment-and-shopping complex, Midtown Hibiya's curvy glass-meets-greenery design is worth a visit for the architecture itself. The complex has six floors of shopping and dining, focusing on high-end and smaller brands. Two floors are devoted to Toho Cinema's premier theater. Outside, the grassy lawn of the sixth-floor garden often hosts events and is a great place to relax outside. ✉ *1–1–2 Yurakucho, Chiyoda-ku* ☎ *03/5157–1251* 🌐 *www.hibiya.tokyo-midtown.com* Ⓜ *Hibya Station (Exit A11, A12); JR Yurakucho Station (South Exit).*

Nihonbashi

Sights

Artizon Museum
(アーティゾン美術館; *Achizon bijutsukan*)
ART MUSEUM | Formerly the Bridgestone Museum of Art, the Artizon Museum is one of Japan's best private collections of French impressionist art and sculpture and of post-Meiji Japanese painting in Western styles by such artists as Shigeru Aoki and Tsuguharu Foujita. The collection, assembled by Bridgestone Tire Company founder Shojiro Ishibashi, also includes works by Picasso, Utrillo, and Van Gogh. In addition, the museum mounts exhibits featuring works from other private collections and museums abroad. ✉ *1–7–2 Kyobashi, Chuo-ku* ☎ *050/5541–8600* 🌐 *www.artizon.museum* 🎫 *From ¥1,200 depending on exhibition* 🕒 *Closed Mon.* Ⓜ *Ginza subway line, Kyobashi Station (Meijiya Exit) or Nihonbashi Station (Takashimaya Exit).*

Bank of Japan Currency Museum
(日本銀行貨幣博物館; *Nihon Ginko Kahei Hakubutsukan*)
SPECIALTY MUSEUM | The older part of the Bank of Japan complex is the work of Tatsuno Kingo, who also designed Tokyo Station. Completed in 1896, on the site of what had been the Edo-period gold mint, the bank is one of the city's few surviving Meiji-era Western-style buildings. An annex houses the Currency Museum, a historical collection of rare gold and silver coins from Japan and other East Asian countries. There's little English-language information on the exhibits, but you can download an audio guide for your phone or pick up a explanatory printout on the second floor—after passing through the airport-like security check at the entrance. ✉ *1–3–1 Nihonbashi Hongokucho, Chuo-ku* ☎ *03/3277–3037* 🌐 *www.imes.boj.or.jp* 🎫 *Free* 🕒 *Closed Mon.* Ⓜ *Ginza and Hanzomon subway lines, Mitsukoshimae Station (Exits B1 and A5).*

Kite Museum
(凧の博物館; *Tako no Hakubutsukan*)
SPECIALTY MUSEUM | **FAMILY** | Kite flying is an old tradition in Japan. The collection here includes examples of every shape and variety from all over the country, hand-painted in brilliant colors with figures of birds, geometric patterns, and motifs from Chinese and Japanese mythology. ✉ *NS Bldg., 1–8–3 Nihonbashi, 2nd fl., Chuo-ku* ☎ *03/3275–2704* 🌐 *www.taimeiken.co.jp/museum.html* 🎫 *¥210* 🕒 *Closed Sun.* Ⓜ *Ginza, Tozai, and Asakusa subway lines, Nihonbashi Station (Exit C5).*

Nihonbashi Bridge (日本橋)
BRIDGE | Originally built in 1603, this was the starting point of Edo Japan's five major highways and the point from which all highway distances were measured. Even today, you'll see signs noting the distance to Nihonbashi. Rebuilt in stone

The Nihonbashi neighborhood is named after its famous 17th-century canal bridge.

n 1911, the structure's graceful double arch, ornate lamps, and bronze Chinese ions and unicorns are unfortunately marred by an expressway running directly overhead. In the rush to relieve traffic congestion in preparation for the 1964 Olympics, city planners ignored the protestations of residents and preservation groups and pushed ahead with construction. Still, the sight of a modern highway running over the old stone bridge makes for interesting photos. ✉ *1–8 Nihonbashi Muromachi, Chuo-ku* Ⓜ *Ginza, Tozai, and Asakusa subway lines, Nihonbashi Station (Exits B5 and B6); Ginza and Hanzomon subway lines, Mitsukoshimae Station (Exits B5 and B6).*

Restaurants

This district is all about legacy and tradition. It was home to Tokyo's original seafood market before it was moved to Tsukiji and then to its current location in Toyosu. Some of the restaurants here have been passed down through generations. Japan's oldest department store, Mitsukoshi, is also here; its basement *depachika* is filled with prepared foods for a quick bite.

Craft Beer Market Mitsukoshimae (クラフトビアマーケット三越前店)

$$ | ECLECTIC | This lively gastro-pub in the Coredo Muromachi complex specializes in local craft beers, with the 20 or so brews on tap covering a range of styles. Though you can stop by for just a pint, there's also a food menu featuring Japanese izakaya staples and lunchtime *teishoku* meals that are great value for money. **Known for:** local craft beers; cheaper than typical craft beer pints in Tokyo; small dishes that pair well with beer. $ *Average main: ¥3,000* ✉ *Coredo Muromachi 3, 1–5–5 Nihonbashi Muromachi, Chuo-ku* ☎ *03/6262–3145* 🌐 *www.craftbeermarket.jp/mitsukoshimae* Ⓜ *Hanzomon and Ginza subway lines, Mitsukoshimae Station (Exit A6).*

Manten Sushi (まんてん鮨)

$$$ | SUSHI | This bustling restaurant in the Coredo Muromachi complex proves that great sushi doesn't have to be super

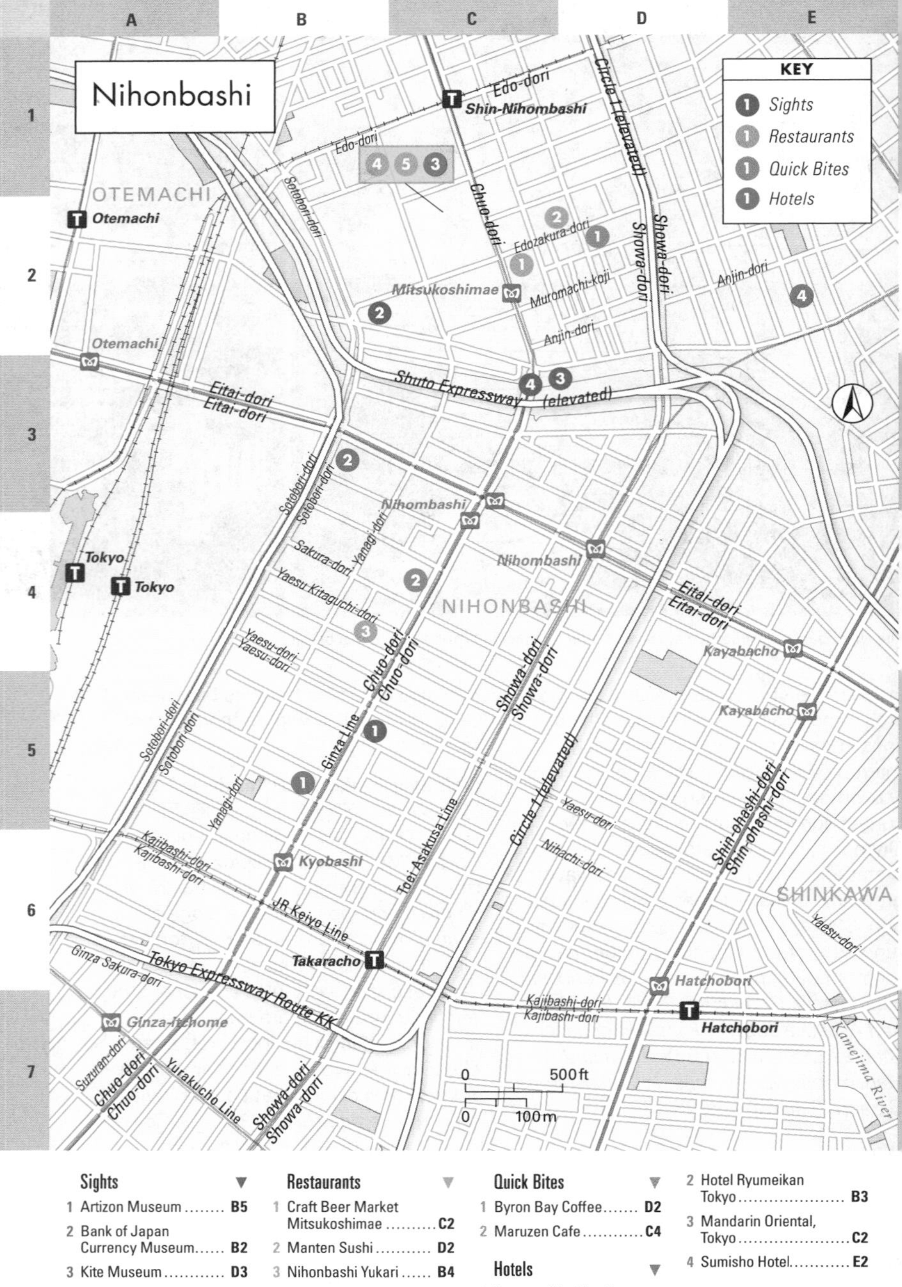

Sights

1 Artizon Museum **B5**
2 Bank of Japan Currency Museum...... **B2**
3 Kite Museum **D3**
4 Nihonbashi Bridge....... **C3**

Restaurants

1 Craft Beer Market Mitsukoshimae **C2**
2 Manten Sushi **D2**
3 Nihonbashi Yukari **B4**
4 Signature **C2**
5 Tapas Molecular Bar.... **C2**

Quick Bites

1 Byron Bay Coffee....... **D2**
2 Maruzen Cafe **C4**

Hotels

1 Courtyard by Marriott Tokyo Station............ **B5**
2 Hotel Ryumeikan Tokyo **B3**
3 Mandarin Oriental, Tokyo **C2**
4 Sumisho Hotel............ **E2**

expensive. Manten does sushi omakase style, meaning you pay for a course and then leave the chefs to choose what to serve, which will vary by season and whatever has been sourced from the market that morning. **Known for:** fresh, seasonal ingredients; lunchtime queues; high-quality sushi in a lively atmosphere. *Average main: ¥7,000* *Coredo Muromachi 2, 2–3–1 Nihonbashi Muromachi, Chuo-ku* *03/3277–6045* *www.manten-sushi.com* *Hanzomon and Ginza subway lines, Mitsukoshimae Station (Exit A6).*

★ **Nihonbashi Yukari** (日本橋ゆかり)
$$$$ | JAPANESE | To enjoy Japanese haute cuisine served in a relaxed atmosphere look to this *kappo-ryori* restaurant, where diners traditionally eat at counters while the chef works in front of them (though Yukari also offers tables and private rooms). Third-generation chef—and 2002 *Iron Chef* champion—Kimio Nonaga displays his artistry in dishes that showcase the freshness and quality of the seasonal ingredients. **Known for:** excellent kappo-style dining; multicourse dinners and affordable lunches; chef Nonaga's creative take on Japanese cuisine. *Average main: ¥20,000* *3–2–14 Nihonbashi, Chuo-ku* *03/3271–3436* *nihonbashi-yukari.com* *Closed Sun.* *Ginza, Tozai, and Asakusa subway lines, Nihonbashi Station (Exit B3).*

Signature (シグネチャー)
$$$$ | FRENCH | This elegant French restaurant on the 37th floor of the Mandarin Oriental Hotel has wonderful views of the Tokyo skyline as well an open kitchen, where you can see the masterful chefs at work. Inspired by Japanese kaiseki, the menu changes with the seasons. **Known for:** fine French cuisine with a Japanese flair; stunning views of the city below; luxurious, modern atmosphere. *Average main: ¥20,000* *Mandarin Oriental Tokyo, 2–1–1 Nihonbashi Muromachi, Chuo-ku* *03/3270–8188* *www.mandarinoriental.com* *Hanzomon and Ginza subway lines, Mitsukoshimae Station (Exit A7).*

Tapas Molecular Bar
(タパス モレキュラーバー)
$$$$ | JAPANESE | Combining aspects of a traditional sushi counter, a tapas bar, a science lab, and a magic show, this award-winning restaurant breaks new ground. In full view of diners, the team of chefs assemble a small parade of bite-size morsels in surprising texture and flavor combinations. **Known for:** a playful take on fine dining; exclusive, intimate atmosphere; watching the chefs is almost as good as the food itself. *Average main: ¥25,000* *Mandarin Oriental Tokyo, 2–1–1 Nihonbashi Muromachi, Chuo-ku* *03/3270–8188* *www.mandarinoriental.com* *Closed Mon and Tues,* *Hanzomon and Ginza subway lines, Mitsukoshimae Station (Exit A7).*

Coffee and Quick Bites

Byron Bay Coffee
$ | CAFÉ | This Australian-style café near Coredo Muromachi is a casual hangout serving potent espressos and milky flat whites. For a quick bite to eat, try a meat pie, or stop by for the money-saving breakfast, which features a coffee and toasted sandwich for ¥650. **Known for:** Aussie meat pies; excellent espresso; flat whites. *Average main: ¥550* *1–5–2 Nihonbashi Muromachi, Chuo-ku* *03/6225–2221* *www.byronbaycoffeejapan.com* *Hanzomon and Ginza subway lines, Mitsukoshimae Station (Exit A6).*

Maruzen Cafe (丸善 カフェ)
$$ | CAFÉ | Known for its classic *hayashi* (hashed beef) rice, lemon herbal tea, and waffles with a side of fluffy ice cream, Maruzen Cafe is the perfect mid-afternoon stop. Its location on the third floor of Maruzen Bookstore and sleek, dark wooden furniture add to the homey atmosphere. **Known for:** hayashi rice; an expansive menu and well-priced dishes;

attentive, polite staff. *Average main: ¥1,580 ✉ Maruzen Nihonbashi, 2–3–10 Nihonbashi, 3F, Chuo-ku ☎ 03/6202–0013 Ⓜ Ginza, Tozai, and Asakusa subway lines, Nihonbashi Station (Exit B1).*

Nihonbashi is primarily a stopover for business travelers. In addition to some high-end accommodations, you can also find good budget options away from the center.

Courtyard by Marriott Tokyo Station (コートヤード・バイ・マリオット 東京ステーション)
$$ | **HOTEL** | Situated on the first four floors of the sleek Kyobashi Trust Tower, the Courtyard by Marriott is a convenient option for business travelers. **Pros:** convenient; many nearby dining options; fitness center. **Cons:** small rooms; closet space limited; somewhat generic atmosphere. *Rooms from: ¥41,000 ✉ 2–1–3 Kyobashi, Chuo-ku ☎ 03/3516–9600 🌐 www.cytokyo.com 150 rooms No Meals Ⓜ Ginza subway line, Kyobashi Station (Exit 1); JR lines, Tokyo Station (Yaesu Exit).*

Hotel Ryumeikan Tokyo (ホテル龍名館東京)
$ | **HOTEL** | One of the most affordable hotels near Tokyo Station (a mere three-minute walk away), the Ryumeikan is a great option for business travelers or those making side trips outside the city. **Pros:** great, convenient location; good breakfast; English-speaking staff. **Cons:** busy area during the week; rooms can feel small; basic amenities. *Rooms from: ¥19,500 ✉ 1–3–22 Yaesu, Chuo-ku ☎ 03/3271–0971 🌐 www.ryumeikan-tokyo.jp/english 135 rooms No Meals Ⓜ JR Tokyo Station (Yaesu North Exit).*

★ **Mandarin Oriental, Tokyo** (マンダリン オリエンタル 東京)
$$$$ | **HOTEL** | Occupying the top nine floors of the glistening Nihonbashi Mitsui Tower, this modern hotel has harmonious rooms, tastefully decorated in shades of brown and featuring such touches as down bedding, luxury linens, in-room newspaper delivery, and large picture windows with city-lights panoramas. **Pros:** wonderful spa and concierge service; superb dining options; attractive room interiors and city views. **Cons:** pricey; area feels a little less lively on the weekends; no pool. *Rooms from: ¥101,000 ✉ 2–1–1 Nihonbashi Muromachi, Chiyoda-ku ☎ 03/3270–8800 🌐 www.mandarinoriental.com 179 rooms No Meals Ⓜ Ginza and Hanzomon subway lines, Mitsukoshimae Station (Exit A7).*

Sumisho Hotel (住庄ほてる)
$ | **HOTEL** | This hotel is popular with budget-minded foreign visitors who prefer to stay near the small Japanese restaurants and bars of the Ningyocho area of Nihonbashi. **Pros:** nicely priced for the area; friendly staff; neighborhood restaurants and pubs have great food for a good price. **Cons:** small rooms and baths; not particularly stylish; quiet area on weekends. *Rooms from: ¥11,000 ✉ 9–14 Nihonbashi Kobunacho, Chuo-ku ☎ 03/3661–4603 🌐 sumisho-hotel.co.jp 83 rooms No Meals Ⓜ Hibiya and Asakusa subway lines, Ningyocho Station (Exit A5).*

Performing Arts

Suigian (水戯庵)
THEATER | The Suigan offers a taste of traditional Japanese Noh and Kyogen plays and geisha performances over a full-course dinner or drinks. While Noh and Kyogen plays can often run hours and be difficult to comprehend, the short performances at Suigan focus on the climactic scenes and give explanations of the story and artistry of the performance. Tickets must be reserved in advance on the website. *✉ B1F, 2–5–10 Nihonbashi Muromachi, Chuo-ku ☎ 03/3527–9378 🌐 suigian.jp Full dinner plans from ¥15,400 Closed Mon.*

With its own subway stop, bronze entrance lions, and an atrium sculpture of the goddess Magokoro, the flagship Mitsukoshi store merits a visit even if you're not planning to shop.

Ⓜ *Ginza and Hanzomon subway lines, Mitsukoshimae Station.*

Shopping

Nihonbashi has 21st-century malls and historical department stores, as well as some of Tokyo's oldest independent shops.

DEPARTMENT STORES

★ **Mitsukoshi Main Store** (三越本店; *Mitsukoshi honten*)

DEPARTMENT STORE | Founded in 1673 as a dry-goods store, Mitsukoshi later played one of the leading roles in introducing Western merchandise to Japan. It has retained its image of quality and excellence, with a particularly strong representation of Western fashion designers. The store also stocks fine traditional Japanese goods and, in the basement, has excellent deli counters and prepared foods—if the weather is good, take your *bento* to the rooftop garden. With its own subway stop, bronze lions at the entrance, and an atrium sculpture of the Japanese goddess Magokoro, this flagship store merits a visit even if you're not planning on buying anything. ✉ *1–4–1 Nihonbashi Muromachi, Chuo-ku* ☎ *03/3241–3311* 🌐 *www.mistore.jp/store/nihombashi.html* Ⓜ *Ginza and Hanzomon subway lines, Mitsukoshimae Station (Exits A3 and A5).*

FOOD

Yamamoto Seaweed (山本海苔店; *Yamamoto Noriten*)

FOOD | The Japanese are resourceful in their uses of products from the sea. Nori, the paper-thin dried seaweed used to wrap maki sushi and *onigiri* (rice balls), is the specialty here. If you plan to bring some home with you, buy unroasted nori and toast it yourself at home; the flavor will be far better than that of the pre-roasted sheets. ✉ *1–6–3 Nihonbashi Muromachi, Chuo-ku* ☎ *03/3241–0290* 🌐 *www.yamamoto-noriten.co.jp/english* Ⓜ *Hanzomon and Ginza subway lines, Mitsukoshimae Station (Exit A1).*

MALLS AND SHOPPING CENTERS

Coredo Muromachi (コレド室町)

MALL | **FAMILY** | Housed in three sleek buildings, simply named 1, 2 and 3, this fashionable complex combines restaurants, artisanal food purveyors, craft stores, boutiques, and cultural facilities such as a tea ceremony center. The complex is across the road from the Mandarin Oriental hotel. There's also a smaller Coredo (Coredo Nihonbashi) a short distance away on the other side Nihonbashi Bridge. ✉ *2–2–1 Nihonbashi Muromachi, Chuo-ku* ☎ *03/3242–0010* 🌐 *mitsui-shopping-park.com/urban/muromachi* Ⓜ *Hanzomon and Ginza subway lines, Mitsukoshimae Station (Exit A6).*

PAPER

★ **Haibara** (榛原)

STATIONERY | Founded elsewhere in 1806, but now located in this sleek, modern grey cube just off Chuo-dori in Nihonbashi, Haibara specializes in gorgeous notebooks, letter sets, fans, and traditional washi paper. Among the examples of the latter, look for *gampi*, an artisanal paper known for its delicate appearance yet high durability. ✉ *2–7–1 Nihonbashi, Chuo-ku* ☎ *03/3272–3801* 🌐 *www.haibara.co.jp* Ⓜ *Ginza, Tozai, and Asakusa subway lines, Nihonbashi Station.*

★ **Ozu Washi** (小津和紙)

STATIONERY | This shop, which was opened in 1653, has one of the largest *washi* showrooms in the city and its own gallery of antique papers and calligraphy. It also offers a variety of cultural classes each day (see the website for times), including a washi paper workshop for ¥800. ✉ *3–6–2 Nihonbashi Honcho, Chuo-ku* ☎ *03/3662–1184* 🌐 *www.ozuwashi.net* Ⓜ *Ginza and Hanzomon subway lines, Mitsukoshimae Station (Exit A4).*

SWORDS AND KNIVES

Kiya Blades (木屋本店; *Kiya Honten*)

SPECIALTY STORE | Workers shape and hone blades in one corner of this shop, which carries cutlery, pocketknives, saws, and more. Scissors with handles in the shape of Japanese cranes are among the many unique gift items sold here, and custom-made knives are available, too. ✉ *Coredo Muromachi, 2–2–1 Nihonbashi Muromachi, Chuo-ku* ☎ *03/3241–0110* 🌐 *www.kiya-hamono.co.jp* Ⓜ *Hanzomon and Ginza subway lines, Mitsukoshimae Station (Exit A6).*

Chapter 5

GINZA AND TSUKIJI

Updated by
Rob Goss

Sights
★★☆☆☆

Restaurants
★★★★☆

Hotels
★★★★☆

Shopping
★★★★★

Nightlife
★★★★☆

NEIGHBORHOOD SNAPSHOT

TOP EXPERIENCES

■ **Take a leisurely stroll.** On weekend afternoons, see the historic Wako department store and glitzy shops along Ginza's Chuo-dori without fear of traffic.

■ **Indulge in a feeding frenzy.** Check out the basement food halls in Ginza's Mitsukoshi and Matsuya department stores, where you will find hundreds of delicious desserts and prepared foods.

■ **Experience traditional performance.** Take in a show of Kabuki, Noh, geisha dance, and other traditional arts at one of the area's famous theaters.

■ **Browse a lively market.** Visit several blocks of food stalls at the Tsukiji Outer Market before grabbing a super-fresh sushi lunch.

GETTING HERE

Ginza is on the other side of the Yamanote Line from the Marunouchi district and the Imperial Palace. It can be reached via the Yamanote's Yurakucho Station, or, more conveniently, by Ginza Station on the Ginza, Hibiya, and Marunouchi subway lines. Tsukiji is a 15-minute walk southeast of central Ginza and is directly served by Tsukiji-shijo Station on the Oedo Line and Tsukiji Station on the Hibiya Line.

PLANNING YOUR TIME

If you plan to explore both Ginza and Tsukiji, start with the latter, as the Tsukiji Outer Market is best visited mid-morning. After that, you could stop at the Tsukiji Hongan-ji Temple, before heading into Ginza, where most stores will be open from 11 am until evening.

On weekend afternoons (October–March, noon–5; April–September, noon–6), Chuo-dori is closed to traffic from Shimbashi to Kyobashi and becomes a pedestrian mall with tables and chairs set out along the street.

A VIEW OF NEW MEETS OLD

■ A short walk from Tsukiji Outer Market, Hama Rikyu Garden (⇨ *see the Shiodome and Odaiba chapter*) is one of Tokyo's classic landscaped spaces. Originally developed in the Edo era (1603–1868), it now provides views of Tokyo old and new. Looking across its main pond toward the Nakajima-no-Ochaya teahouse, you also see the shiny skyscrapers of the Shiodome business district towering above the garden. It makes a great photo.

PAUSE HERE

■ For a free-of-charge break from Ginza's busy shopping streets, head to the rooftop garden at the plush Ginza Six complex. Spread over 4,000 square meters (13,123 square feet), this green space—with benches scattered amid lawns, trees, and bushes—provides a 360-degree view over Ginza. It's a lovely spot to enjoy a coffee or bento.

Ginza was originally the city's banking district. In 1612, Ieyasu Tokugawa moved a plant making silver coins to reclaimed land east of his castle. The area soon came to be known as Ginza (Silver Mint).

Today, the neighborhood is Tokyo's most upscale retail district. The luxury manifests itself in giant department stores, exclusive boutiques, Michelin-starred restaurants, and refined bars.

Until 2018, Tsukiji, a kilometer (just over a half-mile) southeast of Ginza, was home to Japan's biggest wholesale seafood market, where the draw for many was the early morning tuna auctions. That market has moved to a less interesting location in Toyosu, but many stalls still operate in Tsukiji's older outer market, which is near the traditionally landscaped Hama Rikyu Gardens.

Ginza

Sights

Art Aquarium (アートアクアリウム)
AQUARIUM | **FAMILY** | Aquarium meets futuristic art gallery on the eighth floor of Mitsukoshi department store in Ginza. Overseen by innovative artist Hidetomo Kimura, the aquarium features thousands of ornamental fish on display in artistically arranged glass tanks, accompanied by digital art and vivid projections. Among the installations is the Bamboo Grove Seven Sages, comprised of cylindrical tanks illuminated green to mimic the gentle light of a bamboo grove. ✉ *Mitsukoshi Department Store, 8F., 4–6–16 Ginza, Chuo-ku* ✣ *Entrance is on 9F, but aquarium is on 8F.* ☎ *03/3528–6721* 🌐 *artaquarium.jp* 🎫 *¥2,300 advance ticket, ¥2,500 same-day ticket* Ⓜ *Ginza, Marunouchi, and Hibiya subway lines, Ginza Station (Exits A6, A7, and A8).*

Kabuki-za Theater (歌舞伎座)
PERFORMANCE VENUE | After the Meiji Restoration, Kabuki reestablished itself in this part of the city. The first Kabuki-za was built in 1889, with a European facade. In 1912, it was taken over by the Shochiku theatrical management company, which replaced the old building in 1925; it was damaged during World War II but restored soon thereafter. The most recent iteration retains a classic architecture—until you notice the office tower looming above it. Regardless, this is *the* place to see a Kabuki show. For a short 15- to 30-minute sampling, get a single-act ticket; the final act usually provides the best spectacle. Tickets are best bought in advance online. English Earphone Guides are available for a small fee and provide explanations and commentary. ✉ *4–12–15 Ginza, Chuo-ku* ☎ *03/3545–6800* 🌐 *www.kabuki-za.co.jp* 🎫 *From ¥4,000 for full performances; single act tickets typically ¥1,000 to ¥2,000* Ⓜ *Hibiya and Asakusa subway lines, Higashi-Ginza Station (Exit 3).*

Nissan Crossing
OTHER ATTRACTION | On one corner of the Ginza Crossing, across from Mitsukoshi and Wako, this incredibly slick two-floor showroom highlights Nissan's latest

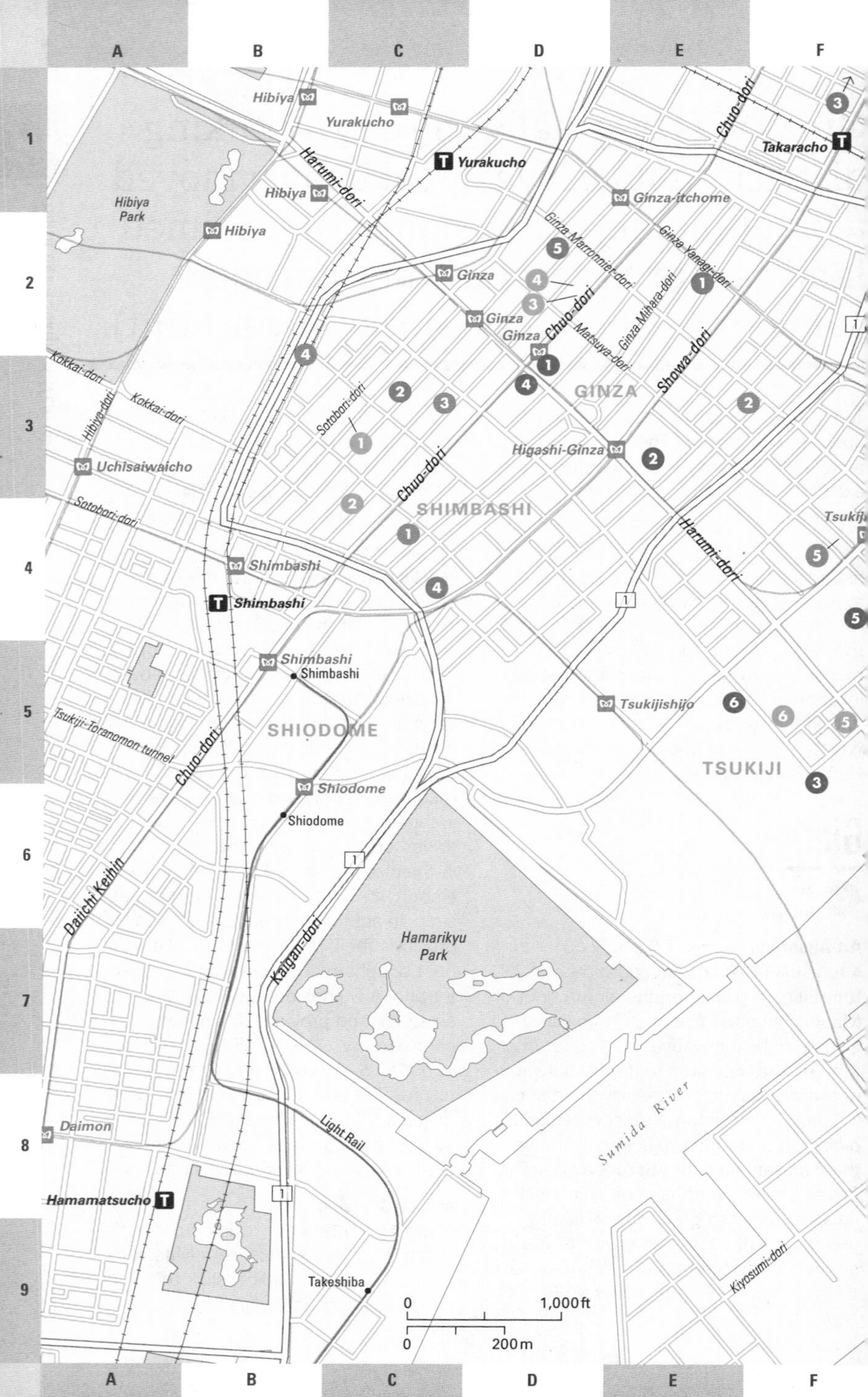

A
B
C
D
E
F
1
2
3
4
5
6
7
8
9
Hibiya
Yurakucho
Yurakucho
Takaracho
Harumi-dori
Chuo-dori
Hibiya
Hibiya Park
Hibiya
Ginza-itchome
Ginza-Marronnier-dori
Ginza-Yanagi-dori
Ginza
Ginza-Mihara-dori
Ginza
Ginza
Chuo-dori
Matsuya-dori
Kokkai-dori
Kokkai-dori
Hibiya-dori
Sotobori-dori
GINZA
Showa-dori
Higashi-Ginza
Uchisaiwaicho
Chuo-dori
SHIMBASHI
Sotobori-dori
Tsukiji
Harumi-dori
Shimbashi
Shimbashi
Shimbashi
Shimbashi
Tsukijishijo
Tsukiji-Toranomon tunnel
SHIODOME
TSUKIJI
Chuo-dori
Shiodome
Shiodome
Daiichi Keihin
Kaigan-dori
Hamarikyu Park
Light Rail
Sumida River
Daimon
Hamamatsucho
Kiyosumi-dori
Takeshiba
0
1,000 ft
0
200 m

Ginza and Tsukiji

G H I J

NIHONBASHI
Hatchobori
Hatchobori
Shin-ohashi-dori
Kyoryuchi Chuo-dori
Teppozu-dori
Shintomicho
CHUO
Tsukuda-ohashi Bridge
Sumida River
Tsukuda-ohashi-dori
Tsukishima
Nishinaka-dori
Kiyosumi-dori
Higashi Naka-dori
Harumi-dori
KACHIDOKI
Kachidoki
Kiyosumi-dori
Higashinaka-dori
HARUMI
Harumi-dori
Reimeibashi Koen-dori

KEY

- Sights
- Restaurants
- Quick Bites
- Hotels

G H I J

Sights

1 Art Aquarium D3
2 Kabuki-za Theater E3
3 Namiyoke Shrine F5
4 Nissan Crossing D3
5 Tsukiji Hongan-ji Temple F4
6 Tsukiji Outer Market E5

Restaurants

1 Kitafuku C3
2 Kyubey C4
3 Rangetsu D2
4 Sake no Ana D2
5 Takeno Shokudo F5
6 Tsukiji Kagura Sushi Honten F5

Quick Bites

1 Cafe de l'Ambre C4
2 Ginza Hachigou E3
3 Rose Bakery Ginza C3
4 Tachinomi Marugin B2
5 Turret Coffee F4

Hotels

1 Hotel Monterey Ginza E2
2 Hyatt Centric Ginza Tokyo C3
3 Lyf F1
4 Mitsui Garden Hotel Ginza Premier C4
5 Muji Hotel Ginza D2

The Power of Tea

Green tea is ubiquitous in Japan; it contains antioxidants twice as powerful as those in red wine that help reduce high blood pressure, lower blood sugar, and fight cancer. A heightened immune system and lower cholesterol are other benefits attributed to green tea.

In Japan pay attention to tea varietals, which are graded (and priced) by the quality and parts of the plant used. For the very best Japanese green tea, take a trip to the Uji region of Kyoto or to Shizuoka Prefecture, just west of Tokyo.

***Bancha* (common tea).** This second-harvest variety ripens between summer and fall, producing leaves larger than those of sencha and a weaker-tasting tea.

***Genmaicha* (brown rice tea).** This is a mixture sencha and roasted brown rice.

***Gyokuro* (jewel dew).** Derived from a grade of green tea called *tencha* (divine tea), the name comes from the light-green color the tea develops when brewed. Gyokuro is grown in the shade, an essential condition to develop its signature savory flavor and high caffeine content.

***Hojicha* (roasted tea).** A roasted green tea with a brown appearance and a slightly lower caffeine hit.

***Kabusecha* (covered tea).** Similar to gyokuro, kabusecha leaves are grown in the shade, though for a shorter period, giving it a refined flavor.

***Kukicha* (stalk tea).** A tea made from stalks by harvesting one bud and three leaves.

***Matcha* (rubbed tea).** Most often used in the tea ceremony, matcha is a high-quality powdered green tea. It has a thick, paint-like consistency when mixed with hot water. It is also a popular flavor of ice cream and other sweets in Japan.

***Sencha* (steamed tea).** This is the green tea you are most likely to find at a supermarket, a local restaurant, or your ryokan inn. Its leaves are grown under direct sunlight, giving it a different flavor from more expensive cousins like gyokuro.

concept vehicles and technological innovations. Cars on display change every few months or so, with recent examples having included a futuristic-looking Disaster Support Mobile Hub and an X-Trail G E-4ORCE four-wheel drive. On the second floor, you can shop for Nissan goods and model cars in a boutique or linger with a latte in a café. ✉ *5–8–1 Ginza, Chuo-ku* ☎ *03/3573–0523* 🌐 *www.nissan.co.jp/crossing/en* 🎫 *Free* Ⓜ *Ginza, Hibiya and Marunouchi subway lines, Ginza Station (Exits A3 to A5).*

Restaurants

At night, neon lights fills the streets with the names of eateries and bars. For a quick bite, head into a department store basement, where you'll find a dizzying array of prepared foods.

Kitafuku (きた福)

$$$$ | **SEAFOOD** | If you're going to splurge on crab in Tokyo, do it at this exclusive restaurant. Chefs serve a choice of kaiseki-like crab courses, featuring in-season delicacies such as red king crab served in a variety of ways—from sashimi to shabu-shabu. **Known for:** sumptuous crab courses; cozy private rooms; eye-watering prices. *Average main: ¥40,000* *7–4–5 Ginza, Chuo-ku* *03/6280–6368* *kanikitafuku.com/ginza* *Ginza, Hibiya and Marunouchi subway lines, Ginza Station (Exit B3); JR Lines, Shinbashi Station (Ginza Exit).*

Kyubey (久兵衛)
$$$$ | **SUSHI** | This world-famous spot proves that a high-end sushi restaurant doesn't have to be solemn to be refined. In addition to having excellent knife skills, many of the chefs speak English and are happy to chat with you about the food, making Kyubey a great choice for a first-time high-end sushi experience. **Known for:** originator of gunkan-maki style sushi rolls; excellent sushi since 1935; easier to book than other high-end sushi restaurants, though reservations are still essential. *Average main: ¥22,000* *8–7–6 Ginza, Chuo-ku* *03/3571–6523* *www.kyubey.jp/en* *Closed Sun. and Mon.* *Ginza, Hibiya and Marunouchi subway lines, Ginza Station (Exit B3); JR Lines, Shinbashi Station (Ginza Exit).*

Rangetsu (銀座らん月)
$$$$ | **JAPANESE** | Japan enjoys a special reputation for its lovingly raised, tender, marbled domestic beef (Wagyu), and if your budget can bear the weight, Rangetsu serves excellent dishes with this beef as a star ingredient. Try the signature shabu-shabu or sukiyaki course for a primer. **Known for:** high-quality Wagyu; wide selection of sake; affordable lunch sets. *Average main: ¥21,000* *3–3–1 Ginza, Chuo-ku* *On the 5th floor of Zoe Building, next door to Muji.* *03/3567–1021* *www.ginza-rangetsu.com* *Marunouchi, Hibiya and Ginza subway lines, Ginza Station (Exit A9).*

Sake no Ana (酒の穴)
$$$ | **JAPANESE** | With more than 100 varieties of sake from all over Japan, Sake no Ana (literally, "the sake hole") has a sake sommelier who can help you make a selection. Though most sake-specialty restaurants are open only for dinner, this one is also open for lunch, and the food is classic izakaya fare. **Known for:** great for sake novices; welcoming atmosphere; simple, hearty food. *Average main: ¥5,000* *3–3–1 Ginza, Chuo-ku* *On the 5th floor of Zoe Building, next to Muji.* *03/3567–1133* *www.sakenoana.com* *Marunouchi, Hibiya and Ginza subway lines, Ginza Station (Exit A9).*

Coffee and Quick Bites

Café de l'Ambre (カフェ・ド・ランブル)
$ | **COFFEE** | In business since 1948, Café de l'Ambre is a legendary haunt for Tokyo's coffee aficionados. The retro decor provides a snapshot of an older Tokyo, and the caffeine-fix options include a dozen or so single-origin beans, including some that have been aged for years. **Known for:** aged coffee beans; retro vibe; doesn't open until noon. *Average main: ¥700* *8–10–15 Ginza, Chuo-ku* *03/3571–1551* *www.cafedelambre.com* *No credit cards* *Closed Mon.* *Ginza, Hibiya and Marunouchi subway lines, Ginza Station (Exit A3).*

Ginza Hachigou (銀座八五)
$ | **RAMEN** | This lunch-only restaurant not far from the Kabuki-za Theater has received a Michelin Bib Gourmand for its subtle take on ramen. The key is the soup, which foregoes soy for a light broth that takes inspiration from consommé, using vegetables, duck, chicken, and sea salt. **Known for:** subtle ramen broth; accepts reservations; value for money. *Average main: ¥1,250* *3–14–2 Ginza, Chuo-ku* *katsumoto-japan.com/en/ginza_hachigou.html* *Closed Mon and some Tues.* *Hibiya and Asakusa subway lines, Higashi-Ginza Station (Exit 7).*

Rose Bakery Ginza
(ローズベーカリー銀座)
$$ | **CAFÉ** | Satisfying the need for light, healthy food that is neither raw nor fried, this airy but rather nondescript bakery and café in the ultra-trendy Dover Street

Market serves up a tasty selection of salads, quiches, vegetables, and other deli-style dishes. Although the interior's rows of tables and blank white walls can feel a bit too much like a hip reinterpretation of a school cafeteria, Rose Bakery is a good bet for a quick lunch or pastry while out wandering the Ginza area. **Known for:** lighter fare; flavorful sweets; crisp, fresh salads. *Average main: ¥2,000 ✉ 6–9–5 Ginza, Ginza Komatsu West Wing 7F, Chuo-ku ☎ 03/6274–6211 🌐 ginza.doverstreetmarket.com/pages/rose-bakery Ⓜ Ginza, Hibiya and Marunouchi subway lines, Ginza Station (Exit A2).*

Tachinomi Marugin (立呑みマルギン)
$$ | JAPANESE | This *yakitori* (grilled chicken) restaurant is an ideal place for a short stop inside Ginza. Skewered chicken breasts, small salads, and sausages are sure to put a smile on the face of even the weariest shopper. **Known for:** char-grilled chicken skewers (yakitori); opens nightly from 5 pm to 6 am; cheap whiskey highballs. *Average main: ¥2,500 ✉ 7–2 Ginza, Chuo-ku ☎ 03/3571–8989 No credit cards ⏲ No lunch Ⓜ Yamanote Line, Yurakucho Station (Ginza Exit).*

Hotels

Domestic hotel chains are reasonably priced bets in Ginza, although there are also luxury options in its outskirts.

Hotel Monterey Ginza
(ホテルモントレ銀座)
$ | HOTEL | The faux-stone exterior that attempts to replicate 20th-century Europe might seem cheesy, but this hotel is a true Ginza bargain. **Pros:** lots of nearby shopping; central location; reasonable prices for the area. **Cons:** design lacks elegance; rooms are a tad small and a bit outdated; limited on-site dining options. *Rooms from: ¥24,000 ✉ 2–10–2 Ginza, Chuo-ku ☎ 03/3544–7111 🌐 www.hotelmonterey.co.jp/ginza 224 rooms No Meals Ⓜ Ginza, Hibiya and Marunouchi subway lines, Ginza Station (Exit A13) and Yurakucho subway line, Ginza-itchome Station (Exit 11).*

Hyatt Centric Ginza Tokyo (ハイアット セントリック 銀座 東京;)
$$$ | HOTEL | Situated in the heart of Ginza, this hotel is a chic place to unwind after a day of shopping and before a night on the town. **Pros:** close to shops and nightspots; spacious, well-designed rooms; helpful, English-speaking staff. **Cons:** far better value breakfast options at cafés in Ginza; aimed at travelers in their 30s and 40s rather than families; gym is a little cramped. *Rooms from: ¥64,000 ✉ 6–6–7 Ginza, Chuo-ku ☎ 03/6837–1234 🌐 www.hyatt.com 164 rooms No Meals Ⓜ Ginza, Hibiya and Marunouchi subway lines, Ginza Station (Exits B5 and B6).*

Lyf (Lyf銀座東京)
$ | HOTEL | Trendy yet budget-friendly, this hotel on the edge of Ginza seems geared to a younger crowd, with pop-art throughout and guest rooms done in light blues and oranges. **Pros:** fun design; hotel with a friendly hostel vibe; good range of facilities. **Cons:** a little removed from the center of Ginza; small rooms; will feel too youthful for some. *Rooms from: ¥16,000 ✉ 2–5–4 Kyobashi, Chuo-ku 🌐 www.discoverasr.com/en/lyf 140 rooms No Meals Ⓜ Ginza subway line, Kyobashi Station.*

Mitsui Garden Hotel Ginza Premier
(三井ガーデンホテル銀座プレミア)
$$ | HOTEL | Both chic and reasonable, this hotel occupies the top nine floors of the 24-story Ginza Mitsui Building in a convenient location at the edge of the bustling neighborhood. **Pros:** affordable; sharp design; plenty of nearby shopping. **Cons:** small rooms; in-hotel restaurant a tad pricey; geared more to business travelers. *Rooms from: ¥31,000 ✉ 8–13–1 Ginza, Chuo-ku ☎ 03/3543–1131 🌐 www.gardenhotels.co.jp 361 rooms No Meals Ⓜ Ginza subway line, Ginza Station (Exit A3) or JR Shimbashi Station (Ginza Exit).*

Muji Hotel Ginza

$$ | **HOTEL** | Smack in the center of Ginza, this hotel was created in 2019 by budget Japanese retailer Muji, a company known for its natural toned, minimalist approach to interiors and fashion. **Pros:** smart, fresh design; superb central Ginza location; well-maintained rooms. **Cons:** no gym or business center; very small rooms, especially the "A" singles; cheaper options available nearby. *$ Rooms from: ¥42,000 ✉ 3–3–5 Ginza, Chuo-ku ☎ 03/3538–6101 🌐 hotel.muji.com 79 rooms No Meals M JR Yamanote Line and Yurakucho subway line, Yurakucho Station (Central Exit); Ginza, Marunouchi, Hibiya subway lines, Ginza Station (Exit A9).*

Nightlife

Ginza Lion (銀座ライオン)

PUB | Japan's oldest beer hall, in business since 1899 and occupying the same stately Chuo-dori location since 1934, is remarkably affordable for one of Tokyo's toniest addresses. Ginza shoppers and office workers alike drop by for beer and ballast—anything from Japanese-style fried chicken to spaghetti. *✉ 7–9–20 Ginza, Chuo-ku ☎ 03/3571–2590 🌐 www.ginzalion.jp/shop/brand/lionginza M Ginza, Hibiya, and Marunouchi subway lines, Ginza Station (Exit A3).*

Star Bar Ginza

BARS | It's said that Ginza has all the best bars, and this may be the best of the lot. Owner, bartender, and mixologist Hisashi Kishi is the president of the Japan Bartenders Association, and his attention to detail in the narrow, dark, and calm room is staggering. *✉ 1–5–13 Ginza, B1 fl., Chuo-ku ☎ 03/3535–8005 🌐 www.starbar.jp/en M Yurakucho subway line, Ginza-itchome Station (Exits 3 or 6).*

Performing Arts

Kanze Noh-gakudo (観世能楽堂)

THEATER | At one of the most important of Japan's Noh family schools, the current *iemoto* (head) is the 26th in his line. Kanze's stylish new theater is in the basement of the Ginza Six complex. English-language plot summaries are available upon request. *✉ Ginza Six Bldg., 6–10–1 Ginza, B3 fl., Chuo-ku ☎ 03/6274–6579 🌐 kanze.net From ¥4,000 for reserved seats ☞ Opens only on performance days (see website for schedule) M Ginza, Hibiya, and Marunouchi subway lines, Ginza Station (Exit A2).*

Shimbashi Enbujo (新橋演舞場)

THEATER | Dating from 1925, this theater was built for the geisha of the Shimbashi quarter to present their spring and autumn performances of traditional music and dance. It remains one of the best spots in Tokyo to see traditional performing arts, although the theater is now also the home of "Super Kabuki," a faster, jazzier modern version of kabuki. *✉ 6–18–2 Ginza, Chuo-ku ☎ 03/6745–0888 🌐 www.shinbashi-enbujo.co.jp Seats commonly run ¥3,000–¥17,500. M Hibiya and Asakusa subway lines, Higashi-Ginza Station (Exit 6).*

Shopping

Shops here—including flagships of Tiffany & Co., Harry Winston, and Mikimoto—are often expensive and exclusive. Still, in recent years, affordable fashion chains have built towers in the area, creating a mix of high- and low-brow style that defines modern Tokyo's taste.

TIP→ Don't plan a Ginza shopping excursion for too early in the day; most stores and cafés don't open until 11 am. On Sunday, the main strip of Chuo-dori is closed to car traffic, and umbrella-covered tables dot the pavement.

In business since 1899 and in its current location since 1934, the beloved Ginza Lion is Japan's oldest beer hall.

CLOTHING

★ Dover Street Market

CLOTHING | This multistory fashion playhouse is a shrine to exclusives, one-offs, and other hard-to-find pieces from luxury brands all over the world. Curated by Comme des Garçons, the selection may leave all but the most dedicated fashion fans scratching their heads, but the unique interior sculptures alone warrant a visit. ✉ *6–9–5 Ginza, Chuo-ku* ☎ *03/6228–5080* 🌐 *ginza.doverstreetmarket.com* Ⓜ *Ginza, Hibiya, and Marunouchi subway lines, Ginza Station (Exit A2).*

Uniqlo (ユニクロ)

CLOTHING | **FAMILY** | Here's your chance to stock up on the company's own brand of simple, low-priced clothing staples. This 12-story location is the world's largest Uniqlo, and sells men's, women's, and children's clothing right on the main Ginza drag. ✉ *6–9–5 Ginza, Chuo-ku* ☎ *03/6252–5181* 🌐 *www.uniqlo.com* Ⓜ *Ginza, Hibiya, and Marunouchi subway lines, Ginza Station (Exit A2).*

DEPARTMENT STORES

Ginza Six

DEPARTMENT STORE | Below upper-floor office spaces, you'll find eight floors that are home to outposts of swanky brands like Celine, Fendi, and Jimmy Choo. There are also cosmetic stores, deli foods, restaurants, art installations, and even the Kanze Noh theater in the basement. It's immediately across from the 12-story flagship of budget fashion brand Uniqlo. ✉ *6–10–1 Ginza, Chuo-ku* ☎ *03/6891–3390* 🌐 *ginza6.tokyo* Ⓜ *Ginza, Hibiya, and Marunouchi subway lines, Ginza Station (Exit A2).*

Matsuya (松屋)

DEPARTMENT STORE | The second-floor of this slick major department store has the European-designer boutiques (Prada, Luis Vuitton, Balenciaga) that are popular with Tokyo's brand-obsessed shoppers. The rooftop terrace is a welcome respite for the weary. ✉ *3–6–1 Ginza, Chuo-ku* ☎ *03/3567–1211* 🌐 *www.matsuya.com/ginza* Ⓜ *Ginza, Marunouchi, and Hibiya subway lines, Ginza Station (Exit A12).*

Mitsukoshi Ginza (三越銀座)
DEPARTMENT STORE | The Ginza branch of Japan's first department-store chain has been open since 1930 and remains the largest department store in the area, with a sprawling grass-covered terrace on the ninth floor that provides a respite from the shopping bustle. Away from the multiple floors of fashion and style, the two basement floors have an impressive selection of delicacies, while the eighth floor is home to the Art Aquarium (fee required), where fish are displayed in a vibrant collection of tanks. ✉ *4–6–16 Ginza, Chuo-ku* ☎ *03/3562–1111* 🌐 *www.mistore.jp/store/ginza.html* Ⓜ *Ginza, Marunouchi, and Hibiya subway lines, Ginza Station (Exits A6, A7, and A8).*

★ **Muji** (無印良品; *Mujirushi ryohin*)
DEPARTMENT STORE | **FAMILY** | The global flagship store of this minimalist, design-focused interiors and clothing brand is home to a large selection of furniture, appliances, bedding, and clothes for the whole family. The store also houses a café–bakery, a diner, and a sleek hotel. ✉ *3–3–5 Ginza, Chuo-ku* ☎ *03/3538–1311* 🌐 *www.muji.com* Ⓜ *Ginza, Marunouchi, and Hibiya subway lines, Ginza Station (Exit B4).*

Wako (和光)
DEPARTMENT STORE | This grand old department store is well known for its high-end watches (it's owned by Seiko), glassware, and jewelry, as well as having some of the most sophisticated window displays in town. The clock atop the curved 1930s-era building is illuminated at night, making it one of Ginza's more recognized landmarks. ✉ *4–5–11 Ginza, Chuo-ku* ☎ *03/3562–2111* 🌐 *www.wako.co.jp* Ⓜ *Ginza, Marunouchi, and Hibiya subway lines, Ginza Station (Exits A9 and A10).*

ELECTRONICS

Sukiya Camera (スキヤカメラ)
CAMERAS & PHOTOGRAPHY | The cramped Nikon House branch of this two-store operation features so many Nikons—old and new, digital and film—that it could double as a museum to the brand. Plenty of lenses and flashes are available as well. ✉ *4–3–7 Ginza, Chuo-ku* ☎ *03/3561–6000* 🌐 *www.sukiya.co.jp* Ⓜ *JR Yamanote Line, Yurakucho Station (Ginza Exit); Ginza, Hibiya, and Marunouchi subway lines, Ginza Station (Exit B10).*

JEWELRY

Ginza Tanaka (銀座田中)
JEWELRY & WATCHES | One of the finest jewelers in Japan, founded in 1892, specializes in precious metals and diamond jewelry. It also sells a wide variety of art objects in gold, like those found on Buddhist altars. ✉ *1–7–7 Ginza, Chuo-ku* ☎ *03/5561–0491* 🌐 *www.ginzatanaka.co.jp/en* Ⓜ *Yurakucho subway line, Ginza-itchome Station (Exit 7).*

★ **Mikimoto Ginza Main Store** (ミキモト銀座本店; *Mikimoto Ginza honten*)
JEWELRY & WATCHES | Since 1893, Kokichi Mikimoto has been associated with the best quality cultured pearls in the industry, and this flagship store is devoted to them. The building, like the pearls it holds, dazzles shoppers with a facade decorated with 40,000 small glass plates. A few streets away, the exterior design of the sister branch, Mikimoto Ginza 2, is even more striking: it resembles a block of Swiss cheese. ✉ *4–5–5 Ginza, Chuo-ku* ☎ *03/3535–4611* 🌐 *www.mikimoto.com* Ⓜ *Ginza, Hibiya, and Marunouchi subway lines, Ginza Station (Exit A9).*

Tasaki Pearls Ginza Main Store (田崎銀座本店; *Tasaki Ginza honten*)
JEWELRY & WATCHES | At this pearl retailer's glittery flagship tower by the Ginza Crossing, there's a large collection of both pearl and gem items, from costume to bridal and fine jewelry to watches. The fifth-floor events space often hosts art exhibits. ✉ *5–7–5 Ginza, Chuo-ku* ☎ *03/3289–1111* 🌐 *www.tasaki.co.jp* Ⓜ *Ginza, Hibiya, and Marunouchi subway lines, Ginza Station (Exit A2).*

KIMONOS

Tansu-ya (たんす屋)

SPECIALTY STORE | This small but pleasant Ginza shop has attractive used kimono, yukata, and other traditional clothing in many fabrics, colors, and patterns. The helpful staff can acquaint you with the somewhat complicated method of putting on the garments. Other locations are scattered throughout the city, including Asakusa, Aoyama, and Shinjuku. ✉ *3–4–5 Ginza, Chuo-ku* ☎ *03/3561–8529* 🌐 *tansuya.jp* Ⓜ *Ginza, Hibiya, and Marunouchi subway lines, Ginza Station (Exit A13).*

PAPER

Itoya (伊東屋)

STATIONERY | This 12-storey paper emporium brims with locally crafted and imported stationery, as well as contemporary office accessories. For a distinctive souvenir, check out the traditional washi and origami paper on the eighth floor and the calligraphy goods on the seventh. ✉ *2–7–15 Ginza, Chuo-ku* ☎ *03/3561–8311* 🌐 *www.ito-ya.co.jp* Ⓜ *Ginza, Hibiya, and Marunouchi subway lines, Ginza Station (Exit A13).*

Kyukyodo (鳩居堂)

STATIONERY | In business since 1663—and in this spacious location since 1880—Kyukyodo sells wonderful handmade Japanese papers, paper products, incense, brushes, and other materials for calligraphy. ✉ *5–7–4 Ginza, Chuo-ku* ☎ *03/3571–4429* 🌐 *www.kyukyodo.co.jp* Ⓜ *Ginza, Hibiya, and Marunouchi subway lines, Ginza Station (Exit A2).*

SWORDS AND KNIVES

Token Shibata (刀剣柴田)

SPECIALTY STORE | This tiny, somewhat modest looking shop incongruously situated near Ginza's glittering department stores sells expensive antique swords. Staffers can also sharpen your blade for you. ✉ *5-6-8 Ginza, Chuo-ku* ☎ *03/3573–2801* 🌐 *www.tokensibata.co.jp* Ⓜ *Ginza, Hibiya, and Marunouchi subway lines, Ginza Station (Exit A1).*

Tsukiji

Sights

Namiyoke Shrine
(波除神社; *Namiyoke Jinja*)

RELIGIOUS BUILDING | Built in the mid-1600s to house and honor a Shinto spirit that calmed the waters of Tokyo Bay, this little shrine is worth a stop on your way to Tsukiji Outer Market. The name literally means "protection from waves," and it is an unofficial guardian shrine for the marketplace and its workers. ✉ *6–20–37 Tsukiji, Chuo-ku* ☎ *03/3541–8451* 🌐 *www.namiyoke.or.jp* Ⓜ *Oedo subway line, Tsukiji-shijo Station (Exit A1); Hibiya subway line, Tsukiji Station (Exit 1).*

Tsukiji Hongan-ji Temple (築地本願寺)

TEMPLE | Disaster seemed to follow this temple, an outpost of Kyoto's Nishi Hongan-ji. Since it located here in 1657, it was destroyed at least five times, and reconstruction in wood was finally abandoned after the Great Kanto Earthquake of 1923. The present stone building, dating from 1935, was designed by Chuta Ito, a pupil of Tokyo Station architect Tatsuno Kingo. Ito's other credits include the Meiji Shrine in Harajuku; he also lobbied for Japan's first law to preserve historic buildings. Ito traveled extensively in Asia; the evocations of classical Hindu architecture in the temple's domes and ornaments were his homage to India as the cradle of Buddhism. But with stained-glass windows and a pipe organ as well, the building is nothing if not eclectic. Talks in English are held on the final Saturday of the month at 5:30. The final Friday sees lunchtime concerts of classical and Buddhist music (from 12:30 pm). ✉ *3–15–1 Tsukiji, Chuo-ku* ☎ *03/3541–1131* 🌐 *tsukijihongwanji.jp* 🎫 *Free* ☞ *Daily services at 7 am and 4 pm* Ⓜ *Hibiya subway line, Tsukiji Station (Exit 1).*

Stalls with fresh seafood for sale at the Tsukiji Outer Market

★ **Tsukiji Outer Market**
(築地場外市場; *Tsukiji jyogai shijo*)
MARKET | **FAMILY** | Enjoying a sushi breakfast at this famous fish market is an integral part of any trip to Tokyo, even now that its famed inner market has been relocated to nearby Toyosu. If you have time for only one market, this is the one to see, as the shopkeepers maintain the feeling of the original Tsukiji area. The three square blocks between the former site of Tokyo Central Wholesale Market and Harumi-dori have scores of fishmongers, plus shops and restaurants. Stores sell pickles, tea, crackers and snacks, cutlery (what better place to pick up a professional sushi knife?), baskets, and kitchenware. Many of the sushi bars here have set menus ranging from ¥1,000 to ¥2,500; look for the plastic models of food in glass cases out front. The area includes a row of little counter restaurants, barely more than street stalls, under the arcade along the east side of Shin-Ohashi-dori, each with its specialty. Come hungry, and be sure to stop for *maguro donburi*—a bowl of fresh raw tuna slices served over rice and garnished with bits of dried seaweed. ✉ *Tsukiji 4–chome, Chuo-ku* 🌐 *www.tsukiji.or.jp/english* Ⓜ *Toei Oedo subway line, Tsukiji-shijo Station (Exit A1); Hibiya subway line, Tsukiji Station (Exit 1).*

Restaurants

A visit to the Tsukiji Outer Market is a must for foodies. Small restaurants and stalls serve sushi, ramen, and other quick bites, and shops sell kitchenware.

Takeno Shokudo (多け乃食堂)
$$ | **JAPANESE** | Expect generous portions of fresh, reasonably priced seafood at this neighborhood restaurant. Sashimi and simmered fish are the staples, but there's also a wonderful *tendon* bowl with shrimp and eel tempura on rice. À la carte prices are not posted because they vary with the costs that morning in the Toyosu Market. **Known for:** cheap, delicious seafood; popular with locals; a menu based on what the cooks found in the market that morning. $ *Average*

main: ¥2,000 ✉ *6–21–2 Tsukiji, Chuo-ku* ☎ *03/3541–8698* 🌐 *tsukijitakeno.owst.jp/en* 💳 *No credit cards* 🕒 *Closed Sun.* Ⓜ *Hibiya subway line, Tsukiji Station (Exit 1); Oedo subway line, Tsukiji-shijo Station (Exit A1).*

Tsukiji Kagura Sushi Honten (築地神楽寿司本店)
$$$$ | **SUSHI** | This no-frills sushi restaurant with wooden interiors serves up excellent Tokyo-style (Edomae) sushi, the classic *nigiri* topped with seafood. Á la carte is an option, but it's easier to opt for a set meal, which will be substantially cheaper during lunch than at dinner. **Known for:** friendly, local vibe; good value sushi sets; rustic interiors. 💲 *Average main: ¥7,700* ✉ *4–14–13 Tsukiji, Chuo-ku* ☎ *03/3541–4180* 🌐 *tukijikagura.jp* 🕒 *Closed Mon.* Ⓜ *Hibiya subway line, Tsukiji Station (Exit 1); Oedo subway line, Tsukiji-shijo Station (Exit A1).*

Coffee and Quick Bites

Turret Coffee (ターレットコーヒー;)
$ | **COFFEE** | Tucked on a side street, this friendly café takes its name from the little "turret" trucks that carted produce around the old Tsukiji Market. The owner serves a powerful espresso in ceramic sake cups and also creates delightful latte art—all for similar prices to the far less enjoyable Starbucks on the corner. **Known for:** excellent espresso; artful lattes; early opening by Tokyo standards (from 7 am Monday to Saturday, from 9 am Sunday). 💲 *Average main: ¥490* ✉ *2–12–6 Tsukiji, Chuo-ku* ☎ *080/3344–8819* 🌐 *www.instagram.com/turretcoffee* 💳 *No credit cards* 🕒 *Some irregular closing days (listed on Instagram)* Ⓜ *Oedo subway line, Tsukiji-shijo Station; Hibiya subway line, Tsukiji Station (Exit 2).*

Activities

Yakatabune Harumiya (屋形船晴海屋)
BOAT TOURS | As in the time of the samurai, cruising in a roof-topped boat, or *yakatabune,* is the perfect way to relax. You're treated like royalty and are entertained while floating along the gentle Sumida or Arakawa River. Hosts within the cabin serve multiple courses of tempura and sushi and pour beer, sake and whiskey while the boats. When the *shoji* (paper blinds) are opened, the illuminated Tokyo nightscape is a sight to behold. Observation decks offer even better views. Boats accommodate groups of 20 to 350, and regular tours run nightly year-round from 7 pm. ✉ *Harumi Josenba, 4–6–1 Kachidoki, Chuo-ku* ☎ *03/3644–1344* 🌐 *yakatabune-tokyo.com* 🎫 *Dinner cruises from ¥12,500* Ⓜ *Oedo subway line, Kachidoki Station (Exit A3).*

Chapter 6

6

SHIODOME AND ODAIBA

Updated by
Randall Grace

Sights	Restaurants	Hotels	Shopping	Nightlife
★★★☆☆	★★★☆☆	★★★★☆	★★★★☆	★★☆☆☆

NEIGHBORHOOD SNAPSHOT

TOP EXPERIENCES

■ **Barbecue or sushi?** Toyosu might be home to Tokyo's bustling fish market and a parade of sushi options, but it has also become a hot spot for grilled meat and lively get-togethers.

■ **Traditional garden landscaping.** Settle into a lovely traditional garden and old teahouse surrounded by skyscrapers and concrete at Hama Rikyu Garden.

■ **Retro design.** See historical advertisements dating from the Edo period (1603–1868) at the Ad Museum Tokyo.

■ **Play time.** With a fake Statue of Liberty, man-made beach, game, and theme restaurants, Odaiba is a good destination for kitsch-lovers.

■ **Hit the mall.** A succession of malls in Tokyo Bay might hurt your purse strings.

■ **Meet a robot.** Interact with humanoid robots at Miraikan (the National Museum of Emerging Science and Innovation).

GETTING HERE AND AROUND

Shiodome is easily accessed by public transport: JR lines and Yurikamome Line at Shimbashi Station, Toei Oedo Line to Shiodome Station, and Asakusa Line and Ginza Line to Shimbashi Station. To visit Toyosu Fish Market, continue on the Yurikamome Monorail from Shimbashi Station.

The best way to reach Odaiba is via the fully automated Yurikamome Line. From Shimbashi Station you can take the JR Karasumori Exit, Asakusa subway line Exit A2, or the Ginza subway line Exit 4—follow the blue seagull signs to the station entrance. You can pick up a map of Odaiba in English at the entrance. The JR Rinkai Line also serves the area from Osaki Station on the Yamanote Line.

PLANNING YOUR TIME

■ Spend the morning strolling around Hama Rikyu Gardens and exploring the Ad Museum before having lunch in Shiodome. If you still have energy, take yourself across the bay to Odaiba. Alternatively, start your morning at Toyosu Market and continue on to Ariake in the afternoon.

WHAT IS PURI-KURA?

■ In Odaiba's malls and game centers, there are rows of sticker photo booths, often occupied by gaggles of giggling teenage girls. These machines are known as *puri-kura* and don't take run-of-the-mill photos. The inside of the booth is large enough for a small group to stand, and, once the snapping is done, there are endless options to customize your photo. After filters, icons, and text have been added, the results are often unrecognizable.

Now a redeveloped business district, Shiodome (literally "where the tide stops") was once an area of saltwater flats where the Meiji government built the Tokyo terminal in 1872—the original Shimbashi Station—on Japan's first railway line.

In the period after the Meiji Restoration, Shimbashi (also sometimes transliterated as "Shinbashi") was one of the most famous geisha districts of the new capital. Its reputation as a pleasure quarter is even older. In the Edo period, when there was a network of canals and waterways here, it was the height of luxury to charter a covered boat (called a *yakatabune*) from one of the Shimbashi boathouses for a cruise on the river; a local restaurant would cater the excursion, and a local geisha house would provide companionship. Almost nothing remains in Shimbashi to recall that golden age, but as its luster has faded, adjacent Shiodome has risen—literally—in its place.

In 1997, an urban renewal plan for the area evolved, and the land was auctioned off. Among the buyers were Nippon Television and Dentsu, the largest advertising agency in Asia. In 2002, Dentsu consolidated its scattered offices into the centerpiece of the Shiodome project: a 47-story tower and annex designed by Jean Nouvel. With the annex, known as the Caretta Shiodome, Dentsu created an "investment in community"—a complex of cultural facilities, shops, and restaurants that has turned Shiodome into one of the most fashionable places in the city.

Odaiba is a man-made peninsula in Tokyo Bay, with its beginnings dating from the Edo period (1603–1868), when various fortifications were constructed for protection from attacks by ships. As a result of Japan's rapidly expanding economy in the 1980s, the area became a target location for a number of flamboyant and futuristic-looking development projects. Today, 1,000 acres of landfill are home to various leisure, corporate, and commercial complexes, as well as the new Toyosu Fish Market, which replaced the historic Tsukiji Market in 2018.

Shiodome

Sights

Ad Museum Tokyo (アドミュージアム東京)
SPECIALTY MUSEUM | The distinctive Japanese sensibility in graphic and commercial design comes into historical perspective in these exhibits featuring everything from 18th-century woodblock prints to contemporary fashion photographs and videos. The museum is maintained by a foundation established in honor of Hideo Yoshida, fourth president of the mammoth Dentsu Advertising Company, and includes a digital library of some 130,000 entries and articles on everything you ever wanted to know about hype. ✉ *Caretta Shiodome, 1–8–2 Higashi-Shinbashi, B1F–B2F, Minato-ku*

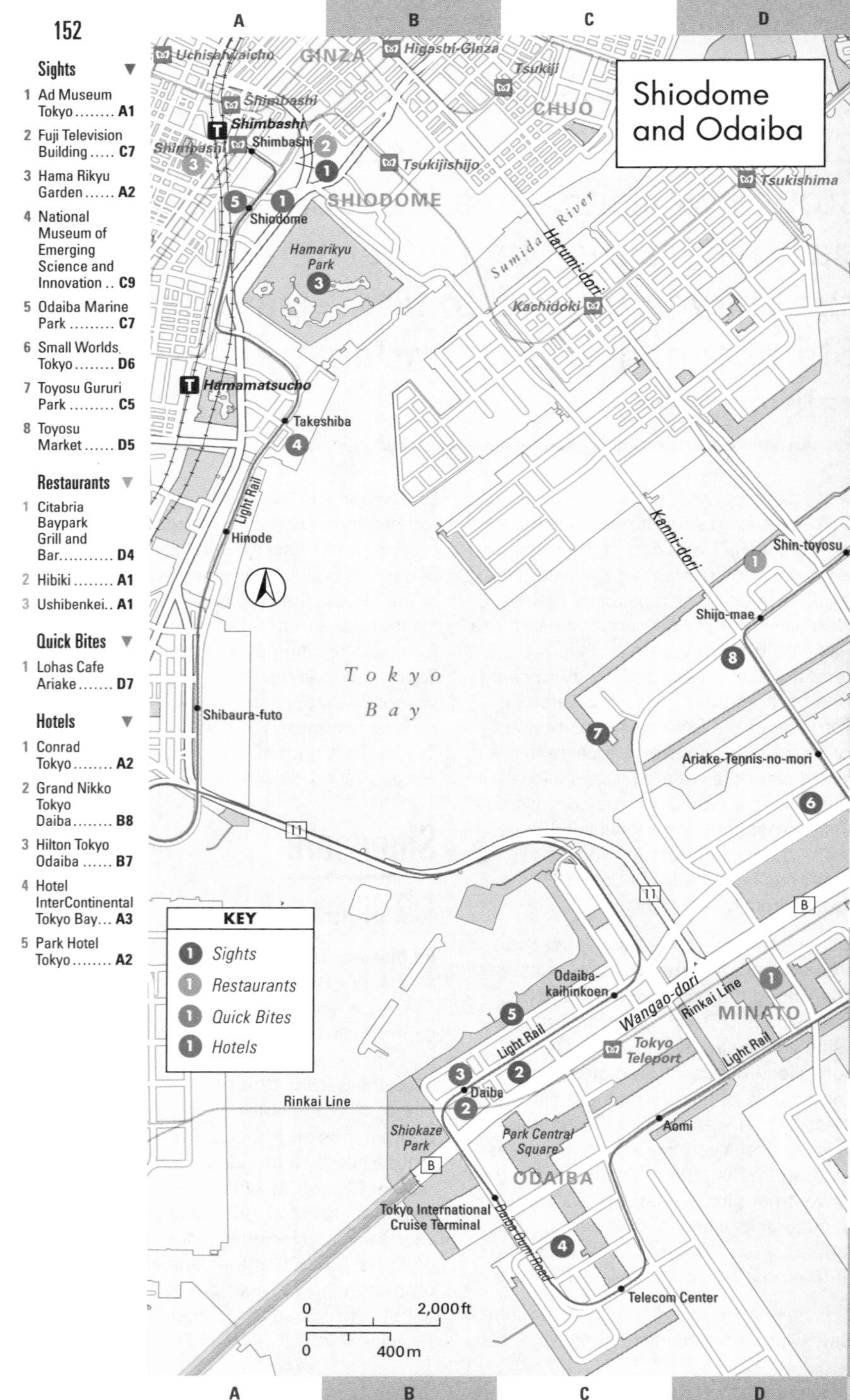
Sights
1 Ad Museum Tokyo........ A1
2 Fuji Television Building..... C7
3 Hama Rikyu Garden...... A2
4 National Museum of Emerging Science and Innovation.. C9
5 Odaiba Marine Park......... C7
6 Small Worlds Tokyo........ D6
7 Toyosu Gururi Park......... C5
8 Toyosu Market...... D5
Restaurants
1 Citabria Baypark Grill and Bar........... D4
2 Hibiki........ A1
3 Ushibenkei.. A1
Quick Bites
1 Lohas Cafe Ariake....... D7
Hotels
1 Conrad Tokyo........ A2
2 Grand Nikko Tokyo Daiba........ B8
3 Hilton Tokyo Odaiba...... B7
4 Hotel InterContinental Tokyo Bay... A3
5 Park Hotel Tokyo........ A2
A
B
C
D
Shiodome and Odaiba
Uchisaiwaicho
GINZA
Higashi-Ginza
Tsukiji
CHUO
Shimbashi
Shimbashi
Shimbashi
Shimbashi
Tsukijishijo
Tsukishima
SHIODOME
Shiodome
Sumida River
Harumi-dori
Hamarikyu Park
Kachidoki
Hamamatsucho
Takeshiba
Light Rail
Hinode
Kanni-dori
Shin-toyosu
Shijo-mae
Tokyo Bay
Shibaura-futo
Ariake-Tennis-no-mori
11
11
B
KEY
Sights
Restaurants
Quick Bites
Hotels
Odaiba-kaihinkoen
Wangan-dori
Rinkai Line
MINATO
Light Rail
Tokyo Teleport
Light Rail
Daiba
Rinkai Line
Shiokaze Park
B
Park Central Square
Aomi
ODAIBA
Tokyo International Cruise Terminal
Daiba-Dumi Road
Telecom Center
0
2,000 ft
0
400 m

03/6218–2500 www.admt.jp Free Closed Sun. and Mon. Toei Oedo subway line, Shiodome Station (Exit 7); JR (Shiodome Exit) and Asakusa and Ginza lines (Exit 4), Shimbashi Station.

Hama Rikyu Garden
(浜離宮庭園; *Hama Rikyu Teien*)
GARDEN | FAMILY | A tiny sanctuary of Japanese tradition and nature that's surrounded by towering glass buildings is a great place to relax or walk off a filling sushi meal. The land here was originally owned by the Owari branch of the Tokugawa family from Nagoya, and, when a family member became shogun in 1709, his residence was turned into a palace—with pavilions, ornamental gardens, pine and cherry groves, and duck ponds. The garden became a public park in 1945, although a good portion of it is fenced off as a nature preserve.

None of the original buildings have survived, but on the island in the large pond is a reproduction of the pavilion where the former U.S. president Ulysses S. Grant and Mrs. Grant had an audience with Emperior Meiji in 1879. The Hobai-tei meeting house can now be rented for parties, and the stone linings of the saltwater canal work and some of the bridges have been restored. The path to the left as you enter the garden leads to the "water bus" ferry landing, from which you can cruise up the Sumidagawa to Asakusa. Note that you must pay the admission to the garden even if you're just using the ferry. *1–1 Hamarikyu–Teien, Chuo-ku 03/3541–0200 www.tokyo-park.or.jp/teien/en/hama-rikyu ¥300 Toei Oedo subway line, Shiodome Station (Exit 8).*

Restaurants

Hibiki (響)
$$$$ | JAPANESE | Perched on the 46th floor of the Carretta Shiodome Building overlooking Tokyo Bay, this seafood-focused izakaya is a nice escape from the chaotic frenzy below. Specialties include grilled fish and house-made tofu. **Known for:** Hibiki whiskey; seasonal ingredients; open, big glass windows. *Average main: ¥8,500 Carretta Shiodome, 46F, 1–8–2 Higashi-Shimbashi, Minato-ku 050/3200–0679 www.dynacjapan.com/brands/hibiki/shops/shiodome/.*

Ushibenkei (牛弁慶)
$$$$ | JAPANESE | High-quality marbled beef is taken quite seriously in Japan—cuts are ranked based on the ratio, distribution, and sweetness of the fat in relation to the meat. At Ushibenkei, you can sample some pieces of the highest rank at reasonable prices in a charmingly rustic atmosphere. **Known for:** high-grade Japanese beef; sukiyaki and other beef hotpots; beef sushi. *Average main: ¥9,000 3–18–7 Shimbashi, Minato-ku 03/3459–9318 www.dd-holdings.jp/shops/ushibenkei/shinbashi No lunch weekdays JR Yamanote Line, Shimbashi Station (Kasumori Exit); Ginza subway line, Shimbashi Station (Exit A1).*

Hotels

Shiodome has a number of medium- and high-end lodging options, many of them perched above the city, on the upper floors of the area's skyscrapers.

Conrad Tokyo (コンラッド東京)
$$$ | HOTEL | Elevators shoot up 28 floors in the slick, green-hued Tokyo Shiodome Building to a lobby of dark oak paneling and bronze lattices at the luxurious Conrad, which artfully mixes ultramodern and traditional Japanese aesthetics. **Pros:** modern design; fantastic bay view; fine restaurants. **Cons:** pricey; finding the entrance to the elevator is troublesome; extra charge to use pool and gym. *Rooms from: ¥60,000 1–9–1 Higashi-Shinbashi, Minato-ku 03/6388–8000 conrad-tokyo.hilton-japan.co.jp 291 rooms No Meals JR Yamanote Line, Shimbashi Station (Shiodome Exit); Oedo subway line, Shiodome Station (Exit 9).*

Cherry blossoms bloom at Hama Rikyu garden.

Hotel InterContinental Tokyo Bay (ホテルインターコンチネンタル 東京ベイ)
$$$ | **HOTEL** | The InterContinental offers lovely views of the Rainbow Bridge, Tokyo Bay, and surrounding Odaiba and has large rooms featuring soft neutral textiles and bathrooms with separate showers and tubs—all of which offsets a somewhat isolated location, wedged between Tokyo Bay and an expressway, with nothing in the way of nearby entertainment options. **Pros:** sweeping views; large, nicely appointed rooms; quiet area. **Cons:** no pool; some might find it too removed for sightseeing; the gym is small. *Rooms from: ¥70,400* *1–16–2 Kaigan, Minato-ku* *03/5404–2222* *www.interconti-tokyo.com* *330 rooms* *No Meals* *Yurikamome rail line, Takeshiba Station.*

★ **Park Hotel Tokyo** (パークホテル東京)
$$ | **HOTEL** | Rates at this boutique hotel are reasonable for rooms—many of them decorated by local artists—that have large bathrooms and great city or (even better) bay views. **Pros:** great value; stylish, artsy decor throughout; bar has more than 100 kinds of single malt whisky. **Cons:** small rooms; few in-room frills; no pool or gym. *Rooms from: ¥42,000* *1–7–1 Higashi Shimbashi, Minato-ku* *03/6252–1111* *parkhotel-tokyo.com* *270 rooms* *No Meals* *JR Yamanote Line, Shimbashi Station (Shiodome Exit); Oedo subway line, Shiodome Station (Exit 10).*

Nightlife

Shinshu Osake Mura (信州おさけ村)
BARS | Although it's primarily a liquor store specializing in products from Nagano prefecture, this place also functions as a casual, standing-room-only bar where you can sample more than 100 kinds of sake (paying per 110-milliliter glass), more than 60 craft beers from brewers such as Shiga Kogen, and interesting snacks like spiced cow's tongue. A great option is one of the many reasonably priced three-sake sampler sets. It's tricky to find, being on the first floor of a very dated office building opposite the

west exit of Shimbashi Station, but look for the big statue of a *tanuki* (raccoon dog) with extremely large testicles that's outside the building, then go in and turn right. Staffers are very friendly and speak enough English to help with the sake choices. The clientele spills into the hallway when it gets crowded, and plastic hand fans are cached around the place for customer use on warm evenings. ✉ *Shimbashi Ekimae Bldg. 1, 2–20–15 Shinbashi, 1st fl., Minato-ku* ☎ *03/3572–5488* 🌐 *www.nagano-sake.com/vil* Ⓜ *JR Yamanote Line, Shimbashi Station (West Exit); Ginza subway line, Shimbashi Station (Exit A3).*

Odaiba

Connected to the city by the Yurikamome monorail from Shimbashi and the Rinkai Line from Osaki, Odaiba is known to tourists for its arcades, hotels, shopping malls, and museums. It also has the city's longest (albeit artificial) stretch of sandy beach, along the boat harbor (high levels of pollution preclude swimming here, though), and the Rainbow Bridge, which becomes a multicolored neon beacon at night. The exhibition halls at the Tokyo Big Sight (✉ *3–11–1 Ariake, Koto-ku*), whose entrance is beneath four large upside-down pyramids, host numerous conventions, trade shows, and fairs.

At the foot of the Rainbow Bridge, you can walk out onto the diamond-shape Odaiba Park, which juts out into the bay. Alternatively, you can stroll over the bridge itself for an amazing view of what is certainly one of Tokyo's most diverse megaprojects.

Sights

Fuji Television Building (フジテレビ)
FILM/TV STUDIO | **FAMILY** | Make time for a visit to Odaiba if only to contemplate this futuristic building, designed by Kenzo Tange and completed in 1996. In addition, the 25th-floor observation deck affords a spectacular view of the bay and the graceful curve of the Rainbow Bridge. ✉ *2–4–8 Daiba, Minato-ku* 🌐 *www.fujitv.com* 🎫 *Observation deck: ¥800* 🕒 *Closed Mon.* Ⓜ *Rinkai Line, Tokyo Teleport Station; Yurikamome Line, Odaiba-kaihinkoen Station.*

National Museum of Emerging Science and Innovation (日本科学未来館; *Nihon Kagaku Miraikan*)
SCIENCE MUSEUM | **FAMILY** | Be sure to visit the third floor of the museum known as Miraikan (Future Hall), where you will get to meet and control a humanoid robot. This hands-on facility has areas focusing on humans' relationship to the planet, the frontiers of outer space and the deep sea, and our life in the near future. There's also a special theater with planetarium and 3-D shows (reservations required). ✉ *2–3–6 Aomi, Koto-ku* ☎ *03/3570–9151* 🌐 *www.miraikan.jst.go.jp* 🎫 *¥630* 🕒 *Closed Tues.* Ⓜ *Yurikamome Line, Tokyo International Cruise Terminal Station.*

Odaiba Marine Park (お台場海浜公園; *Odaiba Kaihin Koen*)
BEACH | **FAMILY** | This artificial beach and its boardwalk are home to a small replica of the Statue of Liberty and, for many strolling couples, a wonderful evening view of the Rainbow Bridge. ✉ *1–4–1 Daiba, Minato-ku* Ⓜ *Yurikamome Line, Odaiba-kaihinkoen Station.*

Small Worlds Tokyo (ミニチュアミュージアム スモールワールズ)
THEME PARK | **FAMILY** | At this novel and surprisingly spacious indoor theme park dedicated to miniatures, you can imagine what it's like to be a giant while wandering through various countries, time periods, and fantasy lands. Watch a small rocket launch, search for hidden characters, or create a mini-me and become a permanent resident. ✉ *Ariake Butsuryu Center, 1–3–33 Ariake, Koto-ku* 🌐 *www.smallworlds.jp* 🎫 *¥2,700* Ⓜ *Yurikamome Line, Ariake-Tennis-no-mori Station; Rinkai Line, Kokusai-Tenjijo Station.*

Officially named the Tokyo Bay Connector Bridge, this white bridge is illuminated with colorful solar-powered lights by night, hence its more common name, the Rainbow Bridge.

Toyosu Gururi Park (豊洲ぐるりパーク)
CITY PARK | **FAMILY** | From an alternative view of the Rainbow Bridge, head to this park on the other side of Tokyo Bay. Here you'll find families playing football, barbecuing, and having picnics. If you don't have your own gear, The BBQ Beach in Toyosu can supply meat to grill and seats in which to unwind. ✉ *6–5 Toyosu, Koto-ku* 🌐 *www.toyosugururi.jp* 🎫 *Free* Ⓜ *Yurikamome Line, Shijo-mae Station.*

Toyosu Market (豊洲市場; *Toyosu Shijo*)
MARKET | **FAMILY** | Opened in October 2018 as the replacement to the legendary Tsukiji Market, the 40-hectare (99 acres) Toyosu Market, like its predecessor, is one of the busiest seafood markets in the world, with more than 400 merchants hard at work. The new market is an upgrade in terms of size and facilities, but, sadly, a downgrade in terms of experience and charm. Visitors also have far less market access than they once did: you're restricted to viewing the early morning auctions from behind glass (you need to apply for a spot online before going), and you can no longer stroll the inner market. Rather you must follow a fixed route through the three main buildings, two of which are for seafood, the other for fruit and vegetables.

Afterward, head up to the rooftop lawn on the Fisheries Intermediate Wholesale Market Building for bay and city views, then check out the market's restaurants for a sushi or seafood breakfast; some popular Tsukiji eateries, like Sushi Dai, have made the move to Toyosu. ■ TIP→ **Don't access the market by traveling to Toyosu Station, which is a 20-minute walk away; instead, head to Shijo-mae Station on the Yurikamome Line.** ✉ *6–1 Toyosu, Koto-ku* ☎ *03/3520–8205* 🌐 *www.shijou.metro.tokyo.jp/english/toyosu* ⏲ *Closed Sun.* Ⓜ *Yurikamome Line, Shijo-mae Station.*

Restaurants

Citabria Baypark Grill and Bar (サイタブリア ベイパーク グリル＆バー)
$$ | **FAST FOOD** | Stop off near the end of the Yurikamome Line and have dinner along the riverbank before heading back to your hotel. The live DJ (on weekends), order-at-bar service, and strong cocktails create a lively ambience, and the location along a popular walking path makes for excellent people- and dog-watching. **Known for:** outdoor-only dining; pizza and fish-and-chips; fairy lights with river and city views. *Average main: ¥3,000* *6–4–26 Toyosu, Koto-ku* *080/9179–5151* *citabria-baypark.com* *Closed Mon. and Tues.; no lunch weekdays* *Yurikamome Line, Shijo-mae Station.*

Coffee and Quick Bites

Lohas Cafe Ariake (ロハスカフェ)
$ | **BISTRO** | If you venture across the broad Yumeno Ohashi Bridge between Odaiba and Ariake, it might be time for a break. Attached to Musashino University's Ariake Campus is a cheap, bright, and fun café with good weekly specials and a wide variety of dishes including pasta and rice bowls. **Known for:** open space and high ceilings; café dishes at student prices; veranda with tree views. *Average main: ¥1,000* *Musashino University Ariake Campus, 3–3–3 Ariake, 2F, Koto-ku* *03/6457–1150* *www.lohascafe-ariake.net* *No dinner* *Yurikamome Line, Tokyo Big Sight Station.*

Hotels

Thanks to its secluded location, the Odaiba area is a lovely place to stay on a romantic getaway. (The hotels that line Tokyo Bay are known for their views.) Business travelers also stay here to be close to the convention center grounds.

Grand Nikko Tokyo Daiba (グランドニッコー東京 台場)
$$ | **HOTEL** | **FAMILY** | As soon as you enter the grand, extravagant lobby, you and your luggage will be immediately taken care of, and, although rooms are spacious, the real highlights are the bathrooms with luxurious sinks and bathtubs big enough for two. **Pros:** great views of Rainbow Bridge; large, clean rooms; romantic setting. **Cons:** reception can get busy; slightly old-fashioned rooms; not much to do in the evening. *Rooms from: ¥30,000* *2–6–1 Daiba, Minato-ku* *03/5500–6711* *www.tokyo.grand-nikko.com* *884 rooms* *No Meals* *Yurikamome Line, Daiba Station.*

Hilton Tokyo Odaiba (ヒルトン東京お台場)
$$ | **HOTEL** | **FAMILY** | With a facade that follows the curve of the Tokyo Bay shoreline, the 15-story Hilton Tokyo Odaiba presents itself as an "urban resort" with European style. **Pros:** great views of Tokyo Bay; friendly staff; romantic setting. **Cons:** isolated location isn't ideal for sightseeing; room interiors are a tad bland; expensive pool fees for guests. *Rooms from: ¥30,000* *1–9–1 Daiba, Minato-ku* *03/5500–5500* *hilton-hotels.jp* *453 rooms* *No Meals* *Yurikamome Line, Daiba Station.*

Shopping

Unlike the narrow streets of central Tokyo, Odaiba's wide, open spaces are well suited for multistory shopping complexes. It's no surprise, then, that this area has four of them, three of which—Decks Tokyo Beach, Aqua City, and Diver City—are within walking distance of one another.

Aqua City Odaiba (アクアシティお台場)
MALL | **FAMILY** | Aqua City, with stores selling wide selection of Japanese and international brand-name items, is almost indistinguishable from its next-door neighbor, Decks Tokyo Beach. What does set it apart from a regular shopping mall,

though, is its variety of food options—a food court in the basement, a barbecue spot on the roof, and a ramen theme park—and the fact that it has its own shrine. There's also a cinema. ✉ *1–7–1 Daiba, Minato-ku* ☎ *03/3599–4700* 🌐 *www.aquacity.jp* Ⓜ *Rinkai Line, Tokyo Teleport Station; Yurikamome Line, Odaiba-kaihinkoen Station.*

Ariake Garden (有明ガーデン)
MALL | **FAMILY** | Opened in June 2020, Ariake Garden is a large-scale shopping mall with more than 100 stores, a hotel, a spa with hot-spring access, a theater, a rooftop terrace, and—of course—a garden. ✉ *2–1–8 Ariake, Koto-ku* ☎ *050/3111–4850* 🌐 *www.shopping-sumitomo-rd.com* Ⓜ *Yurikamome Line, Ariake and Ariake-tennis-no-mori Station; Rinkai Line, Kokusai-tenjijo Station.*

★ **Decks Tokyo Beach**
(デックス東京ビーチ)
MALL | **FAMILY** | Overlooking the harbor, this six-story complex of shops, restaurants, and boardwalks is really two connected malls: Island Mall and Seaside Mall. For kids (or nostalgic adults), check out the LEGO Discovery Center, Joypolis mega-arcade, Trick Art Museum, and Madame Tussauds Tokyo. At the Seaside Mall, a table by the window in any of the restaurants looks out over the harbor, a view that's particularly delightful at sunset, when the *yakatabune* (traditional-roofed pleasure boats) drift down the Sumida-gawa from Yanagibashi and Ryogoku. ✉ *1–6–1 Daiba, Minato-ku* ☎ *03/3599–6500* 🌐 *www.odaiba-decks.com* Ⓜ *Rinkai Line, Tokyo Teleport Station; Yurikamome Line, Odaiba-kaihinkoen Station.*

Diver City Tokyo Plaza
(ダイバーシティ東京 プラザ)
MALL | **FAMILY** | Diver City gets a lot of foot traffic, mainly due to the life-sized Gundam robot statue welcoming shoppers at the door. It also has a wide selection of stores and a food court with many dining options. ✉ *1–1–10 Aomi, Koto-ku* ☎ *0570/012–780* 🌐 *mitsui-shopping-park.com/divercity-tokyo* Ⓜ *Rinkai Line, Tokyo Teleport Station.*

Chapter 7

AOYAMA, HARAJUKU, AND SHIBUYA

WITH AKASAKA, OMOTESANDO, AND SHIMOKITAZAWA

Updated by
Jay Farris

Sights
★★★★★

Restaurants
★★★★★

Hotels
★★★★★

Shopping
★★★★★

Nightlife
★★★★★

NEIGHBORHOOD SNAPSHOT

TOP EXPERIENCES

■ **Tokyo street style.** Street fashion may now be more understated elsewhere, but Shibuya, Harajuku, and Omotesando are still trendy.

■ **A national treasure and an intersection.** On the connector between Shibuya Station and Mark City you can see the huge *Myth of Tomorrow* mural by avant-garde artist Taro Okamoto, then turn around for a view of the famous Shibuya Scramble Crossing.

■ **Prayers and picnics.** The beautiful Meiji Shrine and more lively Yoyogi Koen offer a refreshing bit of green amid the concrete, crowds, and neon.

■ **Chill out in Shimokitazawa.** This neighborhood is filled with vintage shops, periodic outdoor markets, a linear park, and a calmer vibe than Shibuya.

■ **People-watch.** From casual indoor-outdoor spots between Shibuya and Harajuku and Omotesando or cafés in Aoyama you can watch the world go by.

■ **See fantastic Asian art.** The Nezu Museum has a vast collection of calligraphy, paintings, sculptures, bronzes, and lacquerware.

GETTING HERE

The looping JR Yamanote Line connects Shibuya with Ebisu and Harajuku Stations, though you can walk between Shibuya and Harajuku. The Fukutoshin subway line runs from Shibuya north through Shinjuku and onto Ikebukuro. The Hanzomon and Ginza lines stop at Omotesando and Aoyama-Itchome Stations en route to Shibuya Station from central Tokyo, with the Ginza line passing through Akasaka-Mitsuke. The Keio Inokashira railway travels to Shimokitazawa and on to Kichijoji, home to Inokashira Park, and the Toyoko railway connects the area to Yokohama. The Hachiko Exit is often swarmed with people. Just next to it is the famous Shibuya Scramble Crossing, which leads from the station to restaurants and shops. Buses provide service to Roppongi in the east and Meguro and Setagaya in the west.

PAUSE HERE

■ If you need a break from the crowds on Tokyo's celebrated boulevards, try the shady deck area on the roof of the Tokyu Plaza Omotesando mall, at the intersection of Omotesando and Meiji-dori. Just look up and you can't miss the trees.

PLANNING YOUR TIME

■ In a day, you could visit Meiju Shrine, which you can see in about an hour, and browse shops along Takeshita-dori and Ometesando.

■ With two days you can explore more of the area, including Aoyama, where you could spend a couple hours at the Nezu Museum and its gardens, and Shibuya, where time spent getting lost and finding new things amid all the construction is part of the experience.

■ If you like browsing vintage stores or want to take a quiet walk before or after a meal, allow time to explore the farther-afield Shimokitazawa neighborhood.

Since 1885, when the original train station opened, Shibuya has been the hub for this part of Tokyo. Neighborhoods here developed organically and now seem to flow together seamlessly, especially the shopping meccas of Aoyama, Harajuku, and Omotesando, as well as Shibuya.

In upscale Aoyama, to the northeast of Shibuya, high-end shopping is a sport, as is people-watching, which is easily done from the area's many cafés and restaurants. A bit farther northeast, the Akasaka district is physically close to Aoyama, but, with its government ministries and corporate headquarters, feels more culturally connected to the business-like east side of town. It is, however, a good lodging base, given its proximity to both Aoyama and the sights near the Imperial Palace and its good mix of hotels, *izakaya,* and bars.

Northwest of Aoyama are Harajuku and the grand shopping boulevard known as Omotesando, which together comprise an area that's as trendy and eclectic as it is geographically confounding. It's bookended by the Harajuku Station on one end and the Omotesando Metro Station on the other. The two stations are connected by Omotesando, considered by many to be the Champs-Élysées of Tokyo. Some people consider only the area nearest Harajuku Station to be Harajuku. Younger people tend to call the wider area Harajuku, while their elders might refer to it as Omotesando. It's hard to know where the line between them really is.

For years, Shibuya has been a construction zone, gradually morphing into someone's vision of a future Tokyo. It has, more recently, started taking on a much more vertical form. If, for instance, you travel here via the Ginza Line, you'll depart from beneath ground but will arrive several stories above the street. The elevated pathways and interconnected developments surrounding the station create a labyrinth of shops, restaurants, and other amenities—perfect for rainy day explorations, as you can spend most of your time sheltered and not run out of things to do. Although Shibuya's layout can be confusing, try not to let its maze of shops and sights overwhelm you and, instead, just roll with it.

Directly connected via public transit to Shibuya (as well as to the northern neighborhood of Shinjuku) is low-key Shimokitazawa, which is known for its *furugiya* (vintage clothing stores) whose merchandise is far more curated and expensive than that at your average thrift shop. The neighborhood's newest feature is a linear park that was created after one of the train lines was made an underground route.

Aoyama

There's plenty of money in Aoyama, as evidenced by the area's classy, leafy streets lined with high-end boutiques, cafés, and restaurants. This neighborhood not only showcases high fashion, but also the latest concepts in commercial architecture and interior design.

Akasaka, which separates Aoyama from the sights in the Imperial Palace area, has some outstanding hotels, as well as a mix of bars of eateries near Akasaka-Mitsuke Station.

Sights

★ Nezu Museum
(根津美術館; *Nezu Bijutsukan*)
ART MUSEUM | On view are traditional Japanese and Asian works of art owned by Meiji-period railroad magnate and politician Kaichiro Nezu. For the main building, architect Kengo Kuma designed an arched roof that rises two floors and extends roughly half a block through this upscale Minami Aoyama neighborhood. At any one time, the vast space houses a portion of the 7,400 works of calligraphy, paintings, sculptures, bronzes, and lacquerware that make up the museum's collection. The site is also home to one of Tokyo's quietest gardens, featuring ponds, rolling paths, waterfalls, and a restaurant. ⊠ *6–5–1 Minami-Aoyama, Minato-ku* ☎ *03/3400–2536* 🌐 *www.nezu-muse.or.jp/en* 🎫 *From ¥1,300 depending on exhibit* ⏲ *Closed Mon.* Ⓜ *Ginza and Hanzomon subway lines, Omotesando Station (Exit A5).*

Restaurants

★ Cicada (シカダ)
$$$$ | **MEDITERRANEAN** | With an outdoor patio dining area and bar—the perfect place to relax with a nightcap—Cicada has a resortlike atmosphere that makes it feel a world away from Aoyama's busy shopping streets. Craft beers and wine from the extensive list complement dishes that range from Spanish tapas and Middle Eastern mezze to hearty grilled meats and seafood. **Known for:** terrace dining; flavorful Mediterranean dishes; stylish bar. $ *Average main: ¥12,000* ⊠ *5–7–28 Minami-Aoyama, Minato-ku* ☎ *03/6434–1255* 🌐 *www.tysons.jp/cicada/en* Ⓜ *Ginza, Chiyoda, and Hanzomon subway lines, Omotesando Station (Exit B1).*

Darumaya (だるまや)
$ | **RAMEN** | Although a classic bowl of ramen is topped with slices of pork, here it's often topped with grilled vegetables. Other specialties to try include the *tsukemen,* with the noodles served in one bowl and the broth into which you dip them served in another, or the chilled noodles topped with vegetables and ham in a sesame dressing. **Known for:** refreshing takes on ramen; a quick, affordable lunch in a high-end area; one of the neighborhood's few noodle shops. $ *Average main: ¥1,000* ⊠ *Murayama Bldg., 5–9–5 Minami-Aoyama, 1F, Minato-ku* ☎ *03/3499–6295* 💳 *No credit cards* ⏲ *Closed Sun. and Mon.* Ⓜ *Ginza, Chiyoda, and Hanzomon subway lines, Omotesando Station (Exit B1).*

Maisen Aoyama (まい泉 青山店)
$$$ | **JAPANESE** | Bouquets of flowers are lovely seasonal touches in the airy dining room of this restaurant, which was converted from a *sento* (public bathhouse) and still has the original high ceiling (built for ventilation) and the signs instructing bathers where to change. The specialty is the *tonkatsu* set—tender, juicy, deep-fried pork cutlets served with a tangy sauce, shredded cabbage, miso soup, and rice. **Known for:** retro-chic decor; hearty lunch sets; succulent deep-fried pork. $ *Average main: ¥3,500* ⊠ *4–8–5 Jingumae, Shibuya-ku* ☎ *03/3470–0073* 🌐 *mai-sen.com* Ⓜ *Ginza, Chiyoda, and Hanzomon subway lines, Omotesando Station (Exit A2).*

Tempura Tensho (てんぷら天翔)
$$$$ | **JAPANESE** | Beyond the rather nondescript entrance are counter seats where you can watch the chef expertly prepare and fry exceptional tempura. Although this is a great place for dinner, the lunch sets are far more reasonably priced yet still give you a proper tempura experience. **Known for:** elaborate lunch and dinner sets; an airy atmosphere; fresh, seasonal ingredients. *$ Average main: ¥15,000 ✉ 2–7–13 Kitaaoyama, Minato-ku ✣ On the ground floor of Hotel Allamanda Aoyama ☎ 050/3184–3600 Reservations only 🌐 tempura-tensho.jp Ⓜ Ginza subway line, Gaienmae Station (Exit 2b or 4a).*

Coffee and Quick Bites

Café Kitsuné Aoyama
$ | **CAFÉ** | **FAMILY** | Associated with the funky clothing shop just around the corner and part of an international chain, this bright, open café serves high-quality coffee, cakes, snacks, and gelato. It also has some Kitsuné-branded goods on hand. **Known for:** quality coffee; Kitsuné-branded small gifts; lively and airy atmosphere. *$ Average main: ¥1,500 ✉ 3–15–9 Minami-Aoyama, Minato-ku ☎ 03/5786–4842 🌐 maisonkitsune.com ⏲ No dinner Ⓜ Ginza, Chiyoda, and Hanzomon subway lines, Omotesando Station (Exit A4).*

Hotels

As an entertainment and business district in a central location—close to both Aoyama and the sights near the Imperial Palace—Akasaka has accommodations that range from international luxury brands to pared-down capsule hotels.

ANA InterContinental Tokyo (インターコンチネンタルホテル東京; *ANA*)
$$$ | **HOTEL** | With a central location and stylish, bright, and relatively spacious guest rooms, this hotel is a reliable choice for business travelers and families alike. **Pros:** great concierge; wonderful city views; acclaimed French restaurant on-site. **Cons:** a bit of a corporate feel; bathrooms a bit small; few sightseeing options within walking distance. *$ Rooms from: ¥60,000 ✉ 1–12–33 Akasaka, Minato-ku ☎ 03/3505–1111 🌐 anaintercontinental-tokyo.jp/en ⇨ 844 rooms 🍽 No Meals Ⓜ Ginza and Namboku subway lines, Tameike-Sanno Station (Exit 13); Namboku subway line, Roppongi-itchome Station (Exit 3).*

★ **Andaz Tokyo Toranomon Hills** (アンダーズ東京)
$$$$ | **HOTEL** | Set in the revitalized Toranomon district, this Hyatt boutique property occupies the top six floors of one of the city's tallest towers and offers chic guest rooms, considerate service, an airy spa, and views, views, views. **Pros:** contemporary design with Japanese aesthetics; stylish rooftop bar; swimming pool overlooks the Imperial Palace. **Cons:** finding entrance can be hard; long corridors on guestroom floors; high fees to use the pool and gym. *$ Rooms from: ¥85,000 ✉ 1–23–4 Toranomon, Minato-ku ☎ 03/6830–1234 🌐 www.hyatt.com ⇨ 164 rooms 🍽 No Meals Ⓜ Ginza subway line, Toranomon Station (Exit 1).*

The Capitol Hotel Tokyu (ザ・キャピトルホテル東急)
$$$$ | **HOTEL** | Direct connection to the metro lines makes this a great place to stay, as do the tastefully decorated rooms and lobby designed by renowned architect Kengo Kuma. **Pros:** convenient location; beautiful, spacious, indoor pool; nice amenity-filled rooms. **Cons:** a bit expensive; government district might not appeal to tourists; the immediate area is very quiet on weekends. *$ Rooms from: ¥110,000 ✉ 2–10–3 Nagatacho, Minato-ku ☎ 03/3503–0109 🌐 www.tokyuhotels.co.jp ⇨ 251 rooms 🍽 No Meals Ⓜ Ginza and Namboku subway lines, Tameike-Sanno Station (Exit 5).*

A
B
C
D
E
F
1
2
3
4
5
6
7
8
9
0
500 ft
0
100 m
Yoyogi Park
Chiyoda Line
Inokashira-dori
Shonan Shinjuku Line
Meiji-dori
Fukutoshin Line
Harajuku Street
HARAJUKU
Meiji-jingumae 'Harajuku'
Omotesando
Fire Street
Cat Street
Koen-dori Pkwy
Park Street
Aoyama-dori
KEY
Sights
Restaurants
Quick Bites
Hotels
Aoyama and Harajuku

Sights

1 Meiji Jingu Museum C3
2 Meiji Jingu Shrine B1
3 Nezu Museum J9
4 Ota Memorial Museum of Art.... D5
5 Yoyogi Park......................... A5

Restaurants

1 Baird Beer Harajuku Taproom D4
2 Barbacoa Churrascaria Aoyama G6
3 Brown Rice Tokyo Omotesando........................ G7
4 Cicada.............................. H8
5 Darumaya G8
6 Heiroku Sushi Omotesando......................... F6
7 Maisen Aoyama G6
8 Red Pepper......................... H7
9 Sakuratei F4
10 Tempura Tensho J4

Quick Bites

1 Café Kitsuné Aoyama I8
2 The Roastery by Nozy Coffee D7

Hotels

1 ANA InterContinental Tokyo...... G3
2 Andaz Tokyo Toranomon Hills..... I3
3 The Capitol Hotel Tokyu........... G1
4 Hotel New Otani Tokyo............ G1
5 The Okura Tokyo H3

Hotel New Otani Tokyo (ホテルニューオータニ東京)
$$$$ | HOTEL | A central location in a bustling complex with restaurants and shopping arcades can make the New Otani feel frantic, but its spectacular, 10-acre Japanese garden can help you find peace. **Pros:** beautiful garden; first-rate concierge; spa and outdoor pool. **Cons:** complex layout could be off-putting; some areas a bit dated; few sightseeing options within walking distance. *$ Rooms from: ¥100,000 ✉ 4–1 Kioi-cho, Chiyoda-ku ☎ 03/3265–1111 🌐 www.newotani.co.jp 🛏 1,474 rooms 🍽 No Meals Ⓜ Ginza and Marunouchi subway lines, Akasaka-mitsuke Station (Exit 7).*

The Okura Tokyo (オークラ東京)
$$$$ | HOTEL | The rebuilt Okura combines modern, 21st-century luxury with the retro charm and stylish design of its predecessor, an iconic property that was constructed before the first Tokyo Olympics and featured a blend of traditional Japanese and modernist aesthetics. **Pros:** many dining options; retro-modern design and feel; large rooms. **Cons:** retro design not for everyone; not ideal for families; expensive. *$ Rooms from: ¥120,000 ✉ 2–10–4 Tora-no-mon, Minato-ku ☎ 03/3582–0111 🌐 theokura-tokyo.jp/en 🛏 508 rooms 🍽 No Meals Ⓜ Hibiya subway line, Kamiya-cho Station (Exit 4B); Ginza subway line, Tora-no-mon Station (Exit 3).*

Nightlife

BARS

Radio (バー・ラジオ)
COCKTAIL BARS | Creative, beautifully crafted cocktails served in gorgeous glasses perfectly accompany the wooden interior of this bar, which has been serving drinks since its superstar bartender, Koji Ozaki, opened the place in 1972. He might still turn up depending on the night. You can't miss the sign outside what looks like an inviting house, where the ambience is elegant (so dress to match it). *✉ 3–10–34 Minami-Aoyama, Shibuya-ku ☎ 03/3402–2668 🌐 www.bar-radio.com ⏲ Closed Sun. Ⓜ Chiyoda, Ginza, and Hanzomon subway lines, Omotesando Station (Exit A4).*

Two Rooms
COCKTAIL BARS | This establishment—serving everything from standard beers to fruity cocktails—is a little pricier than many other bar–eateries, but the service, atmosphere, terrace, and city views make up for it. The restaurant is also open for lunch on weekdays and brunch on weekends. *✉ AO Bldg., 3–11–7 Kita-Aoyama, 5th fl., Shibuya-ku ☎ 03/3498–0002 🌐 www.tworooms.jp Ⓜ Chiyoda, Ginza, and Hanzomon subway lines, Omotesando Station (Exit B2).*

JAZZ CLUBS

Blue Note Tokyo (ブルーノート東京)
LIVE MUSIC | This premier live-jazz venue isn't for everyone: prices are high, sets short, and patrons packed in, sometimes sharing a table with strangers. But if you check what is on and want to catch someone in a relatively small venue, this is the place. Expect to pay upward of ¥10,000 or more to see major acts. *✉ Raika Bldg., 6–3–16 Minami-Aoyama, Minato-ku ☎ 03/5485–0088 🌐 www.bluenote.co.jp Ⓜ Chiyoda, Ginza, and Hanzo-mon subway lines, Omotesando Station (Exit A5).*

Shopping

Here, you'll find boutiques with pricey clothes, accessories, and housewares created by many leading Japanese and other designers. There are also elegant and equally pricey antiques stores on Kotto-dori.

CERAMICS

Tatsuya Shoten (つたや商店)
CERAMICS | *Ikebana* (flower arrangement) and *sado* (tea ceremony) goods are the only items sold at this shop, but variety of items on offer is stunning. Colorful vases in surprising shapes and traditional

What to Drink in Tokyo

This rundown of Japan's various liquor offerings will give you an idea of what to expect during your night on the town. Regardless of your selection, remember to shout *kanpai!* (sounds like "kaan-pie") instead of *cheers!* when you raise your glass.

Sake

More than 2,000 brands of sake, called *nihonshu* in Japanese, are produced throughout the country. Sake comes in sweet (*amakuchi*) and dry (*karakuchi*) varieties, both of which are graded based on how much the rice has been polished down before brewing and whether additional brewer's alcohol has been blended in. *Junmai Daiginjo-shu* is the highest grade, with no extra alcohol added and a rice polishing rate over 50%, meaning only the purest, inner part of each grain is used.

Sake is often drunk at room temperature (*nurukan*) or slightly chilled so as not to alter the flavor. Although heat can ruin some top brews, sake is also served heated (*atsukan*) in winter. It's usually poured from *tokkuri* (small ceramic vessels) into tiny cups called *choko*. Despite the diminutive size of these cups, you can end up drinking too much, given the custom of ensuring that no one's cup never runs dry.

Apart from the *nomiya* (bars) and restaurants, the place to sample sake is the *izakaya*, a drinking establishment that usually serves food along with dozens of kinds of sake, including a selection of *jizake*, the kind created in limited quantities by small regional producers.

Heavenly Spirits

Shochu, which is made from a variety of base ingredients such as buckwheat, sweet potatoes, or rice, is associated with the southern island of Kyushu. It's served hot or cold—mixed with water or on the rocks. Sometimes, a wedge of lemon or a small pickled apricot, known as *umeboshi*, is added as well. Shochu can also be blended with club soda and juice, creating the popular cold drink called *chuhai*. At an izakaya, this drink is often called "a sour."

Havin' a Biiru

Beers made by Japan's heavyweight breweries, Asahi and Kirin, are everywhere, and the two companies are constantly battling for the coveted title of "Japan's No. 1 Brewery." Many beer fans, however, rate Suntory's Malts brand and Sapporo's Yebisu brand as the most flavorful. In addition, national brand Orion makes a light brew. In recent years, Belgian beers have become more popular and readily available, as have the offerings produced by Japanese microbreweries. In terms of domestic craft beer (*kurafuto bi-ru*) good choices include Shiga Kogen, Minoh, and Baird.

ceramic tea sets make unique souvenirs. ✉ *6–3–10 Minami-Aoyama, Minato-ku* ☎ *03/3400–3815* 🌐 *www.instagram.com/tsutayashouten* Ⓜ *Ginza, Chiyoda, and Hanzomon subway lines, Omotesando Station (Exit B1).*

CLOTHING

BAPExclusive Aoyama (青山; *Bapexclusive*)

CLOTHING | FAMILY | Since the late 1990s, no brand has been more coveted by young scenesters than the BATHING APE label (shortened to BAPE) founded

Mix with Tokyo's most glamorous residents at Prada's architecturally dazzling Aoyama store.

by DJ–fashion designer NIGO. At the height of the craze, hopefuls would line up outside NIGO's well-hidden boutiques and pay ¥7,000 for a T-shirt festooned with a simian visage or *Planet of the Apes* quote. BAPE has since gone aboveground, with the brand expanding across the globe. You can see what the fuss is all about in this spacious two-story shop or in other locations around the city. ✉ *5–5–8 Minami-Aoyama, Minato-ku* ☎ *03/6805–0691* 🌐 *en.jp.bape.com/* Ⓜ *Ginza and Hanzomon subway lines, Omotesando Station (Exit A5).*

★ **Comme des Garçons** (コムデギャルソン)
CLOTHING | Sinuous low walls snake through Comme des Garçons founder Rei Kawakubo's flagship store, a minimalist labyrinth that is one of Tokyo's funkiest retail spaces. Here you can shop for the designer's signature clothes, as well as shoes and accessories. ✉ *5–2–1 Minami-Aoyama, Minato-ku* ☎ *03/3406–3951* 🌐 *www.comme-des-garcons.com* Ⓜ *Ginza, Chiyoda, and Hanzomon subway lines, Omotesando Station (Exit A5).*

★ **Issey Miyake** (イッセイミヤケ)
CLOTHING | The otherworldly creations of internationally renowned brand Issey Miyake are on display at his Tokyo flagship store, which carries the full Paris line. Just a stone's throw away are other Miyake stores, among them Issey Miyake Men, Pleats Please, and Reality Lab. The latter showcases Miyake's most experimental creations including incredible origami-like clothing and Bao-Bao totes. ✉ *3–18–11 Minami-Aoyama, Minato-ku* ☎ *03/3423–1408* 🌐 *www.isseymiyake.com* Ⓜ *Ginza, Chiyoda, and Hanzomon subway lines, Omotesando Station (Exit A4).*

Maison Kitsuné
CLOTHING | **FAMILY** | The half-Japanese, half-French duo who make this brand are former DJs and music producers, which may explain why the funky clothes have such a cool edge to them. The Kitsuné Café, which is just up the street and around a corner, serves some great coffee and sells some Kitsuné-branded goods. ✉ *3–15–1 Minami-Aoyama,*

Minato-ku ☏ 03/5786-4841 ⊕ www.maisonkitsune.com Ⓜ Ginza, Chiyoda, and Hanzomon subway lines, Omotesando Station (Exit A4).

★ Prada

CLOTHING | This fashion landmark, designed by Herzog & de Meuron, is one of the city's most buzzed-about architectural wonders in the city. Its facade is a mosaic of green glass "bubble" windows with alternating convex and concave panels that create distorted reflections of the surrounding area. Many world-renowned, nearby boutiques have tried to replicate the significant impact the Prada building has had on the area, but none have been unable to match this tower. Don't miss the cavelike entrance that leads into the basement shoe floor. ✉ *5–2–6 Minami-Aoyama, Minato-ku* ☏ *03/6418–0400* ⊕ *www.prada.com* Ⓜ *Ginza, Chiyoda, and Hanzomon subway lines, Omotesando Station (Exit A5).*

Sou-Sou Kyoto (そうそう青山店)

CLOTHING | *Tabi* are the traditional cloth boots with a cleft-toe shape requiring special socks, which are sold here among other cloth goods and clothing. This Kyoto-based brand creates graphic, cute, and funky patterns that are so of this era that you'd never know they based on traditional things. Across the street is its sister shop, which sells Westernized items made with the same fabrics. ✉ *5–4–24 Minami-Aoyama, Minato-ku, Minato-ku* ☏ *03/3407–7877* ⊕ *www.sousou.co.jp* Ⓜ *Ginza, Hanzomon, and Chiyoda subway lines, Omotesando Station (Exit B1).*

Undercover Aoyama
(アンダーカバー青山店)

CLOTHING | Here, racks of Jun Takahashi's cult clothing sit under a ceiling adorned with thousands of hanging lightbulbs. ✉ *5–3–22 Minami-Aoyama, Minato-ku* ☏ *03/5778–4405* ⊕ *www.undercoverism.com* Ⓜ *Ginza, Chiyoda, and Hanzomon subway lines, Omotesando Station (Exit A5).*

CRAFTS

Japan Traditional Crafts Aoyama Square (伝統工芸 青山スクエア; *Dento Kogei Aoyama Sukuea*)

CRAFTS | You don't have to travel around the country to see a collection of the best artisan crafts from different regions. Tea kettles, bows, knives, scarves, fans—this shop almost feels like a museum where all the items are on sale. It also hosts events highlighting artisans or regions, so you might see pottery being made or get a chance to make something of your own. ✉ *8–1–22 Akasaka, Minato-ku* ☏ *03/5785–1301* ⊕ *kougeihin.jp* Ⓜ *Hanzomon, Ginza, and Oedo subway lines, Aoyama-Itchome Station (Exit 4).*

HOUSEWARES

Francfranc Aoyama (フランフラン青山)

HOUSEWARES | This popular chain sells very reasonably priced kitchen goods and housewares that are favored by young, trendy Tokyoites. Expect to see everything from utilitarian items like chopsticks to funky offerings like waffle irons shaped like cartoon characters. ✉ *3–1–3 Minami-Aoyama, Minato-ku, Minato-ku* ☏ *03/4216–4021* ⊕ *www.francfranc.com* Ⓜ *Ginza subway line, Gaienmae Station (Exit 1A).*

MALLS AND SHOPPING CENTERS

Glassarea Aoyama (グラッセリア青山)

SHOPPING CENTER | Virtually defining Aoyama elegance is this small cobblestone shopping center, which draws well-heeled young professionals to its handful of fashion boutiques and its specialty store selling Japanese crafts and foods from Fukui Prefecture on the Sea of Japan. ✉ *5–4–41 Minami-Aoyama, Minato-ku* ⊕ *www.glassarea.com* Ⓜ *Ginza, Chiyoda, and Hanzomon subway lines, Omotesando Station (Exit B1).*

Activities

IKEBANA COURSES

Sogetsu Ikebana School
(草月会館; *Sogetsu Kaikan*)
CRAFT CLASSES | The schools of *ikebana* (flower arranging), like those of other traditional arts, are highly stratified organizations. Students rise through levels of proficiency, paying handsomely for lessons and certifications as they go, until they can become teachers themselves. At the top of the hierarchy is the *iemoto,* the head of the school, a title often held within a family for generations. The Sogetsu school of flower arrangement is a relative newcomer to all this, being founded by Sofu Teshigahara in 1927, and, compared to the older schools, it embraces even radical styles. Regular classes are offered as are private demonstrations. Some of the shorter, 90-minute classes are geared to travelers and have an English-speaking assistant. Reservations must be made in advance. A rock garden in the Sogetsu Kaikan, created by the late Isamu Noguchi, one of the masters of modern sculpture, is worth a visit. Additionally, the school holds rotating ikebana exhibitions throughout the year and has a shop on the 4th floor. Sogetsu Kaikan is a 10-minute walk west on Aoyama-dori from the Akasaka-mitsuke intersection or east from the Aoyama-itchome subway stop. ✉ *7–2–21 Akasaka, Minato-ku* ☎ *03/3408–1154* 🌐 *www.sogetsu.or.jp* 🎫 *¥5,600 per person for 2-hour introductory lesson* ☞ *Reservations essential* Ⓜ *Ginza and Marunouchi subway lines, Akasaka-mitsuke Station; Ginza and Hanzomon subway lines, Aoyama-itchome Station (Exit 4).*

Harajuku

On weekends, young Tokyoites flock to Harajuku to shop for clothes and accessories along Takeshita-dori, where giggling teens show off their cute and often brightly colored outfits and stop for a bite in fast-food restaurants, ice-cream shops, and creperies. Trendy thirty- and forty-somethings come here for the hip backstreet boutiques and similarly hip eateries and cafés on and around Omotesando, the boulevard considered by many to be the Champs-Élysées of Tokyo.

The distinction between Harajuku and Omotesando—which is the name of the name of an area as well as a grand boulevard and a metro station—is hard to pin down. A *sando* is a path, typically lined with lanterns, that leads to a temple or shrine. In this case, Omotesando runs northwest from its namesake metro station and intersection, past Louis Vuitton and Dior, and to the entrance of Meiji Shrine, which is adjacent to Harajuku Station.

Sights

Meiji Jingu Museum
(明治神宮ミュージアム)
HISTORY MUSEUM | **FAMILY** | The newest feature in the Meiji Shrine complex is this museum designed by renowned architect Kengo Kuma. The museum's location inside the shrine's forest is part of the attraction, but those interested in the lives of the emperor and empress will really enjoy the artifacts on display. ✉ *1–1 Yoyogi Kamizono-cho, Shibuya-ku* ☎ *03/3379–5511* 🌐 *www.meijijingu.or.jp/en* 🎫 *¥1000* 🕒 *Closed Thurs.*

★ **Meiji Jingu Shrine** (明治神宮)
RELIGIOUS BUILDING | This shrine honors the spirits of Emperor Meiji, who died in 1912, and Empress Shoken. It was established by a resolution of the Imperial Diet the year after the emperor's death to commemorate his role in ending the long isolation of Japan under the Tokugawa Shogunate and setting the country on the road to modernization. Virtually destroyed in an air raid in 1945, it was rebuilt in 1958.

When you arrive at Meiji Shrine area, pay your respects by purifying your body and mind at the water basin area called the temizuya.

A wonderful spot for photos, the mammoth entrance gates (*torii*), rising 40 feet high, are made from 1,700-year-old cypress trees from Mt. Ari in Taiwan; the crosspieces are 56 feet long. Torii are meant to symbolize the separation of the everyday secular world from the spiritual world of the Shinto shrine. The buildings in the shrine complex, with their curving, green, copper roofs, are also made of cypress wood. The surrounding forest is home to thousands of flowering shrubs and trees donated from around Japan.

An annual festival at the shrine takes place on November 3, Emperor Meiji's birthday. On New Year's Day, as many as a million people come to offer prayers and pay their respects. Several other festivals and ceremonial events are held here throughout the year. Even on a normal weekend the shrine draws thousands of visitors, but this seldom disturbs its air of serenity.

The peaceful Meiji Jingu Gardens (Meiji Jingu Gyoen), where the irises are in full bloom in the latter half of June, is on the left as you walk in from the main gates, before you reach the shrine. Designed by Kengo Kuma, the architect behind Tokyo's new Olympic stadium, the Meiji Jingu Museum displays personal effects and clothes of Emperor and Empress Meiji. ✉ *1–1 Yoyogi-kamizonocho, Shibuya-ku* ☎ *03/3379–5511* 🌐 *www.meijijingu.or.jp* 🎫 *Shrine free, Meiji Jingu Garden ¥500, museum ¥1,000* Ⓜ *Chiyoda and Fukutoshin subway lines, Meiji-Jingumae Station; JR Yamanote Line, Harajuku Station (Exit 2).*

Ota Memorial Museum of Art (太田記念美術館; *Ota Kinen Bijutsukan*)
ART MUSEUM | The gift of former Toho Mutual Life Insurance chairman Seizo Ota, this is probably the city's best private collection of *ukiyo-e,* traditional Edo-period woodblock prints. Ukiyo-e (pictures of the floating world) flourished in the 18th and 19th centuries. The works on display are selected and changed periodically from the 12,000 prints in the collection, which includes some extremely rare work by artists

Tokyo's Commercial Architecture

With Tokyo's impressive array of high-end fashion and jewelry stores has come an equally astonishing collection of beautiful buildings. A 20-minute walk along Omotesando from Aoyama to Harajuku Station takes you past several standout structures. Start at the **Prada** flagship in Aoyama, just southeast of Omotesando Crossing. The Swiss-based Herzog & de Meuron team created this building of concave and protruding diamond-shape glass panels, which give it a honeycomblike effect. Across the street they reprised their hit with the **Miu Miu** flagship, made of aluminum and brass.

At Omotesando Crossing, look beyond the lanterns flanking the road, and you'll catch a glimpse of Kengo Kuma's **One Omotesando** with its wooden-slat facade. Heading toward Shibuya on Aoyama-dori, you'll see the **Ao Building** on the right. At night, the glass exterior becomes a curtain of blue, green, and purple lights, recalling the aurora borealis. Alternatively, proceed on Omotesando toward Harajuku, where you'll find the "squeezed" building that is **Hugo Boss** almost embraced by Toyo Ito's L-shaped Bottega Veneta Omotesando building that dramatically recreates tree shapes in concrete blending into the street.

Farther along is the white translucent box that is **Dior**, designed by Pritzker Architecture Prize recipients Kazuyo Sejima and Ryue Nishizawa of SANAA. Across the street, it's hard to miss the **Omotesando Hills** complex, more impressive from the inside with its six-floor atrium connected by a spiral ramp. One end of the building incorporates one of the much-loved structures it replaced—the last remaining example of Donjunkai architecture, one of Japan's early modern movements.

Make a left on Meiji-dori at Jingumae Crossing to see the **"Iceberg" Building**. The sharp geometry of the blue glass structure was inspired by ice, crystal, and plastic bottles. Across from the mirrored entrance to Tokyu Plaza Omotesando, on the northeast side of that same crossing, is the new **Tokyu Plaza Harajuku** decorated with greenery.

such as Hiroshige, Hokusai, Sharaku, and Utamaro. ✉ *1–10–10 Jingumae, Shibuya-ku* ☎ *03/3403–0880* 🌐 *www.ukiyoe-ota-muse.jp* 🎫 *From ¥1,000 (cash only)* ⏲ *Closed Mon.* Ⓜ *Chiyoda and Fukutoshin subway lines, Meiji-Jingumae Station (Exit 5); JR Yamanote Line, Harajuku Station (Omotesando Exit).*

Yoyogi Park (代々木公園; *Yoyogi Koen*)
CITY PARK | FAMILY | This park is the perfect spot for a picnic. On Sunday, people come to play music, practice martial arts, and ride bicycles (rentals are available) on the bike path. From spring through fall there are events, concerts, and festivals most weekends. Although the front half of the park makes for great people-watching, farther along the paths it is easy to find a quiet spot to slip away from the crowds. ✉ *2–1 Yoyogi-mizonocho, Shibuya-ku* ☎ *03/3469–6081* Ⓜ *Chiyoda and Fukutoshin subway lines, Meiji-Jingumae Station (Exit 2); JR Yamanote Line, Harajuku Station (Omotesando Exit).*

Restaurants

★ Baird Beer Harajuku Taproom (原宿タップルーム)
$$$ | **JAPANESE** | Founded by American Bryan Baird in 2000, Baird Brewing has become one of the leaders in Japan's booming craft-beer movement, with a range of creative seasonal beers as well as such year-round brews as the hop-heavy Suruga Bay IPA. The Taproom combines Baird's excellent lineup of microbrews with Japanese *izakaya* (pub) fare like *yakitori* (grilled chicken skewers). **Known for:** Japanese craft beer; hand-pumped ales on tap; blend of Western and Japanese pub fare. *$ Average main: ¥4,000 ✉ No Surrender Bldg., 1–20–13 Jingumae, 2nd fl., Shibuya-ku ☎ 050/5456–2648 🌐 bairdbeer.com/taprooms/harajuku ⏲ No lunch weekdays Ⓜ JR Yamanote Line, Harajuku Station.*

Barbacoa Churrascaria Aoyama (バルバッコア青山本店;)
$$$$ | **BRAZILIAN** | Carnivores flock here for the all-you-can-eat Brazilian grilled chicken and barbecued beef, which the efficient waiters will bring to your table until you tell them to stop, so be sure to pace yourself at the impressive, self-serve salad bar. With drinks (including, perhaps, Brazilian cocktails), dinner can easily run ¥10,000 per person, but the weekday lunch buffet offers largely the same selection at a fraction of the price. **Known for:** meat lover's paradise; range of wines; excellent salad buffet. *$ Average main: ¥8,000 ✉ REIT Omotesando Sq., 4–3–2 Jingumae, Shibuya-ku ☎ 03/3796–0571 🌐 www.barbacoa.jp/aoyama Ⓜ Ginza, Chiyoda, and Hanzomon subway lines, Omotesando Station (Exit A2).*

Brown Rice Tokyo Omotesando (ブラウンライス)
$$ | **VEGETARIAN** | Inside Neal's Yard Green Square, this laid-back café has all-natural wooden interiors and a menu of dishes that will make the health-conscious happy. While shopping along Omotesando, it's a great place to stop for a snack or a lunch that might include a Japanese *teishoku* set, vegetable curry, tofu lemon cake, or other vegan fare. **Known for:** relaxed atmosphere; Japanese-style vegan dishes; affordable lunch sets. *$ Average main: ¥2,000 ✉ 5–1–8 Jingumae, Shibuya-ku ☎ 03/5778–5416 🌐 brownrice.jp/en Ⓜ Ginza and Hanzomon subway lines, Omotesando Station (Exit A1).*

Heiroku Sushi Omotesando (平禄寿司 表参道店)
$$ | **SUSHI** | **FAMILY** | Sushi restaurants can be expensive, but a rock-bottom alternative is an assembly line–style *kaiten-zushi,* where chefs inside a circular counter put sushi on plates color-coded for price onto a revolving belt, you choose what you'd like as it passes, and a staffer counts up the plates and calculates the bill when you're done. It's all about the fresh fish—and clearly not about the interior design—at this bustling branch of a kaiten-zushi chain opposite Omotesando Hills. **Known for:** fresh, cheap sushi; quintessential Japan experience; wide selection of classic and original sushi. *$ Average main: ¥2,500 ✉ 5–8–5 Jingumae, Shibuya-ku ☎ 03/3498–3968 🌐 www.heiroku.jp Ⓜ Ginza, Chiyoda, and Hanzomon subway lines, Omotesando Station (Exit A1).*

Red Pepper (レッドペッパー)
$$$$ | **FRENCH** | After a short walk down a narrow alley from Omotesando Crossing, diners squeeze into this cozy bistro, perch on tiny antique school chairs, and order from the daily recommendations (mostly in Japanese) chalked onto blackboards—ignoring the ever-changing printed menu. Specials lean toward French-accented comfort food. **Known for:** cozy atmosphere; seasonal specials; a constantly changing menu. *$ Average main: ¥6,000 ✉ 1F Shimizu Bldg., 3–5–25 Kita-Aoyama, Shibuya-ku ☎ 03/3478–1264 🌐 take-5.co.jp/brand/redpepper Ⓜ Ginza, Chiyoda, and Hanzomon subway lines, Omotesando Station (Exit A3).*

Elements of Japanese Cuisine

It starts with soup, often followed by raw fish, and then by what might be consider the main dish (grilled, steamed, simmered, or fried fish, chicken, or vegetables). It ends with rice and pickles and, perhaps a dessert of fresh fruit and a cup of green tea. It's as simple as that—almost. There are, admittedly, a few twists to the story, including some regional variations. There are also a few basic rules that add complexity to the creation of a "simple" traditional Japanese meal.

Freshness is first. There's little tolerance for poor food quality, and much of a Japanese chef's reputation relies on the ability to obtain the finest ingredients at the peak of season: fish brought in from the sea this morning (not yesterday) and vegetables from the earth (not the hothouse)—including more exotic options such as *take-no-ko* (bamboo shoots), *renkon* (lotus root), or the treasured *matsutake* mushrooms (which grow wild in jealously guarded forest hideaways and sometimes sell for obscene prices).

Simplicity is next. The Japanese chef eschews heavy spices and rich sauces, preferring to enhance or accent, rather than conceal, flavors. Without a heavy sauce, fish, for instance, is permitted a degree of natural fishiness, and a garnish of fresh red ginger might be provided to offset the flavor rather than to disguise it.

The third prerequisite is beauty. Simple, natural foods must appeal to the eye as well as to the palate. You might see green peppers on a vermilion dish, an egg custard in a blue bowl, round eggplant in a rectangular dish. The importance of seasonality in Japanese cooking comes into play with Japanese presentation as well. Maple leaves and pine needles might accent an autumn dish. In summer, a pair of freshwater *ayu* fish might be grilled with a purposeful twist to their tails to make them "swim" across a crystal platter and thereby suggest the coolness of a mountain stream on a hot August night.

Of course, then there is mood, which can make or break the entire meal. Japanese connoisseurs, for example, go to great lengths to find the perfect yakitori stand—a smoky, lively place offering a night of grilled chicken, cold beer, and camaraderie. In fancier places, mood becomes a seeming competition to impress diners perhaps by serving something in a creative way or providing a background of soothing water sounds.

Sakuratei (さくら亭)

$$ | JAPANESE | FAMILY | At this restaurant specializing *okonomiyaki* (a savory pancake made with egg, meat, and vegetables), you choose the ingredients and cook them on the *teppan* (grill) yourself. Flipping the pancake can be challenging—potentially messy but still fun—and, fortunately, you're not expected to wash the dishes. **Known for:** cooking at your table; artsy, DIY interior; vegetarian, vegan, and gluten-free options. *Ⓢ Average main: ¥2,500 ✉ 3–20–1 Jingumae, Shibuya-ku ☎ 03/3479–0039 🌐 www.sakuratei.co.jp Ⓜ Chiyoda subway line, Meiji-Jingumae (Harajuku) Station (Exit 5).*

Takeshita-dori is a crowded pedestrian street lined with boutiques and cafes.

Coffee and Quick Bites

The Roastery by Nozy Coffee
(ザ・ロースタリー)
$ | **CAFÉ** | The Roastery serves up some good single-origin coffee. Tucked away along Cat Street, a shopping street connecting Omotesando to Shibuya, it offers outdoor seating, giving you a place to watch the shoppers stream by. **Known for:** single-origin coffee; relaxed atmosphere; clean restrooms that smell like roasting coffee. *$ Average main: ¥1,000 ✉ Jingumae 5–17–13, Shibuya-ku ☎ 03/6450–5755 🌐 www.tysons.jp/roastery/en Ⓜ Chiyoda subway line, Meiji-Jingumae (Harajuku) Station (Exit 7).*

Shopping

The average shopper in Harajuku is on the younger side, so many stores focus on moderately priced, sometimes kitschy, clothing and accessories. Shops that target the youngest consumers are concentrated on the narrow street called Takeshita-dori. As you head southeast along Omotesando from Harajuku Station and toward Aoyama, the merchandise gets pricier. Be sure to explore some of the area's back streets, where you might find shops with items created by local, up-and-coming designers.

CLOTHING

★ **Beams Harajuku** (ベームス原宿)
CLOTHING | **FAMILY** | Shopping at Beams ensures that you or your kids will be properly stocked with the city's coolest wares. Indeed, there's such a variety of merchandise—ranging from street wear to high-end imports—that it won't fit into just one store. In Harajuku, you'll find a cluster of shops, including Beams T for T-shirts, Beams Plus for casual wear, a record store, a funky "from Tokyo" souvenir shop that sells anime figurines, and more. *✉ 3–24–7 Jingumae, Shibuya-ku ☎ 03/3470–3947 🌐 www.beams.co.jp Ⓜ JR Harajuku Station (Takeshita-Dori Exit); Chiyoda and Fukutoshin subway lines, Meiji-Jingumae Station (Exit 5).*

Graniph Harajuku (グラニフ原宿)
CLOTHING | FAMILY | Cool and quirky tops and T-shirts are the main focus of this store, but you can find other items (umbrellas, mugs, hats, bags, socks) in the frequently changing lineup of designs that feature anything from cartoon characters and abstract graphic images to odd quotes. There's also a café upstairs. ✉ *4–25–13 Jingumae, Shibuya-ku* ✣ *Just behind Ralph Lauren* 🌐 *www.graniph.com* Ⓜ *Chiyoda and Fukutoshin subway lines, Meiji-Jingumae Station (Exit 5).*

6%DokiDoki (ロクパーセントドキドキ; *Roku pasento dokidoki*)
CLOTHING | FAMILY | *Kawaii* (cute) Harajuku fashion lives on at this pastel, doll-house-like shop on the second floor of a nondescript building. Browsing the colorful items and glittery accessories—part of a style called "kawaii anarchy"—might be one of Tokyo's most unique shopping experiences. Even the shop clerks dress the part. ✉ *4–28–16 Jingumae, Shibuya-ku* ☎ *03/3479–6116* 🌐 *6dokidoki.com* Ⓜ *Chiyoda and Fukutoshin subway lines, Meiji-Jingumae Station (Exit 5).*

CRAFTS

★ **Ginza Natsuno** (銀座夏野)
CRAFTS | FAMILY | This two-story boutique sells an incredible range of chopsticks, from those with traditional to pop motifs to wooden or crystal-encrusted sticks that can be personalized. The kid-focused second floor is a must-see no matter your age. ✉ *4–2–17 Jingumae, Shibuya-ku* ☎ *03/3403–6033* 🌐 *www.e-ohashi.com* Ⓜ *Ginza, Chiyoda, and Hanzomon subway lines, Omotesando Station (Exit A2).*

★ **Musubi** (むす美)
CRAFTS | You might not expect to find classic crafts in the vicinity of trendy Harajuku, but this charming boutique specializes in traditional *furoshiki* cloths—beautifully decorated squares used to wrap anything and everything. You'll find up to 500 options here made from a variety of fabrics and featuring traditional, seasonal, and modern designs. The store also offers workshops on the various ways to use the cloths. ✉ *2–31–8 Jingumae, Shibuya-ku* ☎ *03/5414–5678* 🌐 *www.musubi-furoshiki.com* Ⓜ *Tokyo Metro Meiji-jingumae (Harajuku) Station.*

Oriental Bazaar (オリエンタルバザー)
CRAFTS | Established in 1916 and very successful serving members of the post-war occupation forces, this shop is the perfect place to find reasonably priced, traditional handicrafts—painted screens, pottery, chopsticks, dolls—that make great souvenirs. Like many area businesses of late, this shop has moved off of the main drag of Omotesando and onto a back street between Dior and Chanel. ✉ *5–9–8 Jingumae, Shibuya-ku, Shibuya-ku* ☎ *03/3400–3933* 🌐 *www.orientalbazaar.co.jp* Ⓜ *Chiyoda and Fukutoshin subway lines, Meiji-Jingumae Station (Exit 4).*

MALLS AND SHOPPING CENTERS

Gyre (ジャイル)
MALL | At the corner of Omotesando and Cat Street leading to Shibuya, this mall houses luxury-brand shops such as Chanel and Maison Martin Margiela, a food floor, concept shops by Comme des Garçons, and one of only three Museum of Modern Art Design Stores outside New York City. ✉ *5–10–1 Jingumae, Shibuya-ku* ☎ *0570/056–990* 🌐 *gyre-omotesando.com* Ⓜ *Chiyoda and Fukutoshin subway lines, Meiji-Jingumae Station (Exit 4).*

Laforet (ラフォーレ)
MALL | FAMILY | Teen trends are born in this mall's stores, where merchandise genres range from Gothic Lolita to bohemian chic. It's even rumored that designers frequent this place to see where fashion is headed. ✉ *1–11–6 Jingumae, Shibuya-ku* ☎ *03/3475–0411* 🌐 *www.laforet.ne.jp* Ⓜ *Chiyoda and Fukutoshin subway lines, Meiji-Jingumae Station (Exit 5).*

Continued on page 184

Shoppers mill around the entrance to Tokyo's Louis Vuitton

SHOP TOKYO

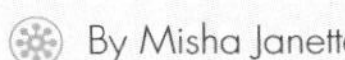
By Misha Janette

Tokyo, the most retail-dense city in the world, lures even very reluctant shoppers with promises of every product imaginable. Travel back in time at department and specialty stores selling traditional ceramics and lacquerware, or leap into the future in Akihabara and other gadget-oriented neighborhoods. Fashionistas watch trends in Harajuku morph before their eyes, while those with more highbrow sensibilities browse the jewelry at stalwarts like Mikimoto.

Each Tokyo neighborhood has its own specialty, style, mood, and type of customer. Local production still thrives in the city's backstreets despite an influx of global chains and mega-corporations. Keep in mind, however, that nearly all of the locally produced goods will cost a pretty penny; the Japanese are meticulous in design and quality, and tend to prefer small-scale production to large output. Here in Tokyo you will find that one-offs and limited-edition items are often the norm rather than the exception.

For clothing, sizing is still the biggest roadblock to really getting the most from Tokyo boutiques. But with the abundance of quirky trends, sometimes it's enough just to window-shop.

WHAT TO BUY

MANGA

Manga, or Japanese comic books, have had an incredible influence on pop culture around the world. The inherently Japanese-style illustrations are fun to look at, and the simple language is great for studying. Book-Off, a well-known used manga chain, sells comics at rock-bottom prices, sometimes ¥100 each.

INNERWEAR

The Japanese are known for their electronics, but did you know their textile and fiber industry is also one of the most advanced in the world? The sweat-repelling, heat-conducting, UBAV/UVB-blocking and aloe-vera dispensing underthings available at Tokyo department stores are probably already in every Japanese person's top drawer at home.

FLAVORED SNACKS

Japan is the land of limited-edition products, and every season brings new, adventurous flavors in finite quantities. All it takes is a trip to the local convenience store to find melon- or Sakura-flavored Kit-Kat bars, or sweet Mont Blanc-flavored Pepsi. We dare you to try them.

PHONE ACCESSORIES

Cell phones and their accoutrements have become a fashion statement all their own. Phone straps, small plastic models that hang from one's phone, are the most popular. They come in all forms, from Asahi beer bottles to Hello Kitty dolls. There are also matching plastic "no peek" sheets that prevent others from spying on your phone's screen.

HOUSEWARES

Tokyoites appreciate fine design, and this passion is reflected in the exuberance of the city's *zakka* shops—retailers that sell small housewares. The Daikanyama and Aoyama areas positively brim with these stores, but trendy zakka can be found throughout the city. Handmade combs, chopsticks, and towels are other uniquely Japanese treasures to consider picking up while in Tokyo.

RECORDS

Tokyo's small specialty music stores are a real treat: local music and imports from around the world are usually available on both vinyl and CD. Out-of-print or obscure vinyl editions can run well over ¥10,000, but collectors will find the condition of the jackets to be unmatched.

SOCKS

As it's customary in Japanese houses to remove one's shoes, socks are more than mere padding between foot and shoe. It's no surprise, then, that the selection of socks goes well beyond black and white. Stripes, polka-dots, Japanese scenery, and monograms are just some of the depictions you'll find at the high-end sock boutiques. The complicated weaving techniques mean they will also cost more than the average cotton pair.

SAKE SETS

Sake is a big deal here, and the type of sake presented to another can make or break business deals and friendships. Better than just a bottle are the gift sets that include the short sake glasses and oversized bottles in beautiful packaging fit for royalty.

JEWELRY

Japan has always been known for its craftsmen who possess the ability to create finely detailed work. Jewelry is no exception, especially when cultured pearls are used. Pearls, which have become something of a national symbol, are not inexpensive, but they are much cheaper in Japan than elsewhere.

WASHLETTE TOILET SEATS

It may seem ludicrous, but the Japanese "washlette" toilet seat is perhaps the best innovation of this millennium. The seats are heated, come with deodorizers, and may even play music to mask any "rude" sounds. Even better, some can be retrofitted to old toilets—just be sure to check your seat measurements before leaving home.

CHARCOAL

Japanese women have been using charcoal, or *takesumi*, in their beauty routines for centuries, believing it cleans out the pores and moisturizes the skin. Charcoal-infused formulas are used in soaps, cleansers, cremes, and masques, and often are naturally colored pitch-black like squid ink.

FOLK CRAFTS

Japanese folk crafts, called *mingei*—among them bamboo vases and baskets, fabrics, paper boxes, dolls, and toys—achieve a unique beauty in their simple and sturdy designs. Be aware, however, that simple does not mean cheap. Long hours of labor go into these objects, and every year there are fewer craftspeople left, producing their work in smaller and smaller quantities. Include these items in your budget ahead of time: The best—worth every cent—can be fairly expensive.

EXPERIENCING JAPANESE DEPATO

Japanese *depato* (department stores) offer eye candy inside and out.

A visit to a Japanese *depato* (department store) is the perfect Cliffs Notes introduction to Japanese culture. Impeccable service combines with the best luxury brands, gourmet food, and traditional goods—all displayed as enticing eye candy.

These large complexes are found around major train stations and are often owned by the conglomerate rail companies who make their profit when visitors take the train to shop there. The stores themselves commonly have travel agencies, theaters, and art galleries on the premises, as well as reasonably priced and strategically placed restaurants and cafés.

ARRIVE EARLY

The best way to get the full experience is to arrive just as the store is opening. Err on the early side: Tokyo's department stores are exacting in their opening times. White-gloved ladies and gents bow to waiting customers when the doors open on the hour. Early birds snatch up limited-edition food and goods before they sell out. There's never a dearth of reasons to come: local celebrity appearances, designer Q&A sessions, and fairs.

ANATOMY OF A DEPATO

The first floors typically house cosmetics, handbags, and shoes, with the next few floors up going to luxury import brands. On many a top floor you'll find gift packages containing Japan's best-loved brands of sake, rice crackers, and other foods. Department stores also typically devote one floor to traditional Japanese crafts, including ceramics, paintings, and lacquerware.

Don't miss the *depachika* (food departments) on the basement levels, where an overwhelming selection of expensive Japanese and Western delicacies are wrapped with the utmost care. More affordable versions come packed deli-style to be taken home for lunch or dinner.

Shibuya's depato attract trendsetters.

BEST DEPATO FOR...

Most department stores are similar and house the same brands. But some have distinctive characteristics.

The trendy dresser: Seibu in Shibuya and Ikebukuro is known for its collection of fashion-forward tenants.

Emerging designers: Isetan in Shinjuku oozes style and has ample space on the fourth floor dedicated to up-and-coming designers.

Gifts: Shinjuku's Takashimaya is the place to buy souvenirs for discerning friends back home.

Traditional crafts: Mitsukoshi in Nihonbashi will leave those looking for a bit of Old Japan wide-eyed.

Depato interiors are often dramatic.

TIPS FOR DEPATO SHOPPING

- Major department stores accept credit cards and provide shipping services.
- It's important to remember that, unlike most of the Western world, goods must be purchased in the department where they were found. This goes for nearly every multi-level shop in Japan.
- Nowadays, most salesclerks speak some English. If you're having communication difficulties, someone will always come to the rescue.
- On the first floor you'll invariably find a general information booth with maps of the store in English.
- Some department stores close one or two days a month. To be on the safe side, call ahead.

FASHIONABLE TOKYO

The Japanese fashion scene has gone through many changes since Yohji Yamamoto's solemn, deconstructed garments and Rei Kawakubo's Comme des Garçons clothing lines challenged norms in the 1980s. While these designers and their ilk are still revered, it's Tokyo's street fashion that keeps the city on the world's radar.

Top left: modern street fashion; Top right: classic Lolita fashion; Bottom: Fashions on Takeshita Street

Harajuku fashion is a mix of cute, sweet, pop, punk, goth, and anime.

Thanks to Gwen Stefani's "Harajuku Girls" and Quentin Tarantino's *Kill Bill*, images of the Gothic Lolita—a fashion subculture typified by a Victorian porcelain-doll look punctuated by dark makeup and macabre accessories—have seeped into Western popular culture. New subcultures, or "tribes," like the Harajuku Girls emerge, take hold in Tokyo, and evolve (or get thrown aside) with blazing speed. The "forest girl" tribe's aesthetic draws from sources such as the American prairie and traditional German attire in loose layers, often in organic and vintage materials. The "skirt boys" are among the mens' tribes. These cool boys stomp around in boots and skirts that Japanese menswear designers have been favoring on the runway in recent years.

Japanese fashion continues to awe and inspire; international designers come to Tokyo for ideas. This means you might already be wearing something from Tokyo without even knowing it!

SIZING UP JAPANESE SIZES

Japanese garments, even if they are not a troublesome and common "one-size-fits-all," run considerably smaller than American items. The female aesthetic tends to favor loose and roomy shapes and is far more forgiving than the menswear, which is often cut impossibly small and tight.

Shibuya brands often carry items in nothing more than an arbitrary "one-size-only" on the racks that may not fit many Westerners at all. Many designers, in deference to the growing foreign market, are starting to offer larger sizes. The internationally recognized brands, department stores, and bigger boutiques, including Opening Ceremony in Shibuya, are the best bets for finding a range of sizes.

Shoes tend to run small, often stopping at 27 cm (U.S. size 9) for men and 24 cm (U.S. size 8) for women. What's more, Japanese shoes are often made a little wider than their Western counterparts.

Omotesando Hills (表参道ヒルズ)
MALL | Despised and adored with equal zeal, another of Tadao Ando's adventures in concrete is this controversial project, which replaced the charming Dojunkai Aoyama Apartments and its selection of small shops and galleries. The mall's six, wedge-shape floors have a mix of brand-name heavy hitters and smaller stores with mid- to high-end shoes, bags, and other fashions. After checking out the latest in Japanese outure, you can take a break in one of the on-site restaurants or cafés. ✉ *4–12–10 Jingumae, Shibuya-ku* ☎ *03/3497–0310* 🌐 *www.omotesandohills.com* Ⓜ *Hanzomon, Ginza, and Chiyoda subway lines, Omotesando Station (Exit A2), Chiyoda and Fukutoshin subway lines, Meiji-Jingumae Station (Exit 4).*

Tokyu Plaza Harajuku
(東急プラザ原宿 *Harakado*)
MALL | The newest addition to an already architecturally impressive intersection, greenery-covered Tokyu Plaza stands across from its sister building, Tokyu Plaza Omotesando. The two complexes, which are redefining what it means to shop in this area, even have nicknames, both incorporating the Japanese word *kado* (corner). This one is called "Harakado," and its more-established counterpart to the northeast is "Omokado," as it's on Omotesando. ✉ *6–31–21 Jingumae, Shibuya-ku* ☎ *03/6427–9634* 🌐 *harakado.tokyu-plaza.com/en/* Ⓜ *Chiyoda subway line, Meiji-Jingumae (Harajuku) Station (Exit 4 or 7).*

Tokyu Plaza Omotesando
(東急プラザ表参道 *Omokado*)
MALL | Right at the intersection of Omotesando and Meiji-dori (don't miss the lanterns leading you to Meiji Shrine) and across from its newer sister complex, Tokyu Plaza Harajuku (aka Harakado), Tokyu Plaza Omotesando (aka Omokado) was designed by award-winning Hiroshi Nakamura's NAP architectural firm. It contains numerous shops and eateries, but its biggest draw might be the shady roof garden, which has great views. ✉ *4–30–3 Jingumae, Shibuya-ku* ☎ *03/3497–0418* 🌐 *omokado.tokyu-plaza.com* Ⓜ *Chiyoda subway line, Meiji-Jingumae (Harajuku) Station (Exit 5).*

TOYS

★ **Kiddy Land** (キデイランド)
TOYS | **FAMILY** | Considered by many to be Tokyo's best toy store, this Omotesando landmark carries the cutest and kitschiest of items, including some character-themed wares that are being test-marketed. The store can become quite crowded and the atmosphere chaotic, but that's part of the experience of shopping for toys that are unique, new, or both. ✉ *6–1–9 Jingumae, Shibuya-ku* ☎ *03/3409–3431* 🌐 *www.kiddyland.co.jp/harajuku* Ⓜ *JR Yamanote Line, Harajuku Station (Omotesando Exit); Chiyoda and Fukutoshin subway lines, Meiji-Jingumae Station (Exit 4).*

Shibuya

Shibuya is a shopper's paradise that's constantly changing, so there's always something new. It's also a popular entertainment district loaded with restaurants, karaoke lounges, bars, and nightclubs.

Although the neighborhood once had a reputation for attracting a younger crowd, its offerings have recently become more varied. In addition, calmer shopping and higher-end dining can be found toward Shibuya's southern neighbor, Ebisu.

Sights

Myth of Tomorrow
(明日の神話; *Asu no Shinwa*)
PUBLIC ART | This once-lost mural by avant-garde artist Taro Okamoto has been restored and mounted inside Shibuya Station. With 14 colorful panels depicting the moment of an atomic bomb detonation, the painting is often compared to

The statue of Hachiko, Japan's most loyal canine, stands immediately outside Shibuya Station, where he waited for his deceased master every day for seven years.

Picasso's *Guernica*. It was discovered in 2003 in Mexico City, where, in the late 1960s, it was to be displayed in a hotel but was misplaced following the bankruptcy of the developer. Walk up to the Inokashira Line entrance; the mural is mounted along the hallway that overlooks the Hachiko statue and that famous Shibuya Scramble Crossing. ✉ *Shibuya Mark City, Dogenzaka 1–12–12, Shibuya-ku* ✥ *Follow signs to Mark City* Ⓜ *JR Shibuya Station.*

Shibuya Sky

VIEWPOINT | Located atop a giant shopping and entertainment complex is Shibuya's, and, perhaps, Tokyo's, most celebrated viewpoint—one you'll want to make reservations to visit. There's also the option of mixing the whole experience with a glass of Champagne. ✉ *Shibuya 2–24–12, Shibuya-ku* 🌐 *www.shibuya-scramble-square.com/sky* 🎫 *¥2,200.*

Statue of Hachiko (ハチ公像)

PUBLIC ART | This Shibuya landmark and popular meeting place features Hachiko, a dog that has been portrayed in a few heart-wrenching films. As the story goes, every morning, Hachiko would accompany his master, a professor at Tokyo University, as far as Shibuya Station and then return to the station every evening to greet him. In 1925, the professor died of a stroke. Every evening for the next seven years, Hachiko went to the station and waited there until the last train had pulled out. The story of his loyalty spread, and Hachiko's fame grew. During the dog's lifetime, a handsome bronze statute of him was installed in front of the station at the exit that now bears his name. The present version is a replica—the original was melted down for its metal in World War II. ✉ *2–1 Dogenzaka, Shibuya-ku* Ⓜ *JR Shibuya Station (Hachiko Exit).*

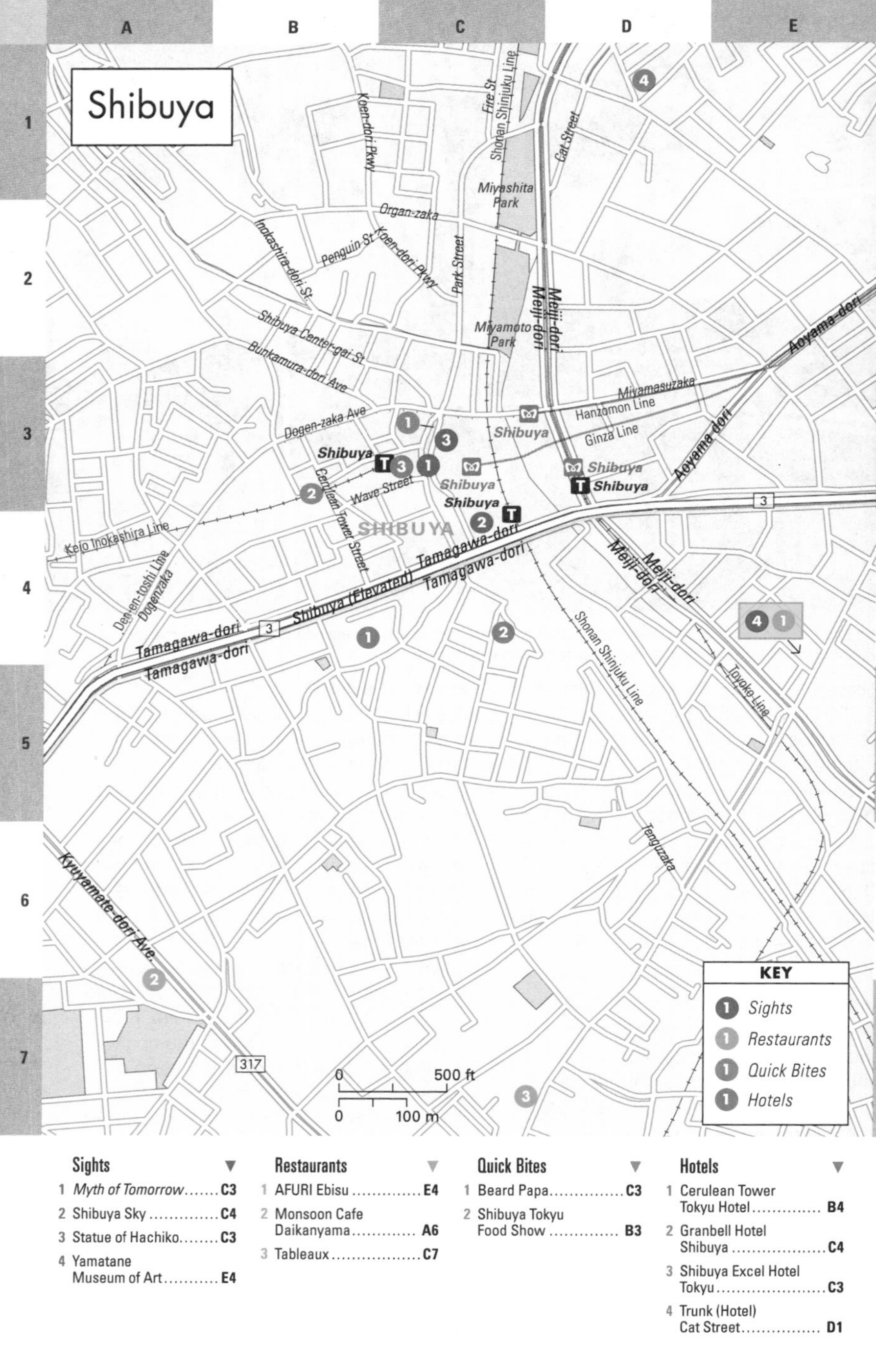

Sights	**Restaurants**	**Quick Bites**	**Hotels**
1 *Myth of Tomorrow*....... **C3**	1 AFURI Ebisu **E4**	1 Beard Papa............... **C3**	1 Cerulean Tower Tokyu Hotel.............. **B4**
2 Shibuya Sky **C4**	2 Monsoon Cafe Daikanyama............. **A6**	2 Shibuya Tokyu Food Show **B3**	2 Granbell Hotel Shibuya **C4**
3 Statue of Hachiko........ **C3**	3 Tableaux **C7**		3 Shibuya Excel Hotel Tokyu...................... **C3**
4 Yamatane Museum of Art........... **E4**			4 Trunk (Hotel) Cat Street................ **D1**

Yamatane Museum of Art
(山種美術館; *Yamatane Bijutsukan*)
ART MUSEUM | This museum, which specializes in *Nihonga* (a modernized form of traditional Japanese painting) from the Meiji Period, also has a collection of *ukiyoe* (woodblock prints) and oil paintings. Exhibits change seven or eight times a year and sometimes include works borrowed from other collections. You can take a break at Café Tsubaki, which offers tea and *wagashi* (a type of local sweets) as well as cake sets. *Hiroo 3–12–36, Shibuya-ku* *047/316–2772* *www.yamatane-museum.jp/english* *¥1,100 (special exhibit prices vary)* *Closed Mon.* *Hibiya subway line, Ebisu Station (Exit 2); JR Yamanote Line, Ebisu Station (West Exit).*

AFURI Ebisu (阿夫利らーめん恵比寿; *AFURI* 恵比寿)
$ | **RAMEN** | **FAMILY** | Ramen is the quintessential Japanese fast food—thick noodles in a bowl of savory broth topped with sliced grilled *chashu* (pork loin)—and each neighborhood in Tokyo has its go-to ramen restaurant. In Ebisu, near Shibuya, the hands-down favorite is this branch of Afuri, where you choose and pay for your ramen at a machine, find a seat, and hand over your payment ticket to the cooks, who prepare your ramen then and there. **Known for:** quick, affordable meals; refreshing shio ramen with yuzu; vegan ramen. *Average main: ¥1,200* *117 Bldg., 1–1–7 Ebisu, 1st fl., Shibuya-ku* *03/5795–0750* *afuri.com* *JR Yamanote Line (Nishi-guchi/West Exit) and Hibiya subway line (Exit 1), Ebisu Station.*

Monsoon Cafe Daikanyama
(モンスーンカフェ代官山)
$$$ | **ASIAN** | At the original branch of Monsoon Cafe, which has a dozen locations (including in Shinjuku and Omotesando), the pan-Asian menu is complemented by rattan furniture, brass Thai tableware, colorful papier-mâché parrots, Balinese carvings, and ceiling fans. The best seats in the house are on the balcony that runs around the four sides of an atrium-style space. **Known for:** spicy Southeast Asian dishes; stylish interior; lively atmosphere. *Average main: ¥5,000* *Hachiyama-cho 15–4, Shibuya-ku* *050/5444–9110* *monsoon-cafe.jp/daikanyama/* *Tokyu Toyoko private rail line, Daikanyama Station (Kita-guchi/North Exit).*

Tableaux (タブローズ)
$$$$ | **ECLECTIC** | Although some might find the glitzy decor at this restaurant to be over the top, the service is cordial and professional; the food, which is centered on Tokyo's version of international cuisine, is superb; and the wine list has more than 200 bottles, ranging from affordable house wines to real rarities. There might be a DJ during your dinner, and if you feel like some live music and a drink after, check out the Tableaux Lounge in the same building. **Known for:** decor that feels like stepping into a French picture book; classic high-end European fare; impressive wine list. *Average main: ¥8,000* *Sunroser Daikanyama Bldg., 11–6 Sarugakucho, B1, Shibuya-ku* *050/544–5125* *www.tableaux.jp* *No lunch* *Tokyu Toyoko private rail line, Daikanyama Station (Kita-guchi/North Exit).*

Coffee and Quick Bites

Beard Papa (ビアードパパ)
$ | **BAKERY** | **FAMILY** | Many long lines outside Shibuya's eateries are more about trendiness than quality, but Beard Papa makes a wide variety of genuinely good cream puffs. Pick up a single or a six-pack of freshly made pastries. **Known for:** cream puffs in seasonal flavors; buttery smells; fresh pastries. *Average main: ¥800* *2–2–1 Dogenzaka, Shibuya-ku* *03/6427–8817* *www.beardpapa.jp* *JR Shibuya Station (connected to the underground passageways).*

Shibuya Tokyu Food Show (渋谷東急フードショー)
$$ | **JAPANESE** | **FAMILY** | Inside Shibuya's underground Shibuchika shopping area is this huge array of stalls selling all kinds of foods. In addition to enjoying a snack or buying a bento to enjoy on a picnic, you can shop for gifts galore. **Known for:** variety of quick bites; reasonable prices; great people-watching. *Average main: ¥1,000 ✉ 2–2–1 Dogenzaka, Basement level, Shibuya-ku 🌐 www.tokyu-dept.co.jp/shibuya_foodshow Ⓜ Shibuya Station, Hachiko Exit.*

Hotels

Cerulean Tower Tokyu Hotel (セルリアンタワー東急ホテル)
$$$$ | **HOTEL** | Occupying the 19th to 37th floors of a tower that is, itself, on a slope above Shibuya's chaos, this hotel has an expansive, welcoming lobby, as well as spacious, tastefully designed rooms with neutral color schemes and fantastic views of Tokyo Tower or Mt. Fuji (when weather cooperates). **Pros:** attentive service; great city views; convenient location. **Cons:** pricey rates; not great for families with young kids; in a crowded area. *Rooms from: ¥60,000 ✉ 26–1 Sakuragaokacho, Shibuya-ku ☎ 03/3476–3000 🌐 www.tokyuhotels.co.jp 411 rooms No Meals Ⓜ JR Shibuya Station (South Exit).*

Granbell Hotel Shibuya (渋谷グランベルホテル)
$$ | **HOTEL** | At this understated hotel not far from the West Exit of Shibuya Station, guest rooms are done in neutral tones and have interesting decor features and/or pops of bright color. **Pros:** great location; funky design; 2nd floor steakhouse gets great reviews. **Cons:** small rooms; neighborhood can be noisy; difficult to find hotel entrance. *Rooms from: ¥28,000 ✉ 15–17 Sakuragaokacho, Shibuya-ku ☎ 03/5457–2681 🌐 www.granbellhotel.jp 105 rooms No Meals Ⓜ JR Shibuya Station (West Exit).*

Shibuya Excel Hotel Tokyu (渋谷エクセルホテル東急)
$$ | **HOTEL** | Location is key to this otherwise unremarkable hotel in the towering Mark City complex—not only does the Narita Express depart from nearby Shibuya Station regularly but the Shinjuku neighborhood is just a five-minute train ride north, and there are plenty of shops and affordable restaurants outside the door. **Pros:** affordable; convenient location; efficient. **Cons:** small, uninspired rooms; crowds in the area can be intimidating; few amenities. *Rooms from: ¥40,000 ✉ 1–12–2 Dogenzaka, Shibuya-ku ☎ 03/5457–0109 🌐 www.tokyuhotels.co.jp 408 rooms No Meals Ⓜ JR Shibuya Station (Hachiko Exit).*

Trunk (Hotel) Cat Street (トランクホテル)
$$$ | **HOTEL** | Just off Cat Street, which connects trendy Shibuya with equally trendy Harajuku (aka Omotesando), this boutique hotel has an open terrace, a lobby-lounge bar, and other common areas where guests have the opportunity to interact with locals and feel a part of Tokyo's creative scene. **Pros:** one of Tokyo's most unique boutique hotels; excellent location amid the city's coolest neighborhoods; hotel design, service, and layout foster a sense of community. **Cons:** wedding events can be disruptive; can be noisy, especially on weekends; expensive for the quality of the rooms. *Rooms from: ¥50,000 ✉ 5–31 Jingumae, Shibuya-ku ☎ 03/5766–3210 🌐 catstreet.trunk-hotel.com 15 rooms No Meals Ⓜ JR Harajuku; Jingumae (Exit 7); Omotesando (Exit A1); Shibuya (Exit A13).*

Nightlife

BARS

Akaoni (赤鬼)
WINE BAR | The emphasis here is on *nama*, unrefined, unpasteurized sake. Tons of types of sake from over 60 breweries are available daily. Since *nama* is short-lived, too delicate and fresh to transport or

export, it's not widely available overseas. You can accompany your choices with Japanese fare, served here as small bites in the *izakaya* style. Reservations are recommended. ✉ *2–15–3 Sangenjaya, Shibuya-ku* ☎ *03/3410–9918* 🌐 *www.akaoni39.com* Ⓜ *Denenchofu and Tokyu Setagaya lines, Sangenjaya Station.*

buri (立喰酒場; *Tachigui Sakaba buri*)
WINE BAR | Buri serves tasty *ji-zake* (local sake) from around Japan in the one-cup style. Imagine sake in a mini mason jar, paired with a range of tapas-like servings of sashimi, yakitori, salads, and prosciutto, albeit in a mostly standing-room-only setting. There's also beer on tap. Just a five-minute walk from Ebisu Station, this casual bar fills up quickly on weekends, so it's best to stop in early to grab that bench by the window. ✉ *1–14–1 Ebisu-Nishi, Shibuya-ku* ☎ *03/3496–7744.*

DANCE CLUBS

Womb
DANCE CLUB | Well-known techno, breakbeat, and drum-and-bass DJs often stop by this place on their way through town. The turntable talent, local and international, and multiple floors of dance and lounge space make Womb a consistently rewarding club experience. Drawing adults from their late twenties to forties, the place gets packed sometimes after 1 in the morning. Entry costs around ¥3,000 or so depending on the event. ✉ *2–16 Maruyamacho, Shibuya-ku* ☎ *03/5459–0039* 🌐 *www.womb.co.jp/en* Ⓜ *JR Yamanote Line, Ginza and Hanzomon subway lines, Shibuya Station (Hachiko Exit for JR and Ginza, Exit 3A for Hanzomon).*

IZAKAYA

Tatemichiya (立道屋)
PUB | The concrete walls are adorned with rock musicians' autobiographies and posters of the Sex Pistols and Ramones, who also provide the sound track. Artist Yoshitomo Nara has been known to show up here, so if you're lucky, you can drink with him and watch him draw on the walls. This is a storied place, so if you're in the area and looking for a drink, it's not a poor choice. ✉ *B1, 30–8 Sarugakucho, Shibuya-ku* ☎ *03/5459–3431* Ⓜ *Tokyu Toyoko Line, Daikanyama Station.*

KARAOKE

Karaoke Pasela (カラオケパセラ渋谷店)
KARAOKE | FAMILY | This large, glitzy karaoke joint has plenty of English songs and private rooms for small and large groups. Daytime weekday rates (noon to 5 pm) are quite cheap, but at other times, expect to pay about ¥580 per 30 minutes per person on weekends and evenings (5 pm to 5 am). You can order all kinds of surprisingly good food and drinks and have it delivered to your room. There are also all-you-can-drink plans if you're feeling frisky. If you have a large group and want to make reservations, you can do so in English at the very top of the website by pressing the tiny "English" button. ✉ *1–22–9 Jinnan, Shibuya-ku* ☎ *0120/428–875* 🌐 *www.pasela.co.jp/shop/shibuya* Ⓜ *JR Yamanote Line and Ginza and Hanzomon subway lines, Shibuya Station (Hachiko exit).*

PUBS

What the Dickens!
PUB | This spacious pub in Ebisu feels more authentically British than many of its rivals, thanks partly to a menu of traditional pub grub, including steak pies. Aged logs make the second floor feel like a nice tree house. The place hosts regular live music (funk, folk, jazz, rock, reggae—anything goes here) and other events, so it can be very loud, particularly on Friday and Saturday. ✉ *Roob 6 Bldg., 1–13–3 Ebisu-Nishi, 4th fl., Shibuya-ku* ☎ *03/3780–2099* 🌐 *www.whatthedickens.jp* ⏲ *Closed Mon.* Ⓜ *Hibiya subway line, Ebisu Station (Nishi-guchi/West Exit).*

FILM

Eurospace (ユーロスペース)

FILM | One of the best venues for art-house films in Japan screens independent European and Asian hits and small-scale Japanese movies. Directors and actors often appear on the stage, greeting fans on opening days. Occasionally Japanese films run with English subtitles, but ask ahead of time. ✉ *1–5 Maruyama-cho, 3rd fl., Shibuya-ku* ☎ *03/3461–0211* 🌐 *www.eurospace.co.jp* Ⓜ *JR Yamanote Line and Ginza and Hanzomon subway lines, Shibuya Station (Hachiko Exit).*

MUSIC

NHK Hall (ホール; *NHK*)

MUSIC | The home base for the Japan Broadcasting Corporation's NHK Symphony Orchestra, known as N-Kyo, is probably the auditorium most familiar to Japanese lovers of classical music, as performances here are routinely rebroadcast on the national TV station. Other performances are held here, too, from professional acts to high school groups. ✉ *2–2–1 Jinnan, Shibuya-ku* ☎ *03/3465–1751* 🌐 *www.nhk-fdn.or.jp/nhk_hall* Ⓜ *JR Yamanote Line, Harajuku Station (Omotesando Exit).*

TRADITIONAL THEATER

National Noh Theater (国立能楽堂; *Kokuritsu No Gaku Do*)

THEATER | **FAMILY** | One of the few public halls to host Noh performances provides basic English-language summaries of the plots at performances. Individual screens placed in front of each seat also give an English translation. There are other types of performances at the same theater, so check what is on. ✉ *4–18–1 Sendagaya, Shibuya-ku* ☎ *03/3230–3000 reservations* 🌐 *www.ntj.jac.go.jp/en/theatre/noh/* 🎫 *¥5,000 depending on event* Ⓜ *JR Chuo Line, Sendagaya Station (Minami-guchi/South Exit); Oedo subway line, Kokuritsu-Kyogijo Station (Exit A4).*

Shopping

Although Shibuya has traditionally been retail district geared to teenagers and young adults, the shifting tides of late have resulted into a shopping scene that caters to all kinds with many reasonably priced shops, vertical malls, and a few department stores.

At the neighborhood's southern edges you can unleash your inner fashionista in Daikanyama, a boutique-laden area with shops selling retro T-shirts, skate-punk wear, and premium denim that makes jeans fans giddy.

BOOKS

★ **Daikanyama T-Site** (代官山; *T-Site*)

BOOKS | This is a calming respite, complete with a leafy garden, a trendy terrace eatery, a gallery, and, of course, the main business—a shop selling books, music, and videos with a focus on art and design. One of the lounges has 30,000 books and a large selection of foreign magazines you can read there with a drink. There's also a pet boutique, so some locals bring their designer-dud-clad dogs with them to enjoy the on-site amenities. ✉ *17–5 Sarugakucho, Shibuya-ku* ☎ *03/3770–2525* 🌐 *store.tsite.jp/daikanyama/english/* Ⓜ *Tokyu Toyoko Line, Daikanyama Station (Central Exit).*

CRAFTS

★ **Tokyu Hands** (東急ハンズ渋谷店)

CRAFTS | **FAMILY** | This chain carries a wide and varied assortment of goods, including hobby and crafts materials, art supplies, and knitting and sewing materials, as well as jewelry, household goods, stationery, even cosmetics. There is also the related Hands Do within the store that hosts events on how to make things. It's not unusual for local hobbyists to spend an entire afternoon browsing in here. ✉ *12–18 Udagawacho, Shibuya-ku* ☎ *03/5489–5111* 🌐 *hands.net* Ⓜ *JR Yamanote Line and Ginza, Fukutoshin, and Hanzomon subway lines, Shibuya Station (Hachiko Exit for JR, Exits 6 and 7 for subway).*

CLOTHING

Bingo Shibuya Modi Used Clothing
(渋谷モディ店; *Bingo*)
SECOND-HAND | If you're looking for vintage fashion and don't feel like making the trek to Shimokitazawa, Bingo is your place. It's on the third floor of the Modi building, which is just north of Shibuya Scramble Crossing and which also houses a variety of other stores. ✉ *1–21–3 Jinnan, 3rd Floor, Shibuya-ku* ☎ *03/5428–4812.*

HOUSEWARES

★ **Yamada Heiando** (山田平安堂)
HOUSEWARES | With a spacious, airy layout and lovely lacquerware goods, this fashionable shop is a must for anyone who appreciates fine design. Rice bowls, sushi trays, bento lunch boxes, *hashioki* (chopstick rests), and jewelry cases come in traditional blacks and reds, as well as patterns both subtle and bold. Prices are fair—many items cost less than ¥10,000—but these are the kinds of goods for which devotees of Japanese craftsmanship would be willing to pay a lot. ✉ *Hillside Terrace, 18–12 Sarugakucho, G Block #202, Shibuya-ku* ☎ *03/3464–5541* 🌐 *www.heiando1919.com* Ⓜ *Tokyu Toyoko Line, Daikanyama Station (Komazawa-dori Exit).*

MALLS AND SHOPPING CENTERS

Shibuya 109
MALL | **FAMILY** | A teenage girl's dream, this nine-floor outlet is filled with small stores where the merchandise screams kitsch and trendy. On weekends, dance concerts and fashion shows are often staged at the front entrance. ✉ *2–29–1 Dogenzaka, Shibuya-ku* ☎ *03/3477–5111* 🌐 *www.shibuya109.jp* Ⓜ *JR Yamanote Line and Ginza, Fukutoshin, and Hanzomon subway lines, Shibuya Station (Hachiko Exit for JR, Exit 3A for subway lines).*

Shibuya Parco (渋谷パルコ)
MALL | **FAMILY** | These vertical malls filled with small retail shops and boutiques are all within walking distance of one another in the commercial heart of Shibuya. Shopping options range from stores carrying designer brands to an entire floor with game and anime goods. There's a rooftop garden and a basement full of restaurants. ✉ *15–1 Udagawa-cho, Shibuya-ku* ☎ *03/3464–5111* 🌐 *shibuya.parco.jp* Ⓜ *Ginza, Fukutoshin, and Hanzo-mon subway lines, Shibuya Station (Exits 6 and 7).*

Shibuya Scramble Square
(渋谷スクランブルスクエア)
MALL | **FAMILY** | Inside the building immediately adjacent to the station is one of Shibuya's newest landmarks—home not only to the Shibuya Sky viewpoint, but also to numerous stores (carrying some brands you know and others you don't), restaurants, and constantly changing pop-up shops. It also has a roster of special events. ✉ *3–21–3 Shibuya, Shibuya-ku* 🌐 *www.shibuya-scramble-square.com.*

MUSIC

Manhattan Records
(マンハッタンレコード)
MUSIC | Whatever you're looking for in music—hip-hop, reggae, house, R&B—can be found at this shop, where a DJ booth in the center of the room pumps out the jams. ✉ *10–1 Udagawacho, Shibuya-ku* ☎ *03/3477–7166* 🌐 *manhattanrecords.jp* Ⓜ *JR Yamanote Line and Ginza, Fukutoshin, and Hanzomon subway lines, Shibuya Station (Hachiko Exit for JR, Exits 6 and 7 for subway).*

Tower Records Shibuya
(タワーレコード渋谷)
MUSIC | This huge emporium carries one of the most diverse selections of CDs and DVDs in the world, in addition to new and used vinyl records. You can take a break from shopping in the second-floor café. ✉ *1–22–14 Jinnan, Shibuya-ku* ☎ *03/3496–3661* 🌐 *tower.jp/store/kanto/shibuya* Ⓜ *JR Yamanote Line and Ginza, Fukutoshin, and Hanzomon subway lines, Shibuya Station (Hachiko Exit for JR, Exit 7 for subway).*

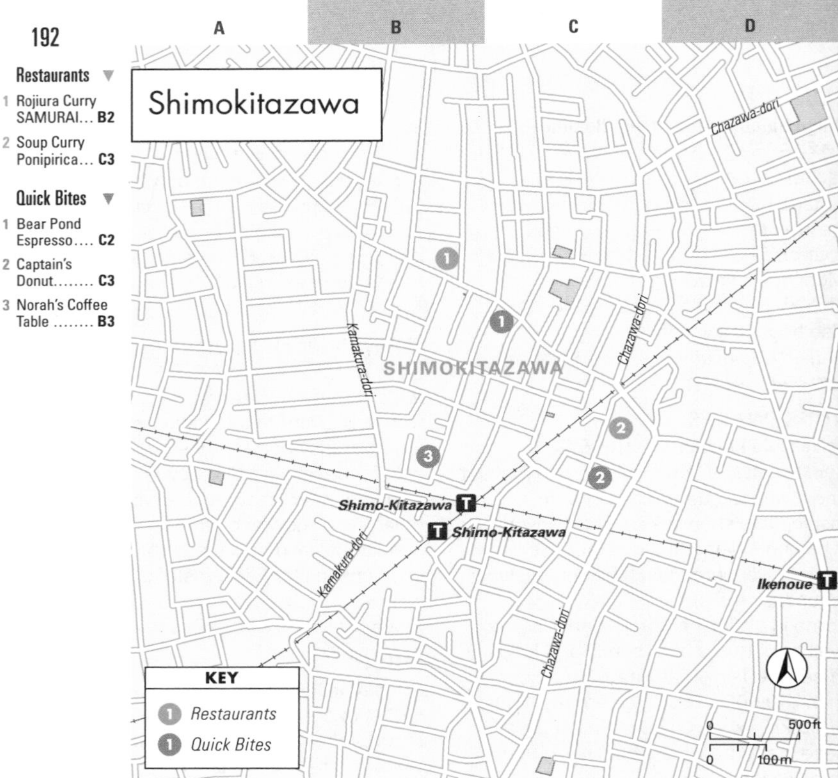

Shimokitazawa

Shimokitazawa, where two of Tokyo's suburban lines cross, is in transition. Since the burial of one train line left in its wake a new linear park that's now dotted with shops and restaurants, Shimokita (as it's often called) has become trendy. And yet, it retains an overall low-key atmosphere. Streets here are still lined with curry eateries and vintage clothing stores.

Note that although most of the neighborhood is accessible, people with limited mobility might have problems with the elevation changes. In addition, although Shimokita is compact, its maze of streets can be confusing. Be prepared to get lost and let serendipity take hold.

Restaurants

Rojiura Curry SAMURAI
(ロジウラカリィ サムライ下北沢店)
$$ | **JAPANESE** | Off a main shopping street, one of Shimokitazawa's many curry shops has a cute entrance, table seating, and a couple of counter seats so you can watch the cooks at work. Unlike most Japanese curries, those served here tend to be heavy on the vegetables. **Known for:** Japanese curries with the freshest ingredients; adjustable spice levels; creative additional toppings to customize your meal. *Average main: ¥1,500* *3–31–14 Kitazawa, Setagaya-ku* *03/5453–6494* *samurai-curry.com* *Odakyu and Keio lines, Shimokitazawa Station.*

Soup Curry Ponipirica
(スープカレーポニピリカ)
$$ | **JAPANESE** | What's a soup curry? You'll find out here when you choose your curry (a wide variety with vegetables); your soup base (tomato, shrimp, or the base that's used to make many soupy Japanese dishes); your spice level (from 0 to 7); your toppings (perhaps avocados, an egg, or fried mushrooms); and, finally, the amount of rice you'd like. **Known for:** curries you can customize; vegetables from Hokkaido; crispy fried chicken wings in the soup. *Average main: ¥1,500* *Kitazawa 2–8–8, 2nd floor, Setagaya-ku* *Look for "Soup Curry" written by the stairs leading in.* *03/6804–8802* *ponipirica.com* *Odakyu and Keio lines, Shimokitazawa Station.*

Coffee and Quick Bites

Bear Pond Espresso
(ベアポンド エスプレッソ)
$ | **CAFÉ** | Look for the cute neon bear sign to find what is possibly the neighborhood's best coffee shop, since, aside from some branded merchandise, coffee is the only thing that's sold. It's a tiny, low-key place with a simple design, including old wooden benches that make the place feel as if it's both in the now and from long ago. **Known for:** quality coffee; unique atmosphere; cute merchandise. *Average main: ¥900* *2–36–12 Kitazawa, Setagaya-ku* *03/5454–2486* *www.bearpondespresso.com* *No credit cards* *Odakyu and Keio lines, Shimokitazawa Station.*

Captain's Donut
(キャプテンズドーナツ 下北沢本部)
$ | **BAKERY** | **FAMILY** | Stop by and watch specialty donuts being fried before your eyes. They come in many flavors, and although they're on the "healthy" side, don't worry—they're still donuts. **Known for:** fresh donuts made with soybean fiber left over from tofu-making; great soft-serve ice cream; coffee. *Average main: ¥600* *Kitazawa 2–7–5, Setagaya-ku* *03/6407–9691* *captain-d.com* *No credit cards* *Odakyu and Keio lines, Shimokitazawa Station.*

Norah's Coffee Table
$ | **CAFÉ** | **FAMILY** | Situated near Shimokitazawa Station, Norah's is a great place to do some people-watching while enjoying a coffee (including an Irish coffee if you'd like) and a snack. It also serves tea, wine, and beer. **Known for:** locally roasted coffee; fluffy pancakes with dessert toppings; cozy atmosphere. *Average main: ¥900* *Kitazawa 2–26–25, Setagaya-ku* *03/3468–2014* *No credit cards* *Closed Tues.* *Odakyu and Keio lines, Shimokitazawa Station.*

Nightlife

DANCE CLUBS

Shelter (下北沢; *Shelter*)
LIVE MUSIC | All kinds of acts play at this "live house" and bar in Shimokitazawa. Admission runs ¥2,000 to ¥6,000 depending on the act. Check the website to see what's on. *Senda Bldg., 2–6–10 Kitazawa, basement level, Setagaya-ku* *03/3466–7430* *www.loft-prj.co.jp/shelter* *Odakyu and Keio lines, Shimokitazawa Station.*

Shopping

If you like to shop, you won't be bored here. Small stores occupy spaces above the station, under the elevated train tracks, and along streets extending from the station. The area is known for its vintage clothing stores, which are the most concentrated on the north side of the station.

One-of-a-kind secondhand goods include designer fashions, jeans of all types, shoes, hats from all eras, outlandish sweaters, and quality imported goods, as well as rare knickknacks here and there. Be sure to explore the linear park that extends from the station or to check out whatever outdoor market might be set up outside the station's East Exit.

Antique Life Jin II
(アンティークライフ・ジン II)
ANTIQUES & COLLECTIBLES | The most interesting of a pair of two shops that are about a minute away from one another is a great place to browse for, say, one of those aprons worn at an izakaya, an old tool box, or maybe an antique sake container. All kinds of knickknacks fill the tiny space and spill out onto the street. If you want to hunt for still more treasure, make a right as you walk out of the store and then another right at the corner; up on your left, you'll see the original Antique Life Jin. ✉ *2–35–15 Kitazawa, Setagaya-ku* ☎ *03/5454–3545* 🌐 *antique-life-jin.com* Ⓜ *Odakyu and Keio lines, Shimokitazawa Station.*

Gallery Hana Shimokitazawa
(ギャラリー; *Hana* 下北沢)
ART GALLERY | Hana is the oldest gallery in Shimokitazawa, a neighborhood that's not particularly well known for art. Here, however, the eclectic collections and shows, which change about every other week and typically feature up-and-coming Japanese artists, are noteworthy. ✉ *3–26–2 Kitazawa, Setagaya-ku* ☎ *03/6380–5687* 🌐 *www.g-hana.jp* Ⓜ *Odakyu and Keio lines, Shimokitazawa Station.*

Tamaiya Senbei Shop (玉井屋)
FOOD | **FAMILY** | If you're looking for a snack while shopping, check out this purveyor of *senbei* (a type of grilled rice cracker), which has has been in Shimokitazawa since the Meiji Period. Theoretically, senbei are gluten-free since they're made of rice, but the soy-sauce coating often includes some wheat. ✉ *Kitazawa 2-31-1, Setagaya-ku* ☎ *03/3466–9191* Ⓜ *Odakyu and Keio lines, Shimokitazawa Station.*

Chapter 8

ROPPONGI

8

Updated by
Rob Goss

Sights ★★★☆☆
Restaurants ★★★★☆
Hotels ★★★★★
Shopping ★★★★☆
Nightlife ★★★★★

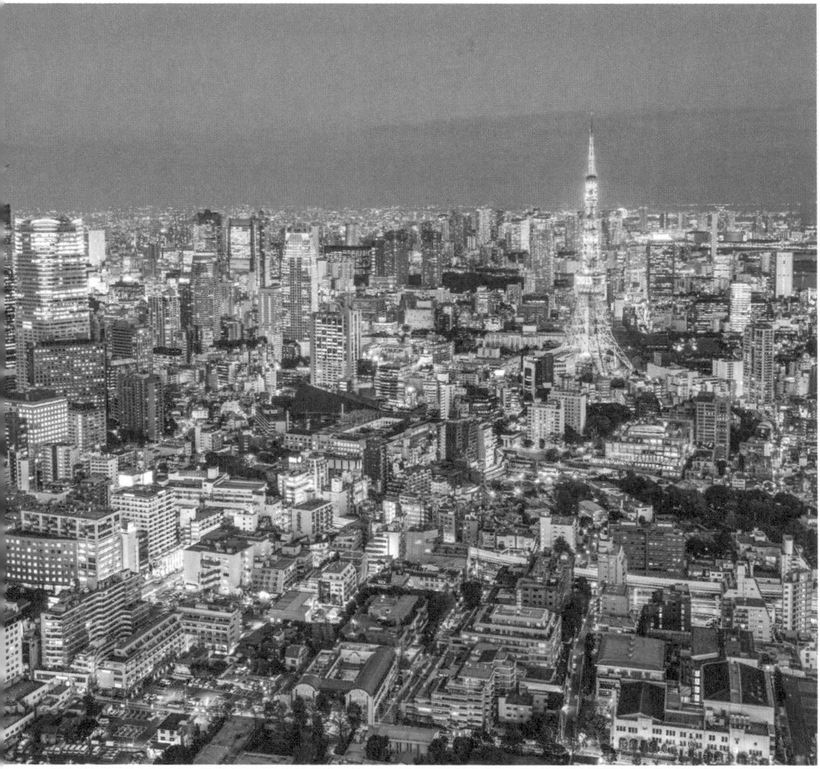

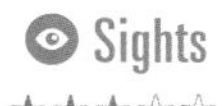

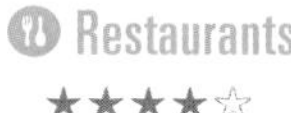

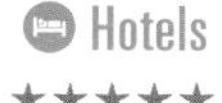

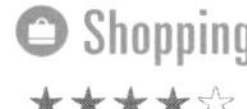

NEIGHBORHOOD SNAPSHOT

TOP EXPERIENCES

■ **See Tokyo's top art.** With the National Art Center, Tokyo, the Mori and Suntory art museums, and 21_21 Design Sight, Roppongi has become the place for Tokyo's top art exhibitions.

■ **Hit the heights.** Take in the view from one of two observation decks atop the Tokyo Tower, an unabashed knockoff of Paris's Eiffel Tower.

■ **Eat your fill.** From Michelin-starred Japanese and international cuisines to simple yet addictive ramen, Roppongi has an incredible concentration of great places to eat.

GETTING HERE

Roppongi is just east of Shibuya and Aoyama, and southwest of the Imperial Palace.

The best way to get to Roppongi is by subway, and there are two lines that travel to Roppongi Station: the Hibiya Line, which takes you right into the complex of Roppongi Hills, or the Oedo Line, with exits convenient to Tokyo Midtown.

PLANNING YOUR TIME

There are ATMs and currency-exchange services at Roppongi Hills and Tokyo Midtown shopping complexes, as well as family- and kid-friendly activities, such as small parks and sculptures. Combine those with the area's excellent art venues, and you could easily spend a full afternoon and early evening here, before indulging in dinner at one of Roppongi's many excellent restaurants.

OFF THE BEATEN PATH: AZABU JUBAN

■ Wander into the adjoining residential enclave of Azabu Juban, about 1 km (0.6 miles) southeast, to observe everyday life for the most well-heeled Tokyoites, along with some nice café sitting. This is a neighborhood where some toy poodles have bigger fashion budgets than most humans. While people-watching is fun here any time of year, the best time to visit is in August, during the Azabu Juban Noryo Festival, one of the biggest festivals in Minato-ku. Over a weekend near the end of the month, the streets, which are closed to car traffic, are lined with food vendors selling delicious international fare and drinks. Everyone wears their nicest summer *yukatas* (robes) and watches live performances.

VIEWPOINT

■ Head up Mori Tower in the Roppongi Hills complex for superb city views. Looking across Tokyo from the 52nd-floor indoor observation deck brings into focus just how vast and sprawling Tokyo is. The view at night is particularly mesmerizing, with Tokyo illuminated below.

Roppongi, once known for its clubs, bars, and nightlife, has become one of Tokyo's major shopping, dining, and art districts. The area is abuzz with shoppers, tourists, and office workers throughout the day and evening. As the clock inches closer to the last train, the crowd changes to young clubbers and barhoppers staying out until sunrise.

or many travelers, the lure of the eighborhood is the shopping on offer in tzy developments like Roppongi Hills, zabudai Hills, and Tokyo Midtown. In ddition, though, there are the three oints of what's known as Art Triangle oppongi—the National Art Center, Mori rt Museum, and Suntory Museum of rt. The neighborhood is also home to ne Fujifilm Square photo gallery, 21_21 esign Sight, and many art and cultural vents.

Sights

ujifilm Square (フジフイルムスクエア)
RT GALLERY | Located within Tokyo Aidtown, the Fujifilm Photo Salon hosts otating photography exhibits across nultiple genres, albeit with a strong mphasis on landscapes, while the hoto History Museum is a showcase f cameras and prints dating back to the nid-19th century. Although the salon and istory museum are on the small side, it s a good stop while visiting Roppongi's arger galleries, especially as its free. *9–7–3 Akasaka, Minato-ku* *03/6271–3350* *fujifilmsquare.jp* *Free* *Hibiya nd Oedo subway lines, Roppongi Station (Exit 8); Chiyoda subway line, Nogizaka Station (Exit 3).*

★ **Mori Art Museum**
(森美術館; *Mori Bijutsukan*)
ART MUSEUM | Occupying the 52nd and 53rd floors of Mori Tower, this museum is one of the leading contemporary art showcases in Tokyo. The space is well designed (by American architect Richard Gluckman), intelligently curated, diverse in its media, and hospitable to big crowds. The nine galleries host exhibits that rotate every few months and tend to focus on leading contemporary art, architecture, fashion, design, and photography. *6–10–1 Roppongi, Minato-ku* *050/5541–8600* *www.mori.art.museum/en* *Weekdays ¥2,000, weekends ¥2,200* *Oedo and Hibiya subway lines, Roppongi Station (exits 1c and 3).*

Mori Tower (森タワー)
VIEWPOINT | When it opened in 2003, the Roppongi Hills complex was the epitome of Tokyo opulence, with the shimmering, 54-story Mori Tower as its main showpiece. Though no longer a unique skyscraper, the tower still outclasses most with the Tokyo City View observation deck on the 52nd floor, where the

The Mori Art Museum presents temporary contemporary art exhibitions in a sky-high space.

panorama extends all the way to Mt. Fuji on a clear day. ✉ *6–10–1 Roppongi, Minato-ku* ☎ *03/6406–6652* 🌐 *tcv.roppongihills.com/en* 🎫 *Tokyo City View: Weekdays ¥2,000, weekends and public holidays ¥2,200* Ⓜ *Oedo and Hibiya subway lines, Roppongi Station (exits 1c and 3).*

The National Art Center, Tokyo (国立新美術館; *Kokuritsu Shin Bijutsukan*)
ART MUSEUM | Tokyo's largest rotating exhibition space, which hosts major international modern and contemporary exhibits as well as smaller shows, is worth visiting for the architecture alone. Architect Kisho Kurokawa, a cofounder of the influential metabolist movement in 1960, created a stunning facade that shimmers in undulating waves of glass, and entering the bright exposition space, with its soaring ceilings, feels a bit like stepping inside the set of a utopian sci-fi movie. The building houses seven gallery areas; a library; a museum shop; a trio of cafés; and a restaurant, Brasserie Paul Bocuse Le Musée, offering fine French dishes. ✉ *7–22–2 Roppongi, Minato-ku* ☎ *050/5541–8600* 🌐 *www.nact.jp/englis* 🎫 *Admission fee varies with exhibit* ⏱ *Closed Tues.* Ⓜ *Toei Oedo and Hibiya lines, Roppongi Station (exits 4a and 7); Chiyoda line, Nogizaka Station (Exit 6).*

Suntory Museum of Art (サントリー美術館; *Santori Bijutsukan*)
ART MUSEUM | Based on the principle of dividing profits three ways, Suntory, Japan's beverage giant, has committed a third of its earnings to what it feels is its corporate and social responsibility: environmental conservation and providing the public with art and education. The establishment of the Suntory Art Museum in 1961 was just one of the fruits of this initiative, and the museum's current home at Tokyo Midtown Galleria is a beautiful place to view some of Tokyo's finest fine-art exhibitions. Past displays have included everything from works by Picasso and Toulouse-Lautrec to fine kimonos from the Edo period. The museum also runs occasional tea ceremonies in its traditional Gencho-an

eahouse; check the website for the nonthly schedule. ✉ *Tokyo Midtown Galeria, 9–7–4 Akasaka, 3rd fl., Minato-ku* ☎ *03/3479–8600* 🌐 *www.suntory.com/sma* 🎫 *From ¥1,300 (varies by exhibition); tea ceremony additional ¥1,000* ⏱ *Closed Tues.* Ⓜ *Hibiya and Oedo subway lines, Roppongi Station (Exit 8); Chiyoda subway line, Nogizaka Station (Exit 3).*

★ **teamLab Borderless**
(チームラボボーダレス)

ART GALLERY | **FAMILY** | Opened in 2024 in the Azabudai Hills complex, Borderless is the latest permanent outpost of pioneering digital-art collective teamLab. The sprawling installations are like a psychedelic fantasy—all rendered in real-time, as the art reacts to the movements of visitors. This concept even extends to the on-site teahouse, where digital branches grow wherever you place your teacup. ✉ *Azabudai Hills, 1–2–4 Azabudai, Minato-ku* ☎ *03/6230–9666* 🌐 *www.teamlab.art/e/tokyo* 🎫 *¥4,000 to ¥4,800, depending on the day* ⏱ *Closed twice a month on irregular dates; check website for details.* ✍ *Tickets must be bought online in advance.* Ⓜ *Hibiya subway line, Kamiyacho Station (Exit 5).*

Tokyo Tower (東京タワー)

VIEWPOINT | **FAMILY** | In 1958, Tokyo's fledgling TV networks needed a tall antenna array to transmit signals. Trying to emerge from the devastation of World War II, the nation's capital was also hungry for a landmark—a symbol for the aspirations of a city still without a skyline. The result was the 1,093-foot-high Tokyo Tower, an unabashed knockoff of Paris's Eiffel Tower, complete with great views of the city. The Main Observatory, set at 492 feet above ground, and the Top Deck, up an additional 330 feet, quickly became major tourist attractions. Both observation decks were renovated in 2018 and are still major draws. On weekends and holidays, ambitious visitors can make the 600-stair climb up to the Main Observatory. ✉ *4–2–8 Shiba-Koen, Minato-ku* ☎ *03/3433–5111* 🌐 *en.tokyotower.co.jp* 🎫 *Main Deck only ¥1,200, Main and Top Deck ¥2,800* Ⓜ *Hibiya subway line, Kamiyacho Station (Exit 1).*

21_21 Design Sight

ART GALLERY | This low-slung building in the garden at Tokyo Midtown hosts rotating exhibitions focused on cutting-edge art and design. Designed by architect Tadao Ando, the subdued exterior belies the expansive and bright gallery space, where exhibits focus on presenting the world of design in an exciting and accessible light. ✉ *9–7–6 Akasaka, Minato-ku* ☎ *03/3475–2121* 🌐 *www.2121designsight.jp/en* 🎫 *¥1,400* ⏱ *Closed Tues.* Ⓜ *Toei Oedo and Hibiya lines, Roppongi Station (Exit 6).*

Zenpuku-ji Temple
(麻布山善福寺 *Azabusan Zenpuku-ji*)

TEMPLE | This temple, just south of the Ichinohashi Crossing, dates back to the 800s and was, in the 1200s, converted to the Jodo Shinshu school of Buddhism. When Consul-General Townsend Harris arrived from the Americas in 1859, he lived on the temple grounds. It's also home to what's said to be the oldest tree in Tokyo, a 750-year-old giant gingko. ✉ *1–6–21 Moto-Azabu, Minato-ku* ☎ *03/3451–7402* 🌐 *www.azabu-san.or.jp/eng* 🎫 *Free* Ⓜ *Oedo and Namboku subway lines, Azabu Juban Station (Exits 1 and 7).*

Restaurants

The opulent Roppongi has outgrown its disco days and matured into a district with Western hotels and business skyscrapers. Serving an array of Japanese and international flavors, restaurants run the gamut from lunch spots to quick bites to Michelin-starred options in the evening.

A
B
C
D
E
F
1
2
3
4
5
6
7
8
9
Aoyama-itchome
Aoyama-dori
Akasaka
AKASAKA
Sanpun-zaka
Akasaka-dori
Akasaka-dori
Hinokicho Park
Nogizaka
Chiyoda Line
Toei Oedo Line
Tokyo Metropolitan Aoyama Park
Shibuya (elevated)
Roppongi
Roppongi
Hibiya Line
Roppongi-dori
Stars and Stripes Street
Gaien Nishi
ROPPONGI
Gaien Higashi
Shibuya (elevated)
Roppongi-dori
Roppongi-dori
Keyaki-zaka
Sakura-zaka
Gaien Nishi-dori
Gaien Nishi-dori
Torii-zaka
Toei Oedo Line
Azabu-Juban
AZABU-JUBAN
Azabu-Jub
KEY
Sights
Restaurants
Quick Bites
Hotels

G H I J

Roppongi

Tameike-sanno
Tameike-sanno
Roppongi-itchome
Kamiyacho
Sakurada-dori
AZABUDAI
Gaien Higashi-dori
Akabanebashi
0 500 ft
0 100 m

G H I J

Sights

1 Fujifilm Square D4
2 Mori Art Museum.................. D6
3 Mori Tower D6
4 The National Art Center, Tokyo.... C4
5 Suntory Museum of Art........... D4
6 teamLab Borderless............... H6
7 Tokyo Tower.......................... J7
8 21_21 Design Sight D3
9 Zenpuku-ji Temple.................. E9

Restaurants

1 Homework's.......................... E8
2 Kushiyaki Ganchan.................. E6
3 Roppongi Inakaya F5
4 Sushisho Masa A6
5 Tony Roma's.......................... E6
6 Towers D4

Quick Bites

1 Falafel Brothers...................... E5
2 Ippudo.................................. E5
3 Menya Musashi Kosho D4
4 Mercer Brunch Roppongi E4
5 Verve Coffee Roasters Roppongi.............................. F6

Hotels

1 Grand Hyatt Tokyo C6
2 Hotel Asia Center of Japan........C2
3 Janu Tokyo H5
4 The Prince Park Tower Tokyo J8
5 The Ritz-Carlton, Tokyo.............E4

Homework's (ホームワークス)

$$ | **AMERICAN** | **FAMILY** | Every so often, even on foreign shores, you've got to have a burger, and the Swiss-and-bacon special at Homework's is an incomparably better choice than anything you can get at one of the global chains. Hamburgers come in three sizes on white or wheat buns, with a variety of toppings. **Known for:** burgers you can sink your teeth into; hearty deli sandwiches; relaxed atmosphere. *Average main: ¥2,000* ✉ *1–5–8 Azabu Juban, Minato-ku* ☎ *03/3405–9884* 🌐 *homeworks-1.com* Ⓜ *Namboku and Oedo subway lines, Azabu Juban Station (Exit 4).*

★ **Kushiyaki Ganchan** (串焼がんちゃん)

$$$$ | **JAPANESE** | Smoky, noisy, and cluttered, Ganchan is exactly what the Japanese expect of their yakitori joints—restaurants that specialize in bits of charcoal-broiled chicken and vegetables. The counter here seats barely 15 (you have to squeeze to get to the chairs in back), and festival masks, paper kites, lanterns, and greeting cards from celebrity patrons adorn the walls. **Known for:** eclectic decor; cozy, down-to-earth atmosphere; skewer sets that make ordering easier. *Average main: ¥6,000* ✉ *6–8–23 Roppongi, Minato-ku* ☎ *03/3478–0092* ⏲ *Closed Sun. No lunch.* Ⓜ *Hibiya and Oedo subway lines, Roppongi Station (Exit 1A).*

★ **Roppongi Inakaya** (六本木田舎家)

$$$$ | **JAPANESE** | The style here is *robatayaki,* a dining experience that segues into pure theater. Seated on cushions behind a grill, traditionally attired cooks prepare fresh vegetables, seafood, and skewers of beef and chicken. **Known for:** entertaining service; fresh ingredients grilled just right; fun, lively atmosphere. *Average main: ¥10,000* ✉ *3–14–17 Roppongi, Minato-ku* ☎ *03/3408–5040* 🌐 *www.roppongiinakaya.jp* ⏲ *No lunch* Ⓜ *Hibiya and Oedo subway lines, Roppongi Station (Exit 3).*

Sushisho Masa (すし匠 まさ)

$$$$ | **SUSHI** | Here you need a dose of luck—there are only seven counter seats and reservations book up fast (ask your hotel concierge to make one for you)—and a full wallet, as high-end sushi comes at a pretty price. The interior is unpretentious, putting the focus squarely on the gorgeous presentations for each course, but what really makes a meal here subline is the extreme quality of the cuts of fish and garnishes featuring such rare ingredients as *zha cai* (pickled stem of the mustard plant). **Known for:** impeccable attention to detail; extremely high-quality, fresh fish with rare garnishes; great service. *Average main: ¥33,000* ✉ *Nishi-Azabu Bldg., B1 fl., 4–1–15 Nishi Azabu, Minato-ku* ☎ *03/3499–9178* 🌐 *www.sushisyomasa.com* ⏲ *Closed Mon. No lunch* Ⓜ *Hibiya and Oedo subway lines, Roppongi Station (exits 4b and 1c).*

Tony Roma's (トニーローマ)

$$$ | **AMERICAN** | **FAMILY** | This casual American chain is world-famous for its barbecued ribs. It also serves kid-size (and much larger) portions of burgers, chicken strips, and fried shrimp. **Known for:** a taste of the States; large portions of barbecued ribs; friendly service. *Average main: ¥3,500* ✉ *5–4–20 Roppongi, Minato-ku* ☎ *03/3408–2748* 🌐 *tonyromas.jp/en* Ⓜ *Oedo and Hibiya subway lines, Roppongi Station (Exit 3).*

Towers (タワーズ)

$$$$ | **ASIAN FUSION** | When you're looking for a break from all the ramen, tempura, and yakitori, this restaurant on the 45th floor of the Ritz-Carlton Hotel serves a fusion of French and Japanese cuisines. The prix-fixe lunches include a three-course business lunch (¥6,500), and there are dinners with four and five courses (¥12,200 and ¥16,500). **Known for:** views over Tokyo; sophisticated fusion dishes; luxurious weekend brunches. *Average main: ¥12,000* ✉ *Ritz Carlton Hotel, 9–7–1 Akasaka, 45th fl.,*

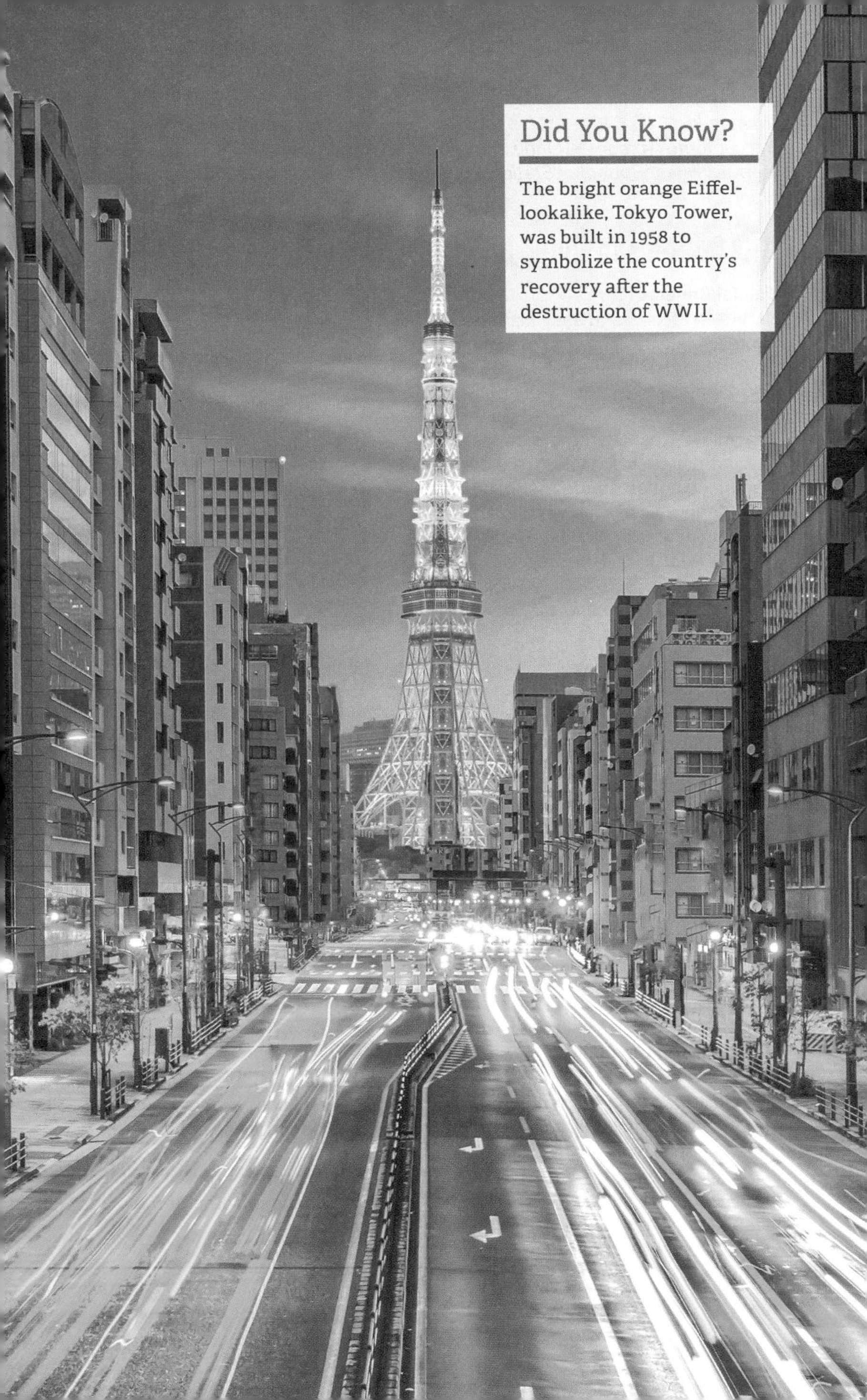

Did You Know?

The bright orange Eiffel-lookalike, Tokyo Tower, was built in 1958 to symbolize the country's recovery after the destruction of WWII.

Minato-ku ☎ *03/6434–8711* 🌐 *towers.ritzcarltontokyo.com* Ⓜ *Oedo and Hibiya subway lines, Roppongi Station (exits 4a and 7).*

Coffee and Quick Bites

Falafel Brothers (ファラフェルブラザーズ)
$ | **VEGAN** | Quick and easy plant-based food isn't always easy to come by in Tokyo, but this small spot serves up excellent vegan fast food—namely, falafel, veggies burgers, and plant-based brownies. Most customers buy takeout, but there are a few tables, plus craft beers and coffee on the menu, if you fancy lingering. **Known for:** veggie burgers; falafel in pita; vegan desserts. $ *Average main: ¥1,450* ✉ *5–1–1 Roppongi, Minato-ku* ☎ *03/6459–2844* 🌐 *www.falafel-brothers.jp* Ⓜ *Oedo and Hibiya subway lines, Roppongi Station.*

Ippudo (一風堂)
$ | **RAMEN** | Open from 11 am to 11 pm, this ever-busy ramen joint, now an international chain with almost 30 locations in Tokyo alone, is an ideal quick stop on or after a night out. The classic ramen is the Shiromaru, which features a creamy pork-based stock, thin yet slightly firm noodles, and a topping of *chashu* (braised) pork slices. **Known for:** Shiromaru ramen; late hours; gyoza (dumplings). $ *Average main: ¥780* ✉ *4–9–11 Roppongi, Minato-ku* ☎ *03/5775–7561* 🌐 *www.ippudo.com* Ⓜ *Hibiya and Oedo subway lines, Roppongi Station (Exit 6).*

Menya Musashi Kosho (麺屋武蔵虎嘯)
$ | **RAMEN** | **FAMILY** | Serving both ramen and *tsukemen* (noodles with the broth on the side for dipping), this sleek ramen shop is a great stop for a quick and hearty bowl of noodles. The fusion broths—a hearty chicken/pork or lighter seafood stock made from dried bonito and sardines—are a specialty. **Known for:** quick and affordable meals; ramen in a hip, modern interior; rich, flavorful bowls of noodles. $ *Average main: ¥1,000* ✉ *4–12–6 Roppongi, Minato-ku* ☎ *03/3497–0634* ▭ *No credit cards* Ⓜ *Hibiya and Oedo subway lines, Roppongi Station (exits 4a and 7).*

Mercer Brunch Roppongi (マーサーブランチ六本木)
$$ | **CAFÉ** | By day, this pleasant café offers outdoor seating and brioche French toast with great coffee just minutes from Tokyo Midtown and the museums of the Roppongi Art Triangle. From 5 pm, the menu changes to more expensive grilled meats and pastas. **Known for:** reasonably priced brunch; terrace seating; convenient location. $ *Average main: ¥2,200* ✉ *4–2–35 Roppongi, Minato-ku* ☎ *03/3470–6551* 🌐 *www.mercer-brunch.com* Ⓜ *Oedo and Hibiya subway lines, Roppongi Station (Exits 5 or 7).*

Verve Coffee Roasters Roppongi (六本木店)
$ | **CAFÉ** | **FAMILY** | For a quick caffeine break, Verve serves coffee made using single-origin beans from around the world in fashionable, but laidback surrounds. They also have herb teas, sandwiches, and sweet treats like carrot cake and vegan cookies. **Known for:** single-origin coffee; light bites like sandwiches; opens early (7 am). $ *Average main: ¥750* ✉ *5–16–7 Roppongi, Minato-ku* ☎ *03/6427–5403* 🌐 *vervecoffee.jp* Ⓜ *Oedo and Hibiya subway lines, Roppongi Station.*

Hotels

A boisterous entertainment district by night and cosmopolitan cultural hub by day, Roppongi has hotels for travelers who want to be in the thick of the action. Lodgings run the gamut from low-end budget inns to some of the world's top brands.

Grand Hyatt Tokyo (グランドハイアット東京)
$$$$ | **HOTEL** | Japanese refinement and a contemporary design come together perfectly at the Grand Hyatt, a centrally located hotel where no expense has been spared on materials—from the Frette bed linens to the red-granite pool in the Nagomi spa. **Pros:** great spa; wide range of restaurants; spacious rooms. **Cons:** rooms lack distinctive character; easy to get lost in the building's complicated layout; in a busy complex. *Rooms from: ¥104,000* *6–10–3 Roppongi, Minato-ku* *03/4333–1234* *www.hyatt.com* *387 rooms* *No Meals* *Hibiya and Oedo subway lines, Roppongi Station (exits 1a and 3).*

Hotel Asia Center of Japan (ホテルアジア会館; *Hoteru Ajia Kaikan*)
$ | **HOTEL** | Established in 1957 and renovated in 2015, these budget accommodations offer both good value for the money and easy access (a 15-minute walk) to the nightlife of Roppongi. **Pros:** affordable; great area for those who love the nightlife; free Wi-Fi. **Cons:** just one restaurant; no room service; mostly small rooms. *Rooms from: ¥17,300* *8–10–32 Akasaka, Minato-ku* *03/3402–6111* *www.asiacenter.or.jp* *173 rooms* *No Meals* *Ginza and Hanzo-mon subway lines, Aoyama-itchome Station (Exit 4).*

Janu Tokyo (ジャヌ東京)
$$$$ | **HOTEL** | Situated in a tower of the glistening Azabudai Hills complex, the Janu is one of the newest and swankiest luxury hotels in Tokyo. **Pros:** excellent spa; a peaceful retreat despite being in a busy urban complex; spacious rooms with a range of modern amenities. **Cons:** bars and restaurants not for guests only; one of the city's most expensive hotels; service might feel too hushed and formal for some. *Rooms from: ¥140,000* *Azabudai Hills Residence A, 1–2–2 Azabudai, Minato-ku* *03/6731–2333* *www.janu.com/janu-tokyo* *122 rooms* *No Meals* *Hibiya subway line, Kamiyacho Station (Exit 5).*

The Prince Park Tower Tokyo (ザ・プリンス パークタワー東京)
$$ | **HOTEL** | **FAMILY** | The surrounding parkland and the absence of any adjacent structures make the Park Tower a peaceful urban retreat, where a vertically impressive atrium lobby, with two glass elevators, gives a clear look into the building's hollow core. **Pros:** park nearby; well-stocked convenience store on first floor; fun extras like a bowling alley and pool. **Cons:** a tad isolated; extra fee for pool and fitness center (except Premium Club guests); few dining options in immediate area. *Rooms from: ¥45,000* *4–8–1 Shiba-koen, Minato-ku* *03/5400–1111* *www.princehotels.com/parktower* *603 rooms* *No Meals* *Oedo subway line, Akabanebashi Station (Akabanebashi Exit).*

★ **The Ritz-Carlton, Tokyo** (ザ・リッツ・カールトン東京)
$$$$ | **HOTEL** | Installed in the top floors of the 53-story Midtown Tower, the Ritz-Carlton provides some of Tokyo's most luxurious accommodations squarely in the middle of the city. **Pros:** great views of Tokyo; romantic setting; stunning rooms loaded with luxurious goodies. **Cons:** high prices; a bit of a walk to the subway; club lounge extras don't live up to the Ritz's reputation. *Rooms from: ¥112,000* *9–7–1 Akasaka, Minato-ku* *03/3423–8000* *www.ritzcarlton.com* *247 rooms* *No Meals* *Hibiya and Oedo subway lines, Roppongi Station (exits 4 and 7).*

BARS

Agave (アガヴェ)

BARS | In this authentic Mexican cantina, your palate will be tempted by a choice of more than 550 kinds of tequila and mezcal—Japan's largest selection. Most of the varieties here aren't available anywhere else in the country, so the steep prices may be worth paying. Foods options are mostly Mexican appetizers. Just be aware this place also offers cigars, so things can get smoky. ✉ *7–18–11 Roppongi, Minato-ku* ☎ *03/3497–0229* 🌐 *agave.jp* Ⓜ *Hibiya and Oedo subway lines, Roppongi Station (Exit 3).*

Gen Yamamoto (ゲンヤマモト)

COCKTAIL BARS | Tucked on a side street of Azabu Juban, this stylish cocktail bar has just eight counter seats, so it's worth booking ahead if you fancy trying some of the most innovative tipples in Tokyo. The bartender uses in-season Japanese produce like Okinawan pineapple and ume (apricots) from Wakayama, along with fine liquor, to produce superb cocktail tasting menus. ✉ *1–6–4 Azabu Juban, Minato-ku* ☎ *03/6434–0652* 🌐 *www.genyamamoto.jp* ⏲ *Closed Sun.–Mon.* Ⓜ *Oedo and Namboku subway lines, Azabu Juban Station (Exit 2).*

KARAOKE

Pasela Roppongi (カラオケ パセラ)

THEMED ENTERTAINMENT | This 10-story entertainment complex on the main Roppongi drag of Gaien-Higashi-dori has seven floors of karaoke rooms, some Bali-themed, with more than 10,000 foreign-song titles. Both large and small groups can be accommodated. A darts bar and a restaurant are also on-site. Rates start from ¥760 per hour, and there are also all-you-can drink deals to keep your tonsils nicely lubricated for singing. ✉ *5–16–3 Roppongi, Minato-ku* ☎ *0120/911–086* 🌐 *www.pasela.co.jp* Ⓜ *Hibiya and Oedo subway lines, Roppongi Station (Exit 3).*

MUSIC CLUBS

Billboard Live Tokyo (ビルボードライブ東京)

LIVE MUSIC | With everything from jazz and J-pop to soul and funk, this three-story joint offers one of the best food-and-live music experiences in Tokyo, all with panoramic views of Roppongi. Patrons love this venue partly because they're so close to performers like George Clinton, Neneh Cherry, and Howard Jones. Shows usually kick off at 7 and 9:30 pm on weekdays, 6 and 9 pm on Saturday, and 4:30 and 7:30 pm on Sunday. ✉ *Tokyo Midtown Garden Terr., 9–7–4 Akasaka, 4th fl.* ☎ *03/3405–1133* 🌐 *www.billboard-live.com.*

Performing Arts

FILM

Toho Cinemas Roppongi Hills (東宝シネマズ六本木ヒルズ)

FILM | **FAMILY** | This nine-screen complex has about 2,100 seats that include very comfortable, "first-class," VIP seats. It also has an extra-large screen and MediaMation MX4D technology. There are plenty of bars in the area for post-movie discussions. Late shows screen on weekends. ✉ *Keyakizaka Complex, 6–10–2 Roppongi, Minato-ku* ☎ *03/6868–5024* 🌐 *www.roppongihills.com/en/cinema* 🎟 *From ¥2,000; ¥1,300 on Wed.* Ⓜ *Hibiya and Oedo subway lines, Roppongi Station (Exits 1c and 3).*

MUSIC

Suntory Hall (サントリーホール)

CONCERTS | This lavishly appointed concert auditorium in the Ark Hills complex has probably the best acoustics in the city, and its great location allows theatergoers to extend their evening out: there's an abundance of great restaurants and bars nearby. ✉ *1–13–1 Akasaka, Minato-ku* ☎ *03/3505–1001* 🌐 *www.suntory.com/culture-sports/suntoryhall* Ⓜ *Ginza subway line, Tameike-Sanno Station (Exit 13); Namboku subway line, Roppongi-Itchome Station (Exit 3).*

CLOTHING

Restir (リステア)

CLOTHING | Next to the Midtown Tokyo complex, this fashion-forward boutique brings together a cluster of stores, with three floors of cutting-edge clothing, some of which looks like it came straight from a Tokyo or Paris catwalk, and accessories for men and women. ✉ *9–6–17 Akasaka, Minato-ku* ☎ *03/5413–3708* 🌐 *www.restir.com/en* Ⓜ *Hibiya and Oedo subway lines, Roppongi Station (Exit 8); Chiyoda subway line, Nogizaka Station (Exit 3).*

CRAFTS

Japan Traditional Crafts Aoyama Square (伝統工芸青山スクエア; *Dento Kogei Aoyama Sukuea*)

CRAFTS | North of Roppongi, near Aoyama-itchome Station, this store showcases Japan's best craft work, from paper to tools to pottery. Although prices can be high (often deservedly so), this is an excellent place to find one-of-a-kind, high-quality items. In addition to the gift shop, the center hosts rotating crafts exhibit, workshops, and demonstrations. ✉ *8–1–22 Akasaka, Minato-ku* ☎ *03/5785–1301* 🌐 *kougeihin.jp* Ⓜ *Oedo, Hanzomon and Ginza subway lines, Aoyama-itchome Station (Exit 4).*

MALLS AND SHOPPING CENTERS

Axis (アクシス)

MALL | Classy and cutting-edge furniture, electronics, fabrics, ceramics, and books are sold at this multistory design center on the main Roppongi drag of Gaien-Higashi-dori. Nuno specializes in Japanese fabrics; Le Garage has accessories for high-end cars. On the fourth floor, the JIDA Design Museum shows the best of what's current in Japanese industrial design. ✉ *5–17–1 Roppongi, Minato-ku* ☎ *03/3587–2781* 🌐 *center.axisinc.co.jp/english* Ⓜ *Hibiya and Oedo subway lines, Roppongi Station (exits 3 or 5); Namboku subway line, Roppongi Itchome Station (Exit 2).*

★ **Azabudai Hills** (麻布台ヒルズ)

SHOPPING CENTER | **FAMILY** | The area's latest ultra-sleek urban complex opened in late 2023. Like Tokyo Midtown and Roppongi Hills, it mixes office spaces with cafés, restaurants, a luxury hotel, art galleries, and plenty of high-end shops—all spread across two skyscrapers and a cluster of smaller buildings and plazas. Shop-wise, it's known for it's brand-name boutiques, such as Bulgari, Cartier, Celine, and Dior. The most notable art venue is the digital teamLab gallery, although there's also a small manga museum and the contemporary art-focused Azabudai Hills Gallery. ✉ *1–3–1 Azabudai, Minato-ku* 🌐 *www.azabudai-hills.com* Ⓜ *Hibiya subway line, Kamiyacho Station (Exit 5).*

Roppongi Hills (六本木ヒルズ)

SHOPPING CENTER | **FAMILY** | You could easily spend a whole day exploring the retail areas of this complex of shops, restaurants, residential and commercial towers, a nine-screen cineplex, the Grand Hyatt Tokyo hotel, and the Mori Art Museum—all wrapped around the TV Asahi studios and sprawled out in five zones located between the Roppongi intersection and Azabu Juban. The shops here emphasize eye-catching design and chichi brands, although finding a particular shop can be a hassle given the building's Escher-like layout. To navigate, go to the information center to retrieve a floor guide with color-coded maps in English. ✉ *6–10–1 Roppongi, Minato-ku* ☎ *03/6406–6000* 🌐 *www.roppongihills.com* Ⓜ *Hibiya and Oedo subway lines, Roppongi Station (exits 1c and 3).*

Tokyo Midtown (東京ミッドタウン)

SHOPPING CENTER | This huge complex is an architectural statement with sweeping glass roofs and a large walkable garden in the back. The airy, open spaces house exclusive boutiques, a Ritz-Carlton, galleries, and a concentration of cafés by the world's top pâtissiers on the first few floors. ✉ *9–7–1 Akasaka, Minato-ku*

☎ *03/3475–3100* 🌐 *en.tokyo-midtown.com* Ⓜ *Hibiya and Oedo subway lines, Roppongi Station (Exit 8); Chiyoda subway line, Nogizaka Station (Exit 3).*

SWORDS AND KNIVES

Japan Sword Co.

(日本刀剣; *Nippon Tokken*)

SPECIALTY STORE | Aspiring samurai can learn how to tell their *toshin* (blades) from their *tsuka* (sword handles) with help from the staff at this small shop, which has been open since the Meiji era (1868–1912). Items range from genuine antique samurai swords to inexpensive or decorative reproductions. ✉ *3–8–1 Toranomon, Minato-ku* ☎ *03/3434–4321* 🌐 *www.japansword.co.jp* Ⓜ *Hibiya and Ginza subway lines, Toranomon Station (Exit 2).*

Chapter 9

SHINJUKU

WITH IKEBUKURO

Updated by
Jay Farris

Sights	Restaurants	Hotels	Shopping	Nightlife
★★★☆☆	★★★☆☆	★★★★☆	★★★☆☆	★★★★★

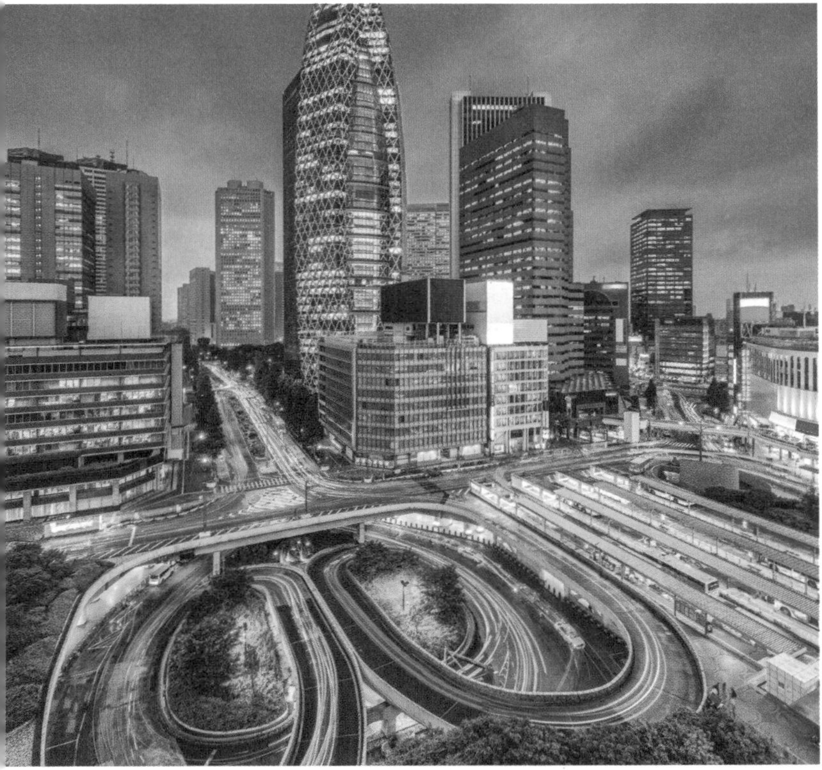

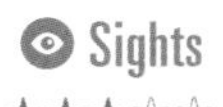

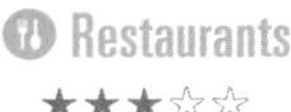

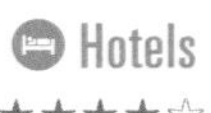

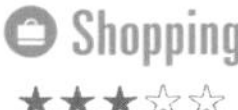

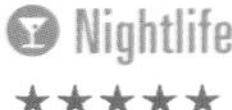

NEIGHBORHOOD SNAPSHOT

TOP EXPERIENCES

■ **The observation deck of Tokyo Metropolitan Government Building.** Gaze at Japan's most famous mountain from this observation deck. The complex also hosts open-air concerts and exhibitions.

■ **Sompo Museum of Art.** Originally founded to showcase the work of Western-style Japanese painter Seiji Togo, the gallery has since expanded to include pieces by other iconic names like Gauguin, Cezanne, and van Gogh. Van Gogh's *Sunflowers* is a highlight here.

■ **Kabuki-cho.** Tokyo is a safe metropolis, but if you wanted to see some of its seedier side, then this is the place at night. And during the day, there is all kinds of fun to be had in game centers.

GETTING HERE

From Shibuya to the south and Ikebukuro to the north, the JR Yamanote Line is one of the more common ways to reach Shinjuku Station. The Saikyo Line travels the same path less frequently, but continues out of town. The Keio and Odakyu lines serve destinations to the west. Subway lines, like the Marunouchi, Shinjuku, and Toei Oedo, are best for connections in the center of the city, such as Ote-machi, Kudanshita, or Roppongi. On foot, Kabuki-cho is accessible in minutes to the northeast. For the forest of office-building skyscrapers, go through the underground passage to the west.

PLANNING YOUR TIME

Plan at least a full day for Shinjuku if you want to see both the east and west sides. Don't rule out walking, but check your maps, and use trains for a break. Near Shinjuku Station, many underground paths are worth exploring on their own and can be a way to avoid rain. The Shinjuku Gyoen National Garden is worth at least an hour, more if you come in early April during *sakura* (cherry blossom) season. The Tokyo Metropolitan Government Building complex can take longer than you might expect as lines for the elevators to the observation decks can be long.

PAUSE HERE

■ While the name Shinjuku Southern Terrace is slightly misleading, the elevated pedestrian pathways along and across the tracks just south of Shinjuku Station can help you get between points A and B and surprise you along the way. Kids might like Suica Penguin Square (you'll see the character a lot around Tokyo's JR stations), where they can watch trains come and go. Or stroll down the path on the west side of the tracks and find Petit Delirium Tap Cafe, where you can have a beer sitting outside.

SHINJUKU BY NIGHT

■ By day, Shinjuku is a bustling center of business and government where office workers move in droves during rush hour. Although the neighborhood's rough edges have been polished to a more tourist friendly shine, Shinjuku is still a fascinating place at night. The area is inundated with flashing signs, and a darker side of Tokyo emerges, has hordes leave their offices and head out for drinks, food, and sometimes, sex.

If you like the grittiness and chaos of big cities, you're bound to love Shinjuku: Come here, and Tokyo begins to seem *real*: all the celebrated virtues of Japanese society—its safety and order, its grace and beauty, its cleanliness and civility—fray at the edges.

To be fair, the area has been on the fringes of respectability for centuries. When Ieyasu, the first Tokugawa shogun, made Edo his capital, Shinjuku was at the junction of two important arteries leading into the city from the west. It became a thriving post station, where travelers would rest up for the last leg of their journey; the appeal of this suburban pit stop was its "teahouses," where the waitresses dispensed a bit more than tea.

When the Tokugawa dynasty collapsed in 1867, reformers restored direct power to the 16-year-old emperor, Meiji, who moved his residence from Kyoto to Edo, which was renamed Tokyo by 1868. Modern Shinjuku became the railroad hub connecting Edo to Japan's western provinces. In the 1930s, Shinjuku was the bohemian quarter, a haunt for artists, writers, and student. The area was virtually leveled during the fire bombings of 1945—a blank slate on which developers could write, as Tokyo surged west after the war.

Now, by day the east side of Shinjuku Station has an astonishing concentration of retail stores, vertical malls, and discounters of every stripe. By night, activity shifts to the nearby red-light quarter of Kabuki-cho, which has an equally astonishing collection of bars and clubs, strip joints, hole-in-the-wall restaurants, pachinko parlors (an upright pinball game), and peep shows—just about anything that amuses, arouses, alters, or intoxicates is for sale. Police have attempted to crack down and limit some of the adult activity, but whatever you're after is probably still here if you know where to look.

North of the area is Ikebukuro, a bustling neighborhood that is the nearest urban center to Tokyo's northern suburbs. Many Shinjuku stores have set up shop in Ikebukuro, too, but here they are often larger (like the main branch of the Seibu department store, which is undergoing renovations) to accommodate the suburban crowds.

Shinjuku

Sights

Hanazono Jinja Shrine (花園神社)
RELIGIOUS BUILDING | Prayers offered at this shrine, originally constructed in the early Edo period, are believed to bring prosperity in business. Although it isn't among Tokyo's most beautiful shrines, it does host festivals, and it has a long history and an interesting location. It's a five-minute walk north on Meiji-dori from the Shinjuku-sanchome subway station, and the back of it is adjacent to

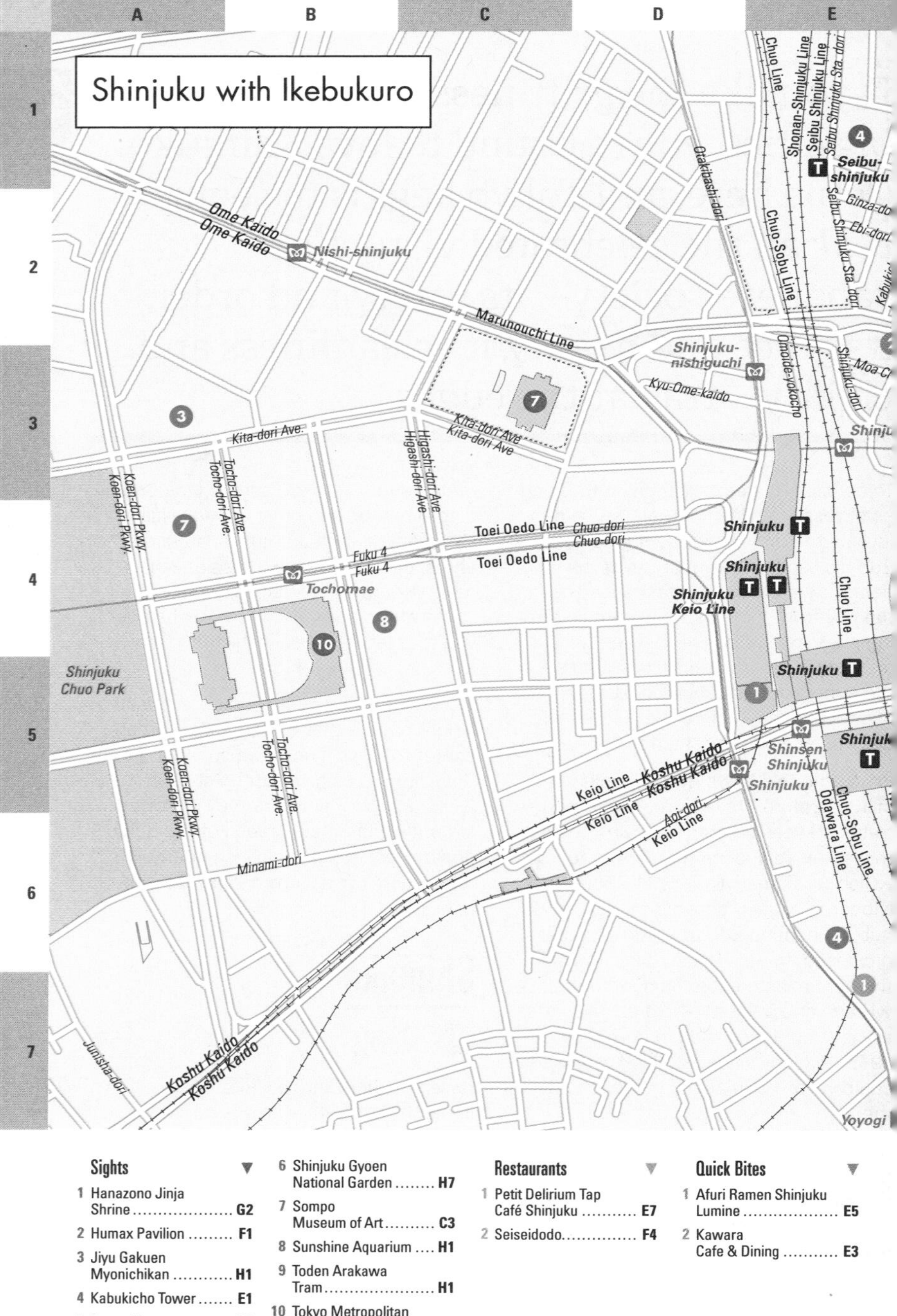

Sights

1 Hanazono Jinja Shrine **G2**

2 Humax Pavilion **F1**

3 Jiyu Gakuen Myonichikan **H1**

4 Kabukicho Tower **E1**

5 Paper Museum **H1**

6 Shinjuku Gyoen National Garden **H7**

7 Sompo Museum of Art **C3**

8 Sunshine Aquarium **H1**

9 Toden Arakawa Tram **H1**

10 Tokyo Metropolitan Government Building... **B4**

Restaurants

1 Petit Delirium Tap Café Shinjuku **E7**

2 Seiseidodo............... **F4**

Quick Bites

1 Afuri Ramen Shinjuku Lumine **E5**

2 Kawara Cafe & Dining **E3**

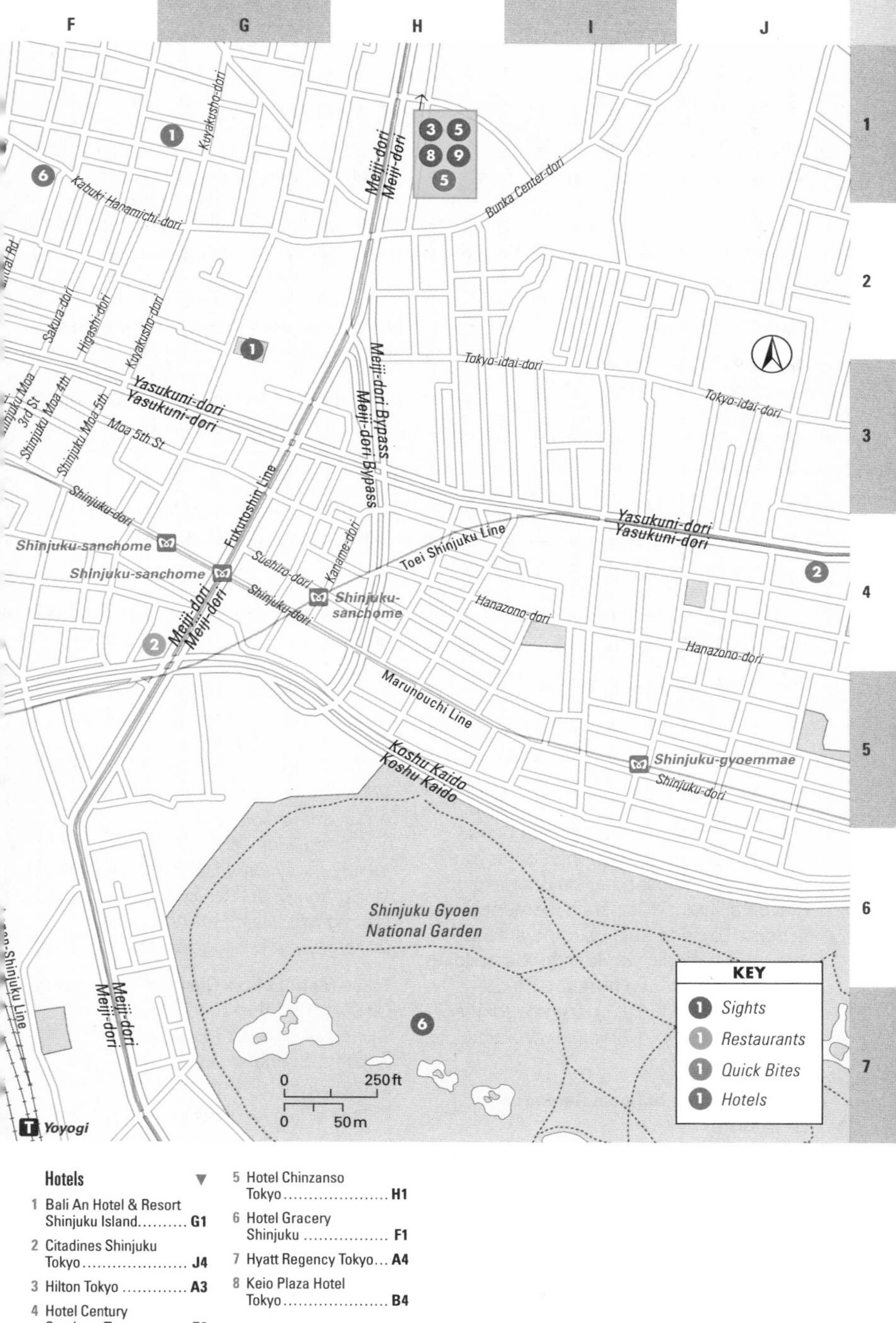

Hotels ▼

1 Bali An Hotel & Resort Shinjuku Island.......... **G1**

2 Citadines Shinjuku Tokyo...................... **J4**

3 Hilton Tokyo **A3**

4 Hotel Century Southern Tower......... **E6**

5 Hotel Chinzanso Tokyo...................... **H1**

6 Hotel Gracery Shinjuku **F1**

7 Hyatt Regency Tokyo... **A4**

8 Keio Plaza Hotel Tokyo...................... **B4**

the so-called Golden-Gai, a district of tiny, fascinating *nomiya* (bars) that, in the '60s and '70s, commanded the fierce loyalty of fiction writers, artists, freelance journalists, and expat Japanophiles—all the city's hard-core outsiders. ✉ *5–17–3 Shinjuku, Shinjuku-ku* ☎ *03/3209–5265* 🎫 *Free* Ⓜ *Marunouchi and Fukutoshin subway lines, Shinjuku-san-chome Station (Exits B2 and B3).*

Humax Pavilion (ヒューマックスパビリオン)
ARCADE | **FAMILY** | Set amid the chaos of Kabuki-cho, this multilevel entertainment complex is a place where you can shoot a few games of pool, recline in a sauna, indulge in karaoke, or sharpen your skills at any number of video games. ✉ *1–20–1 Kabuki-cho, Shinjuku-ku* Ⓜ *JR Shinjuku Station (Higashi-guchi/East Exit) and Marunouchi subway line (Exits B10, B11, B12, and B13).*

Kabukicho Tower (東急歌舞伎町タワー)
ARCADE | **FAMILY** | Kabukicho Tower is just next to the Humax Pavillion and has some of the same offerings, albeit on a much larger scale and at slightly higher prices. Need a snack? Want to play some video games? See a movie or a band? With a food floor and game floors, you could probably spend all day here—and maybe all night, too. The basement level is home to Zepp Shinjuku, the area's largest live-music venue, and the building is also home to two hotels. ✉ *1–29–1 Kabukicho, Shinjuku-ku* 🌐 *www.tokyu-kabukicho-tower.jp* Ⓜ *Shinjuku or Seibu Shinjuku stations.*

Shinjuku Gyoen National Garden (新宿御苑)
GARDEN | **FAMILY** | This lovely, 144-acre garden was once the estate of the powerful Naito family of feudal lords, who were among the most trusted retainers of the Tokugawa shoguns. After World War II, the grounds were opened to the public. It's a perfect place for leisurely walks: paths wind past ponds and bridges, artificial hills, thoughtfully placed stone lanterns, and more than 3,000 kinds of plants, shrubs, and trees. There are different gardens in Japanese, French, and English styles, as well as a greenhouse (the nation's first, built in 1885) filled with tropical plants. The best times to visit are April, when 75 different species of cherry trees—some 1,500 trees in all—are in bloom, and the first two weeks of November, during the chrysanthemum exhibition. ✉ *11 Naito-machi, Shinjuku-ku* ☎ *03/3350–0151* 🌐 *www.env.go.jp/garden/shinjukugyoen* 🎫 *¥500* ⏲ *Closed most Mon.* Ⓜ *Marunouchi subway line, Shinjuku Gyo-en-mae Station (Exit 1).*

Sompo Museum of Art (東郷青児美術館 *Sompo Japan Togo Seiji Bijutsukan*)
ART MUSEUM | The multilevel museum began its life as a place to showcase works by painter Seiji Togo (1897–1978), who was a master at capturing grace on canvas. Today, it exhibits his work alongside pieces by other Japanese and Western artists, such as Gauguin and Cezanne. The museum is also home to van Gogh's *Sunflowers.* ✉ *1–26–1 Nishi-Shinjuku, Shinjuku-ku* ☎ *03/5777–8600* 🌐 *www.sompo-museum.org/en* 🎫 *Admission fees vary by exhibit* ⏲ *Closed Mon.* Ⓜ *Marunouchi and Shinjuku subway lines, JR rail lines; Shinjuku Station (Exit A18 for subway lines, Nishi-guchi/West Exit or Exit N4 from the underground passageway for all others).*

Tokyo Metropolitan Government Building (東京都庁; *Tokyo Tocho*)
VIEWPOINT | **FAMILY** | Dominating the western Shinjuku skyline, this grandiose, Kenzo Tange–designed complex seems to serve as a reminder that Tokyo's annual budget is bigger than that of some countries. Several other area skyscrapers have free observation floors, but those—on the 45th floors of both towers (663 feet above ground)—at city hall are the best. On a clear day, you can see all the way to Mt. Fuji, as well as to the Boso Peninsula in Chiba Prefecture. The Metropolitan Government website, incidentally,

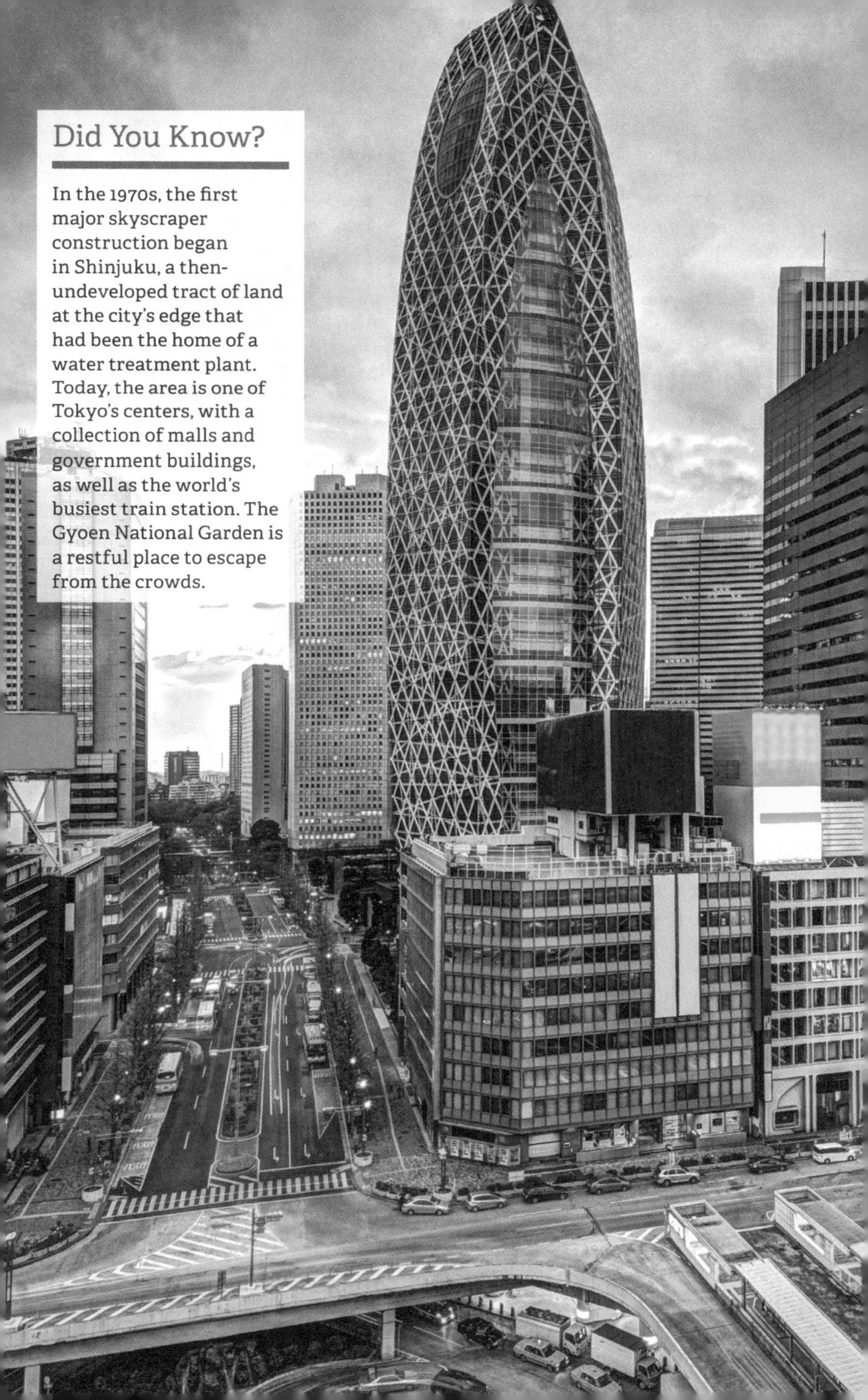

Did You Know?

In the 1970s, the first major skyscraper construction began in Shinjuku, a then-undeveloped tract of land at the city's edge that had been the home of a water treatment plant. Today, the area is one of Tokyo's centers, with a collection of malls and government buildings, as well as the world's busiest train station. The Gyoen National Garden is a restful place to escape from the crowds.

is an excellent source of information on sightseeing and current events in Tokyo. *✉ 2–8–1 Nishi-Shinjuku, Shinjuku-ku ☎ 03/5321–1111 🌐 www.metro.tokyo.jp/english/offices/observat.html 🎫 Free ⏲ South Observation Deck closed 1st and 3rd Tues. North Observation Deck closed 2nd and 4th Mon. Ⓜ ToeiOedo subway line, Tocho-mae Station (Exit A4).*

Restaurants

Huge varieties of cuisine are available at local restaurants, tucked into narrow lanes or on upper floors of buildings. Also, department stores in the area have impressive *depachika* basement food levels.

Petit Delirium Tap Café Shinjuku
$$$ | **EUROPEAN** | This could be considered a drinking establishment, thanks to its wine selection and its surprising variety of mostly Belgian and craft beers, but its range of meat plates, tapas, and appetizers also makes it a great place for a full meal at lunch or dinner. It's housed in an unimposing building at the far end of Shinjuku Station's outdoor Southern Terrace. **Known for:** wide variety of beers; eclectic European-focused fare; comfortable outdoor seating. *$ Average main: ¥5,000 ✉ 2–2–1 Yoyogi, Shinjuku-ku ✣ Walk to the end of Shinjuku Southern Terrace west of the tracks. ☎ 03/6300–0807 🌐 www.deliriumcafe.jp/shinjuku Ⓜ Shinjuku Station.*

Seiseidodo (正々堂々)
$$$$ | **JAPANESE** | If you're feeling adventurous, check out this *izakaya*'s seafood-focused dishes, which pair nicely a cup of sake and which do not disappoint. The daily menu is often hand-written, though, so unless you read Japanese, be nice to the wait staff, and trust them to help you make a selection. **Known for:** large variety of seasonal dishes; particularly busy on weekends; close to Shinjuku Sanchome Station. *$ Average main: ¥7,000 ✉ Shinjuku 3–9–7, T&T Building, Shinjuku-ku ✣ A few steps away from Shinjuku Sanchome's C6 exit. ☎ 03/5368–0640 ⏲ Closed Mon. No lunch Ⓜ Shinjuku Sanchome Station, Marunouchi and Shinjuku subway lines.*

Coffee and Quick Bites

Afuri Ramen Shinjuku Lumine
(新宿ルミネ; *Afuri*)
$ | **JAPANESE** | Just south of the Shinjuku station, on a basement food level of Shinjuku's Lumine I department store, this branch of a ramen-house chain serves its noodles with a broth that has hints of citrus, turning what can be a heavy dish into something more refreshing (and even free of meat if you like). **Known for:** a light version of the sometimes heavy ramen; very unusual citrusy broth; lively atmosphere. *$ Average main: ¥1,000 ✉ 1–1–2 Nishishinjuku, Lumine I, Basement Level 2, Shinjuku-ku ☎ 03/5990–5182 🌐 www.afuri.com Ⓜ Shinjuku Station.*

Kawara Cafe & Dining (新宿東口店)
$$ | **JAPANESE FUSION** | Offering a bird's eye view of happenings below, this 8th-floor restaurant combines Japanese and Western ingredients to create modern home cooking–style dishes. A picture menu before the elevator let's you decide on your selection before you even go in. **Known for:** hearty lunches; great street views; modern Japanese home-cooking. *$ Average main: ¥1,500 ✉ Pandora Building, 3–23–12 Shinjuku, 8th fl., Shinjuku-ku ☎ 03/3355–3180 🌐 www.dd-holdings.jp/shops/kawaracafedining/shinjuku-higashiguchi# Ⓜ Shinjuku Station.*

Hotels

Home to what is known to be the world's busiest train hub, Shinjuku attracts business and leisure travelers. The west side of the station includes numerous big-name international chains, while the opposite side offers a number of domestic chains.

Bali An Hotel & Resort Shinjuku Island (ホテルバリアン新宿アイランド)
$ | **HOTEL** | If you need a vacation from your vacation, then step off of Shinjuku's streets and into this Balinese-themed fantasy island, one of Tokyo's many "love hotels" that happens to offer both nice overnight accommodations and a quintessential Japanese experience (in general, people come to a love hotel for fun rather as a place to stay). **Pros:** a whole variety of interesting food and drinks available; all kinds of amenities on offer as you check in; activities like karaoke in your room. **Cons:** the neighborhood can be sketchy at night; not a place to stay for multiple nights; time limits on use and extra fees for staying longer. *Rooms from: ¥20,000 2–22–10 Kabukicho, Shinjuku-ku 0120/759–184 www.balian.jp/shop/shinjuku_island 79 rooms No Meals Fukutoshin, Marunouchi, and Shinjuku lines, Shinjuku Sanchome Station (Exit E1).*

Citadines Shinjuku Tokyo (シタディーン新宿)
$$ | **HOTEL** | While short-term guests can appreciate the amenities, the Citadines Shinjuku is also a bright bit of value for long-term travelers—a place where primary colors and attentive staffers greet you in the lobby, and guest rooms are cheerfully decorated and practically outfitted. **Pros:** away from the congestion of Shinjuku Station; sizable rooms; contemporary rooms with pops of color. **Cons:** a little difficult to find; limited on-site dining options; a bit of a walk to Shinjuku's sights. *Rooms from: ¥30,000 1–28–13 Shinjuku, Shinjuku-ku 03/5379–7208 www.discoverasr.com 160 apartments No Meals Marunouchi subway line, Shinjuku Gyoemmae Station (Exit 2).*

Hilton Tokyo (ヒルトン東京)
$$ | **HOTEL** | At this behemoth hotel, the lobby—where a staircase leads to a mezzanine floor and a bar-lounge—has a surprisingly human scale, and sizable guest rooms have soft, relaxing color schemes and such Japanese touches as the shoji screen, a constant since the hotel's opening in 1963. **Pros:** great gym; convenient location; free shuttle to Shinjuku Station. **Cons:** hotel lobby can get busy; restaurants are pricey; few sightseeing options nearby. *Rooms from: ¥50,000 6–6–2 Nishi-Shinjuku, Shinjuku-ku 03/3344–5111 www.hilton.com 811 rooms No Meals Shinjuku Station (Nishi-guchi/West Exit); Marunouchi subway line, Nishi-Shinjuku Station (Exit C8); Oedo subway line, Tocho-mae Station (all exits).*

Hotel Century Southern Tower (小田急ホテルセンチュリーサザンタワー)
$$ | **HOTEL** | A wonderful location—atop the 35-floor Odakyu Southern Tower, minutes on foot from Shinjuku Station—and several on-site dining options are the main draws at this hotel. **Pros:** convenient location; great views; simple but tasteful rooms. **Cons:** room amenities are basic; business hotel feel; small rooms. *Rooms from: ¥40,000 2–2–1 Yoyogi, Shibuya-ku 03/5354–0111 global.southerntower.co.jp/hotel 375 rooms No Meals Shinjuku Station (Minami-guchi/South Exit); Oedo and Shinjuku subway lines, Shinjuku Station (Exit A1).*

Hotel Gracery Shinjuku (ホテルグレイスリー新宿)
$$ | **HOTEL** | With a giant Godzilla head on the eighth-floor lobby terrace and one special guest room with movie posters, a rubber monster suit, and a giant claw emerging from a headboard, the Gracery is a good choice for fans of the silver screen's top prehistoric creature. **Pros:** convenient to Shinjuku Station; easy access to bars and restaurants; Godzilla theme. **Cons:** noise from construction by day and red-light-district crowds at night; kitsch might not appeal to everyone; rooms on small side. *Rooms from: ¥30,000 1–19–1 Kabukicho, Shinjuku-ku 03/6833–2489 shinjuku.*

The Red Lights of Kabuki-cho

Tokyo has more than its fair share of red-light districts, but the leader of the pack is unquestionably Kabuki-cho, located just north of Shinjuku Station. The land was once a swamp, although its current name refers to an aborted post–World War II effort to bring culture to the area in the form of a landmark Kabuki theater. Most of the entertainment has traditionally been the insalubrious kind, with strip clubs, love hotels, host and hostess clubs, and thinly disguised brothels all luridly advertising their presence.

Since the mid-2000s, however, the area has undergone a clean-up (similar to the one done to New York's Times Square in the 1990s) to draw in more tourists. Nowadays, despite its sordid reputation, Kabuki-cho does have attractions beyond the red lights, including eateries—from chain diners to designer restaurants—galore,

The area was also once home to throngs of Japanese and Chinese gangsters, giving rise to its image domestically as a danger zone. But in truth, the Kabuki-cho of today poses little risk even to the solo traveler. The sheer volume of people in the area each night, combined with a prominent security-camera presence, means that crime stays mostly indoors.

gracery.com ⇨ *970 rooms* 🍽 *No Meals* Ⓜ *JR subway lines, Shinjuku Station (East Exit).*

Hyatt Regency Tokyo (ハイアットリージェンシー 東京)
$$ | **HOTEL** | Snuggled amid the skyscrapers of Shinjuku, this hotel has Hyatt's trademark, atrium-style lobby—seven stories high, with glass elevators soaring upward—and as well as rooms that are spacious rooms, if somewhat unremarkable in design. **Pros:** friendly staff; familiar surroundings; spacious rooms. **Cons:** rather generic exteriors and common areas; restaurant options are limited outside hotel; a bit sterile. Ⓢ *Rooms from: ¥38,000* ✉ *2–7–2 Nishi-Shinjuku, Shinjuku-ku* ☎ *03/3348–1234* 🌐 *www.hyatt.com* ⇨ *744 rooms* 🍽 *No Meals* Ⓜ *Marunouchi subway line, Nishi-Shinjuku Station (Exit C8); Oedo subway line, Tocho-mae Station (all exits).*

Keio Plaza Hotel Tokyo (京王プラザホテル)
$$ | **HOTEL** | Although some areas of this hotel are nondescript, it has a remarkable variety of contemporary accommodations, including fully accessible rooms and those with as many as four beds. **Pros:** nice pool and gym; fairly reasonable rates; convenient location. **Cons:** not all guests can use the pool for free; dining options outside the hotel are limited; can be crowded with conventioneers. Ⓢ *Rooms from: ¥40,000* ✉ *2–2–1 Nishi-Shinjuku, Shinjuku-ku* ☎ *03/3344–0111* 🌐 *www.keioplaza.com* ⇨ *1,436 rooms* 🍽 *No Meals* Ⓜ *Shinjuku or Nishi-Shinjuku on the Marunouchi subway line.*

Nightlife

Shinjuku has everything, but don't forget to look up. East of the station, the area is littered with *izakayas* and other varieties of gastropubs serving the many office workers looking to loosen up. A bit farther east takes you to Shinjuku Sanchome (Shinjuku 3), where many more casual bars—some that are set up for just standing around—and restaurants spill onto the streets. And a trip a bit farther east from there lands you in Shinjuku Nichome (Shinjuku 2), which probably has one of the world's highest concentration of gay bars, many of them, like the rest of Shinjuku, occupying upper floors.

There are also many tucked-away enclaves that have their own charms. Golden-gai, long the haunt of artists and misfits, is the perfect example of Tokyo's history still on display. Between Hanazono Jinja Shrine and the much more in-your-face hawking of Kabuki-cho, Golden-gai is a series of narrow alleys and tiny bars you might find yourself wedging yourself into for a unique vibe, music, or the conversation. Whatever you're looking for after dark, Shinjuku can likely provide it.

BARS

Bar Albatross

BARS | An eclectic clientele is drawn to this tiny, artsy bar decorated with gilt-framed paintings, deer heads, and numerous chandeliers. Luckily, its sign will light your way in Golden-Gai's tiny alleys. ✉ *1–1–7 Kabuki-cho, 5th Golden Gai St., Shinjuku-ku* ☎ *03/3203–3699* 🌐 *www.alba-s.com/#/f2* Ⓜ *JR and Marunouchi subway lines, Shinjuku Station (East Exit).*

Donzoko (どん底)

BARS | This venerable bar claims to be Shinjuku's oldest—established in 1951—and has hosted actors and filmmakers like Yukio Mishima and Akira Kurosawa among many other luminaries. It's also one of several bars that claim to have invented the popular *chu-hai* cocktail (*shochu*, a distilled grain spirit, with juice and soda). The atmosphere is vibrant, the four floors are almost always packed, and food is served. There is a small outdoor seating area, but keep in mind that smoking is allowed in some areas. ✉ *3–10–2 Shinjuku, Shinjuku-ku* ☎ *03/3354–7749* 🌐 *www.donzoko.co.jp* Ⓜ *Marunouchi and Shinjuku subway lines, Shinju-ku-san-chome Station (Exit C3).*

La Jetée

BARS | Covered in Euro-cinema posters and named after a French movie, La Jetée is a tiny bar, which makes conversing (in Japanese, French, or English) a challenge. To find it, look for the he cats painted on the door, and head up the narrow staircase. If you can't find it, Golden Gai has hundreds of other equally quirky and hard-to-find places you might stumble upon. ✉ *1–1–6 Kabuki-cho, 2nd fl., Shinjuku-ku* ☎ *03/3208–9645* 🌐 *www.lajetee.org* Ⓜ *JR and Marunouchi subway lines, Shinjuku Station (East Exit).*

GAY BARS

Aiiro Cafe (藍色酒場; *Aiiro Sakaba*)

BARS | Many great gay nights out begin at this welcoming street-corner bar, which is hard to miss because of its *torii* shrine gate and all the patrons spilling out onto the street. This is the perfect place to put back a few cocktails, meet new people, and get a feeling for where to go next. The crowd is mixed, with locals and visitors mingling for hours or just meeting up for a quick drink. ✉ *Tenka Bldg., 2–18–1 Shinjuku, Shinjuku-ku* ☎ *03/6273–0740* 🌐 *aliving.net/aiirocafe* Ⓜ *Shinjuku Sanchome Station, Marunouchi and Shinjuku subway lines.*

Arty Farty (アーティファーティ)

BARS | Cheap and cheesy, Arty Farty is hit or miss. It's a good spot to go with a group of friends to kind of take over the place. Or it might be a nice spot for single travelers to find a group of like-minded folks. Be ready to pay to get in, though this cover charge does include a drink. ✉ *Kyutei Bldg., 2–11–7 Shinjuku, 2nd fl., Shinjuku-ku* ☎ *03/5362–9720* 🌐 *artyfarty.jp* Ⓜ *Shinjuku Sanchome Station, Marunouchi and Shinjuku subway lines.*

Dragon Men

DANCE CLUB | This might be Tokyo's swankiest gay lounge—just over-the-top enough to put you in the mood for a great night out. It hosts a variety of DJs, as well as nights with go-go boys, and the staff will

Kabuki-cho is a brightly lit hub for izakaya, pachinko parlors, and karaoke.

whip you up a cocktail as soon as you can make your way to the bar. ✉ *Stork Nagasaki, 2–11–4 Shinjuku, Shinjuku-ku* ☎ *03/3341–0606* 🌐 *www.instagram.com/dragon.men* Ⓜ *Marunouchi subway line, Shinjuku-san-chome Station.*

GB

BARS | Claiming to be the one of the friendliest bars in the neighborhood, GB has been a fixture in the Ni-chome gay district for decades. On weekends, rather quiet and reserved gentlemen, mostly in their thirties and forties, gather around the wooden bar, and it is also quite popular among foreign residents and visitors—especially before a night out. ✉ *Shinjuku Plaza Bldg., 2–12–3 Shinjuku, B1 fl., Shinjuku-ku* ☎ *03/3352–8972* 🌐 *gb-tokyo.com* Ⓜ *Marunouchi subway line, Shinjuku-san-chome Station.*

Gold Finger

BARS | With vintage lamps and a café-like ambience, this is a relaxed, cozy bar for women. Men accompanied by women are welcome on most days, but Saturday is a women-only night. The location on a lively corner in the center of the Ni-chome LGBTQ+ area makes it another good starting point for a night out. It also hosts events that you might want to stay for. ✉ *Hayashi Bldg., 2–12–11 Shinjuku, Shinjuku-ku* ☎ *03/6383–4649* 🌐 *www.goldfingerparty.com/bar* Ⓜ *Marunouchi subway line, Shinjuku Sanchome Station.*

JAZZ CLUBS

Café Cotton Club

LIVE MUSIC | Though there's jazz here most nights, on Friday evenings, the basement of this club is the place to be for nearby, sister-property Jazz Spot Intro's jam sessions. You can enjoy Tokyo's take on Italian food while you're waiting for the music to start. ✉ *1–17–14 Takadanobaba, Sounds Bldg., Shinjuku-ku* ☎ *03/3207–3369* 🌐 *www.cafecottonclub.com* Ⓜ *Takadanobaba Station, JR Yamanote Line, Tozai subway line.*

Jazz Spot Intro (イントロ)

LIVE MUSIC | This small basement jazz joint hosts many up-and-coming acts from around Tokyo nightly. Though these jam sessions often don't cost more than the

Tokyo's LGBTQ+ Scene

Though Tokyo's late-April Rainbow Pride event attracts hundreds of thousands and the LGBTQ+ presence on TV is increasing, most gay life still takes place under the radar. Even so, there's less prejudice than you might experience elsewhere. Farther afield, some are more likely to be baffled than upset by same-sex couples, and some hotels may "not compute" that a same-sex couple would like a double bed. With a little digging you'll find a scene more vibrant than you—or many Tokyoites—might expect.

The primary LGBTQ+ hub is Ni-chome in the Shinjuku area (take the Shinjuku or Marunouchi subway line to Shinjuku-Sanchome Station; Exit C7). Although the neighborhood is sometimes likened to its more notorious neighbor, Kabuki-cho, and its name might be spoken in hushed tones by some people, Ni-chome is calmer and safer than the red-light district.

LBGTQ+ establishments can be found sprinkled in other areas, too, among them Shibuya, Asakusa, Ueno, and, notably, Shinbashi—where clusters of gay bars near the station are cheek-by-jowl with establishments that cater to hard-drinking businessmen out for a night on the town.

price of a drink; other nights, when well-known acts are playing, there's a cover charge. Either way, this place provides some of the best jazz experiences in Tokyo, particularly during Saturday evening jam sessions. A Friday night jam session and other events are held at its sister location, the Cotton Club, which has more space and serves Italian food. ✉ *NT Bldg., 2–14–8 Takadanobaba, B1 fl., Shinjuku-ku* ☎ *03/3200–4396* 🌐 *www.intro.co.jp* Ⓜ *JR Takadanobaba Station (Waseda Exit).*

Shinjuku Pit Inn (ピットイン)
LIVE MUSIC | They say that most major jazz musicians have played at least once in this classic Tokyo club now tucked into a basement. It stages mostly mainstream fare with the odd foray into the avant-garde. The emphasis here is strictly on jazz—and the place resembles a small concert hall. Entry runs ¥3,000 in the evenings and includes a drink. Some shows are pricier, and you might want a reservation. ✉ *Accord Shinjuku Bldg., 2–12–4 Shinjuku, B1 fl., Shinjuku-ku* ☎ *03/3354–2024* 🌐 *pit-inn.com/e* Ⓜ *Marunouchi subway line, Shinju-ku-san-chome Station.*

Performing Arts

DANCE

Samurai Restaurant Time
OTHER DANCE | With all the neon and flashes of light, this dance performance with dubious foundations in historical reality is outrageous in all the right ways. During breaks between acts, which can last a while, you can grab the food or the sake on offer, but you're likely better off doing so elsewhere before or after the show. Reservations can be made online or by phone. ✉ *Kabukicho 1–7–7, Shinjuku-ku* ☎ *03/6205–6100* 🌐 *samurai-restaurant.tokyo/reservation/index.php* Ⓜ *Shinjuku Station.*

MUSIC

New National Theater and Tokyo Opera City Concert Hall (新国立劇場; *Shin Kokuritsu Gekijo*)
CONCERTS | With its 1,632-seat main auditorium, this venue nourishes Japan's fledgling efforts to make a name for itself in the world of opera and other performing arts. The Opera City Concert Hall has a massive pipe organ and hosts Tokyo's symphony, domestic and international

visiting orchestras, and other performers. The complex also includes an art gallery. ✉ *1–1–1 Honmachi, Shibuya-ku, Shinjuku-ku* ☎ *03/5353–0788, 03/5353–9999 ticket center* 🌐 *www.nntt.jac.go.jp/english* 🎫 *From ¥3,500* Ⓜ *Keio Shin-sen line, Hatsudai Station (Higashi-guchi/East Exit).*

Zepp Shinjuku

MUSIC | Occupying the lower levels of Kabukicho Tower, Zepp claims to be the areas largest live music venue. Mostly hosting domestic artists, the four-story, underground facility might be a place for you to discover your next favorite Japanese band. Check their online schedule. Entry prices vary by event. ✉ *Kabukicho 1–29–1, Basement levels 1–4, Shinjuku-ku* ✥ *Basement levels of Kabukicho Tower* ☎ *03/6380–3741* 🌐 *www.zepp.co.jp/hall/shinjuku* Ⓜ *Shinjuku Station.*

Shopping

Shinjuku might have its grit and sleaze, but it also has some of the city's most popular department stores. Shoppers here are a mix of Tokyo youth and office workers.

BOOKS

Books Kinokuniya Tokyo (紀伊国屋)

BOOKS | Not to be confused with its flagship store near the East Exit of Shinjuku Station, this bookstore is connected to Takashimaya department store and is accessible via Shinjuku's Southern Terrace. The sixth floor is devoted to non-Japanese texts with predominantly English titles. It also has excellent selection of travel guides, magazines, and books on Japan. ✉ *Takashimaya Times Sq., 5–24–2 Sendagaya, 6th floor, Shibuya-ku* ☎ *03/5361–3316* 🌐 *store.kinokuniya.co.jp/store* Ⓜ *JR Yamanote Line, Shinjuku Station (Minami-guchi/South Exit); Fukutoshin subway line, Shinjuku Sanchome Station (Exit E8).*

CRAFTS

Bingo-ya (備後屋)

CRAFTS | You could almost do all your souvenir shopping here, where the inventory features tastefully selected and displayed traditional handicrafts from all over Japan. Look for ceramics, toys, lacquerware, Noh mask, fabrics, and lots more. ✉ *10–6 Wakamatsucho, Shinjuku-ku* ☎ *03/3202–8778* 🌐 *bingoya.tokyo* Ⓜ *Oedo subway line, Wakamatsu Kawada Station (Kawada Exit).*

★ **Kukuli** (くくり)

CRAFTS | This tiny store in charming Kagurasaka sells scarves, wraps, and linens made of all kinds of fabrics—sometimes even vintage textiles—from different regions of Japan. ✉ *1–10 Tsukudocho, Shinjuku-ku* ☎ *03/6280–8462* 🌐 *kukuli.co.jp* Ⓜ *Chuo-Sobu subway line, Iidabashi Station.*

DEPARTMENT STORES

Don Quijote (ドンキホーテ)

DEPARTMENT STORE | **FAMILY** | This massive store with branches all over the country is a bargain-hunters dream, though shopping here can be a claustrophobic experience. It's packed with eclectic discount merchandise—watches, used luxury handbags, costumes, cosmetics, family-size bags of Japanese snacks—that is stacked haphazardly from floor to ceiling. The store is also open 24 hours, which means there's ample opportunity for both shopping and people-watching. ✉ *1–16–5 Kabuki-cho, Shinjuku-ku* ☎ *03/5291–9211* 🌐 *www.donki.com/en* Ⓜ *Marunouchi, Oedo, and Shinjuku subway lines, JR Yamanote Line, Keio and Odakyu lines, Shinjuku Station (Higashi-guchi/East Exit).*

Isetan (伊勢丹)

DEPARTMENT STORE | Shopping at Isetan, which was established in 1886 and is known in Japan and abroad for its high-end fashions, is one of the most pleasant retail experiences in the city. Its upper floors are a mix of clothes, cosmetics, foods, and drinks; its basement food court, which has both traditional and modern offerings, is the largest one inside a Tokyo department store. In addition, Isetan is directly connected to Shinjuku's maze of underground pathways. ✉ *3–14–1 Shinjuku, Shinjuku-ku* ☎ *03/3225–2514* 🌐 *www.mistore.jp* Ⓜ *JR Yamanote Line, Marunouchi subway line, Shinjuku Station (Higashi-guchi/East Exit for JR, Exits B2, B3, B4, and B5 for subway line).*

★ **Shinjuku Marui - Main Building** (新宿マルイ本館)
DEPARTMENT STORE | **FAMILY** | Almost ubiquitous at Tokyo's major stations and easily recognized by its giant O|O| logo, Marui burst onto the retail scene in the 1980s, when it was one of the first department stores in Japan to offer an in-store credit card. With four buildings—Marui Honkan, Marui Annex, Marui One, and Marui Mens—this branch is by far the area's largest department store, and the variety on offer makes each building worth a visit. Of course, as with all Tokyo shopping adventures, there are also dining options. ✉ *3–30–13 Shinjuku, Shinjuku-ku* ☎ *03/3354–0101* 🌐 *www.0101.co.jp* Ⓜ *JR Yamanote Line, Shinjuku Station (Higashi-guchi/East Exit); Marunouchi, Shinjuku, and Fukutoshin subway lines, Shinjuku San-chome Station (Exit A1).*

Takashimaya Shinjuku (高島屋)
DEPARTMENT STORE | **FAMILY** | Like many Japanese department stores, each of Takashimaya's floors is dedicated to labels with similar price points, but here, the north half of each floor is for women and south half is for men, so couples and families can shop on the same floors. The basement-level food court carries every gastronomic delight imaginable, and the whole complex is linked to ground- and terrace-level shops as well as to the station. In addition, Kinokuniya book shop is nearby, as is the Ikea-like Japanese retailer, Nitori. ✉ *Takashimaya Times Sq., 5–24–2 Sendagaya, Shibuya-ku* ☎ *03/5361–1111* 🌐 *www.takashimaya.co.jp/shinjuku* Ⓜ *JR Yamanote Line, Shinjuku Station (Minami-guchi/South Exit); Fukutoshin subway line, Shinjuku San-chome Station (Exit E8).*

ELECTRONICS

Bic Camera Shinjuku East Exit (ビックカメラ新宿東口店; *Bikku Kamera Shinjuku Higashi-guchi ten*)
ELECTRONICS | One of Tokyo's largest discount electronics stores, Bic Camera is one has multiple locations around the city and the station. Although you can shop for cameras and parts, this retailer also has everything from beauty products you never knew existed to the latest in rice cookers. ✉ *3–29–1 Shinjuku, Shinjuku-ku* ☎ *03/5312–1111* 🌐 *www.biccamera.com* Ⓜ *Marunouchi, Oedo, and Shinjuku subway lines, JR Yamanote Line, Keio and Odakyu lines, Shinjuku Station (Higashi-guchi/East Exit).*

Yodobashi Camera (ヨドバシカメラ)
ELECTRONICS | Another of Tokyo's electronics superstores is made up of several annexes, including a watch, hobby, and professional camera building, that together span several surrounding blocks. ✉ *1–11–1 Nishi-Shinjuku, Shinjuku-ku* ☎ *03/3346–1010* 🌐 *www.yodobashi.com* Ⓜ *Marunouchi, Shinjuku, and Oedo subway lines, JR Yamanote Line, Keio and Odakyu lines, Shinjuku Station (Nishi-guchi/West Exit).*

JEWELRY AND WATCHES

Komehyo Shinjuku (コメ兵新宿)
JEWELRY & WATCHES | Reselling a variety of name-brand goods, this retailer's three separate stores—one for men, one for women, and one for watches and jewelry—occupy a block east of Shinjuku Station and are like well-curated and uncluttered secondhand shops. If you want a bit more cash for shopping, the watch and jewelry store also buys merchandise. ✉ *3–19–4 Shinjuku, Shinjuku-ku* ☎ *03/5363–9588 watches, bags, jewelry* 🌐 *www.komehyo.co.jp* Ⓜ *Shinjuku.*

Takashimaya department store is a mecca for gift-givers and foodies. Its basement-level food court stocks everything from Japanese crackers to Miyazaki beef to gourmet desserts.

MUSIC

★ **Disk Union** (ディスクユニオン)

MUSIC | Music lovers rejoice: the Shinjuku flagship of this chain has floors devoted to different genres of music, selling vinyl and more from around the world. Other branches even specialize in just one type of music, so if you have a preference—be it Latin, rock, indie, jazz, or something else—grab a store flyer that lists all the outlets. ✉ *3–31–4 Shinjuku, Yamada Bldg, Shinjuku-ku* 🌐 *diskunion.net* Ⓜ *Marunouchi, Oedo, and Shinjuku subway lines, JR Yamanote Line, Keio and Odakyu lines, Shinjuku Station (Higashi-guchi/East Exit).*

PAPER

Kami no Takamura
(紙のたかむら; *Kami no Takamura*)

STATIONERY | Although this shop specializes in *washi* and other papers printed in traditional Japanese designs, it also carries brushes, inkstones, and other calligraphy tools. In addition, a gallery at the entrance showcases a seasonal selection of traditional stationery as well as works by local artists. ✉ *1–1–2 Higashi-Ikebukuro, Toshima-ku* ☎ *03/3971–7111* 🌐 *www.wagami-takamura.com* Ⓜ *JR Yamanote Line, Marunouchi and Fukutoshin subway lines, Ikebukuro Station (East Exit for JR, Exit 35 for subway).*

Ikebukuro

A major crossroads and entry point for people from the northern and northwestern suburbs, Ikebukuro is Shinjuku's oft-overlooked cousin. The bustling neighborhood has many shopping options, including the main branch of the Seibu department store, which is undergoing a years-long renovation, and the Sunshine City shopping and entertainment complex, which has an aquarium and the Gashapon Department Store, where some 3,000 gachapon (or gashapon) capsule machines spit out perfectly quirky and affordable souvenirs—from tiny anime figurines to bags specifically for green onions.

)ther area attractions include a Frank .loyd Wright–designed school, a muse-ım dedicated to paper and paper-making, ınd a historical tram line.

kebukuro Station is the center of the ıction. The easiest access is via the JR 'amanote Line, but it's also served by the Marunouchi, Yurakucho, and Fukutoshin ubway lines.

Sights

iyu Gakuen Myonichikan
自由学園明日館)
IOTABLE BUILDING | Frank Lloyd Wright vas popular in Japan. Indeed, Japanese ırchitects both influenced and were influ-enced by his designs. Fans will enjoy the ınmistakable example of his distinctive 'rairie style at this off-the-beaten-path school building. When Wright was in 'okyo designing the Imperial Hotel in he 1920s, he was commissioned to uild this schoolhouse, which is now pen to the public. Its use of local stone eeps it in harmony with its location. t is, however, a bit difficult to find, so our journey to the building will take you hrough a small neighborhood. The brick street the building occupies is a helpful narker. Call ahead to be sure the site sn't closed to the general public for a rivate event. ✉ *2–31–3 Nishi Ikebukuro, 'oshima-ku* ✣ *Use the Metropolitan Hotel as a landmark, then head directly south onto a narrow street heading into neighborhood, following the street until ou see a small, brick-paved road on your ight.* ☎ *03/3971–7535* 🌐 *jiyu.jp* 🎫 *¥500 o enter, ¥800 includes a drink and snack n the café* 🕙 *Closed Mon.* Ⓜ *Ikebukuro JR Station (Metropolitan Exit).*

'aper Museum
紙の博物館 *Kami no Hakubutsukan*)
IISTORY MUSEUM | **FAMILY** | The mill that ınce stood here was Japan's first to roduce Western-style paper, starting in 1875. The museum now occupying the location celebrates paper-making and paper of all kinds, including domestic *washi*, in permanent and special exhibits covering 2,000 years of history. Some exhibits also illustrate the astonishing variety of products that can be made from paper. ✉ *1–1–3 Oji, Kita-ku* ☎ *03/3916–2320* 🌐 *papermuseum.jp/en* 🎫 *¥400* 🕙 *Closed Mon.* Ⓜ *Toden Arakawa Line, Asukayama Station; JR Keihin-Tohoku Line, Oji Station (South Exit).*

Sunshine Aquarium (サンシャイン水族館; *Sanshain Suizokukan*)
AQUARIUM | **FAMILY** | Part of the Sunshine City shopping and entertainment complex, which is housed in what was once Tokyo's tallest building, this aquarium is a good rainy day sight, especially if you have kids in tow. Although it's a bit of a trek from Ikebukuro Station, the way is lined with restaurants, shops, and arcades. There are 750 kinds of sea creatures on display, plus daily special events. English-language pamphlets are available, though most exhibits have some English explanation. Generally, its easy to buy entrance tickets in person, but, on holidays and weekends, you might want to make advance reservations via the website. ✉ *3–1–3 Higashi-Ikebukuro, Toshima-ku* ☎ *03/3989–3466* 🌐 *sunshinecity.jp/en/aquarium* 🎫 *¥2,600* Ⓜ *JR Yamanote Line, Ikebukuro Station (East Exit); Yurakucho subway line, Ikebukuro Station (Exit 35).*

Toden Arakawa Tram
(都電荒川線; *Toden Arakawa-sen*)
TRAIN/TRAIN STATION | **FAMILY** | Tokyo was once crisscrossed by tram lines, and this is its last surviving one. Also known as the Tokyo Sakura Tram, for its views during the cherry blossom season (*sakura* means "cherry blossom"), the tram runs for 12 km (7.5 miles) and makes 30 stops. A ride on it is a great way to

experience some Tokyo history and see what everyday life in the city is like. You can access the tram from directly under the Yamanote Loop Line's Otsuka Station. ✉ *Otsuka, Toshima-ku* 🌐 *www.kotsu.metro.tokyo.jp/toden* 🎫 *Single ride ¥170, day pass ¥400.*

Hotel Chinzanso Tokyo (ホテル椿山荘東京)
$$$ | **HOTEL** | When you have had enough of feeling that you're in a city, try this sheltered haven of a hotel surrounded by a 17-acre garden nestled onto the former estate of an imperial prince. **Pros:** gorgeous, sprawling grounds; large rooms with huge bathrooms; glamorous pool. **Cons:** limited dining options nearby; isolated location; might be overly formal for some. $ *Rooms from: ¥70,000* ✉ *2–10–8 Sekiguchi, Bunkyo-ku* ☎ *03/3943–1111* 🌐 *www.hotel-chinzanso-tokyo.com* *260 rooms* 🍽 *No Meals* Ⓜ *Yurakucho subway line, Edogawabashi Station (Exit 1A).*

Chapter 10

WEST TOKYO

Updated by
Jonathan DeLise

Sights ★★★☆☆
Restaurants ★★★☆☆
Hotels ★☆☆☆☆
Shopping ★★☆☆☆
Nightlife ★★★☆☆

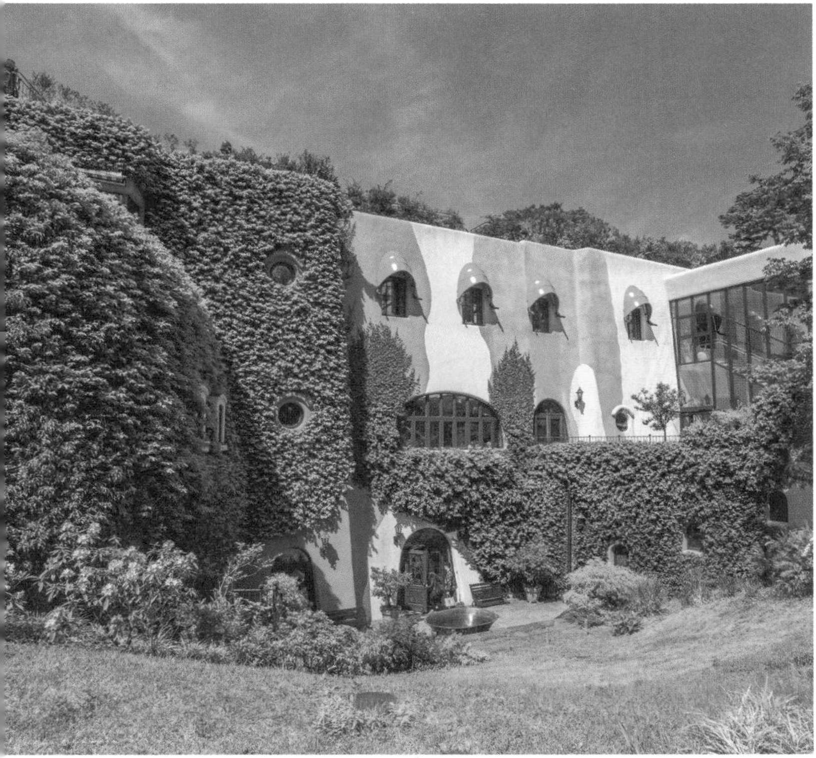

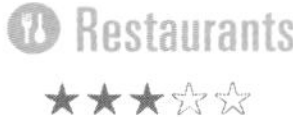

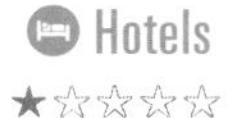

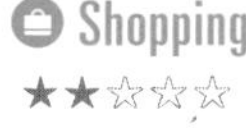

NEIGHBORHOOD SNAPSHOT

TOP EXPERIENCES

■ **Hang out with Hello Kitty.** Head to Tama for a day at the Sanrio Puroland theme park, the wonderfully kitschy home of the famous feline.

■ **Dance in the streets.** In late August, the hip neighborhood of Koenji hosts the vibrant Koenji Awa-Odori dance festival.

■ **Go back in time.** Visit Jindai-ji in Chofu, a temple first built in AD 733 that houses a priceless gilded bronze statue of the Buddha dating from the late Asuka period (592–710).

■ **Get geeky in Nakano.** Akihabara may be Tokyo's main hub for *otaku* (geek) culture, but the hundreds of anime- and manga-related stores in the Nakano Broadway mall make it an otaku destination, too.

■ **Explore the world of Ghibli.** This museum-slash-theme park in Mitaka transports you into the fantastical worlds of animator Miyazaki Hayao and his Studio Ghibli team.

■ **Amble one of Tokyo's largest greenspaces.** From maple and gingko trees to cherry and plum blossoms, Tachikawa's Showa Kinen Park has something different in bloom each month of the year.

GETTING HERE

The areas of West Tokyo covered in this chapter are easily reached by train from central Tokyo. Either the JR Chuo Line or the Keio Line, both of which can be taken from Shinjuku, access Nakano, Suginami, Chofu, Tachikawa, Tama, Mitaka, and Musashino. Within West Tokyo, bus routes connect stations to sights that might otherwise require a long walk, such as the Ghibli Museum and Jindai-ji Temple. Taxis wait outside all major stations.

PLANNING YOUR TIME

West Tokyo is an expansive area. It's best to pick one area at a time and tackle it as a half- or full-day trip while basing yourself in one of Tokyo's 23 wards, as that's where most hotels are located.

OFF THE BEATEN PATH

■ The main attraction of Koganei, just west of Mitaka and Musashino, the Edo-Tokyo Open-air Architectural Museum preserves 30 historical buildings relocated from around Tokyo. The structures range from Edo-era thatched farmhouses that give insights into how West Tokyo would have looked before urbanization to early 20th-century soy sauce and cosmetics shops from central Tokyo. To get here, take the Chuo Line to Higashi-Koganei Station (two stops west of Mitaka Station).

PAUSE HERE

■ Scattered around West Tokyo are hundreds of places to stop and have a relaxing soak in piping-hot water, ranging from modest neighborhood *sento* (public bathhouses) to more indulgent *onsen* (natural hot-spring baths). You could try Gokuraku Yu in Tama for the latter or Kotobuki Yu in Nakano for the former. It's a very Japanese way to decompress from just another day in the world's largest metropolis.

West Tokyo offers up less touristy experiences than the city center and gives you a chance to embark on day trips that genuinely veer off paths well-trodden by international travelers, yet without having to uproot and leave the higher-quality accommodations or conveniences of the capital behind.

Also known as the Tama Area, West Tokyo is vast. Spreading westward from the central 23 wards (*-ku*), the region covers almost 1,160 square km (720 square miles), encompassing everything from built-up extensions of the city's urban sprawl to leafy suburbs and mountains. Within that are 26 municipalities called *-shi* (cities), three *-machi* (towns), and even a *-mura* (village), which all together are home to more than 4 million people. This section looks at some of the most accessible and worthwhile trips into West Tokyo, including highlights of less-visited west-side *-ku* such as Nakano and Suginami. Mount Takao in Tokyo's far west is covered in the Side Trips chapter.

Starting with the western parts of the 23 *-ku*, Nakano, a few stops from Shinjuku, provides a fun alternative to the *otaku* (geek culture) center of Akihabara: the Nakano Broadway mall has everything an anime- or manga-loving traveler needs. Directly west of Nakano, Suginami is home to the thrift stores and bohemian hangouts of Koenji, a neighborhood that also hosts one of Tokyo's most energetic summer festivals, the Koenji Awa-Odori.

West of there are the neighboring *-shi* of Mitaka and Musashino, which share the lovely green expanse of Inokashira Park. In addition to a small zoo and boating pond, the park is the site of the Studio Ghibli animation studio's wonderful Ghibli Museum. Quite a contrast, the lively neighborhood of Kichijoji nearby is great for bar hopping, dining in casual restaurants, and taking breaks in hip cafés.

To the south, another *-shi* is Chofu, which, despite being less than 20 minutes by train from Shinjuku, feels a million miles apart thanks to the natural surrounds of the historic Jindai-ji Temple and flora and fauna of Jindai Botanical Gardens. Farther west then comes Tama, a quiet residential area full of spacious parks. Here, you could spend a day in the colorful world of Hello Kitty and friends at the Sanrio Puroland theme park or unwind in natural hot-spring baths at Gokuraku Yu.

A 33-minute train ride west from Shinjuku gets you to Tachikawa, a *-shi* that's home to Showa Kinen Park, one of Tokyo's largest greenspaces. It was built on land formerly part of Tokyo's first civil international airport. To the northwest lies the *-shi* known as Ome, where you'll find Shiofune Kannon Temple, remarkable for its springtime azalea bloom. Given Ome's small-town atmosphere, you'll probably find it hard to believe that you're still within one of the world's largest cities.

Nakano

The name of both a station and one of the 23 *-ku* (districts) that make up the heart of West Tokyo, Nakano goes under-the-radar for most travelers, despite being Shinjuku's neighbor. If, however, you're interested in otaku (a term used to describe big fans of anime/manga and video games), the district's vast, five-floor Nakano Broadway complex makes it a fantastic addition—or alternative—to Tokyo's super-busy Akihabara, a neighborhood also known for its otaku culture. To get here, take the JR Chuo or Chuo-Sobu line or the Tozai line of the Tokyo metro.

Sights

★ **Nakano Broadway** (中野ブロードウェイ)
STORE/MALL | **FAMILY** | Visiting Nakano Broadway is like visiting Akihabara, but with everything under one roof. When it opened in 1966, it was presented as luxury complex, but it has since has morphed into a center for all things otaku, with five floors of roughly 300 stores largely focused on manga, anime, gaming, and related collectibles—everything from figurines to cosplay outfits. Mandarake, Japan's largest manga- and anime-related retailer, alone has close to 30 stores here, all divided by specialty. Down in the basement are plenty of places for lunch or a quick snack, including the stomach-busting Daily Chiko, which offers an eight-scoop soft-serve, as well as udon. ✉ *5–52–15 Nakano, Nakano-ku* ✢ *Due north of JR Nakano station* ☎ *03/3388–7004* 🌐 *nakano-broadway.com* Ⓜ *JR Chuo Line and Tozai subway line, Nakano Station (North Exit).*

Nakano Kotobuki-Yu Onsen (中野寿湯温泉 *Kotobuki Yu Onsen*)
HOT SPRING | If the frenetic energy of Shinjuku, or the otaku epicenter of Nakano Broadway have left you feeling defeated, stop by Kotobuki-yu (just to the north of J Nakano station) for a refreshing soak. Tokyo's neighborhood baths have been in steady decline in recent decades as only the oldest of homes lack a bath or shower. Kotobuki-yu, albeit modest, maintains the tradition of being a casual place to socialize and unwind. Just note that it opens late: from 4 pm until 1:30 am, so it's definitely something to do once you've gotten your shopping out of the way.

Once you've located Kotobuki Yu's orange building and have found your way to the gender-separated baths, the key thing, as at any public bath, is to follow the basic etiquette. First, you need to be completely naked in the baths, and make sure your wash towel doesn't go in the communal bathtub. You also need to wash and rinse well in the seated shower area, before getting into the baths. After that, just enjoy a piping-hot soak, then try the on-site sauna. ✉ *1–14–13 Arai, Nakano-ku* ✢ *Short walk north from JR Nakano station* ☎ *03/3387–2047* 🎫 *¥460* ⏲ *Closed Tues.* Ⓜ *JR Chuo Line and Tozai subway line, Nakano Station (North Exit).*

Coffee and Quick Bites

Daily Chiko (デイリーチコ)
$ | **ICE CREAM** | **FAMILY** | This basement-level ice cream store has become a Nakano Broadway institution for its soft-serve ice cream, which comes in flavors that vary from simple vanilla to matcha (powdered green tea), horse chestnut, and *ramune* (a popular citrus soda flavor). The specialty is the eight-layered, 20-cm (8-inch) *tokudai sofuto*, or extra-large soft serve, though small cups and cones are also on the menu. **Known for:** flavors like matcha; served in cups or cones; 8-layer soft-serve ice cream. Ⓢ *Average main: ¥280* ✉ *Nakano Broadway, 5–52–15 Nakano, B1 Floor, Nakano-ku* ☎ *03/3386–4461* 🌐 *nakano-broadway.com* 💳 *No credit cards* Ⓜ *JR Chuo Line and Tozai subway line, Nakano Station (North Exit).*

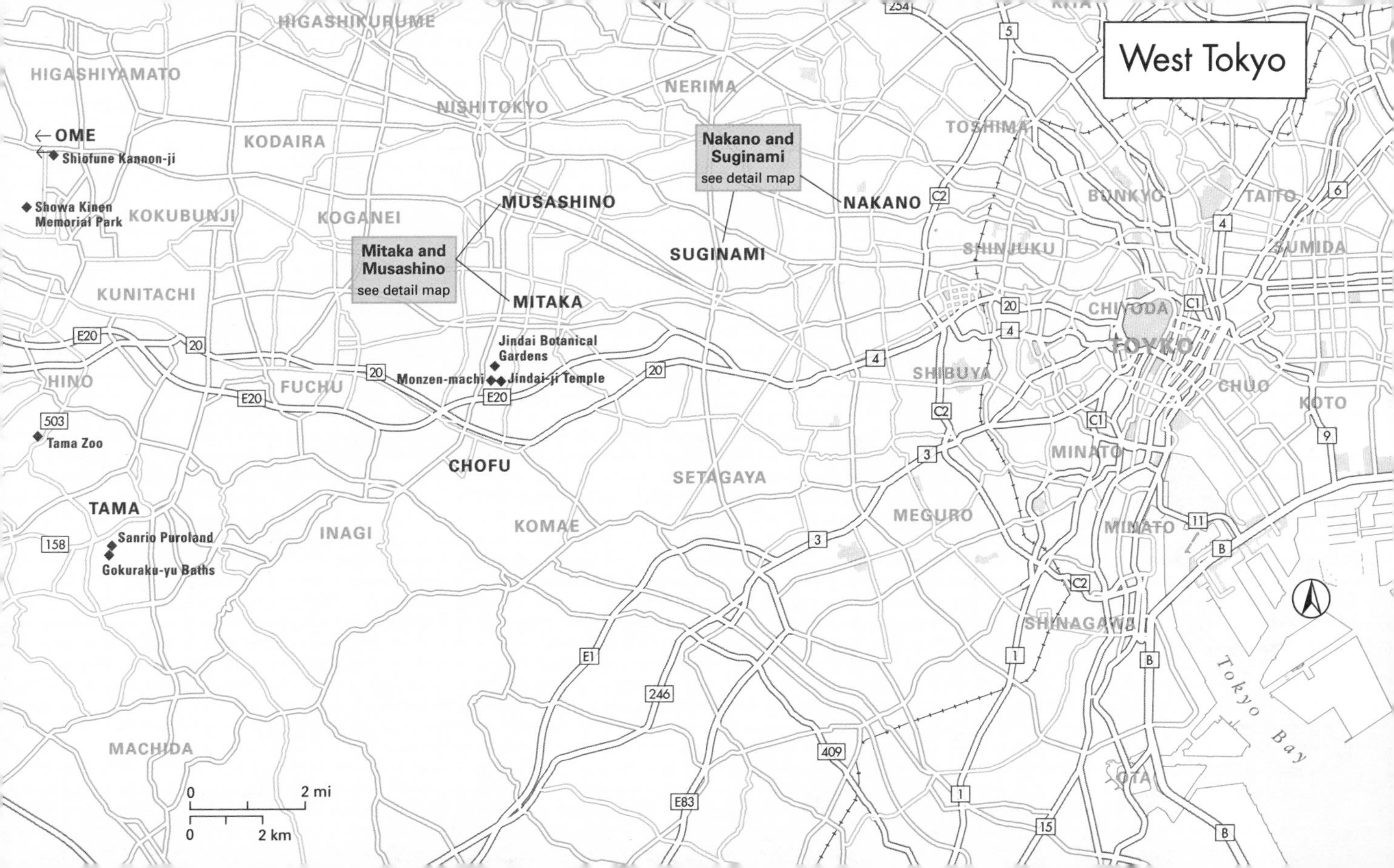
West Tokyo
HIGASHIKURUME
HIGASHIYAMATO
NERIMA
NISHITOKYO
TOSHIMA
← OME
Shiofune Kannon-ji
KODAIRA
Nakano and Suginami
see detail map
Showa Kinen Memorial Park
KOKUBUNJI
KOGANEI
MUSASHINO
NAKANO
BUNKYO
TAITO
Mitaka and Musashino
see detail map
SUGINAMI
SHINJUKU
SUMIDA
KUNITACHI
MITAKA
CHIYODA
TOKYO
Jindai Botanical Gardens
HINO
FUCHU
Monzen-machi
Jindai-ji Temple
SHIBUYA
CHUO
KOTO
Tama Zoo
MINATO
CHOFU
SETAGAYA
TAMA
MEGURO
Sanrio Puroland
INAGI
KOMAE
Gokuraku-yu Baths
SHINAGAWA
Tokyo Bay
MACHIDA
OTA
0
2 mi
0
2 km

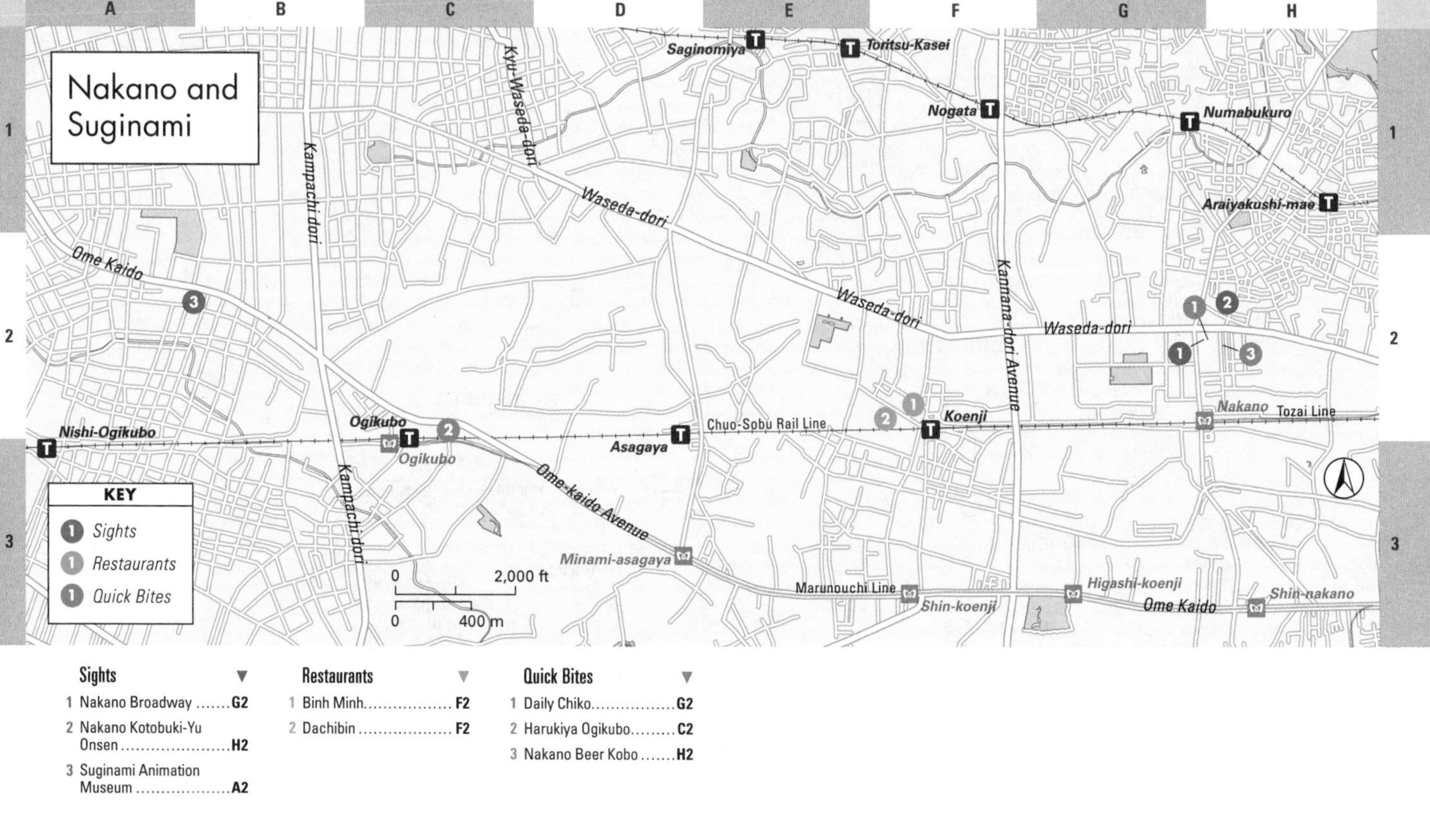

Sights

1 Nakano Broadway **G2**

2 Nakano Kotobuki-Yu Onsen **H2**

3 Suginami Animation Museum **A2**

Restaurants

1 Binh Minh **F2**

2 Dachibin **F2**

Quick Bites

1 Daily Chiko **G2**

2 Harukiya Ogikubo **C2**

3 Nakano Beer Kobo **H2**

Nakano Beer Kobo (中野ビール工房)
$$ | ECLECTIC | For a post-shopping drink and a bite to eat, stop by this tiny brewpub amid the side streets just east of Nakano Broadway. The rustic decor makes the place seem as if a carpentry enthusiast has made a bar in their garage (the name *kobo* translates to "workshop," after all), but you're really here for the beer. **Known for:** range of craft beers; light-bite comfort foods; no-frills wooden interior. *Average main: ¥1,500* ✉ *5–53–4 Nakano, Nakano-ku* ☎ *03/3385–3301* *www.beerkobo.com* *Closed Mon.* Ⓜ *JR Chuo Line and Tozai subway line, Nakano Station (North Exit).*

Shopping

Mandarake (まんだらけ)
SPECIALTY STORE | FAMILY | Not one Mandarake store, but nearly *30* of them, each with a distinct focus, can be found in the Nakano Broadway shopping plaza. Nearly every otaku culture need is catered to here. If you want a Kamen Rider figurine, head to Mandarake Special 3 on the third floor. If you're a fan of tabletop role-playing games like Warhammer, make a beeline for the Kojosen branch on the fourth floor. Or, maybe you've outgrown otaku culture, and want to sell your goods? Try the third floor buy-back stand. ✉ *Nakano Broadway, 5–52–15 Nakano, Nakano-ku* ☎ *03/3228–5787* *www.mandarake.co.jp* Ⓜ *JR Chuo Line and Tozai subway line, Nakano Station (North Exit).*

Robot Robot (ロボットロボット)
SPECIALTY STORE | FAMILY | Another brand with multiple Nakano Broadway outlets, Robot Robot is the place otaku go for figurines and action figures. On the third-floor Robot Robot 1 specializes in Japanese anime and manga characters, such as Gundam, Dragonball, and One Piece, while Robot Robot 2 is packed with U.S. favorites, with heaps of choices from the Star Wars, Disney, and Marvel franchises. Down on the second floor, Robot Robot 3 is a bit more of a mishmash, though it's a good stop for anyone into Studio Ghibli productions such as *My Neighbor Totoro* and *Spirited Away.* ✉ *Nakano Broadway, 5–52–15 Nakano, Nakano-ku* ☎ *03/5345–7553* *robotrobot.com* Ⓜ *JR Chuo Line and Tozai subway line, Nakano Station (North Exit).*

Suginami

Located next to Nakano, on the edge of Tokyo's 23 *-ku*, Suginami oozes rough-around-the-edges cool. Around Koenji Station, you will find hip eateries, quirky watering holes, modish thrift stores, and underground music venues. Then there's Ogikubo, which is a must-visit for anyone with a penchant for ramen; some ramen connoisseurs consider insist that this area has some of the city's best ramen spots. Neither area has much in the way of major sightseeing attractions; rather, they're places you visit to soak in the atmosphere.

Koenji, in particular, always has an energy about it, but if you come on the last weekend of August, it will be absolutely pulsating because of the superb Koenji Awa-Odori dance festival. A spin-off of the 440+ year-old Awa-Odori in Tokushima on Shikoku island, this version started in the 1950s and now sees troupes of dancers and musicians (almost 10,000 people in all) performing energetic routines in the streets as hundreds of thousands look on.

Sights

Suginami Animation Museum (杉並アニメーションミュージアム)
SPECIALTY MUSEUM | FAMILY | Suginami is home to more than 100 animation studios, making it by far the animation creation center of Tokyo. Although you can't visit any studios, exhibits at this small but highly interactive museum highlight the history of animation and demonstrate production processes. You

Nakano Broadway is one of the world's best shopping complexes for all things related to otaku culture, including anime, manga, and cosplay.

can even sign up for workshops (for a fee) that enable you to create your own anime using digital screens. *3–29–5 Kamiogi, Suginami-ku* *From Ogikubo Station take any bus from bus stop 0 or 1 to the Ogikubo Keisatsusho-mae bus stop.* *03/3396–1510* *www.sam.or.jp* *Free* *Closed Mon.* *JR Chuo Line, Ogikubo Station and Marunouchi subway line, Ogikubo Station.*

Restaurants

Binh Minh (ビンミン)
$$ | **VIETNAMESE** | *Kushiyaki* (grilled skewers), Vietnamese-style, are on the menu at the bustling restaurant that is the Tokyo branch of a popular barbecue chain in Hanoi. The skewers here include chicken thigh on or off the bone, chicken feet, and gizzards, as well as seafood, vegetables such as okra, and sweet treats like banana. **Known for:** lively vibe; Vietnamese grilled chicken; Vietnamese beer. *Average main: ¥1,800* *3–22–8 Koenji Kita, Suginami-ku* *03/3330–3992* *namamen.com* *Closed Tues. No lunch weekdays* *JR Chuo Line, Koenji Station.*

Dachibin (抱瓶)
$$ | **JAPANESE** | Koenji has many culinary bases covered, and with this izakaya it delivers Okinawan food and drink as authentic as any you'd find in Japan's southern islands (you can thank the Okinawan owner for that). Dachibin, whose name refers to a portable ceramic container for sake, specializes in regional classics such as *goya champuru* (a stir-fry of bitter gourd, spam, and tofu) and *soki soba* (noodles with pork sparerib meat), which can be chased down with a pint of Orion Beer or a shot of Okinawan firewater *awamori*. **Known for:** Okinawan dishes; awamori spirits; open until 5 am. *Average main: ¥3,000* *3–2–13 Koenji Kita, Suginami-ku* *03/3337–1352* *www.dachibin.com* *No lunch* *JR Chuo Line, Koenji Station.*

Coffee and Quick Bites

Harukiya Ogikubo (春木屋)
$ | JAPANESE | Having started as a street stall in Ogikubo in the late 1940s, Harukiya is now a *ramenya* (ramen restaurant) that often has patrons lining up along the street. The noodles are freshly made by hand every morning, come in a soy and *niboshi* (dried sardine)–based stock, and are served with a topping of *chashu* (roast pork). **Known for:** long lines; chuukasoba (Chinese noodle soups, e.g., ramen); quick turnover of diners. *Average main: ¥1,250 1–4–6 Kamiogi, Suginami-ku 03/3391–4868 www.haruki-ya.co.jp No credit cards JR Chuo Line, Ogikubo Station and Marunouchi subway line, Ogikubo Station.*

Nightlife

BARS

Bar Mugen
BARS | A drink in this dimly lit, late-night, basement haunt favored by anime fans, would be the perfect way to finish a day of shopping at Nakano Broadway. Beer, whiskey, and cocktails are on the menu, anime figurines dot the counter, and anime plays endlessly on the bar's TV. Indeed, the bar's name, *mugen*, means "infinite," and the owners have several thousand DVDs in their collection. *3–58–17 Koenji Minami, USA Building, B1, Suginami-ku 03/6383–1643 www.facebook.com/mugen0127 JR Chuo Line, Koenji Station.*

Cocktail Shobo (コクテイル書房)
BARS | A 100-year-old tenement house, all dark woods and creaking sounds, houses one of Koenji's most unique bars. You can pick up and read any of the hundreds of books that are on hand in addition to ordering snacks and cocktails, some of them inspired by literary legends. Occasionally, the bar hosts events featuring authors or sketch artists. *3–8–13 Koenji Kita, Suginami-ku 03/3310–8130 www.koenji-cocktail.info JR Chuo Line, Koenji Station.*

Koenji Beer Kobo
(高円寺麦酒工房 *Koenji Bakushu Kobo*)
BREWPUBS | This small brewpub offers a frequently changing line-up of craft creations, often including pale ales and white beers. Chalkboards on the walls indicate the nine staple brews as well as whatever else is on tap. Comfort foods, such as Japanese fried chicken (*karaage*) or homemade sausage, pair nicely with the beer. *2–24–8 Koenji Kita, Suginami-ku 03/5373–5301 www.beerkobo.com JR Chuo Line, Koenji Station.*

LIVE MUSIC

Manhattan
LIVE MUSIC | Local musicians jam at this narrow, ramshackle but well-established jazz café every night. It's a very friendly hangout with a reputation for great music. Cover charges vary by performance. *2–2–7 Asagaya Kita, Suginami-ku 03/3336–7961 ateliermw.com/manhattan JR Chuo Line, Asagaya Station.*

Showboat (ショーボート)
LIVE MUSIC | A small, basic venue that been going strong since the late 1990s, Showboat attracts semi-professional and professional performers. Tickets run from ¥2,000 to ¥5,000, depending on the show and whether they're purchased in advance or at the door. *Oak Hill Koenji, 3–17–2 Koenji Kita, B1, Suginami-ku 03/3337–5745 www.showboat1993.com JR Sobu and JR Chuo lines, Koenji Station (Kita-guchi/North Exit).*

Performing Arts

Asagaya Jazz Street Festival
(阿佐谷ジャズストリート)
FESTIVALS | Held the last weekend of October, this predominantly mainstream festival, which first started in 1995, takes places in some less-than-mainstream venues, ranging from a Shinto shrine to a Lutheran church. Fortunately, most

venues are within walking distance of JR Asagaya Station. More than 200 bands and 1,300 musicians play, with previous headliners having included the Mike Price Jazz Quintet and pianist Yosuke Yamashita. The festival gets crowded, so come early to have a better chance at entry. Note: Outdoors events are free, but indoor events have a charge. ✉ *4F, Wagafurusato-kan, 1–36–10 Asagaya-Minami, Suginami-ku* ☎ *03/5305–5075* 🌐 *asagayajazzstreets.com* 🎫 *Indoor event tickets from ¥2000* Ⓜ *JR Chuo Line, Asagaya Station.*

Shopping

Asagaya Pearl Center (阿佐谷パールセンター)

SHOPPING CENTER | FAMILY | Despite the name, this isn't a pearl store but rather a classic *shotengai* (covered shopping arcade) running for just over ½ kilometer (⅓ mile) on the south side of Asagaya Station. Like many shotengai, it houses a mix of options, from cafés and small restaurants to everyday-goods and clothing shops. You will also find kimonos, crafts, and *wagashi* (traditional Japanese sweets), making this a great place to buy souvenirs as well as to soak up some local flavor. Most stores open around 11 am. Also, for fans of *matsuri* (festivals), every August, the Asagaya Tanabata Festival, which originated in China as the Qixi Festival, takes place here. It celebrates the once-a-year reunion of two stars otherwise separated by the Milky Way. ✉ *1–36–7 Asagaya Minami, Suginami-ku* 🌐 *www.asagaya.or.jp* Ⓜ *JR Chuo Line, JR Asagaya station.*

Mitaka and Musashino

Directly west of Suginami, one of Tokyo's central 23 *-ku* (districts), are two of the closest of West Tokyo's 26 *-shi* (cities), Mitaka and Musashino, which, by and large, feel like extensions of the central sprawl. The main exception is leafy Inokashira Park, which straddles the Mitaka–Musashino border. In its southern Mitaka section, you will find the superb Ghibli Museum, while the Musashino side includes a small zoo and boating pond. Then there's the fun neighborhood of Kichijoji immediately to the north of the park, a place packed with bars, cafés, and places to eat. Locals will tell you it's the best place for a night out in all of western Tokyo.

Look Down

As a tourist in a big city, you're often looking up at the skyscrapers. But in Japan, you might also want look down at the sewer covers. First introduced in Okinawa in 1977 to raise awareness of the country's sewer systems, there are now thousands of unique designs scattered across all 47 prefectures. What's more, since 2016 sewer-cover trading cards have been issued!

Sights

Edo-Tokyo Open-Air Architectural Museum (江戸東京たてもの園; *Edo-Tokyo Tatemono-en*)

MUSEUM VILLAGE | FAMILY | Located in Koganei, just west of Mitaka, this outdoor museum has brought together 30 historic buildings, mostly from Tokyo but also from other parts of Japan. Across West, Center, and East zones are structures such as thatched farmhouses from the late Edo period, one-time residences of politicians and magnates, and central Tokyo grocery and cosmetics stores, as well as a traditional bathhouse, an old-fashioned bar, and a soy sauce shop. It's best to wear slip-on footwear as some buildings require you to remove your shoes before entering. Also, the visitor center has free lockers in case you

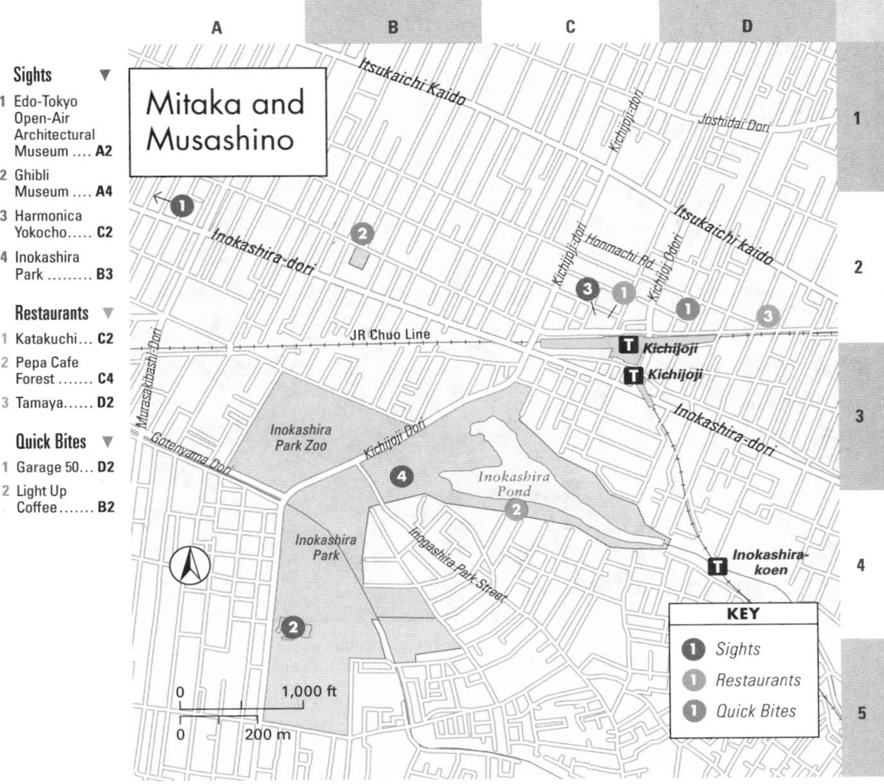

want to stash your stuff while exploring. ✉ *3–7–1 Sakuracho, Koganei* ✥ *From Mitaka, take the Chuo Line two stops west to Higashi-Koganei Station. Buses run from outside the station to the Tatemono-en Iriguchi bus stop, from there it's a 7-min walk.* ☎ *042/388–3300* 🌐 *www.tatemonoen.jp* 🎫 *¥400* 🕒 *Closed Mon.* Ⓜ *JR Chuo Line, Higashi-Koganei Station.*

Ghibli Museum (三鷹の森ジブリ美術館; *Mitaka no Mori Ghibli Bijutsukan*)
SPECIALTY MUSEUM | **FAMILY** | With classics like *Spirited Away* and *My Neighbor Totoro*, Miyazaki Hayao's Studio Ghibli has created some of the most beloved animated movies in history, Japanese or otherwise. At this museum/theme park in suburban Mitaka—located within the sprawling Inokashira Park—exhibits trace the creative process taking initial concepts to screen, all amid designs inspired by Ghibli films. A real bonus is the on-site cinema that shows museum-exclusive animated shorts. As the museum is extremely popular, advance reservations for visits are required; book well ahead on the website. ✉ *1–1–83 Shimorenjaku, Mitaka* ✥ *It's a 15-min walk from either Mitaka Station or Kichijoji Station, but a Ghibli bus also runs every 10 to 20 min from bus stop number 9 outside Mitaka Station (¥310 return, ¥210 one-way)* ☎ *0570/055–777* 🌐 *www.ghibli-museum.jp* 🎫 *¥1000* ✍ *Reservations required* Ⓜ *JR Chuo Line, Mitaka Station or Kichijoji Station.*

Harmonica Yokocho (ハーモニカ横丁)
NEIGHBORHOOD | This cramped warren of alleys on the north side of Kichijoji Station started life as a flea market in the 1940s. In the 1990s, the down-on-its-luck maze was given a new lease on life when bars

The Edo-Tokyo Open-Air Architectural Museum brings together about 30 historical structures from Tokyo and beyond that survived both the Great Kanto Earthquake of 1923 and the destruction of World War II.

and restaurants began opening. Fairly compact, and with a down-to-earth, old Tokyo vibe, it's a less-touristy alternative for bar-hopping than Shinjuku's more famous Golden Gai district or the hectic area with izakaya just west of Shimbashi Station. Some places open as early as 11 am, and most don't close until midnight. ✉ *1–1 Kichijoji Honcho, Musashino* 🌐 *hamoyoko.jp/hamonika_kichijoji* 🎫 *Free* Ⓜ *JR Chuo Line, Kichijoji Station.*

★ **Inokashira Park** (井の頭公園; *Inokashira Koen*)

CITY PARK | **FAMILY** | South of Kichijoji Station, with one foot in Mitaka and another in Musashino, this large, laidback, leafy park, founded in 1917, has activities and attractions for all ages. In addition to the Ghibli Museum in its southernmost reaches, there's a small zoo with a guinea pig petting area, playground equipment, and a pond with row boats and swan-shaped paddle boats. On weekends, buskers perform in the park, which is repainted pink during spring's cherry-blossom season. It's a lovely place to picnic, though the surrounding area also has small cafés and restaurants. ✉ *1–18–31 Gotenyama, Musashino* 🎫 *Park free, zoo ¥400* ⏲ *Zoo closed Mon.* Ⓜ *JR Chuo Line, Mitaka Station or Kichijoji Station.*

Restaurants

Katakuchi (片口)

$$ | **SUSHI** | This laidback joint in the lively Harmonica Yokocho neighborhood proves that an intimate sushi experience doesn't have to be overly formal or expensive. Grab a seat at the counter, and use the picture menu to help you order, or enjoy a three-, eight-, or twelve-piece set menu—perhaps paired with nihonshu sake selected from the short beverage list. **Known for:** good-value sushi sets; oden (small stewed dishes) for dinner on Wednesday; laidback atmosphere. Ⓢ *Average main: ¥3,000* ✉ *1–1–1 Kichijoji Honcho, Musashino* ☎ *0422/21–3066* 🌐 *www.hamoyoko.jp/menu/kichijoji_katakuchi* 💳 *No credit cards* ⏲ *No lunch Wed.* Ⓜ *JR Chuo Line, Kichijoji Station.*

Pepa Cafe Forest (ペパカフェフォレスト)
$$ | **THAI** | A good option for lunch, dinner, or a quick bite smack dab in the middle of Inokashira Park, Pepa Cafe Forest cooks up Thai staples such as green curry, pad Thai noodles, and tom yum kung soup. Other Southeast Asian options include fresh spring rolls, Vietnamese coffee, and bottled beer. **Known for:** Thai staples; Vietnamese coffee; outdoorsy vibe. *Average main: ¥2,500* ✉ *4–1–5 Inokashira, Mitaka* ☎ *0422/42–7081* ⊕ *www.instagram.com/pepacafe_forest* Ⓜ *JR Chuo Line, Mitaka Station or Kichijoji Station.*

Tamaya (たまや)
$$$ | **JAPANESE** | **FAMILY** | Yakitori and other skewers of chargrilled meat and vegetables are the name of the game at this hip, local-favorite izakaya. To make ordering easier, select one of the set menus, which feature multiple skewers and a few side dishes such as tofu. **Known for:** Japanese wines; chargrilled yakitori; good nihonshu (sake) selection. *Average main: ¥4,000* ✉ *1–34–2 Kichijoji Honcho, Musashino* ☎ *050/5462–5145* ⊕ *tamaya-kichijyoji.foodre.jp* Ⓜ *JR Chuo Line, Kichijoji Station.*

Coffee and Quick Bites

Garage 50 (ガレージ50)
$ | **PIZZA** | **FAMILY** | Amid a sea of dilapidated buildings, thin-crust pizza specialist Garage 50 stands out for its retro camper van equipped with a brick-oven. Numerous toppings—from seafood to ham or chorizo—are available, and all the pies cost the same. **Known for:** dry-cured ham and egg, basil, and mascarpone pies; Italian ingredients; quirky (but limited) outdoor seating. *Average main: ¥700* ✉ *1–23–5 Honmachi, Musashino* ✣ *Short walk northeast of JR Kichijoji Station* ⊕ *www.facebook.com/Garage50* ▭ *No credit cards* ⏲ *Closed Wed.* Ⓜ *JR Chuo, JR Sobu, Keio Inokashira lines to JR Kichijoji Station.*

Light Up Coffee
$ | **CAFÉ** | Drop by this branch of a hipster chain for hand-dripped coffee made with house-roasted beans or lattes with artistic patterns in the foam. If you're really into your coffee, try the taster set to compare three different beans. **Known for:** house-roasted beans; coffee taster sets; low-key ambience. *Average main: ¥600* ✉ *4–13–15 Kichijoji Honcho, Musashino* ✣ *Walk down Nakamichi dori from the north exit of JR Kichijoji station* ☎ *0422/27–2094* ⊕ *lightupcoffee.com* Ⓜ *JR Chuo Line, Kichijoji Station.*

Nightlife

Ahiru Beer Hall (アヒルビアホール)
BARS | Unlike most beer halls—but like many of Japan's best watering holes—this Harmonica Yokocho neighborhood institution is shoulder-to-shoulder snug, which actually helps to make it a very convivial place to enjoy Belgian draft beers or Japanese spirits. To go with your drinks, try the fish and chips. The bar is on the second floor; the ground floor has a well-stocked liquor shop. ✉ *1–1–2 Kichijoji Honcho, Musashino* ✣ *Diagonally across from the northern exit of JR Kichijoji station* ☎ *0422/20–6811* ⊕ *hamoyoko.jp/menu/kichijoji_ahiru* Ⓜ *JR Chuo Line, Kichijoji Station.*

Kichijoji Taproom
(ベアードタップルーム吉祥寺)
BREWPUBS | Owned by Baird Beer, one of Japan's leading microbrewers, this small, hip Kichijoji taproom serves a fantastic line-up of the company's limited-release and year-round offerings, including the hop-heavy Suruga Bay IPA, the rich Kurofune Porter, and the refreshing Wheat King Witte. Everything goes well with the Tex-Mex food menu's tacos, burritos, and nachos. ✉ *2–10–15 Kichijoji Minamicho, Musashino* ✣ *A short hop east of JR Kichijoji station* ☎ *0422/24–8691* ⊕ *bairdbeer.com/taprooms/kichijoji* Ⓜ *JR Chuo Line, Kichijoji Station.*

The pond in Inokashira Park is famous for its swan-shaped paddleboats, which draw locals from all over the city on weekends, especially during cherry blossom season.

Chofu

One of the 26 *-shi* (cities) in West Tokyo, Chofu is only 17 minutes by express train from high-octane Shinjuku, yet its small cluster of attractions—the sylvan Jindai-ji Temple, neighboring Jindai Botanical Gardens, and traditional eateries featuring soba noodles—feel worlds apart from more central Tokyo districts. A visit is best done as a morning or afternoon side-trip. Just take the Keio Line from Shinjuku Station to Chofu Station; from there, buses (or taxis) make the short trip to Jindai-ji Temple.

Sights

Jindai Botanical Gardens (神代植物公園; *Jindai Shokubutsu Koen*)

GARDEN | FAMILY | These large gardens, just a few minutes' walk from Jindai-ji Temple, make a visit to Chofu well worth your time. The grounds, which have roughly 100,000 plants, are divided into sections featuring azaleas, plum blossoms, cherry blossoms, begonias, wisterias, and more. From spring to autumn, there's always something beautiful in bloom. Other highlights include Tokyo's largest rose garden, a greenhouse with tropical and aquatic plants, and the engaging exhibits on flora in the Center for Plant Diversity. ✉ *5–31–10 Jindaiji-motomachi, Chofu* ✣ *From the station, take buses from bus stop 12 to Jindai Shokubutsu Koen.* ☏ *042/483–2300* 🌐 *www.tokyo-park.or.jp/jindai* 🎫 *¥500* ⏲ *Closed Mon.* Ⓜ *Keio Line, Chofu Station.*

★ **Jindai-ji Temple** (深大寺)

TEMPLE | FAMILY | Established in 733 BC, Jindai-ji is Tokyo's second-oldest temple site after Senso-ji in Asakusa. Much like Senso-ji, multiple fires have caused it to undergo several different eras of reconstruction, mostly recently in the early 1900s, but its large, wooden *sanmon* (main gate) dates from 1695. However, where Senso-ji sits amid urban sprawl and the frenzied Nakamise-dori street, Jindai-ji is more tranquil, surrounded by trees and shrubs in an area with *monzen-machi* (traditional temple town) streets lined with old wooden buildings selling soba noodles and other Japanese treats.

The site also feels more spiritual, particularly during the main hall's daily Goma fire ceremonies, where monks set alight sticks representing human desires to burn away the root of suffering. Arguably the highlight, however, is the bronze gilded statue of the Hakuhoh Buddha dating from the late Asuka Period (AD 592–710), which was thought to have been lost until 1909, when a monk found it buried beneath one of the temple's floorboards. Although it's only 84 cm (33 inches) in height, it's nevertheless priceless.

Goma ceremonies last 30 minutes and are held at 11 and 2 on weekdays, 11, 1, and 2 on weekends. To have an *ofuda* (talisman) burned on your behalf, inquire at the main hall (¥3,000). ✉ *5–15–1 Jindaiji-motomachi, Chofu* ✥ *From the station, take bus number 34 (from bus stop 14) to the Jindai-ji bus stop.* ☎ *042/486–5511* 🌐 *www.jindaiji.or.jp/en* 🎫 *Free* Ⓜ *Keio Line, Chofu Station.*

Monzen-machi (門前町)
STREET | **FAMILY** | Small communities or streets filled with restaurants and inns serving the needs of pilgrims developed near many of Japan's important temples. At Jindai-ji Temple, a short, pleasant, rustic street lined with small soba restaurants and places selling souvenirs, steamed buns gives you a sense of just such a traditional *monzen-machi* (temple- or gate-front town). ✉ *5–11–2 Jindaiji-motomachi, Chofu* Ⓜ *Keio Line, Chofu Station.*

Restaurants

Ikkyu-An (一休庵)
$ | **JAPANESE** | **FAMILY** | Soba noodles, which are made from buckwheat, are a signature of the restaurants along the bucolic *monzen-machi* approach to Jindai-ji temple, perhaps because buckwheat was traditionally easier to grow in this area than rice. Here, toppings for the handmade soba, which is served in a variety of ways—including in warm broths or cold with a dipping sauce—change according to the season. **Known for:** close to the main sights; soba noodles; rustic vibe. Ⓢ *Average main: ¥1,200* ✉ *5–11–2 Jindaiji-motomachi, Chofu* ☎ *042/482–6773* 🌐 *jindaiji19an.com* 💳 *No credit cards* ⏲ *Closed Mon. No dinner* Ⓜ *Keio Line, Chofu Station.*

Coffee and Quick Bites

Ameya (あめや)
$ | **JAPANESE** | **FAMILY** | Situated along the *monzen-machi* approach to Jindai-ji temple, this traditional-looking spot has its own spin on soba dishes. Here, you don't get soba noodles, but rather "soba bread"—basically, a steamed bun made with buckwheat (soba) flour, sugar, and rice flour that comes with your choice of fillings consisting of sweet red bean paste (*anko*), mustard greens (*takana*), daikon radish, or the very nontraditional *keema*, or mince-meat curry. **Known for:** soba bread (steamed buns); traditional setting; takeout only. Ⓢ *Average main: ¥350* ✉ *5–15–10 Jindaiji-motomachi, Chofu* ✥ *From either Keio Chofu/Tsutsujigaoka station, or JR Kichijoji station, take a bus to "Jindaiji." It's a one-minute walk from that stop.* ☎ *042/485–2768* 💳 *No credit cards* ⏲ *Closed Mon.* Ⓜ *Keio Line, Chofu Station.*

Tama

West of Chofu, Tama City is another suburban area that you can visit on a half- or full-day trip from central Tokyo. Tama is known for its peaceful residential areas, leafy parks, and attractions like the Sanrio Puroland theme park (a mecca for all things Hello Kitty) and the Tama Zoo. To get here, take the Keio Line or Odakyu Line from Shinjuku Station to Tama Center Station (30 minutes).

Sanrio Puroland is devoted to the famously cute Hello Kitty.

Sights

Gokuraku-yu Baths (極楽湯)
HOT SPRING | **FAMILY** | For some traditional Japanese relaxation, head to this smart hot-spring facility a couple of minutes south of Sanrio Puroland. It has nine indoor and outdoor, gender-separated baths, a sauna, and a salon that offers massages and facials. There's also an on-site restaurant that serves soba noodles, simple set menus, and sweet treats. ✉ *1–30–1 Ochiai, Tama* ☎ *042/357–8626* 🌐 *www.gokurakuyu.ne.jp/tempo/tamacenter* 🎫 *¥880 weekdays, ¥980 weekends and public holidays; towel rental ¥220* Ⓜ *Keio, Odakyu, and Tama Monorail lines, Tama Center Station.*

Sanrio Puroland (サンリオピューロランド)
AMUSEMENT PARK/CARNIVAL | **FAMILY** | As a theme park dedicated to the world's most famous white feline—Hello Kitty, of course—Sanrio Puroland is effectively a shrine to the concept of cuteness. An all-day passport allows for unlimited access to multiple attractions, including three theaters, a boat ride, and the Lady Kitty House—one of many park features seemingly designed for taking selfies. Pens, packaged snacks, and plush toys are readily available so you don't have to leave empty-handed. ✉ *1–31 Ochiai, Tama-shi, Tama* ☎ *042/339–1111* 🌐 *www.puroland.jp* 🎫 *¥3,600 weekdays, ¥3,900 weekends and holidays* Ⓜ *Keio Line, Tama Center Station.*

Tama Zoo (多摩動物園; *Tama Dobutsuen*)
ZOO | **FAMILY** | More a wildlife park than a zoo, this facility in Hino City (just north of Tama) gives animals room to roam; moats typically separate them from you, although, for an additional fee, you can take a bus ride through the lion enclosure for an up-close experience. To get here from Tama's main sights, take the Tama Monorail four stops from Tama Center Station to Tamadobutsu-koen Station. ✉ *7–1–1 Hodokubo, Hino* ☎ *042/591–1611* 🌐 *www.tokyo-zoo.net* 🎫 *¥600; lion-enclosure bus ¥500* 🕒 *Closed Wed.* Ⓜ *Tama Monorail, Tamadobutsu-koen Station.*

Tachikawa

Tachikawa is one of West Tokyo's major rail hubs, but don't let the fiercely urban area around its train station fool you: just a short walk away is Showa Kinen Park, a very peaceful place to picnic and stroll. One of Tokyo's largest parks, it has a wide variety of flora that changes with the seasons—featuring the colors of cherry blossoms in the spring and gingko trees in the fall.

Sights

Showa Kinen Memorial Park (国営昭和記念公園)
CITY PARK | FAMILY | Opened in the mid-1980s to celebrate the reign of Emperor Showa, this sprawling park, one of Tokyo's largest, is a short walk northwest of the JR Tachikawa station. Depending on the time of year, you'll be treated to seas of hydrangeas, tulips, and nemophilas or to paths covered in cherry blossoms or gingko leaves. A museum dedicated to Emperor Showa is at the southeastern entrance of the park, which also has a small Japanese garden, a replica of a Showa Era (1926–89) farmhouse, and a number of sports facilities and fountains. *Midoricho 3173, Tachikawa 042/528–1751 www.showakinen-koen.jp/guide-english/ ¥450 Tama Toshi Monorail and JR Chuo, JR Ome, or JR Nambu lines to JR Tachikawa Station.*

Restaurants

Harvest Tachikawa (はーべすと立川店)
$$ | BUFFET | FAMILY | At this all-you-can-eat buffet restaurant, offerings change with the season to highlight the freshest flavors the country has to offer. Options skew heavily toward Japanese favorites, and you can taste the quality in every bite. **Known for:** seasonally appropriate dishes; occasional regional Asian food festivals; bites from throughout Japan. *Average main: ¥1,650 Shibasakicho 3–2–1, Granduo Shopping Center, 7F, Tachikawa Granduo is attached to JR Tachikawa station 042/540–2226 shop.create-restaurants.co.jp/1144 Tama Toshi Monorail and JR Chuo, JR Ome, and JR Nambu lines to JR Tachikawa Station.*

Hotels

★ **Hotel Nikko Tachikawa Tokyo** (ホテル日航立川 東京)
$ | HOTEL | Surrounded by a plethora of shops and restaurants and situated a short walk from JR Tachikawa Station and the two Tachikawa monorail stations on the Tama Toshi line, this hotel makes for an excellent base for exploring West Tokyo. **Pros:** nice staff; good breakfast with local bites; solid location for transportation. **Cons:** no Japanese-style guest rooms; somewhat expensive given the location; no room service. *Rooms from: ¥24,000 1 Chome–12–1 Nishikicho, Tachikawa 10-minute walk east of JR Tachikawa Station 042/521–1111 www.okura-nikko.com 100 rooms No Meals Tama Toshi Monorail and JR Chuo, JR Ome, and JR Nambu lines to JR Tachikawa Station.*

Ome

The rewards for heading this far northwest to Ome include fresh air, a much slower pace of life, and hiking possibilities around the neighboring Mt. Mitake. Be sure to stroll the downtown area near Ome train station to admire some of the nostalgic Japanese movie posters and signs from the 1940s–'60s. Ome is also home to one of Tokyo's underappreciated temples, Shiofune Kannon, where the grounds are awash in red, purple, and pink azaleas from April through May.

Sights

Shiofune Kannon-ji (塩船観音寺)

TEMPLE | **FAMILY** | Counting more than 1,300 years of history, this bucolic temple is best known for its azalea-covered hills. Roughly from the middle of April until early May, hundreds of azalea bushes blossom in vibrant reds, pinks, purples, and whites, providing an uncharacteristically colorful backdrop to typically austere Buddhist grounds. On May 3, there is even an azalea *matsuri,* or festival, with visitors coming from throughout the region to celebrate the fleeting beauty of these spring flowers.

Paths meander around the grounds and lead to a large, hillside statue of Kannon, the goddess of mercy and compassion, where the views are particularly noteworthy. Also of interest is the *hondo,* or main temple hall, dating back from the Muromachi Era (approx.1336–1573). ✉ *194 Shiobune, Ome* ✥ *From Kawabe Station, it is a 35 minute walk. Or hop on the Ume 77 Ko or the Kawa 11 bus to Shiofune Kannon entrance and walk for 10 minutes.* ☎ *0428/22–6677* 🌐 *www.shiofunekannonji.or.jp* 🎫 *Free, except ¥300 during azalea season (approx. Apr. 10 to May 3)* 🕓 *Closures depending on temple events* Ⓜ *JR Ome Line to Kawabe Station.*

Chapter 11

AKIHABARA

Updated by
Randall Grace

Sights
★★☆☆☆

Restaurants
★★☆☆☆

Hotels
★★☆☆☆

Shopping
★★★★☆

Nightlife
★☆☆☆☆

NEIGHBORHOOD SNAPSHOT

TOP EXPERIENCES

■ **Geek out over games.** Known as a mecca for gamers, anime fans, and anyone into electronics, Akihabara is overflowing with shops large and small.

■ **Celebrate in the streets.** A visit in May must include the Kanda Festival—one of Tokyo's major street celebrations. More than 200 portable shrines are carried in a parade towards the grounds of the Kanda Myojin Shrine.

■ **Browse an eccentric collection.** Check out the toys, electronic gadgets, and hobby items at Radio Kaikan, a vertical bazaar.

GETTING HERE

The hub of otaku culture, Akihabara is northeast of the Imperial Palace, right below Ueno and Asakusa. From Tokyo Station, Akihabara is two stops (four minutes) north on the JR Yamanote Line, which also connects Akihabara to Shinjuku in 18 minutes. The Akihabara area is also served by the Hibiya and Tsukuba lines.

Just to the west, the musical instrument shops of Ochanomizu or the used-book district of Jimbocho could be short stopovers before or after an excursion to Akihabara. Ochanomizu is one stop along the JR Chuo and Chuo-Sobu Line from Akihabara, while a taxi is the best way to go directly between Akihabara and Jimbocho, costing about ¥800.

Just north of Jimbocho, Suidobashi is also worth a detour for Koishikawa Korakuen Garden and the Tokyo Dome City amusement park. The JR Sobu Line connects Suidobashi and Akihabara stations, or you could walk there following the Kanda River.

PLANNING YOUR TIME

Most stores in Akihabara do not open until 10 am. Weekends draw hordes of shoppers. This is especially true on Sunday, when the four central blocks of Chuo-dori are closed to traffic and become a pedestrian mall.

OFF THE BEATEN PATH

■ While Akihabara is all about otaku culture and home electronics, neighboring areas provide very different experiences. A couple of miles east, **Koishikawa Korakuen Garden** is a prime example. One of Tokyo's oldest and prettiest gardens, its trails lead you through a succession of scenic spots designed to reproduce famous Japanese and Chinese scenery. It also has some inadvertent "borrowed scenery" now that the Tokyo Dome City entertainment complex looms large next door. If you can, come in fall for the vivid foliage, or in spring when the cherry blossoms are in bloom.

VIEW POINT

■ Akihabara is always full of color, but it feels especially vibrant when parts of Chuo-dori are made pedestrian-only on Sunday afternoons (from 1 to 6 pm). Not only do you have all of Chuo-dori's colorful storefronts and neon signs as a backdrop, but the streets fill up with all sorts of characters, from shoppers to cosplayers to staffers handing out flyers for their cafés.

Akihabara is techno-geek heaven. Also known as Akihabara Electric Town, or more commonly as just Akiba, this district was once a dizzying collection of small, ultra-specialized electronics and computer shops. Today it's the center of Japan's anime, manga, and computer-focused *otaku* (nerd) culture.

More recently, large all-in-one electronics hops have been crowding out many of he small, unique stores. Even so, the rea has stayed true to its roots. Venture ff the main road to see the real Akiba, where maid cafés (where servers are es, dressed as maids and treat their ustomers as "masters and mistresses") nix with computer and hi-fi audio stores lled with dedicated fans searching for omputer parts, rare comics, or tech-o-accessories they can't find anywhere lse. Seeing the subculture and energy of Akiba is as much a draw as the shopping.

or something a little less geeky, head to ither Jimbocho, where family-run shops ell rare and antique books, prints, and naps, or to nearby Ochanomizu with its ows of musical instrument shops. Many f Japan's most prestigious publishing ouses are based in this area, which is lso home to Meiji University and Nihon Jniversity. Ochanomizu is one stop on ne JR Chuo Line from Akihabara, and ne music shops mostly line Meidai-dori Street running south from Ochanomizu Station, leading to Jimbocho's book-tores, which run for ½ km (¼ mile) on asukuni-dori Street beginning at the Surugadaishita intersection.

Sights

Kanda Myojin Shrine (神田明神)

RELIGIOUS BUILDING | This shrine—said to have been founded in AD 730 in a village called Shibasaki, where the Otemachi financial district now stands—was destroyed in the Great Kanto Earthquake of 1923, and the present buildings reproduce, in concrete, the style of 1616. Next door is the Edo Culture Complex, where you check in for your visit and can take in cultural displays on the era when samurai flourished. The shrines in Akihabara are of minor interest unless you are around for the Kanda Festival—one of Tokyo's three great blowouts—in mid-May. (The other two are the Sanno Festival of Hie Jinja in Nagata-cho and the Sanja Festival of Asakusa Shrine.) Some of the smaller buildings you see as you come up the steps and walk around the Main Hall, contain the *mikoshi*—portable shrines that are featured during the festival. ✉ *2–16–2 Soto-Kanda, Chiyoda-ku* ☎ *03/3254–0753* 🌐 *www.kandamyoujin.or.jp* 🎫 *Museum ¥500* Ⓜ *Ginza subway line, Suehiro-cho Station (Exit 3); Marunouchi subway and JR lines, Ochanomizu Station.*

Koishikawa Korakuen Gardens (小石川後楽園)
GARDEN | **FAMILY** | Built in the 1600s as part of a feudal lord's residence, one of Tokyo's oldest gardens incorporates carefully tended trees, manmade hills, rocks, and water features to create miniature versions of famous Japanese and Chinese landscapes. It also changes with the seasons, featuring pink cherry blossoms in spring and the reds, oranges, and yellows of maple and gingko trees in fall. ✉ *1-6-6 Koraku, Bunkyo-ku* ☎ *03/3811–3015* 🌐 *www.tokyo-park.or.jp* 🎟 *¥300* Ⓜ *JR Sobu Line, Toei Oedo Line and multiple Tokyo Metro subway lines, Iidabashi Station.*

Nikolai-do Holy Resurrection Cathedral (ニコライ堂;)
CHURCH | You might be surprised to see a Russian Orthodox cathedral neighboring Tokyo's Electric Town, but this church was established before electronics were even invented. The Holy Resurrection Cathedral was founded by St. Nikolai Kassatkin (1836–1912), a Russian missionary who came to Japan in 1861 and spent the rest of his life here. The building, planned by a Russian engineer and executed by a British architect, was completed in 1891. Heavily damaged in the earthquake of 1923, it was restored with a dome that's much more modest than the original. Even so, the cathedral endows this otherwise featureless part of the city with unexpected charm. ✉ *4–1–3 Kanda Surugadai, Chiyoda-ku* ☎ *03/3295–6879* 🌐 *nikolaido.org* 🎟 *Chapel ¥300* Ⓜ *Chiyoda subway line, Shin-Ochanomizu Station (Exit B1).*

Tokyo Dome City (東京ドームシティ)
AMUSEMENT PARK/CARNIVAL | **FAMILY** | This complex contains restaurants, shops, and Tokyo Dome itself—a major concert venue and home to the Tokyo Giants baseball team and Japan's Baseball Hall of Fame and Museum. Outside, a small amusement park has a selection of kiddie rides, though the Thunder Dolphin roller coaster is a thrill at any age. A visit to the Spa LaQua hot spring, with its various baths and saunas, makes for a relaxing end to a day of sightseeing. ✉ *1–3–61 Koraku, Bunkyo-ku* ☎ *03/5800–9999* 🌐 *www.tokyo-dome.co.jp* 🎟 *Amusement park day-pass ¥4,800, Spa LaQua ¥3,230* Ⓜ *JR Sobu Line, Suidobashi Station; Marunouchi and Namboku subway lines, Korakuen Station.*

Yushima Seido Temple (湯島聖堂)
RELIGIOUS BUILDING | Founded in 1632, this temple originated as a place for the study of the Chinese Confucian classics. Its headmaster was Hayashi Razan, the official Confucian scholar to the Tokugawa government. Moved to its present site in 1691 (and destroyed by fire and rebuilt six times), it became an academy for the ruling elite. In a sense, nothing has changed: in 1872 the Meiji government established the country's first teacher-training institute here, and that, in turn, evolved into Tokyo University, whose graduates still make up much of the ruling elite. The hall is unlike anything you're likely to see in Japan: painted black, weathered, and somber. ✉ *1–4–25 Yushima, Bunkyo-ku* ☎ *03/3251–4606* 🌐 *www.seido.or.jp* 🎟 *Free* Ⓜ *JR Sobu Line and Marunouchi subway line, Ochanomizu Station.*

Restaurants

Bodaijyu (菩提樹 *Linden*)
$$$ | **JAPANESE** | **FAMILY** | Just across the street from Tokyo Dome, this slightly upscale izakaya serves hearty dishes in a comfortable, heavy-timbered basement space. With a menu that includes some of Japanese cuisine's more accessible dishes—curries, fried pork cutlets (*katsudon*) or seafood, hamburgers, steaks—it's a good choice for kids and other less-adventurous eaters. **Known for:** top A5-grade Wagyu-beef hamburgers; Japanese craft beers; choice of booth or tatami-mat seating. Ⓢ *Average main: ¥3,200* ✉ *1–14–3 Hongo, Azumano Bldg.*

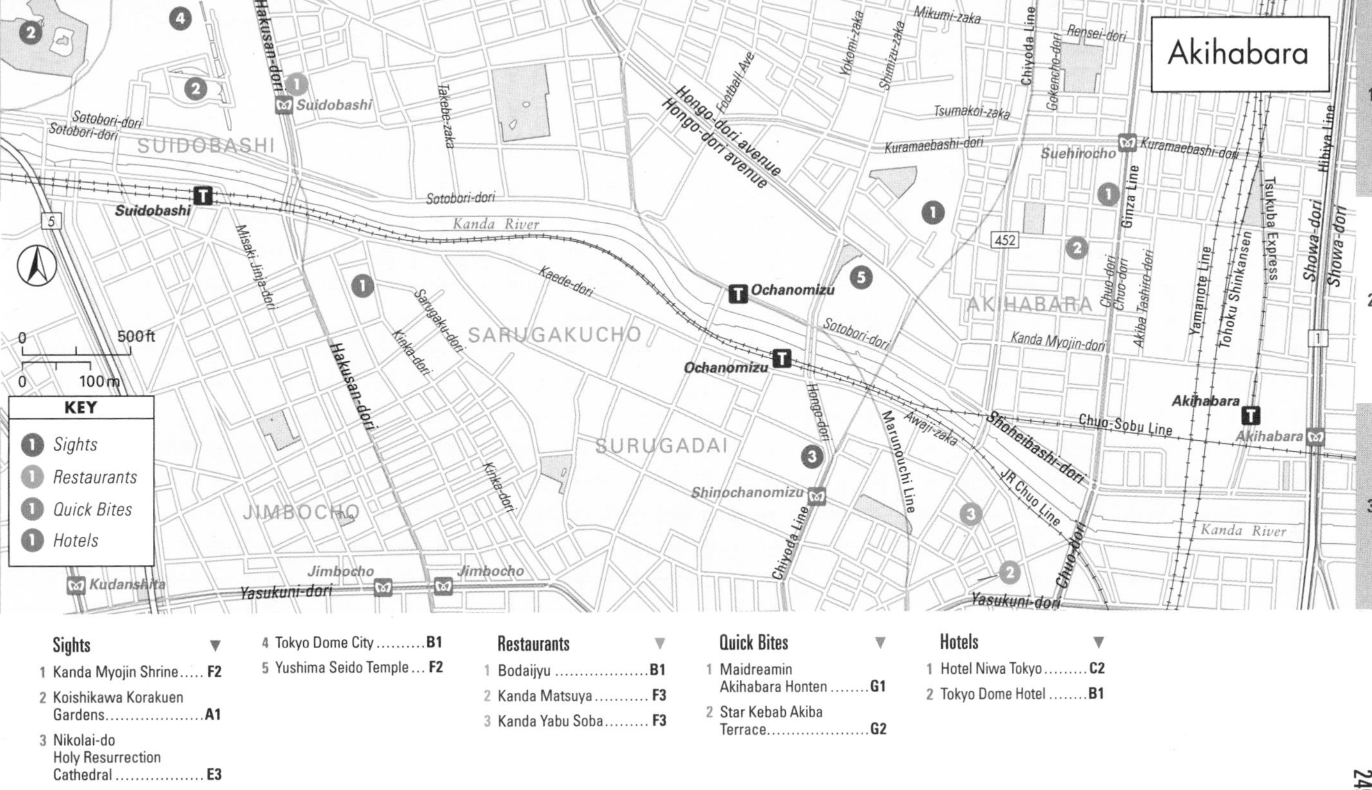

Sights

1 Kanda Myojin Shrine..... **F2**

2 Koishikawa Korakuen Gardens.................... **A1**

3 Nikolai-do Holy Resurrection Cathedral.................. **E3**

4 Tokyo Dome City.......... **B1**

5 Yushima Seido Temple... **F2**

Restaurants

1 Bodaijyu.................... **B1**

2 Kanda Matsuya........... **F3**

3 Kanda Yabu Soba......... **F3**

Quick Bites

1 Maidreamin Akihabara Honten........ **G1**

2 Star Kebab Akiba Terrace...................... **G2**

Hotels

1 Hotel Niwa Tokyo......... **C2**

2 Tokyo Dome Hotel........ **B1**

B1, Bunkyo-ku ☎ 03/3818–1020 🌐 bodai-jyu.owst.jp Ⓜ JR and Mita subway lines, Suidobashi Station.

Kanda Matsuya (神田まつや)
$$ | **JAPANESE** | **FAMILY** | This family-run restaurant serves authentic soba—thin buckwheat noodles, often served chilled in summer and hot in winter in a rustic atmosphere—in a rustic atmosphere. Although a simple soba meal can be quite inexpensive here, it still might be worth spending just a bit more to have your noodles topped with tempura or other goodies. **Known for:** authentic hand-cut noodles; tempura soba; lunchtime crowds. 💲 *Average main: ¥1,500 ✉ 1–13 Kanda Sudacho, Chiyoda-ku ☎ 03/3251–1556 🌐 www.kanda-matsuya.jp 💳 No credit cards 🕑 Closed Sun. Ⓜ Marunouchi Line, Awajicho Station (Exit A3).*

Kanda Yabu Soba (かんだやぶそば)
$$ | **JAPANESE** | **FAMILY** | The ever-popular Kanda Yabu Soba is in a traditional-style building that replaced the original 130-year-old structure after a fire in 2013. It's one of the oldest and best places to sit down and savor freshly made soba noodles—be that on tatami or at one of the tables. **Known for:** excellent rotating seasonal sets; soba sushi rolls; historical atmosphere. 💲 *Average main: ¥2,000 ✉ 2–10 Kanda Awajicho, Chiyoda-ku ☎ 03/3251–0287 🌐 www.yabusoba.net 🕑 Closed Wed. Ⓜ JR and Marunouchi lines, Awajicho Station (Exit A3).*

Coffee and Quick Bites

Maidreamin Akihabara Honten (めいどりーみん秋葉原本店)
$$ | **CAFÉ** | Maid cafés aren't everyone's cup of tea, but, if you want to try one, the main branch of Japan's biggest such chain is as reputable a place as any. All manner of people come to be served by, and have their picture taken with, young women in French maid outfits who affect extreme levels of *kawaii* (cute) and occasionally break into song and dance. **Known for:** quintessential maid café experience; omuraisu (rice omelets) and colorful parfaits; admission fee (¥880). 💲 *Average main: ¥2,500 ✉ 3–16–17 Soto-Kanda, Chiyoda-ku ☎ 0120/229–348 🌐 maidreamin.com/multilp Ⓜ JR Yamanote Line, Akihabara Station.*

Star Kebab Akiba Terrace (スターケバブ)
$ | **FAST FOOD** | **FAMILY** | If you need a break from shopping for electronics and games, stopping to enjoy a spicy kebab sandwich from Star Kebab should do the trick. This and other outlets in the area offer beef, lamb, or chicken strips, as well as lettuce and tomatoes, in pita pockets. **Known for:** inexpensive kebab sandwiches; takeout only; long opening hours (11 am to 9 pm daily). 💲 *Average main: ¥600 ✉ 1–8–10 Soto-Kanda, Chiyoda-ku ☎ 03/6804–8330 🌐 www.kebab.co.jp 💳 No credit cards Ⓜ JR Yamanote Line, Akihabara Station.*

Hotels

Hotel Niwa Tokyo
(庭のホテル 東京; *Niwa no Hoteru Tokyo*)
$$ | **HOTEL** | Traditional and contemporary elements come together to make the Niwa Tokyo a prized little boutique hotel in the middle of the city. **Pros:** quiet area; central location; charming Japanese touches. **Cons:** small rooms; finding entrance is a bit challenging; few major sights within walking distance. 💲 *Rooms from: ¥28,000 ✉ 1–1–16 Misaki-cho, Chiyoda-ku ☎ 03/3293–0028 🌐 www.hotelniwa.jp 🛏 226 rooms 🍽 No Meals Ⓜ JR Chuo or Sobu lines, Suido-bashi Station (East Exit); Mita subway line, Suido-bashi Station (Exit A1).*

Tokyo Dome Hotel (東京ドームホテル)
$$$ | **HOTEL** | **FAMILY** | Most of central Tokyo is readily accessible by train from this hotel beside the city's most popular sports facility (check the summer baseball schedule), where entertainments include a small amusement park and a hot-springs spa. **Pros:** sports motifs;

Did You Know?

Held on odd-numbered years, the Kanda Matsuri is a festival to celebrate health, wealth, and good fortune.

terrific city views; great for kids. **Cons:** surroundings lack charm; rooms are bland; area gets crowded during Tokyo Dome events. $ *Rooms from: ¥54,000* ✉ *1–3–61 Koraku, Bunkyo-ku* ☎ *03/5805–2111* 🌐 *www.tokyodome-hotels.co.jp* *1,006 rooms* 🍽 *No Meals* Ⓜ *JR lines, Suidobashi Station (East Exit); Namboku and Marunouchi subway lines, Korakuen Station.*

Performing Arts

Bunkyo Civic Hall (文京シビックホール)
PERFORMANCE VENUES | This three-story, city-run performance hall showcases classical music, ballet, opera, dance, and drama. Performances puppets, wind music, and Japanese Kabuki dance are especially interesting. ✉ *1–16–21 Kasuga, Bunkyo-ku* ☎ *03/5803–1100, 03/5803–1111 tickets only* 🌐 *www.b-academy.jp/hall* Ⓜ *Marunouchi and Nanboku subway lines, Kourakuen Station (Exit 5).*

Tokyo Dome (東京ドーム)
PERFORMANCE VENUES | **FAMILY** | A 45,852-seat sports arena, the dome also hosts big-name Japanese and international acts. Originally known as "Tokyo Big Egg," the stadium popularly serves as a shorthand unit of measure in Japan, as the size of any large structure might be gauged in terms of how many Tokyo Domes it equals. ✉ *1–3–61 Koraku, Bunkyo-ku* ☎ *03/5800–9999* 🌐 *www.tokyodome.co.jp* Ⓜ *Marunouchi and Namboku subway lines, Koraku-en Station (Exit 2); Mita subway line, Suido-bashi Station (Exit A5); JR Suido-bashi Station (Nishi-guchi/West Exit).*

Shopping

Akihabara was once the only place Tokyoites went to buy cutting-edge electronics. Although it's lost its aura of exclusivity, this foreigner-friendly district is still an essential Tokyo shopping experience for its sheer variety, including video-game and manga shops that cater to the otaku culture. Be sure to poke around the backstreets where smaller stores sell used and unusual electronics.

Kanda Festival 

The mid-May Kanda Festival at Kanda Myojin Shrine began in the early Edo period, and today is held on a grand scale in odd-numbered years (the "Hon-matsuri"), with a smaller version ("Kage-matsuri") in even-numbered years. The floats that lead the procession today move in stately measure on wheeled carts, attended by the shrine's priests and officials. The portable Shinto shrines (*mikoshi*), some 200 of them when the full event is held, follow behind, carried on the shoulders of the townspeople.

BOOKS

With more than 180 used-book stores, the Jimbocho area is a bibliophile's dream. In the ½-km (¼-mile) strip along Yasukuni-dori and its side streets you can find centuries-old Japanese prints, vintage manga, and even complete sets of the Oxford English Dictionary. The large Japanese publisher Sanseido has its flagship store here, and you'll find magazines and postcards on its fifth floor. Most shops stock some foreign titles; a few even devote major floor space to English-language books. Note that smaller shops might be closed on Sunday or Monday.

Kitazawa Bookstore
(北沢書店; *Kitazawa Shoten*)
BOOKS | Recognizable by its stately entryway, Kitazawa has been in business since 1902 and specializes in rare prints, academic texts, and literary works. The dark-wood, floor-to-ceiling bookshelves are overflowing with interesting finds. ✉ *Kitazawa Bldg., 2–5 Kanda Jimbocho, 2F, Chiyoda-ku* ☎ *03/3236–0011* 🌐 *www.*

Akihibara is Tokyo's mecca for electronics, anime, manga, and gaming goods.

kitazawa.co.jp Ⓜ *Hanzomon, Mita, and Shinjuku subway Lines, Jimbocho Station.*

Magnif (マグニフ)
BOOKS | This tiny shop is crammed with vintage magazines—interspersed with photography books—from all over the world. There is a heavy emphasis on fashion, culture, and lifestyle publications. ✉ *1–17 Kanda Jimbocho, Chiyoda-ku* ☎ *03/5280–5911* 🌐 *www.magnif.jp* Ⓜ *Hanzomon, Mita, and Shinjuku subway lines, Jimbocho Station.*

COSTUMES

Cospatio (コスパティオ)
SPECIALTY STORE | **FAMILY** | Serious cosplayers need serious costumes, and this specialty store is where they shop for serious supplies. Anime, manga, video game characters? You'll find them all here, and more—Cospatio shares the fourth floor of its building with a handful of other geeky stores, as well as a maid café. ✉ *Onoden Bldg, 1–2–7 Soto-Kanda, 4F, Chiyoda-ku* ☎ *03/3526–6877* 🌐 *cospatio.com* Ⓜ *JR Yamanote Line, Akihabara Station (Akihabara Electric Town Exit).*

ELECTRONICS

LAOX Akihabara Main Shop (*LAOX* 秋葉原本店; *LAOX Akihabara Honten*)
ELECTRONICS | One of the big Akihabara department stores, LAOX is an outlet for consumer electronics and appliances. The main branch is duty-free, with four floors dedicated to gadgets, (lightweight vacuum cleaners, eco-friendly humidifiers) that come with English instruction booklets. LAOX is also good place to find the latest digital cameras, watches, and games. It has outlets in Narita Airport as well as Sapporo's New Chitose Airport. **■ TIP→ English-speaking staff members are on call.** ✉ *1–2–9 Soto-Kanda, Chiyoda-ku* ☎ *03/3253–7111* 🌐 *laox-globalretailing.co.jp* Ⓜ *JR Yamanote Line, Akihabara Station (Electric Town Exit).*

Radio Kaikan (ラジオ会館)

ELECTRONICS | **FAMILY** | Once a grubby warren of niche electronics merchants, Radio Kaikan has been revitalized as a brightly lit, bustling mall of Japanese pop culture accessories and electronic gizmos. Consider starting at the top and browsing your way down the ten floors of independent vendors selling mini–spy cameras, cell phones disguised as stun guns, manga, plastic models, gadgets, and oddball hobby supplies. ✉ *1–15–16 Soto-Kanda, Chiyoda-ku* ☎ *03/3251–3711* 🌐 *akihabara-radiokaikan.co.jp* Ⓜ *JR Yamanote Line, Akihabara Station (Akihabara Electric Town Exit).*

Sofmap (ソフマップ)

ELECTRONICS | One Akihabara retailer that actually benefited from the bursting of Japan's economic bubble in the early 1990s is this outfit, which was once known as a used-PC and software chain with a heavy presence in Tokyo. Today, its multiple branches sell all sorts of new and used electronics, music, and mobile phones. Most outlets are open daily until 8. ✉ *3–13–12 Soto-Kanda, Chiyoda-ku* ☎ *050/3032–9888* 🌐 *www.sofmap.com* Ⓜ *JR Yamanote Line, Akihabara Station (Electric Town Exit).*

Thanko Rare Mono Shop (サンコー)

ELECTRONICS | **FAMILY** | The king of wacky Japanese electronics sells everything from bamboo smartphone cases and smokeless ashtrays to summer neck coolers and wireless charging stations disguised as jewelry. This showroom and its other branches are musts for gadget geeks. ✉ *3–14–8 Soto-Kanda, Chiyoda-ku* ☎ *03/5297–5783* 🌐 *www.thanko.jp* Ⓜ *JR Yamanote Line, Akihabara Station (Akihabara Electric Town Exit).*

MUSICAL INSTRUMENTS

As Japan's economy roared back from World War II, a homegrown industry of musical instrument manufacturing sprang up, with creations to rival those offered by Western makers in terms of quality and affordability. In Tokyo, the Ochanomizu neighborhood, up the hill from Akihabara, became Japan's capital of musical instrument shops. Places along and around Meidai-dori Street south of Ochanomizu Station sell an astonishing variety of items at every conceivable price point.

Many shops specialize in particular niches, such as traditional Japanese instruments, orchestral brass, woodwinds, strings—even ukuleles. In addition, Tokyo has long been a Mecca for those seeking prized vintage American guitars.

Shimokura Musical Instruments (下倉楽器 *Shimokura Gakki*)

MUSIC | The venerable Shimokura Gakki group has its headquarters and largest presence in Ochanomizu, with five floors of new and used instruments of every type in its main building. There are also two separate secondhand guitar shops on either side of Meidai-dori street, as well as a buttoned-down classical stringed-instrument shop on the same block. ✉ *Kanda Surugadai 2–2–2, Chiyoda-ku* ☎ *03/3293–7706* 🌐 *shimokura-guitar.com* Ⓜ *JR and Marunouchi subway lines, Ochanomizu Station; Chiyoda subway line, Shin-Ochanomizu Station.*

TOYS

Kyugetsu (九月)

SPECIALTY STORE | In business for more than a century, Kyugetsu sells exquisite Japanese dolls that make unique—albeit expensive—souvenirs. Each one is individually handcrafted by an artisan, and prices range from a few hundred to thousands of dollars. ✉ *1–20–4 Yanagibashi, Taito-ku* ☎ *03/5687–5176* 🌐 *www.kyugetsu.com* Ⓜ *Asakusa subway line, JR Sobu Line, Asakusa-bashi Station (Exit A3).*

Chapter 12

UENO AND YANAKA

12

Updated by
Jay Farris

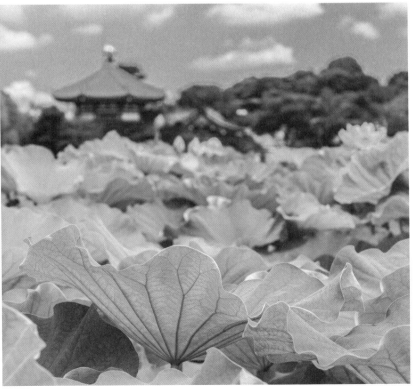

Sights	Restaurants	Hotels	Shopping	Nightlife
★★★★☆	★★☆☆☆	★★☆☆☆	★★★☆☆	★★☆☆☆

NEIGHBORHOOD SNAPSHOT

TOP EXPERIENCES

■ **Hit the top museums.** Some of Tokyo's top museums, including the Tokyo National Museum and the National Museum of Western Art are in Ueno Park.

■ **Get a glimpse of old Tokyo.** Stroll through Yanaka, taking in the temples and old houses, galleries, and cafés in the only Tokyo neighborhood that survived WWII and the earthquake of 1923.

■ **See a shining shrine.** Dating from 1627, the Tosho-gu Shrine is a National Treasure of Japan that houses a priceless collection of historical art and is one of Tokyo's few remaining early-Edo-period buildings.

■ **Witness a lotus display.** From mid-June through August, Shinobazu-ike (Shinobazu Pond) is the only place in Tokyo where you'll see a vast expanse of lotus flowers in bloom.

GETTING HERE

Ueno Station can be accessed by train on the Hibiya Line, Ginza Line, and JR Yamanote and some suburban lines, including directly from Narita Airport. Yanaka is a short walk from the northern end of Ueno Park and can also be accessed from Nippori Station (West Exit). Avoid rush hours in the morning (8–9) and evening (6–9), and, though more and more places are accepting credit cards, bring cash for smaller shops.

PLANNING YOUR TIME

Though the modern Tokyo Skytree transmission tower can be seen from throughout Ueno and Yanaka, these neighborhoods make up a small, historical enclave where life moves at a slower pace. Yanaka, in particular, has an old Tokyo feel with its narrow streets and wooden buildings.

To fully appreciate the area, plan on devoting an entire day—any day but Monday, when most museums are closed—to it. Note, too, that Ueno Park is glorious during April's cherry blossom season, although Yanaka Cemetery is just as spectacular and less crowded.

PAUSE HERE

■ Near Nezu Station and adjacent to the Yanaka neighborhood, Nezu Shrine can be a great resting point on a walk from Ueno Park. The shrine is likely the oldest surviving building in Tokyo and has a fascinating history. Its hillside of azaleas are gorgeous in May, and the shaded, quiet seating areas are a welcome break from summer heat.

YOSHIDA-YA SAKE SHOP

■ Another great place to take a break is Yoshida-ya Sake Shop, which was built in 1910 and is part of the Shitamachi Museum. You'll find it just across from Kayaba Coffee and just south of Yanaka Cemetery. Inside, you can see old barrels of sake and browse leaflets on local spots. Or just enjoy the shade of the courtyard.

JR Ueno Station is the area's beating heart and one of Tokyo's only stations that feels like a European terminus. Since its completion in 1883, the station has served as a gateway for villagers migrating to the city in pursuit of work or to sell their wares.

Ueno was prominent long before the coming of the railroad, however. After 1603, when Tokugawa Ieyasu established his capital in the area, 36 subsidiary temples were erected surrounding the Main Hall, and the city of Edo itself expanded to the foot of the hill where the main gate of Kanei-ji once stood. Some of the temple complex's most important buildings have survived or have been restored and should not be missed. After the railroad terminus was completed, the open space around religious sites became a kind of market area that you can still get a sense of along Ameyokocho. Later, Ueno Park became Tokyo's first city park.

A short walk from the north end of Ueno Park, charming Yanaka is one of city's only areas to have survived both the 1923 earthquake and the WWII firebombing. It was developed during the Edo period, when, to protect them from fires that often broke out in more crowded areas, a number of prominent temples—whose cemeteries often served as firebreaks—were relocated here.

Over time, craftspeople have moved to this neighborhood of temples and traditional wooden houses, and galleries and cafés have opened. Most of what you'll want to see is west of Yanaka Cemetery and south of Yanaka Ginza, a colorful shopping street. As you stroll around, don't be surprised when you turn a backstreet corner and find a quiet temple garden, say, or a Buddhist service in session. During the area's Yanaka Geikoten, a weeks-long arts-and-craft festival typically held in October, artisans open the doors to their workshops, and galleries hold special events.

Ueno

Sights

Ameya Yokocho Market Street (アメヤ横丁)
MARKET | **FAMILY** | In busy seasons, up to a half-million people crowd into the narrow alleys under the railroad tracks to stock up on goods of all kinds. The market dates to World War II, when not much besides Ueno Station survived the bombings. People would travel from the countryside to sell rice at black-market prices. Before long, there were hundreds of stalls selling various kinds of *ame* (confections), most made from sweet potatoes, earning the market its name, *Ame-ya Yoko-cho* (*Ameyoko*, locally), meaning Confectioners' Alley. Shortly before the Korean War, the market was legalized, and soon the stalls were carrying watches, chocolate, ballpoint pens, blue jeans, and T-shirts that had somehow been liberated, as it were, from

"Ame" in Ameya Yokocho Market is associated with "confections," for the sweets sold here, and "American," for the U.S. products sold here during the post-war, black-market era.

American soldiers and the *ame* came to be associated with *Ame*rican. These days you can find anything from beans to shoes in this constantly changing cluster of commerce. ✉ *Ueno 4-chome, Taito-ku* Ⓜ *JR Ueno Station (Hiroko-ji Exit).*

Kiyomizu Kannon-do Temple (清水観音堂)
TEMPLE | This National Treasure was a part of Abbot Tenkai's attempt to build a copy of Kyoto's magnificent Kiyomizu-dera in Ueno. His effort was honorable, but it is still not as impressive as the original. The principal Buddhist image of worship here is the Senju Kannon (Thousand-Armed Goddess of Mercy). Another figure, however, receives greater homage, namely the Kosodate Kannon, who is believed to answer the prayers of women having difficulty conceiving children. If their prayers are answered, they return to Kiyomizu and leave a doll, as both an offering of thanks and a prayer for the child's health. In a ceremony held every September 25, the dolls that have accumulated during the year are burned in a bonfire. ✉ *1–29 Ueno Koen, Taito-ku* ☎ *03/3821–4749* 🌐 *kiyomizu.kaneiji.jp* 🎫 *Free* Ⓜ *JR Ueno Station (Koen-guchi/Park Exit).*

Marishiten Tokudai-ji Temple (摩利支天徳大寺)
TEMPLE | This is a curiosity in a neighborhood of curiosities: a temple on the second floor of a supermarket. Two deities are worshipped here. One is the *bodhisattva* (a being that has deferred its own ascendance into Buddhahood to guide the souls of others to salvation) Jizo, and the act of washing this statue is believed to safeguard your health. The other is the Indian goddess Marici, a daughter of Brahma who is believed to help worshippers overcome difficulties and succeed in business. ✉ *4–6–2 Ueno, Taito-ku* 🌐 *marishiten-tokudaiji.com* Ⓜ *JR Yamanote and Keihin-tohoku lines, Okachi-machi Station (Higashi-guchi/East Exit) or Ueno Station (Hiroko-ji Exit).*

National Museum of Nature and Science (国立科学博物館; *Kokuritsu Kagaku Hakubutsukan*)
SCIENCE MUSEUM | **FAMILY** | This museum houses everything from fossils to moon rocks. The 30-meter (98-foot) model of a blue whale perched at the entrance is a huge hit with children, but, like any self-respecting science museum, this one also has a few kid-pleasing dinosaurs. Although the museum occasionally outdoes itself with special exhibits, it's pretty conventional, with few hands-on learning experiences, so, if time is short, there's no need to linger here for long. To enter, you'll need to make advance reservations online. ✉ *7–20 Ueno Koen, Taito-ku* ☎ *050/5541–8600* 🌐 *www.kahaku.go.jp* 🎫 *¥630; additional fee for special exhibits* ⏲ *Closed Mon.* Ⓜ *JR Ueno Station (Koen-guchi/Park Exit).*

National Museum of Western Art (国立西洋美術館; *Kokuritsu Seiyo Bijutsukan*)
ART MUSEUM | Along with castings from the original molds of Rodin's *Gate of Hell, The Burghers of Calais,* and *The Thinker,* the wealthy businessman Matsukata Kojiro (1865–1950) acquired some 850 paintings, sketches, and prints by such masters as Renoir, Monet, Gauguin, van Gogh, Delacroix, and Cézanne. Matsukata kept the collection in Europe, but he left it to Japan in his will. The French government sent the artwork to Japan after World War II, and the collection opened to the public in 1959 in a building designed by Swiss-born architect Le Corbusier. Since then, the museum has diversified a bit; more recent acquisitions include works by Reubens, Tintoretto, El Greco, Max Ernst, and Jackson Pollock. The Seiyo is one of the best-organized, most pleasant museums to visit in Tokyo. ✉ *7–7 Ueno Koen, Taito-ku* ☎ *03/5777–8600* 🌐 *www.nmwa.go.jp* 🎫 *¥500; additional fee for special exhibits* ⏲ *Closed Mon.* Ⓜ *JR Ueno Station (Koen-guchi/Park Exit).*

Shinobazu Pond (不忍池; *Shinobazu-ike*)
BODY OF WATER | **FAMILY** | When an inlet of Tokyo Bay receded around the 17th century, Shinobazu became a freshwater pond. Abbot Tenkai, founder of Kanei-ji on the hill above the pond, had an island made for Benzaiten, the goddess of the arts. Later improvements included a causeway to the island, embankments, and even a racecourse (1884–93). Today, the pond is in three sections. The first, a wildlife sanctuary, is home to the city's lotus flowers; this is the only place in Tokyo you can see them bloom from mid-June through August. Some 5,000 wild ducks migrate here from as far away as Siberia, sticking around from September to April. The second section, to the north, belongs to Ueno Zoo; the third, to the west, is a small lake for boating. In July, the Ueno *matsuri* (festival) features food stalls and music events at the pond's edge. At the pond's southwestern corner, there is also a bandshell with various music events throughout the year. ✉ *5–20 Uenokoen, Taito-ku* 🎫 *Free* Ⓜ *JR Ueno Station (Koen-guchi/Park Exit); Keisei private rail line, Keisei-Ueno Station (Higashi-guchi/East Exit).*

Shinobazu Pond Bentendo Temple (不忍池辯天堂; *Shinobazu-ike Bentendo*)
TEMPLE | **FAMILY** | Perched in the middle of Shinobazu Pond, this temple is dedicated to the goddess Benten, one of the Seven Gods of Good Luck that evolved from a combination of Indian, Chinese, and Japanese mythology. As matron goddess of the arts, she is depicted holding a lutelike musical instrument called a *biwa.* The temple, built by Abbot Tenkai, was destroyed in the bombings of 1945; the present version, with its distinctive octagonal roof, is a faithful copy. You can rent rowboats and pedal boats at a nearby boathouse. ✉ *2–1 Ueno Koen, Taito-ku* ☎ *03/3828–9502 boathouse* 🎫 *Temple free, boats from ¥700* Ⓜ *JR Ueno Station (Koen-guchi/Park Exit); Keisei private rail line, Keisei-Ueno Station (Ikenohata Exit).*

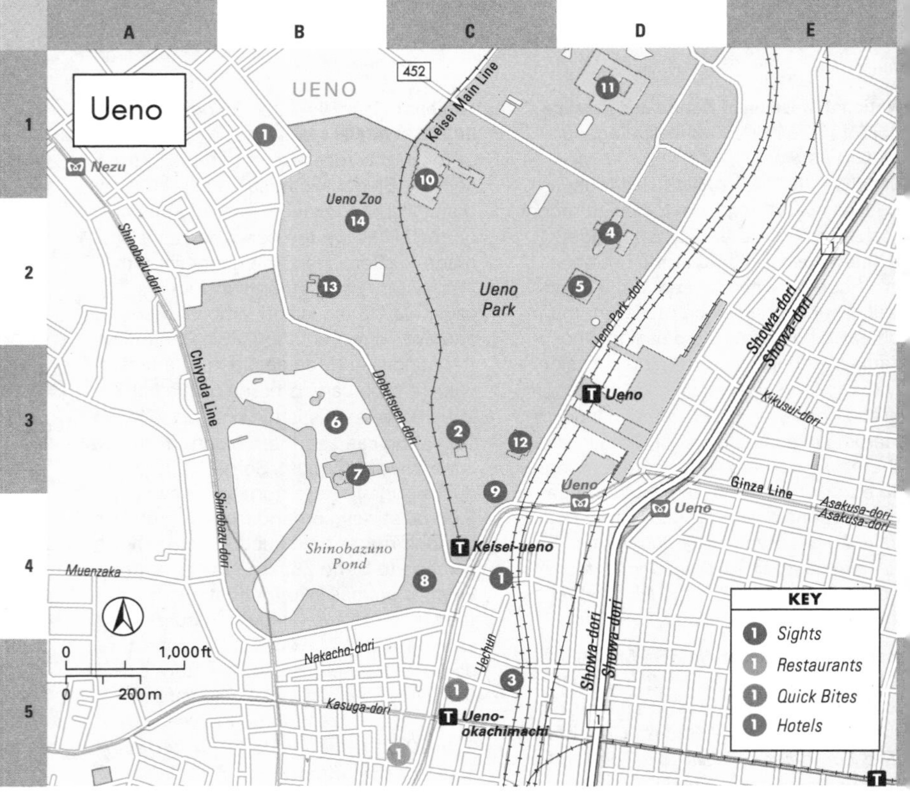

Sights

1 Ameya Yokocho Market Street C4

2 Kiyomizu Kannon-do Temple C3

3 Marishiten Tokudai-ji Temple C5

4 National Museum of Nature and Science.... D2

5 National Museum of Western Art D2

6 Shinobazu Pond......... B3

7 Shinobazu Pond Bentendo Temple....... B3

8 Shitamachi Museum C4

9 Statue of Takamori Saigo C3

10 Tokyo Metropolitan Art Museum.............. C1

11 Tokyo National Museum....... D1

12 Ueno Royal Museum C3

13 Ueno Tosho-gu Shrine B2

14 Ueno Zoo B2

Restaurants

1 Isen Tonkatsu C5

Quick Bites

1 Ichiran Ramen C5

Hotels

1 Ryokan Katsutaro....... B1

he Tokyo National Museum offers not only a huge collection of Japanese artifacts, but its buildings are a tudy in traditional and foreign architecture.

hitamachi Museum (下町風俗資料館; *hitamachi Fuzoku Shiryokan*)

ISTORY MUSEUM | FAMILY | Japanese soci- ty in the days of the Tokugawa shoguns vas rigidly stratified. Most of the city's and was allotted to the warrior class, emples, and shrines. The rest—between eyasu's fortifications on the west, and he Sumida-gawa on the east—was nown as Shitamachi, or "downtown" r the "lower town" (as it expanded, came to include what today consti- utes the Chuo, Taito, Sumida, and Koto vards). It was here that the common, ardworking, free-spending folk, who nade up more than half the population, ved. The Shitamachi Museum preserves nd exhibits what remained of that way f life as late as 1940.

he two main displays on the first floor re a merchant house and a tenement, ntact with all their furnishings. This is hands-on museum: you can take your hoes off and step up into the rooms. On the second floor are displays of toys, ools, and utensils donated, in most cases, by people who had grown up with them and used them all their lives. There are also photographs and video documentaries of craftspeople at work. Occasionally various traditional skills are demonstrated, and you're welcome to take part. This small but engaging museum makes great use of its space, and there are volunteer English-speaking guides. ✉ *2–1 Ueno Koen, Taito-ku* ☎ *03/3823–7451* 🌐 *www.taitogeibun.net/shitamachi* 🎫 *¥300* ⏲ *Closed Mon.* Ⓜ *JR Ueno Station (Koen-guchi/Park Exit).*

Statue of Takamori Saigo (西郷隆盛像; *Saigo Takamori Zo*)

PUBLIC ART | As chief of staff of the Meiji Imperial army, Takamori Saigo (1827–77) played a key role in forcing the surrender of Edo and the overthrow of the shogunate. Interestingly, Saigo himself fell out with the other leaders of the new Meiji government and was killed in an unsuccessful rebellion of his own. The sculptor Takamura Koun's bronze, made in 1893, sensibly avoids presenting Saigo in uniform, but instead with his dog.

Entering Ueno Park from the south, the statue is on the right after climbing the large staircase on your way to Kiyomizu Kanon-do Temple. ✉ *Ueno Park, Taito-ku* Ⓜ *JR Ueno Station (Koen-guchi/Park Exit); Keisei private rail line, Keisei-Ueno Station (Higashi-guchi/East Exit).*

Tokyo Metropolitan Art Museum (東京都美術館; *Tokyo-to Bijutsukan*)
ART MUSEUM | By far the most eclectic of Ueno's art museums, the Tokyo Metropolitan has large-scale exhibitions with themes ranging from classic masterpieces to modern architecture. Smaller galleries often host group exhibitions of painting, photography, calligraphy, sculpture, and nearly any other kind of art you can think of. Many smaller exhibits are free. ✉ *8–36 Ueno Koen, Taito-ku* ☎ *03/3823–6921* 🌐 *www.tobikan.jp* 🎫 *Permanent collection free; fees vary for other exhibits (usually from ¥1,000)* ⏲ *Closed 1st and 3rd Mon. of month* Ⓜ *JR Ueno Station (Koen-guchi/Park Exit).*

★ **Tokyo National Museum** (東京国立博物館; *Tokyo Kokuritsu Hakubutsukan*)
ART MUSEUM | This four-building complex is one of the world's great repositories of East Asian art and archaeology, with some 87,000 objects in its permanent collection and several thousand more on loan from shrines, temples, and private owners. The Hyokeikan, a Western-style building with bronze cupolas that was built in 1909, was once devoted to archaeological finds but is now open to the public only for special exhibitions. The larger Heiseikan, behind the Hyokeikan, was built to commemorate the wedding of crown prince Naruhito in 1993 and now houses Japanese archaeological exhibits. The second floor is used for special exhibitions.

In 1878 the 7th-century Horyu-ji (Horyu Temple) in Nara presented 319 works of art in its possession—sculpture, scrolls, masks, and other objects—to the imperial household. These were transferred to the National Museum in 2000 and now reside in the Horyu-ji Homotsukan (Gallery of Horyu-ji Treasures), which was designed by Yoshio Taniguchi. There's a useful guide to the collection in English, and the exhibits are well explained. Don't miss the hall of carved wooden *gigaku* (Buddhist processional) masks.

The central building in the complex, the 1937 Honkan, houses Japanese art exclusively: paintings, calligraphy, sculpture, textiles, ceramics, swords, and armor. Also here are 84 objects designated by the government as National Treasures. The more attractive Toyokan, to the right of the Honkan, was completed in 1968 and recently renovated; it is devoted to the art and antiquities of China, Korea, Southeast Asia, India, the Middle East, and Egypt. ✉ *13–9 Ueno Koen, Taito-ku* ☎ *03/3822–1111* 🌐 *www.tnm.jp* 🎫 *Regular exhibits ¥1,000, special exhibits from ¥1,600* ⏲ *Closed Mon.* Ⓜ *JR Ueno Station (Koen-guchi/Park Exit).*

★ **Ueno Tosho-gu Shrine** (上野東照宮)
RELIGIOUS BUILDING | This shrine, built in 1627, is dedicated to Ieyasu, the first Tokugawa shogun. It miraculously survived all major disasters that destroyed most of Tokyo's historical structures—the fires, the 1868 revolt, the 1923 earthquake, the 1945 bombings—making it one of the city's few remaining early-Edo-period buildings. The shrine and most of its art are designated National Treasures.

Two hundred *ishidoro* (stone lanterns) line the path from the stone entry arch to the shrine itself. One of them, just outside the arch to the left and more than 18 feet high, is called *obaketoro* (ghost lantern). Legend has it that one night a samurai on guard duty slashed at a ghost (*obake*) that was believed to haunt the lantern. His sword was so strong, it left a nick in the stone, which can be seen today.

The first room inside the shrine is the Hall of Worship. The four paintings in

rightly painted, intricately carved, and trimmed in gold leaf, Tosho-gu is often referred to as Japan's most vishly decorated shrine.

old on wooden panels are by Tan'yu, a ıember of the famous Kano family of rtists, and date from the 15th century. ehind the Hall of Worship, connected y a passage called the *haiden,* is the anctuary where the spirit of Ieyasu is aid to be enshrined.

he real glory of Tosho-gu is its so-called hinese Gate, at the end of the building, nd the fence on either side that has ıtricate carvings of birds, animals, fish, nd shells of every description. The vo long panels of the gate, with their ragons carved in relief, are attributed ɔ Hidari Jingoro, a brilliant sculptor of ıe early Edo period whose real name is nknown (*hidari* means "left"; Jingoro vas reportedly left-handed). ✉ *9–88 Ueno Koen, Taito-ku* ☎ *03/3822–3455* ⊕ *www.uenotoshogu.com* 🎫 *Shrine free; Peony Garden ¥700* Ⓜ *JR Ueno Station (Koen-guchi/Park Exit).*

eno Royal Museum (上野の森美術館; *Ueno-no-Mori Bijutsukan*)
RT GALLERY | With no permanent colection of its own, this museum hosts an interesting temporary exhibits. Most focus on contemporary art, but some highlight more traditional works. Thanks to its manageable size and pleasant atmosphere, the Ueno Royal Museum is a relaxing alternative to Ueno's larger (and more crowded) museums. ✉ *1–2 Ueno Koen, Taito-ku, Taito-ku* ☎ *03/3833–4191* ⊕ *www.ueno-mori.org* 🎫 *Prices vary depending on exhibit* Ⓜ *JR Ueno Station (Koen-guchi/Park Exit).*

Ueno Zoo (上野動物園; *Ueno Dobutsuen*)
ZOO | **FAMILY** | The two main sections of Japan's first zoo, built in 1882, contain an exotic mix of more than 900 species of animals. The giant panda is the biggest draw, but the tigers from Sumatra, gorillas from the lowland swamp areas of western Africa, and numerous monkeys, some from Japan, make a visit to the East Garden worthwhile. The West Garden is highlighted by rhinos, zebras, and hippopotamuses, and a children's area. The process of the zoo's expansion somehow left within its confines the 120-foot, five-story Kanei-ji Pagoda. Built

Ueno Zoo is Japan's oldest zoo and home to about 2,600 animals and 450 species, including the giant panda for which it is famous.

in 1631 and rebuilt after a fire in 1639, the building offers traditional Japanese tea ceremony services. ✉ *9–83 Ueno Koen, Taito-ku* ☎ *03/3828–5171* 🌐 *www.tokyo-zoo.net* 🎫 *¥600* ⏲ *Closed Mon.* Ⓜ *JR Ueno Station (Koen-guchi/Park Exit).*

Restaurants

If you're in the mood for a picnic, there's a large park near Ueno's major railway station; you can pick up provisions at the lively Ameyokocho market along and under the train tracks south of the station. In addition, the streets nearby are home to small eateries, lively izakaya, and *tachinomiya* (low-cost, standing-only bars).

Isen Tonkatsu (井泉本店)
$$ | **JAPANESE** | Down a little side street and behind a tiny door—situated just as all good *tonkatsu* shops should be—Isen has been serving tender, fried pork cutlets since the late 1920s. To avoid the crowds, plan to come right before or after the midday rush, and try to sit at the bar so you can watch the staff place each piece of your set lunch plate with precision. **Known for:** well-established; welcoming atmosphere; a bit hard to find. $ *Average main: ¥2,000* ✉ *3–40–3 Yushima, Bunkyo-ku* ☎ *03/3834–2901* 🌐 *www.isen-honten.jp* 💳 *No credit cards* Ⓜ *Ueno Station.*

Coffee and Quick Bites

Ichiran Ramen (一蘭ラーメン)
$ | **RAMEN** | At Ueno Station is a branch of a raman restaurant chain that has an amusing way of servings its noodles. First, you select your seat and choose and pay for your meal, and then, after you sit down, like magic, a window opens and the food appears. **Known for:** convenient location; unique service method at individual seats; tonkotsu (pork broth) noodles. $ *Average main: ¥1,300* ✉ *Atre Ueno, 7–1–1 Ueno, Taito-ku* ✥ *Entry on the street, under the tracks.* ☎ *03/5826–5861* 🌐 *en.ichiran.com/shop/tokyo/ueno* 💳 *No credit cards* Ⓜ *Ueno Station.*

Hotels

Vhen it comes to lodging, Ueno is onsidered old-fashioned compared to ther neighborhoods, as options here onsist primarily of *ryokans* (traditional ıns with features like communal baths nd tatami-mat rooms) and business otels rather than brand-name interna- ional chains.

yokan Katsutaro (旅館勝太郎)

| **B&B/INN** | Established in the 1980s, his small, simple, economical inn—vhere all the rooms have traditional atami flooring and futon mattresses—is five-minute walk from the entrance to Jeno Koen (Ueno Park) and a 10-minute valk from the Tokyo National Museum. **ros:** a traditional and unique Japanese xperience; reasonable rates; excellent ase for exploring Ueno. **Cons:** no break- ast served; small baths; some rooms ave shared baths. *$ Rooms from: ¥18,000 ✉ 4–16–8 Ikenohata, Taito-ku ☎ 03/3821–9808 8 rooms No Meals Ⓜ Chiyoda subway line, Nezu Station (Exit 2).*

Performing Arts

okyo Bunka Kaikan (東京文化会館)

ERFORMANCE VENUES | Since the 1960s ınd '70s, this hall has been an important venue for classical ballet, orchestral nusic, and visiting soloists. *✉ 5–45 Jenokoen, Taito-ku ☎ 03/3828–2111 ⊕ www.t-bunka.jp Ⓜ JR Yamanote Line, Jeno Station (Koen-guchi/Park Exit).*

Shopping

With an eclectic mix of shops and a few small modern boutiques set amid the many temples, shopping here is a some- what hodgepodge experience.

Jusan-ya (十三や)

SPECIALTY STORE | It's worth slowing down so you don't pass this fascinating shop started by a samurai who couldn't support himself as a feudal retainer and, hence, launched this business selling handmade boxwood combs in 1736. It has been in the same family ever since, and you can still watch as craftspeople create the merchandise. *✉ 2–12–21 Ueno, Taito-ku ☎ 03/3831–3238 Ⓜ Ginza subway line, Ueno Hiroko-ji Station (Exit 3); JR Yamanote Line, Ueno Station (Shinobazu Exit).*

Yanaka

Sights

Asakura Museum of Sculpture (朝倉彫刻館; *Asakura Chosokan*)

ART MUSEUM | Japan's foremost artist of modern sculpture, Fumio Asakura's former house and studio are now home to a selection of the late artist's works, and the building and garden are a lovely stop when wandering through the Yanaka area. Since the museum is housed in an old residence, you'll have to remove your shoes to enter. Note, too, that the museum isn't wheelchair accessible. *✉ 7–18–10 Yanaka, Taito-ku ☎ 03/3821–4549 ⊕ www.taitogeibun.net ¥500 ⏲ Closed most Mon. Ⓜ JR Yamanote Line, Nippori Station.*

Kanei-ji Temple (寛永寺)

TEMPLE | Around 1625, the second Tokugawa Shogun, Hidetada, commis- sioned the priest, Tenkai, to build a tem- ple on the Ueno hill known as Shinobu- ga-oka to defend his city from evil spirits. The original complex encompassed much of what is Ueno Park and while the remaining grounds are beautiful, the most remarkable structure here is the ornately carved vermilion gate to what was the mausoleum of Tsunayoshi, the fifth shogun. Tsunayoshi is famous for his disastrous fiscal mismanagement and his *Shorui Awaremi no Rei* (*Edicts on Com- passion for Living Things*), which, among other things, made it a capital offense for a human being to kill a dog. *✉ 1–14–11*

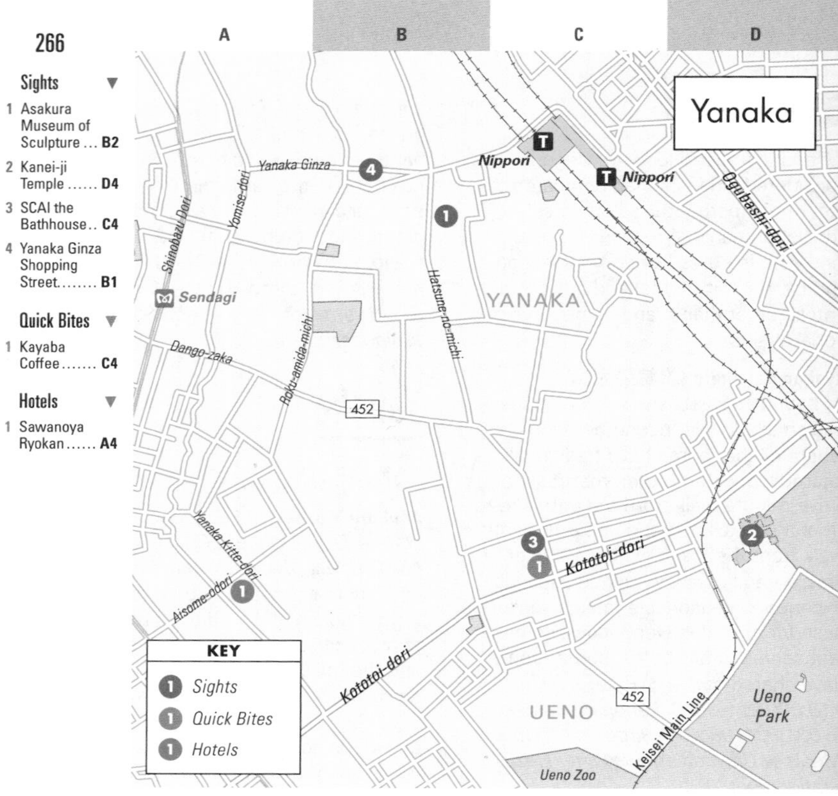

Ueno Sakuragi, Taito-ku ☎ *03/3821–4440* 🌐 *kaneiji.jp* 🎫 *Free (contributions welcome)* Ⓜ *JR Ueno Station (Koen-guchi/Park Exit), JR Uguisudani Station.*

SCAI the Bathhouse (スカイザバスハウス)
ART GALLERY | SCAI exemplifies Yanaka's blend of old and new. The exterior of the building, established in 1787 as a bathhouse, has been well preserved, while the inside is a light and airy space featuring rotating exhibits of contemporary art. Although the gallery is small, the exhibitions are impressive, and it's worth stopping here if only to see the building itself. The surrounding area is also interesting, so even if you arrive before the noon opening time, there's stuff to do. ✉ *Kashiyu-ato, 6–1–23 Yanaka, Taito-ku* ☎ *03/3821–1144* 🌐 *www.scaithebathhouse.com* 🎫 *Free* Ⓜ *Nippori Station for JR Yamanote Line or Nezu Station on the Chiyoda subway line.*

Yanaka Ginza Shopping Street (谷中銀座)
STREET | **FAMILY** | Prior to the rise of supermarkets and convenience stores in the 1980s, Tokyo neighborhoods had vibrant, local shopping streets, with places where you could, say, take a fish to be fried. Thanks to a forward-thinking shopkeepers' and residents' association, Yanaka Ginza not only survived but has flourished. The street is now an interesting mix of shops selling groceries and other goods for locals, as well as sweets, snacks, and crafts. ✉ *3 Yanaka, Taito-ku* Ⓜ *Nippori Station for JR Yamanote Line or Sendagi Station on the Chiyoda subway line.*

Did You Know?

Yanaka Ginza, in the Yanaka area of Tokyo, is one of the best remaining examples of an everyday shopping street still filled with small local stores selling groceries and other daily goods. You won't find any big supermarkets or chains here.

Coffee and Quick Bites

Kayaba Coffee (カヤバ珈琲)
$$ | **CAFÉ** | Prominently standing at the edge of Yanaka, just a short walk to the west from the National Museum, this historical café is a popular stop for lunch or a light snack. A century old, the café has been stylishly renovated and serves homemade sandwiches, curries, cakes, and *kaki gori*, a traditional treat of flavored shaved ice. **Known for:** popular with local residents; retro Japanese drinks and desserts; excellent morning sets. *Average main: ¥1,500* *6–1–29 Yanaka, Taito-ku* *03/3823–3545* *taireki.com* *JR Nippori Station, JR Ueno Station.*

Hotels

Sawanoya Ryokan (澤の屋旅館)
$ | **B&B/INN** | You'll get a full dose of *shitamachi* (lower city) friendliness at the family run Sawanoya, where you'll feel like you're part of an old Tokyo neighborhood and where people might help you plan excursions, say, or book hotels for the next leg of your journey. **Pros:** traditional Japanese experience; affordable rates; friendly management. **Cons:** rooms somewhat small; a bit of a hike to the main station; many rooms share baths. *Rooms from: ¥14,000* *2–3–11 Yanaka, Taito-ku* *03/3822–2251* *www.sawanoya.com* *10 rooms* *No Meals* *Chiyoda subway line, Nezu Station (Exit 1).*

Shopping

★ **Midori-Ya** (翠屋)
CRAFTS | Established in 1908, this family-run shop near the base of the staircase on the traditional Yanaka Ginza shopping street, offers the wares of three generations of bamboo artists. Look for insect cages (with bamboo bugs), flower baskets, chopsticks, cups, lotus-root coasters, and lunchboxes. *3–13–3 Nishi-Nippori, Arakawa-ku* *03/3828–7522* *busekisuikou.com* *Chiyoda line, Nishi-Nippori Station.*

Ueno Sakuragi Atari (上野桜木あたり)
SHOPPING CENTER | A collection of wooden structures at the end of a stone path is home to Yanaka Beer Hall (closed Monday), which has many craft beers on tap, as well as a back garden with a few small shops selling bread, vinegars and olive oils, and other items. It's a good place to stop for a beer and to peek into some wooden structures that just aren't built anymore and are becoming increasingly rare in Tokyo. *2–15–6 Uenosakuragi, Taito-ku* *03/3241–4477* *uenosakuragiatari.jp* *Nippori Station for JR Yamanote Line or Nezu or Sendagi Station, Chiyoda subway line.*

Chapter 13

ASAKUSA AND RYOGOKU

Updated by
Rob Goss

Sights	Restaurants	Hotels	Shopping	Nightlife
★★★★☆	★★★☆☆	★★★☆☆	★★★☆☆	★★★☆☆

NEIGHBORHOOD SNAPSHOT

TOP EXPERIENCES

■ **Visit Senso-ji.** With its giant gateways, impressive pagoda, and steady stream of visitors, this temple complex is arguably the most vibrant in Tokyo.

■ **Wander the backstreets.** The streets to the west of the Senso-ji complex are full of restaurants, cafés, and shops with a wonderfully retro feel.

■ **Sanja Festival.** Drunken people? Loud crowds? Brilliant colors? It's all part of May's Sanja Festival.

■ **Hunt for souvenirs.** Head to Nakamise-dori, where more than 80 shops sell everything from rice crackers to trinkets and T-shirts, or check out the kitchenware stores on Kappabashi-dori.

■ **Go sumo.** Visit Ryogoku to see sumo wrestlers grapple in the ring at a match or practice session.

GETTING HERE

Getting here by subway from Ueno Station (Ginza Line, Ueno Station to Asakusa Station, ¥180, five minutes) or taxi (approximately ¥1,200) is most convenient. Asakusa is the last stop (eastbound) on the Ginza Line. Ryogoku Station on the JR Sobu Line and Toei Oedo Line will get you to all the sumo attractions.

PLANNING YOUR TIME

Asakusa is just east of Ueno and can be explored in a half day. Senso-ji is admirably compact. You can easily see the temple and explore the area surrounding it in a morning. If you decide to include Kappabashi, allow yourself an hour more for the tour. Some of the shopping arcades in this area are covered, but Asakusa is essentially an outdoor experience.

OFF THE BEATEN PATH

■ A several-minute walk east of Senso-ji, Tokyo Cruises (🌐 *www.suijobus.co.jp/en*) boats depart for short trips down the Sumida River, offering a very non-touristy view of the city en route to stops at Hamarikyu Garden, Odaiba, and elsewhere. As the boats sedately work their way down what was once Tokyo's key waterway for trade and commerce, you'll see a mixture of office blocks, apartments, and warehouses, as well as locals unwinding by the river: jogging, walking their dogs, or just relaxing on benches.

VIEWPOINT

■ Looking east over the Sumida River from Asakusa, you'll see one of Tokyo's most striking modern views: the 634-meter (2,080-foot) Tokyo Skytree tower looming large behind the garish offices of Asahi Beer, where a building with a golden glass facade designed to look like a frothy glass of lager sits next to a smaller black building. The latter is topped by what's supposed to be a golden flame; regrettably, it brings something else to mind as the black building has been nicknamed *unchi-biru* (turd building).

If there is one must-visit neighborhood in Tokyo, this is it. Asakusa brings together cultural sights, dining, and entertainment in vibrant surroundings that are at once historic and modern.

Cars make room for the rickshaw drivers who sometimes outpace the motorized traffic as they shuttle around tourists. On the neighborhood's backstreets, neo-French and Italian cafés mix with generations-old soba and tempura shops, while customers in modern fashions sit next to those in traditional kimonos. At Senso-ji Temple and the vibrant Nakamise-dori street leading to it, you hear a global assortment of languages amid the crowds, yet locals still stop by to pray. It is hard not to be swept away by the relaxed energy that pulses through the area.

Historically, the area blossomed after Tokugawa Ieyasu made Edo his capital in 1603, and for the next 300 years it was the wellspring of almost everything we associate with Japanese culture. In the mid-1600s, it became known for its stalls selling toys, souvenirs, and sweets; its acrobats, jugglers, and strolling musicians; and its sake shops and teahouses—where the waitresses often provided more than tea. Then, in 1841, the Kabuki theaters moved to Asakusa. The theaters were here for only a short time, but it was enough to establish Asakusa as *the* entertainment quarter of the city—a reputation it held unchallenged until World War II, when most of the area was destroyed.

After the war, development focused on areas to the west like Shinjuku and Shibuya. In a way, this saved Asakusa from becoming yet another neighborhood filled with neon, concrete, and glass. Here, many of the sides streets retained the charm of an older prewar Tokyo, with low buildings and tiny independent shops. Although the area has since changed—and become dramatically more popular in recent years—tourists usually keep to the main streets and line up at the same restaurants around the Senso-ji Temple complex. Venture a few minutes away from the temple area, though, and the crowds thin out and souvenir shops give way to quiet storefronts selling traditional crafts. Although Senso-ji Temple is well worth seeing, taking the time to wander through the neighborhood gives you a hint of what it may have been like years ago.

If the sport of sumo tickles your fancy, the largest collection of training stables (and the nation's main sumo arena) are in the Ryogoku area, southeast of Asakusa on the other side of the Sumida River. As the center of the world of sumo wrestling, this is the place to watch tournaments as well as eat like a sumo. With the Japanese Sword Museum and Hokusai Museum, it also delivers a sumo-sized amount of culture.

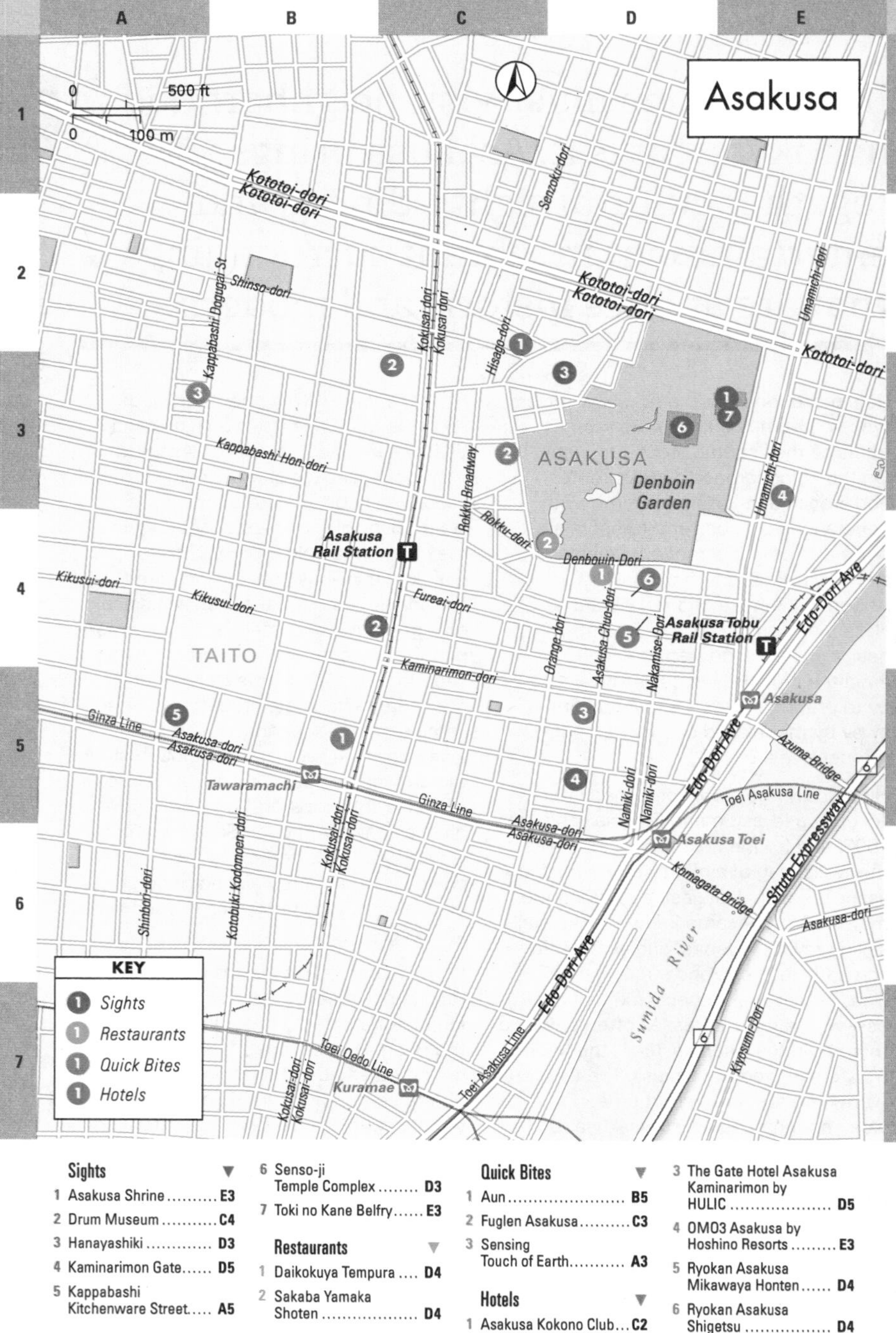

Sights

1 Asakusa Shrine E3
2 Drum Museum C4
3 Hanayashiki D3
4 Kaminarimon Gate...... D5
5 Kappabashi Kitchenware Street..... A5
6 Senso-ji Temple Complex D3
7 Toki no Kane Belfry...... E3

Restaurants

1 Daikokuya Tempura D4
2 Sakaba Yamaka Shoten D4

Quick Bites

1 Aun B5
2 Fuglen Asakusa.......... C3
3 Sensing Touch of Earth........... A3

Hotels

1 Asakusa Kokono Club... C2
2 Asakusa View Hotel..... C3
3 The Gate Hotel Asakusa Kaminarimon by HULIC D5
4 OMO3 Asakusa by Hoshino Resorts E3
5 Ryokan Asakusa Mikawaya Honten...... D4
6 Ryokan Asakusa Shigetsu D4

Asakusa

Sights

Asakusa Shrine (浅草神社)
RELIGIOUS BUILDING | Several structures in the famous Senso-ji temple complex survived the bombings of 1945. The largest, to the right of the Main Hall, is this Shinto shrine to the Hikonuma brothers and their master, Hajino Nakamoto—the putative founders of Senso-ji. In Japan, Buddhism and Shintoism have enjoyed a comfortable coexistence since the former arrived from China in the 6th century. The shrine, built in 1649, is also known as Sanja Sama (Shrine of the Three Guardians). Near the entrance to Asakusa Shrine is another survivor of World War II: the original east gate to the temple grounds, Niten-mon, built in 1618 for a shrine to Ieyasu Tokugawa and designated by the government as an Important Cultural Property. ✉ *2–3–1 Asakusa, Taito-ku* ☎ *03/3844–1575* 🌐 *www.asakusajinja.jp* 🎫 *Free* Ⓜ *Ginza subway line, Asakusa Station (Exit 1) and TOEI Asakusa subway line, Asakusa Station (Exit A4).*

Drum Museum (太鼓館; *Taiko Kan*)
SPECIALTY MUSEUM | **FAMILY** | Become a *taiko* (drum) master for a day as you pound away on the exhibits at this fourth-floor museum dedicated to traditional Japanese and foreign drums. More than 100 instruments can be played, making it a great place for kids. Just make sure their hands remain off the antique instruments, which are carefully marked. A shop on the ground floor of the same building that sells various Japanese drums and festival accessories, which make great souvenirs. ✉ *2–1–1 Nishi-Asakusa, Taito-ku* ☎ *03/3842–5622* 🌐 *www.miyamoto-unosuke.co.jp/taikokan* 🎫 *¥500* ⏲ *Closed Mon.–Tues.* Ⓜ *Ginza subway line, Tawaramachi Station (Exit 3).*

Hanayashiki (花やしき)
AMUSEMENT PARK/CARNIVAL | **FAMILY** | Established in 1853, Tokyo's oldest amusement park has modernized to a degree but still leans heavily in to its retro atmosphere. Think Coney Island: a haunted house, Ferris wheel, and merry-go-round await the kids who will likely be a little tired of Asakusa's historic areas. ✉ *2–28–1 Asakusa, Taito-ku* ☎ *03/3842–8780* 🌐 *www.hanayashiki.net* 🎫 *¥1,200 (rides from ¥400–¥700 each)* Ⓜ *Ginza subway line, Asakusa Station (Exit 1) and TOEI Asakusa subway line, Asakusa Station (Exit A4).*

Kaminarimon Gate (雷門)
HISTORIC SIGHT | The main entryway to Senso-ji's grounds towers above the ever-present throng of tourists and passing rickshaw drivers. With its huge red-paper lantern hanging in the center, this Asakusa landmark is picture perfect. The original gate was destroyed by fire in 1865; the replica you see today was built after World War II. Traditionally, two fearsome guardian gods are installed in the alcoves of Buddhist temple gates to ward off evil spirits. Here, the Thunder God (Kaminari-no-Kami) is on the left with the Wind God (Kaze-no-Kami) on the right. For souvenirs, stop at Tokiwa-do, the shop on the west side of the gate for *kaminari okoshi* (thunder crackers), made of rice, millet, sugar, and beans.

Kaminari-mon marks the southern extent of the shop-lined Nakamise-dori. The area from Kaminari-mon to the inner gate of the temple was once composed of stalls leased to the townspeople who cleaned and swept the temple grounds. This is now kitsch-souvenir central, with key chains, dolls, and (the street's saving grace) snacks. ✉ *2–3–1 Asakusa, Taito-ku* Ⓜ *Ginza subway line, Asakusa Station (Exit 1) and TOEI Asakusa subway line, Asakusa Station (Exit A4).*

Kappabashi Kitchenware Street (かっぱ橋道具街; *Kappa-bashi Dogu-gai*)
STREET | Lined with more than 200 shops selling kitchenware and supplies—from knives to industrial restaurant supplies to the strikingly realistic plastic food models displayed in restaurant windows—this street is shopping heaven for home chefs.

In the 19th century, according to local legend, a river ran through the present-day Kappabashi district. The surrounding area was poorly drained and was often flooded. A local shopkeeper began a project to improve the drainage, investing all his own money, but met with little success until a troupe of *kappa*—mischievous green water sprites—emerged from the river to help him. A more prosaic explanation for the name of the district points out that the lower-ranking retainers of the local lord used to earn extra money by making straw raincoats, also called *kappa*, that they spread to dry on the bridge. ✉ *3–18–2 Matsugaya, Taito-ku* ✣ *The southern end of Kappabashi is a five-minute walk west from exit 3 of Tawaramachi Station* Ⓜ *Ginza subway line, Tawaramachi Station (Exit 3).*

★ **Senso-ji Temple Complex** (浅草寺)
TEMPLE | Even for travelers with little interest in history or temples, this significant complex in the heart and soul of Asakusa is a must-see sight—as much for its five-story pagoda and 17th-century Shinto shrine as for its energy, which is particularly vibrant during the famous Sanja Matsuri festival in May. In addition, the surrounding area has interesting shops, winding backstreets, and an atmosphere unlike any other in Tokyo.

Established in 645, the bright red Main Hall has long been the center of Asakusa, though what you see today is a faithful replica of the original, which burned in the fire raids of 1945. It took 13 years to raise money for the restoration of the beloved Senso-ji, whose large lanterns were donated by the geisha associations of Asakusa and nearby Yanagi-bashi. Kabuki actors still come here to pay their respects before a new performance season, as do sumo wrestlers before a tournament. Indeed, most Japanese climb the stairs to offer prayers, after stopping at the huge bronze incense burner in front to ward off illnesses by bathing their hands and faces in the smoke.

Unlike in many other temples, however, part of the inside has a concrete floor, so you can enter without removing your shoes. In this area hang Senso-ji's chief claims to artistic importance: a collection of 18th- and 19th-century votive paintings on wood. Smaller, simpler versions of such plaques, called *ema,* are still offered to the gods at shrines and temples. The worshipper buys a little tablet of wood with the picture painted on one side and then inscribes a prayer on the other. The temple owns more than 50 of the larger works, which were removed in 1945 to keep them safe during the air raids. Only eight, depicting scenes from Japanese history and mythology, are on display.

Lighting is poor in the Main Hall, and the actual works are difficult to see. One thing that no one can see at all is the holy image of Kannon itself, which is supposedly buried somewhere deep under the temple. Not even the priests of Senso-ji have seen it, and there is, in fact, no conclusive evidence that it actually exists.

Hozo-mon, the temple courtyard gate, also serves as a repository for *sutras* (Buddhist texts) and other Senso-ji treasures. Should either of this gate's guardian gods decide to leave its post for a stroll, it can use the enormous pair of sandals hanging on the back wall—the gift of a Yamagata Prefecture village famous for its straw weaving. ✉ *2–3–1 Asakusa, Taito-ku* ☏ *03/3842–0181* 🌐 *www.senso-ji.jp* 🎫 *Free* Ⓜ *Ginza subway line, Asakusa Station (Exit 1) and TOEI Asakusa subway line, Asakusa Station (Exit A4).*

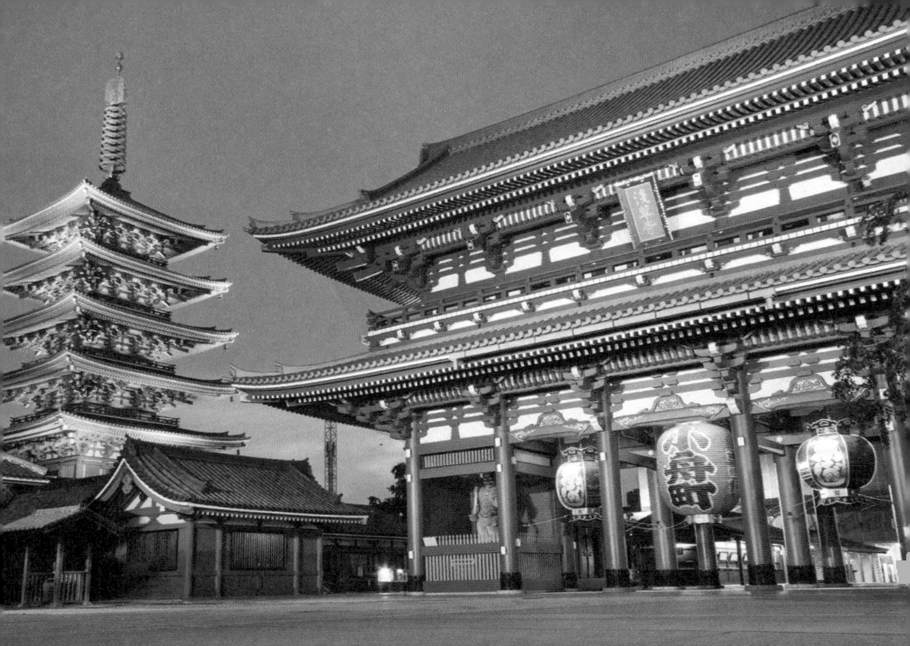

sakusa's heart and soul is the Senso-ji Temple Complex, famous for its pagoda, the Nakamise shopping treet, and 17th-century Shinto shrine, Asakusa Shrine, as well as the wild Sanja Festival in May.

oki no Kane Belfry (時の鐘)

ELIGIOUS BUILDING | The tiny hillock Benten-yama, with its Bentendo temple to he goddess of good fortune, is the site f this 17th-century belfry. The bell here nce tolled the hours for the people of he district, and it was said that you could ear it within a radius of some 6 km (4 niles). The bell still sounds at 6 am every lay, when the temple grounds open. t also rings on New Year's Eve—108 strokes in all, beginning just before nidnight, to "ring out" the 108 sins and railties of humankind and make a clean start for the coming year. Benten-yama nd the belfry are at the beginning of the iarrow street that parallels Nakamise-lori. ✉ *2–3 Asakusa, Taito-ku* Ⓜ *Ginza subway line, Asakusa Station (Exit 1) and TOEI Asakusa subway line, Asakusa Station (Exit A4).*

Restaurants

Historic Asakusa is filled with restaurants specializing in traditional dishes like tempura and *sukiyaki.* Rest and rejuvenate at a café serving Japanese sweets and green tea, or try the very casual *yakitori* restaurants that spill out onto Hoppy Street, a couple of blocks west of Senso-ji. The walk up to the temple is lined with places selling *sembei* (rice crackers), *ningyoyaki* (cakes stuffed with a sweet red-bean paste), and other small bites.

Daikokuya Tempura (大黒家天麩羅)

$$ | **JAPANESE** | Daikokuya, in the center of Asakusa's historic district, is a point of pilgrimage for both locals and tourists. The specialty is shrimp tempura, and the menu choices are simple—*tendon* (tempura shrimp served over rice) or the tempura meal with rice, pickled vegetables, and miso soup. **Known for:** being an Asakusa landmark; Tokyo-style tempura a cut above the rest; long lines. Ⓢ *Average main: ¥3,000* ✉ *1–38–10 Asakusa, Taito-ku* ☎ *03/3844–2222* 🌐 *www.tempura.co.jp/english* 💳 *No credit cards* Ⓜ *Ginza subway line, Asakusa Station (Exit 1) and TOEI Asakusa subway line, Asakusa Station (Exit A4).*

Sakaba Yamaka Shoten (酒場山加商店)
$$ | **JAPANESE** | This lively izakaya on a corner of Hoppy Street's main intersection, a few blocks west of Senso-ji, gets consistently high reviews. Take your pick between the indoor and outdoor seating, then order a chilled beer or some sake to go with the classic izakaya fare on the English menu—perhaps starting with some grilled Atka mackerel or green peppers stuffed with miso-flavored minced beef, before trying the more acquired flavor of the raw beef heart. **Known for:** lively atmosphere on Hoppy Street; outdoor seating; mix of classic izakaya food and less common Japanese dishes. *$ Average main: ¥3,000 ✉ 2–3–14 Asakusa, Taito-ku ☎ 03/6802–8893 Ⓜ Ginza subway line, Asakusa Station (Exit 1) and TOEI Asakusa subway line, Asakusa Station (Exit A4).*

Coffee and Quick Bites

Aun (阿吽)
$ | **RAMEN** | Located near the shops of Kappabashi-dori, the counter-only Aun specializes in *tantanmen* (tantan ramen), a Japanese take on spicy Sichuan dandan noodles. The lip-numbing dish, which routinely score high marks from reviewers, can be ordered here with spice levels that range from gentle to extreme. **Known for:** tantanmen noodles; customizable spice levels; lunchtime lines. *$ Average main: ¥1,100 ✉ 1–1–13 Nishi Asakusa, Taito-ku ☎ 03/5828–5525 ⊕ szechuan-aun.com ⏱ Closed Tues. Ⓜ Ginza subway line, Tawaramachi Station (Exit 3).*

Fuglen Asakusa
$$ | **SCANDINAVIAN** | At the northern end of the izakaya-lined Hoppy Street (a few blocks west of Senso-ji), this hip Scandinavian-style café serves up sweet and savory Norwegian waffles along with coffee made using single-origin beans. In the evenings, there are craft beers and cocktails on the menu, too. **Known for:** craft beer and cocktails at night; Norwegian waffles; coffee made with single-origin beans. *$ Average main: ¥1,500 ✉ 2–6–16 Asakusa, Taito-ku ☎ 03/5811–1756 ⊕ fuglen.no Ⓜ Ginza subway line, Asakusa Station (Exit 1) and TOEI Asakusa subway line, Asakusa Station (Exit A4).*

Sensing Touch of Earth
(センシング・タッチ・オブ・アース)
$ | **CAFÉ** | On Kappabashi-dori, just north of the Kama-Asa knife store, this café has a very hipster feel thanks to its stark concrete walls and occasional in-store art exhibitions. The menu includes specialty coffees as well as organic matcha and ginger lemonade. **Known for:** specialty coffee; hipster vibe; short opening hours (11 to 6 daily). *$ Average main: ¥600 ✉ 3–1–12 Matsugaya, Taito-ku ☎ 03/4400–7678 ⊕ stoe-cafe.tokyo Ⓜ Ginza subway line, Tawaramachi Station (Exit 3).*

Hotels

Thanks to its historic attractions, Asakusa mainly caters to tourists with standard hotels and boutique hotels. There is also, however, a selection of reasonably priced *ryokan* (traditional inns).

Asakusa Kokono Club
(浅草九倶楽部ホテル)
$ | **HOTEL** | A three-minute walk west from Senso-ji, this fairly recent hipster-ish addition to Asakusa's hotel scene has rooms (on its third to tenth floors) that are spacious and modern, with wooden flooring, wide windows, and stark concrete accents. **Pros:** spacious rooms by local standards; modern alternative to Asakusa's many older ryokan; close to the main sights. **Cons:** area can be noisy; restaurant can fill up with nonguests; limited facilities. *$ Rooms from: ¥20,000 ✉ 2–6–12 Asakusa, Taito-ku ☎ 03/5830–6533 ⊕ asakusakokonoclub.com ⇆ 30 rooms 🍽 No Meals Ⓜ Ginza subway line, Asakusa Station (Exit 1).*

Asakusa View Hotel (浅草ビューホテル)
$$ | **HOTEL** | **FAMILY** | Although the box-shaped Asakusa View is the largest

Lined with low-rise buildings housing independent shops and cafés, many of Asakusa's streets have a retro feel.

Western-style hotel in the traditional Asakusa area, it isn't divorced from traditional culture—communal *hinoki* (Japanese-cypress) baths on the sixth floor overlook a Japanese garden. **Pros:** affordable rates; handy base (between Senso-ji and Kappabashi) for exploring the area; pool and gym. **Cons:** room interiors generally basic and a little dated; professional but impersonal service; a long walk from the subway. $ *Rooms from: ¥25,000* *3–17–1 Nishi-Asakusa, Taito-ku* *03/3847–1111* *www.viewhotels.jp* *326 rooms* *No Meals* *Ginza subway line, Tawaramachi Station (Exit 3) or Asakusa Station (Exit 1).*

★ **The Gate Hotel Asakusa Kaminarimon by HULIC** (ザ・ゲートホテル雷門)

$$ | **HOTEL** | This relative newcomer to the historical Asakusa area has a stylish flair that starts at the entrance, where an elevator whisks you up 13 floors to the beautiful, glass-walled lobby, and continues in guest rooms outfitted in deep, dark browns accented with jewel tones and the occasional mod touches. **Pros:** historic area; surrounded with great dining options; lovely views. **Cons:** rooms small by Western standards; not exactly a central location for exploring other parts of Tokyo; can be crowded on weekends. $ *Rooms from: ¥26,000* *2–16–11 Kaminarimon, Taito-ku* *03/5826–3877* *gate-hotels.com* *137 rooms* *No Meals* *Ginza subway line, Asakusa Station (Exit 2) and TOEI Asakusa line, Asakusa Station (Exit A4).*

OMO3 Asakusa by Hoshino Resorts (*OMO3* 浅草 by 星野リゾート)

$ | **HOTEL** | **FAMILY** | This slender tower a couple of minutes east of the Senso-ji complex is part of the affordable yet sleek OMO chain created by luxury brand Hoshino Resorts. **Pros:** close to area sights and the subway; fresh, fashionable design; helpful English-speaking staff and free morning Asakusa tours. **Cons:** on a noisy street; not the biggest rooms; limited dining options. $ *Rooms from: ¥19,000* *1–15–5 Hanakawado, Taito-ku* *50/3134–8095* *hoshinoresorts.com/en/hotels/omo3asakusa* *98 rooms*

No Meals Ⓜ *Ginza subway line, Asakusa Station (Exit 5) and TOEI Asakusa subway line, Asakusa Station (Main Exit).*

Ryokan Asakusa Mikawaya Honten (旅館三河屋本店)
$ | **B&B/INN** | This friendly ryokan has a few modest Western-style twin rooms amid its mostly Japanese-style rooms, and its location—just behind the Kaminari-mon gateway leading to the Senso-ji complex—is convenient for exploring the area. **Pros:** affordable accommodations; traditional Japanese experience; interesting area sights and shops. **Cons:** tatami mats and futons won't appeal to all guests; small rooms; very basic facilities. *$ Rooms from: ¥15,800* ✉ *1–30–12 Asakusa, Taito-ku* ☎ *03/3841–8954* ⊕ *asakusa-mikawaya.com* *15 rooms* *No Meals* Ⓜ *Ginza subway line, Asakusa Station (Exit 1) and TOEI Asakusa subway line, Asakusa Station (Exit A4).*

Ryokan Asakusa Shigetsu (旅館浅草 指月)
$ | **B&B/INN** | Just off Nakamise-dori, this small inn, with both Japanese- and Western-style rooms, could not be better located for a visit to Senso-ji temple. **Pros:** affordable rooms; located in a historic temple area; close to subway station. **Cons:** not convenient to central Tokyo; Western-style rooms are all singles; small rooms. *$ Rooms from: ¥20,000* ✉ *1–31–11 Asakusa, Taito-ku* ☎ *03/3843–2345* ⊕ *www.shigetsu.com* *21 rooms* *No Meals* Ⓜ *Ginza subway line, Asakusa Station (Exit 1) and TOEI Asakusa subway line, Asakusa Station (Exit A4).*

Nightlife

Kamiya Bar (神谷バー)
BARS | Tokyo's oldest Western-style bar hasn't had a face-lift for decades (the main building is registered as a tangible cultural property), and that's part of what draws so many drinkers to this bright, noisy venue. The other major attraction is the Denki Bran, a delicious but hangover-inducing cocktail (essentially, gin, wine, brandy, and curaçao) that was invented here about 100 years ago and is now stocked by bars throughout Japan. ✉ *1–1–1 Asakusa, Taito-ku* ☎ *03/3841–5400* ⊕ *www.kamiya-bar.com* Ⓜ *Ginza subway line, Asakusa Station (Exit 1) and TOEI Asakusa subway line, Asakusa Station (Exit A4).*

Did You Know?

Kamiya Bar, Japan's first drinking establishment to call itself a "bar," opened in 1880 and still stands in Asakusa today. Stop by for a jolt of Denki Bran, a drink that dates from the Meiji Era. Although the full recipe is a secret, the brew contains gin, wine, brandy, and curaçao and is sold in bottles at the bar. It's definitely an acquired taste; some locals wash it down with a beer chaser.

The Tavern in Asakusa
BARS | Asakusa has plenty of izakaya, especially on Hoppy Street, but for just a drink (and without the smokiness of many izakaya), the Tavern is a good choice for its great selection of local and overseas whiskies, as well as sake and cocktails, not to mention Ken, the very cheerful owner–bartender. ✉ *2–14–15 Nishi Asakusa, Taito-ku* ☎ *03/6876–8245* Ⓜ *Next to Asakusa Station on Tsukuba Express Line; Ginza subway line, Asakusa Station (Exit 1).*

Shopping

While visiting the Senso-ji temple complex in Asakusa, take time to stroll through the neighborhood's many arcades. At first glance, many of the goods sold here are the kinds of souvenirs you can find in any tourist trap. Explore a little deeper, though, and you'll find small backstreet shops that have been making beautiful wooden combs, delicate fans, and other fine traditional crafts for generations. Also here are the cookware shops of Kappabashi, with everything from sushi knives to plastic lobsters.

CRAFTS

Omote (仮面屋おもて; *Kamen-ya Omote*)
SPECIALTY STORE | "Omote" means "face" or "mask," and this chic little boutique on the old-fashioned Kirakira Tachibana shopping street a station away from Tokyo Skytree stocks every variety imaginable. The selection includes Japanese-style clown masks and Venetian masks, as well as those from many periods and regions in Japan. There's a broad range of prices too, so you can find unique souvenirs here whatever your budget. Note, though, that the shop is only open Saturday and Sunday from 1 pm to 6 pm. ✉ *3–20–5 Kyōjima, Sumida-ku* ☎ *70/5089–6271* 🌐 *kamenyaomote.com* Ⓜ *Keisei Oshiage Line, Keisei Hikifune Station.*

DOLLS

Marugin
(人形のまるぎん; *Ningyo no Marugin*)
TOYS | **FAMILY** | This well-established emporium by Asakusabashi Station specializes in *hina* (emperor and empress) dolls in extravagant Heian-era clothing. Some families with young girls display these for the month prior to Girls' Day (March 2nd). Asakusabashi is one stop west of Ryogoku on the JR Chuo and Sobu lines or two stops south of Asakusa on the Asakusa subway line. ✉ *1–30–2 Asakusabashi, Taito-ku* ☎ *03/3862–6088* 🌐 *www.marugin.com* 🕒 *Closed Sun.* Ⓜ *JR Chuo and Sobu lines (West Exit), Asakusa subway line, Asakusabashi Station (Exit A3).*

FOOD

Kawahara Shoten (川原商店)
SOUVENIRS | **FAMILY** | The rice crackers, shrimp-flavored chips, and other Japanese snacks in brightly colored packages sold at this ramshackle Kappabashi store make offbeat gifts. ✉ *3–9–2 Nishi-Asakusa, Taito-ku* ☎ *03/3842–0841* Ⓜ *Ginza subway line, Tawaramachi Station (Exit 3).*

Tokiwa-do (常盤堂)
FOOD | **FAMILY** | Come here to buy (and watch the creation of) Asakusa's famous *kaminari okoshi* (thunder crackers), made of rice, millet, sugar, and beans. The shop is on the west side of Asakusa's Thunder God Gate, the Kaminari-mon entrance to Senso-ji. ✉ *1–3–2 Asakusa, Taito-ku* ☎ *03/3841–5656* 🌐 *www.tokiwado.tokyo* Ⓜ *Ginza subway line, Asakusa Station (Exit 1) and TOEI Asakusa subway line, Asakusa Station (Exit A4).*

MARKETS AND SHOPPING ARCADES

Nakamise Street
(仲見世通り; *Nakamise-dori*)
NEIGHBORHOOD | **FAMILY** | Although many shops here now sell cheap knickknacks (often, not made in Japan) rather than traditional Japanese crafts, this street's atmosphere makes it worth a stroll on your way to Senso-ji. Things here are as lively as they were back in the Edo period. The street's entrance is marked by the giant red lantern at the Kaminari-mon; it ends a couple of hundred meters north, shortly before the Hozomon gate. ✉ *Asakusa 1–chome, Taito-ku, Taito-ku* Ⓜ *Ginza subway line, Asakusa Station (Exit 1) and TOEI Asakusa subway line, Asakusa Station (Exit A4).*

Nishi-Sando Arcade
(西参道商店街; *Nishi-Sando Shoten-gai*)
NEIGHBORHOOD | **FAMILY** | Kimono and *yukata* (cotton kimono) fabrics, traditional accessories, swords, and festival costumes at reasonable prices are all for sale at this Asakusa arcade. It runs east of the area's movie theaters, between Rokuku Broadway Street and the Senso-ji Complex. ✉ *2–17–13 Asakusa, Taito-ku, Taito-ku* 🌐 *www.asakusaomatsuri.com* Ⓜ *Ginza subway line, Asakusa Station (Exit 1) and TOEI Asakusa subway line, Asakusa Station (Exit A4).*

SWORDS AND KNIVES

Ichiryo-ya Hirakawa (一両屋平川)
SPECIALTY STORE | This small, cluttered souvenir shop in the Nishi-Sando arcade carries antique swords and reproductions and has some English-speaking salesclerks. ✉ *2–7–13 Asakusa, Taito-ku* ☎ *03/3843–0052* Ⓜ *Ginza subway line, Asakusa Station (Exit 1) and TOEI Asakusa subway line, Asakusa Station (Exit A4).*

★ **Kama-Asa** (釜浅商店)
HOUSEWARES | Specializing in handcrafted knives and kitchen utensils, this elegant store first opened in 1908 in Asakusa's Kappabashi (Kitchen Town). It now occupies two neighboring buildings, one selling more than 80 varieties of knives made by leading makers around Japan, the other focusing on high-grade items like Nambu cast ironware. Allow extra time to have your knives engraved with Japanese symbols or your name at no extra cost. ✉ *2–24–1 Matsugaya, Taito-ku* ☎ *03/3841–9357* 🌐 *kama-asa.co.jp* Ⓜ *Ginza subway line, Tawaramachi Station (Exit 3).*

Tsubaya Knives (つば屋包丁店; *Tsubaya Hocho-ten*)
HOUSEWARES | Just off Kappabashi, this shop has a remarkable selection of high-quality, professional-grade cutlery designed for every imaginable use, as food preparation and presentation in Japan requires a great variety of cutting implements. The best of these are hand-forged tools made with blue carbon steel. Be prepared to pay a premium for these items: a multipurpose *gyuto* kitchen knife can cost as much as ¥50,000. ✉ *3–7–2 Nishi-Asakusa, Taito-ku* ☎ *03/3845–2005* 🌐 *tsubaya.jp* Ⓜ *Ginza subway line, Tawaramachi Station (Exit 3).*

TRADITIONAL WARES

Asakusa Nakaya Honten (浅草中屋本店)
CLOTHING | **FAMILY** | Traditional costumes for the neighborhood's May Sanja Festival are sold here. Best buys include *sashiko hanten,* thick, woven firemen's jackets, and *happi* coats, cotton tunics printed in bright colors with Japanese characters. Some items are available in children's sizes. ✉ *2–2–12 Asakusa, Taito-ku* ☎ *03/3841–7877* 🌐 *www.nakaya.co.jp* Ⓜ *Ginza subway line, Asakusa Station (Exit 6) and TOEI Asakusa subway line, Asakusa Station (Exit A4).*

Ganso Sample (元祖食品サンプル; *Ganso Shokuhin Sanpuru*)
SOUVENIRS | **FAMILY** | Ganso is one of several shops on Kappabashi-dori specializing in *sanpuru*, the replicas of food and drinks seen in many restaurant window displays. Look for fake bottles of beer, plates of noodles, and sushi-shaped trinkets. Or take one of the eight daily workshops (¥3,000 per person) and make your own fake tempura. ✉ *3–7–6 Nishi Asakusa, Taito-ku* ☎ *120/171–839* 🌐 *www.ganso-sample.com/en/shop* Ⓜ *Ginza subway line, Tawaramachi Station (Exit 3).*

Komatsuya (小松屋)
CERAMICS | In business since 1909, this open-fronted store on Kapppabashi almost looks like a garage sale, with its stacks of bowls, plates, hotpots, and other traditional ceramics. Most of it comes with a very affordable price tag. ✉ *2–21–6 Nishi Asakusa, Taito-ku* ☎ *03/3841–2368* 🌐 *kappabashi-komatsuya.com* Ⓜ *Ginza subway line, Tawaramachi Station (Exit 3).*

Tenugui Fuji-ya (てぬぐいふじ屋)
FABRICS | Keiji Kawakami is a master textile creator and expert on the hundreds of traditional towel motifs—geometric patterns, plants and animals, scenes from Kabuki plays and festivals—that have come down from the Edo period. His cotton *tenugui* (pronounced "teh-*noo*-goo-ee") hand towels are collector's items, worthy of being framed. ✉ *2–2–15 Asakusa, Taito-ku* ☎ *03/3841–2283* 🌐 *tenugui-fujiya.jp* Ⓜ *Ginza subway line, Asakusa Station (Exit 1) and TOEI Asakusa subway line, Asakusa Station (Exit A4).*

Sights

1 The Japanese Sword Museum **B3**
2 The Sumida Hokusai Museum **D4**
3 Sumo Museum **B4**
4 Tokyo Skytree...... **D1**

Quick Bites

1 Single O Roastworks. **D4**

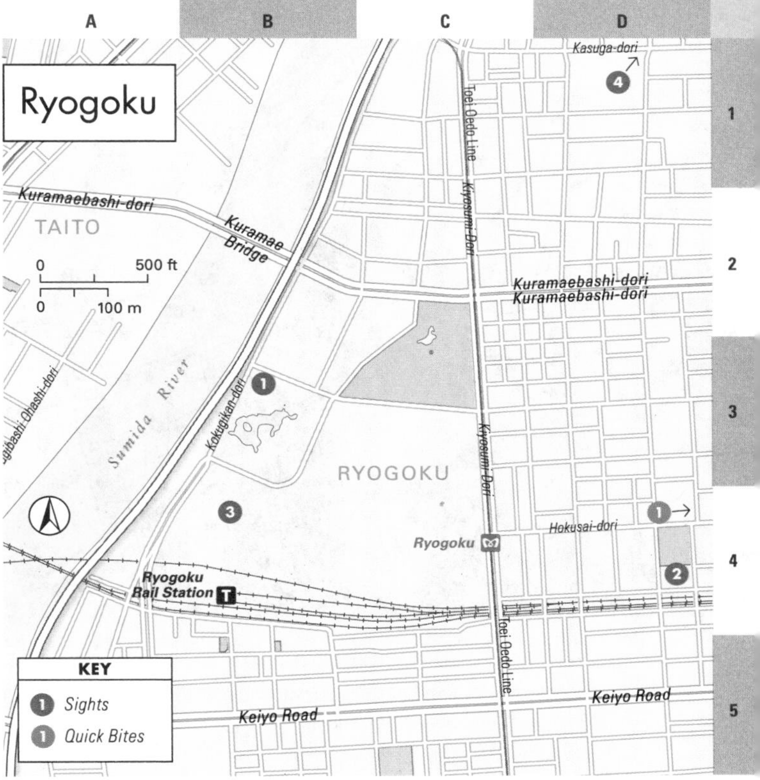

Ryogoku

Sights

The Japanese Sword Museum
(刀剣博物館 *Touken Hakubutsukan*)
SPECIALTY MUSEUM | At one time, Japan had some 200 schools that taught the art of making swords, which were prized not only for their effectiveness in battle but also for the beauty of their blades and fittings. They were also symbols of the higher spirituality of the warrior caste. The Sword Museum's mission is to maintain the knowledge and appreciation of sword making, a craft that's practiced by very few today.

Housed in a sleek, three-story structure designed by Pritzker Prize–winner Fumihiko Maki, the museum has thematic displays ranging from newly made swords to historical katana (single-edge samurai swords), including examples by famous craftsmen such as Sanekage (a 14th-century sword maker). The main third-floor exhibition space treats the swords as objects of beauty, displaying them individually as works of art, enabling visitors to appreciate the detail, creativity, and skill involved in crafting each one. The free rooftop garden, with views over a traditional garden, Kyu-Yasuda Teien, is worth a visit in its own right. ✉ *1–12–9 Yokoami, Sumida-ku* ☎ *03/6284–1000* 🌐 *www.touken.or.jp* 🎫 *Main exhibition (3rd fl.) ¥1,500* 🕒 *Closed Mon.* Ⓜ *Toei Oedo Line and JR Chuo and Sobu lines, Ryogoku Station.*

The Sumida Hokusai Museum (すみだ北斎美術館 *Sumida Hokusai Bijutsukan*)
ART MUSEUM | One of Japan's most famous artists, Katsushika Hokusai

Clear-day views from the Tokyo Skytree broadcast tower are impressive, whether you head to the Tembo Deck 1,155 feet up or pay an extra fee to access the Tembo Galleria, another 330 feet up.

(1760–1849) was born and spent much of his life in what's now Tokyo's Sumida-ku area, where he not only created iconic woodblock prints of Mt. Fuji and life in old Edo, but painted and sketched. Built where Hokusai grew up, this museum traces his life and work with the help of detailed English explanations. Although most pieces here are replicas, there are also a few originals on display, as well as a recreation of Hokusai's cramped workroom. ✉ *2–7–2 Kamezawa, Sumida-ku* ☎ *03/6658–8936* 🌐 *hokusai-museum.jp* 🎫 *Permanent exhibition ¥400, special and permanent exhibitions ¥700* 🕒 *Closed Mon.* Ⓜ *Toei Oedo Line and JR Chuo and Sobu lines, Ryogoku Station.*

Sumo Museum
(相撲博物館; *Sumo Hakubutsukan*)
SPECIALTY MUSEUM | If you can't attend a sumo tournament, visit this museum in the south wing of the arena. There are no explanations in English, but the collection of sumo-related woodblock prints, paintings, and illustrated scrolls includes some nice examples of traditional Japanese fine art. Hours are limited to weekdays 12:30 to 4. ✉ *1–3–28 Yokoami, Sumida-ku* ☎ *03/3622–0366* 🌐 *www.sumo.or.jp/KokugikanSumoMuseum* 🎫 *Free* 🕒 *Closed weekends.*

Tokyo Skytree (東京スカイツリー)
VIEWPOINT | FAMILY | This 2,000-plus-foot-tall broadcast tower and amusement complex is eastern Tokyo's defining landmark. When it opened in 2011, tickets to the observation decks were booked for months in advance. Today, the tower and the adjacent Solamachi shopping complex continue to be big draws. On a clear day, the views from the 1,155-foot-high Tembo Deck observation area are impressive. For an extra fee, you can go to the Tembo Galleria, another 330 feet up. ✉ *1–1–2 Oshiage, Sumida-ku* 🌐 *www.tokyo-skytree.jp* 🎫 *Tembo Deck only ¥2,100; Tembo Deck and Tembo Galleria ¥3,100* ☞ *Tickets are ¥300 to ¥400 cheaper if booked online in advance.* Ⓜ *Tokyo Skytree Station on the Tobu Skytree Line & Oshiage Station on Toei Asakusa, Hanzomon and Tobu Skytree lines.*

A Mostly Naked Free-for-All

Sumo wrestling originated some 1,500 years ago as a religious rite that was held in a shrine and was designed to entertain the harvest gods. To a casual observer, a match might seem like a fleshy free-for-all, but to the trained eye, it's a refined battle. Two wrestlers square off in a dirt ring about 15 feet in diameter before charging straight at each other in nothing but silk loincloths. Their goal is to force their opponent down onto the ground or out of the ring by pushing, grabbing, or throwing him.

Wrestlers aren't allowed to hit an opponent below his belt, strike him with a closed fist, or grab his hair—something that would certainly upset the hairdresser who accompanies every sumo ringside. There are no weight divisions, so a "runt" of merely 250 pounds might face an opponent twice his size. In this sport, having a great technique is key.

To compete, a wrestler must belong to one of the roughly 50 *heya* (stables), many based in Tokyo, that are run by retired wrestlers who have purchased the right from the Japan Sumo Association. Hierarchy and formality rule in the sumo world. Youngsters recruited into the sport live in the stable dormitory, do all the community chores, and wait on their seniors. When they rise high enough in tournament rankings, they acquire their own servant-apprentices.

Most Tokyo stables are concentrated along both sides of the Sumida-gawa near the Kokugikan (National Sumo Arena). Wander, this area, and you might see wrestlers on the streets either in their traditional wooden clogs and kimonos or in more casual clothes. One sumo giveaway is the aroma: the oil they use in their hair smells like baby lotion.

The heya aren't as accessible as they once were, but companies such as Viator.com and Rakuten Travel Experiences (🌐 *experiences.travel.rakuten.com*) offer tours. Otherwise, your best bet for a sumo experience is to attend a match.

When: Of the six Grand Sumo Tournaments (called *basho*) that take place during the year, Tokyo hosts three: in early January, mid-May, and mid-September. Matches go from early afternoon, when the novices wrestle, to the titanic clashes of the upper ranks from around 4:30 to 6 pm.

Where: Tournaments are held in the Kokugikan (✉ *1–3–28 Yokoami, Sumida-ku* ☎ *03/3623–5111* 🚆 *Toei Oedo Line and JR Sobu and Chuo lines, Ryogoku Station*) in Ryogoku, a district in Sumida-ku also famed for its clothing shops and eateries that cater to sumo sizes and appetites.

How: Expensive seats, closest to the ring, are tatami-carpeted boxes for two to four people, called *sajiki*. The boxes are terribly cramped and cost ¥9,000–¥20,000 per person. Cheap seats start as low as ¥2,500 and, despite being high up at the back of the arena, still offer a good view. Tickets sell out fast in advance, but several hundred of the cheapest seats are sold same-day; you should line up by 6 am for those. You can also get tickets through the Ticket Pia website (🌐 *sumo.pia.jp/en*) and at 7-Eleven convenience stores.

 Coffee and Quick Bites

Single O Roastworks
$ | **CAFÉ** | East Tokyo has some serious artisanal coffee credentials, owing to the cafés of the Kiyosumi and Kiba neighborhoods, and now—thanks to this Aussie-run roastery—the Ryogoku neighborhood as well. You'll find this spot in a battered old warehouse, a few minutes northeast of the Sumida Hokusai Museum. **Known for:** ethically sourced coffee; single-origin beans; Australian jaffles (toasted sandwiches). *Average main: ¥500 3–21–5 Kamezawa, Sumida-ku 03/6240–4455 singleo.jp No credit cards Closed Mon. and Tues. Toei Oedo Line and JR Chuo and Sobu lines, Ryogoku Station.*

 Nightlife

Popeye (ポパイ)
BARS | Of the staggering 70 beers on tap here, most are top-quality Japanese microbrews, from pilsners to IPAs to barley wines. The owner is one of Japan's leading authorities on beer, and his passion is reflected in the quality of the offerings. The convivial, sports bar-like atmosphere attracts a mature clientele, making this a great post-sumo spot, but it can fill up quickly. The menu includes chicken ale confit, beery beef stew, beer cake, and beer ice cream. *2–18–7 Ryogoku, Sumida-ku 03/3633–2120 www.70beersontap.com JR Ryogoku Station (West Exit).*

Top of Tree
(天空 ラウンジ; *Tenku Raunji Top of Tree*)
COCKTAIL BARS | Perched atop the Solamachi shopping complex, this bar–restaurant attracts locals and tourists for breathtaking views of Tokyo Skytree. Drink options includes a range of classic cocktails, and, if you are hungry, there's a menu of French-inspired dishes. The music's mostly jazz, and spacious and cushy seats, with sprawling views of Tokyo through the oversized glass windows and ceiling, make you want to linger. *Solamachi complex, Tokyo Skytree Town, 1–1–2 Oshiage, 31st fl., Sumida-ku 03/5809–7377 www.top-of-tree.jp Hanzomon, TOEI Asakusa, and Keisei Oshiage lines, Oshiage (Skytree) Station (Exit B3).*

World Beer Museum (世界のビール博物館; *Sekai no Biru Hakubutsukan*)
BREWPUBS | If you are after a familiar taste, this bar–restaurant serves beers from around the world, including 150 kinds in bottles and 15 more on tap. It's in the Solamachi retail complex and has a large, pleasant outdoor terrace with low-key downtown views. The food menu includes mussels steamed in beer and pickled ham hock. *Solamachi complex, 1–1–2 Oshiage, 7th fl., Sumida-ku 03/5610–2648 www.world-liquor-importers.co.jp/en Hanzomon, TOEI Asakusa, and Keisei Oshiage lines, Oshiage (Skytree) Station (Exit B3).*

Chapter 14

BEYOND CENTRAL TOKYO

Updated by
Jonathan DeLise

Sights	Restaurants	Hotels	Shopping	Nightlife
★★★☆☆	★★☆☆☆	★★☆☆☆	★★☆☆☆	★☆☆☆☆

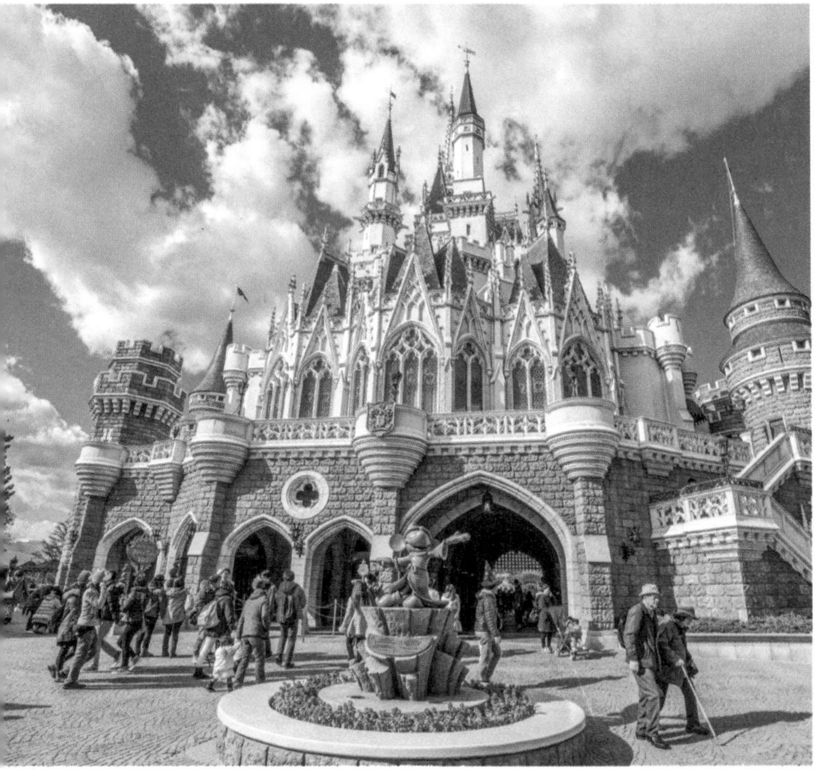

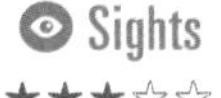

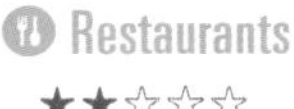

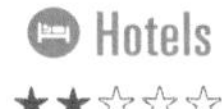

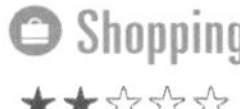

WELCOME TO BEYOND CENTRAL TOKYO

TOP REASONS TO GO

★ **Tokyo Disney Resort:** With a Baymax-themed ride and an accompanying water park, Tokyo Disney Resort, just to the east of Tokyo in Chiba prefecture, is popular with both Japanese and international visitors.

★ **Sengaku-ji Temple:** The 17th-century Buddhist temple in Shinagawa is featured in "47 Ronin," a famous samurai tale of fealty.

★ **Shopping in Shibamata:** The neighborhood's old-school Taishakuten Shopping Street evokes prewar Tokyo.

★ **Kiyosumi Garden:** A lush but often overlooked respite in working-class Fukagawa.

★ **Historic Kawagoe:** With several temples and a shopping street lined with warehouses from a bygone era, this historical area just beyond the city limits in Saitama prefecture has earned its reputation as *Ko-edo*, or "little Edo."

1 **Shibamata.** A quiet residential area northeast of Asakusa.

2 **Fukagawa.** Working-class area east of Nihonbashi with a beautiful garden.

3 **Urayasu.** On the shores of Tokyo Bay and home to the Tokyo Disney Resort.

4 **Nakameguro and Daikanyama.** Upscale areas south of Shibuya known for restaurants and cafés.

5 **Shinagawa.** An important transport hub with hotels and a noteworthy temple.

6 **Kawagoe.** Well-preserved historical town just over the Tokyo border.

7 **Narita Airport.** Over an hour from Tokyo, the country's major international airport has hotels for those with early flights as well as interesting sights in the neighboring town of Narita.

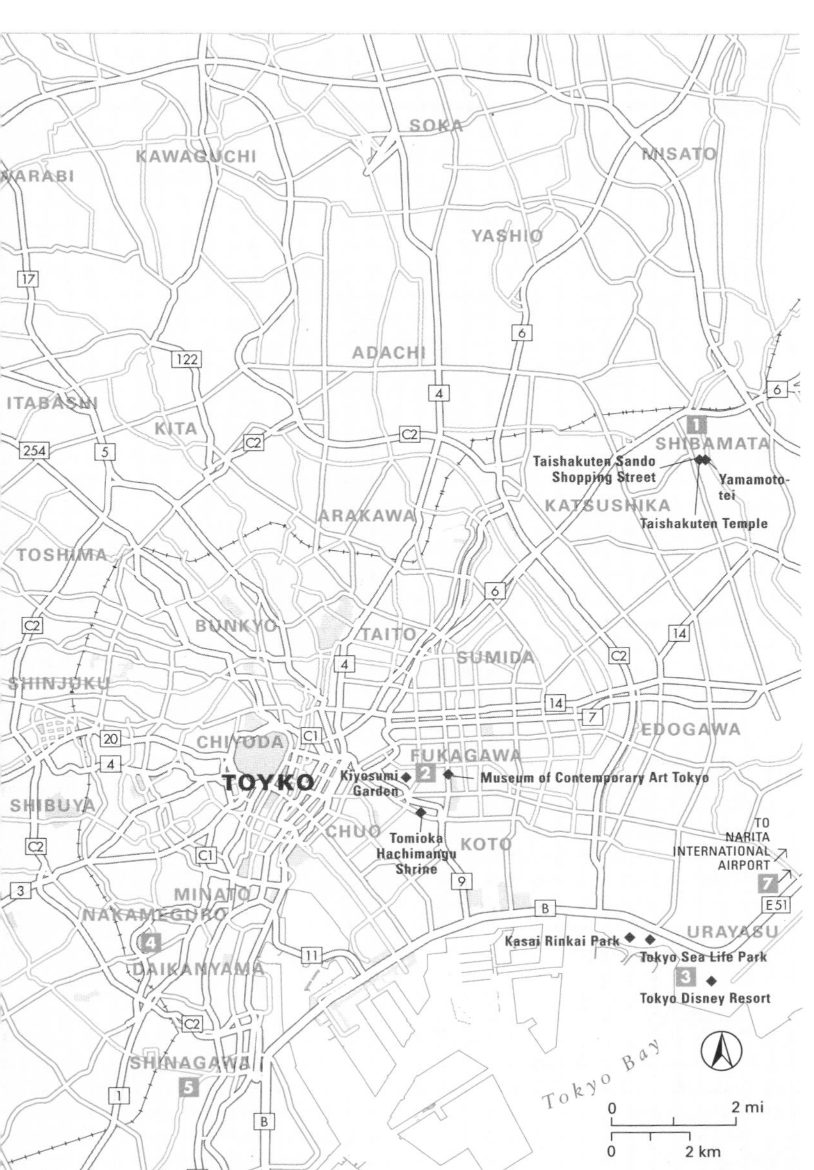
SOKA
KAWAGUCHI
MISATO
WARABI
YASHIO
ADACHI
ITABASHI
KITA
SHIBAMATA
Taishakuten Sando Shopping Street
Yamamoto-tei
KATSUSHIKA
Taishakuten Temple
ARAKAWA
TOSHIMA
BUNKYO
TAITO
SUMIDA
SHINJUKU
EDOGAWA
CHIYODA
FUKAGAWA
TOYKO
Kiyosumi Garden
Museum of Contemporary Art Tokyo
SHIBUYA
CHUO
Tomioka Hachimangu Shrine
KOTO
TO NARITA INTERNATIONAL AIRPORT
MINATO
NAKAMEGURO
URAYASU
Kasai Rinkai Park
Tokyo Sea Life Park
DAIKANYAMA
Tokyo Disney Resort
SHINAGAWA
Tokyo Bay
0
2 mi
2 km

Plenty of places—from Tokyo Disneyland to the historical quarters of Kawagoe—fall outside Tokyo's city limits yet are very much worth exploring.

Central Tokyo—particularly the Ginza, Shibuya, and Shinjuku areas—is routinely described as an endless, neon-lit strip of concrete. There is, however, is far more to discover in and outside the city limits.

To the southwest, near Tokyo's youthful Shibuya area, Daikanyama is an affluent residential enclave likened to Williamsburg, Brooklyn, for its upscale boutiques and hangouts. A bit farther southwest, the train hub of Shinagawa is home to Sengaku-ji, a temple that plays a central role in Japan's most famous tale of samurai loyalty.

To the southeast, in Chiba prefecture, Kasai Seaside Park offers numerous flora and bird-watching opportunities at the edge of Tokyo Bay. To the northeast, in Tokyo's residential district of Katsushika-ku is Shibamata, a charming old neighborhood that retains a 1950s vibe.

Shibamata

In the extreme northeast of Tokyo, within the quiet and mostly residential district of Katsushika-ku, the neighborhood of Shibamata is a charming throwback to early postwar Tokyo. Throughout Japan, the area is best known as a key setting for the long-running *Otoko Wa Tsurai Yo* (*It's Tough Being a Man*) film series, which followed the trials and tribulations of Tora-san, a lovable traveling salesman—and Shibamata denizen—over 48 installments from 1969 to 1995.

Here, you can soak up the retro vibe of Taishakuten Sando, Shibamata's main shopping street. You can also visit the historical temple of Taishakuten and explore the beautifully preserved Yamamoto-tei house and gardens.

To get here, take the Chiyoda subway line to Kanamachi Station. From there, the Keisei Kanamachi Line, which only has three stops and several trains per hour, runs to Shibamata Station. When you come out of the station's only exit, you'll be greeted by a bronze statue of Tora-san. The main attractions are just a short walk away.

Sights

Taishakuten Sando Shopping Street (帝釈天参道)
STREET | FAMILY | This retro shopping street between Shibamata Station and Taishakuten Temple has retained an old-Tokyo vibe, its wooden buildings having avoided both the heavy bombing that flattened much of Tokyo at the end of World War II and the subsequent redevelopment. Although the street developed as the approach to Taishakuten, Shibamata's renowned Buddhist temple, its connection to the eponymous site takes a back seat the items on sale here.

Taishakuten Sando is lined with small, family-run stores selling traditional snacks, such as savory *senbei* (rice crackers), *dorayaki* (sweet pancakes), and the Shibamata classic *kusa-dango* (sticky rice dumplings on skewers colored dark green because they include kudzu, or mugwort, in the mix). For the latter, stop by Monzen Toraya, a rice-dumpling specialist that has been around since 1887. Note that stores and restaurants here generally close sometime between 4 pm and 6 pm. ✉ *7–7–5 Shibamata, Katsushika-ku* 🎫 *Free* Ⓜ *Keisei Kanamachi Line, Shibamata Station.*

Taishakuten Temple (帝釈天)
TEMPLE | Established in 1629, this temple was damaged by the Great Kanto Earthquake of 1923, so its current incarnation dates from 1929. You enter through a towering wooden gateway that connects to Taishakuten Sando, Shibamata's main shopping street. Although admission to the grounds is free, it's worth paying the additional fee to enter the inner sanctuary, adorned with carvings of the life and teachings of Buddha, and the temple garden. ✉ *7–10–13 Shibamata, Katsushika-ku* ☎ *03/3657–2886* 🌐 *www.taishakuten.or.jp* 🎫 *Free; inner sanctuary/gardens, ¥400* Ⓜ *Keisei Kanamachi Line, Shibamata Station.*

Yamamoto-tei (山本亭)
HISTORIC HOME | Once the home of businessman Einosuke Yamamoto, Yamamoto-tei is an attractive example of how Japanese and Western styles merged in the homes of some wealthy Tokyoites in the Taisho era (1912–26). The two-story residence has mostly classic tatami-mat rooms with sliding screen doors (*shouji*), but it also incorporates a British-inspired drawing room with marquetry (wood veneer assembled like a jigsaw puzzle) flooring, white-plaster ceiling, stained-glass windows, and a marble mantel. Arguably the most striking feature is the *shoin*-style garden, whose lush greenery, pond, and waterfall are designed to be viewed from the comfort of the tatami rooms. You can soak up the atmosphere while enjoying green tea or coffee and sweets. ✉ *7–19–32 Shibamata, Katsushika-ku* ☎ *03/3657–8577* 🌐 *www.katsushika-kanko.com/yamamoto* 🎫 *¥100* 🕒 *Closed 3rd Tues. of the month* Ⓜ *Keisei Kanamachi Line, Shibamata Station.*

Restaurants

Monzen Toraya (門前とらや)
$ | JAPANESE | FAMILY | In business since 1887, Monzen Toraya is best known for its skewers of sweet *kusa-dango* rice dumplings, which come topped with red-bean paste and are a popular snack for visitors en route to Taishakuten Temple. The more substantial lunch menu features ramen, udon noodles, and rice bowls topped with seasonal tempura.
Known for: tempura on rice; kusa-dango rice dumplings; ramen. Ⓢ *Average main: ¥900* ✉ *7–7–5 Shibamata, Katsushika-ku* ☎ *03/3659–8111* 🌐 *www.toraya.info* 🕒 *No dinner* Ⓜ *Keisei Kanamachi Line, Shibamata Station.*

Fukagawa

A couple of miles east of Nihonbashi, the Fukagawa area developed as part of Tokyo's Edo-era *shitamachi*—the districts of the common, working people—but gets less attention from travelers than more famous shitamachi like Asakusa and Yanaka. It's a pity because visiting the laid-back overlapping neighborhoods that now comprise Fukagawa—namely, Kiyosumi-Shirakawa (in the north) and Monzen-Nakacho (south)—is a great way to soak up bits of everyday, traditional, and creative Tokyo.

In recent years, the area has gained hipster cred with a wave of coffee roasters and galleries moving in. Monzen-Nakacho has a historical shrine, plus some great down-to-earth restaurants. The best starting points are either Monzen-Nakacho Station on the Oedo and Tozai subway lines or Kiyosumi-Shirakawa Station on the Oedo and Hanzomon subway lines.

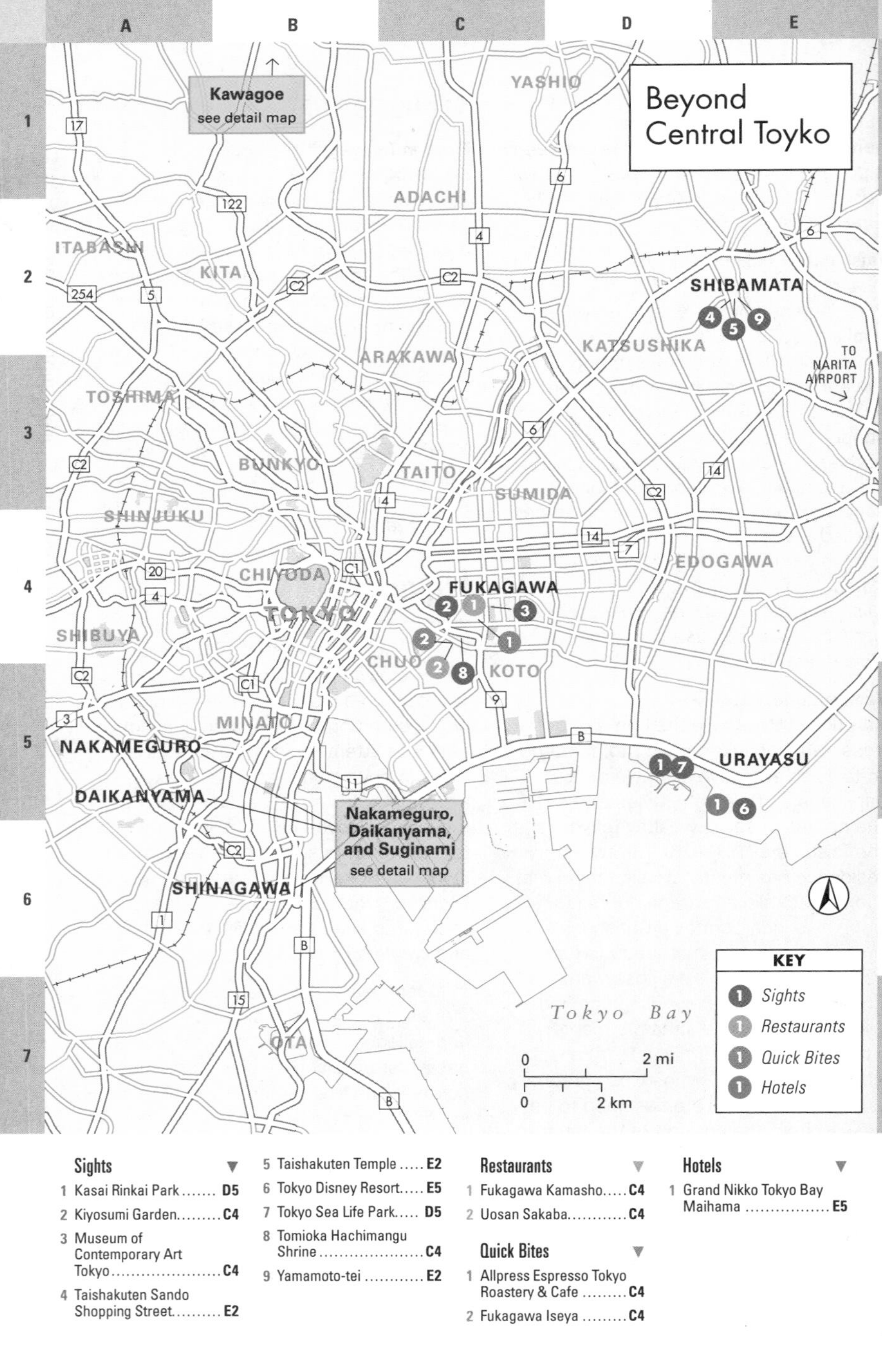

Sights

1 Kasai Rinkai Park **D5**
2 Kiyosumi Garden......... **C4**
3 Museum of Contemporary Art Tokyo....................... **C4**
4 Taishakuten Sando Shopping Street.......... **E2**
5 Taishakuten Temple **E2**
6 Tokyo Disney Resort..... **E5**
7 Tokyo Sea Life Park..... **D5**
8 Tomioka Hachimangu Shrine **C4**
9 Yamamoto-tei **E2**

Restaurants

1 Fukagawa Kamasho..... **C4**
2 Uosan Sakaba............ **C4**

Quick Bites

1 Allpress Espresso Tokyo Roastery & Cafe **C4**
2 Fukagawa Iseya **C4**

Hotels

1 Grand Nikko Tokyo Bay Maihama **E5**

Sights

Kiyosumi Garden
(清澄庭園; *Kiyosumi Teien*)

GARDEN | FAMILY | Defined by its island-accented pond, around which pathways take lead to a succession of carefully landscaped viewpoints with features like manicured trees and ornamental rocks, this traditional garden is one of eastern Tokyo's underappreciated gems. A highlight is the *isowatari*, the stepping stones that meander through the pond, allowing you to appreciate the park's reflections in the lake, as well as the carp and turtles. Part of a feudal lord's residence in the early 1700s, the garden was later owned by the founder of Mitsubishi, who used it to entertain important guests and give staff a place to unwind. Thereafter, it was donated to the city of Tokyo, and opened its doors to everyone in 1932. ✉ *3–3–9 Kiyosumi, Koto-ku* ☎ *03/3641–5892* 🌐 *www.tokyo-park.or.jp* 🎫 *¥150* Ⓜ *Oedo and Hanzomon subway lines, Kiyosumi-Shirakawa Station.*

Museum of Contemporary Art Tokyo (東京現代美術館; *Tokyo Gendai Bijutsukan*)

ART MUSEUM | On the far-eastern end of Kiyosumi-Shirakawa, occupying the northernmost part of the sprawling Kiba Park, this modern museum has spaces for contemporary art from its own collection and special exhibitions. In recent years, the latter have have included shows devoted to artist David Hockney, architect Jean Prouve, composer Sakamoto Ryuichi, and even one focused on the art of language. If you need a break while here, is a café as well as a restaurant on-site. Note that the museum sometimes closes during installations of new exhibitions. ✉ *4–1–1 Miyoshi, Koto-ku* ☎ *03/5245–4111* 🌐 *www.mot-art-museum.jp* 🎫 *From ¥500* 🕒 *Closed Mon.* Ⓜ *Oedo and Hanzomon subway lines, Kiyosumi-Shirakawa Station.*

Tomioka Hachimangu Shrine (富岡八幡宮)

RELIGIOUS BUILDING | This shrine in the heart of Monzen-Nakacho has been a core part of Fukagawa since the 1600s. It's said that some of the earliest sumo tournaments were held here in the 1700s, which explains the sumo-related monuments you'll see. Today, the grounds hold small dawn-to-dusk antiques markets on the first, second, third, and fifth Sundays of each month, while lively flea markets take place on the 15th and 28th of each month. In odd-numbered years, during the month of August, the shrine is also the starting point of Fukagawa Hachiman Matsuri, a festival that sees more than 50 portable shrines paraded energetically through the streets while onlookers pour buckets of water over the carriers (and each other). One more quirk here is that you can bring your car to be blessed. ✉ *1–20–3 Tomioka, Koto-ku* ☎ *03/3642–1315* 🌐 *www.tomiokahachimangu.or.jp* 🎫 *Free* Ⓜ *Oedo and Tozai subway lines, Monzen-Nakacho Station.*

Restaurants

Fukagawa Kamasho (深川釜匠)

$$ | JAPANESE | Kamasho serves the area's traditional signature dish, Fukagawa-meshi—short-neck clams and green onion cooked in a miso broth and poured over a bowl of rice. You can order just a bowl of it or, if you're really hungry, a set meal with a side serving of pickles and miso soup or some sushi. **Known for:** Fukagawa-meshi (clams on rice); lively atmosphere; rustic interiors. $ *Average main: ¥1,800* ✉ *2–1–13 Shirakawa, Koto-ku* ☎ *050/5493–4313* 🌐 *a328700.gorp.jp* 💳 *No credit cards* 🕒 *Closed Mon., no dinner Tues. or Thurs.* Ⓜ *Oedo and Hanzomon subway lines, Kiyosumi-Shirakawa Station.*

Did You Know?

Kiyosumi Garden in workaday Fukagawa is one of Tokyo's hidden gems. Its central feature is a pond with a series of islands and pathways that allow visitors to wander and relax in a natural atmosphere.

Uosan Sakaba (魚三酒場)
$$$ | JAPANESE | Dating back to the 1950s, this classic izakaya is a casual and lively place, where the third and fourth floors have tables, and the first two floors have only counter seats that are ideal for watching and chatting with the chefs. The focus is mostly on seafood, which pairs well the nihonshu on the menu. **Known for:** excellent sashimi; good selection of Japanese spirits; seafood-focused menu. *Average main: ¥4,500* ✉ *1–5–4 Tomioka, Koto-ku* ☎ *03/3641–8071* ▭ *No credit cards* ⏲ *Closed Sun. No lunch* Ⓜ *Oedo and Tozai subway lines, Monzen-Nakacho Station.*

Coffee and Quick Bites

Allpress Espresso Tokyo Roastery & Cafe (オールプレス)
$ | CAFÉ | An outpost of a New Zealand roastery, this small, friendly café serves excellent espressos, flat whites, and cappuccinos, plus simple snacks like cookies and toasted sandwiches. It occupies a repurposed wooden warehouse with indoor seating, but, if the weather is nice, grab a to-go drink and a slice of banana cake and walk a few minutes east to Kiba Park, a lovely green spot to while away an hour. **Known for:** great espresso shots; close to Kiba Park for outdoor coffee; friendly, laid-back staff. *Average main: ¥600* ✉ *3–7–2 Hirano, Koto-ku* ☎ *03/5875–9131* 🌐 *www.allpressespresso.com* Ⓜ *Oedo and Hanzomon subway lines, Kiyosumi-Shirakawa Station.*

Fukagawa Iseya (深川伊勢屋 *Fukagawa Iseya Honten*)
$ | JAPANESE | FAMILY | Preparing *wagashi* (traditional Japanese sweets generally served with tea) since 1907, the main branch (out of six) of Fukagawa Iseya is less than a five-minute walk from Tomioka Hachiman Shrine. Popular choices include *mitarashi dango* (skewers of small rice balls covered in a sweet soy glaze) and *daifuku* (mounds of mochi filled with Hokkaido red bean paste). **Known for:** well-established sweets shop; seasonal offerings; neighboring café. *Average main: ¥500* ✉ *Tomioka 1–8–12, Koto-ku* ✣ *Opposite Exit 1 of Monzen-nakacho station on the Tozai line/Oedo line* ☎ *03/3641–0695* 🌐 *www.iseya-ne.jp* ⏲ *Café closed Tues.* Ⓜ *Monzen-nakacho station on the Tokyo metro Tozai line, Toei metro Oedo line.*

Urayasu

Just east of Tokyo, in Chiba Prefecture, Urayasu is known for one thing: Tokyo Disney Resort, with the twin theme parks of Tokyo Disneyland and Tokyo DisneySea. Because they're so close to the city, most visitors to Tokyo do Disney as a day trip. However, there are a number of lodging options abutting the resort if you want to fully immerse yourself in the Magic Kingdom.

Across the river from Urayasu, in Tokyo's Edogawa district, Kasai Seaside Park is a less crowded alternative for family fun, with a giant Ferris wheel and an aquarium among its attractions.

Sights

Kasai Rinkai Park (葛西臨海公園 *Kasai Rinkai Koen*)
AMUSEMENT PARK/CARNIVAL | FAMILY | The star attraction here is the Diamonds and Flowers Ferris wheel, the second-tallest in Japan. The ride takes you on a 17-minute trip to the apex, 384 feet above the ground, for a spectacular view of the Tokyo bay area. On a clear day you can see all the way to Mt. Fuji; at night, if you're lucky, you reach the top just in time for a bird's-eye view of the fireworks over the Magic Kingdom, across the Kyuedo River. As a bonus, all Ferris wheel gondolas are private. The park also has an observatory looking out over Tokyo Bay, in addition to the Tokyo Sea Life Park aquarium, a bird-watching center, and some so-so beaches. ✉ *6–2*

Rinkai-cho, Edogawa-ku ✣ *From Disney take JR Keiyo Line local train from Maihama to Kasai Rinkai Park Station. The same line also connects to Tokyo Station.* ☎ *03/5696–1331* 🌐 *www.tokyo-park.or.jp* 🎫 *Free, Ferris wheel ¥800* ⏲ *Ferris wheel closes some Wed. in winter* Ⓜ *JR Keiyo Line, Kasai Rinkai Park Station.*

Tokyo Disney Resort
(東京ディズニーリゾート)
AMUSEMENT PARK/CARNIVAL | **FAMILY** | Much like at the original two Disney parks in the United States, Mickey-san and his troupe of Disney characters entertain here at Tokyo Disneyland. When the park was built in 1983, it was much smaller than its American counterparts. In 2001, the construction of the adjacent DisneySea and its seven "Ports of Call," all with different nautical themes and rides, added more than 100 acres and establishing the comprehensive Tokyo Disney Resort. Out of numerous ticket options, most opt for the One-Day Passport, which confers unlimited access to the attractions, as well as shows at one or the other of the two parks. ✉ *1–1 Maihama, Urayasu* ☎ *0570/00–8632* 🌐 *www.tokyodisneyresort.jp* 🎫 *From ¥7,900* Ⓜ *JR Keiyo Line, Maihama Station.*

Tokyo Sea Life Park (葛西臨海水族園; *Kaisai Rinkai Suizoku-en*)
AQUARIUM | **FAMILY** | This three-story dome-like structure houses roughly 600 species of fish and other sea creatures within a dozen zones, including Voyagers of the Sea (Maguro no Kaiyu), with migratory species; Seas of the World (Sekai no Umi), with species from abroad; and the Sea of Tokyo (Tokyo no Umi), devoted to the creatures of the bay and nearby waters. Don't miss the giant 2,200-ton bluefin tuna tank, the rays, or the puffins. ✉ *6–2–3 Rinkai-cho, Edogawa-ku* ✣ *The aquarium is a 10-minute walk from the South Exit at Kasai Rinkai Koen Station.* ☎ *03/3869–5152* 🌐 *www.tokyo-zoo.net/english/kasai* 🎫 *¥700* ⏲ *Closed Wed.* Ⓜ *JR Keiyo Line, Kasai Rinkai Koen Station.*

Hotels

Grand Nikko Tokyo Bay Maihama
(グランドニッコー東京ベイ 舞浜)
$$ | **HOTEL** | **FAMILY** | At one of the closest properties to the Tokyo Disney Resort, lots of natural light shines through a vast atrium, and all the recently renovated rooms rooms have sizable windows with views of either Tokyo Disney or Tokyo Bay. Eating options are limited to the all-day dining spot Le Jardin, a Japanese restaurant, and for guests with access, quick bites and drinks in one of two executive lounges. **Pros:** free shuttles to JR Maihama station/Disney; nice staff; family-friendly. **Cons:** inconvenient breakfast reservation system; no adults-only executive lounge; lack of on-site dining options. $ *Rooms from: ¥41,000* ✉ *1-7 Maihama, Urayasu* ✣ *Take the free hotel shuttle from JR Maihama Station* ☎ *047/350–3533* 🌐 *tokyobay.grandnikko.com* 🛏 *709 rooms* 🍽 *No Meals* Ⓜ *JR Keio or JR Musashino lines to JR Maihama Station.*

Nakameguro and Daikanyama

These two neighborhoods on either side of the Meguro River—one on the quiet edge of the otherwise bustling Shibuya-ku district, the other in the often overlooked Meguro-ku—make for a hip day or night out. Both are residential areas for the well-heeled, with sleek urban complexes and fashionable bars and cafés—places to see and be seen.

In spring, the Meguro River is awash in pink, thanks to the cherry trees that bloom alongside and are reflected in the water. With lanterns up at night and food stalls along the riverbank, it's one of Tokyo's top evening *hanami* (cherry-blossom viewing) spots.

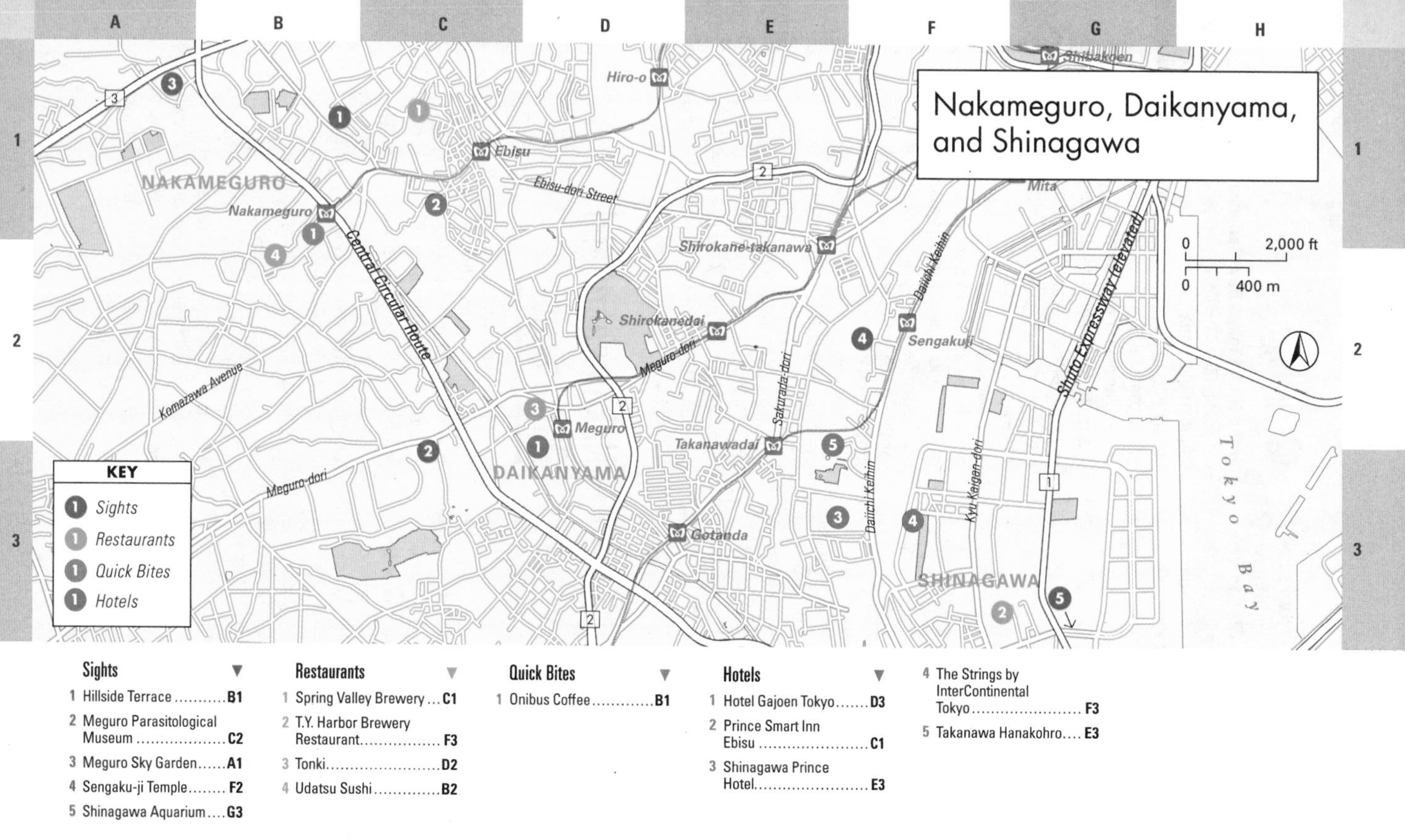

Sights

1 Hillside Terrace B1
2 Meguro Parasitological Museum C2
3 Meguro Sky Garden...... A1
4 Sengaku-ji Temple........ F2
5 Shinagawa Aquarium.... G3

Restaurants

1 Spring Valley Brewery ... C1
2 T.Y. Harbor Brewery Restaurant................. F3
3 Tonki........................ D2
4 Udatsu Sushi.............. B2

Quick Bites

1 Onibus Coffee............. B1

Hotels

1 Hotel Gajoen Tokyo....... D3
2 Prince Smart Inn Ebisu C1
3 Shinagawa Prince Hotel........................ E3
4 The Strings by InterContinental Tokyo....................... F3
5 Takanawa Hanakohro.... E3

The best way to get here is on the Tokyu Toyoko Line from Shibuya Station. From there, it's one stop to Daikanyama and two stops to Naka-Meguro, making either a good destination for a meal out if you are staying in Shibuya.

Sights

Hillside Terrace (ヒルサイドテラス)
STORE/MALL | Designed by famed architect Fumihiko Maki, the Hillside Terrace helped shape Daikanyama as a fashionable neighborhood after it was opened in 1967; since then, it had been expanded through the 1990s. Spread over multiple low-rise buildings, it mixes cafés and restaurants with offices, design (both international and Japanese) and fashion stores, and small galleries. The contemporary art at Art Front Gallery, coffee at Hillside Cafe, and all its other outlets help add to its appeal. ✉ *29–18 Sarugakucho, Shibuya-ku* ☎ *03/5489–3705* 🌐 *hillsideterrace.com* 🎫 *Free* Ⓜ *Tokyu Toyoko Line, Daikanyama Station.*

Meguro Parasitological Museum (目黒寄生虫館; *Meguro Kiseichu-kan*)
SCIENCE MUSEUM | **FAMILY** | Part of a private research facility specializing in the study of parasites, this small but free museum is decidedly not for the squeamish. Some of the specimens preserved in glass jars look like something out of an H.R. Geiger sketchbook. However, if you've ever dreamed of owning a T-shirt with the image of a giant tapeworm on the front, the museum shop has you covered.
✉ *4–1–1 Shimomeguro, Meguro-ku* ✥ *It's a 20-minute walk south of Naka-Meguro Station, or more conveniently 10 minutes west of Meguro Station.* ☎ *03/3716–1264* 🌐 *www.kiseichu.org/e-top* 🎫 *Free* ⏲ *Closed Mon. and Tues.* Ⓜ *JR Yamanote Line and Namboku and Mita subway lines, Meguro Station.*

Meguro Sky Garden (目黒天空庭園)
CITY PARK | **FAMILY** | Encircled by highways, this unabashedly urban park offers a pleasant stroll and superb Tokyo views. In addition to bamboo groves and Japanese maples, depending on the time of year you might see plum and peach blossoms, Chinese redbuds, banana shrubs, or Taiwanese camellias. Meguro Sky Garden is strictly no-smoking.
✉ *1–9–2 Oohashi, Shibuya-ku* ✥ *Under 5 minutes walk from Tokyu Den-en-Toshi Ikejiri Oohashi station* ☎ *03/3464–1612* 🌐 *www.city.meguro.tokyo.jp/shisetsu/index.html* 🎫 *Free* Ⓜ *Tokyu Den-en-Toshi Ikejiri Oohashi station.*

Restaurants

Spring Valley Brewery
(スプリングバレーブルワリー)
$$$ | **AMERICAN** | This microbrewery in Daikanyama produces a core lineup of six ales and lagers, as well as seasonal and limited releases, such as an 8% Belgian "gran cru," Jazzberry made with raspberries and wine yeast, or a 6.5% hop-heavy IPA. But Spring Valley isn't just a place to drink—the menu also lists a good range of burgers, pizzas, and grilled meats, all with beer-pairing suggestions.
Known for: a range of craft beers made in-house; burgers and pizzas; seasonal outdoor terrace. 💲 *Average main: ¥5,000* ✉ *13–1 Daikanyamacho, Shibuya-ku* ☎ *03/6416–4960* 🌐 *www.springvalleybrewery.jp* Ⓜ *Tokyu Toyoko Line, Daikanyama Station.*

Tonki (とんき)
$$ | **JAPANESE** | Just about everybody who comes to this well-established, family-owned restaurant orders the standard course of utterly delicious deep-fried pork cutlets, soup, raw-cabbage salad, rice, pickles, and tea. Although there's a line here every night, right up until closing at 10:45 pm, efficient service means that the wait is usually only about 10 minutes.

Known for: hearty, affordable meals; juicy pork; a line out the door. *Average main: ¥2,100* ✉ *1–1–2 Shimo-Meguro, Meguro-ku* ☎ *03/3491–9928* 🌐 *www.instagram.com/tonkatsu_tonki* ⏲ *Closed Tues. and 3rd Mon. of month. No lunch* Ⓜ *JR Yamanote and Namboku subway lines, Meguro Station (Nishi-guchi/West Exit).*

Udatsu Sushi (宇田津鮨)
$$$$ | **SUSHI** | This compact, counter-only sushi restaurant in Naka Meguro's backstreets just does *omakase*, meaning that you'll be served whatever the owner–chef has sourced each day from Tokyo's Toyosu Market. Although the fish (or hair crab or sea urchin by special request) takes center stage, herbs and vegetables are also incorporated into Udatsu's often-modern takes on sushi. **Known for:** innovative take on traditional sushi; intimate setting; vegetarian sushi options. *Average main: ¥22,000* ✉ *2–48–10 Kamimeguro, Meguro-ku* ☎ *050/3550–5938* 🌐 *www.udatsu-sushi.jp* Ⓜ *Tokyu Toyoko Line, Naka-Meguro Station and Hibiya subway line, Naka-Meguro Station.*

Coffee and Quick Bites

Onibus Coffee (オニバスコーヒー)
$ | **CAFÉ** | Seating is limited at this small stand near Naka Meguro Station, but the baristas are extremely knowledgeable about how to properly prepare espressos, hand-drip coffees, and lattes. And the name of this chain of roasteries isn't a misspelling of "omnibus," but rather a playful mix of "*oni*" (devil) and "bus." **Known for:** adept baristas; excellent hand-drip coffee and espresso; limited seating. *Average main: ¥600* ✉ *2–14–1 Kamimeguro, Meguro-ku* ☎ *03/6412–8683* 🌐 *onibuscoffee.com* 💳 *No credit cards* Ⓜ *Tokyu Toyoko line, Naka-Meguro Station and Hibiya subway line, Naka-Meguro Station.*

Hotels

★ **Hotel Gajoen Tokyo** (ホテル雅叙園東京)
$$$$ | **HOTEL** | If you love art, then this hotel should be your lodestar, as everything—from the ornate entryway and the koi pond to the chapel (the property was a wedding complex in the 1920s) and the Chinese restaurant—features elements seemingly plucked from a renowned art museum. **Pros:** marvelous design and decor; giant rooms; steam bath and whirlpool tub in some accommodations. **Cons:** few homemade options at breakfast; down a steep hill from JR Meguro station; can get crowded with sightseers or event attendees. *Rooms from: ¥90,000* ✉ *1–8–1 Shimomeguro, Meguro-ku* ✥ *Less than 10-min. walk from JR Meguro station* ☎ *03/3491–4111* 🌐 *en.hotelgajoen-tokyo.com* *60 suites* *No Meals* Ⓜ *JR Meguro station; Tokyo Metro Meguro station.*

Prince Smart Inn Ebisu (プリンス スマート イン 恵比寿)
$ | **HOTEL** | If you're all about smart technology and efficient service, try this small Ebisu property, where the lobby has an interactive map, and check-in/out and luggage storage before or after your stay can be done using self-service machines. **Pros:** proximity to public transit; luggage storage lockers; some rooms have "smart" speakers and mirrors. **Cons:** limited albeit free breakfast; impersonal (machine-based) service; small rooms. *Rooms from: ¥23,000* ✉ *Ebisu Minami 3–11–25, Shibuya-ku* ✥ *A 5-min. walk from JR Ebisu station, or a 3-min. walk Ebisu station on the Hibiya metro line* ☎ *03/3161–9550* 🌐 *www.princehotels.co.jp* *82 rooms* *Free Breakfast* Ⓜ *JR Ebisu station; Tokyo Metro Hibiya line Ebisu station.*

Nightlife

abin Naka-Meguro (キャビン中目黒)
ARS | Alongside the Meguro River, a ϶w minutes southeast of Naka Meguro ;tation, the very hip, rustic contempo-ary–style Cabin has an extensive range ·f world whiskies and rare local tipples, s well champagne and cocktails. Since ne inspiration was a *yamagoya*, or moun-ain hut, meat dishes dominate the food nenu. ✉ *1–10–23 Nakameguro, Meguro-'u* ☎ *03/6303–2220* 🌐 *www.cabintokyo. :om* Ⓜ *Tokyu Toyoko Line, Naka-Meguro ;tation and Hibiya subway line, Naka-Me-ɪuro Station.*

ebris (デブリ)
OCKTAIL BARS | Part cocktail bar, part ›vent space with DJ nights, movie ;creenings, recitals, and art exhibitions, ıeon-lit Debris is a stylish hangout for)aikanyama's creative set. The mixolo-jists here can mix up classics, but they ılso get creative with artisanal spirits as ıaried as Cocalero from the Andes or ndonesian Nusa Caña rum made with :loves and nutmeg. Most events have a :over charge. ✉ *11–12 Daikanyamacho, Shibuya-ku* ☎ *03/6416–4334* 🌐 *debris-)ace.com* ⏲ *Closed Sun.* Ⓜ *Tokyu Toyoko ine, Daikanyama Station.*

Shinagawa

Although Shinagawa isn't the most excit-ng part of Tokyo, the numerous hotels and train options make this transport ıub hard to overlook. This isn't to say the area is devoid of attractions—for families, there's the Shinagawa Aquarium, and, ıot far from Shinagawa Station, there's the Sengaku-ji Temple, which is tied to one of Japan's best-known tales from its samurai days.

From Shinagawa Station, the bullet train connects to key destinations west, including Nagoya, Osaka, Kyoto, and Hiroshima. With the Yamanote and other lines, Shinagawa is well connected to Shibuya, Shinjuku, and other popular parts of Tokyo. For anyone flying into or out of Haneda Airport, Shinagawa is only 10 km (6.2 miles); N'Ex, the direct train to Narita Airport, also stops here.

Sights

★ **Sengaku-ji Temple** (泉岳寺)
TEMPLE | **FAMILY** | In 1701, a young provincial baron named Asano Takumi-no-Kami attacked and seriously wounded a royal attendant named Yoshinaka Kira. Asano, for daring to draw his sword in the confines of Edo Castle, was ordered to commit suicide, resulting in his family line being abolished and his estate being confiscated. Forty-seven of Asano's loyal retainers vowed revenge; the death of their leader made them *ronin*—master-less samurai. On the night of December 14, 1702, Asano's ronin stormed Kira's vil-la in Edo, cut off his head, and brought it in triumph to Asano's tomb at Sengaku-ji, the family temple, which dates to 1642. The ronin were sentenced to commit suicide—which they accepted as the reward, not the price, of their honorable vendetta—and were buried in the temple graveyard with their lord.

Through the centuries, this story—known in Japanese as *Chushingura*—has become the last word on the subject of loyalty and sacrifice, celebrated in every medium from kabuki to film. The temple still stands, and the graveyard is wreathed in smoke from the bundles of incense that visitors reverently lay on the tombstones. There is a collection of weapons and other memorabilia from the event in the temple's small museum. One of the items derives from Kira's family's desire to give him a proper burial. The law insisted this could not be done without his head, so they asked for it back. It was entrusted to the temple, and the priests wrote a receipt, which survives even now in the corner of a dusty glass case. "Item," it begins, "One head." ✉ 2–11–1 Takanawa, Minato-ku ☎ 03/3441–5560 🌐 www.sengakuji.or.jp 🎫 Temple and grounds free, museum ¥500 Ⓜ Asakusa subway line, Sengakuji Station (Exit A2).

Shinagawa Aquarium (しながわ水族館; *Shinagawa Suizokukan*)

AQUARIUM | **FAMILY** | The best part of this aquarium in southwestern Tokyo's Shinagawa-ku Residents' Park is walking through a 72-foot underwater glass tunnel while some 450 species of fish swim around and above you. Do your best to avoid weekends, when the dolphin and sea lion shows draw throngs in impossible numbers. As for bilingual signage, don't expect much, save, unironically, for the ticket machines. ✉ *3–2–1 Katsushima, Shinagawa-ku* ✥ *Take the local Kyuko Main Line from Shinagawa to Omori Kaigan Station. Turn left as you exit the station and follow the ceramic fish on the sidewalk to the first traffic light; then turn right.* ☎ *03/3762–3433* 🎫 *¥1,350* ⏲ *Closed Tues.* Ⓜ *Kyuko Main Line, Omori Kaigan Station.*

Restaurants

T.Y. Harbor Brewery Restaurant (*T.Y.*ハーバーブルワリーレストラン)

$$$$ | **ECLECTIC** | In a converted waterfront warehouse, T.Y. Harbor brews five of its own year-round beers and seasonal specials in a tank that reaches all the way to the 46-foot-high ceiling. The restaurant, which is known for its grilled meat and fish, has a California-meets-Asian approach, with such dishes as wheat ale steamed clams, Thai-style gai yang chicken sate, or Indian spice-marinated lamb chops. **Known for:** outdoor seating overlooking Tokyo Bay; craft beers brewed on-site; incorporating pan-Asian elements into classic American fare. $ *Average main: ¥5,500* ✉ *2–1–3 Higashi-Shinagawa, Shinagawa-ku* ☎ *03/5479–4555* 🌐 *www.tysons.jp/tyharbor* Ⓜ *Tokyo Monorail or Rinkai Line, Ten-nozu Isle Station (Exit B).*

Hotels

Shinagawa Prince Hotel (品川プリンスホテル)

$ | **HOTEL** | **FAMILY** | Just a three-minute walk from JR Shinagawa Station, the multi-tower Prince Hotel is in a sprawling entertainment complex with, among other things, an 80-lane bowling alley, an 11-screen movie theater, indoor and outdoor swimming pools, tennis and golf centers, and an aquarium, but crowds definitely detract from the experience of staying here. **Pros:** affordable rates; multiple family-friendly entertainment options; nice view of Tokyo Bay from lounge. **Cons:** complicated layout; the whole complex (especially breakfast area and luggage storage) extremely overcrowded, especially on weekends; rooms can be small and dismal, crying out for a renovation. $ *Rooms from: ¥24,000* ✉ *4–10–30 Takanawa, Minato-ku* ☎ *03/3440–1111* 🌐 *www.princehotels.com/shinagawa* 🛏 *3,560 rooms* 🍽 *No Meals* Ⓜ *JR Yamanote Line, Shinagawa Station (Nishi-guchi/West Exit).*

The Strings by InterContinental Tokyo (ストリングスホテル東京インターコンチネンタル)

$$$ | **HOTEL** | Smoothly blending modernity with traditional Japanese aesthetics, the Strings by InterContinental is one of Shinagawa's top-tier hotels, where the lobby features an artful mix of dark wood and stone—as well as a glass bridge that spans a pond—and where the rooms have high-quality linens, natural wood accents, and astounding city views (it can be mesmerizing to watch the trains pass efficiently through Shinagawa Station). **Pros:** 24-hour room service; convenient location to Shinagawa transport hub; nice skyline views. **Cons:** expensive restaurants; finding elevator entrance is a challenge; no pool or spa. $ *Rooms from: ¥75,000* ✉ *2–16–1 Konan, Minato-ku* ☎ *03/5783–1111* 🌐 *intercontinental-strings.jp* 🛏 *212 rooms* 🍽 *No Meals* Ⓜ *JR Yamanote Line, Shinagawa Station (Konan Exit).*

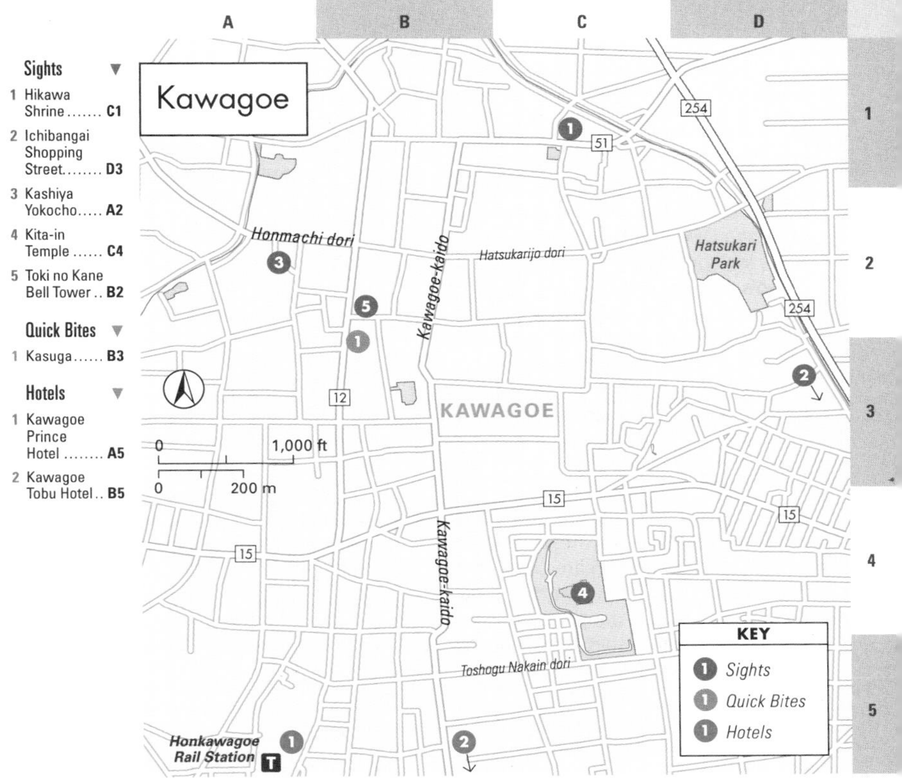

★ **Takanawa Hanakohro** (高輪 花香路)

$$$$ | **HOTEL** | It's as if a traditional ryokan has been transported from rural Japan and delicately placed into this otherwise unremarkable hotel tower, where, after you snake through the Grand Prince Hotel Takanawa, you come to the Takanawa Hanakohro, with its Japanese-style suites and a staff that greets you with the utmost *omotenashi*, or mindful, unobtrusive hospitality. **Pros:** ryokan-style rooms; access to all on-campus Prince hotel lounges; nihonshu tastings and matcha demonstrations. **Cons:** hard to find the entrance elevator; Tayuta Spa requires an additional charge; fitness center is in a neighboring hotel. *Rooms from: ¥110,000* ✉ *3–13–1 Takanawa, Minato-ku* ☎ *03/3447–1117* 🌐 *www.princehotels.com/hanakohro* *16 suites* *Free Breakfast* Ⓜ *5-minute walk from the Takanawa exit of JR Shinagawa station.*

Kawagoe

Sometimes referred to as "Ko-Edo" (Little Edo), the city of Kawagoe was a bustling commercial center in the Edo era (1603–1868). Today, with the Kita-in Temple, Hikawa Shrine, and well-preserved historic quarters, the city retains much of its old-Japan charm. For foodies, big hits include sweet potatoes, freshwater eel, and matcha.

Kawagoe is northwest of and just outside of the Tokyo metropolitan limits, in Saitama Prefecture. Still, it's an easy full- or half-day trip from most parts of the capital on transit options that include Tobu Line express service between Ikebukuro and Kawagoe stations (35 minutes) and the Seibu Line limited express from Seibu-Shinjuku Station to Hon-Kawagoe (55 minutes). Once in Kawagoe, the loop bus (¥400 for a day pass) runs between all the sights.

Day-trippers might be particularly interested in two train passes that can be purchased through Tobu Railway. The Kawagoe Discount Pass, available for ¥710, includes a roundtrip ticket between Tokyo's Ikebukuro station and Kawagoe station, and some exclusive shopping offers once in Kawagoe. The Kawagoe Discount Pass Premium, at ¥1,050, includes those two benefits, plus unlimited Tobu bus rides within Kawagoe.

Sights

Hikawa Shrine (氷川神社; *Hikawa-jinja*)
RELIGIOUS BUILDING | Northeast of Kawagoe's central sightseeing area, this shrine, purportedly founded more than 1,500 years ago, is where people come to pray for love and marital success. If you would like to do so, write a wish on an *ema* (small wooden votive plaque), and hang it in the outdoor tunnel nearly completely covered in ema. There are also two 600-year-old zelkova trees on the grounds, wedded together by an ornately wound rope. It's said that walking around these giant trees in a figure-eight pattern grants good fortune. ✉ *2–11–3 Miyashitamachi, Kawagoe* ☎ *049/224–0589* 🌐 *www.kawagoehikawa.jp* 🎫 *Free* Ⓜ *Seibu Shinjuku Line, Hon-Kawagoe Station; Tobu Line, Kawagoe Station.*

Ichibangai Shopping Street (川越一番街; *Kawagoe Ichibangai*)
STREET | **FAMILY** | The most famous of Kawagoe's old streetscapes, Ichibangai (First Street) is lined with historic, black-and-white-plastered warehouses and dark wooden merchant residences with all sorts of places to shop or stop for a snack. Souvenir options include incense, jewelry, glass beads, and fashion accessories, and street snack choices range from sweet potato brûlée and honey-infused drinks to *wagashi* (traditional sweets meant to be enjoyed with green tea). The street can be crowded, and the shops don't stay open late, but the atmosphere is convivial. ✉ *Saiwaicho area, Kawagoe* 🎫 *Free* Ⓜ *Seibu Shinjuku Line, Hon-Kawagoe Station; Tobu Line, Kawagoe Station.*

Kashiya Yokocho (菓子屋横丁)
STREET | **FAMILY** | Another of Kawagoe's historic enclaves, this cobblestone side street, which translates as "candy store alley," had upwards of 70 different confectioners during the Showa era (1912–26). Although the number of shops has dwindled to about 20, it's still a great place to find colorful hard candies and honeycomb toffee, as well as *dango* (rice dumplings), *karintou* (fried, sugar-covered cookies), *senbei* (savory rice crackers), and other traditional treats. ✉ *Motomachi 2–chome area, Kawagoe* 🎫 *Free* Ⓜ *Seibu Shinjuku Line, Hon-Kawagoe Station; Tobu Line, Kawagoe Station.*

Kita-in Temple (喜多院)
TEMPLE | Established around AD 830, Kita-in has long been an important temple in what was once known as the Kawagoe Domain. Not only is its graveyard the resting place of feudal lords, but it has also accumulated a number of notable features. Several buildings were moved here from Edo Castle in the 1600s, as were 500 *rakan* (a Buddhist term referring to one who has attained enlightenment) statues, which were carved between the 1780s and 1820s and which display a range of emotions—from suffering to sheer delight. There's also a 17th-century shrine, as well as several gardens planted with azaleas, hydrangeas, and plum, cherry, and maple trees that all contribute to the seasonal beauty of the grounds. ✉ *1–20–1 Kosenbamachi, Kawagoe* ☎ *049/222–0859* 🌐 *kitain.net* 🎫 *¥400* Ⓜ *Seibu Shinjuku Line, Hon-Kawagoe Station; Tobu Line, Kawagoe Station.*

Toki no Kane Bell Tower (時の鐘)
HISTORIC SIGHT | The symbol of old Kawagoe is a 17.5-mete (57-foot) bell tower that's the perfect photo-op. Originally

built in the 1600s, the current structure dates to 1893, when it was rebuilt following a fire that destroyed much of the city. It's just north of the Ichibangai shopping street. Although the bell is now automated, it does still ring four times a day. ✉ *15–7 Sawaicho, Kawagoe* 🎫 *Free* Ⓜ *Seibu Shinjuku Line, Hon-Kawagoe Station; Tobu Line, Kawagoe Station.*

Coffee and Quick Bites

Kasuga (かすが)
$ | **JAPANESE** | **FAMILY** | Inside a 120-year-old former merchant house on the prominent Ichibangai shopping street, this casual eatery is good for a quick sit-down lunch or a to-go snack. It's known for its skewers of grilled, soy-basted *dango* (rice dumplings) and its indulgent parfaits, but it also serves bowls of more filling udon or *imo soumen* (thin, wheat-flour noodles thickened with local sweet potatoes). **Known for:** dango; sweet potato soumen noodles; historical location. Ⓢ *Average main: ¥1,100* ✉ *6–1 Saiwaicho, Kawagoe* ☎ *049/226–2392* 🌐 *kanmisaboukasuga.com* Ⓜ *Seibu Shinjuku Line, Hon-Kawagoe Station; Tobu Line, Kawagoe Station.*

Hotels

★ **Kawagoe Prince Hotel** (川越プリンスホテル)
$ | **HOTEL** | **FAMILY** | Attached to Hon-Kawagoe Seibu Station and close to the historical Ichibangai shopping street and JR/Tobu Kawagoe Station, this hotel is a convenient choice for families, couples, and solo travelers alike. **Pros:** close to historical center and new shopping area; ample on-site restaurants; pleasant staff. **Cons:** bland rooms; cramped bathrooms; sterile environment. Ⓢ *Rooms from: ¥19,300* ✉ *Shintomicho 1–22, Kawagoe* ☎ *049/227–1111* 🌐 *www.princehotels.com/kawagoe* 🛏 *110 rooms* 🍽 *No Meals* Ⓜ *Seibu Shinjuku Line, Hon-Kawagoe Station; Tobu Line, Kawagoe Station.*

Kawagoe Tobu Hotel (川越東武ホテル)
$ | **HOTEL** | This hotel is well-located for those who want to be close to Kawagoe train station—just few minutes away on foot via an elevated walkway—and its numerous shops and restaurants. **Pros:** convenient to JR/Tobu Kawagoe station; good breakfast; self-service laundry facilities. **Cons:** pretentious staff; far from historic center; two-elevator system. Ⓢ *Rooms from: ¥15,000* ✉ *8–1 Wakita Honcho, Kawagoe* ☎ *049/241–0111* 🌐 *www.tobuhotel.co.jp* 🛏 *168 rooms* 🍽 *No Meals* Ⓜ *Seibu Shinjuku Line, Hon-Kawagoe Station; Tobu Line, Kawagoe Station.*

Narita Airport

Narita Airport is approximately an hour or more northeast of Tokyo by train, no matter which line you take. By bus or taxi, it could be anywhere from just under an hour to more than two in heavy traffic. For these reasons, an overnight stay is compelling if you have a late arrival or an early departure. For attractions in Narita City, the JR Narita Line and Keisei Main Line connect the airport's terminals with Narita Station in less than 10 minutes.

Sights

Museum of Aeronautical Sciences (航空科学博物館)
TRANSPORTATION MUSEUM | **FAMILY** | Just a short bus ride from either Narita Airport (both terminals) or Narita City lies this little gem. Outside is a collection of light aircraft and helicopters from Japan, the Soviet Union, and the United States. Inside, five floors of exhibit space contain everything from Boeing 747 fuselages to DC-8 flight experiences. There's also a wall detailing international aviation history. Both the fifth-floor observation deck and the fourth-floor restaurant, whose menu is inspired by in-flight meals, have excellent views of Narita Airport runways.

✉ *111–3 Iwayama, Shibayama, Sambu District, Narita* ☎ *0479/78–0557* 🌐 *www.aeromuseum.or.jp* 🎫 *¥700* ⏲ *Closed Mon. except in Aug.*

Naritasan Shinsho-ji Temple (成田山新勝寺)
TEMPLE | One of the Kanto region's oldest temples was founded in the AD 900s to hold a statue of the Buddhist deity Fudo Myoo that was, according to legend, carved by Kobo Daishi, the founder of Shingon Buddhism. That statue alone—still visible in the vast main hall—marks Naritasan out as special to many Japanese, but it also has two impressive pagodas and a spacious wooded park to explore. The oldest extant building was constructed in 1655; other structures have been rebuilt numerous times since then. From JR Narita or Keisei Narita train station, you can reach the temple via Naritasan Omotesando, an 800-meter-long (½-mile) avenue lined with souvenir stores and an eclectic mix of restaurants, some of which serve *unagi* (freshwater eel), a local specialty. ✉ *1 Narita, Narita* ☎ *0476/22–2111* 🌐 *www.naritasan.or.jp/english* 🎫 *Free* Ⓜ *JR Narita Line and Keisei Main Line, Narita Station.*

Coffee and Quick Bites

★ **Kawatoyo** (川豊)
$$ | **JAPANESE** | One of the culinary specialties of the Narita area is freshwater eel (*unagi*)—indeed, on the short stroll along Naritasan Omotesando, you'll see a number of places offering it. This one, close to Naritsan Shinsho-ji, is known for its chargrilled eel, slathered in a savory soy-based sauce and served over rice. **Known for:** unique appetizers such as fried eel bones; in business for more than 100 years; chargrilled and broiled eel. $ *Average main: ¥2,900* ✉ *386 Nakamachi, Narita* ☎ *0476/22–2721* 🌐 *www.unagi-kawatoyo.com* 💳 *No credit cards* ⏲ *No dinner* Ⓜ *JR Narita Line and Keisei Main Line, Narita Station.*

Hotels

Comfort Hotel Narita (コンフォートホテル成田)
$ | **HOTEL** | **FAMILY** | Located in downtown Narita City, a very short walk from both train stations and close to Narita Omotesando, the shopping street leading to the beautiful Naritsan temple grounds, this minimalist property is the perfect base for some last-minute souvenir hunting and sightseeing. **Pros:** self-service laundry facility; convenient location; affordable rates. **Cons:** no airport shuttle; small basic rooms; early checkout time. $ *Rooms from: ¥10,700* ✉ *968 Hanazaki-cho, Narita* ☎ *476/24–6311* 🌐 *www.choice-hotels.jp* 🛏 *142 rooms* 🍽 *Free Breakfast.*

Hilton Tokyo Narita Airport (ヒルトン成田)
$ | **HOTEL** | **FAMILY** | Given its proximity to Narita Airport (15 minutes away on a free shuttle), this hotel is a solid choice for a one-night visit. **Pros:** reasonably priced rooms; spacious lobby; airport and train station shuttles. **Cons:** charge to use the pool and sauna; common areas a bit worn; in-room Wi-Fi isn't free. $ *Rooms from: ¥19,500* ✉ *456 Kosuge, Narita* ☎ *33–1121* 🌐 *www.hilton.com* 🛏 *548 rooms* 🍽 *No Meals.*

nine hours (ナインアワーズ)
$ | **HOTEL** | For a layover at Narita Airport, this capsule hotel, located pre-security in Terminal 2, is a good bet—just pick up your slippers and robe at reception, and make your way to your "sleep pod" (basically, a very narrow sleeping space with a small pillow). **Pros:** in-airport location; reasonably priced; day-use and showers available. **Cons:** confined spaces can seem claustrophobic; limited services; frequently noisy. $ *Rooms from: ¥7,600* ✉ *Narita Airport Terminal 2, 1–1 Furugome, Narita* ☎ *1807–3506* 🌐 *nine-hours.co.jp/narita* 🛏 *129 capsules (71 for men, 58 for women)* 🍽 *No Meals.*

Chapter 15

SIDE TRIPS FROM TOKYO

Updated by
Rob Goss

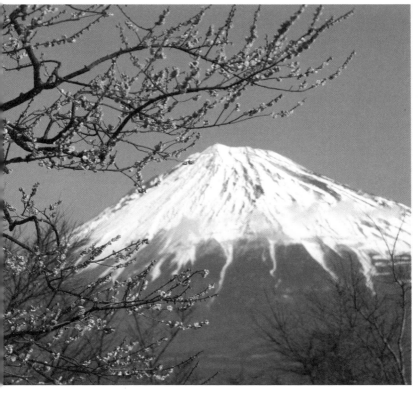

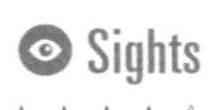

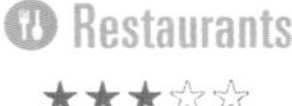

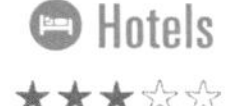

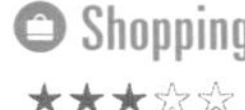

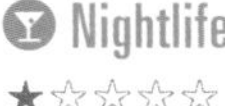

WELCOME TO SIDE TRIPS FROM TOKYO

TOP REASONS TO GO

★ **Peer at Fuji:** Climb Japan's tallest mountain or catch a glimpse of it from Fuji-Hakone-Izu National Park.

★ **Escape into rustic Japan:** The endless modernity of Tokyo seems worlds away in Nikko, where the Toshogu area shrines and temples transport you centuries back into the country's past and the Kegon Falls just transport you.

★ **Get into a Zen-like state:** Kita-Kamakura is home to two preeminent Zen temples, Engaku-ji and Kencho-ji. In Hase, gaze on the Great Buddha or explore inside the giant statue.

★ **Visit China without boarding a plane:** In the port city of Yokohama, sample authentic Chinese goods, spices, and crafts in Chinatown. For a bit of whimsy and a great view, ride Yokohama's Ferris wheel.

1 **Yokohama.** A busy port, Yokohama also has a cultured, relaxed atmosphere and Japan's largest Chinatown.

2 **Kamakura.** A city filled with temples and hiking as well as a bustling town center.

3 **Mt. Fuji (Fuji-san).** Japan's tallest and most sacred mountain.

4 **Fuji Five Lakes (Fuji Go-ko).** The five lakes and surrounding mountains offer a quiet getaway and a staging point for visiting Mt. Fuji.

5 **Hakone.** Filled with hot springs and hiking, cafes, and museums.

6 **Izu.** From the town of Atami's retro vibe to the laid-back beach town of Shimoda, visitors come to Izu for the hot springs, beaches, and coastal views.

7 **Mt. Takao.** The most-hiked mountain in Japan is an hour's train ride from Shinjuku.

8 **Nikko.** Crowds flock to Nikko to see Toshogu Shrine, the resting place of Ieyasu Tokugawa.

Mt. Nantai
Tosho-Gu
Nikko
Chuzenji-Ko
Imaichi
8
Ashio
Utsunmiya
Karasuyama
Higashidate
Daigo
Isohara
Hitachi
Kuji
Nakaminato
Shibukawa
Kiryu
Tochigi
Kasama
Mito
Ashikaga
Oyama
Shimodate
Kurogo
Honjo
Isezaki
Hase
Kumagaya
Koga
Ishioka
Hokota
Konosu
Matsuyama
HONSHU ISLAND
Hamatsuga
Kashimanada Sea
Noda
Kashima
Kawagoe
Omiya
Omigawa
Narita Int'l Airport
Hanno
Ichikawa
Sakura
Tako
Asahi
Choshi
Inubo-saki
Tachikawa
TOKYO
Yokoshiba
Mt. Takao
7
Hachioji
Chiba
Naruto
Tokyo Bay
Kawasaki
Haneda Int'l Airport
Oami
Katakai
1
Atsugi
Yokohama
Mobara
Kisarazu
Fujisawa
2
Kamakura
Hiratsuka
Yokosuka
Ohara
Odawara
Fujioayashi
Kazusaminato
Sagami Bay
Misaki
Kamogawa
Atami
Tateyama
Chikura
Ito
Sagaminada Sea
TAIHEIYO (PACIFIC OCEAN)
JAPAN
Tokyo
Fuji-Hakone-Izu National Park
Ōshima
ŌSHIMA
TO-SHIMA

As diverse and exciting as the neighborhoods of Tokyo are, the city is also a great base for several short excursions—either day or overnight trips—that offer refreshingly different perspectives on Japan.

The port city of Yokohama has the country's largest Chinatown and an international character all its own. Kamakura, the capital from 1192 to 1333, has great historical and cultural sights. The iconic Fuji-san (Mt. Fuji) and Fuji Go-ko (Fuji Five Lakes) are also popular resort areas that are readily accessible from the city. Within Fuji-Hakone-Izu National Park, Hakone offers hot springs and relatively easy access to the mountain area. There are still more hot springs on the Izu Peninsula, a resort area appreciated by both Japanese and foreign travelers. Nikko is home to the Toshogu, an astonishing shrine to the first Tokugawa shogun, Ieyasu.

One caveat: the term "national park" does not quite mean what it does elsewhere in the world. Near Tokyo, pristine grandeur is hard to come by; there are few places where intrepid hikers can go to contemplate the beauty of nature in solitude for very long. If a thing's worth seeing, it's worth developing. This worldview tends to fill Japan's national parks with bus caravans, ropeways, gondolas, scenic overlooks with coin-fed telescopes, signs that tell you where you may or may not walk, fried-noodle joints and vending machines, and shacks full of kitschy souvenirs. That's true of Nikko, and it's true as well of Fuji-Hakone-Izu National Park.

MAJOR REGIONS

Yokohama is Japan's largest port. Its waterfront park, vibrant Chinatown, and Minato Mirai bayside development project draw visitors from all over.

Kamakura is an ancient city—the birthplace of the samurai way of life. The country's first shogun chose this site as the seat of his military government. The warrior elite took much of their ideology from Zen Buddhism, endowing splendid temples. As a religious center, Kamakura presents an extraordinary legacy. Most of its temples and shrines are in settings of remarkable beauty; many are designated National Treasures.

Fuji-san (Mt. Fuji), southwest of Tokyo between Suruga and Sagami bays, is one of Japan's most popular resort areas. The main attraction, of course, is Mt. Fuji, a dormant volcano—it last erupted in 1707—rising to a height of 12,388 feet. The mountain is truly beautiful; utterly captivating in the ways it can change in different light and from different viewpoints. Its symmetry and majesty have been immortalized by poets and artists for centuries. Keep in mind, though, that, in spring and summer, Mt. Fuji often hides behind a blanket of clouds.

To the north of Mt. Fuji, the **Fuji Go-ko (Fuji Five Lakes)** area affords an unbeatable view of the mountain on clear days and makes the best base for a climb to the summit. With its various outdoor

Mt. Fuji is an active volcano that last erupted in 1707.

activities, such as skating and fishing in winter and boating and hiking in summer, this is a popular resort area for families and business conferences. The five lakes are, from the east, Yamanaka-ko, Kawaguchi-ko, Sai-ko, Shoji-ko, and Motosu-ko. Yamanaka and Kawaguchi are the largest and most-developed resort areas, with Kawaguchi more or less the centerpiece of the group.

Hakone has mountains, volcanic landscapes, and lake cruises, plus onsen (hot springs) of its own.

The Izu Peninsula is popular for its beaches and scenically rugged coastline.

Mt. Takao is in a densely wooded area with hiking trails, beautiful scenery, an interesting temple, and a monkey zoo. It's actually within the limits of metropolitan Tokyo, just an hour from the center of the city.

Nikko, which means "sunlight," is a popular Japanese vacation spot for good reason: its gorgeous sights include a breathtaking waterfall and one of the country's best-known shrines. In addition, Nikko combines the rustic charm of a countryside village (complete with wild monkeys that have the run of the place) with a location close to Tokyo. It's also the site of the magnificent Toshogu Shrine and Nikko National Park, where highlights include Lake Chuzenji and the famous Kegon Falls.

Planning

Hotels

Although Nikko, Fuji-Hakone-Izu, and other resort areas have modern, Western-style hotels, more common are the traditional ryokan (inns) with Japanese-style rooms and less-central locations. After a full day of sightseeing, it's truly a pleasure to return to a ryokan, where you can luxuriate in a hot-spring bath, put on a *yukata* (cotton kimono), and sit down to an exquisite, multicourse Japanese dinner.

The price categories listed here are for double occupancy, but most ryokan normally quote per-person rates, which typically include breakfast and dinner (although more ryokan are now offering room-only options). The typical ryokan takes great pride in its cuisine, usually with good reason: the evening meal is an elaborate affair of 10 or more different dishes, based on the fresh produce and specialties of the region and served on a wonderful variety of trays and tableware that celebrate the season.

Restaurants

Befitting an international port city with almost 4 million inhabitants, Yokohama has restaurants offering almost every imaginable cuisine. Your best bet is Chinatown—Japan's largest Chinese community—where more than 100 restaurants represent every regional style. If, however, you fancy Italian, Indian, or Thai, you'll find an eminently satisfying meal here.

Three things about Kamakura make it a good place to dine. It's on Sagami Bay, which means that there's lots of fresh seafood; it's a major stop for travelers; and it has long been a prestigious place to live among Japan's worldly and well-to-do (many writers, artists, and intellectuals call Kamakura home). You can confidently pick a place to eat at random.

The local specialty in Nikko is a soybean-based concoction known as *yuba* (tofu skin); dozens of its restaurants serve it in a variety of dishes. Other local favorites are soba (buckwheat) and udon (wheat-flour) noodles—both inexpensive, filling, and tasty.

RESTAURANT AND HOTEL PRICES

Restaurant prices are the average cost of a main course at dinner, or if dinner is not served, at lunch. Hotel prices are the lowest cost of a standard double room in high season. Be aware that hotels add a 10% in consumption tax and a small accommodation tax (usually ¥100–¥300, depending on the room rate). In the hot-spring areas, you might also be asked to pay roughly ¥150/day in hot-spring tax at checkout.

⇨ *Restaurant and hotel reviews have been shortened. For full information, visit Fodors.com.*

What It Costs in Yen

$	$$	$$$	$$$$
RESTAURANTS			
under ¥1,500	¥1,500–¥3,000	¥3,001–¥5,000	over ¥5,000
HOTELS			
under ¥15,000	¥15,000–¥30,000	¥30,001–¥45,000	over ¥45,000

Yokohama 横浜

30 km (24 miles) southwest of Tokyo.

In 1853, four American warships under Commodore Matthew Perry sailed into the bay of Tokyo (then Edo) and presented the reluctant Japanese with the demands of the U.S. government for the opening of diplomatic and commercial relations. The following year, Perry returned and first set foot on Japanese soil at Yokohama—then a small fishing village on the mudflats of Tokyo bay.

Two years later, New York businessman Townsend Harris became America's first diplomatic representative to Japan, and, in 1858, he negotiated a commercial treaty between the two countries. Part of the deal designated four locations—one of them Yokohama—as treaty ports. In 1859, the shogunate created a special settlement in Yokohama for the growing community of merchants, traders, missionaries, and other assorted adventurers drawn to this exotic new land of opportunity.

The foreigners (predominantly Chinese and British, with a smattering of French, Americans, and Dutch) were confined here to a guarded compound about 5 square km (2 square miles)—placed, in effect, in isolation. Within a few years, though, the shogunal government collapsed, and Japan began to modernize. Western goods and ideas were welcomed, and the little treaty port became Japan's principal gateway to the outside world.

In 1872, Japan's first railway linked Yokohama and Tokyo. By the time Yokohama became a city in 1889, its population had grown to 120,000. Yokohaman and its international community continued to prosper, and, by the early 1900s, it was East Asia's busiest and most modern international trade hub.

Then Yokohama came tumbling down. On September 1, 1923, the Great Kanto Earthquake devastated the city. The ensuing fires destroyed some 60,000 homes and took more than 40,000 lives. During the six years it took to rebuild, many foreign businesses took up quarters elsewhere, primarily in Kobe and Osaka, and did not return.

Over the next 20 years, Yokohama steadily grew as an industrial center—until May 29, 1945, when, in a span of four hours, some 500 American B-29 bombers leveled nearly half the city and left more than half a million people homeless. When the war ended, what remained became—in effect—the center of the Allied occupation. General Douglas MacArthur set up headquarters here, briefly, before moving to Tokyo; the entire port facility and about a quarter of the city remained in the hands of the U.S. military throughout the 1950s.

By the 1970s, Yokohama was once more on the rise; in 1978, it surpassed Osaka as the nation's second-largest city, and the population is now inching up to the 3.7-million mark. Boosted by Japan's postwar economic miracle, Yokohama has extended its urban sprawl north to Tokyo and south to Kamakura—in the process creating a whole new subcenter around the Shinkansen Station at Shin-Yokohama.

With its bustling modern side combined with remnants of its early international days, a vibrant waterfront, and attractions like Yokohama Chinatown, Yokohama is at least worth a day trip while you are in Tokyo.

GETTING HERE AND AROUND

From Narita Airport, a direct limousine-bus service (¥3,700 one-way) departs once or twice an hour between 8:05 am and 9:45 pm for Yokohama City Air Terminal (YCAT). YCAT is a five-minute taxi ride from Yokohama Station. JR Narita Express trains going on from Tokyo to Yokohama leave the airport every hour from 7:44 am to 9:44 pm. The fare is ¥4,370 (¥6,640 for the first-class Green Car coaches). Or you can take the limousine-bus service from Narita to Tokyo Station and continue on to Yokohama by train. Either way, the journey from Narita takes two to three hours.

The Airport Limousine Information Desk phone number provides information in English daily from 9 to 6; you can also get timetables and book tickets on its website. For information in English on Narita Express trains, call the JR East Info Line (☎ *050/2016–1603*), available daily from 10 to 6.

JR trains from Tokyo Station leave approximately every 10 minutes, depending on the time of day. Take the Yokosuka, the Tokaido, or the Keihin Tohoku Line to Yokohama Station (the Yokosuka and Tokaido lines take 30 minutes; the Keihin Tohoku Line takes 40 minutes and cost ¥490). From there the Keihin Tohoku Line (Platform 3) continues as the Negishi Line to Kannai and Ishikawacho, Yokohama's business and downtown areas. ■ TIP→ **If you're going directly to downtown Yokohama from Tokyo, the blue commuter trains of the Keihin Tohoku Line are best.**

The private Tokyu Toyoko Line, which runs from Shibuya Station in Tokyo directly to Yokohama Station, is a good alternative if you leave from the western part of Tokyo. **■ TIP→ The term "private" is important because it means that the train does not belong to JR and is not a subway line. If you have a JR Pass, you'll have to buy a separate ticket.**

Depending on which Tokyu Toyoko Line you catch—the Limited Express, Semi Express, or Local—the trip takes between 25 and 44 minutes and costs ¥310.

Yokohama Station is the hub that links all the train lines and connects them with the city's subway and bus services. Kannai and Ishikawacho are the two downtown stations, both on the Keihin Tohoku Line/Negishi Line; trains leave Yokohama Station every two to five minutes from Platform 3. From Sakuragicho, Kannai, or Ishikawacho, most of Yokohama's points of interest are within easy walking distance; the one notable exception is Sankei-en, which you reach via the JR Keihin Tohoku Line/Negishi Line to Negishi Station and then a local bus.

The Yokohama Municipal Subway's Blue Line connects Azamino, Shin-Yokohama, Yokohama, Sakuragicho, Totsuka, and Shonandai (with many other stops in between). The basic fare is ¥210. One-day passes are also available for ¥740 (¥830 for a subway-bus one-day pass). The Minato Mirai Line, a spur of the Tokyu Toyoko Line, runs from Yokohama Station to all the major points of interest, including Minato Mirai, Chinatown, Yamashita Park, Motomachi, and Bashamichi. The fare is ¥200–¥220, and one-day unlimited-ride passes are available for ¥460.

Most of Yokohama's sights are within easy walking distance of a JR or subway station, but this city is so much more negotiable than Tokyo that exploring by bus is a viable alternative. The city map available in local visitor centers shows most major bus routes, and the important stops on the tourist routes are announced in English. The fixed fare is ¥220; one-day passes are also available for ¥600. Check with the Sightseeing Information Office at Yokohama Station (JR, East Exit) for more information and ticket purchases.

There are taxi stands at all the train stations, and you can always flag a cab on the street. The basic fare is ¥730 for the first 2 km (1 mile), then ¥90 for every additional 293 meters (0.2 mile). Traffic is heavy in downtown Yokohama, however, and it's often faster to walk. **■ TIP→ Vacant taxis show a red light in the windshield.**

AIRPORT TRANSPORTATION Airport Limousine Information Desk. ☎ *03/3665–7220* 🌐 *webservice.limousinebus.co.jp/web/en.*

Sights

As large as Yokohama is, its central area is easy to navigate. Though areas of interest have expanded to include the waterfront, which is on the west side of Tokyo Bay, and Ishikawacho to the south, the heart of the city is still its downtown, which is called Kanai, meaning "within the checkpoint"—a remnant of the period under the shogunate when Yokohama's foreign residents were confined to this area.

The old district of Kannai, which now actually contains the offices of the modern city, is bounded by Bashamichi to the northwest and Nihon-odori to the southeast, the Negishi Line tracks to the southwest, and the waterfront to the northeast. An adjacent area of Kannai extends southeast from Nihon-odori to the Motomachi shopping street and the International Cemetery, bordered by Yamashita Koen and the waterfront to the northeast. In the center is Chinatown, with Ishikawacho Station to the southwest.

Get a taste of China in Japan with a visit to the restaurants and shops of Yokohama's Chinatown.

■ TIP→ **Whether you're coming from Tokyo, Nagoya, or Kamakura, make Ishikawacho Station your starting point. Take the South Exit from the station and head in the direction of the waterfront.**

Bashamichi Street (馬車道)
STREET | **FAMILY** | Running southwest from Shinko Pier to Kannai is Bashamichi, which translates to "Horse-Carriage Street," a name it was given in the 19th century, when it was widened to accommodate the conveyances of the city's new European residents. This red-brick-paved thoroughfare and the streets parallel to it have been partially restored to evoke that past, with faux-antique phone booths and imitation gas lamps. Here you'll find coffee shops, patisseries, boutiques, and places for dinner. ✉ *Naka-ku* Ⓜ *JR lines and Yokohama Subway Blue Line, Kannai Station; Minato Mirai Line, Bashamichi Station.*

Chinatown (中華街; *Chuka-gai*)
NEIGHBORHOOD | **FAMILY** | Once Japan's largest Chinese settlement, Yokohama's Chinatown draws more than 18 million visitors a year. Its narrow streets and alleys are lined with some 350 shops selling foodstuffs, herbal medicines, cookware, toys and ornaments, and clothing and accessories. If China exports it, you'll find it here. Wonderful aromas waft from the spice shops. Even better aromas drift from the quarter's 160-odd restaurants, which serve every major style of Chinese cuisine: this is the best place for lunch in Yokohama. ✉ *Naka-ku* Ⓜ *JR lines, Ishikawacho Station; Minato Mirai Line, Motomachi-Chukagai Station.*

Cup Noodles Museum Yokohama
(カップヌードルミュージアム 横浜)
SPECIALTY MUSEUM | **FAMILY** | At this hands-on museum, you can create your own instant-ramen flavors and packaging and learn all about one of Japan's biggest culinary exports. Kids love running through the Cup Noodle Park, a playground simulating the noodle-making process, complete with a "noodle net" and "seasoning pool" ball pit. ✉ *2–3–4 Shinko, Naka-ku* ☎ *045/345–0918* 🌐 *www.cupnoodles-museum.jp* 🎫 *Entry ¥500,*

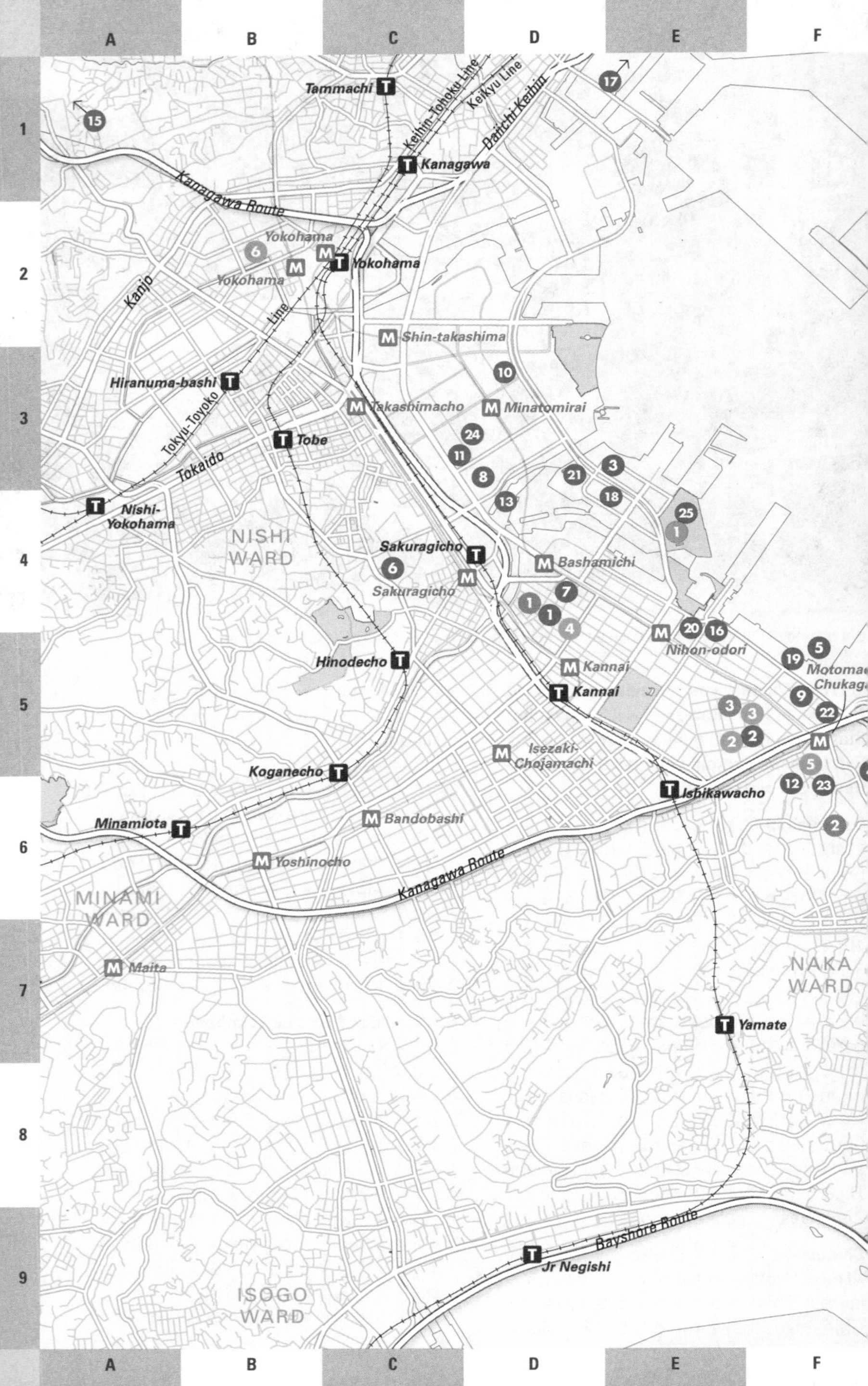

A B C D E F
1 2 3 4 5 6 7 8 9
Tammachi
Kanagawa
Keihin-Tohoku Line
Keikyu Line
Daiichi Keihin
Kanagawa Route
Yokohama
Kanjo
Line
Shin-takashima
Hiranuma-bashi
Takashimacho
Minatomirai
Tokyu-Toyoko
Tobe
Tokaido
Nishi-Yokohama
NISHI WARD
Sakuragicho
Bashamichi
Hinodecho
Nihon-odori
Kannai
Motoma
Chukag
Isezaki-Chojamachi
Koganecho
Ishikawacho
Minamiota
Bandobashi
Yoshinocho
Kanagawa Route
MINAMI WARD
Maita
NAKA WARD
Yamate
Bayshore Route
Jr Negishi
ISOGO WARD

Yokohama

Port of Yokohama

Bayshore Route

Honmoku dori

0 1/2 mi

0 1/2 km

KEY

Sights

Restaurants

Quick Bites

Sights

1 Bashamichi Street.................D4

2 Chinatown...........................F5

3 Cup Noodles Museum Yokohama............................E3

4 Harbor View Park...................F5

5 Hikawa Maru.........................F5

6 Iseyama Kotai Jingu Shrine.......C4

7 Kanagawa Prefectural Museum of Cultural History......D4

8 Landmark Tower...................D3

9 Marine Tower........................F5

10 Minato Mirai 21....................D3

11 Mitsubishi Minatomirai Industrial Museum.................C3

12 Motomachi...........................F6

13 Nippon Maru........................D4

14 Sankei-en............................G9

15 Shin Yokohama Ramen Museum............................A1

16 Silk Museum.........................E5

17 Soji-ji.................................E1

18 World Porters........................E4

19 Yamashita Park.....................F5

20 Yokohama Archives of History Museum.................E4

21 Yokohama Cosmo World..........D3

22 Yokohama Doll Museum...........F5

23 Yokohama Foreign General Cemetery..................F6

24 Yokohama Museum of Art.......D3

25 Yokohama Red Brick Warehouses.........................E4

Restaurants

1 Chano-ma............................E4

2 Kakin Hanten........................E5

3 Kaseiro...............................E5

4 Seryna Roman-chaya.............D4

5 Shunotei Hira........................F5

6 Yokohama Cheese Cafe...........B2

Quick Bites

1 Baird Beer Bashamichi Taproom............................D4

2 Enokitei Honten.....................F6

3 Houtenkaku Shinkan...............E5

then separate fees for some experiences (from ¥500) ⏲ Closed Tues. Ⓜ JR lines and Yokohama Subway Blue Line, Sakuragicho Station; Minato Mirai Line, Minato Mirai Station.

Harbor View Park (港の見える丘公園; *Minato-no-Mieru-Oka Koen*)

CITY PARK | FAMILY | The park—a major landmark in this part of the city, known, appropriately enough, as the Bluff (*yamate*)—once contained the barracks of the British forces. Come here for spectacular nighttime views of the waterfront, the floodlit gardens of Yamashita Park, and the Bay Bridge. Foreigners were first allowed to build here in 1867, and it has been prime real estate ever since—an enclave of churches, international schools, private clubs, and palatial Western-style homes. ✉ *114 Yamatecho, Naka-ku* Ⓜ *JR lines, Ishikawacho Station; Minato Mirai Line, Motomachi-Chukagai Station.*

Hikawa Maru (氷川丸)

NAUTICAL SIGHT | FAMILY | Moored on the waterfront, more or less in the middle of Yamashita Park, is the *Hikawa Maru*. The ocean liner was built in 1929 by Yokohama Dock Co. and launched on September 30, 1929. For 31 years, it shuttled passengers between Yokohama and Seattle, Washington, making a total of 238 trips. A tour of the ship evokes the time when Yokohama was a great port of call for the transpacific liners. In summer, there's a beer garden on the upper deck. ✉ *Yamashita-koen, Naka-ku* ☎ *045/641–4362* 🌐 *hikawamaru.nyk.com* 🎟 *¥300* ⏲ *Closed Mon.* Ⓜ *JR lines, Ishikawacho Station; Minato Mirai Line, Motomachi-Chukagai Station.*

Iseyama Kotai Jingu Shrine (伊勢山皇大神宮)

RELIGIOUS BUILDING | A branch of the nation's revered Grand Shrines of Ise, this is the most important Shinto shrine in Yokohama—but it's worth a visit only if you've seen most everything else in town. ✉ *64 Miyazakicho, Nishi-ku* ✣ *The shrine is a 10-min. walk west of Sakuragicho Station* ☎ *045/241–1122* 🌐 *www.iseyama.jp* 🎟 *Free* Ⓜ *JR lines and Yokohama Subway Blue Line, Sakuragicho Station.*

Kanagawa Prefectural Museum of Cultural History (神奈川県立歴史博物館; *Kanagawa Kenritsu Rekishi Hakubutsukan*)

HISTORY MUSEUM | This museum is housed in one of the few Yokohama buildings to have survived both the Great Kanto Earthquake of 1923 and World War II. Although most exhibits have no explanations in English, the third-floor galleries showcase some remarkable medieval wooden sculptures (including one of the first Kamakura shogun, Minamoto no Yoritomo), hanging scrolls, portraits, and armor. The exhibits of prehistory and of Yokohama in the early modern period are of much less interest. ✉ *5–60 Minami Nakadori, Naka-ku* ☎ *045/201–0926* 🌐 *ch.kanagawa-museum.jp* 🎟 *¥300* ⏲ *Closed Mon.* Ⓜ *JR lines and Yokohama Subway Blue Line, Kannai Station; Minato Mirai Line, Bashamichi Station.*

Landmark Tower (ランドマークタワー)

VIEWPOINT | FAMILY | Although no longer Japan's tallest building—that title now goes to Tokyo's Azabudai Hills Mori JP Tower—this 70-story tower in Yokohama's Minato Mirai is the tallest in Greater Tokyo. The 69th-floor Sky Garden observation deck has a spectacular view of the city, especially at night; you reach it via a high-speed elevator that carries you up at an ear-popping 45 kph (28 mph). The complex's Dockyard Garden is a restored dry dock with stepped sides of massive stone blocks. The long, narrow floor of the dock, with its water cascade at one end, makes a wonderful year-round open-air venue for concerts and other events; in summer (July–mid-August), the beer garden installed here is a perfect refuge from the heat. The Yokohama Royal Park Hotel occupies the building's top 20 stories, and the courtyard on the northeast side connects to Queen's Square, a huge atrium-style vertical mall with dozens of shops (mainly for clothing and accessories) as well as cafés and restaurants. ✉ *2–2–1 Minatomirai, Nishi-ku* ☎ *045/222–5015* 🌐 *www.yokohama-landmark.jp* 🎫 *Elevator to observation deck ¥1,000* Ⓜ *JR lines and Yokohama Subway Blue Line, Sakuragicho Station; Minato Mirai Line, Minato Mirai Station.*

Marine Tower (マリンタワー)
VIEWPOINT | **FAMILY** | For an older generation of Yokohama residents, the 348-foot-high decagonal tower, which opened in 1961, was the city's landmark structure; civic pride prevented them from admitting that it falls lamentably short of an architectural masterpiece. The tower has a navigational beacon at the 338-foot level and purports to be the world's tallest lighthouse. At the 328-foot level, an observation gallery provides 360-degree views of the harbor and the city, and, on clear days in autumn or winter, you can often see Mt. Fuji in the distance. ✉ *15 Yamashitacho, Naka-ku* ☎ *045/664–1100* 🌐 *marinetower.yokohama* 🎫 *Daytime ¥1,000, nighttime ¥1,200* Ⓜ *JR lines, Ishikawacho Station; Minato Mirai Line, Motomachi-Chukagai Station.*

Minato Mirai 21 (みなとみらい21; *Minato Mirai Nijyu-ichi*)
BUSINESS DISTRICT | **FAMILY** | If you want to see Yokohama urban development at its most self-assertive, then this is it. The aim of this project, launched in the mid-1980s, was to turn some three-quarters of a square mile of waterfront property, lying east of the JR Negishi Line railroad tracks between Yokohama and Sakuragicho stations, into a model "harbor of the future." As a hotel, business, international exhibition, and conference center, it's been a smashing success. ✉ *Nishi-ku* 🌐 *minatomirai21.com* 🎫 *Free* Ⓜ *JR lines and Yokohama Subway Blue Line, Sakuragicho Station; Minato Mirai Line, Minato Mirai Station.*

Mitsubishi Minatomirai Industrial Museum (三菱みなとみらい技術館; *Mitsubishi Minatomirai Gijutsukan*)
SCIENCE MUSEUM | **FAMILY** | Filling galleries directly across from the Landmark Tower are rocket engines, power plants, a submarine, various gadgets, and displays that simulate piloting helicopters. ✉ *3–3–1 Minatomirai, Nishi-ku* ☎ *045/200–7351* 🌐 *www.mhi.com/company/overview/museum/minatomirai* 🎫 *¥500* 🕒 *Closed Tues. and Wed.* Ⓜ *JR lines and Yokohama Subway Blue Line, Sakuragicho Station; Minato Mirai Line, Minato Mirai Station.*

Motomachi (元町)
STREET | **FAMILY** | Within a block of Ishikawacho Station is the beginning of this street, which follows the course of the Nakamura-gawa (Nakamura River) to the harbor where the Japanese set up shop 100 years ago to serve the foreigners living in Kannai. The street is now lined with smart boutiques and jewelry stores. A network of side streets leading from Motomachi contain a nice selection of cafés and restaurants. ✉ *Motomachi, Naka-ku* Ⓜ *JR lines, Ishikawacho Station; Minato Mirai Line, Motomachi-Chukagai Station.*

Nippon Maru (日本丸)
NAUTICAL SIGHT | **FAMILY** | The centerpiece of the park immediately southeast of Landmark Tower is the *Nippon Maru*, a full-rigged three-mast ship popularly called the "Swan of the Pacific." Built in 1930, it served as a training vessel and although it's now retired, it's an occasional participant in tall-ships festivals. It's also open as a museum, with enough English explanations to help bring its nicely preserved quarters to life. Adjacent to the ship is the Yokohama Port Museum, a two-story collection of ship models, displays, and archival materials that celebrates the achievements of the Port of Yokohama from its earliest days to the present. There are also a couple of boat and gantry crane simulators there, if you fancy a hands-on taste of

port life. ✉ *2–1–1 Minatomirai, Nishi-ku* ☎ *045/221–0280* 🌐 *www.nippon-maru.or.jp* 🎫 *¥800 combo ticket for Nippon Maru and Yokohama Port Museum; ¥400 for Nippon Maru only.* ⏲ *Closed Mon.* Ⓜ *JR lines and Yokohama Subway Blue Line, Sakuragicho Station; Minato Mirai Line, Minato Mirai Station.*

Sankei-en (三渓園)
GARDEN | **FAMILY** | Opened to the public in 1906, this was once the estate and gardens of Tomitaro Hara (1868–1939), one of Yokohama's wealthiest men, who made his money as a silk merchant before becoming a patron of the arts. On the estate's extensive grounds, he created is a kind of open-air museum of traditional Japanese architecture, some of which was brought here from Kamakura and the western part of the country. Especially noteworthy is Rinshun-kaku, a villa built for the Tokugawa clan in 1649. There's also a tea pavilion, Choshu-kaku, built by the third Tokugawa shogun, Iemitsu. Other buildings include a small temple transported from Kyoto's famed Daitoku-ji and a farmhouse from the Gifu district in the Japan Alps (around Takayama). If you need some refreshments while in the gardens, you'll find three tea shops serving tea, Japanese sweets, and light meals like soba noodles. ✉ *58–1 Honmoku Sannotani, Naka-ku* ☎ *045/621–0634* 🌐 *www.sankeien.or.jp* 🎫 *¥900* Ⓜ *JR Keihin Tohoku Line/Negishi Line to Negishi Station and a local bus (No. 58 or 101) bound for Honmoku; Yokohama Station (East Exit) and take the bus (No. 8 or 168) to Sankei-en Mae (the trip takes about 35 min).*

Shin Yokohama Ramen Museum
(新横浜ラーメン博物館)
SPECIALTY MUSEUM | **FAMILY** | Calling this a museum might be a little misleading: it's home to a collection of ramen restaurants (seven currently), each serving a different style of Japan's favorite noodle, all packaged together in a streetscape designed to replicate 1950s Yokohama. While here, you could also try a noodle-making class or create your own instant ramen. There are also a few old-fashioned sweet shops for a post-noodle snack. ✉ *2–14–12 Shin Yokohama, Yokohama* ↔ *Two blocks northwest of Shin Yokohama Station* ☎ *045/471–0503* 🌐 *www.raumen.co.jp/english* 🎫 *¥450 entry; separate fees for food and workshops* Ⓜ *JR lines, Shinkansen lines, Tokyu lines, Shin Yokohama Station.*

Bloomin' Season

Walking through Sankei-en is especially delightful in spring, when the flowering trees are at their best: plum blossoms in February and cherry blossoms in early April. In June come the irises, followed by the water lilies. In autumn the trees come back into their own with tinted golden leaves.

Silk Museum
(シルク博物館; *Shiruku Hakubutsukan*)
SPECIALTY MUSEUM | From the opening of its borders to the beginning of the 20th century, silk was Japan's most sought-after export, and nearly all of it went through Yokohama. This museum, which pays tribute to this period, houses a collection of silk fabrics and an informative exhibit on the silk-making process. The hands-on exhibits include silk reeling and weaving machines. The museum is near the northwestern end of the Yamashita Park promenade, on the second floor of the Silk Center Building. ✉ *1 Yamashitacho, Naka-ku* ☎ *045/641–0841* 🌐 *www.silkcenter-kbkk.jp/museum* 🎫 *¥500* ⏲ *Closed Mon.* Ⓜ *Minato Mirai Line, Nihon-odori Station.*

Soji-ji (總持寺)
TEMPLE | One of the two major centers of the Soto sect of Zen Buddhism, Soji-ji, in

'okohama's Tsurumi ward, was founded ו 1321. The center was moved here from shikawa, on the Noto Peninsula (on the ;ea of Japan, north of Kanazawa), after fire in the 19th century. There's also Soji-ji monastic complex at Eihei-ji in ukui Prefecture. The Yokohama Soji-ji s one of Japan's largest and busiest 3uddhist institutions, with more than 00 monks and novices in residence. he 14th-century patron of Soji-ji was he emperor Go-Daigo, who overthrew he Kamakura Shogunate; the emperor s buried here, but his mausoleum is ff-limits to visitors. Nevertheless, you an see the Buddha Hall, the Main Hall, nd the Treasure House. English tours of he complex are available by reservation. *2–1–1 Tsurumi, Tsurumi-ku 045/581–;021 www.sojiji.jp Entry is free, but ¥400 for guided tour Treasure House losed Mon. JR Keihin Tohoku Line, 'surumi Station (three stops north of 'okohama Station).*

Vorld Porters (ワールドポーターズ)
TORE/MALL | **FAMILY** | This shopping enter, on the opposite side of Yokohama ;osmo World, is notable chiefly for its estaurants, which overlook the Minato Airai area. Try arriving at sunset; the pectacular view of twinkling lights and he Landmark Tower, the Ferris wheel, nd hotels occasionally include Mt. Fuji in he background. *2–2–1 Shinko, Naka-u 045/222–2121 www.yim.co.jp JR lines and Yokohama Subway Blue ine, Sakuragicho Station; Minato Mirai ine, Minato Mirai Station.*

'amashita Park
山下公園; *Yamashita Koen*)
ITY PARK | **FAMILY** | This park is perhaps he only positive legacy of the Great ;anto Earthquake of 1923. The debris of he warehouses and other buildings that nce stood here were swept away, and he area was made into a 17-acre oasis f green along the waterfront. On spring nd summer weekends, the park fills ıp with families, couples, and groups of friends, making it one of the best people-watching spots in town. In the rose garden at the park's center is a fountain, representing the Guardian of the Water, presented to Yokohama by San Diego, California, one of its sister cities. *279 Yamashitacho, Naka-ku Free JR lines, Ishikawacho Station; Minato Mirai Line, Motomachi-Chukagai Station and Nihon-Odori Station.*

Yokohama Archives of History Museum
(横浜開港資料館; *Yokohama Kaiko Shiryokan*)
HISTORY MUSEUM | Within the archives, housed in a small complex that once also included the British Consulate, are two rooms of items recording the history of Yokohama since the opening of the port to international trade in the mid-19th century. It's worth a quick look if you like old photos and newspaper clippings. Across the street is a monument to the U.S.–Japanese Friendship Treaty. *3 Nihonodori, Naka-ku 045/201–2100 www.kaikou.city.yokohama.jp/en ¥200 Closed Mon. Minato Mirai Line, Nihon-odori Station.*

Yokohama Cosmo World
(よこはまコスモワールド)
AMUSEMENT PARK/CARNIVAL | **FAMILY** | This amusement-park complex has—among its 30 or so very retro rides and attractions—everything from a four-story water-chute ride to sedate rides for toddlers. The Ferris wheel, which was once the world's tallest, towers over Yokohama. The park is east of Minato Mirai and Queen's Square, on both sides of the river. *2–8–1 Shinko, Naka-ku 045/641–6591 cosmoworld.jp Park entry free, rides from ¥400 each Closed Thurs. JR lines and Yokohama Subway Blue Line, Sakuragicho Station; Minato Mirai Line, Minato Mirai Station.*

Yokohama Doll Museum
(横浜人形の家; *Yokohama Ningyo no Ie*)
SPECIALTY MUSEUM | **FAMILY** | This museum houses a collection of roughly 3,500 dolls from all over the world. In Japanese

tradition, dolls are less to play with than to display—either in religious folk customs or as the embodiment of some spiritual quality. The museum is worth a quick visit, with or without a child in tow, although the puppet shows that sometimes take place on the fourth floor are especially good for kids. It's just across from the southeast end of Yamashita Park. ✉ *18 Yamashitacho, Naka-ku* ☎ *045/671–9361* 🌐 *www.doll-museum.jp* 🎫 *¥400, but additional fees for special exhibitions* 🕙 *Closed Mon.* Ⓜ *JR lines, Ishikawacho Station; Minato Mirai Line, Motomachi-Chukagai Station.*

Yokohama Foreign General Cemetery (横浜外国人墓地; *Yokohama Gaikokujin Bochi*)
CEMETERY | This landmark is a reminder of Yokohama's heritage as a port city. It was established in 1854 with a grant of land from the shogunate. The inscriptions on the crosses and headstones attest to some 40 different nationalities whose citizens lived and died in Yokohama. Although the first foreigners to be buried here were Russian sailors assassinated by xenophobes in the early days of the settlement, most of the 4,500 graves are English and American; about 120 are of the Japanese wives of foreigners. ✉ *96 Yamatecho, Naka-ku* ✥ *From the eastern end of Motomachi, it's a short walk uphill to northern end of the cemetery* 🌐 *www.yfgc-japan.com* 🎫 *¥200* 🕙 *Closed Mon. and Tues.* Ⓜ *JR lines, Ishikawacho Station; Minato Mirai Line, Motomachi-Chukagai Station.*

Yokohama Museum of Art (横浜美術館 *Yokohama Bijutsukan*)
ART MUSEUM | Designed by Kenzo Tange and housed at Minato Mirai 21, this museum has 5,000 works in its permanent collection. You'll see paintings by both Western and Japanese artists, including Picasso, Dalí, Yoshitomo Nara, and Yokoyama Taikan. ✉ *3–4–1 Minatomirai, Nishi-ku* ☎ *045/221–0300* 🌐 *yokohama.art.museum/eng* 🎫 *Varies with exhibition* 🕙 *Closed Thurs.* Ⓜ *JR lines and Yokohama Subway Blue Line, Sakuragicho Station; Minato Mirai Line, Minato Mirai Station.*

★ **Yokohama Red Brick Warehouses** (赤レンガ倉庫; *Aka-Renga Soko*)
STORE/MALL | **FAMILY** | History meets entertainment at Yokohama's Red Brick Warehouses, just a few minutes from World Porters Mall. Constructed in 1911 and 1913 to accommodate trade, partially destroyed ten years later in the Kanto earthquake, and then used for military storage in World War II before being taken over by the United States upon Japan's surrender, today these two redbrick warehouses are a fashionable hangout. You'll find event spaces and unique shops, as well as cafés, restaurants, and bars (some with balcony seating). There are also seasonal fairs and markets, and the seafront areas are perfect picnic spots. ✉ *1–1 Shinko, Naka-ku* 🌐 *www.yokohama-akarenga.jp* Ⓜ *JR lines and Yokohama Subway Blue Line, Sakuragicho Station; Minato Mirai Line, Minato Mirai Station.*

Restaurants

Chano-ma (チャノマ)
$$$ | **JAPANESE** | This stylish eatery serves Japanese-Italian fusion pasta that you enjoy while lounging on bedlike seats as a house DJ spins tunes. There's also a lengthy drinks menu (alcohol and soft drinks), if you want to settle in for a longer stay. **Known for:** Japanese-Italian pasta; laidback setting; weekend crowds 💲 *Average main: ¥3,500* ✉ *Red Brick Warehouse Bldg. 2, 1–1–2 Shinkou, 3rd fl., Naka-ku* ☎ *045/650–8228* Ⓜ *JR lines and Yokohama Subway Blue Line, Sakuragicho Station; Minato Mirai Line, Minato Mirai Station.*

Kakin Hanten (華錦飯店)
$$$$ | **CANTONESE** | In contrast to many of the meat-heavy choices in Chinatown, this Cantonese restaurant specializes in fresh, flavorful seafood dishes. Menu

ighlights include the shrimp-shiso spring olls, steamed Sakhalin surf clams with arlic, and a rotating selection of fresh ish caught that day. **Known for:** some of hinatown's freshest seafood; excellent uality at reasonable prices; wide selecion of Cantonese dishes. *Average main: ¥6,000 126–22 Yamashitacho, Naka-ku 050/5485–4599 kakinhanten.gorp.jp JR lines, Ishikawacho Station; Minato Mirai Line, Motomachi-Chukagai Station.*

aseiro (華正樓)

$$$ | **CHINESE** | Chinese food can be it-or-miss in Japan, but not at Kaseiro. his elegant restaurant, with red carpets nd gold-toned walls, is the best of its ind in the city, serving authentic Beijing uisine, including, of course, Peking uck and shark-fin soup. **Known for:** okohama's flagship Chinese restaurant; rand atmosphere; excellent multicourse neals. *Average main: ¥16,500 186 amashita-cho, Chinatown, Naka-ku 045/681–2918 www.kaseiro.com/onten JR lines, Ishikawacho Station; Ainato Mirai Line, Motomachi-Chukagai tation.*

eryna Roman-chaya (瀬里奈 浪漫茶屋;)

$$$ | **JAPANESE** | The hallmarks of this resaurant—in business since 1973—are *ishiaki* steak, which is grilled on a hot stone, nd *shabu-shabu*—thin slices of beef ooked in boiling water at your table and ipped in one of several sauces (sesame, inegar, or soy). Fresh vegetables, noodles, nd tofu are also dipped into the seasoned roth for a filling yet healthful meal. **Known r:** high-grade Wagyu beef; rustic atmoshere; excellent service. *Average main: 15,000 Shin-Kannai Bldg., 4–45–1 Sumoshicho, 1st fl., Naka-ku 045/681–2727 www.seryna.com/romanjaya/romanjaya.tml JR lines and Yokohama Subway lue Line, Kannai Station.*

hunotei Hira (春鶯亭ひら)

$$$ | **JAPANESE** | The area of Motomachi known as the wealthy, posh part of okohama, so restaurants here tend to be exclusive and expensive, with service and quality justifying the price. This restaurant in an old-style Japanese house—complete with a Japanese garden and five private tatami rooms—serves dinners that are more akin to a banquet, with dishes that (depending on the season) could include traditional Japanese delicacies such as sashimi, shiitake mushrooms, and chicken in white sauce; deep-fried burdock; or broiled sea bream. **Known for:** seasonally focused multicourse meals; traditional atmosphere; long dinners. *Average main: ¥16,500 1–55 Motomachi, Naka-ku walk uphill from the eastern end of Motomachi and you'll find it opposite the cemetery 045/662–2215 shunoutei.com Closed Mon. JR lines, Ishikawacho Station; Minato Mirai Line, Motomachi-Chukagai Station.*

Yokohama Cheese Cafe (横浜チーズカフェ)

$$$ | **ITALIAN** | **FAMILY** | The interior of this cozy, inviting, casual restaurant feels like an Italian country home, one with candles on the tables and an open kitchen. On the menu are Neopolitan-style wood fired pizzas, pastas, fondue, and other dishes that include—you guessed it—cheese. **Known for:** a cheese lover's paradise; rich, creamy fondue; affordable multicourse meals. *Average main: ¥3,500 2–1–10 Kitasaiwai, Nishi-ku 045/290–5656 cheesecafe-yokohama.com No lunch Multiple lines, JR Yokohama Station.*

Coffee and Quick Bites

Baird Beer Bashamichi Taproom (ベアードビール馬車道タップルーム)

$$ | **AMERICAN** | Baird, one of the first craft brewers to find success in Japan, now has several taprooms in and near Tokyo, including this one on a side street just off of Bashamichi. You'll find almost a dozen Baird beers on tap—from year-round IPAs to seasonal specials like a summer mikan ale and warming imperial stouts—and the bar menu features Texas barbecue. **Known for:** their own range of year-round

craft beers; seasonal beers; excellent brisket sandwich. *Average main: ¥3,000 5–63–1 Sumiyoshicho, Naka-ku bairdbeer.com/taprooms/bashamichi JR lines and Yokohama Subway Blue Line, Kannai Station; Minato Mirai Line, Bashamichi Station.*

Enokitei Honten (えの木てい本店)
$$ | **CAFÉ** | **FAMILY** | Located in one of the area's few remaining historic Western-style houses, Enokitei is a relaxing stop for sweets or a light meal. The interior has the feel of a British-style tea room, with dark wood and antiques, while the garden terrace is surrounded by greenery and flowers much of the year. **Known for:** elegant yet casual atmosphere; people-watching in the shade; afternoon tea. *Average main: ¥1,600 89–6 Yamatecho, Naka-ku 045/623–2288 www.enokitei.co.jp No credit cards JR lines, Ishikawacho Station; Minato Mirai Line, Motomachi-Chukagai Station.*

Houtenkaku Shinkan (鵬天閣 新館)
$$ | **SHANGHAINESE** | This no-frills eatery serves excellent *sheng jian bao* (Shanghai-style fried dumplings) and other casual Shanghai cuisine all day long. The kitchen is behind glass so you can admire the speed with which the chefs cook up this Shanghai staple. **Known for:** authentic Shanghai dumplings; quick and satisfying street food; lines for takeout service. *Average main: ¥3,000 192–15 Yamashitacho, Naka-ku 045/681–9016 houtenkaku.com/shinkan JR lines, Ishikawacho Station; Minato Mirai Line, Motomachi-Chukagai Station.*

Kamakura 鎌倉

40 km (25 miles) southwest of Tokyo.

If you have time for just one day trip away from Tokyo, spend it at this religious center. Kamakura's temples and shrines, many designated National Treasures, are beautifully situated.

For the aristocrats of Heian-era Japan (794–1185), life was defined by the Imperial Court in Kyoto, where there was grace and beauty and poignant affairs of the heart—everything beyond was howling wilderness. By the 12th century two clans—the Taira (pronounced "*ta-ee-ra*") and the Minamoto, themselves both offshoots of the imperial line—had come to dominate the affairs of the court and were at each other's throats in a struggle for supremacy.

The rivalry between the two clans became an all-out war, and, by 1185, the Minamoto were masters of all Japan. Yoritomo no Minamoto forced the Imperial Court to name him shogun, making him the de facto and de jure the military head of state. The emperor was left as a figurehead in Kyoto, and the little fishing village of Kamakura, a superb natural fortress surrounded on three sides by hills and guarded on the fourth by the sea, became—and for 141 years remained—the seat of Japan's first shogunal government.

After 1333, when the center of power returned to Kyoto, Kamakura reverted to being a sleepy backwater town. After World War II, it began to develop as a residential area for the well-to-do. Though the religious past is much in evidence, nothing secular survives from the shogunal days; there wasn't much there to begin with. The warriors of Kamakura had little use for courtiers, or their palaces and gardened villas; the shogunate's name for itself, in fact, was the Bakufu—literally, the "tent government."

GETTING HERE AND AROUND

Traveling by train is by far the best way to reach Kamakura. Trains run from Tokyo Station (and Shimbashi Station) every 10 to 15 minutes during the day. The trip takes 56 minutes to Kita-Kamakura and one hour to Kamakura. Take the JR Yokosuka Line from Track 1 downstairs in Tokyo Station (Track 1 upstairs is on a different line and does not go to Kamakura). The cost is ¥830 to Kita-Kamakura, ¥950 to Kamakura. For more comfort, an additional ¥1,010 gets you a seat in the first-class Green Car.

It's now also possible to take a train from Shinjuku, Shibuya, or Ebisu to Kamakura on the Shonan-Shinjuku Line, but these trains depart less frequently than those departing from Tokyo Station. Local train services connect Kita-Kamakura, Kamakura, Hase, and Enoshima.

Buses run from the East Exit of Kamakura Station to many of the temples and shrines in downtown Kamakura and Kita-Kamakura, and even to Hase. The Kamakura Tegata one-day bus pass gives unlimited rides on these buses, as well as the Enoden Railway to Hase, for ¥900.

Kamakura is also a pleasant city for walking. With a full day and good weather, you could start with the sights near Kita-Kamakura Station, then work your way south to Tsurugaoka Hachimangu Shrine and then Kamakura Station.

TOURS

KSGG Club Volunteer Guides

GUIDED TOURS | The KSGG Club Volunteer Guides has a free guide service and regular events. Arrangements must be made in advance through the group's website. *volunteerguide-ksgg.jp* *Tours are free, but guests pay their own admission fees.*

VISITOR INFORMATION

The Kamakura City Tourist Information Center at Kamakura Station has a useful brochures and maps.

CONTACTS Kamakura City Tourist Information Center. *Kamakura Station, 1–1–1 Komachi, Kamakura* *0467/22–3350* *www.trip-kamakura.com.*

Kita-Kamakura

40 km (25 miles) southwest of Tokyo.

Hierarchies were important to the Kamakura Shogunate. In the 14th century, it established a ranking system called Go-zan (literally, "Five Mountains") for the Zen Buddhist monasteries under its official sponsorship. These are clustered in the Kita-Kamakura district.

Sights

Engaku-ji Temple (円覚寺)

TEMPLE | The largest of the Zen monasteries in Kamakura, Engaku-ji was founded in 1282 and ranks second in the Five Mountains hierarchy. Here, prayers were to be offered regularly for the prosperity and well-being of the government; Engaku-ji's special role was to pray for the souls of those who died resisting the Mongol invasions in 1274 and 1281. The temple complex currently holds 18 buildings, but once contained as many as 50. Often damaged in fires and earthquakes, it has been completely restored.

Engaku-ji belongs to the Rinzai sect of Zen Buddhism. The ideas of Zen were introduced to Japan from China at the beginning of the Kamakura period (1192–1333). The samurai especially admired the Rinzai sect, with its emphasis on the ascetic life as a path to self-transcendence. The monks of Engaku-ji played an important role as advisers to the shogunate in matters spiritual, artistic, and political.

Among the National Treasures at Engaku-ji is the Hall of the Holy Relic of Buddha (Shari-den), with its Chinese-inspired thatched roof. Built in 1282, it was destroyed by fire in 1558 but rebuilt in its original form soon after, in 1563. The hall is said to enshrine a tooth of the Gautama Buddha himself, but it's not on display. In fact, except for the first three

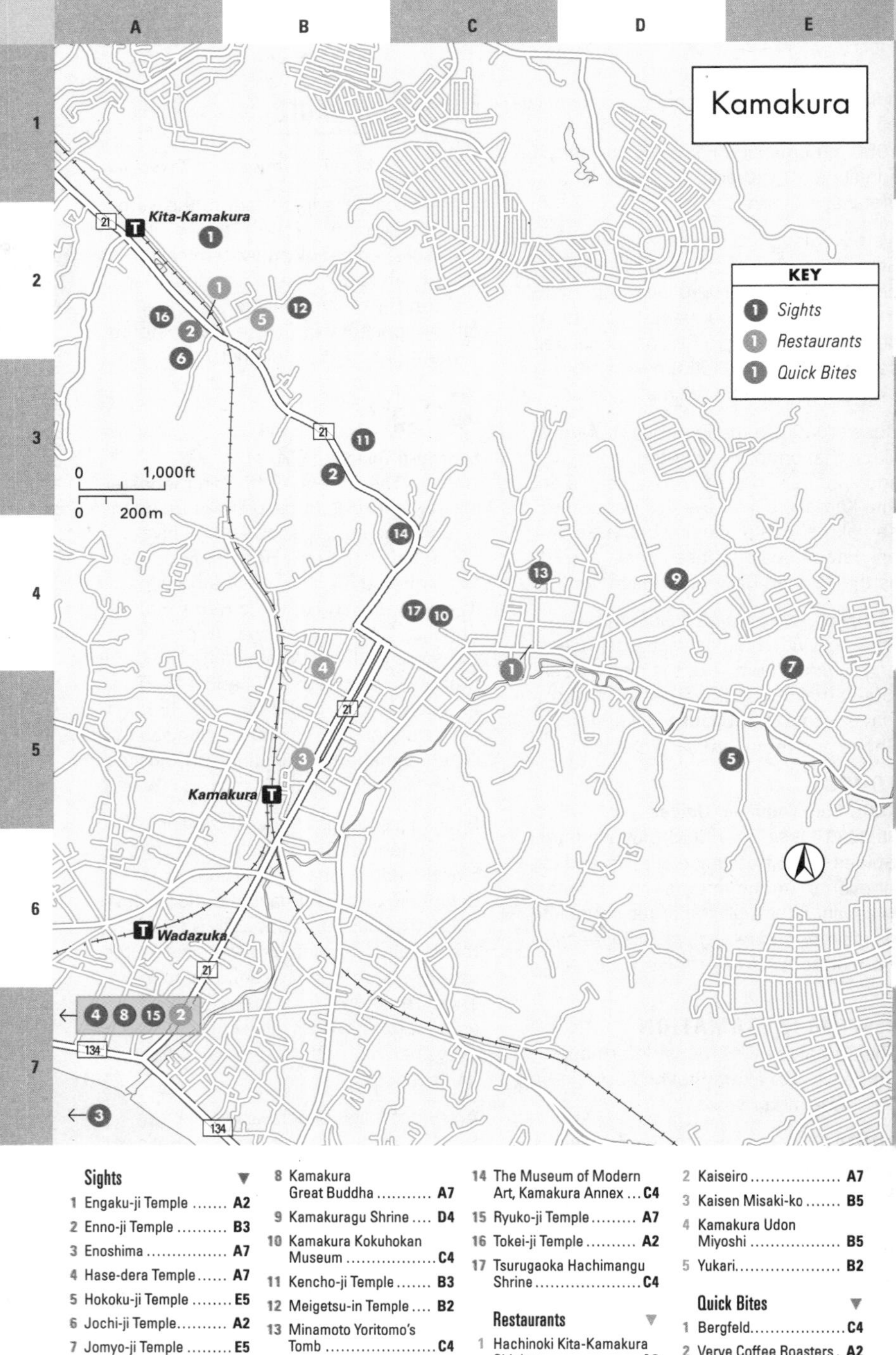

Sights

1 Engaku-ji Temple **A2**
2 Enno-ji Temple **B3**
3 Enoshima **A7**
4 Hase-dera Temple...... **A7**
5 Hokoku-ji Temple **E5**
6 Jochi-ji Temple.......... **A2**
7 Jomyo-ji Temple **E5**
8 Kamakura Great Buddha **A7**
9 Kamakuragu Shrine **D4**
10 Kamakura Kokuhokan Museum **C4**
11 Kencho-ji Temple **B3**
12 Meigetsu-in Temple **B2**
13 Minamoto Yoritomo's Tomb **C4**
14 The Museum of Modern Art, Kamakura Annex ... **C4**
15 Ryuko-ji Temple **A7**
16 Tokei-ji Temple **A2**
17 Tsurugaoka Hachimangu Shrine **C4**

Restaurants

1 Hachinoki Kita-Kamakura Shinkan **A2**
2 Kaiseiro **A7**
3 Kaisen Misaki-ko **B5**
4 Kamakura Udon Miyoshi **B5**
5 Yukari...................... **B2**

Quick Bites

1 Bergfeld.................. **C4**
2 Verve Coffee Roasters. **A2**

days of the New Year, you won't be able to go any farther into the hall than the main gate. Such is the case, alas, with much of the Engaku-ji complex: this is still a functioning monastic center, and many of its most impressive buildings are not open to the public.

The accessible National Treasure at Engaku-ji is the Grand Bell (Ogane), on the hilltop on the southeast side of the complex. The bell—Kamakura's most famous—was cast in 1301 and stands 8 feet tall. It's rung only on special occasions, such as New Year's Eve. Reaching it requires a trek up a long staircase, but once at the top, you can enjoy tea and traditional Japanese sweets at a small outdoor café.

The standout buildings open to the public at Engaku-ji are the Butsu-den (main hall), which houses a 2.5-meter-high statue of the Hokan Shaka Nyorai Buddha, and the Obai-in. The latter is the mausoleum of the last three regents of the Kamakura Shogunate: Tokimune Hojo, who led the defense of Japan against the Mongol invasions; his son Sadatoki; and his grandson Takatoki. Off to the side of the mausoleum is a quiet garden with apricot trees, which bloom in February. As you exit Kita-Kamakura Station, you'll see the stairway to Engaku-ji just in front of you. ✉ *409 Yamanouchi, Kamakura* ☎ *0467/22–0478* 🌐 *www.engakuji.or.jp/en* 🎫 *¥500.*

Enno-ji Temple (円応寺)
TEMPLE | In the feudal period, Japan acquired from China a belief in Enma, the lord of hell, who, with his court attendants, judged the souls of the departed and determined their destination in the afterlife. Kamakura's otherwise undistinguished Enno-ji Temple houses some remarkable statues of these judges—as grim and merciless a court as you're ever likely to confront. To see them is enough to put you on your best behavior, at least for the rest of your excursion. Enno-ji is a minute's walk or so from Kencho-ji Temple, on the opposite (south) side of the main road to Kamakura. ✉ *1543 Yamanouchi, Kamakura* ☎ *0467/25–1095* 🌐 *kamakura-ennouji.jp* 🎫 *¥300.*

Timing Tip

If your time is limited, you may want to visit only Engaku-ji and Kencho-ji in Kita-Kamakura before riding the train one stop to Kamakura. If not, follow the main road all the way to Tsurugaoka Hachimangu and visit four additional temples en route.

Jochi-ji Temple (浄智寺)
TEMPLE | In the Five Mountains hierarchy, Jochi-ji Temple was ranked fourth. The buildings now in the complex are thoughtful reconstructions (the Great Kanto Earthquake of 1923 destroyed the originals), while older features include a small garden and bamboo grove. Jochi-ji is on the south side of the railway tracks, a few minutes' walk farther southwest of Tokei-ji in the direction of Kamakura. ✉ *1402 Yamanouchi, Kamakura* ✥ *Turn right off main road (Rte. 21) and cross over small bridge; flight of moss-covered steps leads up to temple* ☎ *0467/22–3943* 🌐 *jochiji.com* 🎫 *¥300.*

Kencho-ji Temple (建長寺)
TEMPLE | Founded in 1250, Kencho-ji was the foremost of Kamakura's five great Zen temples, and it lays claim to being the oldest Zen temple in all of Japan. It was modeled on one of the great Chinese monasteries of the time and built for a distinguished Zen master who had just arrived from China. Over the centuries, disasters have taken their toll; indeed, the Main Gate and the Lecture Hall (Hatto) are the only two structures to have survived the devastating Great Kanto Earthquake of 1923. Although many buildings have been authentically reconstructed, the complex today is half

Did You Know?

Engaku-ji Temple belongs to the Rinzai sect of Zen Buddhism. Introduced by China at the beginning of the Kamakura period (1192–1333), Zen was quickly embraced by the emerging warrior class. The samurai especially admired Rinzai's emphasis on the ascetic life as a path to self-transcendence. The monks of Engaku-ji advised the shogunate in matters spiritual, artistic, and political.

its original size. Near the Main Gate (Sanmon) is a bronze bell cast in 1255; it's the temple's most important treasure.

Like Engaku-ji, Kencho-ji is a functioning temple of the Rinzai sect, where novices train and laypeople can come to take part in Zen meditation. Nearly hidden at the back of the temple is a long stairway and hiking trail that leads to Zuisen-ji, another of Kamakura's major temples. The hike takes about 90 minutes. ✉ *8 Yamanouchi, Kamakura* ✣ *Entrance to Kencho-ji is about halfway along main road from Kita-Kamakura Station to Tsurugaoka Hachimangu, on left* ☎ *0467/22–0981* 🌐 *www.kenchoji.com* 🎫 *¥500.*

Meigetsu-in Temple (明月院)
TEMPLE | This temple is also known as Ajisai-dera ("the hydrangea temple"), and when the flowers bloom in June, it becomes one of the most popular places in Kamakura. The gardens transform into a sea of color—pink, white, and blue—and visitors can number in the thousands. The rainy season drizzle that accompanies the flowers shouldn't deter you; it only showcases this incredible floral display to its best advantage. Meigetsu-in features Kamakura's largest *yagura* (a tomb cavity enclosing a mural) on which 16 images of Buddha are carved. ✉ *189 Yamanouchi, Kamakura* ✣ *To reach Meigetsu-in from Engaku-ji, follow the train tracks southeast for about 5 min. then follow the sign left, tracing the course of a little stream called Meigetsu-gawa to temple gate* ☎ *0467/24–3437* 🎫 *¥500.*

Tokei-ji Temple (東慶寺)
TEMPLE | A Zen temple of the Rinzai sect, Tokei-ji provides an example of feminism in medieval Japan. More popularly known as the Enkiri-dera, or Divorce Temple, it was founded in 1285 by the widow of the Hojo regent Tokimune as a refuge for the victims of unhappy marriages. Under the shogunate, a husband of the warrior class could obtain a divorce simply by sending his wife back to her family. Not so for the wife: no matter what cruel and unusual treatment her husband meted out, she was stuck with him. If she ran away, however, and managed to reach Tokei-ji without being caught, she could receive sanctuary at the temple and remain there as a nun. After three years (later reduced to two), she was officially declared divorced.

The temple survived as a convent through the Meiji Restoration of 1868. The last abbess died in 1902; her headstone is in the cemetery behind the temple, beneath the plum trees that blossom in February. Tokei-ji was later reestablished as a monastery. The Matsugaoka Hozo (Treasure House) of Tokei-ji displays several Kamakura-period wooden Buddhas, ink paintings, scrolls, and works of calligraphy, some of which have been designated by the government as Important Cultural Objects. The library, called the Matsugaoka Bunko, was established in memory of the great Zen scholar D. T. Suzuki (1870–1966).

Tokei-ji is on the southwest side of the JR tracks (the side opposite Engaku-ji), less than a five-minute walk south from the station on the main road to Kamakura (Route 21), on the right. ✉ *1367 Yamanouchi, Kamakura* ☎ *0467/22–1663* 🌐 *tokeiji.com* 🎫 *¥200* ⏲ *Matsugaoka Treasure House closed Mon.*

Restaurants

Hachinoki Kita-Kamakura Shinkan (鉢の木北鎌倉新館)
$$$$ | **JAPANESE** | **FAMILY** | Traditional *kaiseki ryori* and pretty *bento* boxes are served at this restaurant on Route 21, near the entrance to Jochi-ji Temple. While the full kaiseki courses can get expensive, the lunchtime kaiseki taster sets are a very affordable way to try this refined culinary style. **Known for:** Kaiseki cuisine for all budgets; beautiful presentation; kids meals available. [$] *Average main: ¥5,500* ✉ *350 Yamanouchi, Kamakura* ☎ *0467/23–3723* 🌐 *www.hachinoki.co.jp* ⏲ *Closed Thurs.*

Yukari (ゆかり)

$$ | **FRENCH** | The special at this restaurant and café, housed in an old Japanese building on the approach to Meigetsu-in, is beef bourguignon, which can be ordered à la carte or in a set along with soup, salad, and rye bread. For a lighter bite, you can order coffee and cheesecake. **Known for:** beef bourguignon; cheesecake; peaceful setting. *Average main: ¥2,700 ✉ 187 Yamanouchi, Kamakura ✣ On the approach to Meigetsu-in, on the right, behind the gateway with a purple noren curtain. ☎ 050/5487–9717 🌐 kitakamakurayukari.gorp.jp ⏲ Closed Thurs.*

Coffee and Quick Bites

Verve Coffee Roasters

$ | **CAFÉ** | **FAMILY** | On Route 21, a few minutes south of Tokei-ji, Verve serves up single-origin coffee in fashionably airy surroundings and in an outdoor seating area. You'll also find waffles and toasted sandwiches on the menu. **Known for:** single-origin coffee; waffles; toasted sandwiches. *Average main: ¥780 ✉ 1395 Yamanouchi, Kamakura ☎ 0467/81-4495 🌐 vervecoffee.jp.*

Downtown Kamakura

Downtown Kamakura is a good place to stop for lunch and shopping. Restaurants and stores selling local crafts, especially the carved and lacquered woodwork called Kamakura-bori, abound on Wakamiya Oji and the street parallel to it on the east, Komachi-dori.

When the first Kamakura shogun, Minamoto no Yoritomo, learned he was about to have an heir, he had the tutelary shrine of his family moved to Kamakura from nearby Yuigahama and ordered a stately avenue to be built through the center of his capital from the shrine to the sea. Along this avenue would travel the procession that brought his son—if there were a son—to be presented to the gods. In 1182, Yoritomo's consort did, indeed, bear him a son, Yoriie (pronounced "yo-*ree*-ee-eh"), who was brought in great pomp to the shrine and then consecrated to his place in the shogunal succession. Alas, the blessing of the gods did Yoriie little good. He was barely 18 when Yoritomo died, and the regency established by his mother's family, the Hojo, kept him virtually powerless until 1203, when he was banished and later assassinated. The Minamoto were never to hold power again, but Yoriie's memory lives on in the street that his father built for him: Wakamiya Oji, "the Avenue of the Young Prince."

Sights

Hokoku-ji Temple (報国寺)

TEMPLE | This lovely, little, often-overlooked Zen temple of the Rinzai sect that was built in 1334 is truly worth a visit. Over the years it had fallen into disrepair and neglect, until an enterprising priest took over, cleaned up the gardens, and began promoting the temple for meditation sessions, calligraphy exhibitions, and tea ceremony. Behind the main hall are a thick grove of bamboo and a small tea pavilion—a restful oasis and a fine place to go for *matcha* (green tea).

The temple is about 1.5 km (1 mile) east on Route 204 from the main entrance to Tsurugaoka Hachimangu. Turn right at the traffic light by the Hokokuji-iriguchi bus stop and walk about three minutes south to the gate. *✉ 2–7–4 Jomyo-ji, Kamakura ☎ 0467/22–0762 🌐 houkokuji.or.jp/en Admission ¥400; matcha and sweets ¥600.*

Jomyo-ji Temple (浄妙寺)

TEMPLE | Founded in 1188, this is the fifth of the Five Mountains Zen monasteries. Though this modest single-story monastery belonging to the Rinzai sect lacks the grandeur and scale of Engaku-ji and Kencho-ji, it still merits the status of an Important Cultural Property. It is nestled inside an immaculate garden that is particularly beautiful in spring, when the cherry trees bloom. The monastery's only distinctive features are its green roof and the statues of Shaka Nyorai and Amida Nyorai, who represent truth and enlightenment, in the main hall. There's also a tearoom serving Japanese tea and sweets. ✉ *3–8–31 Jomyo-ji, Kamakura* ✢ *From Hokoku-ji, cross main street (Rte. 204) that brought you the mile or so from Tsurugaoka Hachimangu, and take first narrow street north. The monastery is about 100 yd from corner* ☎ *0467/22–2818* 🎫 *Admission ¥100; tea and sweets from ¥660.*

Kamakuragu Shrine (鎌倉宮)

SHRINE | This Shinto shrine was built after the Meiji Restoration of 1868 and was dedicated to Prince Morinaga (1308–36), the first son of Emperor Go-Daigo. When Go-Daigo overthrew the Kamakura Shogunate and restored Japan to direct imperial rule, Morinaga—who had been in the priesthood—was appointed supreme commander of his father's forces.

The prince lived in turbulent times and died young: when the Ashikaga clan in turn overthrew Go-Daigo's government, Morinaga was taken into exile, held prisoner in a cave behind the present site of Kamakuragu, and eventually beheaded. The Homotsu-den (Treasure House), on the northwest corner of the grounds, next to the shrine's administrative office, is of interest mainly for its collection of paintings depicting the life of Prince Morinaga. ✉ *154 Nikaido, Kamakura* ✢ *From Yoritomo's tomb walk to Rte. 204 and turn left; at next traffic light, a narrow street on left leads off at an angle to shrine, about 5-min. walk west* ☎ *0467/22–0318* 🌐 *www.kamakuraguu.jp* 🎫 *Shrine free, Treasure House ¥300.*

Kamakura Kokuhokan Museum (鎌倉国宝館)

ART MUSEUM | This museum was built in 1928 as a repository for many important objects belonging to area shrines and temples; many of these are designated Important Cultural Properties. Located along the east side of the Tsurugaoka Hachimangu shrine precincts, the museum has an especially fine collection of devotional and portrait sculpture in wood from the Kamakura and Muromachi periods; the portrait pieces may be among the most expressive and interesting in all of classical Japanese art. ✉ *2–1–1 Yukinoshita, Kamakura* ☎ *0467/22–0753* 🌐 *www.city.kamakura.kanagawa.jp/kokuhoukan* 🎫 *From ¥400* ⏲ *Closed Mon.*

Minamoto Yoritomo's Tomb (源頼朝の墓; *Minamoto no Yoritomo no Haka*)

TOMB | The man who put Kamakura on the map, so to speak, chose not to leave it when he died: it's only a short walk from Tsurugaoka Hachimangu to the tomb of the man responsible for its construction, Minamoto no Yoritomo. If you've already been to Nikko and have seen how a later dynasty of shoguns sought to glorify its own memories, you may be surprised at the simplicity of Yoritomo's tomb. ✉ *2–5–2 Nishimikaido, Kamakura* ✢ *Exit Tsurugaoka Hachimangu, turn left and then left again, and follow small road up to Yoritomo's tomb* 🎫 *Free.*

The Museum of Modern Art, Kamakura Annex (神奈川県立近代美術館 鎌倉別館; *Kanagawa Kenritsu Kindai Bijutsukan Kamakura Bekkan*)

ART MUSEUM | Just a few minutes' walk north of Tsurugaoka Hachimangu, this museum houses a collection of Japanese oil paintings and watercolors, woodblock prints, and sculpture. ✉ *2–8–1 Yukinoshita, Kamakura* ☎ *0467/22–5000* 🌐 *www.moma.pref.kanagawa.jp/en/annex* 🎫 *From ¥700, depending on exhibition* ⏲ *Closed Mon.*

Tsurugaoka Hachimangu Shrine (鶴岡八幡宮)

SHRINE | This shrine is dedicated to the legendary emperor Ojin, his wife, and his mother, from whom Minamoto no Yoritomo claimed descent. At the entrance, the small, steeply arched, vermilion

An Ancient Soap Opera

Once a year, during the week-long Spring Festival (early to mid-April, when the cherry trees are in bloom), the Mai-den hall at Tsurugaoka Hachiman-gu is used to stage a heartrending drama about Minamoto no Yoritomo's brother, Yoshitsune. Although Yoritomo was the tactical genius behind the downfall of the Taira clan and the establishment of the Kamakura Shogunate in the late 12th century, it was his dashing half brother who actually defeated the Taira in battle. In so doing, Yoshitsune won the admiration of many, and Yoritomo came to believe that his sibling had ambitions of his own. Despite Yoshitsune's declaration of allegiance, Yoritomo had him exiled and sent assassins to have him killed. Yoshitsune spent his life fleeing from one place to another until, at the age of 30, he was betrayed in his last refuge and took his own life.

Earlier in his exile, Yoshitsune's lover, the dancer Shizuka Gozen, had been captured and brought to Yoritomo and his wife, Masako. They commanded her to dance for them as a kind of penance. Instead she danced for Yoshitsune. Yoritomo was furious, and only Masako's influence kept him from ordering her death. When he discovered, however, that Shizuka was carrying Yoshitsune's child, he ordered that if the child were a boy, he was to be killed. A boy was born. Some versions of the legend have it that the child was slain; others say he was placed in a cradle, like Moses, and cast adrift in the reeds.

Taiko-bashi (Drum Bridge) crosses a stream between two lotus ponds, which were made to Yoritomo's specifications. His wife, Masako, suggested placing islands in each. In the larger Genji Pond, to the right, filled with white lotus flowers, she placed three islands, a number that signifies birth and prosperity. In the smaller Heike Pond, to the left, she put four islands. Heike (pronounced "*heh*-ee-keh") was another name for the rival Taira clan, which the Minamoto had destroyed, and four—homophonous in Japanese with the word for "death"—is very unlucky indeed. Directly north of the Heike pond is the Kamakura Tsurugaoka Museum, where exhibitions focus on traditional arts and crafts.

Beyond the museum is the track where traditional horseback archery (yabusame) takes place during the shrine's spring and autumn festivals. Following the pathway north, you'll then see the Mai-den. This hall is the setting for a story of the Minamoto celebrated in Noh and Kabuki theater. Beyond the Mai-den, a flight of steps leads to the shrine's Hon-do (Main Hall). To the left of these steps is a ginkgo tree that—according to legend—was witness to a murder that ended the Minamoto line in 1219. From behind this tree, a priest named Kugyo leapt out and beheaded his uncle, the 26-year-old Sanetomo, Yoritomo's second son and the last Minamoto shogun. The priest was quickly apprehended, but Sanetomo's head was never found. As at all other Shinto shrines, the Hon-do is unadorned; the building itself, an 1828 reconstruction, is not particularly noteworthy. ✉ *2–1–31 Yukinoshita, Kamakura* ☎ *0467/22–0315* 🌐 *www.hachimangu.or.jp* 🎫 *Shrine free; Kamakura Museum from ¥600* 🕓 *Museum closed Mon.*

Restaurants

Kaisen Misaki-ko (海鮮三崎港)
$$ | **SUSHI** | This *kaiten-zushi* (sushi served on a conveyor belt that lets you pick the dishes you want) restaurant serves eye-poppingly large fish portions that hang over the edge of their plates. All the standard sushi creations, including tuna, shrimp, and egg, are prepared here. **Known for:** friendly, helpful staff and sushi chefs; inexpensive, quality sushi; fast service. *Average main: ¥2,000* *1–7–1 Komachi, Kamakura* *0467/22–6228* *No credit cards.*

Kamakura Udon Miyoshi (鎌倉みよし)
$$ | **JAPANESE** | **FAMILY** | Serving up some of Kamakura's best handmade udon noodles and tempura, this unpretentious restaurant is a good bet for quick and satisfying lunch. Miyoshi also has a selection of local sakes to pair with your meal. **Known for:** fresh noodles made before your eyes; reliability amid the tourist traps in the area; tempura that won't weigh you down. *Average main: ¥1,850* *1–5–38 Yukinoshita, Kamakura* *0467/61–4634* *kamakuraudon.jp* *No credit cards.*

Coffee and Quick Bites

Bergfeld (ベルグフェルド)
$ | **BAKERY** | **FAMILY** | This German bakery serves cakes and cookies that are surprisingly authentic—the baker trained in Germany. There are a few small tables outside, and cozy tables inside where you can enjoy coffee and cakes before resuming your tour. **Known for:** authentic German pastries and desserts; a good break between seeing sights; tasty sandwiches. *Average main: ¥1,500* *3–9–24 Yukinoshita, Kamakura* *0467/24–7616* *bergfeld-kamakura.com* *No credit cards* *Closed Mon. and Tues.*

Hase

On hydrangea-clad hillsides just outside downtown Kamakura are two of the town's main attractions, the Great Buddha and Hase-dera Temple. To get there, take the tram-like Enoshima Electric Railway (aka Enoden) from Kamakura Station three stops to Hase Station (¥200, 7 minutes).

Sights

Enoshima (江ノ島)
ISLAND | **FAMILY** | Although, like the beaches of Sagami Bay, the tiny island of Enoshima can be mobbed in summer and on sunny holidays, it's still worth a visit outside those times. While the island is only 4 km (2½ miles) around, with a hill in the middle and a long causeway connecting it to the mainland, there's quite a bit to see.

Partway up the hill is a shrine where the local fisherfolk used to pray for a bountiful catch—before it became a tourist attraction. Once upon a time it was quite a hike up to the shrine; now there are escalators, flanked by the inevitable stalls selling souvenirs and snacks. Some of the island's cafés and restaurants have spectacular views of Mt. Fuji and the Izu Peninsula.

To reach the causeway from Enoshima Station, walk south from the station for about 1 km (0.6 miles), keeping the Katase-gawa (Katase River) on your right. To return to Tokyo from Enoshima, take a train to Shinjuku on the Odakyu line. From the island walk back across the causeway, and take the second bridge over the Katase-gawa. Within five minutes you'll come to the Odakyu's Katase-Enoshima Station. Or you can retrace your steps to Kamakura and take the JR Yokosuka Line to Tokyo Station. *Kamakura* *Head to Enoshima Station on the Enoden Line, six stops from Hase (nine from Kamakura).*

Hase-dera, in Kamakura, is dedicated to unborn children. The beautiful temple faces the sea.

★ Hase-dera Temple (長谷寺)

TEMPLE | This temple is one of the most beautiful, and saddest, places of pilgrimage in the city. On a landing partway up the stone steps that lead to the temple's main hall are hundreds of small stone images of Jizo, one of the *bodhisattvas* in the Buddhist pantheon. Jizo is the savior of children, particularly the souls of the stillborn, aborted, and miscarried; the mothers of these children dress the statues of Jizo in bright red bibs and leave them small offerings of food, heartbreakingly touching acts of prayer.

The Kannon Hall (Kannon-do) at Hase-dera enshrines one of the largest carved-wood statues in Japan: the votive figure of Juichimen Kannon, the 11-headed goddess of mercy. Standing 30 feet tall, the goddess bears a crown of 10 smaller heads, symbolizing her ability to search in all directions for those in need of her compassion. No one knows for certain when the figure was carved. According to the temple records, a monk named Tokudo Shonin carved two images of the Juichimen Kannon from a huge laurel tree in 721. One was consecrated to the Hase-dera in present-day Nara Prefecture; the other was thrown into the sea to go wherever the waters decided that there were souls in need, and that image washed up on shore near Kamakura. Much later, in 1342, Takauji Ashikaga—the first of the 15 Ashikaga shoguns who followed the Kamakura era—had the statue covered with gold leaf.

The Amida Hall of Hase-dera enshrines the image of a seated Amida Buddha, who presides over the Western Paradise of the Pure Land. Minamoto no Yoritomo ordered the creation of this statue when he reached the age of 42; popular Japanese belief, adopted from China, holds that your 42nd year is particularly unlucky. Yoritomo's act of piety earned him another 11 years—he was 53 when he was thrown by a horse and died of his injuries. The Buddha is popularly known as the *yakuyoke* (good luck) Amida, and many visitors—especially students facing entrance exams—come here to pray.

To the left of the main halls is a small restaurant where you can buy good-luck candy and admire the view of Kamakura Beach and Sagami Bay. ✉ *3–11–2 Hase, Kamakura* ✣ *From Hase Station, walk north about 5 min. on main street (Rte. 32) toward Kotoku-in and Great Buddha, and look for signpost to temple on side street to left* ☎ *0467/22–6300* 🌐 *www.hasedera.jp* 🎫 *¥400.*

★ **Kamakura Great Buddha**
(鎌倉大仏; *Kamakura Daibutsu*)
PUBLIC ART | The single biggest attraction in Hase is the Great Buddha—a strong candidate for the quintessential image of Japan. The statue of the compassionate Amida Buddha sits cross-legged in the temple courtyard. The 37-foot bronze figure was cast in 1252, three centuries before Europeans reached Japan; the concept of the classical Greek lines in the Buddha's robe must have come over the Silk Route through China during the time of Alexander the Great. The casting was probably first conceived in 1180, by Minamoto no Yoritomo, who wanted a statue to rival the enormous Daibutsu in Nara. Until 1495 the Amida Buddha was housed in a wooden temple, which washed away in a great tidal wave.

It may seem sacrilegious to walk inside the Great Buddha, but for ¥50 you can enter the figure from a doorway in the right side and explore his stomach, with a stairway that leads up to two windows in his back, offering a nice view of the temple grounds (open until 4:15 pm). To reach Kotoku-in and the Great Buddha, take the Enoden Line from the west side of JR Kamakura Station three stops to Hase. From the main exit, turn right onto the main street (Route 32) and walk north about 10 minutes. ✉ *4–2–28 Hase, Kamakura* ☎ *0467/22–0703* 🌐 *www.kotoku-in.jp* 🎫 *¥300.*

Ryuko-ji Temple (龍口寺)
TEMPLE | The Kamakura story would not be complete without the tale of Nichiren (1222–82), the monk who founded the only native Japanese sect of Buddhism and is honored here. Nichiren's rejection of both Zen and Jodo (Pure Land) teachings brought him into conflict with the Kamakura Shogunate, and the Hojo regents sent him into exile on the Izu Peninsula in 1261. Later allowed to return, he continued to preach his own interpretation of the Lotus Sutra—and to assert the "blasphemy" of other Buddhist sects, a stance that finally persuaded the Hojo regency, in 1271, to condemn him to death.

What Is a Bodhisattva?

A *bodhisattva* is a being that has deferred its own ascendance into Buddhahood to guide the souls of others to salvation. It is considered a deity in Buddhism.

The execution was to take place on a hill to the south of Hase. As the executioner swung his sword, legend has it that a lightning bolt struck the blade and snapped it in two. Taken aback, the executioner sat down to collect his wits, and a messenger was sent back to Kamakura to report the event. On his way, he met another messenger, who was carrying a writ from the Hojo regents commuting Nichiren's sentence to exile on the island of Sado.

Followers of Nichiren built Ryuko Temple in 1337, on the hill where he was to be executed, marking his miraculous deliverance from the headsman. There are other Nichiren temples closer to Kamakura—Myohon-ji and Ankokuron-ji, for example. But Ryuko has not only the typical Nichiren-style main hall, with gold tassels hanging from its roof, but also a beautiful pagoda, built in 1904. ✉ *3–13–37 Katase, Fujisawa* ✣ *Take Enoden train line west from Hase to Enoshima—a short, scenic*

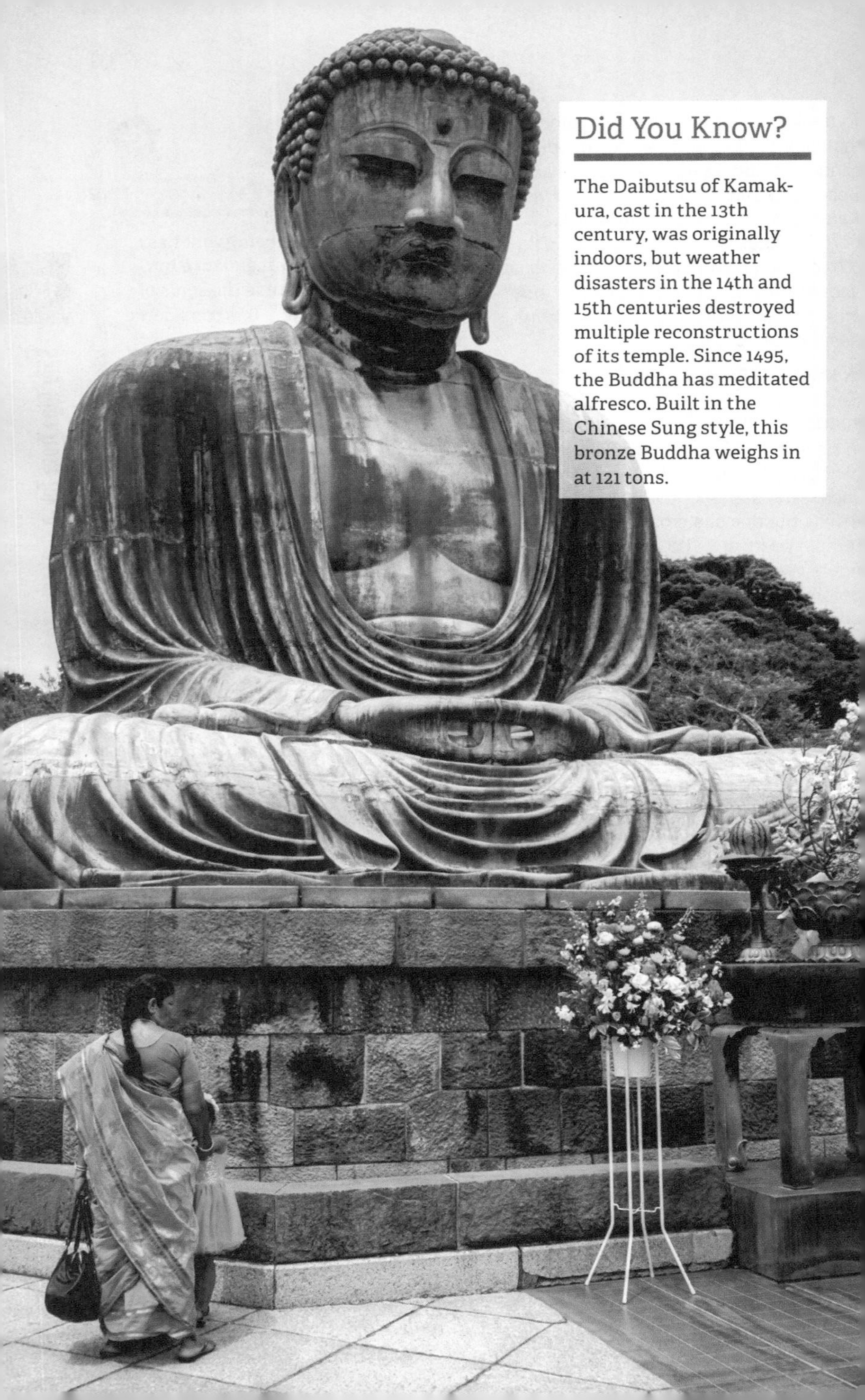

Did You Know?

The Daibutsu of Kamakura, cast in the 13th century, was originally indoors, but weather disasters in the 14th and 15th centuries destroyed multiple reconstructions of its temple. Since 1495, the Buddha has meditated alfresco. Built in the Chinese Sung style, this bronze Buddha weighs in at 121 tons.

ride that cuts through hills surrounding Kamakura to shore. From Enoshima Station walk about 100 yards east, keeping train tracks on your right ☎ 0466/25–7357 🎫 Free.

Restaurants

Kaiseiro (華正樓)

$$$$ | **CHINESE** | This establishment, in an elegant old Japanese house, serves the best Chinese food in the city. The dining-room windows look out on a small, restful garden. **Known for:** elegant atmosphere; substantially more affordable courses at lunch; excellent Peking duck and other multicourse meals. 💲 *Average main: ¥11,000* ✉ *3–1–14 Hase, Kamakura* ☎ *0467/22–0280* 🌐 *www.kaseiro-kamakura.com.*

Mt. Fuji (Fuji-san) 富士山

100 km (62 miles) southwest of Tokyo.

Mt. Fuji is the crown jewel of Fuji-Hakone-Izu National Park and an incredibly popular destination for both Japanese and international travelers. There are four main routes to the summit of the 12,388-foot-high (3,776-meter) mountain but the most recommendable (and most accessible) is the Yoshida Trail (sometimes called Kawaguchiko Trail), which starts from the Fuji-Subaru Line 5th Station and is on the peak's north side.

GETTING HERE AND AROUND

Take one of the daily buses directly to the Fuji-Subaru Line 5th Station from Tokyo; they run July through mid-September and leave from Shinjuku Station. The journey takes between 2½ to 3 hours from Shinjuku and costs ¥3,800. Reservations are required; book seats through the Fuji Kyuko Highway Bus Reservation Center or the Keio Highway Bus Reservation Center.

There are no direct trains between Mt. Fuji and Tokyo; as a result, buses are more affordable and convenient. But if you want to return from Mt. Fuji to Tokyo by train, take a 50-minute bus ride from Fuji-Subaru Line 5th Station to Kawaguchiko (¥1,780). From there, the fastest rail option is the Fuji Excursion express, which gets to Shinjuku in just under two hours (¥4,130).

CONTACTS Fuji Kyuko Highway Bus Reservation Center. ☎ *0555/73–8181* 🌐 *bus-en.fujikyu.co.jp.* **Keio Highway Bus Reservation Center.** ☎ *03/5376–2222* 🌐 *highway-buses.jp.*

TOURS

JTB Sunrise Tours

BUS TOURS | For an up-close look at Fuji that doesn't involve hiking, JTB Sunrise Tours operates a one-day tour to Mt. Fuji and Hakone from Tokyo, departing from (and returning to) Shinjuku. The tour includes a stop at the Fuji-Subaru Line 5th Station, before continuing to Hakone for a cruise on Lake Ashi and a trip on the gondola over Owakudani. ✉ *Tokyo* ☎ *03/5796–5454* 🌐 *www.sunrise-tours.jp/en* 🎫 *From ¥22,000.*

Sights

★ **Mt. Fuji** (富士山; *Fuji-san*)

MOUNTAIN | Rising from the surrounding plains, the single, flat-topped peak of Mt. Fuji is a sight to behold. Spending a day—or more commonly an afternoon and the following morning—to hike Mt. Fuji can be a once-in-a-lifetime experience with a fascinating variety of terrain and a stunning view of the sunrise from the peak—provided you go into it with the right expectations.

Unlike Japan's more remote mountains like the Japan Alps, Fuji is crowded, and the summer hiking season, when trails are open and accessible is short (roughly July to mid-September). Timing your hike to see the sunrise might mean that the final stretch to the summit feels

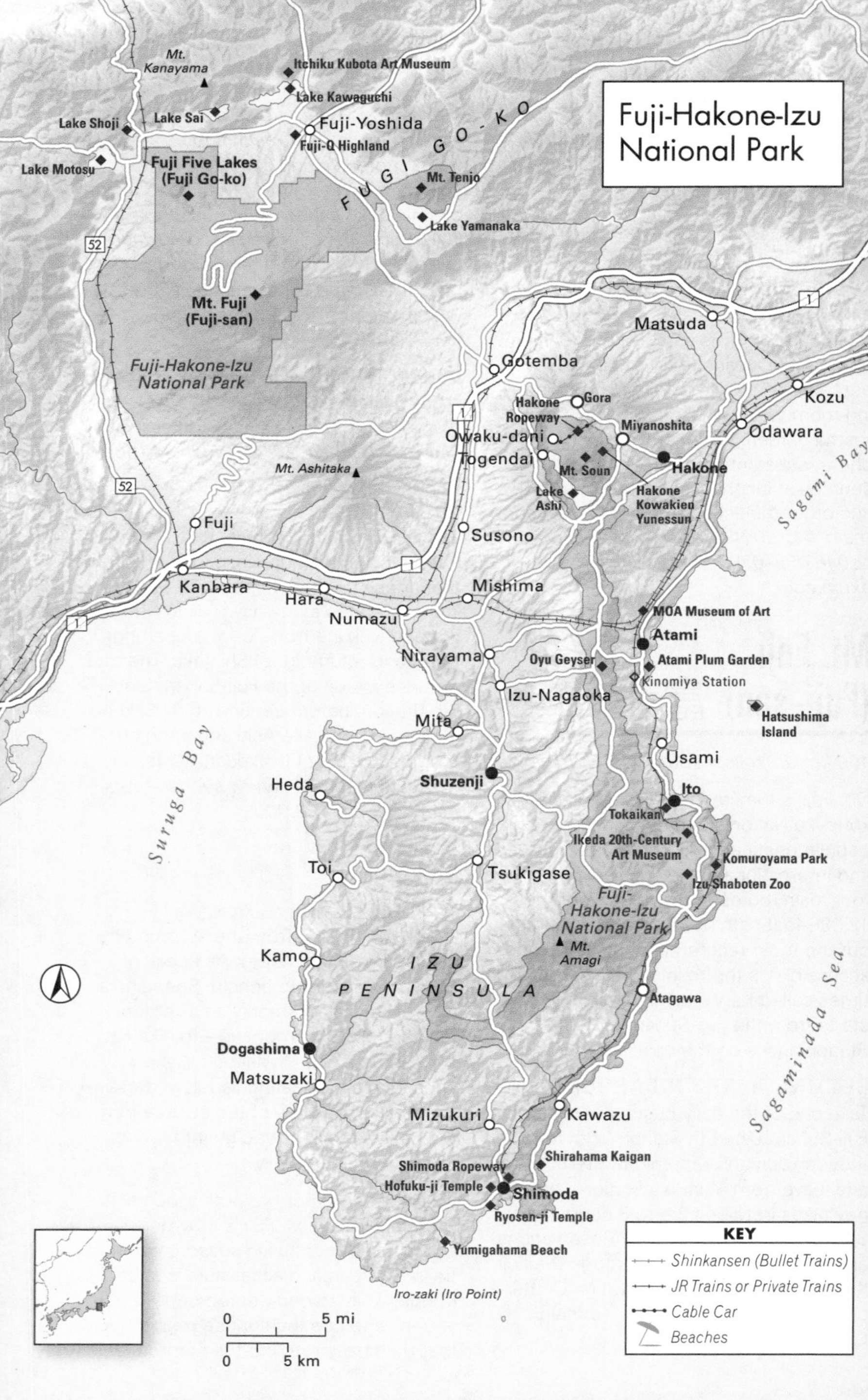

Fuji-Hakone-Izu National Park
Mt. Kanayama
Itchiku Kubota Art Museum
Lake Kawaguchi
Lake Sai
Lake Shoji
Fuji-Yoshida
Fuji-Q Highland
Lake Motosu
Fuji Five Lakes (Fuji Go-ko)
FUJI GO-KO
Mt. Tenjo
Lake Yamanaka
52
Mt. Fuji (Fuji-san)
Fuji-Hakone-Izu National Park
Matsuda
1
Gotemba
Kozu
Hakone Ropeway
Gora
Miyanoshita
Odawara
Owaku-dani
Togendai
Hakone
Mt. Soun
Sagami Bay
Mt. Ashitaka
Lake Ashi
Hakone Kowakien Yunessun
Fuji
Susono
Kanbara
Mishima
Hara
Numazu
MOA Museum of Art
Atami
Nirayama
Oyu Geyser
Atami Plum Garden
Kinomiya Station
Izu-Nagaoka
Hatsushima Island
Mita
Suruga Bay
Usami
Shuzenji
Heda
Ito
Tokaikan
Ikeda 20th-Century Art Museum
Komuroyama Park
Toi
Tsukigase
Izu Shaboten Zoo
Fuji-Hakone-Izu National Park
Mt. Amagi
Kamo
IZU PENINSULA
Sagaminada Sea
Atagawa
Dogashima
Matsuzaki
Kawazu
Mizukuri
Shirahama Kaigan
Shimoda Ropeway
Hofuku-ji Temple
Shimoda
Ryosen-ji Temple
Yumigahama Beach
Iro-zaki (Iro Point)
0
5 mi
0
5 km
KEY
Shinkansen (Bullet Trains)
JR Trains or Private Trains
Cable Car
Beaches

more like waiting in line than hiking. Still, making the trek to the top and watching the sunrise from Japan's most sacred mountain is a singularly incredible experience, and there is fun to be had climbing with the crowd.

There are four trails up Fuji, but the most common starting point is the Fuji-Subaru Line 5th Station (aka Kawaguchiko 5th Station), which is easily accessed by direct buses from Tokyo, Hakone, and many other cities. From here it takes between five to seven hours to reach the summit via the Yoshida Trail. The descent takes another three to four hours. There are numerous mountain huts on the way up to sleep for a few hours and adjust to the altitude (¥12,000–¥16,000 per person for a dorm spot, which includes dinner and breakfast), but they fill up quickly during peak times. Spots can be reserved for some huts online, but others require a phone call. The length and altitude require a decent level of fitness but no technical climbing skills. ✉ *Fuji-Hakone-Izu National Park* 🌐 *www.fujisan-climb.jp* 🎫 *¥1,000* ☞ *Outside of hiking season, the weather is highly unpredictable and extremely dangerous, so climbing is strongly discouraged.*

Fuji Five Lakes (Fuji Go-ko) 富士五湖

55 km (34 miles) northwest of Hakone.

To the north of Mt. Fuji, the Fuji Go-ko area affords an unbeatable view of the mountain on clear days and makes the best base for a climb to the summit. With its various outdoor activities, such as skating and fishing in winter and boating and hiking in summer, this is a popular resort area for families and business conferences.

The five lakes are, from the east, Yamanaka-ko, Kawaguchi-ko, Sai-ko, Shoji-ko, and Motosu-ko. Yamanaka and Kawaguchi are the largest and most developed as resort areas, with Kawaguchi more or less the centerpiece of the group.

GETTING HERE AND AROUND

The transportation hub, as well as one of the major resort areas in the Fuji Five Lakes area, is Kawaguchi-ko. The easiest rail option from Tokyo is the Fuji Excursion express, which runs between Shinjuku Station and Kawaguchi-ko Station in just under two hours (¥4,130) four times a day. A more frequent rail option is the JR Chuo Line's Kaiji and Azusa express trains, which run from Shinjuku Station to Otsuki (one hour), where you change to the private Fuji-Kyuko Line for Kawaguchi-ko (50 minutes). The total the fare is ¥3,990.

A direct bus service runs daily from Shinjuku Station in Tokyo to Lake Kawaguchi at least every hour between 7:15 am and 10:25 pm, costing ¥3,800 and taking about 2½ to 3 hours. You can also get buses to Kawaguchi-ko from Tokyo Station. Buses go from Kawaguchi-ko Station to Fuji-Subaru Line 5th Station (the start of the climb up Mt. Fuji) in about an hour (¥2,800 return); there are five departures a day until the climbing season (July 15 to September 10) starts, when there are 12 departures daily.

TIMING

With an early start, you can visit this area on a day trip from Tokyo, but unless you want to spend most of your time on buses and trains, it's better to plan an overnight stay.

VISITOR INFORMATION

CONTACTS Fuji-Kawaguchiko Tourist Information Center. ✉ *3641–1 Funatsu, Fujikawaguchiko, Minami-Tsuru-gun* ☎ *0555/72–6700* 🌐 *www.fujisan.ne.jp.*

Continued on page 346

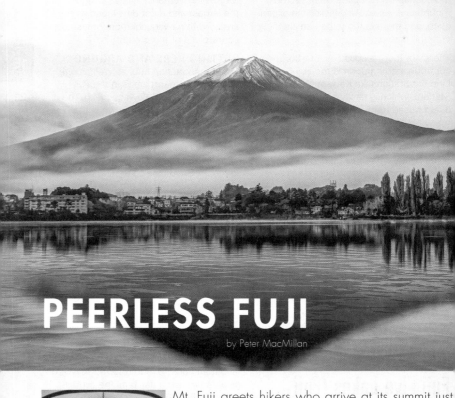

PEERLESS FUJI

by Peter MacMillan

Camping near Mt. Fuji

Mt. Fuji greets hikers who arrive at its summit just before dawn with the *go-raiko,* or the Coming of the Light. The reflection of this light shimmers across the sky just before the sun first appears, giving the extraordinary sunrise a mystical feel. Fuji-san's early morning magic is just one of the characteristics of the mountain that has captured the collective imagination of the Japanese, along with its snowy peak, spiritual meaning, and propensity to hide behind clouds. The close-to-perfectly symmetrical cone is an object to conquer physically and to admire from afar.

Japan is more than 70% mountainous, and Fuji is its tallest mountain. It appears in literature, art, and culture from the highest level to the most ordinary in countless ways. In a word, Fuji is ubiquitous.

Since ancient times, Mt. Fuji has been an object of worship for both Shinto and Buddhist practitioners. Shrines devoted to Konohana-Sakuya Hime, Mt. Fuji's goddess, dot the trails. So sacred is Fuji that the mountaintop torii gate at the Okumiya of Sengen Taisha Shrine (though at Fuji's foot, the shrine also encompasses the mountain above the 8th station) states that this is the greatest mountain in the world. Typically the gate would provide the shrine's name. Here, the torii defines not the shrine but the sacred space of the mountain.

Rising to 12,385 feet (3,776 meters), Mt. Fuji is an active volcano, but the last eruption was in 1707. Located on the boundaries of Shizuoka and Yamanashi prefectures, the mountain is an easy day trip west of Tokyo, and on clear days you can see the peak from the city. In season, hikers clamber to the peak, but it is gazing upon Fuji that truly inspires awe and wonder. No visit to Japan would be complete without at least a glimpse of this beautiful icon.

(Top left) Mt. Fuji's famous morning light draws visitors, (Top right): Climbing Mt. Fuji, (Bottom right): Hikers on one of the steep, forested trails

THE SYMBOLISM OF FUJI-SAN

ARTISTIC FUJI

Mt. Fuji is one of the world's most painted and photographed mountains. But rising above all the visual depictions are Katsushika Hokusai's *Thirty-Six Views of Mt. Fuji* and his *One Hundred Views of Mt. Fuji*. The latter is a stunning series and considered his masterpiece. However, the *Thirty-Six Views* is more famous because the images were printed in full color, while the *One Hundred Views* was printed in monochrome black and gray. His *Great Wave off Kanagawa* is one of the most famous prints in the history of art.

Hokusai believed that his depictions would get better and better as he got older, and they did; his *One Hundred Views* was completed when he was 75. He was also obsessed with achieving immortality. In creating the *One Hundred Views of Mt. Fuji,* a mountain always associated with immortality, he hoped to achieve his own. History proved him right.

LITERARY FUJI

There are thousands of literary works related to Fuji, including traditional and modern poems, haiku, Noh dramas, novels, and plays. In the *Man'yoshu*, 8th-century poet Yamabe no Akahito famously extolled Fuji: "When I sail out / on the Bay of Tago / every where's white / Look! Snow's piling up / on the peak of Fuji" Matsuo Basho, in another well known poem, wrote about not being able to see the mountain: "How lovely and intriguing / Covered in drifting fog / The day I could not see Fuji." There are many times of the year when Fuji hides behind the clouds, so don't be disappointed if you miss it. Like the great haiku poet, see the mountain in the eye of your heart.

(Top) Katsushika Hokusai's *Red Fuji*, (Bottom) *Great Wave off Kanagawa* by Katsushika Hokusai

SEE FUJI-SAN FROM AFAR

Like the poets and artists who have found inspiration in gazing at Fuji-san, you, too, can catch a glimpse of the snow-capped cone on the horizon. On a clear day, most likely in winter when the air is dry and the clouds lift, the following experiences provide some of the best Fuji views.

SEE FUJI

Atop Tokyo. Visit the Tokyo City View observation promenade on the 52nd floor of the Mori Tower in Roppongi. You can walk all around this circular building and take in the spectacular views of Tokyo and, when the weather is fine, Fuji.

While you're here, don't miss the sky-high Mori Art Museum, a contemporary art space on the 52nd and 53rd floors. The evening view of the city is also splendid, but Fuji will be slumbering under the blanket of nightfall.

From Hakone. Part of Fuji-Hakone-Izu National Park, the same park Fuji calls home, and an easy day trip from Tokyo, Hakone is a playground of hiking trails, small art museums, an onsen, and more. Head to the beautiful garden at Hakone Detached Palace for scenic views of Fuji-san. Early morning and late evening will provide the best chance for clear skies and stellar views of Fuji-san.

Speeding out of town. While traveling aboard the Shinkansen between Tokyo and Kyoto, try not to let the hum of some of Japan's fastest transportation technology lull you to sleep or you'll miss the classic view of Fuji. The world's most beautiful and sacred mountain will appear suddenly on the left.

(Top) Shinkansen speeding past Fuji,
(Bottom) Detached Palace Park in Hakone

CLIMBING FUJI-SAN

FROM YOSHIDA TRAIL

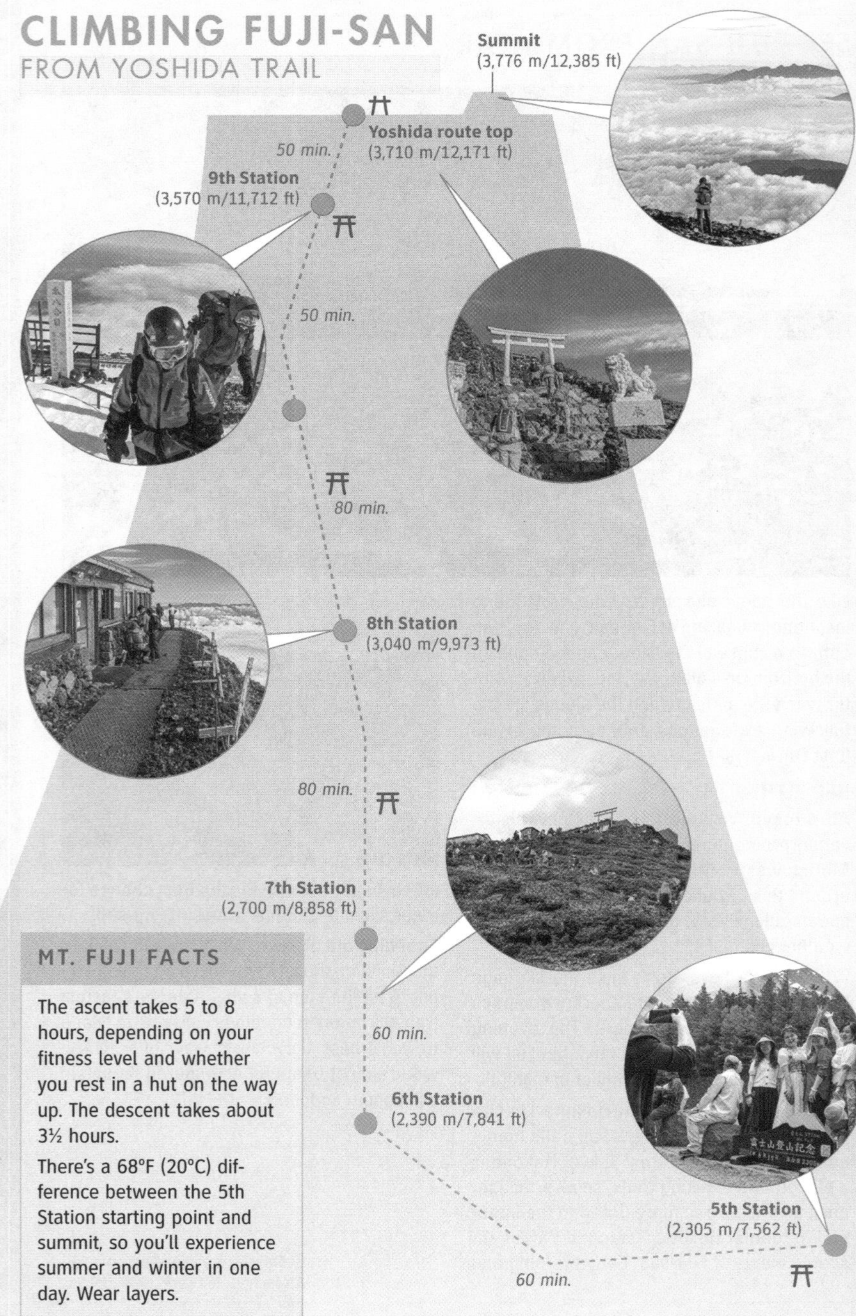

MT. FUJI FACTS

The ascent takes 5 to 8 hours, depending on your fitness level and whether you rest in a hut on the way up. The descent takes about 3½ hours.

There's a 68°F (20°C) difference between the 5th Station starting point and summit, so you'll experience summer and winter in one day. Wear layers.

Although many Japanese like to climb Mt. Fuji once in their lives, there's a saying in Japanese that only a fool would climb it twice. You, too, can make a once-in-a-lifetime climb during the mountain's official open season from July through August. Unless you're an experienced hiker, do not attempt to make the climb at another time of year.

TRAIL CONDITIONS

Except for the occasional cobblestone path, the routes are unpaved and at times steep, especially toward the top. Near the end of the climb there are some rope banisters to steady yourself, but for the most part you'll have to rely on your own balance.

Fuji draws huge crowds in season, so expect a lot of company on your hike. The throngs grow thicker in August during the school break and reach their peak during the holiday Obon week in mid-August; it gets so crowded that hikers have to queue up at certain passes. Trails are less crowded overnight. Go during the week and in July for the lightest crowds (though the weather is less reliable). Or accept the crowds and enjoy the friendships that spring up among strangers on the trails.

TRAILS OVERVIEW

If you're in good health you should be able to climb from the base to the summit. That said, the air is thin, and it can be humbling to struggle for oxygen while some 83-year-old Japanese grandmother blithely leaves you in her dust (it happens).

Most visitors take buses as far as the Fifth Station and hike to the top from there (⇨ *See Mt. Fuji listing in this chapter for more information on buses*). The paved roads end at this halfway point.

Four routes lead to Mt. Fuji's summit—the **Yoshida (aka Kawaguchiko)**, **Subashiri**, **Gotemba**, and **Fujinomiya**—and each has a corresponding Fifth Station that serves as the transfer point between bus and foot. Depending on which trail you choose, the ascent takes between 5 and 10 hours. Fujinomiya is closest to the summit; Gotemba is the farthest.

We recommend the Yoshida Trail in Yamanashi, as its many first-aid centers and lodging facilities (huts) ensure that you can enjoy the climb. **TIP→ Those interested in experiencing Fuji's religious and spiritual aspects should walk this trail from the mountain's foot. Along the way are small shrines that lead to the torii gate at the top, which signifies Fuji's sacred status.** While the food and cleanliness standards at mountain huts are subpar, they provide valuable rest spots and even more valuable camaraderie and good will among travelers.

AT THE TOP

Once you reach the top of Mt. Fuji, you can walk along the ridge of the volcano. A torii gate declares that Fuji is the greatest mountain in the world. It also marks the entrance to the **Fuji-san Hon-miya Sengen Taisha Shrine** (at the foot of the mountain near the Yoshida Trail is the shrine's other facility). Inside the shrine, head to the post office where you can mail letters and postcards with a special Mt. Fuji stamp. There's also a chalet at the top for those captivated enough to stay the night.

(Above) A photographer capturing the view from Mt. Fuji

NIGHT HIKES

The most spectacular way to hike Mt. Fuji is to time the climb so that you arrive at sunrise. Not only is the light famously enchanting, but the sky is also more likely to be clear, allowing for views back to Tokyo. Those who choose this have a few options. Start from the Yoshida 5th Station on the Yoshida Trail around 10 pm (or later, depending on the sunrise time) and hike through the night, arriving at the summit between 4:30 and 5 am, just as the sun begins to rise. A better alternative is to begin in the afternoon or evening and hike to the 7th or 8th Station, spend a few hours resting there, and then depart very early in the morning to see the sun rise. ■ **TIP→ The trail isn't lit at night, so bring a headlamp to illuminate the way. Avoid carrying flashlights, though, as it is important to keep your hands free in case of a fall.**

(Top) First glimpse of the *go-raiko*, (Bottom) Mt. Fuji at dawn

COMMEMORATE YOUR VISIT

Purchase a walking stick at the base of Mt. Fuji and, as you climb, have it branded at each station. By the time you reach the top you'll have the perfect souvenir to mark your achievement.

Walking sticks for sale

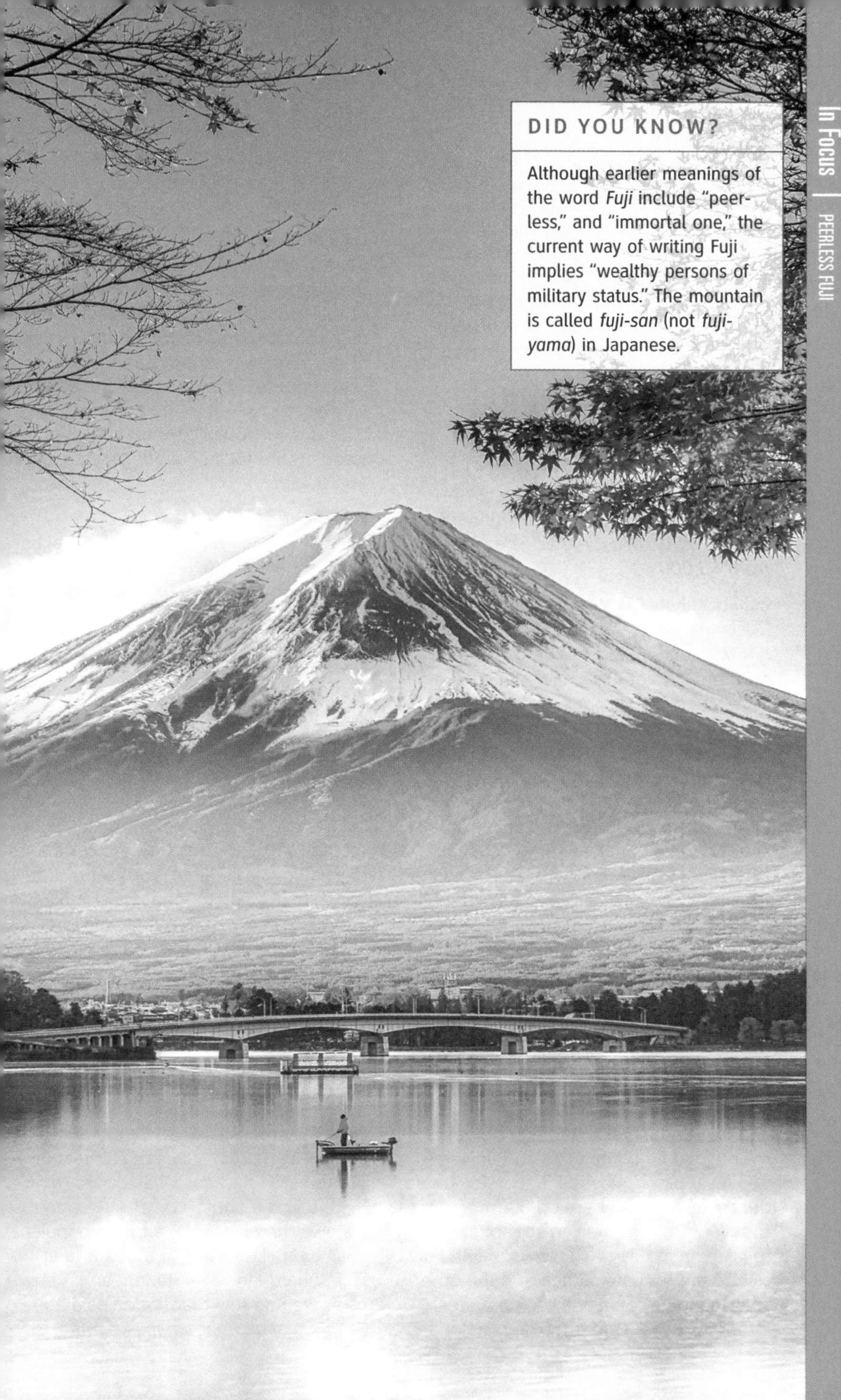

DID YOU KNOW?

Although earlier meanings of the word *Fuji* include "peerless," and "immortal one," the current way of writing Fuji implies "wealthy persons of military status." The mountain is called *fuji-san* (not *fuji-yama*) in Japanese.

Sights

Fuji-Q Highland (富士急ハイランド)
AMUSEMENT PARK/CARNIVAL | **FAMILY** | The largest of the recreational facilities at Lake Kawaguchi has an impressive assortment of rides, roller coasters, and other amusements, but it's probably not worth a visit unless you have children in tow. In winter, there's superb skating here, with Mt. Fuji for a backdrop. Fuji-Q Highland is about a 20-minute walk southeast from Kawaguchi-ko Station. In addition to the entry fee, there are charges for various attractions, so it's best to get the one-day free pass. ✉ *5–6–1 Shinnishihara, Fujiyoshida* ☎ *0555/23–2111* 🌐 *www.fujiq.jp/en* 🎫 *1-day pass from ¥6,000.*

Itchiku Kubota Art Museum (久保田一竹美術館 *Kubota Itchiku Bijutsukan*)
ART MUSEUM | **FAMILY** | Located on the northern side of Lake Kawaguchi, this museum displays a superb collection of elaborately decorated kimono created by the late Itchiku Kubota. All the work is beautiful, but the standout is an unfinished piece called Symphony of Light, which combines several dozen kimono to depict a seasonally changing Mt. Fuji. It's all housed in a Gaudi-inspired facility that's worth a look in its own right. ✉ *2255 Kawaguchi, Fujikawaguchiko* 🌐 *thekubotacollection.com/museum* 🎫 *¥1,500* ⏲ *Closed Tues.*

Lake Kawaguchi (河口湖; *Kawaguchi-ko*)
BODY OF WATER | **FAMILY** | A 5- to 10-minute walk north from Kawaguchi-ko Station, the most developed of the five lakes is ringed with weekend retreats and traditional ryokan—many of them maintained by companies and universities for their employees. Excursion boats depart from a pier here on 30-minute lake tours (¥1,000). The promise, not always fulfilled, is to have two views of Mt. Fuji: one of the mountain itself and the other inverted in its reflection on the water. Other attractions near the lake include Fuji-Q Highland amusement park and the impressive kimono collection at the Itchiku Kubota Museum. ✉ *Kawaguchiko, Fujikawaguchiko.*

Lake Motosu (本栖湖; *Motosu-ko*)
BODY OF WATER | **FAMILY** | Lake Motosu is the deepest, clearest, and farthest west of the five lakes (about 50 minutes by bus from Kawaguchi-ko). As it's also one of the least developed of the lakes, it's a good spot for hikers and nature lovers. If you want to see it without visiting, take a look at a ¥1,000 bill; Motosu is pictured on the reverse side. ✉ *Motosuko, Fujikawaguchiko.*

Lake Sai (西湖; *Sai-ko*)
BODY OF WATER | **FAMILY** | Between lakes Shoji and Kawaguchi, Sai is the third-largest lake of the Fuji Go-ko, with only moderate development. From the western shore there is an especially good view of Mt. Fuji. Near Sai-ko there are three natural caves, an ice cave, a bat cave, and a wind cave. You can either take a bus or walk to them. ✉ *Saiko, Fujikawaguchiko.*

Lake Shoji (精進湖; *Shoji-ko*)
BODY OF WATER | **FAMILY** | Many consider Lake Shoji, the smallest of the lakes, to be the prettiest. There are still remnants of lava flow jutting out from the water, which locals perch upon while fishing. The 17-km-long (10.5 miles) Shoji Trail leads from Lake Shoji to Mt. Fuji's Fuji-Subaru Line 5th Station through Aokiga-hara (Sea of Trees). This forest has an underlying magnetic lava field that makes compasses go haywire. Be prepared with a good trail map before taking this hike. ✉ *Shojiko, Fujikawaguchiko.*

Lake Yamanaka (山中湖; *Yamanaka-ko*)
BODY OF WATER | **FAMILY** | The largest lake of the Fuji Go-ko, Yamanaka is 35 minutes by bus to the southeast of Kawaguchi. It's also the closest lake to the popular Yoshida Trail up Mt. Fuji that starts at Fuji-Subaru Line 5th Station, and many climbers use this resort area as a base. ✉ *Yamanakokoko, Yamanaka-ko-mura.*

Mt. Tenjo (天上山; *Tenjo-san*)
MOUNTAIN | From the shore of Lake Kawaguchi (near the pier), the Mt. Fuji Panoramic Ropeway quickly brings you to the top of the 3,622-foot-tall Mt. Tenjo. From the observatory here, the whole of Lake Kawaguchi lies before you, and beyond the lake is a classic view of Mt. Fuji. ✉ *1163–1 Azagawa, Fujikawaguchiko* ☎ *0555/72–0363 ropeway* 🌐 *www.mtfujiropeway.jp* 🎫 *Round-trip ¥1,000, one-way ¥500.*

Hotels

Fuji View Hotel (富士ビューホテル)
$$$ | **HOTEL** | **FAMILY** | Accommodations are comfortable (if a little threadbare) at this lakefront hotel, where a terrace lounge affords fine views of the lake and of Mt. Fuji beyond and amenities include hot-spring baths, tennis courts, pitch-and-putt golf, and rental bicycles. **Pros:** lower weekday rates; excellent views from many rooms; convenient shuttle bus to town and the station. **Cons:** rooms are rather small; crowded with tour groups during peak seasons; meals are average. $ *Rooms from: ¥32,800* ✉ *511 Katsuyama, Fujikawaguchiko* ☎ *0555/83–2211* 🌐 *www.fujiview.jp* *70 rooms* 🍽 *Free Breakfast.*

Hotel Mount Fuji (ホテルマウント富士)
$$$ | **HOTEL** | **FAMILY** | This is the biggest resort hotel on Lake Yamanaka, with European-style rooms, hot-spring baths, on-site game and karaoke rooms, and a nature walk on the grounds. **Pros:** comfortable rooms; open-air hot-springs with Fuji views; friendly and helpful staff. **Cons:** one of the more expensive options in the area; convenient location and large banquet halls make it a favorite among tour groups; some guest rooms are dated. $ *Rooms from: ¥40,000* ✉ *1360–83 Yamanaka, Yamanaka-ko-mura* ☎ *055/62–2111* 🌐 *www.mtfuji-hotel.com* *150 rooms* 🍽 *Free Breakfast.*

Mizno Hotel (湖のホテル)
$$ | **HOTEL** | Not only does the Mizno have a stylish lodge aesthetic and stunning views of Lake Kawaguchiko but nearly every part of the hotel—from the restaurant and rooftop bar to the guest rooms and private onsen—is designed to offer stellar Mt. Fuji views as well. **Pros:** mountain and lake views from all rooms; great rooftop bar and terrace; private onsen. **Cons:** onsen bath is functional but simple; much of the appeal depends on having good weather; dinner is expensive. $ *Rooms from: ¥26,000* ✉ *187 Azagawa, Fujikawaguchiko* ☎ *0555/72–1234* 🌐 *mzn.jp* *27 rooms* 🍽 *Free Breakfast.*

Ryokan Fujitomita (旅館ふじとみた)
$ | **B&B/INN** | One of the closest lodging options to the Mt. Fuji hiking trails isn't much to look at from the outside, but the interior is spacious and homey, and the English-speaking staff speak can help you plan an area sightseeing itinerary. **Pros:** spacious rooms; pleasant surrounding grounds; excellent home cooking. **Cons:** books out quickly during climbing season; rooms are clean but simple; somewhat isolated. $ *Rooms from: ¥11,000* ✉ *3235 Shibokusa, Oshinomura, Minami-Tsuru-gun* ☎ *0555/84–3359* 🌐 *innfujitomita.com* 💳 *No credit cards* *9 rooms* 🍽 *Free Breakfast.*

Hakone 箱根

85 km (52 miles) southwest of Tokyo.

The national park and resort area of Hakone is a popular day trip from Tokyo and a good place for a close-up view of Mt. Fuji (assuming the mountain is not swathed in clouds, as often happens in summer).

TIP→ On summer weekends it often seems as though all of Tokyo has come out to Hakone with you. Expect long lines at cable cars and traffic jams everywhere.

DISCOUNTS AND DEALS

Many places in Hakone accept the Hakone Free Pass issued by the privately owned Odakyu Railways. It's valid for two or three days (¥6,100 or ¥6,500); covers roundtrip train fare between Shinjuku and Hakone; and allows you to use any mode of transportation in Hakone, including the Hakone Tozan Cable Car, the Hakone Ropeway, and the Hakone Cruise Boat.

In addition to transportation, Free Pass holders get discounts at 70 facilities, including the Hakone Museum of Art, restaurants, and shops. Although the list of participants is extensive, it often changes, so check the website for the latest list and the current terms and conditions. You can buy the pass at the Odakyu Sightseeing Service Center or online.

CONTACT Odakyu Sightseeing Service Center. ✉ *Shinjuku Station B1F, Odakyu Railway West Underground Exit, Odawara* ☎ *03/5909–0211* 🌐 *www.odakyu.jp/english/support.*

GETTING HERE AND AROUND

The typical Hakone route might seem complex, but it is, in fact, one excursion from Tokyo so well defined that you really can't get lost—no more so, at least, than any of the thousands of Japanese tourists ahead of and behind you. The first leg of the journey is from Odawara or Hakone-Yumoto by a trundling switchback railway (Hakone Tozan Line) followed by a cable car through the mountains to Togendai, on the north shore of Ashi-no-ko (Lake Ashi).

The long way around distance-wise, from Odawara to Togendai by bus, takes 60 to 90 minutes, depending on traffic. The trip over the mountains, on the other hand, takes about two hours. Credit the difference to the Hakone Tozan Line—possibly the slowest train you'll ever ride. Using three switchbacks to inch its way up the side of the mountain, the train takes 54 minutes to travel the 16 km (10 miles) from Odawara to Gora (38 minutes from Hakone-Yumoto). The steeper it gets, the grander the view.

■ TIP→ **Due to concerns about volcanic activity, sections of the ropeway may be closed and buses will run from Sounzan to Togendai. The Hakone Ropeway's English site is not always up to date, so check with the tourist information office before you go.**

Trains do not stop at any station en route for any length of time, but they do run frequently enough to allow you to disembark, visit a sight, and catch another train.

Within the Hakone area, buses run every 15 to 30 minutes from Hakone-machi to Hakone-Yumoto Station on the private Odakyu Line (40 minutes, ¥1,080) and Odawara Station (one hour, ¥1,340). From either, you can take the Odakyu Romance Car back to Shinjuku Station. From Odawara, you can also take a JR Shinkansen (bullet train) to Tokyo Station.

TIMING

You can cover the best of Hakone in a one-day trip out of Tokyo, but if you want to try the curative powers of the thermal waters or do some hiking, then stay overnight. Two of the best areas are around the old hot-springs resort of Miyanoshita and the western side of Komagatake-san (Mt. Komagatake).

TOURS

Hakone Sightseeing Cruise (箱根海賊船; *Hakone Kaizoku-sen*)

BOAT TOURS | FAMILY | This ride is free with your Hakone Free Pass; otherwise, buy a ticket at the office in the terminal. A few ships of conventional design ply Lake Ashi; the rest are astonishingly corny Disney knockoffs. One, for example, is rigged like a 17th-century warship. ✉ *181 Hakone, Ashigarashimo District, Hakone* ☎ *0460/83–6325* 🌐 *www.hakonenavi.jp/hakone-kankosen* 🎫 *¥2,220 round-trip (without Hakone Free Pass).*

The Road to the Shogun

In days gone by, the town of Hakone was on the Tokaido, the main highway between the imperial court in Kyoto and the shogunate in Edo (present-day Tokyo). The road was the only feasible passage through this mountainous country, which made it an ideal place for establishing a checkpoint. The Tokugawa Shogunate built the Hakone Sekisho (checkpoint) here in 1618; its most important function was to monitor the *daimyo* (feudal lords) passing through—to keep track, above all, of weapons coming into Edo, and women coming out.

When Ieyasu Tokugawa came to power, Japan had been through nearly 100 years of bloody struggle among rival coalitions of daimyo. Ieyasu emerged supreme because some of his opponents had switched sides at the last minute, in the Battle of Sekigahara in 1600. The shogun was justifiably paranoid about his "loyal" barons—especially those in the outlying domains—so he required the daimyo to live in Edo for periods of time every two years. When they did return to their own lands, they had to leave their wives behind in Edo, hostages to their good behavior. A noble lady coming through the Hakone Sekisho without an official pass, in short, was a case of treason.

The checkpoint served the Tokugawa dynasty well for 250 years. It was demolished only when the shogunate fell, in the Meiji Restoration of 1868. An exact replica, with an exhibition hall of period costumes and weapons, was built in 1965.

VISITOR INFORMATION

CONTACTS Hakone Tourist Information Center. ✉ *Opposite Hakone-Yumoto Station, 706–35 Yumoto, Hakone* ☎ *0460/85–5700* 🌐 *hakone-japan.com.*

Lake Ashi (芦ノ湖; *Ashino-ko*)
VIEWPOINT | FAMILY | From Owakudani, the descent by gondola to Togendai (via Ubako) on the shore of Lake Ashi takes 25 minutes. There's no reason to linger at Togendai; it's only a terminus for buses to Hakone-Yumoto and Odawara and to the resort villages in the northern part of Hakone. Head straight for the pier, a few minutes' walk down the hill, where boats set out on the lake for Hakonemachi. With still water and good weather, you'll get a breathtaking reflection of the mountains in the waters of the lake. ✉ *Motohakone, Hakone.*

Gora (強羅)
TOWN | This small town is at the end of the train line from Odawara and at the lower end of the Hakone Tozan Cable Car. It's a good jumping-off point for hiking and exploring. Ignore the little restaurants and souvenir stands here: get off the train as quickly as you can and make a dash for the cable car at the other end of the station. If you let the other passengers (and, perhaps, those from a tour bus or two as well) get there before you, you may stand 45 minutes in line. ✉ *Gora, Hakone.*

★ **Hakone Kowakien Yunessun** (箱根小涌園 ユネッサン)
HOT SPRING | FAMILY | This hillside complex overlooking Hakone has more than the average onsen. In addition to all the water-based attractions, amenities include a shopping mall modeled on a European outdoor market, a swimsuit rental shop, a massage salon, and a

Passengers floating over the Owakudani valley on the Hakone Ropeway can see Fuji looming—on a clear day, of course.

game center. The park is divided into two main zones, called Yunessun and Mori no Yu (Forest Bath). When signing in at reception, get a waterproof digital wristband that allows you to pay for lockers and drink machines within the complex.

In the Yunessun side, where you must wear a swimsuit, you can visit somewhat tacky re-creations of Turkish and ancient Roman baths or take a dip in coffee or red wine. It's all a bit corny, but fun. Younger visitors enjoy the waterslides on Rodeo Mountain. In the more secluded Mori no Yu side, you can go au naturel in a variety of indoor and outdoor, single-sex baths. ✉ *1297 Ninotaira, Hakone* ☎ *0460/82–4126* 🌐 *www.yunessun.com* 🎫 *Yunessun zone ¥2,500, Mori no Yu zone ¥1,500; both for ¥3,500.*

Hakone Museum of Art
(箱根美術館; *Hakone Bijutsukan*)
ART MUSEUM | A sister institution to the MOA Museum of Art in Atami, Hakone Museum of Art is at the second stop (Koen-kami) of the Hakone Tozan Cable Car. The museum, which consists of two buildings set in a beautiful Japanese garden, houses a modest collection of porcelain and ceramics from China, Korea, and Japan. ✉ *1300 Gora, Hakone* ☎ *0460/82–2623* 🌐 *www.moaart.or.jp/hakone* 🎫 *¥1,430* ⏲ *Closed Thurs.*

★ **Hakone Open-Air Museum**
(彫刻の森美術館; *Hakone Chokoku-no-mori Bijutsukan*)
ART MUSEUM | Only a few minutes' walk from the Miyanoshita Station (directions are posted in English), this museum houses an astonishing collection of 19th- and 20th-century Western and Japanese sculpture, most of it on display in a spacious, handsome garden. There are works here by Rodin, Moore, Taro Okamoto, and Kotaro Takamura. One section of the garden is devoted to Emilio Greco. Inside are works by Picasso, Léger, and Manzo, among others. ✉ *1121 Ninotaira, Hakone* ☎ *0460/82–1161* 🌐 *www.hakone-oam.or.jp* 🎫 *¥2,000.*

Hakone Ropeway (箱根ロープウェイ)
TRANSPORTATION | **FAMILY** | At the cable-car terminus of Sounzan, a gondola called

Scrambled or Boiled in Sulfur?

No, your eyes aren't playing tricks on you: those vendors are, indeed, boiling eggs in the sulfur pits in Owakudani. Locals make a passable living selling the eggs, which turn black, to tourists at exorbitant prices. A popular myth suggests that eating one of these eggs can extend your life by seven years.

the Hakone Ropeway swings up over a ridge and crosses the Owakudani Valley (aka the Great Boiling Valley) on its way to Togendai. The landscape here is desolate, with sulfurous billows of steam escaping through holes from some inferno deep in the earth—yet another reminder that Japan is a chain of volcanic islands.

Atop the ridge is one of the two stations where you can leave the gondola. From here, a ¾-km (½-mile) walking course wanders among the valley's sulfur pits. Just below the station is a restaurant; the food here isn't great, but, on a clear day, the view of Mt. Fuji is. Remember that if you get off the gondola at any stage, you will have to wait for someone to make space on a later gondola before you can continue down to Togendai and Ashi-no-ko. The good news is that gondolas come by every minute.

⚠ **Due to concerns about volcanic activity, sections of the ropeway may be closed and buses will run from Sounzan to Togendai. The Hakone Ropeway's English site is not always up-to-date, so check with the tourist information office before you go.** ✉ *1–15–1 Shiroyama, Odawara* ☎ *0460/32–2205* ⊕ *www.hakonenavi.jp/international/en/transportation/hakone-ropeway* 🎫 *¥2,500 round-trip from Sounzan Station to Owakudani Station, ¥1,500 one-way Sounzan Station to Togendai Station (without Hakone Free Pass).*

Hakone Checkpoint Museum (箱根関所; *Hakone Sekisho*)
HISTORIC SIGHT | FAMILY | This barrier, a checkpoint on the road with a guardhouse and lookout tower, was originally built in 1618 to inspect incoming and outgoing traffic but was demolished during the Meiji Restoration of 1868. This exact replica was constructed in 1965 and is only a few minutes' walk from the pier, along the lakeshore in the direction of Moto-Hakone. The hilltop guardhouse offers excellent views of Lake Ashi and the surrounding area. ✉ *1 Hakone-machi, Hakone* ☎ *0460/83–6635* ⊕ *www.hakonesekisyo.jp/english* 🎫 *¥500.*

Miyanoshita (宮ノ下)
TOWN | The third stop on the train route from Hakone-Yumoto, this is a small but very pleasant and popular resort village. In addition to hot springs, it has antiques shops along its main road and several trailheads for hiking routes up the ¾-km-(½-mile-) tall Mt. Sengen. If you get to the top, you'll be rewarded with a great view of the gorge. ✉ *Hakone.*

Mt. Soun (早雲山; *Soun-zan*)
MOUNTAIN | Mt. Soun is a good starting point for an afternoon of hiking. From here, trails around Mt. Hakone and Mt. Kamiyama lead towards the lake. Before heading out, pick up a trail map at the tourist information office. ✉ *Hakone.*

Hotels

Fuji-Hakone Guest House (富士箱根ゲストハウス)
$$ | GUESTHOUSE | This small, family-run Japanese inn has simple tatami rooms with the bare essentials. **Pros:** friendly staff; inexpensive rates; private onsen baths for guests. **Cons:** difficult to access from nearest transportation, especially at night; comfortable but basic accommodations; lacks the charm of a traditional ryokan. $ *Rooms from: ¥16,500* ✉ *912*

Sengokuhara, Hakone ☎ 0460/84–6577 🌐 fujihakone.com 🛏 14 rooms 🍴 Free Breakfast.

Fujiya Hotel (富士屋ホテル)

$$$$ | HOTEL | Built in 1878 and most-recently renovated in 2020, this hotel combines the best of traditional Western design with the exceptional hospitality of a fine Japanese inn—one that has, over the years, welcomed VIPs like Charlie Chaplin and John Lennon and Yoko Ono. There are both Western and Japanese restaurants, and, in the gardens behind the hotel is an old imperial villa that serves as a dining room. **Pros:** wonderful, friendly service; Hakone's most historical hotel; hot-spring water pumped right in guest rooms. **Cons:** often full of noisy tour groups; hotel onsen (spa) can't compete with others in the area; price reflects the hotel's history rather than its comfort and amenities. *$ Rooms from: ¥60,000 ✉ 359 Miyanoshita, Hakone ☎ 0460/82–2211 🌐 www.fujiyahotel.jp 🛏 149 rooms 🍴 No Meals.*

The Prince Hakone Lake Ashinoko (箱根プリンスホテル芦ノ湖)

$$ | HOTEL | FAMILY | This resort hotel has the lake in front and the mountains of Komagatake in back. **Pros:** outdoor activities such as kayaking; views of Mt. Fuji over the lake; spacious guest rooms. **Cons:** a bit remote; popular with groups and business conferences; guest rooms are a bit dated. *$ Rooms from: ¥33,600 ✉ 144 Motohakone, Hakone ☎ 0460/83–1111 🌐 www.princehotels.com/the-prince-hakone 🛏 258 rooms 🍴 Free Breakfast.*

Tensui Saryo (天翠茶寮)

$$ | B&B/INN | Upon entering this cross between a luxury Western-style hotel and traditional inn, you'll remove your shoes and socks, sit at a counter bar with your tired feet resting in a hot-mineral-spring bath under the bar, and enjoy a tea or beer while checking in. **Pros:** four rooms have a private onsen on a terrace; excellent service; easy access from Gora Station. **Cons:** rates with dinner plans are substantially more expensive; some rooms have limited views; lacks the secluded ryokan atmosphere. *$ Rooms from: ¥29,000 ✉ 1320–276 Gora, Hakone ☎ 0570/062–302 🌐 www.tensui-saryo.com 🛏 17 rooms 🍴 No Meals.*

Izu Peninsula 伊豆半島

Shimoda is 190 km (118 miles) southwest of Tokyo.

Izu is defined by its rugged coastline, beaches, and onsen (hot springs), but it also holds a place in history as the region where Japan reopened to the West in the 1850s.

GETTING HERE AND AROUND

Having your own car makes sense for touring the Izu Peninsula, but only if you're prepared to cope with less-than-ideal road conditions, lots of traffic (especially on holiday weekends), and the paucity of road markers in English. It takes some effort—but exploring the peninsula *is* a lot easier by car than by public transportation.

From Tokyo take the Tomei Expressway as far as the Atsugi Interchange (about 50 km [31 miles]); then pick up the Seisho Bypass and Route 135 to Atami (approximately 50 km [31 miles]). From Atami drive another 70 km (47 miles) on Route 135 down to Shimoda.

■ TIP→ **One way to save yourself some trouble is to book a car through the Nippon or Toyota rental agency in Tokyo and arrange to pick it up at the Shimoda branch.**

You can then simply take a train to Shimoda and use it as a base. From Shimoda, you can drive back up the coast to Kawazu (35 minutes) and then to Shuzenji (45 minutes). It is possible to drop off the car in Tokyo, but only at specific branches, so visit your rental-car company's website or call them in advance.

Trains are by far the easiest and fastest ways to reach the Izu Peninsula and the rest of the Fuji-Hakone-Izu National Park area. The gateway station of Atami is well served by comfortable express trains from Tokyo, on both JR and private railway lines. These in turn connect to local trains and buses that can get you anywhere in the region you want to go. Download a route planning app or call the JR East Info Line (10–6 daily, except December 31–January 3) for assistance in English.

The Kodama Shinkansen runs from JR Tokyo Station to Atami (¥4,270, 45 minutes) and Mishima (¥4,600, 52 minutes); JR (Japan Railways) passes are valid. The JR local from Atami to Ito takes 25 minutes and costs ¥330. Ito, Atami and Shimoda are also served by the JR Odoriko Express (not a Shinkansen train) also departing from Tokyo Station. The Tokyo–Ito run takes 1¾ hours and costs ¥3,890, while Tokyo–Shimoda takes 2¾ hours and costs ¥6,180 (JR passes can be used to cover the fare up to Ito).

To get to Shuzenji by train, take the private Izu–Hakone Railway from Mishima (¥550, 35 minutes).

RENTAL-CAR CONTACTS Nippon Rent-a-Car. ☎ *03/6859–6234 Head office, 050/1712–2586 Shimoda Branch* 🌐 *www.nipponrentacar.co.jp.* **Toyota Rent-a-Car.** ☎ *0800/7000–815 toll-free in Japan; English operator available, 0558/27–0100 Shimoda Branch* 🌐 *rent.toyota.co.jp.*

TRAIN CONTACTS Izukyu Corporation. ☎ *0557/53–1115 main office, 0558/22–3202 Izukyu Shimoda Station* 🌐 *www.izukyu.co.jp.* **JR East Info Line.** ☎ *050/2016–1603 English info line* 🌐 *www.jreast.co.jp.* **Odakyu Sightseeing Service Center.** ✉ *Shinjuku Station B1F, Odakyu Railway West Underground Exit* ☎ *03/5909–0211* 🌐 *www.odakyu.jp/english/support.*

TOURS

If you have limited time and want to see the highlights of Fuji-Hakone-Izu National Park on a day-trip from Tokyo, there are several bus options from JTB Sunrise Tours. You'll also find plenty of options for boat tours along the Izu coastline.

Dogashima Marine (堂ヶ島マリン)

BOAT TOURS | Once you are on the Izu Peninsula itself, sightseeing excursions by boat are available from several picturesque small ports. From Dogashima, you can take the Dogashima Marine short (20 minutes) or long (45 minutes) tours of Izu's rugged west coast. ☎ *0558/52–0013* 🌐 *dogashimamarine.jp* 🎫 *From ¥1,500.*

Fuji Kyuko (富士急行)

BOAT TOURS | The Fuji Kyuko company operates a daily ferry to Hatsushima from Atami (25 minutes). ☎ *0557/81–0541* 🌐 *www.hatsushima.jp* 🎫 *¥2,800 round-trip.*

Izu Cruise (伊豆クルーズ)

BOAT TOURS | Izukyu Marine offers a 40-minute tour by boat from Shimoda to the coastal rock formations at Iro-zaki. ☎ *0558/22–1151* 🌐 *www.izu-kamori.jp/izu-cruise* 🎫 *From ¥1,500.*

JTB Sunrise Tours

BUS TOURS | For an up-close look at Fuji that doesn't involve hiking, JTB Sunrise Tours operates a one-day tour to Mt. Fuji and Hakone from Tokyo, departing from (and returning to) Shinjuku. The tour includes a stop at the Fuji-Subaru Line 5th Station, before continuing to Hakone for a cruise on Lake Ashi and a trip on the gondola over Owakudani. ✉ *Tokyo* ☎ *03/5796–5454* 🌐 *www.sunrise-tours.jp/en* 🎫 *From ¥22,000.*

Atami 熱海

100 km (60 miles) southwest of Tokyo Station.

Many travelers make it no farther into the peninsula than this lively gateway town on Sagami Bay. In addition to a fair number of hotels and traditional inns, Atami has frequent and short (30 minutes) but stunning firework shows over the bay. When you arrive, pick up a map from the Atami Information Center at the train station.

GETTING HERE AND AROUND

From Tokyo Station, the fastest way to Atami is to catch the Kodama shinkansen (45 minutes, ¥4,270). Another Tokyo–Atami rail option is the Odoriko Limited Express (1 hour, 20 minutes; ¥3,560) or the first class-only Saphir Odoriko Limited Express (1 hour, 15 minutes; ¥6,640). If you're on a tight budget, the regular JR Tokaido Line also does Tokyo Station to Atami (1 hour, 55 minutes; ¥1,980).

VISITOR INFORMATION

CONTACTS Atami Information Center. ✉ *Atami Station, 11–1 Tawarahoncho, Atami* ☎ *0557/81–5297* 🌐 *www.ataminews.gr.jp.*

Sights

Atami Plum Garden
(熱海梅園; *Atami Bai-en*)
GARDEN | The best time to visit this garden is in late January or early February, when its 850 trees bloom. Be sure to stop by the small Kinomiya Shrine that's in the shadow of an enormous old camphor tree. The shrine is more than 1,000 years old and is popular with people who are asking the gods for healing and longevity. The tree is more than 2,000 years old and has been designated a National Monument. It's believed that if you walk around the tree once, another year will be added to your life. Atami Plum Garden is always open to the public and is 15 minutes by bus from Atami or an eight-minute walk west from Kinomiya Station, the next stop south of Atami served by local trains. Kinomiya Shrine is just northeast of Kinomiya Station. ✉ *8–11 Baiencho, Atami* ☎ *0557/86–6218* 🎫 *¥300 Jan.–early Mar.; free the rest of the year.*

Hatsushima Island (初島)
ISLAND | **FAMILY** | If you have the time and the inclination for a beach picnic, take the 25-minute high-speed ferry (¥2,800 round-trip) from the pier. There are ten departures daily between 7:30 and 5:20 from Atami, though the times can vary if one of the two boats is under maintenance. You can easily walk around the island, which is only 4 km (2½ miles) in circumference, in less than two hours. There is also an obstacle course adventure park, great for travelers with kids. ✉ *6–11 Wadahama Minamicho, Atami* ☎ *0557/81–0541 ferry* 🌐 *www.hatsushima.jp.*

MOA Museum of Art
(*MOA美術館; MOA Bijutsukan*)
ART MUSEUM | This museum houses the private collection of messianic religious leader Mokichi Okada (1882–1955), who founded a movement called the Sekai Kyusei Kyo (Religion for the Salvation of the World). He also acquired more than 3,000 works of art; some are from the Asuka period (6th and 7nth centuries). Among the collection are several particularly fine *ukiyo-e* (Edo-era woodblock prints) and ceramics. On a hill above the station and set in a garden full of old plum trees and azaleas, the museum also affords a sweeping view over Atami and the bay. ✉ *26–2 Momoyama, Atami* ✣ *The easiest way to reach the museum is to take a 5-min. taxi ride from the station. Buses also run several times an hour from Bus Rank 8 by Atami Station.* ☎ *0557/84–2511* 🌐 *www.moaart.or.jp/en* 🎫 *¥1,760* 🕒 *Closed Thurs.*

Oyu Geyser
(大湯間歇泉; *Oyu Kanketsusen*)
NATURE SIGHT | **FAMILY** | Just a 15-minute walk southwest from Atami Station, this geyser used to gush on schedule once every 24 hours but stopped after the Great Kanto Earthquake of 1923. Not happy with this, the local chamber of commerce rigged a pump to raise the geyser every five minutes. ✉ *4–3 Kami-jukucho, Atami.*

Hotels

Atami Taikanso (熱海大観荘)
$$$$ | **B&B/INN** | Exquisite furnishings, indoor and outdoor hot-springs baths, and spacious, predominately Japanese-style rooms with floor-to-ceiling windows are among this hotel's draws. **Pros:** seaside rooms have beautiful views; luxurious traditional experience; impeccable service. **Cons:** eating dinner may take most of your evening; easy to get lost in the complex layout of the hotel; one of Atami's more expensive options. *Rooms from: ¥71,000* ✉ *7–1 Hayashigaoka-cho, Atami* ☎ *0557/81–8137* 🌐 *www.atami-taikanso.com/en* *44 rooms* *All-Inclusive.*

Ito 伊東

20 km (12 miles) south of Atami.

Although the area's 700 thermal springs and the beautiful, rocky, indented coastline nearby are Ito's main draws, it also has plenty of other interesting sights, as well as a good number of inns and hotels.

Ito's history of association with the West is tied to William Adams (1564–1620), the Englishman whose adventures served as the basis for James Clavell's novel *Shogun.*

In 1600, Adams beached his disabled Dutch vessel, *De Liefde,* on the shores of the southwestern island of Kyushu, becoming the first Englishman to set foot on Japan. Believing that he and his men were Portuguese pirates, the authorities put them in prison. But Adams was eventually befriended by the shogun Ieyasu Tokugawa, who brought him to Edo (present-day Tokyo), granted him an estate, and made him an adviser on foreign affairs.

The English castaway taught mathematics, geography, gunnery, and navigation to shogunate officials, and, in 1604, was ordered to build an 80-ton Western-style ship. Pleased with this venture, Ieyasu ordered the construction of a larger oceangoing vessel. These two ships were built at Ito, where Adams lived from 1605 to 1610.

This history was largely forgotten until British Commonwealth occupation forces began coming to Ito for rest and recuperation after World War II. Adams's memory was revived, and, since then, the Anjin Festival (the Japanese gave Adams the name *anjin,* which means "pilot") has been held in his honor every August. A monument to the Englishman stands at the mouth of the river.

GETTING HERE AND AROUND

From JR Tokyo Station, take the Odoriko Limited Express (1 hour, 45 minutes; ¥3,890) or the first class-only Saphir Odoriko Limited Express (1 hour, 35 minutes; ¥6,970) to Ito Station. It's also possible to take the Kodama shinkansen (bullet train) from Tokyo Station to Atami (45 minutes, ¥4,270) and then transfer to the JR Ito Line to Ito (23 minutes, ¥330).

VISITOR INFORMATION

CONTACTS Ito Onsen Information Center. (伊東観光協会; *Ito Kanko Kyoukai*) ✉ *JR Ito Station, 3–12–1 Yukawa, Ito* ☎ *0557/37–6105* 🌐 *itospa.com.*

Sights

Atagawa (熱川)

TOWN | South of Ito the coastal scenery is lovely—each sweep around a headland reveals another picturesque sight of a rocky, indented shoreline. There are several spa towns en route to Shimoda. Higashi-Izu (East Izu) has numerous hot-springs resorts, of which Atagawa is the most popular. South of Atagawa is relatively peaceful Kawazu, which is known for its spring cherry blossoms and forested mountainside where waterfalls plunge through lush greenery. ✉ *Ito* 🌐 *atagawa.net.*

Ikeda 20th-Century Art Museum (池田20世紀美術館; *Ikeda 20-Seiki Bijutsukan*)

ART MUSEUM | The museum, between Mt. Omuro and Lake Ippeki, houses works by Picasso, Dalí, Chagall, and Matisse, plus a number of woodblock prints. ✉ *614 Totari, Ito* ✥ *Buses run from JR Ito Station (30 min.) and Izukyu Izu-Kogen Station (20 min.). Get off at the Ikeda Bijutsukan bus stop.* ☎ *0557/45–2211* 🌐 *ikeda20.or.jp/en* 🎫 *¥1,000* ⏲ *Closed Wed.*

Izu Shaboten Zoo (伊豆シャボテン動物公園; *Izu Shaboten Dobutsukoen*)

ZOO | **FAMILY** | A semi–free-range petting zoo and cactus park might not seem like the best combination, but Izu Shaboten Zoo makes it work. In addition to viewing some of the 1,500 varieties of cactus, you can feed, pet, or otherwise get up close and personal with more than 140 different animals, including the capybara onsen (animals like hot springs too). Next to the zoo is 580-meter (1,903-foot) Mt. Omuro, a distinctive cinder cone volcano worth the hike (or the ropeway fee) for the panoramas from the trail around its crater. ✉ *1317–13 Futo, Ito* ✥ *At the base of Omuro-san (Mt. Omuro), the park is 35 min. by bus from JR Ito Station or 20 min. by bus from Izukyu Izu-Kogen Station.* ☎ *0557/51–1111* 🌐 *izushaboten.com* 🎫 *¥2,800 weekends and holidays, ¥2,700 weekdays.*

Komuroyama Park (小室山公園; *Komuroyama Koen*)

GARDEN | **FAMILY** | Komuroyama is known for its views of Mt. Fuji to the northwest and the 100,000 azaleas that bloom on and around Mt. Komuro in April. You can take a ski-lift style cable to the top of the mountain, which has a lovely view of the sea below. ✉ *1260–1 Kawana, Ito* ✥ *20 min. south of JR Ito Station by bus.* ☎ *0557/45–1444* 🌐 *www.tokaibus.jp/business/lift.html* 🎫 *Free; round-trip lift to mountaintop ¥800.*

Tokaikan (東海館)

HISTORY MUSEUM | Built in the 1920s as a traditional inn (ryokan), this creaking old building south of JR Ito Station is now a local history museum and culture center. It's worth the small fee just to see the tatami-mat ryokan rooms and their traditional decor, but you can also pay extra for a soak in Tokaikan's modest hot-spring baths. ✉ *12–10 Higashimatsubaracho, Ito* ☎ *0557/36-2004* 🌐 *itospa.com/spot/detail_52002.html* 🎫 *Admission ¥200, baths ¥500* ⏲ *Closed 3rd Tues. of the month.*

Coffee and Quick Bites

Chit Chat Cafe

$ | **CAFÉ** | **FAMILY** | This little café in the backstreets near Ito's main shopping arcade specializes in drinks, including green-tea latte, made with tea grown in Izu. You'll also find coffee, soda floats, and snacks like waffles and green-tea cheesecake. **Known for:** drinks and snacks using local teas; waffles; baked cheesecake. 💲 *Average main: ¥600* ✉ *8–13 Chuocho, Ito* ☎ *0557/28–0394* 🌐 *chit-chat-izu.com.*

Hotels

Hanafubuki (花吹雪)

$$$$ | **B&B/INN** | Set in the Jogasaki forest, this traditional Japanese inn has modern, comfortable rooms, but still retains classic elements like tatami mats, sliding

Hot-Spring Resorts

Earthquakes may be an unsettling aspect of life in Japan, but they also provide one of the country's greatest delights: thermal baths. Wherever there are volcanic mountains—and there are a lot—you're sure to find *onsen*, springs of hot water that's rich in all sorts of restorative minerals. Any place where lots of spas have tapped these waters is an *onsen chiiki* (hot-springs resort area), and the Izu Peninsula is with particularly rich with them in towns such as Shuzenji, Ito, Shimoda, Atami, and Dogashima.

Spas take several forms, but for many people nothing is better than a small secluded, Japanese mountain inn with a *rotemburo* (an open-air mineral-spring pool). Open only to inn guests, these pools are usually in a screened-off nook with a panoramic view. Book rooms in such accommodations months in advance for stays on weekends or in high-season, generally late December to early January, late April to early May, the second and third weeks of August, and the second and third weeks of October.

More typical is the large resort hotel, with one or more spacious indoor (and sometimes outdoor) mineral baths of its own. Where whole towns and villages have developed to exploit a local supply of hot water, there will be several of sizeable properties, an assortment of smaller inns, and probably a few modest public bathhouses, with no accommodations, where you just pay an entrance fee for a soak of whatever length you wish.

screen doors, and *chabudai* (low dining tables) with *zabuton* (cushion seating). **Pros:** an authentic Japanese experience; the seven private hot-spring baths are free for guests; excellent dinners. **Cons:** meals are available to nonguests, so the dining room can be crowded; not as quiet as more secluded onsen; regular room rates are high for the area. $ *Rooms from: ¥61,600* ✉ *1041 Yawatano Isomichi, Ito* ✥ *200 meters east of Izukyu Izu-Kogen Station* ☎ *0557/54–1550* 🌐 *www.hanafubuki.co.jp/e* *17 rooms* *All-Inclusive*.

Yokikan (陽気館)
$$$ | **B&B/INN** | Overlooking the town of Ito and the sea, Yokikan has been catering to visitors for more than a century. **Pros:** views of Ito and the sea from the open-air bath; friendly, welcoming service; understated Japanese aesthetic perfect for a relaxing getaway. **Cons:** simple, somewhat dated furnishings; not much to do in the immediate vicinity; no private bath in standard rooms. $ *Rooms from: ¥30,800* ✉ *2–24 Suehirocho, Ito* ☎ *0557/37–3101* 🌐 *www.yokikan.co.jp* *19 rooms* *All-Inclusive* ☞ *It's possible to book without meals, making a stay far cheaper.*

Shimoda 下田

35 km (22 miles) south of Ito city.

Of all the resort towns south of Ito along the Izu Peninsula's eastern coast, none can match the distinction of Shimoda. The town's encounter with the West began when Commodore Matthew Perry anchored his fleet of black ships off the coast here in 1853. To commemorate the event, the three-day Black Ship Festival (Kurofune Matsuri) is held here every year in mid-May. Shimoda was also the site, in 1856, of the first American consulate.

The town's tourist office, on the main intersection just southeast of the station, has a good selection of English-language brochures and can give advice on getting around town.

GETTING HERE AND AROUND

From JR Tokyo Station, take the Odoriko Limited Express (2 hours, 45 minutes; ¥6,180) or the first class-only Saphir Odoriko Limited Express (3 hours; ¥10,060) to Izukyu Shimoda Station. Alternatively, take the Kodama shinkansen (bullet train) from Tokyo Station to Atami (45 minutes, ¥4,270) and then transfer to the JR Ito Line–Izukyu Line (joint service) to Izukyu Shimoda Station (1 hour, 40 minutes, ¥2,020).

VISITOR INFORMATION

CONTACTS Shimoda Tourist Association. (伊豆下田観光ガイド) ✉ *1–4–27 Shimoda, Shimoda* ☎ *0558/22–1531* 🌐 *www.shimoda-city.com.*

Sights

Hofuku-ji Temple (宝福寺)

TEMPLE | The first American consul to Japan was New York businessman Townsend Harris. Soon after his arrival in Shimoda, he asked the Japanese authorities to provide him with a female servant; they sent him a young girl named Okichi Saito, who was engaged to be married. The arrangement brought her a new name—Tojin (the Foreigner's) Okichi—much disgrace, and a tragic end: she drowned herself in 1892. Her tale is recounted in Rei Kimura's biographical novel *Butterfly in the Wind* and inspired Puccini's *Madame Butterfly,* although some skeptics say the story is more gossip than fact. Hofuku-ji was Okichi's family temple. The museum annex displays a life-size image of her, and, just behind the temple, is her grave, where incense is still kept burning in her memory. ✉ *1–18–26 Shimoda, Shimoda* ☎ *0558/22–0960* 🎫 *¥400 for the museum.*

Ryosen-ji Temple (了仙寺)

TEMPLE | **FAMILY** | This temple, which is especially pretty when its jasmines are in bloom in May, is where the negotiations took place that eventually led to the United States–Japan Treaty of Amity and Commerce of 1858. A museum on the grounds contains more than 300 original artifacts relating to Commodore Perry and the "black ships" that opened Japan to the West. Also don't miss Perry Road, a quaint but short canal-side street leading from the temple's gate toward the port. Some of its old buildings house cafés and restaurants. ✉ *3–12–12 Shimoda, Shimoda* ☎ *0558/22–0657* 🌐 *ryosenji.net/english* 🎫 *Museum ¥500.*

Shirahama Kaigan (白浜海岸)

BEACH | **FAMILY** | This attractive stretch of coast running east and then north out of Shimoda is ideal for some beach time. On an inlet a short distance from town, the white sands of Sotoura Beach provide a calm point for swimming, paddling with kids, or even sea kayaking. A little ways north is Shirahama Beach, an 800-meter (875-yard) belt of sand that has become one of Izu's most popular beach spots: good for swimming and tanning in summer and surfing year-round. For the latter, you'll find several surf shops renting gear near the beach. There are also convenience stores and café–restaurants in the area. ✉ *Shirahama Kaigan, Shimoda* ✥ *Take any bus from bus stop #9 by Izukyu Shimoda Station, but be aware that they don't run more than hourly. Sotoura Beach is the Sotoura Guchi stop, while Shirahama is the Shirahama Kaigan stop.*

Shimoda Ropeway (下田ロープウェイ)

VIEWPOINT | **FAMILY** | Shimoda's ropeway takes you to the top of 200-meter (656-foot) Mt. Nesugata, a stone's throw from Izukyu Shimoda Station. From the peak's observation decks you're treated to vistas of Shimoda and its picturesque bay, with clear days allowing views across the water to the Izu Islands. A café at the top serves light meals; there's also a small temple, called Aizendo, where you can try throwing small clay stones through a distant hoop in the hope of achieving a sense of *wa* (peace and harmony). ✉ *1–3–2 Higashihongo, Shimoda* ☎ *0558/22–1211* 🌐 *www.ropeway.co.jp/wp* 🎫 *Round-trip ¥1,500, one-way ¥900.*

Yumigahama Beach (弓ヶ浜)
BEACH | FAMILY | If you love the sun, make sure you stop at Yumigahama. It's one of the nicest sandy stretches on the whole Izu Peninsula. Although the water is usually warm enough to swim from June, the crowds come out during Japan's beach season in July and August, which is when the beach has food and drink options as well as lifeguards. The bus from Izukyu Shimoda Station stops here before continuing to Iro-zaki, the last stop on the route. **Amenities:** food and drink; lifeguards; toilets; parking (fee). **Best for:** swimming; solitude. ✉ *Shimoda* ✢ *11 km (7 miles) southwest of Shimoda, just south of highway 136.*

Hotels

Pension Sakuraya (ペンション桜家)
$ | B&B/INN | The best lodgings at this family-run inn just a few minutes' walk from Shimoda's main beach are the Japanese-style corner rooms, which have nice views of the hills surrounding Shimoda. **Pros:** very homey atmosphere; close to the beach; friendly and helpful staff. **Cons:** rooms are a bit cramped; clean but simple; buses from station are infrequent. $ *Rooms from: ¥11,000* ✉ *2584–20 Shirahama, Shimoda* ☎ *0558/23–4470* 🌐 *izu-sakuraya.jp/english* *9 rooms* *No Meals.*

Shimoda Prince Hotel
(下田プリンスホテル)
$$ | HOTEL | At this V-shaped resort hotel that faces the Pacific, the decor is more functional than it is aesthetically pleasing, but the white sand of Shirahama Beach is just steps away, and there are oceans views from all rooms and the public onsen baths, which open early enough for you to catch the sunrise while soaking. **Pros:** excellent sea views; some staffers speak English; spacious rooms. **Cons:** restaurants are pricey; some areas feel worn and dated; very little nearby. $ *Rooms from: ¥29,000* ✉ *1547–1 Shirahama, Shimoda* ✢ *10-minute taxi or hourly local bus (15 min.) from Izukyu Shimoda Station* ☎ *0558/22–2111* 🌐 *www.princehotels.com/shimoda* *76 rooms* *No Meals.*

Shimoda Tokyu Hotel (下田東急ホテル)
$$$ | HOTEL | Perched just above the bay, the Shimoda Tokyu has impressive views of the Pacific from one side (where rooms cost more) and mountains from the other. **Pros:** nice ocean views; easy access to Shimoda Station and sights; spacious guest rooms (except for mountain-side standard rooms). **Cons:** restaurants are expensive; rooms are a bit dated; service can be hit or miss. $ *Rooms from: ¥38,500* ✉ *5–12–1 Shimoda, Shimoda* ☎ *0558/22–2411* 🌐 *www.tokyuhotels.co.jp/shimoda-h* *115 rooms* *No Meals.*

Dogashima 堂ヶ島

30 km (19 miles) northwest of Shimoda, 45 km (28 miles) southwest of Shuzenji.

The sea has eroded the coastal rock formations into fantastic shapes near the little port town of Dogashima. Here you'll find a *tombolo*, or a narrow band of sand, that connects the mainland to a small peninsula with a scenic park.

GETTING HERE AND AROUND

There's no direct train access, but buses run from other areas of the Izu Peninsula, making Dogashima best suited as an add-on rather than a standalone destination. Tokai Bus runs an express bus from Izukyu Shimoda Station to Dogashima (55 minutes, ¥1,680) as well as a bus from Shuzenji to Dogashima (85 minutes, ¥2,480).

TOURS

Dogashima Marine Sightseeing Boat (堂ヶ島マリン遊覧船; *Dogashima Marin Yugansen*)

BOAT TOURS | FAMILY | Small sightseeing boats from Dogashima Pier make runs to see the rocks. Depending on the course, trips last 20 to 45 minutes. *☎ 0558/52–0013 🌐 dogashimamarine.jp ¥1,500 to ¥2,200.*

Hotels

Dogashima New Ginsui (堂ヶ島ニュー銀水)

$$$ | HOTEL | As this hotel is perched above the water and a secluded beach, all of its Japanese-style guest rooms overlook the sea. **Pros:** the area's best luxury resort; stunning views; open-air hot-spring baths. **Cons:** a bit far from sightseeing spots; some rooms (Western-style especially) are dated; busy with families during peak summer season. *$ Rooms from: ¥39,000 ✉ 2977–1 Nishina, Nishiizu-cho, Kamo-gun ☎ 0558/52–2211 🌐 www.dougashima-newginsui.jp 121 rooms All-Inclusive.*

Shuzenji 修善寺

25 km (15 miles) south of Mishima by Izu-Hakone Railway.

Shuzenji—a hot-springs resort in the center of the Izu Peninsula, along the valley of the Katsura-gawa (Katsura River)—has a certain historical notoriety as the place where the second Kamakura shogun, Minamoto no Yoriie, was assassinated in the early 13th century on the orders of his own grandfather.

Don't judge the town by the area around the station. Most of the hotels and hot springs are 2 km (1.2 miles) to the west, in a peaceful riverside area where you'll also find a pretty bamboo grove and the historic Shuzen-ji Temple.

GETTING HERE AND AROUND

The train is by far the easiest way to get to Shuzenji. The fastest option from Tokyo Station is to take the Kodama Shinkansen to Mishima (42 minutes, ¥4,600), then change to the Izu-Hakone Railway to Shuzenji (35 minutes, ¥550). A direct Tokyo-Shuzenji option is the Odoriko Express (2 hours, 5 minutes, ¥6,870).

Hotels

Goyokan (五葉館)

$$$ | B&B/INN | This family-run ryokan on Shuzenji's main street has rooms that look out on the Katsura-gawa, plus gorgeous stone- and wood-lined indoor hot springs. **Pros:** modern take on a ryokan; excellent service with English-speaking staff; private onsen baths free for guests. **Cons:** lacks cozy feel of a traditional ryokan; decor can be a bit over the top; no bath in rooms. *$ Rooms from: ¥44,000 ✉ 765–2 Shuzenji ☎ 0558/72–2066 🌐 www.goyokan.co.jp 8 rooms All-Inclusive.*

Ochiairou (おちあいろう)

$$$$ | B&B/INN | This traditional ryokan was built in the 1870s, and though it has been renovated and modernized, the main wooden structure remains true to its original design, with spacious, comfortable rooms overlooking gardens. **Pros:** free pickup from Yugashima bus terminal; lovely garden; stunning surroundings. **Cons:** very expensive; remote; some parts of the hotel show their age. *$ Rooms from: ¥80,000 ✉ 1887–1 Yugashima, Izu ☎ 055/885–0014 🌐 www.ochiairo.co.jp 14 rooms All-Inclusive.*

Ryokan Sanyoso (旅館三養荘)

$$$$ | B&B/INN | At the former villa of the Iwasaki family, founders of the Mitsubishi conglomerate, this hotel has rooms furnished with museum-quality antiques. **Pros:** authentic ryokan and furnishings; Japanese bath available; as luxurious and beautiful a place as you'll find on the Izu

Ryokan Etiquette

You're expected to arrive at ryokan in the late afternoon. Upon arrival, you'll probably be asked to change into slippers that are provided, and then a member of staff will escort you to your room. Remember to remove your slippers before entering your room; never step on the tatami (straw mats) with shoes or slippers. Each room will be simply decorated—typically one small, low table, cushions on the tatami, a scroll on the wall, and *shoji* (sliding paper-paneled walls).

In ryokan with hot-spring baths (onsen), you can take to the waters anytime after arrival, though the onsen doors are usually locked from 11 pm to 6 am. In ryokan with small public bathing areas, you might have to reserve a time. As other guests will be using the same bath water, it's customary to wash and rinse off *thoroughly* before getting into an onsen. It's bad manners to get soap in the bath water, to splash the bath water, to take drinks into the bath, or to make much noise. After your soak, change into the *yukata* (cotton robe) provided in your room. Don't worry about walking around in it—other guests will be doing the same.

Dinner is served around 6 or 7 pm. At the larger, newer ryokan, it will be in the dining room; at smaller, more personal ryokan, it will most likely served in your room. When you're finished, a staffer will clear away the dishes and lay out your futon. In Japan *futon* means bedding, and, in ryoken, it consists of a thin cotton mattress; a small, hard pillow filled with grain; and a heavy comforter in cool months or a light quilt in summer. Around 7 to 8 am, a staffer will gently wake you, clear away the futon, and bring in your Japanese-style breakfast, which will probably consist of fish, pickled vegetables, and rice. If this isn't appealing, politely ask if you can have coffee and toast—just don't be surprised if the answer is no. Ryokan aren't known for flexibility. Checkout is at 10 am.

Some ryoken don't offer online booking, which means you must book by phone or email. Do so as far in advance as possible, and be aware that some inns don't accept foreign guests because of language and cultural barriers. That said, more ryokan now list themselves on popular hotel booking websites, so finding and booking a room isn't as hard as it used to be.

Peninsula. **Cons:** most expensive ryokan in the area; not easy to get to without a car; less intimate than smaller area ryokan. $ *Rooms from: ¥95,000* ✉ *270 Mamanoue, Izunokuni* ☎ *055/947–1111* 🌐 *www.princehotels.com/sanyo-so* *40 rooms* *All-Inclusive.*

Mt. Takao 高尾山

50 km (31 miles) west of central Tokyo.

There are eight hiking trails within Mori Memorial Forest Park. The three main routes that lead to the top of Mt. Takao begin at Kiyotaka Station, the base station of the mountain's funicular railway. To determine which hike is best for you, check out the large billboard with a map of the mountain and its trails.

GETTING HERE AND AROUND

It is very easy to access the Mt. Takao area by train. From Keio Shinjuku Station, take the semi-express train on the Keio Line and get off at Takaosanguchi Station (53 minutes, ¥430). Or take the JR Chuo Line to Takao Station (44 minutes, ¥570), and change to the Keio Line for one station to Takaosanguchi (three minutes, ¥140).

The Takao Tozan Cable is a funicular railway that is Japan's steepest train line. From Takaosanguchi Station, walk five minutes west to Kiyotaka Station, and the cable car will bring you halfway up the mountain in six minutes (¥490 one-way, ¥950 round-trip). The trains run every 15 minutes from 8 am until around 5 or 6 pm, depending on the season. When the beer garden at the top of the mountain is open, from mid-June through mid-October, the last train down is at 9:15 pm. Many visitors take the cable car halfway, then hike up one of the paved paths to the top, which takes about 30 minutes, walking down one of the paths before sunset.

The Takao Tozan Chair Lift is a somewhat more scenic way to get up the mountain. From Takaosanguchi Station, walk to Sanroku Station, which is only a few yards from the cable car station. It takes around 12 minutes to get to Sanjo Station at the top (¥490 one-way, ¥950 round-trip), which is about 100 yards from the cable car station. The lift runs from 9 am to 4:30 pm May to November, and until 4 pm December to April.

CONTACT Takao Tozan Dentetsu. ☎ *042/666–3572* 🌐 *www.takaotozan.co.jp.*

VISITOR INFORMATION

The Takao Visitor Center is at the top of the mountain. Takao Tozan Dentetsu, the company that operates the funicular and lift, has a great deal of information in English on its website.

CONTACTS Takao Visitor Center. ✉ *2176 Takao-machi, Hachioji, Tokyo* ☎ *042/664–7872* 🌐 *www.ces-net.jp/takaovc.*

Sights

★ **Mt. Takao** (高尾山; *Takao-san*)
MOUNTAIN | When Shinjuku's concrete skyscrapers become too much, in about an hour, you can escape to the foot of 599-meter (1,965-foot) Mt. Takao and the heavily wooded Meiji Memorial Forest Park that surrounds it. While heading to the top of the peak—which is associated with *tengu,* one of the best known *yokai* (monster-spirits) of Japanese folklore—it's hard to believe that you're still within Tokyo's metropolitan area.

On weekends, the mountain gets unpleasantly crowded. Although there are still plenty of hikers, weekday excursions are pleasant. If you start early, you can get in a hike; stop at some viewpoints, temples, or shrines; perhaps visit the Monkey Zoo and Wild Plant Garden (¥500 for entrance to both)—which has indigenous primates and wild native plants—and be back in central Tokyo by nightfall. Note, too, that the Tokai Nature Trail, which runs all the way to Osaka, also starts at the mountain.

The Mt. Takao climb isn't nearly as grueling as that of Mt. Fuji, especially along Trail 1. This popular, fairly direct, paved route starts at Kiyotaka Station, the cable-car base station, and leads to the visitor center at the top. The 3.8-km (2.4-mile) hike takes about 1¾ hours. If you take the cable car or chairlift up, you'll join this trail a third of the way up.

Comfortable sneakers are fine, unless you plan to tackle unpaved trails, which get quite slippery and require hiking boots. In either case, dress in layers, and bring a raincoat. Although there's a seasonal beer hall and overpriced vending machines and food stalls, there's no running water, so bring plenty of your own water and snacks. **TIP→ It is mountain-climbing etiquette to greet people you overtake or meet coming the opposite direction. Smile and say "konnichiwa."**

Near the start of Trail 1 is a short detour to *konpira-dai,* one of the mountain's several small shrines, where there is a clear view of central Tokyo. After backtracking to Trail 1, continue past Sanjo Station (the upper chairlift station) and Takaosan Station (the cable-car terminus) to reach the *tenbodai,* an observatory with another view of the Tokyo skyline.

Here you have choices. You could detour to Trail 2, a 30-minute loop that meets back up with Trail 1 farther up the mountain; heading to the right on Trail 2 means your first stop will be the *hebitaki,* a picturesque waterfall; head to the left to stop at the Monkey Zoo and Wild Plant Garden first. Alternatively, you could just continue on Trail 1 to the *takosugi* (octopus cedar), a tree with exposed roots so fantastical that they resemble a giant sea monster, and the Joshinmon Gate, the entrance to Takao's sacred grounds.

Continue to the *busharito,* a stone pagoda that literally means "Buddha's bone," and is said to mark one of the spots where pieces of Buddha's remains were spread around the world after his cremation. Just past this is Yakuoin Temple, dedicated to Yakushi Nyorai, the Buddha of Medicine, believed to have been built in 744. The 2,500 historical documents surviving in the temple explain Japanese religious beliefs during the Warring States (mid-1400s–1603) and Edo (1603–1868) periods. Trail 1 then continues on to the visitor center at the peak, passing beech, oak, and Japanese nutmeg trees along the way. ✉ *Takao-machi, Tokyo.*

Restaurants

The best thing to do upon reaching the top of Mt. Takao is to eat lunch while enjoying the breathtaking view. On a clear day, you get a nice view of Mt. Fuji, and at the very least you can see the massive urban sprawl of Tokyo. There are food stands selling boxed lunches, rice balls, and other snacks, but it is a good idea to bring your own lunch.

Beer Mountain (ビアマウント)
$$$ | **INTERNATIONAL** | This seasonal beer hall serves a prix-fixe two-hour, all-you-can eat, all-you-can drink buffet meal that is a hodgepodge of sausages, pasta, Japanese dishes, and desserts. Of course, there are also a number of Japanese beers on tap. **Known for:** filling post-hike meal; views over the mountains and Western Tokyo; lively outdoor atmosphere. *$ Average main: ¥4,300* ✉ *2205 Takao-machi, Tokyo* ☎ *042/665–9943* 🌐 *www.takaotozan.co.jp* ⏲ *Closed mid-Oct.–mid-June* ☞ *Also opens for lunch on weekends only Apr.–mid-June.*

Nikko 日光

150 km (92 miles) north of Tokyo.

"Think nothing is splendid," asserts an old Japanese proverb, "until you have seen Nikko." Nikko, which means "sunlight," is a popular vacation spot for the Japanese, for good reason: its sights include a breathtaking waterfall and one of the country's best-known shrines. In addition, Nikko's Chuzenji area combines the rustic charm of a countryside village (complete with wild monkeys that have the run of the place) with a convenient location not far from Tokyo.

If you are just going to see Toshogu Shrine and the surrounding area, Nikko is best as a long day-trip from Tokyo as there is little to do in the town proper after dark. The scenic Lake Chuzenji, however, makes for a relaxing overnight stop.

GETTING HERE AND AROUND

It's possible, but unwise, to travel by car from Tokyo to Nikko. The trip takes at least three hours, and merely getting from central Tokyo to the toll-road system can be a nightmare. Coming back, especially on a Saturday or Sunday evening, is even worse.

There is no bus service between Tokyo and Nikko, but there is good rail service. The Spacia X limited express train of the Tobu Railway has six direct connections from Tokyo to Nikko daily, starting at 7:50 am from Tobu Asakusa Station, a minute's walk from the last stop on Tokyo's Ginza subway line (1 hour, 45 minutes; ¥3,340; online bookings via 🌐 *www.tobu.co.jp/spaciax/en*). During summer, fall, and weekends, buy tickets a few days in advance. If you're visiting Nikko on a day trip, note that the last return Spacia X is at 5:44 pm.

More expensive, but only slightly faster, is taking the Shinkansen to Utsunomiya and changing for the local JR train to Nikko Station; the total one-way fare is ¥5,150. The first train leaves Tokyo Station at 6:04 am (or Ueno at 6:10) and takes about 1 hour, 40 minutes to Nikko, including transfer time. The latest return is the 9:52 pm train from Nikko to Utsunomiya to catch the last Shinkansen back at 10:54 pm.

Buses and taxis can take you from Nikko to the village of Chuzenji and nearby Lake Chuzenji; one-way cab fare from Tobu Nikko Station to Chuzenji is about ¥8,000.

Local buses leave Tobu Nikko Station for Lake Chuzenji, stopping just above the entrance to Toshogu, approximately every 30 minutes from 6:11 am until 6:55 pm. The fare to Chuzenji is ¥1,250, and the ride takes about 45 minutes. The last return bus from the lake leaves at 8:00 pm, arriving back at Tobu Nikko Station at 8:38 pm.

The Peerless Japanese Blade

In the corner of the enclosure where Toshogu's Chinese Gate and Sanctum are found, an antique bronze lantern stands some 7 feet high. Legend has it that the lantern would assume the shape of a goblin at night; the deep nicks in the bronze were inflicted by swordsmen of the Edo period—on guard duty, perhaps, startled into action by a flickering shape in the dark. This proves, if not the existence of goblins, the incredible cutting power of the Japanese blade, a peerlessly forged weapon.

The town of Nikko is essentially one long avenue—Sugi Namiki (Cryptomeria Avenue)—extending for about 2 km (1 mile) from the railway stations to Toshogu. You can easily walk to most places within town. Tourist inns and shops line the street, and if you have time, you might want to make this a leisurely stroll. The antiques shops along the way may turn up interesting—but expensive—pieces like armor fittings, hibachi, pottery, and dolls. The souvenir shops here sell ample selections of local wood carvings.

VISITOR INFORMATION

Both Nikko and Tobu Nikko stations have small tourist information centers. There's also the Mekke Nikko Kyodo Center, about halfway up the main street of town between the railway stations and Toshogu, on the left; the center has a good array of English information about local restaurants and shops, registers of inns and hotels, and mapped-out walking tours. It also has bicycle rentals and a coworking space.

CONTACTS Mekke Nikko Kyodo Center. ✉ *591 Gokomachi, Nikko* ☎ *0288/25–5715* 🌐 *www.mekke-nikko.com.*

Toshogu 東照宮

150 km (92 miles) north of Tokyo.

The Toshogu area encompasses three UNESCO World Heritage sites—Toshogu Shrine, Futarasan Shrine, and Rinno-ji Temple. These are known as *nisha-ichiji* (two shrines and one temple) and are Nikko's main draw. Signs and maps clearly mark a recommended route that will allow you to see all the major sights, which are within walking distance of each other. You should plan for at least half a day to explore the area around Toshogu Shrine.

Sights

Edo Wonderland
(日光江戸村; *Nikko Edo Mura*)
MUSEUM VILLAGE | **FAMILY** | Edo Wonderland, a living-history theme park on the northeastern outskirts of Nikko, re-creates an 18th-century Japanese village. The complex includes sculpted gardens with waterfalls and ponds and vintage buildings, where actors in traditional dress stage martial arts exhibitions, historical theatrical performances, and comedy acts. You can even observe Japanese tea ceremony rituals in gorgeous tatami-floor houses, as well as people dressed as geisha and samurai. Strolling stuffed animal characters and acrobatic ninjas keep kids happy. Edo Wonderland also has restaurants and small food stalls serving cuisine like *yakisoba* (fried soba) and *dango* (dumplings). ✉ *470–2 Karakura, Nikko* ☎ *0288/77–1777* 🌐 *edowonderland.net* 🎫 *¥5,800 unlimited day pass includes rides and shows* ⏲ *Closed Wed.*

Torii

Symbolizing the boundary between the world of the everyday and a sacred space of the gods, *torii* gates mark the entrance to Shinto shrines. Although they come in various shapes and colors, they all share the same basic design making them the easiest way to differentiate between a Shinto shrine and Buddhist temple.

Futarasan-jinja Shrine (二荒山神社)
SHRINE | Nikko's holy ground is far older than the Tokugawa dynasty, in whose honor it was improved upon. Founded in AD 782, Futara-san Jinja (Futura-san Shrine) is a peaceful contrast to the more elaborate Toshogu Shrine. Futarasan has three locations: the Main Shrine at Toshogu; the Chugushi (Middle Shrine) at Lake Chuzenji; and the Okumiya (Inner Shrine) on top of Mt. Nantai.

The bronze torii at the entrance to the shrine leads to the gilded and elaborately carved Kara-mon (Chinese Gate); beyond it is the Hai-den, the shrine's oratory. The Hai-den, too, is richly carved and decorated, with a dragon-covered ceiling. The Chinese lions on the panels at the rear are by two distinguished painters of the Kano school.

From the oratory of the Taiyu-in a connecting passage leads to the Honden (Sanctum)—the present version of which dates from 1619. Designated a National Treasure, it houses a gilded and lacquered Buddhist altar some 9 feet high, decorated with paintings of animals, birds, and flowers, in which resides the object of all this veneration: a seated wooden figure of Iemitsu himself. ✉ *2307 Sannai, Nikko* ✥ *Take avenue to left as you're standing before stone torii at Tosho-gu and follow it to end* 🌐 *www.futarasan.jp* 🎫 *¥300.*

Nikko Toshogu Museum (日光東照宮宝物館; *Nikkō Tōshōgū Homotsu-kan*)
ART MUSEUM | An unhurried visit to the precincts of Toshogu should definitely

Edo Wonderland is a living history museum that re-creates an 18th-century Japanese village.

include this treasure house, as it contains a collection of antiquities from its various shrines and temples. From the west gate of Rinno-ji temple, turn left off Omote-sando, just below the pagoda, onto the cedar-lined avenue to Futarasan-jinja. A minute's walk brings you to the museum, on the left. ✉ *2301 Sannai, Nikko* ☎ *0288/54–2558* 🌐 *www.toshogu.or.jp/english/museum* 🎫 *¥1,000.*

★ **Nikko Toshogu Shrine** (東照宮)

SHRINE | With its riot of colors and carvings, inlaid pillars, red-lacquer corridors, and extensive use of gold leaf, this 17th-century shrine to Ieyasu Tokugawa is one of the most elaborately decorated in Japan.

The Hon-den (Main Hall) of Toshogu is the ultimate purpose of the shrine. You approach it from the rows of lockers at the far end of the enclosure; here you remove and store your shoes, step up into the shrine, and follow a winding corridor to the Oratory (Hai-den)—the anteroom, resplendent in its lacquered pillars, carved friezes, and coffered ceilings bedecked with dragons. Over the lintels are paintings by Tosa Mitsuoki (1617–91) of the 36 great poets of the Heian period, with their poems in the calligraphy of Emperor Go-Mizunoo. At the back of the Oratory, is the Inner Chamber (Nai-jin)—repository of the Sacred Mirror that represents the spirit of the deity enshrined here. The hall is enclosed by a wall of painted and carved panel screens; opposite the right-hand corner of the wall, facing the shrine, is the Kito-den, a hall where annual prayers were once offered for the peace of the nation.

Behind the Inner Chamber is the Innermost Chamber (Nai-Nai-jin). No visitors come this far. Here, in the very heart of Toshogu, is the gold-lacquer shrine where the spirit of Ieyasu resides, along with two other deities, who the Tokugawa later decided were fit companions. One was Toyotomi Hideyoshi, Ieyasu's mentor and liege lord in the long wars of unification at the end of the 16th century. The other was Minamoto no Yoritomo, a brilliant military tactician and founder of the earlier (12th-century) Kamakura Shogunate (Ieyasu claimed Yoritomo for an ancestor).

Between the Goma-do and the Kagura-den (a hall where ceremonial dances are performed to honor the gods) is a passage to the Sakashita-mon (Gate at the Foot of the Hill). Above the gateway is another famous symbol of Toshogu: the Sleeping Cat—a small panel said to have been carved by Hidari Jingoro (Jingoro the Left-handed), a late-16th-century master carpenter and sculptor credited with important contributions to numerous Tokugawa-period temples, shrines, and palaces. Head up the flight of 200 stone steps through a forest of cryptomeria to arrive at Ieyasu's tomb. The climb is worth it for the view of the Yomei-mon and Kara-mon from above.

The centerpiece of Toshogu is the Yomei-mon (Gate of Sunlight), atop the second flight of stone steps. A designated National Treasure, it's also called the Higurashi-mon (Twilight Gate), implying that you could gape at its richness of detail all day, until sunset. And rich it is indeed: 36 feet high and dazzling white, the gate has 12 columns, beams, and roof brackets carved with dragons, lions, clouds, peonies, Chinese sages, and demigods, painted vivid hues of red, blue, green, and gold. On one of the central columns, there are two carved tigers; the natural grain of the wood is used to bring out the "fur." As you enter the Yomei-mon, there are galleries running east and west; their paneled fences are also carved and painted with nature motifs.

The portable shrines that appear in the Toshogu Grand Spring Festival, held yearly on May 17–18, are kept in the Shinyosha, a storeroom to the left as you come through the Twilight Gate into the heart of the shrine. The paintings on the ceiling, of *tennin* (Buddhist angels) playing harps, are by Tan-yu Kano (1602–74).

Fortune Gods

Make sure you visit Gohoten-do, in the northeast corner of Rinno-ji Temple, behind the Sanbutsu-do. Three of the Seven Gods of Good Fortune, derived from Chinese folk mythology, are enshrined here. These three Buddhist deities are Daikoku-ten and Bishamon-ten, who bring wealth and good harvests, and Benzai-ten, patroness of music and the arts.

Mere mortals may not pass through the Chinese Gate (Kara-mon), which is the "official" entrance to the Toshogu inner shrine. Like its counterpart, the Yomei-mon, on the opposite side of the courtyard, the Kara-mon is a National Treasure—and, like the Yomei-mon, is carved and painted in elaborate detail with dragons and other auspicious figures. ✉ *2301 Sannai, Nikko* ☎ *0288/54–0560* 🌐 *www.toshogu.jp* 🎫 *Toshogu ¥1,600, Treasure House ¥1,000; combo ticket ¥2,400.*

Rinno-ji Temple (輪王寺)

TEMPLE | This temple belongs to the Tendai sect of Buddhism, the head temple of which is Enryaku-ji, on Mt. Hiei near Kyoto. The main hall of Rinno-ji Temple, called the Sanbutsu-do (or Hondo), is the largest single building at Toshogu. It enshrines an image of Amida Nyorai, the Buddha of the Western Paradise, flanked on the right by Senju (Thousand-Armed) Kannon, the goddess of mercy, and on the left by Bato-Kannon, the protector of animals. These three images are lacquered in gold and date from the early part of the 17th century. The original Sanbutsu-do is said to have been built in 848 by the priest Ennin (794–864), also known as Jikaku-Daishi. The present building dates from 1648.

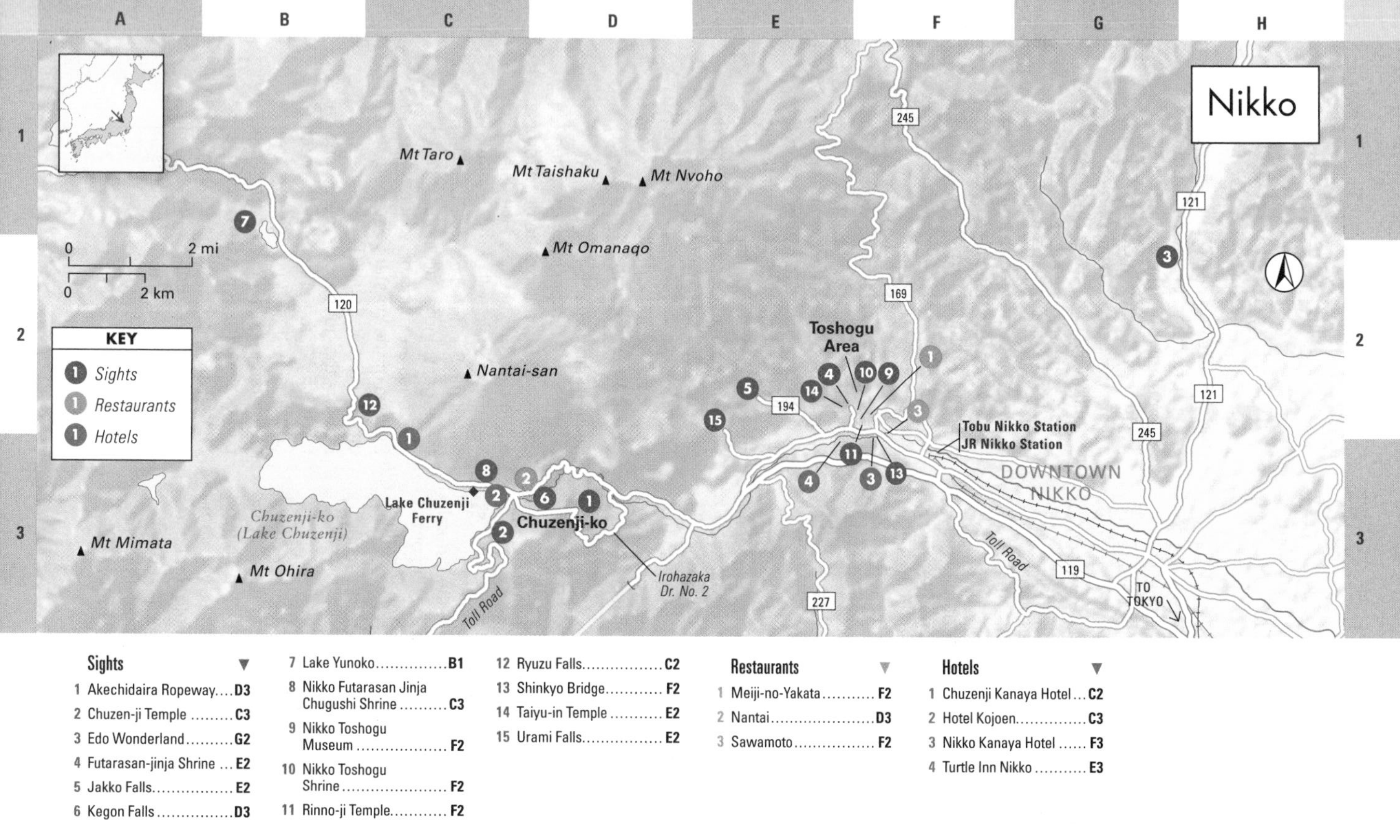

Sights	
1 Akechidaira Ropeway	D3
2 Chuzen-ji Temple	C3
3 Edo Wonderland	G2
4 Futarasan-jinja Shrine	E2
5 Jakko Falls	E2
6 Kegon Falls	D3
7 Lake Yunoko	B1
8 Nikko Futarasan Jinja Chugushi Shrine	C3
9 Nikko Toshogu Museum	F2
10 Nikko Toshogu Shrine	F2
11 Rinno-ji Temple	F2
12 Ryuzu Falls	C2
13 Shinkyo Bridge	F2
14 Taiyu-in Temple	E2
15 Urami Falls	E2

Restaurants	
1 Meiji-no-Yakata	F2
2 Nantai	D3
3 Sawamoto	F2

Hotels	
1 Chuzenji Kanaya Hotel	C2
2 Hotel Kojoen	C3
3 Nikko Kanaya Hotel	F3
4 Turtle Inn Nikko	E3

In the temple compound's southwest corner, behind the abbot's residence, is an especially fine Japanese garden called Shoyo-en, created in 1815 and thoughtfully designed to present a different perspective of its rocks, ponds, and flowering plants along every turn on its path. To the right of the garden entrance is the Homotsu-den (Treasure Hall) of Rinno-ji Temple, a museum with some 30,000 works of lacquerware, painting, and Buddhist sculpture. The museum is rather small, so only a few of the pieces in the collection—many of them designated National Treasures and Important Cultural Properties—are on display at any given time. ✉ *2300 Sannai, Nikko* ☎ *0288/54–0531* 🌐 *www.rinnoji.or.jp/en* 🎫 *Temple ¥400; Treasure Hall ¥500.*

Shinkyo Bridge (神橋)

BRIDGE | Built in 1636 for shoguns and imperial messengers visiting the shrine, the original bridge was destroyed in a flood; the present red-lacquer wooden structure dates to 1907. Buses leaving from either railway station at Nikko go straight up the main street to the bridge, opposite the first of the main entrances to Toshogu. The Sacred Bridge is just to the left of a modern bridge, where the road curves and crosses the Daiya-gawa (Daiya River). ✉ *2307 Sannai, Nikko* 🎫 *¥300 to stand on the bridge, free to view.*

Taiyu-in Temple (大猷院廟)

TEMPLE | This grandiose building is the resting place of the third Tokugawa shogun, Iemitsu (1604–51), who imposed a policy of national isolation on Japan that was to last more than 200 years. Iemitsu, one suspects, had it in mind to upstage his illustrious grandfather: he marked the approach to his own tomb with no fewer than six different decorative gates. The first is another Nio-mon—a Gate of the Deva Kings—like the one at Toshogu. The dragon painted on the ceiling is by Yasunobu Kano. A flight of stone steps leads from here to the second gate, the Niten-mon, a two-story structure protected front and back by carved and painted images of guardian gods. Beyond it, two more flights of steps lead to the middle courtyard.

As you climb the last steps to Iemitsu's shrine, you'll pass a bell tower on the right and a drum tower on the left; directly ahead is the third gate, the remarkable Yasha-mon, so named for the figures of *yasha* (she-demons) in the four niches. This structure is also known as the Peony Gate (Botan-mon) for the carvings that decorate it.

Just before the main building is the fourth gate, the Chinese-style Kara-mon, known for its gold-leaf and carvings of a crane and dragon. As you exit the shrine, on the west side, you come to the fifth gate: the Koka-mon, built in the style of the late Ming dynasty of China. The gate is normally closed, but from here another flight of stone steps leads to the sixth and last gate—the cast copper Inuki-mon, inscribed with characters in Sanskrit—and Iemitsu's tomb. ✉ *2300 Sannai, Nikko* 🎫 *¥550.*

Restaurants

Meiji-no-Yakata (明治の館)

$$$$ | **EUROPEAN** | Not far from the east entrance to Rinno-ji Temple, Meiji-no-Yakata is in an elegant 19th-century Western-style stone house, originally built as a summer retreat for an American diplomat. The food, too, is Western-style, with house specialties that include fresh rainbow trout from Lake Chuzenji, roast lamb with green pepper sauce, and melt-in-your-mouth Tochigi beef steak. **Known for:** classic high-end Japanese–Western cuisine; excellent desserts; lovely outdoor seating. [$] *Average main: ¥6,000* ✉ *2339–1 Sannai, Nikko* ☎ *0288/53–3751* 🌐 *www.meiji-yakata.com/en/meiji.*

Toshogu honors Ieyasu Tokugawa, the first shogun.

Sawamoto (澤本)
$$$ | **JAPANESE** | Charcoal-broiled *unagi* (eel) is an acquired taste, but there's no better place in Nikko to acquire it than at this small, unpretentious place with only five plain-wood tables. Service can be lukewarm, but Sawamoto is reliable for a light lunch or very early dinner of unagi served on a bed of rice in an elegant lacquered box. **Known for:** simple, beautifully prepared unagi; 90 years of history; simple, comfortable atmosphere. *Average main: ¥4,000* *1037–1 Kami Hatsuishimachi, Nikko* *0288/54–0163* *No dinner.*

Hotels

Nikko Kanaya Hotel (日光金谷ホテル)
$$ | **RESORT** | This classic hotel is a little worn around the edges after a century of operation, but it still has the best location in town—across the street from Toshogu—and the main building is a delightful, rambling Victorian structure that has hosted royalty and other important personages from around the world. **Pros:** spacious; helpful staff; perfect location for sightseeing in Nikko. **Cons:** best rooms are rather pricey; very touristy: daytime visitors browse through the old building and its gift shops; some annex rooms lack historic charm. *Rooms from: ¥25,000* *1300 Kami Hatsuishimachi, Nikko* *0288/54–0001* *www.kanayahotel.co.jp* *70 rooms* *No Meals.*

Turtle Inn Nikko (タートルイン日光)
$ | **HOTEL** | At this hotel, modest, cost-conscious Western- and Japanese-style accommodations come with or without a private bath. **Pros:** cozy atmosphere; English-speaking staff; good location for sightseeing in Nikko and Chuzenji. **Cons:** rooms dated and a bit small; no frills; few dining options nearby after dark. *Rooms from: ¥11,000* *2–16 Takumicho, Nikko* *0288/53–3168* *www.turtle-nikko.com* *No credit cards* *12 rooms* *No Meals.*

Ieyasu's Legacy

In 1600 Ieyasu Tokugawa (1543–1616) won a battle at a place in the mountains of south-central Japan called Sekigahara. This victory left him the undisputed ruler of the archipelago. He died 16 years later, but the Tokugawa Shogunate would last another 252 years.

The founder of such a dynasty required a fitting resting place. Ieyasu ("ee-eh- *ya*-su") had provided for one in his will: a mausoleum at Nikko, in a forest of tall cedars, where a religious center had been founded more than eight centuries earlier. The year after his death, in accordance with Buddhist custom, he was given a *kaimyo*—an honorific name to bear in the afterlife. Thenceforth he was Tosho-Daigongen: the Great Incarnation Who Illuminates the East. The Imperial Court at Kyoto declared him a god, and his remains were taken in a procession of great pomp and ceremony to be enshrined at Nikko.

The dynasty he left behind was enormously rich. Ieyasu's personal fief, on the Kanto Plain, was worth 2½ million *koku* of rice. One koku, in monetary terms, was equivalent to the cost of keeping one retainer in the necessities of life for a year. The shogunate itself, however, was still an uncertainty. It had only recently taken control after more than a century of civil war. The founder's tomb had a political purpose: to inspire awe and to make manifest the power of the Tokugawas. It was Ieyasu's legacy, a statement of his family's right to rule.

Toshogu was built by his grandson, the third shogun, Iemitsu (it was Iemitsu who established the policy of national isolation, which closed the doors of Japan to the outside world for more than 200 years). The mausoleum and shrine required the labor of 15,000 people for two years (1634–36). Craftsmen and artists of the first rank were assembled from all over the country. Every surface was carved and painted and lacquered in the most intricate detail imaginable. Toshogu shimmers with the reflections of 2,489,000 sheets of gold leaf. Roof beams and rafter ends with dragon heads, lions, and elephants in bas-relief; friezes of phoenixes, wild ducks, and monkeys; inlaid pillars and red-lacquer corridors: Toshogu is everything a 17th-century warlord would consider gorgeous, and the inspiration is very Chinese.

Chuzenji-ko 中禅寺湖

120 km (75 miles) north of Tokyo.

More than 4,000 feet above sea level, at the base of the volcano known as Nantai-san, is Chuzenji-ko (Lake Chuzenji), renowned for its clean waters and fresh air. People come to boat and fish and to enjoy the surrounding scenic woodlands, waterfalls, and hills.

TOURS

Lake Chuzenji Ferry (中禅寺湖機船 *Chuzenjiko Kisen*)

BOAT TOURS | **FAMILY** | From mid-April through November, you can explore Lake Chuzenji on chartered 60-minute boat rides. ✉ *2478–21 Chugushi, Nikko* ☎ *0288/55–0360* 🌐 *chuzenjiko-cruise.com* 🎫 *¥1,680.*

Sights

Akechidaira Ropeway (明智平ロープウェイ)
VIEWPOINT | FAMILY | If you want to avoid the hairpin turns, try the ropeway that runs from Akechidaira Station directly to the 1,372-meter (4,500-foot) Akechidaira lookout. It takes three minutes, and the panoramic views of Nikko and Kegon Falls are priceless. *703 Hosomachi, Nikko* *0288/55–0331* *www.nikko-kotsu.co.jp/en/ropeway* *¥1,000 round-trip.*

Chuzen-ji Temple (中禅寺)
TEMPLE | At this, a subtemple of Rinno-ji Temple at Tosho-gu, the principal object of worship is the Tachiki Kannon, a 5-meter (17-foot) standing statue of the Buddhist goddess of mercy, said to have been carved more than 1,200 years ago by the priest Shodo (the temple's founder) from the living trunk of a single Judas tree. *2578 Chugushi, Nikko* *Located on the lake's eastern shore, 1.2 km (.75 miles) south of the Chuzenji Onsen bus terminal* *0288/55–0013* *www.rinnoji.or.jp/en/spot/08.html* *¥500.*

Jakko Falls (寂光滝; *Jakko-no-taki*)
WATERFALL | FAMILY | Falling water is one of the special charms of the Nikko National Park area, and people traveling from Toshogu to Lake Chuzenji often stop off to see these cascades. They descend in a series of seven terraced stages, forming a sheet of water about 30 meters (100 feet) high. About 1 km (½ mile) west from the shrine precincts, at the Tamozawa Imperial Villa bus stop, a narrow road to the right leads to an uphill walk of some 3 km (2 miles) to the falls. *Nikko.*

★ **Kegon Falls (華厳滝; *Kegon-no-taki*)**
WATERFALL | FAMILY | More than anything else, the country's most famous falls are what draw the crowds to Chuzenji. Fed by the eastward flow of the lake, the falls drop 97 meters (318 feet) into a rugged gorge; an elevator takes you to an observation platform at the bottom. The volume of water over the falls is carefully regulated, but it's especially impressive after a summer rain or a typhoon. In winter, the falls do not freeze completely, but they still transform into a beautiful cascade of icicles. The elevator is just a few minutes' walk east from the Chuzenji Onsen bus stop, downhill and off to the right at the far end of the parking lot. *2479–2 Chugushi, Nikko* *0288/55–0030* *www.kegon.jp* *Elevator ¥570.*

Lake Yunoko (湯ノ湖; *Yuno-ko*)
BODY OF WATER | FAMILY | On the northern shore of peaceful Yunoko (Lake Yuno), a series of isolated hot springs were a popular with 14th-century aristocrats. Today, the area is still known for its hot springs—being able to soak in an onsen even when temperatures drop below zero is a major plus—but they are now controlled by separate resorts. Besides the healing and relaxing effects of the baths, visitors come for the hiking trails, fishing, camping, skiing, bird-watching, and mountain-climbing opportunities. Try to avoid the fall season, as it's peak visitor time and there are always delays. *Yumoto Onsen, Nikko* *You can get to the Yumoto onsen by taking the Tobu*

Did You Know? 

Under the policy of national seclusion, the Dutch were the only Westerners who retained trading privileges with Japan. Even then, they were confined to the tiny artificial island of Dejima, in the port of Nagasaki. To keep their precarious monopoly, they regularly sent the shogunate tokens of their esteem, including the two bronze items found in the Sacred Stable, which were sent in 1636. The 200-year-plus monopoly was dissolved when Japan decided to open its borders to other Western countries in 1858.

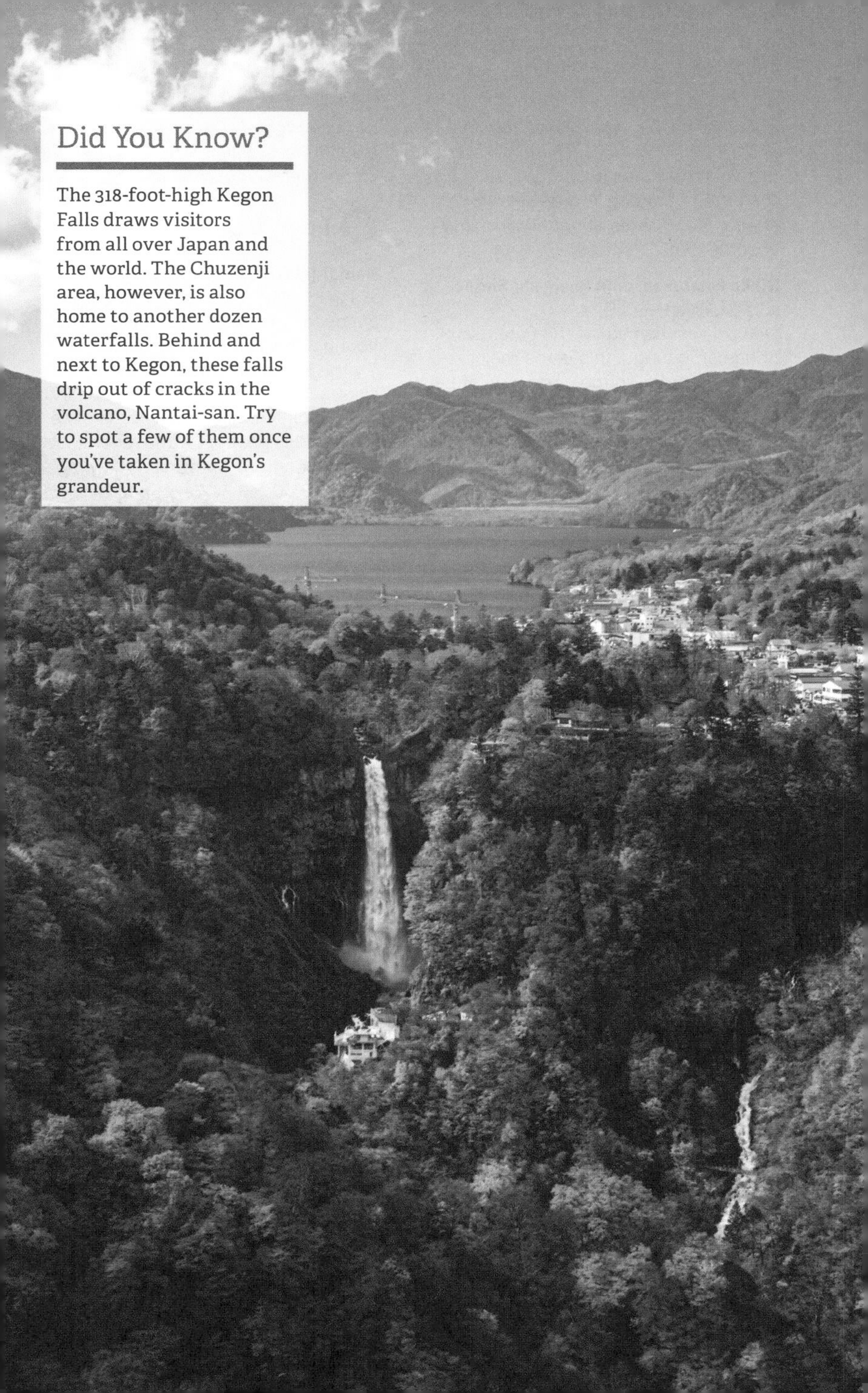

Did You Know?

The 318-foot-high Kegon Falls draws visitors from all over Japan and the world. The Chuzenji area, however, is also home to another dozen waterfalls. Behind and next to Kegon, these falls drip out of cracks in the volcano, Nantai-san. Try to spot a few of them once you've taken in Kegon's grandeur.

operated buses, which leave Tobu Nikko and JR Nikko Stations. There are one or two services an hour, depending on the time of the day. A one-way trip from central Nikko takes about 80 min. and costs ¥1,950.

Nikko Futarasan Jinja Chugushi Shrine (二荒山神社中宮祠)
SHRINE | A subshrine of the Futarasan Shrine at Toshogu, this is the major religious center on the north side of Lake Chuzenji, about 1½ km (1 miles) west of Kegon Falls. The Homotsu-den (Treasure House) contains an interesting historical collection, including swords, lacquerware, and medieval shrine palanquins. ✉ *2484 Chugushi, Nikko* ☎ *0288/55–0017* *Homotsu-Den ¥500; shrine free.*

Ryuzu Falls (竜頭滝; *Ryuzu-no-taki*)
WATERFALL | **FAMILY** | If you've budgeted a second day for Nikko, you might want to consider a walk around the lake. A paved road along the north shore extends for about 8 km (5 miles), one-third of the whole distance, as far as the "beach" and campsite at Shobu-ga-hama. Here, where the road branches off to the north for the Senjogahara Marsh, are the lovely cascades of Ryuzu no Taki, literally Dragon's Head Falls. If you don't fancy retracing your steps, Tobu buses running between Yumoto Onsen and Tobu Nikko stop here. ✉ *Nikko.*

Urami Falls (裏見ノ滝; *Urami-no-taki*)
WATERFALL | **FAMILY** | A poetic description says it all and still holds true: "The water," wrote the great 17th-century poet Basho, "seemed to take a flying leap and drop a hundred feet from the top of a cave into a green pool surrounded by a thousand rocks. One was supposed to inch one's way into the cave and enjoy the falls from behind." The falls and the gorge are striking—but you should make the climb only if you have good hiking shoes and are willing to get wet in the process. ✉ *Nikko* *Take the bus that runs between Tobu-Nikko and Chuzenji Onsen. It's a 50-min. walk to the falls from the Urami-no-taki Iriguchi bus stop.*

Restaurants

Nantai (なんたい)
$$ | **JAPANESE** | The wooden tables, antiques, and patches of raised tatami flooring give Nantai a very rustic feel. Try the Nikko specialty, *yuba* (tofu skin), which comes with the *nabe* (hot pot) for dinner. **Known for:** home-style hot-pot cuisine; cozy atmosphere; local specialties from Chuzen-ji. *Average main: ¥3,000* ✉ *2478–8 Chugushi, Nikko* ☎ *080/7091–3200* *www.dining-nantai.com* *Closed Thurs.*

Hotels

Chuzenji Kanaya Hotel (中禅寺金谷ホテル)
$$ | **RESORT** | Floor-to-ceiling windows overlook the lake or the grounds, and pastel colors decorate the simple rooms at this outpost of the Nikko Kanaya on the road from Chuzenji Onsen to Shobu-ga-hama. **Pros:** relaxing resort feel; spacious rooms; excellent food. **Cons:** bland and dated room interiors; no outside dining options nearby after dark; not easy to access without a car. *Rooms from: ¥24,000* ✉ *2482 Chugushi, Nikko* ☎ *0288/51–0001* *www.kanayahotel.co.jp/en/ckh* *57 rooms.*

Hotel Kojoen (湖上苑)
$$ | **B&B/INN** | Located at the entrance to Lake Chuzenji, Hotel Kojoen is an excellent middle ground between the area's larger luxury hotels and bare-bones pensions. **Pros:** easy access; relaxing; excellent meals included. **Cons:** Western-style rooms are clean but dated; outdoor hot spring crowded during peak times; rooms are on the small side. *Rooms from: ¥22,000* ✉ *2478 Chugushi, Nikko* ☎ *0288/55–0500* *www.kojoen.com* *10 rooms* *All-Inclusive.*

Index

D

E

F

G

H

S

T

Photo Credits

Front Cover: Jordan Banks/Sime/eStock Photo [Descr.: Japan, Kanto, Tokyo, Meguro River, Lanterns and cherry blossom.] **Back cover, from left to right:** Phattana Stock/Shutterstock. Pandara/Shutterstock. Sean Pavone/Shutterstock. **Spine:** Ilolab/Shutterstock. **Interior, from left to right:** Blanscape/Shutterstock (1). SeanPavonePhoto/iStockphoto (2-3). Stockmelnyk/Shutterstock (5). **Chapter 1: Experience Tokyo:** Sean Pavone/Shutterstock (6-7). Benny Marty/Shutterstock (8-9). HappyTogether/Shutterstock (9). MichaelBK/Shutterstock (9). Akashi/Tokyo Convention & Visitors Bureau (10). MMpai/Shutterstock (10). Yury Zap/Dreamstime (10). Björkdahl Per/Dreamstime (10). Kavram/Shutterstock (11). Sean Pavone/Shutterstock (11). Stray Toki/Shutterstock (12). Tokyo Convention & Visitors Bureau (12). Tokyo Convention & Visitors Bureau (12). Tokyo Convention & Visitors Bureau (12). Sanniely/GettyImages (13). NavinTar/Shutterstock (13). J.Henning Buchholz/Shutterstock (13). Mark Bassett/Alamy Stock Photo (13). Tokyo Convention & Visitors Bureau (14). Cowardlion/Shutterstock (14). Sergio Delle Vedove/Shutterstock (14). Tokyo Convention & Visitors Bureau (14). Kuremo/iStockphoto (15). Aimuse/Shutterstock (15). Tommyakky/iStockphoto (20). Hideo Kurihara/Alamy (20). 2nix/iStockphoto (20). Tokyo Convention & Visitors Bureau (20). Gyro/iStockphoto (21). Pablo Hidalgo/Dreamstime (22). Phurinee Chinakathum/Shutterstock (22). Image_vulture/Shutterstock (22). Walter Lim/Flickr (22). Anutr Yossundara/Shutterstock (23). Yujistyle/Shutterstock (24). Naruto4836/Dreamstime (24). Sean Pavone/Shutterstock (24). Zerobug2000/Dreamstime (24). 3331 Arts Chiyoda (25). Laika AC/Meguro Parasitological Museum (25). Norikko/Shutterstock (25). Nissan/Tokyo (25). Mint Images Limited/Alamy (26). Fuminari Yoshitsugu (27). Melpomenem/Dreamstime (28). Eakkarat Rangram/Shutterstock (29). Tanya Jones/Shutterstock (30). Page Light Studios/Shutterstock (30). Guy William/Shutterstock (30). KenSoftTH/Shutterstock (31). Stephen Kelly/Flickr (31). Fotogrin/Shutterstock (35). Luciano Mortula - LGM/Shutterstock (36). Sean Pavone/Shutterstock (36). Public Domain/WikimediaCommons (36). My name is boy/Shutterstock (37). Rolf52/Dreamstime (37). Razvanjp/Dreamstime (37). Sean Pavone/GettyImages (38). Zorrillocojo/Shutterstock (38). Library of Congress/WikimediaCommons (38). JWCohen/Shutterstock (39). Nguyen Hoand Kha/Shutterstock (39). Tataroko/Wikimedia Commons (39). Sueddeutsche Zeitung Photo/Alamy Stock Photo (40). Jonathan William Cohen/GettyImages (40). Lokyo Multimedia JP/Shutterstock (40). **Chapter 2: Travel Smart:** Ned Snowman/Shutterstock (51). Retirementbonus/Shutterstock (51). **Chapter 3: A Japanese Culture Primer:** Cowardlion/Shutterstock (69). Stockmelnyk/Shutterstock (71). Kazoka/Shutterstock (72-73). Kazoka/Shutterstock (73). Volodymyr Platonov/GettyImages (74). Hiroamano/Shutterstock (74). Again Peace/Shutterstock (75). Nishihama/Shutterstock (75). Hihitetlin/Shutterstock (75). Podsawat.dew/Shutterstock (76). Chiristsumo/Shutterstock (76). Gontabunta/Shutterstock (77). Aao nori/Shutterstock (77). Tondo Soesanto Soegondo/Shutterstock (78). Urban Napflin/Shutterstock (78). Jon Chica/Shutterstock (79). Ishikawa Prefecture Tourist Association and Kanazawa Convention Bureau/JNTO (80). Su.bo/Flickr (81). Nagano Prefecture/JNTO (81). Jim Epler/Flickr (82). Iwate Prefecture/JNTO (83). Onemu/Shutterstock (84). JNTO (85). Nagano Prefecture/JNTO (85). Narongsak Nagadhana/Shutterstock (86). Kai keisuke/Shutterstock (87). Antonina Polushkina/Shutterstock (88). Ekaterina McClaud/Shutterstock (89). Julianne.hide/Shutterstock (89). Hannari_eli/Shutterstock (90). Enchanted_fairy/Shutterstock (91). Spatuletail/Shutterstock (91). Sean Pavone/Shutterstock (92). Mirko Kuzmanovic/Shutterstock (93). Picture cells/Shutterstock (93). Oneinchpunch/Shutterstock (94). Alexander Gatsenko/Shutterstock (95). Vladimir Vasiltvich/Shutterstock (95). J. Henning Buchholz/Shutterstock (96). J. Henning Buchholz/Shutterstock (97). Bluehand/Shutterstock (97). Osaze Cuomo/Shutterstock (98). Juri Pozzi/Shutterstock (99). Patrick Foto/Shutterstock (99). Dach_chan/Shutterstock (100). Joe1971/Dreamstime (101). Kajohnwit Boonsom/Shutterstock (101). Chen Min Chun/Shutterstock (102). Pxhidalgo/Dreamstime (103). Cambo01/Dreamstime (103). JNTO (104). Gorosan/Shutterstock (105). JNTO (105). Muhammad Mahfuzh Huda/Shutterstock (106). Ishikawa Prefecture/JNTO (107). Nyiragongo70/ Dreamstime (108). Jean-Pierre Dalbéra/Flickr (109). Nikitu/Dreamstime (109). PSno7/Shutterstock (110). Beeboys/Shutterstock (111). Adaychou/Dreamstime (112). **Chapter 4: Marunouchi and Nihonbashi:** DoctorEgg/iStockphoto (113). Pop Navy/Shutterstock (116). Kristi Blokhin/Shutterstock (125). Yoshi0511/Shutterstock (129). Tktktk/Dreamstime (133). **Chapter 5: Ginza and Tsukiji:** Cendhika/Shutterstock (135). DakerboyDreamstime (144). Naruto4836/Dreamstime (147). **Chapter 6: Shiodome and Odaiba:** Sangapark118/Dreamstime (149). Bennymarty/Dreamstime (154). ESB Professional/Shutterstock (156). **Chapter 7: Aoyama, Harajuku, and Shibuya with Akasaka, Omotesando, and Shimokitazawa:** SeanPavonePhoto/iStockphoto (159). Andres Garcia Martin/Shutterstock (168). Phurinee Chinakathum/Dreamstime (171). SeanPavonePhoto/iStockphoto (175). 2p2play/Shutterstock (177). Andrew Currie/Flickr (178). Brunocoelhopt/iStockphoto (178). Everyday polkadot/Shutterstock (178). Pakpoom Phummee/Shutterstock (178). Naruto4836/Dreamstime (179). Foxxy63/Shutterstock (179). Akiyoko/Shutterstock (179). Dzimmu/Shutterstock (179). Kokoroimages/GettyImages (180). Ned Snowman/Shutterstock (181). Vtt Studio/Shutterstock (181). Jayson_Photography/Shutterstock (182). Alex Segre/Shutterstock (182). Blanscape/Dreamstime (182). FiledImage/iStockphoto (183). Huytonthat/Dreamstime (185). **Chapter 8: Roppongi:** ESB Professional/Shutterstock (195). Witaya ratanasirikulchai/Shutterstock (198). F11photo/Shutterstock (203). **Chapter 9: Shinjuku with Ikebukuro:** Sean Pavone/iStockphoto (209). SeanPavonePhoto/iStockphoto (215). TwilightShow/iStockphoto (220). Yu_photo/Shutterstock (224). **Chapter 10: West Tokyo:** Cowardlion/Shutterstock (227). Cowardlion/Shutterstock (234). Jessedyck/Flickr (238). Picture cells/Shutterstock (240). Asiangrandkid/Shutterstock (242). **Chapter 11: Akihabara:** Aleksandar Todorovic/Shutterstock (245). Brett Laybutt/Shutterstock (251). Luciano Mortula - LGM/Shutterstock (253). **Chapter 12: Ueno and Yanaka:** Minokku/iStockphoto (255). Richie0703/Dreamstime (258). Alexirina27000/Dreamstime (261). Luciano Mortula - LGM/Shutterstock (263). SenpaiSama/Shutterstock (264). Cowardlion/Dreamstime (267). **Chapter 13: Asakusa and Ryogoku:** Galina Savina/Shutterstock (269). MeeRok/Shutterstock (275). Simonlong/GettyImages (277). Foodforthoughts/Shutterstock (282). **Chapter 14: Beyond Central Tokyo:** Komang Arjana/Dreamstime (285). Travelling-light/Dreamstime (292-293). **Chapter 15: Side Trips from Tokyo:** Yujiro/Dreamstime (305). Kazu8/Shutterstock (309). Cowardlion/Dreamstime (313). Manuel Ascanio/Shutterstock (326). Engineer story/Shutterstock (332). Samuel Ponce/Shutterstock (334). Warasit phothisuk/Shutterstock (338-339). Anek.soowannaphoom/Shutterstock (338). Nackoper/Shutterstock (339). Sandra Foyt/Shutterstock (339). Public Domain/Wikimedia Commons (340). Public Domain/WikimediaCommons (340). Blanscape/Shutterstock (341). Tanya Jones/Shutterstock (341). Miroboudny/Shutterstock (342). Christian Schmutz/Flickr (342). Madsolar/Shutterstock (342). Picturesque Japan/Shutterstock (342). Hachi888/Shutterstock (342). JwCohen/Shutterstock (342). Azlan DuPree/Flickr (343). Balky79/Dreamstime (344). Wongkarho/Shutterstock (344). Dowraik/Shutterstock (344). DoctorEgg/GettyImages (345). Aleksandar Todorovic/Shutterstock (350). Stray Toki/Shutterstock (366). Masterlu/Dreamstime (370). Taweep Tang/Shutterstock (373). **About Our Writers:** All photos are courtesy of the writers except for the following: Jay Farris, courtesy of Takuya Ishikawa; Randy Grace, courtesy of Ena Miyazaki Jr.; Robert Morel, courtesy of Claire van der Lee. *Every effort has been made to trace the copyright holders, and we apologize in advance for any accidental errors. We would be happy to apply the corrections in the following edition of this publication.

Fodor's TOKYO

Publisher: Stephen Horowitz, *General Manager*

Editorial: Douglas Stallings, *Editorial Director*; Jill Fergus, Amanda Sadlowski, *Senior Editors*; Brian Eschrich, Alexis Kelly, *Editors;* Angelique Kennedy-Chavannes, Yoojin Shin, *Associate Editors*

Design: Tina Malaney, *Director of Design and Production*; Jessica Gonzalez, *Senior Designer*, Jaimee Shaye, *Graphic Design Associate*

Production: Jennifer DePrima, *Editorial Production Manager*, Elyse Rozelle, *Senior Production Editor;* Monica White, *Production Editor*

Maps: Rebecca Baer, *Map Director*, David Lindroth, Mark Stroud (Moon Street Cartography), *Cartographers*

Photography: Viviane Teles, *Director of Photography;* Namrata Aggarwal, Neha Gupta, Payal Gupta, Ashok Kumar, *Photo Editors;* Jade Rodgers, *Photo Production Intern*

Business and Operations: Chuck Hoover, *Chief Marketing Officer;* Robert Ames, *Group General Manager*

Public Relations and Marketing: Joe Ewaskiw, *Senior Director of Communications and Public Relations*

Fodors.com: Jeremy Tarr, *Editorial Director;* Rachael Levitt, *Managing Editor*

Technology: Jon Atkinson, *Executive Director of Technology;* Rudresh Teotia, *Associate Director of Technology;* Alison Lieu, *Project Manager*

Writers: Jonathan DeLisle, Jay Farris, Rob Goss, Randy Grace, Robert Morel, Alexandra Ziminski

Editor: Laura M. Kidder

Production Editor: Elyse Rozelle

9th Edition

ISBN 978-1-64097-750-1

ISSN 1554-5881

SPECIAL SALES

This book is available at special discounts for bulk purchases for sales promotions or premiums. For more information, e-mail SpecialMarkets@fodors.com.

PRINTED IN CANADA

10 9 8 7 6 5 4 3 2 1

About Our Writers

Originally from the New York City area, **Jonathan DeLise** has lived in Tokyo, Jakarta, Jeddah, Shenzhen, Hong Kong, and Orizaba (Mexico) for varying lengths of time. As a freelance writer, he has covered a wide range of food, history, and travel topics. One of his hobbies is studying languages—primarily so he can decipher menus. His dream title would be Fluent Eater. You can follow him on YouTube (@findingfoodfluency) and/or on one of his two blogs (NoWorkAllTravel and FindingFoodFluency).

Jay Farris has spent most of his life getting acquainted with Japan and now calls Tokyo home after a stint in Yamagata's Shonai region. He gardens, writes, bikes around the countryside, and, having graduated from the University of Tokyo with a master's degree in urban engineering, also leads around curious people interested in urban history and Tokyo's rich backstory.

Rob Goss has lived in Tokyo since 1999. In that time, Rob has worked with more than 100 publications around the globe, including *Time, National Geographic,* and BBC Travel. He is also the author of seven occasionally award-winning books on Japan.

Randy Grace has lived more than half his life in Japan. Following an almost entirely unnoticed departure from the world of music, he now splits his time between Tokyo, where he works, and the Izu Peninsula, where he also works. His current creative endeavor is getting his wife on board with his latest innovation, his-and-hers wine-drinking caps.

Robert Morel has been exploring Japan since 2003 and still thinks the best way to get from Hokkaido to Okinawa is by bicycle. He currently writes about, photographs, and lives in Tokyo's Shitamachi neighborhood.

Alexandra Ziminski has been living in Japan since 2016. As well as being a travel writer, she has thrown in the towel (literally) as a life model, izakaya waitress, and hostel receptionist. When she isn't keeping up to date with the latest events, happenings, and drama in Tokyo, she's venturing outside the capital to her favorite seasonal spots in Japan: summer in Yakushima, spring in Hakone, autumn in Fukushima, and winter in Hakodate.

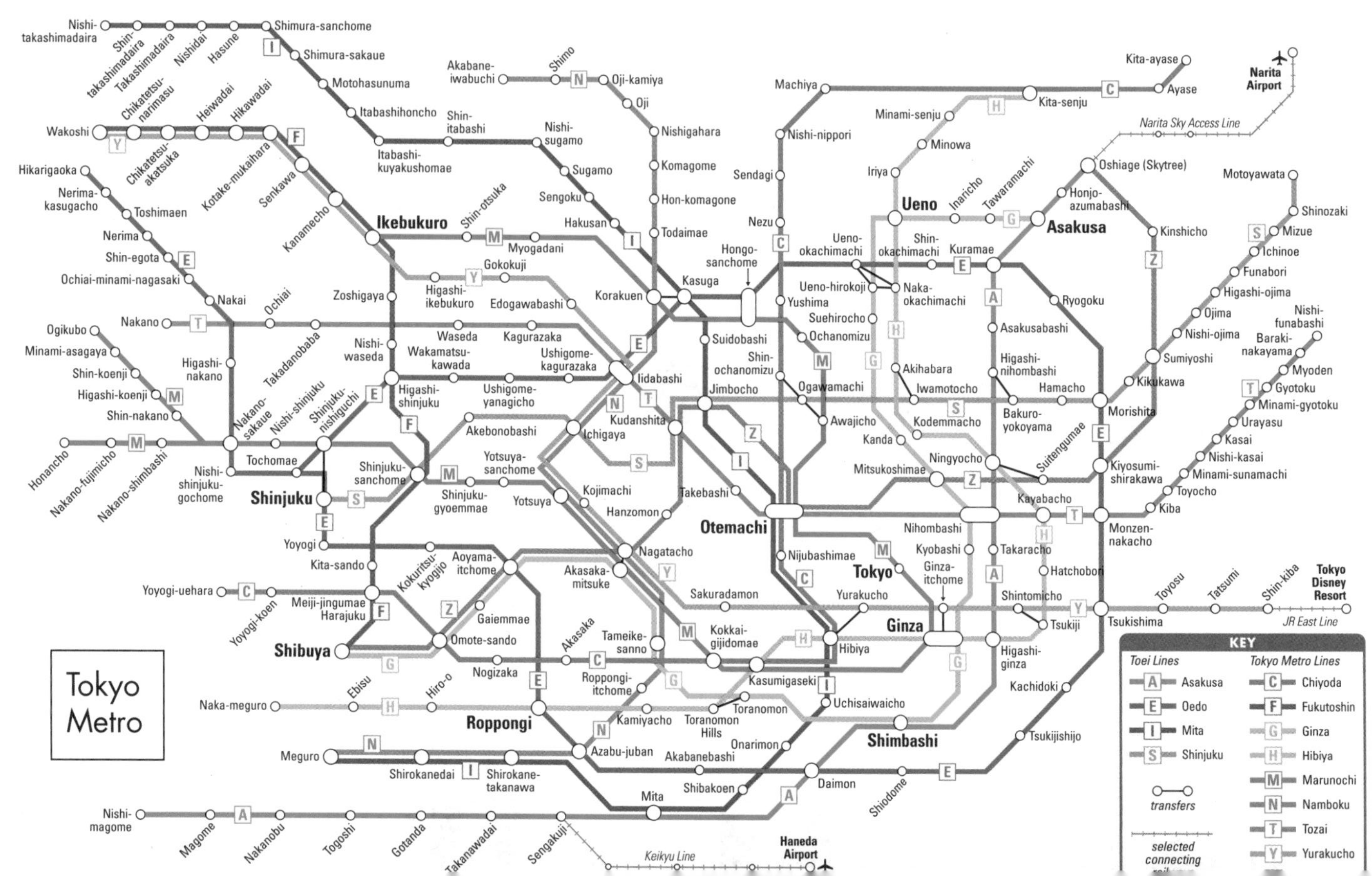
Tokyo Metro
KEY
Toei Lines
A Asakusa
E Oedo
I Mita
S Shinjuku
transfers
selected connecting
Tokyo Metro Lines
C Chiyoda
F Fukutoshin
G Ginza
H Hibiya
M Marunochi
N Namboku
T Tozai
Y Yurakucho
Narita Airport
Narita Sky Access Line
Haneda Airport
Keikyu Line
Tokyo Disney Resort
JR East Line
Nishi-takashimadaira
Shin-takashimadaira
Takashimadaira
Nishidai
Hasune
Shimura-sanchome
Shimura-sakaue
Motohasunuma
Itabashihoncho
Shin-itabashi
Itabashi-kuyakushomae
Nishi-sugamo
Sugamo
Sengoku
Hakusan
Wakoshi
Chikatetsu-narimasu
Chikatetsu-akatsuka
Heiwadai
Hikawadai
Kotake-mukaihara
Senkawa
Kanamecho
Ikebukuro
Hikarigaoka
Nerima-kasugacho
Toshimaen
Nerima
Shin-egota
Ochiai-minami-nagasaki
Nakai
Nakano
Ochiai
Takadanobaba
Ogikubo
Minami-asagaya
Shin-koenji
Higashi-koenji
Shin-nakano
Higashi-nakano
Nakano-sakaue
Nishi-shinjuku
Shinjuku-nishiguchi
Honancho
Nakano-fujimicho
Nakano-shimbashi
Nishi-shinjuku-gochome
Tochomae
Shinjuku
Yoyogi
Kita-sando
Yoyogi-uehara
Yoyogi-koen
Meiji-jingumae Harajuku
Shibuya
Akabane-iwabuchi
Shimo
Oji-kamiya
Oji
Nishigahara
Komagome
Hon-komagone
Todaimae
Shin-otsuka
Myogadani
Gokokuji
Higashi-ikebukuro
Edogawabashi
Zoshigaya
Nishi-waseda
Waseda
Kagurazaka
Wakamatsu-kawada
Ushigome-kagurazaka
Higashi-shinjuku
Ushigome-yanagicho
Akebonobashi
Shinjuku-sanchome
Yotsuya-sanchome
Shinjuku-gyoemmae
Yotsuya
Kojimachi
Hanzomon
Kokuritsu-kyogijo
Aoyama-itchome
Gaiemmae
Omote-sando
Nogizaka
Akasaka
Akasaka-mitsuke
Nagatacho
Tameike-sanno
Roppongi-itchome
Kamiyacho
Roppongi
Ebisu
Hiro-o
Naka-meguro
Meguro
Shirokanedai
Shirokane-takanawa
Azabu-juban
Nishi-magome
Magome
Nakanobu
Togoshi
Gotanda
Takanawadai
Sengakuji
Mita
Shibakoen
Akabanebashi
Onarimon
Toranomon Hills
Toranomon
Daimon
Shiodome
Korakuen
Kasuga
Hongo-sanchome
Iidabashi
Ichigaya
Kudanshita
Suidobashi
Jimbocho
Takebashi
Otemachi
Machiya
Nishi-nippori
Sendagi
Nezu
Yushima
Ueno-okachimachi
Ueno-hirokoji
Shin-okachimachi
Naka-okachimachi
Suehirocho
Ochanomizu
Shin-ochanomizu
Ogawamachi
Awajicho
Akihabara
Iwamotocho
Kanda
Kodemmacho
Mitsukoshimae
Nijubashimae
Tokyo
Sakuradamon
Kokkai-gijidomae
Kasumigaseki
Uchisaiwaicho
Hibiya
Yurakucho
Ginza
Ginza-itchome
Kyobashi
Nihombashi
Kayabacho
Takaracho
Hatchobori
Shintomicho
Tsukiji
Higashi-ginza
Shimbashi
Kachidoki
Tsukijishijo
Minami-senju
Kita-senju
Ayase
Kita-ayase
Minowa
Iriya
Ueno
Inaricho
Tawaramachi
Asakusa
Honjo-azumabashi
Oshiage (Skytree)
Kinshicho
Kuramae
Asakusabashi
Higashi-nihombashi
Bakuro-yokoyama
Hamacho
Ningyocho
Suitengumae
Ryogoku
Morishita
Kikukawa
Sumiyoshi
Kiyosumi-shirakawa
Monzen-nakacho
Kiba
Toyocho
Minami-sunamachi
Nishi-kasai
Kasai
Urayasu
Minami-gyotoku
Gyotoku
Myoden
Baraki-nakayama
Nishi-funabashi
Nishi-ojima
Ojima
Higashi-ojima
Funabori
Ichinoe
Mizue
Shinozaki
Motoyawata
Tsukishima
Toyosu
Tatsumi
Shin-kiba